I0816799

AMERICAN STEAM LOCOMOTIVES

Design and Development, 1880–1960

WILLIAM L. WITHUHN

INDIANA UNIVERSITY PRESS AND THE RAILWAY & LOCOMOTIVE HISTORICAL SOCIETY, INC.

This book is a joint publication of

Indiana University Press
Office of Scholarly Publishing
Herman B Wells Library 350
1320 E. 10th St.
Bloomington, IN 47405-3707

iupress.indiana.edu

The Railway & Locomotive Historical Society, Inc.
PO Box 2913
Pflugerville, TX 78691-2913

rlhs.org

IUP Acquisitions Editor
Ashley Runyon

R&LHS Editor
Peter A. Hansen

Design, typesetting, and layout
Kevin J. Holland

The paper used in this book meets the minimum requirements of the American National Standard for Information Sciences – Permanence of Paper for Printed Library Materials, ANSI Z39.48–1992.

8 25

Printed in the United States of America

Cataloging information is available from the Library of Congress.

ISBN 978-0-253-03933-0 (cloth)
ISBN 978-0-253-03934-7 (ebook)

TO JOHN H. WHITE, JR.

CAUTION
WATER COLUMN WILL
NOT CLEAR A MAN ON
SIDE OF CAR
454

Contents

Central Vermont Railway No. 454, a 2-8-0 Consolidation-type engine, takes on water at Amherst, Mass.

Courtesy Kalmbach Media

1361

Foreword

by Kevin P. Keefe

THE TRANSPORTATION SCHOLAR WAS HAVING a hard time with his 154-ton beast. It was a hot, humid Sunday afternoon in July 1987, all the more miserable if you were inside the cab of Pennsylvania Railroad K4s steam locomotive No. 1361, where close confines and a boiler full of steam at 205 psi had caused the temperature to soar well past 100 degrees. William L. Withuhn, on Monday through Friday the curator of transportation at the Smithsonian Institution's National Museum of American History, was moonlighting this particular weekend, sweating it out in heavy denim overalls, gauntlet gloves, and a Kromer engineer's cap.

The normally gregarious Withuhn was all business, especially now that his immense charge appeared to be stuck on the tracks of the Nittany & Bald Eagle, a central Pennsylvania short line. Only an occasional one-word instruction or epithet emerged from his mouth as he went about his business. He was the classic grumpy hogger. And for good reason: a torrential rain had struck moments after the train stopped for a photo opportunity. Now, with the rails covered in slick-as-grease dead leaves, the big 4-6-2's 80-inch driving wheels were having difficulty getting traction, even with a short passenger train. With a schedule to keep, and a short window ahead on Conrail's always-busy main line, Withuhn and his fireman were under the gun.

Bill Withuhn eventually got his burly Pacific rolling, of course, thanks to his skill at the throttle and his patience with everyone else in the cab. Later, in the yard at Altoona, he could allow himself a moment to relax. His visitor relaxed, too, having witnessed a rare moment in which the grimy engineer, the credentialed museum executive, the restless journalist, and the unabashed steam fan somehow synthesized all his passions into one successful moment – just as he has with the monumental book you now hold in your hands.

A master of the art

A central fact of Bill's career is that he was a licensed locomotive engineer, something that brought him not only a singular sense of pride but also informed his work as a historian and curator, probably in ways even he could not fully understand. Bill knew what it meant to take on the responsibility of a trainload

Restored Pennsylvania Railroad Class K4s 4-6-2 Pacific No. 1361 on one of its early fantrips, taken on Conrail in April 1987, near Altoona, Pa.
Ken Murry, Courtesy Kalmbach Media

of passengers as he used the throttle and reverse lever and brake handle to coax the most out of a recalcitrant machine. In those experiences, he internalized both the ethos and the techniques of generations of steam engineers.

Bill's career as an engineer began in 1966, when he first volunteered to work at New Jersey's Black River & Western tourist line. His duties included running the BR&W's diesels, but he also mastered the railroad's two steam locomotives, 2-8-0 No. 60 and 4-6-2 No. 148. The apprentice performed well. That same year, he was certified as an engineer by the Pennsylvania Railroad's New York Division examiner, who handed him a qualification card he kept for the rest of his life. A few years later, Bill timed his resignation from the Air Force so he could work on the tourist trains until attending Cornell University's graduate business school. Years later, he would put in much more time on the right-hand side of the cabs of other mainline engines, notably PRR 1361, the entire stable of locomotives at the Steamtown National Historic Site, and in what became his favorite charge, Milwaukee Road 4-8-4 No. 261.

The man who oversees the 261, Steve Sandberg, spent long hours in the cab with Bill and appreciated his skills at handling the engine. "Bill always approached the locomotive as a very simple machine with a very complex historical significance," says Sandberg. "When he ran the engine, he was pretty gentle with it. He knew these machines are treasures and should be treated properly. He also saw the 261 as a product of World War II, and he was a military man himself. He almost saw the engine as an extension of himself."

An essential book on steam

That notion – the locomotive as an extension of the man – is a familiar theme running through steam locomotive culture, and it's apt in the case of this, Bill's highest achievement as an author. This book fills a significant gap. Not that steam hasn't gotten its due in some form – the shelves of railroad libraries groan under the weight of hundreds of books covering the subject. Alas, so many of them are narrow in scope. Some simply are picture books, depicting the visual drama of steam, but in the end, not telling the reader very much. Others are in the tradition of the single-railroad "power" book, typically an exhaustive review of every single locomotive on a given railroad, loaded with pictures and roster data but lacking in larger context, as if no other railroad but the XY&Z ever fielded a decent 4-8-4.

Bill's comprehensive approach to the subject has precedents, but even those serve to underscore the depth of his achievement. The standard reference on steam, Alfred W. Bruce's exhaustive but dry *The Steam Locomotive in America: Its Development in the Twentieth Century*, first published in 1952, was impressive in its analysis of technology but necessarily missed all the perspective developed in the decades since. Bill's predecessor and mentor at the Smithsonian, John H. "Jack" White, authored a landmark book, *American Locomotives: An Engineering History, 1830-1880*, first published in 1968 and updated with a second edition in 1997, but the book ends when, for many readers, steam was just beginning to get exciting – a bit like reading a book on military aviation that ends with the Sopwith Camel. This book of Bill's is explicitly intended as a complement to Jack White's monumental work, picking up where the earlier book left off.

The legendary editor of *Trains* magazine, David P. Morgan, took a stab at the entirety of modern steam with his *Steam's Finest Hour* of 1961, an oversize coffee-table book distinguished by Morgan's pithy insights but otherwise a showcase of black-and-white action photography. More informative is Kalmbach Books' *Guide to North American Steam Locomotives*, a useful compendium of individual railroad rosters fleshed out with a concise narrative by George H. Drury, first published in 1993 and released in revised form in 2015. But the book is very much a digest. Other notable titles are Albert J. Churella's *From Steam to Diesel: Managerial Customs and Organizational Capabilities in the Twentieth-Century American Locomotive Industry*, and J. Parker Lamb's *Perfecting the American Steam Locomotive*, both fine works that explore essential aspects of steam.

The mystique of technology

Which brings us to this wonderful volume. There are so many reasons to recommend it. One is Bill's peerless ability to explain the machine in clear language, always exhibiting technical credibility balanced with accessibility. Somehow, he manages to connect with the roundhouse master mechanic as easily as he does the casual fan. Yet the book is solid in its scholarship: Just read Bill's exhaustive and often quite entertaining chapter notes, nearly as enlightening as the narrative itself.

The book is certain to become a standard in the field for its treatment of engineering development alone. Bill was around technology his entire life – as a young man obsessed with cars in 1960s California, as an Air Force major, and, of course, as a railroader – and here he shows an innate sense of the importance of problems and breakthroughs both obvious and obscure. He eloquently unravels the central problem locomotive designers faced, the everlasting challenge of getting the most out of a boiler and its attendant components. Bill follows the quest for thermal efficiency, a tale filled with twists and turns, including the wide adoption of superheaters just before World War I; the big firebox made possible by Lima's four-wheel trailing truck of 1925; the move away from the compound Mallet to the simple articulated; breakthroughs in metallurgy, interrupted by War Production Board restrictions of the early 1940s.

But with steam, there's so much more than the boiler. Thus we get Bill's fascinating excursions into such arcana as the debate over the best engine hinge for an articulated, Baldwin's solution versus Norfolk & Western's; or the on-again, off-again fascination some railroads had with three-cylinder power delivery, culminating with Union Pacific's 4-12-2 of 1926; or the astonishingly fast impact of roller bearings after the success of Timken's "Four Aces" 4-8-4. Alone worth the price of the book, at least for some, will be Bill's brilliant take on the tricky business of driving-wheel counterbalancing, a field he aptly describes as "science, pseudoscience, and black art."

For all his enthusiasm for technology, Bill thinks carefully about the various audiences that will be drawn to this book and their relative ability to grasp, or care about, some of the details. Thus, in Chapter 7, his analysis of Alco's pioneering designer Francis Cole, we get a surprising bit of advice from an author: If what follows is heavy going, "skip ahead," he says, to the next chapter. Cole's quest was to find a locomotive's top sustainable output, and his model for determining it was a mixture of theories and practices involving such minutiae as evaporation rates, cylinder horsepower, and combustion losses. Actually, Bill's explanation should satisfy most readers, but I still found his advice thoughtful and generous.

Beyond technology

Two other aspects of this book really struck me, and both are related directly to what were priorities in Bill's career as a historian. One was his interest in the role of people. Not just their objective contributions, but also the way their personalities – their strengths and fallibilities, their sheer humanness – affected the course of technology. His characters include Samuel Vauclain, the onetime Pennsylvania Railroad apprentice who landed at Baldwin in 1883 and subsequently drove his company to the top of the industry. Or William G. McAdoo, the cunning political animal who, nearly despite himself, made the first significant advancement in the standardization of steam during his reign at the United States Railroad Administration. Or Will Woodard, the genius of Lima Locomotive Works and father of Super Power, whose design principles made possible the "steam's finest hour" era of the 1930s and '40s.

Bill's other great passion was safety, influenced by his own experiences running steam engines and the resulting kinship he felt for working railroaders. Bill respected and perhaps even feared the steam locomotive. He'd spent long hours on the right-hand seat, watching the water level, checking the boiler-pressure gauge, listening to the exhaust, peering ahead down the track. All his senses served to remind him of the frightful power he held in his gloved hand. In this book, his narrative of the Brotherhood of Locomotive Engineers' push to regulate boilers and the long march to effective federal standards is masterful.

It should be no surprise, then, that this man of action would lead his own crusade for today's safe and sensible regulation of steam locomotive boilers. Bill chaired the Engineering Standards Committee for Steam Locomotives, a group sanctioned by the Federal Railroad Administration to come up with a new framework of rules, regulations, and service intervals for today's tourist-railroad and excursion engines. Bill's colleagues on the task force were a Who's Who of contemporary steam, people with strong personalities and tightly held convictions. Somehow, Bill guided his team through a thicket of debates to reach a point where, in 2000, the FRA was able to adopt a steam policy that reflected the realities of the new millennium, not the 1940s. Later, Union Pacific steam boss Steve Lee, himself no shrinking violet, acknowledged Bill's leadership. "Withuhn is the chairman," said Lee. "He keeps us all honest because he doesn't have an axe to grind."

Author and journalist

Neither did Bill have an axe to grind in his alternate career as a writer. Among all the authors who've attempted to make sense of steam, Bill was probably the best. He had the academic chops, to be sure, as this book and his other books show, but he also had the instincts of a journalist. And it was as a journalist that Bill reached the widest audience in railroading, via his long association with *Trains* magazine. Editor Morgan was one of Bill's many mentors, but he was also a conduit for Bill's restless imagination. The editor liked to provoke, and in Bill he had a kindred spirit.

That relationship blossomed in the June 1974 issue of the magazine, when Bill asked the question, "Did We Scrap Steam Too Soon?" For legions of readers who wanted the answer to be "yes," Bill gave them plenty to think about. His 13-page, 6,000-word story pursued some of the same story lines evident in this book: the last stand of steam on the Norfolk & Western; the quixotic adoption of quick fixes such as poppet valves and the Giesl exhaust; new approaches to coping with dynamic augment. The article was complemented by detailed drawings of exotic "what-if" locomotives derived from Bill's imagination, a series of duplex monsters characterized by multiple sets of drivers, opposed cylinders, and interconnected rod drives. His conclusion: "The future of steam locomotion was unnecessarily aborted."

Bill's restless imagination led to many more bylines in *Trains*. In February 1978, he turned the clock back nearly 25 years when the Southern Railway agreed to his and Morgan's audacious proposal to tack a dynamometer car on the back of leased Texas & Pacific 2-10-4 No. 610 and measure its performance. Bill not only managed the tests on SR's Virginia main line, he also filed a gripping report for the magazine. In 1987, new Editor J. David Ingles dispatched Bill to report from the field on the revival of N&W 2-6-6-4 No. 1218. The resulting article was a showcase for Bill's vivid reportage. In 2000 came a story entitled "Steam, Steel & Safety," Bill's manifesto for creating a new framework for regulating boiler safety. Characteristically, the author soft-pedaled his own contributions and instead focused on other key members of his task force.

The man in the cab

Which brings us to this, Bill's greatest achievement as an author. The fact that it took him more than 30 years to complete it seems fitting, as if the thousands of hours he put into this somehow mirrored the subject of steam itself – constantly evolving, sometimes in fits and starts, occasionally frustrating, always deeply absorbing. What isn't fitting, of course, is the fact that Bill, who passed away on June 29, 2017, isn't here to revel in the finished product. Thank goodness he inspired a team of admirers – led here by the book's editor, Peter A. Hansen – to realize not only his life's vision but also to make a towering contribution to the canon of steam.

A few years ago, I wrote a book about a steam locomotive that figured prominently in my life. I called it *Twelve Twenty-Five: The Life and Times of a Steam Locomotive*, concerning Pere Marquette 2-8-4 No.1225. It was mostly about the successful restoration and operation of a large engine that, for all practical purposes, had been stuck in a park and forgotten. I wanted to tell the story of some intrepid people who brought the 1225 back to life, but I also tried to place the locomotive in the continuum of steam development in the 20th century. For the Foreword, I had only one person in mind.

What Bill wrote for me was perfect. Usually, such an essay would be expected to be serious, sober, and thoughtful, and the scholar in him fulfilled that part of the mission, helping my readers understand 1225 in a larger engineering and industrial context. But the hogger in him also turned the Foreword into something even better, a thrilling, rollicking ride in the cab of a sister Berkshire that was a dead ringer for the 1225. These stories all need red blood, and my guest essayist knew instinctively how to provide it, just as he has in this masterpiece. Bill, I'm honored to return the favor.

Kevin P. Keefe is a Milwaukee-based writer and editor.
He was editor of Trains *magazine, 1992-2000,*
and later served as its publisher.

Acknowledgements

As Bill Withuhn's wife, I recall the origin of this book as coming from a long conversation in Ithaca, N.Y., in the wee hours of a 1970s morning: Bill was mulling his professional educational options if he were to leave Cornell University's PhD program in healthcare policy. The gist was, "If I joined Cornell's PhD program in American History, perhaps the department will let me do a history-of-technology thesis." Of course Bill meant a history of the development of the 20th century steam locomotive. Cornell's history department accepted his application, but Bill never wrote the thesis – at least not in that venue. Instead, after completing the history department's coursework in 1979, Bill saw a notice on a department bulletin board, advertising fellowships at the Smithsonian's National Museum of American History, where Bill never needed an actual PhD. Instead, his extensive number of articles in the railroad press served as his resume, as did his MBA, his work on originating and managing short lines, his congressional staff work on the Regional Rail Reorganization Act of 1973, and, not least, his experience and expertise as a licensed railroad engineer in firing and driving steam locomotives. The Smithsonian fellowship became his job interview for a permanent position at the National Museum of American History.

However, the idea of writing a history of modern American steam locomotives never died. Bill would eventually become Smithsonian's curator of transportation, succeeding John H. "Jack" White, whose 1968 book, *American Locomotives: An Engineering History*, is still the standard reference on locomotives up to 1880. It thus seemed appropriate for Bill to broaden the scope of his proposed manuscript to start where Jack's legendary volume ended.

Knowing that he innately preferred action to solitary, extensive writing, Bill saw to it that his performance objectives for a number of years included chapters in his envisioned engineering/social history of locomotives. But once completed, the drafted chapters remained figuratively and literally in file drawers while Bill pursued projects like installing the permanent exhibit "America on the Move," retrieving Alco PA-1 diesel locomotives from Mexico, and consulting for the National Museum of African American History and Culture in its acquisition and restoration of a Southern Railway Jim Crow coach. Ultimately, with his health failing, Bill realized that he simply had waited too long to finish his book.

However, even in Bill's last days in 2017, I believed that among his admirers and friends were those who would work to bring his manuscript to publication. That faith has been justified fully.

Now, with the posthumous publication of *American Steam Locomotives: Design and Development, 1880-1960*, I acknowledge the many who labored to make Bill's book see the light of day. Among them are Peter A. Hansen and his associates in the Railway & Locomotive Historical Society. Pete has edited the Society's scholarly journal, *Railroad History*, since 2007, and he was instrumental in persuading both the R&LHS and Indiana University Press to participate in publishing this book. Society President Robert Holzweiss took up the cause, seeking approval from his board of directors to assist IUP by funding the editing and layout. Kevin J. Holland, *Railroad History's* design editor, is responsible for the crisp layout you see here; he's among the very best in this specialized business of rail publishing.

Ashley Runyon, the acquisitions editor for IUP's railroads series, believed in the project and was willing to take on a book that was twice the length of most of its other railroad titles.

Others who aided and abetted this publication include Rob McGonigal and Kevin Keefe of Kalmbach Media. Rob edits *Classic Trains*, and he cheerfully allowed Bill and Pete free rein in the magazine's extensive photo archive. Kevin is a former editor of *Trains* and Kalmbach's retired vice president/editorial; he and Bill were friends for decades, and a lot of that regard comes through in Kevin's foreword.

Kurt Bell of the Pennsylvania Historical and Museum Commission located several hard-to-find illustrations, and he also was among the first to read Bill's manuscript and to offer moral support. Jack White and David Oliver, physicist and rail enthusiast, also encouraged Bill to continue rigorously, based on their early readings. Son Harry, from the time he was a teenager to as recently as 2013, transferred computer files several times from operating system to operating system.

Many others shared long conversations with Bill and rooted for his success. Bill conducted several interviews, involving everyone from mechanical engineers to locomotive engineers to patent attorneys, and together, they helped Bill paint a picture of the human striving behind cutting-edge technology. Among the interviews: Lloyd Arkinstall, a former Pennsylvania Railroad locomotive engineer, and the man who taught Bill much of what he learned about firing and running; Ray Delano, a Lima Locomotive Works design engineer, recounted the story of the "Woodard box," as described in Chapter 19; Al Eggerton, a former Southern Railway vice president, shared the perspective from the executive suite on dieselization; Claude Howdyshell, a Chesapeake & Ohio junior mechanical engineer in the 1940s and later the road's chief mechanical officer, provided invaluable information on this company's experimental steam turbine program; Ed King, the recognized guru on Norfolk & Western steam; Julius Kirchhof, who led the design team for the Pennsylvania Railroad's T1 locomotives, peeled back the curtain on the human capital that attended that project; Scott Lindsay, founder of Steam Operations Corp.; Linn Moedinger of the Strasburg Rail Road, who not only shared his knowledge of locomotives, but who recounted his father's experiences as a Pullman Company conductor; James Smith, principal designer of Lima's articulated trailing truck, as related in Chapter 11; Charles Synnestvedt, son of Paul Synnestvedt of Lima's patent-law firm, Synnestvedt & Lechner; Robert F. van der Linden, former chairman of the aeronautics department at the Smithsonian's National Air and Space Museum, for information about the World War II-era transformation in technology and public attitudes about air travel; and George H. Woodard, son of Will Woodard, the driving force behind Lima's Super-Power designs.

Most of these men, like Bill himself, are now deceased, but their legacies will live on through this book. The steam locomotive represents a significant chapter in American history, and each of these men, in his own way, helped to write it.

Gail Withuhn
Burson, Calif., August 2018

Section I: 1880-1920

The Steam Locomotive Comes of Age

RAILROADS DOMINATED LAND TRANSPORTATION in North America for more than 100 years. During the 19th century, transportation costs per mile dropped ten-fold as railroads spread their network across the nation, while the speed of transport increased five and then ten times.[1] At their peak in the early 20th century, railroads employed two million people. In the meantime, almost every job in industry, mining, and agriculture became dependent on the rail distribution system. Enormous wealth was also created, as railroads became the bellwether of the economy. Every community relied on railroads for personal and business travel, for the goods on store shelves, for food on the table, for express shipments, for mail – for the community's physical connections to all the rest of the country. The railroad station was a town's portal to the world.

From 1830 to the mid-1950s, steam powered this indispensable network. In 1920, the midpoint of the period covered in this book, nearly 70,000 steam locomotives rolled in the United States. The railway engine was the preeminent symbol of our national mobility. Lucius Beebe, the popular San Francisco journalist and historian of railroads, wrote in 1955 that "the image of the steam locomotive is engraved in the imagination of every American."

Decades removed from the end of steam, Beebe's words are no longer true. Yet people are still intrigued by human invention. People are also interested in the larger story of technology and its role in the history of industrial and post-industrial society. Therefore I have written for audiences having an interest in technology – but who are not necessarily conversant with either railroading or locomotive development. Clarity for future lay readers is critical, or else this history will soon be lost.

This book is a companion volume to John H. White's now classic 1968 work, *American Locomotives: An Engineering History, 1830-1880*. White covers what he terms the pioneer period of the American locomotive to roughly 1855 and the period of intense development to 1880. The present work treats the phase of rapid maturation from 1880 to 1900, the transitional phase from 1900 to 1920 leading to the "modern" steam locomotive, and the stretching of performance limits through the end of U.S. production in the early 1950s, together with a coda on the final attempts through 1960 to make steam propulsion economically competitive to diesels. An objective of the present book is to render open and accessible, in ordinary language and with sufficient background, the chief concerns and issues that designers faced.

The story is one of invention, of diffusion, and of engineers themselves. People today often have little appreciation beyond lip service that engineers make problematic choices. Decisions affecting all stages of design are rarely so clear-cut as the public often assumes.

As others have said, engineers are human,[2] and they make decisions in a conflicting context of management objectives (designing things for a presumed market, with management objectives well or badly defined), economics (ratios of effectiveness to cost, with imperfect knowledge of either effectiveness as a changing market may define it, or costs), professional goals (how one's work may gain rewards from employers and standing with peers, in the context of engineering practices of the day), and numerous other direct and indirect pressures. Technology and its systems are therefore collectively built, with interacting and formative influences in varying degrees from direct end users, financiers, affected publics, labor, politicians, and many other sectors, all operating within a structure that itself changes.

At the same time, any machine is constrained by limits imposed by physical law. Therefore engineers try to understand materials and the physical, thermal, and chemical processes affecting material properties.

The engineering details are particularly relevant to cracking the ever-present element of *hubris* in all of us. Every generation is, at some level, convinced that it is somehow smarter than those before. We assume that we understand better than past generations, based on accumulated knowledge. The details are a bracing corrective. Only in the details can we appreciate the wisdom that we are no better and no worse than our predecessors in defining design issues and in applying remarkably creative energy and ingenuity to them. To me that is the first responsibility of any historian on any subject: to reveal the subtlety and complexity of issues that confronted the human beings who preceded us. Even if most of those people are anonymous, we understand them more deeply if we grapple a little with the problems they grappled with, in the contexts they faced.

It is always worth remembering that machines are never ends in themselves. They are entirely works made from human thought, conceived by people and crafted by people. If machines are interesting, it is their nature as human conceptions that make them so. In the cases in this book, people created the machines with one central purpose: to provide movement for other people and for their goods, and to do so as economically as possible. Engineering, even when it is engaged in resolving intricate, multi-layered problems – and the reader will find many such episodes in this book – is in service to human goals.

This book tells of people at work, making decisions in context. Along the way, the author hopes, the reader will come to understand the machines as results of those decisions. One may find that, just as an educated "reading the rigging" of a sailing ship can reveal a great deal about a ship's purpose, function, and creation, so also can a reading of the rigging of a locomotive reveal much about its creators, users, and context.

1. G.R. Taylor, *The Transportation Revolution*, Chapter 1.

2. Henry Petroski, *To Engineer is Human: The Role of Failure in Successful Design* (1992).

Entered according to Act of Congress in the year 1871 by the American Bank Note Co. in the Office of the Librarian of Congress at Washin

Chapter 1

High-Wheeled Racers:

The American Standard locomotive at the end of the 19th century

TIMES WERE GOOD IN 1880. The troubles of the previous decade – painful depression capped by the Great Railroad Strike of 1877, the most destructive labor uprising in American history – seemed over. The Baldwin Locomotive Works of Philadelphia, the leading U.S. builder, produced a record 517 engines in 1880, 219 more than in the previous year. Annual locomotive production was an indirect barometer of the economy. Throughout the country, railroads carried the vast bulk of intercity freight – raw materials, manufactured goods, agricultural products. Railroads only bought more locomotives when there was more tonnage for them to pull.[1]

Times were good, too, for locomotive designers. The steam locomotive was by then a reliable, capable machine. Its essential layout of parts and proportions seemed well-established. The adventurous design of previous decades was perhaps over, but the risk that a new engine might not perform as intended had been substantially reduced. The variety of locomotives on American railroads had, in terms of new orders, fairly well settled down to five common types. These included the general-purpose American Standard-type; the Ten-Wheeler for freight and heavy passenger trains; the much less popular Mogul-type for freight and occasional passenger service; and the Consolidation for the heaviest freights. The six-wheel switching locomotive was sorting cars in terminals and yards, supplementing elderly, hand-me-down engines that had been bumped from road to switching use. These five principal types came in all manner of sizes and specific designs, of lesser or greater power and weight.* A smattering of other models, some larger and some smaller as necessary for special kinds of service, rounded out the builders' order books.

The American Standard locomotive of this chapter's title is the 4-4-0, the most popular general type of the 19th century. In the 1880s, engines of this configuration became specialized vehicles for hauling light passenger trains at

This 1873 engraving of an American Standard-type 4-4-0 locomotive, prepared for use by the American Bank Note Co., underscores the ubiquity of this wheel arrangement at the time in the U.S. and its importance to the nation's commerce.

Library of Congress

* Throughout this book, the numerical "Whyte system" of locomotive classification (originated by Frederick M. Whyte of the New York Central) is used where needed. The first digit is the number of pilot or guiding wheels, the second digit is the number of driving wheels, and the third digit is the number of carrying or trailing wheels behind the drivers. Hence the five types in this paragraph are, respectively: 4-4-0, 4-6-0, 2-6-0, 2-8-0, and 0-6-0.

speeds of 60 to 70 mph. Three decades before, designers had come to regard the 4-4-0 layout as inherently stable, with room for an adequate boiler that could be combined with the larger-diameter driving wheels needed for greater speed. By the 1890s, that layout would carry human beings to almost 100 miles per hour for the first time.

In the course of this change, the passenger locomotive rode on the shirttail of the freight. Engines for passenger trains could grow both larger and faster because, on most railroads and in most parts of the country, the railroad infrastructure was pushed by the needs of freight engines and cars, with their heavier total weights. To achieve the highest traction and thus to pull the most revenue-producing lading, a freight locomotive carried as much weight as possible on its driving wheels. Passenger engines did not have to exert as much tractive effort to pull their lighter trains. But as track structure improved, passenger-train speeds could increase. Extra care in rail alignment was needed for high speed, which was not a concern for freight. Since legions of track workers were already employed, however, it was not difficult to insist on better track-alignment standards.

Thus a competitive cycle began in the 1880s and accelerated in the 1890s, as major railroads on similar routes in the same passenger markets vied with one another to field the fastest and most luxurious trains between principal cities.

In 1881, the president of the Master Mechanics' Association commented on freight locomotive design. He observed that, in the mid-1860s,

> ... the recognized standard engine had cylinders 16 by 24 inches, four coupled [*i.e.*, connected] driving-wheels, with a weight of about 30 tons, and from this the standard has been enlarged until we now have cylinders of 20 by 26 inches, eight coupled driving-wheels, with a weight of 50 tons; and these magnificent machines are now in use in all parts of the country where there are heavy grades to overcome for a large traffic.[2]

The statement sounds grand. The reality was that freight trains of the 1870s were slow and usually short, especially when dispatched over hilly districts with grades. For a Mogul, 20 cars would be a sizable train. On level track, which was rare, a 45-ton Consolidation – big for the day – could pull 80-90 cars, or up to about 1,250 tons. On a light grade, however, such an engine might handle 30 to 35 freight cars totaling 500 to 700 tons. The 50-ton behemoth cited by the MMA president was in fact unusual; a few such engines had been built for routes with the steepest grades. In all cases, 10 to 15 miles per hour was a prudent maximum speed.[3] Speed was costly in its wear and tear on rolling stock, and the lack of air brakes and the link-and-pin couplings on freight trains did not permit much speed or train length. Not only was stopping a heavy train difficult, the uncontrolled slack in the couplings could derail its cars during an ordinary attempt to decelerate if speed was too great.

Economic depression held sway from 1873 to 1878. Weak railroads went into receivership. Despite these conditions, new rail mileage and quantities of freight both grew steadily. Since no definitive data exist on railroad freight before 1880, estimates are hazardous. Originated tonnage and ton-mileage (tonnage x distance) rose perhaps three-fold in the 1870s, although from a comparatively tiny base. Traffic fell in 1876 for the biggest Eastern line (the Pennsylvania Railroad), while tonnage on Western carriers was stagnant until the recovery of 1879. Railroads kept up with the traffic by buying a minimum of new locomotives and not retiring older ones. Since rail mileage and tonnage both grew, traffic density per mile of track did not rise dramatically. After 1879, however, freight ton-mileage soared. Railroad mileage also leaped, with 70,000 route-miles added in the 1880s, the peak building decade. Except for the brief recession of 1893-1894, carriage of goods and raw materials expanded at an almost-geometric rate – from 32 billion ton-miles in 1880 to 141 billion in 1900.[4]

As freight trains grew heavier, rails had to be made heavier in cross-section to take the stress, and steel rails (already used by an increasing number of railroads as the 1880s began) replaced iron on main lines.[5] Bridges had to be rebuilt or replaced. Growing traffic, better track structure, heavier freight cars (to increase the load per car and the ratio of lading to tare weight), and larger locomotives all went hand-in-hand in a mutually complementary and accelerating cycle. Air brakes and better couplers for freight trains eventually came, not out of any central concern for safety, but because the greater traffic and longer trains could not be handled otherwise.

Most passenger trains in the 1870s ran no faster than 40 to 45 mph, with five or six cars. Air or vacuum brakes and better couplers on these trains allowed speeds faster than freight, and a few deluxe passenger trains could hit 50 to 60 mph between station stops. Nonetheless, a committee of the MMA assigned in 1880 to investigate locomotives for high-speed passenger service was skeptical about the wisdom of operating such trains faster than 50 mph and concluded:

> While it seems to be a necessity to run passenger trains at high speed, your Committee think [*sic*] it involves increased cost of repairs and requires careful attention on the part of those under whose care this class of engines come, and makes it, as has been said, an expensive luxury.[6]

The mechanical officers reluctantly ceded the necessity of speed to their passenger sales departments, but they doubted the economics. In the meantime, passenger traffic had risen strongly in the 1870s, as shown by the number of passenger cars in use. In that decade, the railroads' fleet increased from 13,000 to 18,400, some 41 percent. From 1880 to 1890, however, the fleet swelled a further 76 percent to 32,400.[7]

With this burgeoning demand, the average size of new locomotives, both freight and passenger, began to grow rapidly in the 1880s. It was not a case of innovators stretching the art, though some innovation attended the growth in size. Designers responded by making locomotives bigger and hence heavier, but they followed design principles found successful in previous years.

The American Standard

This chapter examines three exemplary 4-4-0 designs by three leading engineers. Wilson Eddy, Theodore Ely, and William Buchanan were innovative designers of their day. Eddy served the Western Railroad of Massachusetts and then its successor, the Boston & Albany, from 1840 to 1880.[8] Theodore N. Ely started in 1868 with the Pennsylvania Railroad, and in 1873 became the PRR's superintendent of motive power for its Eastern lines. As the railroad grew, he held various titles that gave him overall charge of the system's locomotives from 1882 to 1911.[9] William Buchanan began on the Albany & Schenectady as a 17-year-old apprentice in 1847, was master mechanic of the Hudson River Railroad in 1859, became system superintendent of motive power of the New York Central & Hudson River Railroad in January 1885, and retired in 1899.[10]

The three locomotives described here were constructed in 1874, 1881, and 1893. An objective of this chapter is to equip the reader to "read the rigging." That is, just as a person skilled in the nautical arts can tell a sailing ship's intended purpose and assess a great deal about the ship's performance from its sail plan and details of masts, spars, and rigging, so can an informed observer interpret the details of a locomotive. The shape and arrangement of each part is not trivial. Each included detail was the result of a severe winnowing over preceding decades.[11]

But a description of details is sterile without the larger, ultimately human context. Each of the locomotives treated in this chapter provides a baseline that ties the state of engineering at the close of the 19th century to the story that follows. The danger in focusing on engineering detail, however, is to relegate designers merely to the status of "problem solvers," working solely in a context of materials and existing practice. Such an interpretation is not enough and would be trivial. Existing design practice always includes a wide range of possibly successful solutions. The core of this book is the story of why and how particular solutions were chosen, in the context – to the extent possible, based on the available evidence – of the engineers themselves. Designers and engineers, after all, make decisions. That means that problems were *not* clear-cut.

Wilson Eddy's engines were famed for reliability, superior fuel economy, and smooth running. Railroaders in New England approvingly dubbed them the "Eddy Clocks." There were two more-or-less standard designs, one for passenger service and one for freight. Eddy supervised their construction in the Springfield, Mass., shops of his railroad, starting in 1852. By 1881, 135 had been built, the last completed a year after Eddy's retirement. Although similar to his earlier engines in many respects, his later engines were larger and heavier. One of the passenger engines – Boston & Albany No. 242, originally the *Crocker* – was delivered in 1874.[12] Its layout of running gear, boiler, and related appliances rewards study.

First, the running gear: pistons, cylinders, valve gear, driving gear, and wheels. The *cylinders* are level, *i.e.*, parallel with the rails. Piston bore and stroke were chosen for the desired tractive force, at the wheels, to be realized from the locomotive's boiler pressure. Wheel diameter was also part of the calculation of tractive force. Because of simple geometry, the larger the wheel, the less the force at the wheel rim. Cylinder dimensions were a standard index to the presumed capacity of a locomotive, and engineers argued frequently about whether a given locomotive was "under-cylindered" or "over-cylindered." The latter term generally meant that an engine could consume more steam at its normal running speeds than the boiler could produce, an embarrassing outcome for a designer. Thus the relations between cylinder size, driving-wheel diameter (since that determined rpm at different speeds), and boiler capacity were central points of concern to both designers and operators.

To transmit piston thrust to the driving wheels, the *crosshead*, *main rod*, and *side rod* are of conventional form, with *wedge* adjustments on the rods to maintain precise alignment of the driving-gear geometry. Driving wheels are fairly large in diameter, marking this as a locomotive for passenger trains. In common with general practice, passenger engines used bigger driving wheels and freight engines used smaller. Although there were no hard-and-fast rules, a

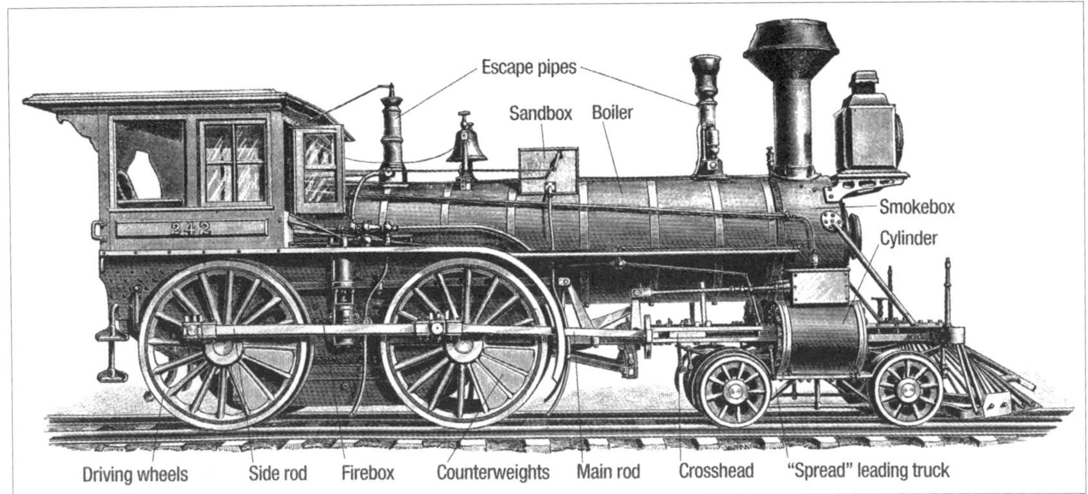

Boston & Albany 4-4-0 No. 242, built at the railroad's Springfield, Mass., shops in 1874, illustrating locomotive design traits favored by Wilson Eddy.

Author's Collection

freighter needed adequate rpm at low speeds to develop its best hauling power. On the other hand, a passenger engine needed to keep rpm within limits at high speed so that machine stresses were not exceeded. The driving-wheel *counterweights* are the "segment" type; note that there is more counterweighting on the first driver on each side, to balance not only the side rod but the back portion of the main rod. The valve gear – the mechanical linkage that operates and times the valve mounted atop each cylinder, providing for steam admission to and exhaust from the cylinder – is the "Stephenson" form of gear used by nearly all engines of the period. The valve itself is a D-type slide valve, and on many of Eddy's engines, this was a balanced valve.

The generous inter-axle distances seen in the No. 242 are a key element of its design. This combination of long wheelbases – the "spread" leading truck together with the separation between the driving axles – was typical by the mid-1850s. More separation between the driving axles accommodated larger fireboxes; more distance from the first pair of drivers to the truck went along with lengthened boilers of higher capacity. As to the spread truck, Eddy helped introduce it.[13] An unexpected payoff of these wheelbase changes was excellent tracking and high stability at all operating speeds – in modern terms, high-quality "train-track dynamics." In the early 1850s, no real theory led to this result; the spread truck was controversial at first. The connection between long wheelbases and running stability, however, was soon recognized. The wheelbase of No. 242's truck is generous.

No. 242's frame, not visible in the engraving above, is unusual. In most contemporary frames, the *top rail* on each side was continuous all the way from the front of the engine to the rear. In contrast, Eddy spliced his frame, just ahead of the front driving wheels. Furthermore, he made the frame's upper and lower rails, between the driving axles, in the form of thin slabs, about one inch thick. These slabs were directly attached to the outside walls of the *firebox* with a large number of tap bolts. This peculiar construction accomplished a number of purposes. First, the spliced connection between front and rear of the frame made frame repairs easier in the event of a collision or serious derailment. Cylinders and front frame could be unbolted and separated from the rest of the locomotive for replacement or realignment. Second, the thin top and bottom rails between the driving axles – combined with underhung springs and equalizers – gave the firebox more lateral room. Eddy's fireboxes were 4 inches to 6½ inches wider than those possible with a conventional frame, gaining grate area and firebox volume for better combustion.

Since the firebox and boiler were firmly attached to the frame at the rear by bolts through the frame rails, Eddy had to deal with boiler expansion in an unconventional way. On most locomotives, the boiler was fixed to the frame at the front, by riveting or bolting, with the back of the boiler carried on the frame's back end via boiler slides or expansion links. These devices allowed for differential expansion between boiler and frame: A boiler "grew" lengthwise (about ¼ to ½ inch in boilers of contemporary size) when fired up from cold. Eddy provided for boiler expansion at the front, in an entirely unorthodox manner. The bottom of the *smokebox* was fixed to a reinforced "arch" of triple-thick iron plate that firmly connected the two cylinders, front frame rails, and smokebox together. The front of the boiler was not rigidly fixed to the smokebox. As in most locomotive boilers, the first boiler course was slightly smaller in diameter than the smokebox; the former fit within the latter. The connection between the two was riveted around the full circumference in conventional construction. In Eddy's design, except for five or six rivets at the very top holding the rear of smokebox onto the boiler, the first boiler course could actually slide within the smokebox.

This joint between boiler and smokebox, not subject to boiler pressure, nevertheless had to be airtight to prevent air from leaking into the smokebox and destroying the locomotive's draft. Therefore the joint was overlaid with a thin iron band held by tap bolts. Surprisingly, this arrangement – despite the sliding action and the obvious flexing stress on the rivets and iron plate joined at the top of the smokebox – apparently gave little trouble in the field. Many of Eddy's engines lasted 40 years.[14]

Other aspects of his boiler design also reflected an independent turn of mind. Most boilers by 1860 were of the "wagon-top" form, so named for the pronounced enlargement in diameter of the boiler over the top of the firebox, compared to the diameter of the boiler courses ahead of the firebox. Eddy believed in a straight boiler, since it was structurally stronger.[15] He also believed that cutting large holes into the boiler shell for a steam *dome* or domes, as well as the connection of the domes to the shell, were sources of weakness. To provide sufficient steam room at the back of the boiler around the firebox, Eddy's straight boilers were larger in diameter by two to four inches at the intermediate courses than similar-sized wagon-top boilers, and tapered slightly toward the front, as each course going forward fit concentrically within the one behind.

In usual practice on most locomotives, the *throttle valve* was placed inside the boiler, up inside a dome. This location, well above the boiler's liquid water, prevented sloshing water from passing through the throttle; entering the *dry pipe*, which carried steam to the cylinders; and thus ruining cylinder lubrication or blowing out a cylinder head. (Incompressible water trapped between a piston and cylinder head after exhaust-port closure could do major damage.) Not liking domes, and feeling he had enough steam room in the boiler without one, Eddy used a perforated dry pipe to collect steam for the cylinders, with a slide-type throttle mounted in the smokebox. This "front-end" throttle was located at the "T" where steam from the drypipe branches to feed the two cylinders. The little oil cup behind the stack seen on No. 242 was to lubricate this throttle. The dry pipe, of copper, was drilled with holes along the tip for its full length (there were no holes along the bottom, to exclude water from entering), giving ample total opening for steam supply. Although Eddy did not invent the perforated dry pipe, he and his contemporary William Mason were the only U.S. designers to use it extensively.[16] In the 20th century, near the end of the steam era, a variation called the slotted dry pipe was used by American Locomotive Co. (Alco) engineer Alfred Bruce in the New York Central 4-8-4 Niagara-type of 1945, one of the most advanced steam locomotives ever built. Bruce's purpose was similar to Eddy's: to provide steam pick-up from the boiler without using a dome. In Bruce's case, a domeless boiler allowed maximum boiler diameter within tight clearance limits of total locomotive height and width. An added benefit, Alco engineers discovered, was less restriction of steam flow into the dry pipe, which helped overall engine performance.

Other Eddy trademarks were the square *sandbox*, supplying the *sand pipe* in front of each front driver, and the two tall *escape pipes*, placed on top of the boiler. The rear one concealed a safety valve, while the front one was a muffled relief valve, manually operated by the engineer in lieu of the safety valve to vent excess boiler pressure at stops. Also visible on No. 242 is an *injector*, to supply feedwater to the boiler from the tender, and a steam-driven *air pump*, to supply compressed air for a Westinghouse air brake system on the tender and coupled passenger cars. Although No. 242 was built in 1874, the illustration of it on page 9 was made in 1891, eleven years after Eddy left the railroad; an injector may not have been original equipment since Eddy favored eccentric-driven pumps for feedwater, and he definitely disliked the Westinghouse air brake, preferring the Smith vacuum brake. No brake shoes are evident for No. 242's own wheels, unremarkable for an engine of the 1870s. There would be brake shoes, however, on 242's tender, so that a "light" engine (*i.e.*, an engine without a train) could be braked.[17]

Eddy advocated a large grate area in the firebox and a generous heating surface in the boiler, the latter including the direct heating surface of *staybolt*-supported firebox sheets and the indirect heating surface of boiler tubes, which together provide the total evaporative surface converting water into steam. Eddy's engines had more heating surface than many 4-4-0s of similar size.

His most controversial design feature was his use of rather short port openings in the valves that admitted and exhausted steam to and from the cylinders. Eddy's were just eight inches long for his freight locomotives and 10 inches long for passenger engines, which ran at higher speeds. In the face of contemporary conventional wisdom, which held that such lengths were

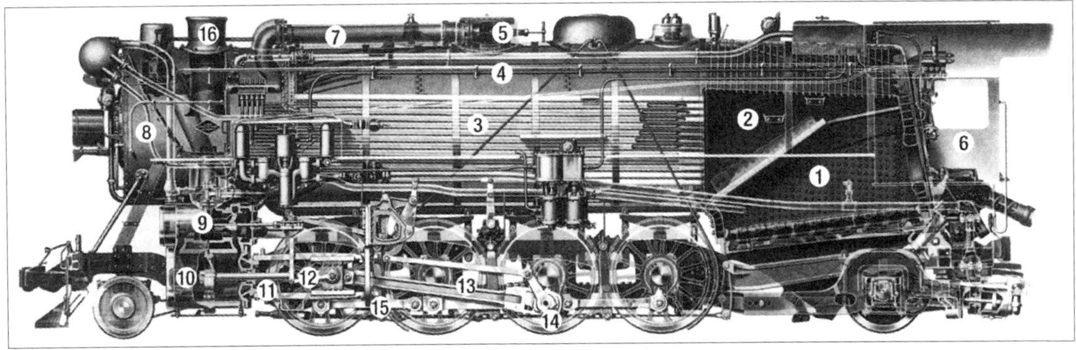

This drawing depicts a 20th century design, but the basic principles of steam locomotives still apply. A fire in the firebox (1) heats the surrounding water (2). The resulting hot gasses pass through the boiler tubes (3), which are also surrounded by water. As the water boils, it rises as steam (4) to the top of the boiler, and to the steam dome (5), which usually houses the throttle, controlled by a lever in the cab (6). The throttle regulates the flow of steam to the dry pipe (7), which conveys the steam to the smokebox (8) and valves (9) on each side of the locomotive. The valve admits steam into the cylinder, where it alternately pushes and pulls a piston (10). Through piston rod (11), crosshead (12), and main rod (13), the reciprocating motion is transmitted to a crankpin (14) on the main driving wheel, converting the reciprocating motion of the piston to the rotating motion of the wheels. The side rod (15) connects all the drivers, enlisting them in the job of turning the wheels. Spent steam is exhausted to the atmosphere through the stack (16).

Author's Collection

small and that large ports gave the least-restricted flow of steam through the valves, Eddy felt that there was an optimal size. His short ports were a bit wider than most, at 1¼ inches, and the travel of his balanced valves was comparatively long, at five to six inches, which gave a quick and sharp port opening. Designers discussed such details endlessly. But without any predictive theory of gas flows, the discussions were always inconclusive.[18]

Eddy was vocal and articulate in his beliefs and, unlike many engineers, he left a rich, first-hand record of his views. He was remarkably inventive, but once he had decided on something, he held to his view with a stubborn rigidity. For example, he resisted using steel in fireboxes, despite the findings of colleagues on other railroads that the type of steel and how it was worked were crucial to success and that well-chosen steel, carefully annealed, gave much-improved firebox longevity. He also felt strongly that vacuum brakes were better for passenger trains than air brakes, though on this point he had some justification. He defended the superiority of the American Standard type for any and all service to the point that most of his peers wondered about his rationality.[19] Revealed in these disputes, however, was the fact that most areas of locomotive design throughout Eddy's time were entirely unsettled, with thoughtful practitioners divided on many such questions.[20]

To understand the question of iron or steel for fireboxes, it is not enough to acknowledge the primitive state of what today we would call metallurgy. One must understand the thermal stress to which a firebox is subjected. Of all the components of a locomotive boiler, the firebox is affected by the most severe and sudden temperature changes. Firing-up from cold is hard enough on a boiler, but varying thermal stress on different parts of the firebox is the rule throughout a day of normal use. The fire, whether of wood or coal, is never entirely even on the grate. And every time the fireman opens the fire door to stoke his fire, an inrush of relatively cold air quickly lowers furnace temperature, which then is made up after the door closes.

Compounding these problems is that of hard water with impurities that hasten formation of deposits called boiler scale on the water side of the boiler shell, tubes, and firebox walls. On the firebox sheets, such deposits cause particularly severe localized stresses and attendant cracking of the plate, since the scale interferes with normal heat flow through the metal. For these reasons, the firebox sheets had to be made of thinner and softer material than the boiler shell, ensuring an adequate degree of flexibility under thermal change. In the 1860s and early 1870s, for example, the Chicago, Burlington & Quincy Railroad used copper for its fireboxes, most roads used iron, and the Illinois Central used iron for firebox crown and flue sheets while using steel for the furnace side and door sheets.[21]

By 1870, however, some railroads were having success with steel from certain mills for making fireboxes. Eddy was not impressed. At the 1872 convention of mechanical officers, Eddy noted that one his peers who had extolled steel a few years previously had just stated an opinion favoring iron in some parts of the firebox when water conditions led to bad scale deposits. Eddy crowed:

> I see he is creeping back a little; not creeping, perhaps, but walking upright, and he is coming round by degrees where I think all roads that have a heavy traffic will soon be – that they will not use any steel for fire-boxes ... I have had considerable experience that way, and I am decidedly opposed to using steel in fire-boxes in any way or shape.[22]

This sort of remark was typical of Eddy – stubborn and verging on *ad hominem*. What his colleague had also said was, "Where you have good water I should say use steel throughout in the whole furnace," and Eddy elsewhere stated that his own experience with "very brittle" steel was with that of only one maker. Other delegates pointed out the obvious – that "We must take into consideration ... that the manufacture of steel only dates back a very short period" and that the methods of working and shaping the metal in the shop greatly affected its qualities of brittleness and strength. Two officers from leading Northeastern railroads concurred that, after long experience with "the best of iron," and with steel from two sources, they felt that "one steel sheet for a crown sheet is worth two iron ones of the best quality" and that "a steel fire-box will ... outwear two made of iron." But every conferee seemed anxious to admit that, in the words of one, "... we all come with different conclusions, with our minds made up" from individual experience. Every conferee save Eddy, who lost his motion to close discussion.[23]

Spirited and inconclusive debate was indeed the rule at such meetings well into the 20th century. The basis for eventual choice in materials or design was empirical: They used what worked. By 1879, the Master Mechanics' Association report on "The Best Material for ... Boilers" concluded that, "Steel is evidently taking the place of iron ... to a greater extent than ever before." Steel was "less liable to furrow, pit, and corrode than iron" and "where, on account of certain impurities in the water used, iron [may be better], yet that fact is not prominently brought out" in reports from the field: "The localities where that seems to be the case [iron reported better] are not numerous or extensive."[24]

Eddy retired a year later. He was made an honorary member of the MMA in 1885 and died in 1898, regarded as one of the great U.S. designers.[25] His most important legacy was his intense interest in the overall economics of locomotive operations. He believed that such economics needed to be fully inclusive of all aspects of capital, maintenance, fuel, labor, and impact on the physical plant, all balanced accurately against the actual work accomplished. Taken together, his stated views showed an early appreciation for cost-benefit analysis – that locomotive costs had to be explicitly analyzed in terms of the revenue they directly produced. He never argued as a theoretician. His impact was in forcefully shaping the ongoing discussion.

Pennsylvania Railroad No. 10

Theodore Ely was never as vocal in public as Eddy. Ely never participated in any of the master mechanics' discussions in the 19th century, and he is rarely cited in the engineering literature. Apparently, as a member of the Pennsylvania Railroad management, he was what that railroad famously demanded: a "company man," loyal, publicly quiet, giving his service exclusively to his employer. Ely's standing among his peers is indicated by the following notice in the leading U.S. railway trade journal upon his 1889 election to membership in the Institution of Civil Engineers, in England:

> American readers do not need to be reminded that it is largely due to Mr. Ely's clear judgment and high mechanical and administrative ability that the mechanical department of the Pennsylvania stands among the very first in the world, and that the Altoona [Pa.] Shops have become a famous training school. The Institution is to be congratulated on its new member.[26]

Pennsylvania Railroad 4-4-0 No. 10, built at the company's Altoona, Pa., shops in 1881.
Author's Collection

Evidently it was the Institution that was honored by Ely's induction rather than the other way around. U.S. authority Angus Sinclair, writing his general history of locomotive development in 1907, highlighted Ely, "whose progressive influence has done so much to make the practice of his department [of motive power] a safe guide for others to follow."[27]

In the spring of 1881, the craftsmen at Altoona constructed a large 4-4-0, one of the biggest conceived to that time. The new American-type was given the railroad's No. 10 and became the prototype for PRR Class K. The engine, less tender, weighed more than 46 tons in working order, that is, with fuel in the firebox and water in the boiler. In comparison, a heavy Consolidation freighter the PRR designed in 1876 weighed about the same. The long-wheelbase No. 10 sported driving wheels a colossal 6' 6" in diameter – a point made visual by the gentleman shown posing in the engine's well-circulated engraving.

Materials were the most advanced for the time: boiler plate and firebox sheets of steel, boiler tubes of wrought iron (for durability under rapid thermal change), and all wheels on the engine and tender made with cast iron centers and steel tires. Boiler pressure was 140 psi. Precedent-shattering for a 4-4-0 was the weight on each driving axle: 16 tons, or 6 tons more per axle than the Consolidation designed just five years before. Making this possible was the fine state of the PRR's mainline track on the Philadelphia-to-New York route for which the K was intended, a line built to one of the finest track-construction standards in the U.S., for the railroad's fastest trains. The 1876 freight engine had been designed for a lesser route. Grate area, a primary determinant of boiler power, was nearly 35 square feet on the K, or 50 percent more than the Consolidation. The difference in grate area, however, was partly based on the different types of coal the two engines burned. The total heating surface of the K's boiler was about the same as the older engine, but the K's boiler put more of that surface in the firebox, with 30 percent more direct heating surface. The increased weight, bigger grate area, and changed ratio of heating surfaces foreshadowed things to come. The K-Class was a benchmark in passenger locomotives, though it was just one of at least 20 distinct 4-4-0 designs on the Pennsylvania, acquired between 1846 and 1910, with many subclasses in addition. [28]

Who played what roles in the creation of No. 10 is no longer recorded. Theodore Ely was then the railroad's superintendent of motive power for the part of the PRR on which the Class K was to be used, and Axel S. Vogt was assistant mechanical engineer. Ely, as presiding locomotive officer, certainly led and approved design, but it is unknown what role he played in creating specifications, or how closely he supervised design decisions. In 1886, Ely was given the formal title of mechanical engineer to signify his clear jurisdiction over all design, apparently in conjunction with the expansion of the PRR's engineering office.[29] Between 1880 and 1882, Alexander Cassatt was first vice-president of the system, and from his formal education in Germany and his first-hand experience in the late 1860s and early 1870s bringing standardization to PRR locomotive design, he always took a keen interest in mechanical engineering issues. Vogt, noted throughout the trade as both theoretician and practical designer, doubtless played a critical part. In contrast to Eddy, both Ely and Vogt worked in a large and highly bureaucratic business enterprise, so that engineering was conducted in a structured manner, with the participation of many staff engineers and draftsmen. (The latter title, through the 1940s, included a lot of detailed problem-solving work assigned today to engineers.)

Using the engraving, one can learn more about No. 10 from reading the rigging. First, the boiler. It is a large wagon-top type, with a less-pronounced change in outer diameter over the firebox, since the forward barrel is also large. (The intermediate barrel course is 50¾ inches in diameter, about the same as on an Eddy straight boiler.) The single large dome contains the throttle valve and a spring-controlled safety valve. The spring to regulate the safety valve is in the cab, below the vertical rod attached to the horizontal actuation lever. The throttle rod, connecting the throttle valve to the engineer's throttle lever, runs in the horizontal tube from the back of the dome at its base through the cab's forward bulkhead. Not seen in the engraving are the firebox's grate bars, which are hollow tubes of heavy section, open to the boiler water at either end, known as water-bar or water grates; the crown-bar support for the firebox crown sheet; and the four expansion links plus two boiler slides supporting the back of the boiler on the frame rails, allowing expansion of the boiler lengthwise from its fully riveted connection at the front on the cylinder saddle. In 1881, all these features were well known.[30]

Water-bar grates helped transfer heat to the boiler water and were successfully used with hard, anthracite coal, which did not burn quite as hot on the grate as bituminous coal. No. 10 was fueled with anthracite – which burned much cleaner than common bituminous – no doubt to minimize smoke. Minimizing smoke was an issue for the upscale clientele that frequented the top-rank trains that the K Class was designed to pull. Anthracite was readily available only from mines in Northeastern Pennsylvania, around Scranton and Hazelton, so it was used on the PRR's New York-Philadelphia corridor only for premier passenger trains. On bituminous-fueled locomotives, water-bar grates were not a success; they warped and burned out from the heat and were difficult to replace.[31]

The type of coal affected firebox design, since anthracite required a larger grate area for the same amount of heat. No. 10's larger grate area, compared to the earlier PRR Consolidation, is partly accounted for by the difference in fuel, because the freight engine burned hotter bituminous. To achieve a wider grate and thus a larger area, No. 10's designers placed its grate entirely above the frame rails, in contrast to most engines, which had their narrower grates down between the frames and rear springs, as seen on Wilson Eddy's No. 242.

Like Eddy's engines, No. 10 also had underhung springs and equalizer, to make room for both the grate and its big ashpan. No. 10's springs are discernible in the engraving, inboard of the drivers and below the axles.

The smokestacks of both No. 242 and No. 10 are tall, to maximize their effect on firebox draft. A fundamental part of any steam locomotive's design was its drafting arrangement. Exhausted steam from the cylinders, directed up an exhaust nozzle in the smokebox and then out the stack, induced a powerful draft through firebox and boiler tubes. The more power required from the locomotive, the wider the throttle opening, the more steam used and exhausted, and the more draft on the fire. It was an elegant feedback loop, basic to any steam locomotive's function since Richard Trevithick's engine of 1804. When properly designed, the exhaust nozzle in the smokebox, combined with the stack, acted like a venturi.

An empirical puzzle for locomotive designers until the end of steam locomotive development was the best configuration of exhaust nozzle and stack. The same lack of predictive theory for gas flows through valves meant that there was no good theory for drafting, either. A tall stack clearly helped, however, like a tall chimney on a fireplace. No. 10's stack is straight, with a decorative cap. No. 242's has a Griggs-type spark deflector at the top to reduce cinders somewhat. Spark-deflecting stacks interfered with draft efficiency but were universal on wood-burners and were used on some coal-burners, too, if fire hazard was high on adjacent rights-of-way. Presumably the mostly rural Boston & Albany had more fire concerns than the Pennsylvania did along its heavily traveled corridors. Though No. 10's anthracite fuel produced far fewer cinders than bituminous coal, the PRR also used straight stacks on its bituminous-fueled engines, as did almost all coal-burning railroads.

No. 10's driver springs are arranged under the engine frame's bottom rail and frame binders. Top and bottom rails connect to the single front rail on both sides by a spliced and bolted connection, very much like Eddy's, but without the slab rails to the rear. The front truck is suspended under the front frame and cylinder saddle on springs and equalizers. It is a rigid-center-type truck, meaning that it can only pivot on its centerplate; no swing links were provided to give a degree of lateral flexibility. The so-called safety truck, with swing links to the truck's bolster or cross-frame, was a well-understood form of truck in 1881.[32] The fact that No. 10's designers did not incorporate such a truck suggests that the K-Class was intended for use only on the broadest curves and long straightaways characteristic of the New York-Philadelphia route.

Another indication that the engine was not intended for sharp curves is that the front pair of drivers is not "blind," or flangeless. Where curves were tight, blind drivers were frequently used on the first pair of drivers of a 4-4-0 (such as Eddy's No. 242 for the curvy Boston & Albany), on the second pair of a Mogul or Ten-Wheeler, and on the second and third pair of a Consolidation.

No. 10 has an early form of the Westinghouse air brake. The required steam-driven air pump is on the left side of the engine, hidden behind the dome in the engraving. The engineer's valve, or "three-way cock" to control the brakes is just visible above the window sill, inside the cab. One can see the air tank – the air-brake system reservoir – lying longitudinally on the engine centerline, just to the rear of the cylinder saddle. The air pump charges the reservoir and maintains it at a set pressure. It is the reservoir that provides the immediate source of compressed air to charge the air-brake line connected to any coupled cars and to operate the engine's own brakes.

The cam-type linkage that operates the engine's brake shoes shows clearly between the driving wheels. The air-brake cylinder for the right-hand side of the locomotive is seen, mounted to the frame, just above the side rod. The piston inside the cylinder moved upward under air pressure to force the shoes against the wheels.

As many authors have pointed out, George Westinghouse did not invent the air brake. In 1869, he patented a form of "straight" air braking. It was simple: Compressed air flowed from the locomotive's air reservoir directly to the brake cylinders throughout the train. The problem was that any leakage anywhere in the air line could lead to a complete loss of braking function. In 1873, Westinghouse worked out his "automatic" air brake, which solved the problem of such brake failure.

The solution was that each car in the train needed a relatively small air reservoir of its own. Additionally, a "triple-valve" was interposed in the air piping of each car. In the automatic system, the line that connected the locomotive and all its coupled cars was kept in a pressurized state. When the locomotive engineer partly vented off, or reduced, the pressure in the line, the triple-valve in each car actuated. The triple-valve then sent compressed air from the car's own reservoir to its brake cylinders, applying the brakes. Any leak in the line resulted in all the brakes on the entire train going on, not off, as on the straight system. In normal operation, the locomotive's reservoir maintained a set pressure in the line and thereby kept each car's reservoir charged and ready for use. The system proved to be extremely reliable and was one of the first truly successful fail-safe devices anywhere in American or European industry, *i.e.*, if it failed, it failed safely.[33]

What is not appreciated by historians is why early forms of the so-called automatic system were hard to control on passenger trains. Applying the brakes smoothly took some skill but was comparatively easy. Once the engineer applied the brakes to his train, however, he had only two more choices: Put on the brakes more strongly, or fully release them. He could not partially release brakes once applied.[34] For passenger trains, that meant that stops at stations were very difficult. The brakes could not be put on too hard because, as the train slowed, wheels would slide. To bring a train down from high speed required a fairly heavy application of short duration, a full release, and then a light application, exquisitely timed so that the train eased to a stop at the right spot at the depot platform. If the last application was a bit too soon or a shade too hard, the engineer could try to work the throttle to partly overcome the braking force, or he had to fully release brakes and try again, usually overshooting the correct spot at the platform or stopping with a jarring abruptness that earned the enmity of travelers.

Following the second of the so-called "Burlington tests" – trials of numerous types of brakes in 1886 and 1887 sponsored by the Master Car Builders Association on the Burlington Route – Westinghouse introduced what he called his quick-action brake. At the same time, he also incorporated a graduated-release feature. But this feature never worked with the kind of fine discrimination characteristic of the system that became the principal alternative to Westinghouse.

The chief rival to the air brake in the mid-1870s was the vacuum brake. Such a system was commercially offered in the U.S. by the Smith & Porter Co., a locomotive builder, starting in late 1872 (the "Smith brake," after its developer, John Y. Smith), and by the Eames Vacuum Brake Co. (the firm of Frederick W. Eames) in 1876. To apply this brake, the locomotive engineer controlled a steam-operated ejector in the cab. The ejector, in turn, partially evacuated air from the line connecting the brake cylinders of the train. A brake cylinder in the Smith brake was in the form of a series of diaphragms with rigid heads; in the Eames, a large cast-iron cup with a rubber diaphragm. As air was drawn from the connected line, atmospheric pressure acted on each brake cylinder, pulling up a linkage to the brake shoes. Like the straight-air brake, a leak degraded or destroyed braking action.

But once applied, a vacuum brake could be partially released, or graduated, at will. The engineer could also ease back on it, to give easy, comfortable, accurate stops. The ejector was a simple apparatus that used a venturi to draw air from the brake line. The system did not need an air pump, which was an expensive item that needed daily maintenance, nor was a reservoir needed for each car. Many locomotive engineers preferred the vacuum brake and, as seen, Wilson Eddy was a partisan. George Westinghouse covered his bets and acquired rights to the Smith brake in about 1875 and offered it under the Westinghouse name along with his air system.[35]

The great advantage of the automatic air brake was its rapid, sure functioning when there was a derailment or a failed coupling that separated cars in the train. The brake's response if an accident occurred was the reason it was called "automatic," not because it was easy to use. The brakes on each separated car, as well as the brakes on the engine and on any cars still coupled, applied immediately at maximum force, as air rushed out of the parted air line. (Hence the Hollywood chestnut of the villain, or hero, uncoupling a car from a moving train without the brakes coming on is nonsense.) In Europe, the vacuum brake and the Westinghouse brake competed over a longer period. In Britain, the vacuum brake was further developed and became a reliable system used there and throughout the Empire.[36]

The Pennsylvania Railroad was one of the first to try air brakes, testing the Westinghouse straight system in September 1869. In 1874, railroads accounting for 57 percent of the route-miles in the U.S. and Canada ran at least some passenger trains with either the straight or automatic air system.[37] About 1878, the automatic brake became a standard part of new locomotives and cars for passenger trains on the PRR and other major carriers. It would take another 15 years, until the passage of the Railway Safety Appliance Act of 1893, before railroads began wide-scale adoption of air brakes on freight trains.

Noteworthy parts of No. 10's running gear are the alligator-type crosshead, the girder-section side rod having non-split bearings without wedge adjustment, and the sector-type counterweights on the driving wheels. Comparison of the engravings on pages 9 and 14 reveals several key differences between No. 10 and Eddy's No. 242. No. 10's crosshead is better suited for stability under high piston thrust than that on Eddy's machine. The simpler bearing at each end of the side rod reduced labor cost a little. Machinery alignment on No. 10 was adjusted by means of the driving-box wedges at the axles and by the wedge adjustment at each end of the main rod. The counterweights on No. 10 are more rational than those on No. 242, placing more of each weight's mass closer to the rim. The counterweight, and thus the wheel, could be lighter for the same balancing effect.

A unique feature of No. 10 is its steam reversing gear, the two small cylinders with associated linkages placed horizontally on the side of the boiler just below the dome. According to a contemporary description, this was the first such installation in the U.S.[38] Locomotives as big and powerful as No. 10 usually had large and heavy valve-gear parts: eccentrics on the first driving axle; eccentric rods connected to Stephenson links; these links were carried by lifting arms, which raised or lowered the links to adjust "valve cutoff," or timing; link blocks and rockers to actuate the valve rods; and a valve rod on each side to move the valve back and forth for each cylinder. Some 20 to 40 horsepower, taken by the eccentrics from the turning of the axle to which they were attached, was consumed in operating the valves. Moving the lifting arms to effect an adjustment of cutoff also took force, and so the lifting arms and the mass attached to them were offset with a counterbalance, usually a spring or a weight.

Basic to running a steam locomotive was adjusting the cutoff. The locomotive engineer adjusted valve cutoff with his reverse lever, which was connected to the lifting arms by a reach rod and intermediate linkage. The reverse lever determined not only whether the engine would go forward or backward, its position also set the timing of the valves when underway in either direction. Precise control of valve timing – the cutoff – was crucial to smooth and economic running. High speed and good economy required a short cutoff, meaning that the engine's valves admitted steam to the cylinders only during a small percentage of each piston stroke. Conversely, low speed required a long cutoff, with steam admitted to the cylinders during a greater percentage of each piston stroke, yielding higher power but at the cost of poor economy. Getting the best in both power and economy demanded continual attention to both throttle and reverse, and to their relationship. A speed change usually required a change to both

On any locomotive but No. 10, adjusting the manual reverse lever (often called the "Johnson bar") while running could be hazardous. The lever was secured in its position by a heavy latch in a toothed quadrant. If the valves were not running smoothly (high friction in the valves causing "kick-back" into the reach rod), or if something broke in the valve gear, the engineer could be thrown when he unlatched the lever from its quadrant. If there were close quarters around the Johnson bar, an engineer could be pinned or seriously injured. (How the Johnson bar got its name is lost in the mists of history, but perhaps it was for the apocryphal engineer who was first maimed by one.) Normally the lever was not hard to move, but good practice was to stand, plant both feet with all parts of one's anatomy away from the arc of the lever, and be ready to move clear if needed.[39]

More-powerful locomotives meant that greater forces could affect an uncontrolled Johnson bar. Clearly needed was an intervening device that would both make the reverse lever easier to move and isolate it from failure of any other part of the valve gear. The steam reversing gear, as seen on No. 10, was an early attempt at a solution. Its operation used differential pressure in the two steam cylinders to adjust cutoff; equilibrium between the cylinders was intended to hold cutoff at its desired setting. Instead of the big, customary lever, the diminutive reverse lever in the cab of No. 10 controlled a valve that acted as a servo.

This reversing gear was apparently not regarded as a success, although No. 10 itself still had the gear in 1895.[40] Ultimately, the air-operated power-reverse gear, introduced around 1912, became virtually universal on U.S. locomotives of all sizes.[41] Probably the same problems that afflicted attempts to develop steam brakes on locomotives in the 1840s applied to the steam reverser: Steam under pressure could be admitted easily enough to a closed cylinder, but once the steam supply was shut off, condensation began and pressure within the cylinder dropped. Holding a steady pressure was impossible without adding more steam. The servo on the steam reversing gear must have oscillated constantly, even when the reverse lever was not moved. Holding the cutoff constant once set – a prerequisite of proper locomotive running – must have been problematic.[42]

Miscellaneous details of No. 10 include its provision for rail-sanding, with sand supply on each side stored in a chamber in the skirt above the first driver. The rod by which the engineer controlled the sand can be seen just above the running board. The cab has been identified as a steel cab by some, probably because of its smooth exterior and rounded corners. As contemporary drawings show, however, it is entirely of wood, as is No. 242's. The two engines share the same basic form of oil headlight.

With its large-diameter driving wheels, the Class K was meant for speed. How fast was that in the early 1880s? For the top trains the Class K pulled on New York-Philadelphia runs, the scheduled average speed was 47 mph, with two stops. That would imply running speeds of 55-60 mph. No. 10 was tested at speeds of up to about 65 mph. Fuel efficiency was better than comparable locomotives. During a week of regular runs in June 1881, No. 10 pulled its trains on 8.32 pounds of coal per car mile.[43] That works out to about 27 pounds per traveler for the 90-mile trip – just 27 pounds of combustible rock for a person to pass at almost a mile a minute between the two biggest cities in America. On such economy was the maturity of the world's Industrial Revolution established.

New York Central No. 999

William Buchanan of the New York Central received more public accolades than the other two designers in this chapter. The Central's locomotive No. 999 hit a claimed speed of 112.5 mph, on a run with four cars in May 1893 from Syracuse to Buffalo in Upstate New York. Proudly, railroad officials then put the engine on display at the World's Columbian Exposition in Chicago. In the massive publicity that followed, probably most adults and every male youngster in the U.S. heard about the engine's world-record run, its locomotive engineer Charlie Hogan, and designer Buchanan. Brand-new No. 999, constructed and numbered especially for the run, then became the star of the fair.[44] The validity of the speed claim is evaluated later in this chapter. First, we can examine its design.

There is little doubt as to the primacy of Buchanan in No. 999's conception. Beginning in 1890, Buchanan supervised the design of a series of large 4-4-0s for his railroad. Called Class I ("Eye"), these 79 engines were all similar, but with small variations. Schenectady Locomotive Works and the railroad's own shops at West Albany, N.Y. and Depew, N.Y. produced them. The initial 1890 model weighed 60 tons and the last, built in 1898-99, 68 tons. Most noticeable were differences among the engines in driving-wheel diameter – some at 70 inches, others 78.[45] Given that these engines all had the same size cylinders and virtually the same boilers – and hence virtually the same horsepower – the great difference in driver size was remarkable.

Designers argued about even minor differences in driver diameter.[46] All else being equal, as it was for the Class I, smaller drivers gave higher tractive effort, both at starting and in the lower part of the engine's speed range. Taller drivers reduced tractive force and power at lower speeds.[47] It was a critical design trade-off that directly impacted daily train operations. A smaller-wheeled engine could start a heavier train and could accelerate better; a taller-wheeled engine was limited in starting ability, had poor acceleration, but could run faster. On the New York Central's famous New York City-to-Buffalo Water Level Route (so-named because it followed the Hudson River to Albany and the Mohawk River valley across the Upstate region), there were few grades. On such a flat profile, the 70-inch-drivered engines could handle any of the scheduled passenger trains on all but the fastest sections of track and, if timetable speeds were not demanding, up to eight or nine cars. The 78-inch-drivered engines could keep the fastest schedules but were limited to five or six cars.[48]

Buchanan's design trademark was his "water-table" firebox.[49] His so-called water table was essentially a water-filled baffle that separated the firebox into upper and lower chambers. Flames from the fire had to pass through the opening at the back of the table. The effect on the combustion pathway was similar to a brick arch.

Starting with the work of Matthew Baird and George Griggs in the 1850s, designers found that an arch constructed of refractory brick, placed in the firebox so as to lengthen the flame path, seemed to improve combustion, reducing smoke and cinders.[50] By the 1880s, it was recognized that an arch significantly reduced fuel loss out the stack, raising combustion efficiency. Later, engineers appreciated that the arch's primary effect was in lengthening the time in which particles of unburned fuel and combustible gas driven off from the fire had opportunity to burn. The so-called "residence time" of fuel in the furnace was increased. What was never appreciated by locomotive designers was the understanding from aerodynamic theory that an arch also produces intense turbulence as combustion gases pass over it. (When any flow of air, or gas, passes around a sharp edge and thus changes direction quickly, a vortex is created.) This turbulence helped combustion go further toward completion.

Buchanan's water table forced the combustion gases through a much smaller passage above the fire than did an arch, which probably increased turbulence in the firebox's upper chamber. The table also added to the direct evaporative heating surface of the firebox, which Buchanan clearly understood. Moreover, as boiler water flowed through the table and was further heated, the rapidity of boiler circulation – the aqueous equivalent of turbulence – was no doubt improved, which speeded evaporation. The downside lay in the construction of the table: the staybolts holding it together were difficult to reach when they needed replacing, and the interior of the table was impossible to clean when boiler scale inevitably built up. While Buchanan was in charge, his type of firebox was used on many New York Central locomotives. His personal influence on design is revealed by the fact that soon after he retired, these fireboxes quickly began disappearing, replaced by conventional furnaces when engines received major overhauls in the railroad's heavy-repair shops.[51]

In many respects, and except for the major increase in weight, Buchanan's 4-4-0 design was quite similar to Ely's Class K of a decade earlier. Note the common features:

- Spliced frames, with angular top rail on No. 999 to accommodate the deeper location of the front of the firebox's foundation ring and grate;
- Placement of the firebox above the frame's top rails for maximum furnace width;
- Wagon-top boilers, with crown-bar support for the crown sheet;
- Steam domes with throttle valve inside, placed over the firebox;
- Straight stacks – appearing deceptively shorter on No. 999 than on No. 10, due to No. 999's larger boiler diameter, but the two engines are only two inches different in total height;
- Cylinders of only slightly different dimension: 18" x 24" for No. 10, 19" x 24" for No. 999;
- Underhung driver springs and equalizers;
- Rigid-center leading trucks.

Note, too, that all three locomotives – Eddy's, Ely's, and Buchanan's – have the Stephenson form of valve gear with slide valves. Valve travel, port openings, and steam passages are slightly more generous on No. 999 than on No. 10. (But compare with Wilson Eddy's practice, previously discussed: No. 999 used 18 x 1¼-inch steam ports and 18 x 2¾-inch exhaust ports – roughly double in size – with a 5¾-inch maximum valve travel, about the same as Eddy. The idea Eddy had of an optimal port size, from his empirical experience, was not borne out in these critical performance dimensions.)

Most of the detail differences between No. 10 and No. 999 seem minor:

- Conventional cast-iron, rocking grates on No. 999 instead of water-bar grates. No. 999 burned bituminous coal instead of anthracite;
- Sand supply located in a sand dome on No. 999;
- Different arrangement of brake rigging, with leading-shoe brakes on No. 999's drivers, and with brakes added to the wheels of No. 999's leading truck. Most of the Class I engines had cam-type brakes on the drivers and no lead-truck brakes, similar to No. 10.

Other differences were more significant. In boiler size, and hence in boiler capacity, the engines vary considerably. Along with the water-table firebox, Buchanan chose a bigger diameter for his boiler: 60⅜ inches at the largest course, compared to 50¾ inches on the K. Inside this greater diameter, Buchanan stuffed 268 boiler tubes, 67 more than the K had. The tubes on No. 999 are also more than one foot longer, since the length of the boiler ahead of the firebox is greater by that amount. The boiler pressure of No. 999, at 190 psi, was 50 psi higher, requiring thicker boiler plate.[52] These factors account for most of the weight difference between the two engines: 62 tons for No. 999, one-third more than No. 10. The enabling condition for this weight increase was, as always, good track structure. By the 1890s, the New York Central and the Pennsylvania vied with one another in setting both civil and mechanical engineering standards, and their great, nationally watched rivalry in attracting customers with faster and more luxurious trains was well underway.[53]

The evaporative heating surface of firebox and tubes on No. 999 is 1,974 square feet, or a comparatively huge 64 percent more than for No. 10. Also important is the larger size of No. 999's boiler at the back end, around the firebox. The back end of No. 999's boiler is even wider than its largest barrel course. The extra foot or so of width around the firebox section on No. 999, along with the firebox being deeper (i.e, having a greater vertical distance between crown sheet and grate), added greatly to furnace volume. Furnace volume is a basic determinant of the limit on combustion rate and hence of boiler power. The other basic determinant of combustion rate is grate area. Surprising to some historians is the comparatively small size of the Class I's grate: just 31 square feet, more than ten percent smaller than No. 10's. The difference is accounted for by fuel type. No. 999 burned much hotter bituminous and so could release more heat into its furnace.[54]

A key determinant of a locomotive's efficiency, both of its boiler and of its cylinders, was its "front end," the locomotive's drafting arrangement. On this point of design, No. 999 and No. 10 differ a good deal. Combustion depends on adequate draft through the firebox and boiler tubes. If drafting is poor, a locomotive has to exert higher back-pressure through its cylinders' exhaust passages in order to generate a given level of draft in the furnace. High back-pressure thus deducts from net piston power to turn the drivers. Conversely, good drafting at lower back-pressure means that net piston power is increased. Thus horsepower generated in the cylinders is increased – for identical levels of draft, combustion rate, and boiler steam production.

No. 10 had a divided steam-exhaust nozzle about four inches in diameter, placed low in the smokebox, with a petticoat pipe (so named for its flared shape), between nozzle and stack. This device was favored by many designers, and it varied somewhat in shape. The petticoat helped channel exhaust steam upward, allowing flue gases to be drawn in at the pipe's open bottom and top. Venturi efficiency was thus increased. No. 999 incorporated an alternative approach. Its steam exhaust nozzles (two 3¼-inch-diameter nozzles in this case) were placed higher in the smokebox. There was no petticoat; instead there was a stack apron, in effect extending the stack partially into the

New York Central 4-4-0 No. 999, built in 1893 and shown soon after construction, was delivered with unusually large 86-inch-diameter driving wheels.

Library of Congress

smokebox. Flue gases were drawn upward through the space between apron and nozzle. Which arrangement worked better was never clear. Many different locomotives with one or the other type of draft apparatus seemed to have equal draft efficiency. In some locomotives, a lot of fiddling was needed to get acceptable results. In engines with a petticoat, adjusting it up or down could equalize the amount of draft through upper and lower boiler tubes. Designers experimented with different steam nozzles. A consistent principle was that a smaller-diameter nozzle increased cylinder back-pressure and a larger nozzle decreased it, but the relation between nozzle size and draft efficiency was not consistent. Dividing the nozzle in different ways or placing the nozzle higher in the smokebox sometimes helped. No. 999's nozzle stand is unusually tall.

Designers probably spent more time discussing the mysteries of drafting than any other topic.[55] There were simply too many variables, each interacting with one or more of the others in too complex a manner: stack size; petticoat vs. apron and their shape; nozzle size, division, shape, and location. The patient, empirical experiments yielded no great improvement, nor did they lead to any clear choice of one arrangement or combination of elements over another.

Since a complete record exists of the materials used in No. 999, the list is wonderfully instructive.[56] This is a much-abbreviated list:

- Boiler and firebox plate: Mild steel. A test piece was cut from each sheet of steel used, to test between 50,000 and 65,000 psi of tensile strength, with not less than 25 percent yield at failure.
- Boiler plate thickness: 9/16-inch for barrel courses, outer shell around the firebox and backhead. Same for front and back tube sheets. Outer throat sheet, 5/8-inch. Dome, ½-inch. Steam dome was insulated with asbestos cement and received a casing of No. 12 sheet iron.
- Firebox plate thickness: Crown sheet, ⅜-inch. Side sheets, door sheet, inner throat sheet, 5/16-inch. Top sheet of water table, 5/16-inch; bottom sheet, 7/16-inch. (Inside width of water spaces, 3 inches at side and back, 4 inches at front.)
- Staybolts and boiler braces: Iron, to test between 50,000 and 65,000 psi ultimate tensile strength, with not less than 30 percent yield at failure, and reduction of the fractured section not to exceed 35 percent. Crown bars were specified to be of "best quality iron," albeit with no particular test given. Staybolts further specified as "Fall's hollow staybolt iron, mandrill rolled, of best quality, 1 in. outside diameter, with a 3/16-in. hole" and "cut with 12 threads per inch ... riveted over at both ends. Hole to be reamed out after riveting."
- Hollow staybolts (each one on No. 999 had its hole all the way through) were a safety feature: A cracked or broken stay leaked water or steam, giving its condition away. A typical engine broke or cracked one or more staybolts every one to three months. Boilermakers then had to replace such stays, generally during an engine's monthly inspection. If two or more adjacent stays cracked or broke, they needed replacing immediately, since the support for that part of the firebox sheet, under boiler pressure, was beginning to fail. Before adoption of the Locomotive Inspection Law in 1911, railroads differed in their practices for timeliness of repair.
- Tubes (also called flues): Of "best-quality steel," with copper "ferrule" at each end to seal the joint between tube and tube sheet.
- Dry pipe: Lap-welded wrought iron.
- Steam and exhaust pipes: Cast iron.
- Boiler insulation, also called lagging: "Asbestos cement." A light metal jacket held the lagging in place and was the visible exterior of the boiler.

- Frames: Of "best hammered iron [*i.e.*, forgings]; main frame in one section with brace welded in." Front frame keyed and bolted to main frame.
- Axle boxes, shoes and wedges: Cast iron. The shoes and adjustable wedges kept the axle boxes in more-or-less accurate alignment fore-and-aft, while allowing vertical motion. The part of the frame in which an axle box is held is called a pedestal, with a pedestal jaw front and rear. For locomotive driving-axle boxes, the term "driving box" was common.
- Driving-axle bearings: Bronze. "3½ parts copper to one of Ajax metal." On No. 999, the lubricant for the driving axles was oil, which was fairly unusual, since most locomotives used grease for driving axles due to the heavy fore-and-aft forces imposed on the drivers by the pistons. Oil was generally used for axles other than driving. The cast iron "cellar," fitted underneath the axle within the bearing box, held the lubricant.
- Springs: Of "best crucible cast steel, oil-tempered." The term "cast" steel here refers to steel rolled from cast ingots, not to steel casting, as would become an important part of locomotive technology after 1900.
- Spring rigging: Equalizers of "best hammered iron," wrought iron fulcrums, "gibs" of steel for fulcrum and hangers.
- Cylinders: Of "close-grained cast iron, as hard as can be worked." Each cylinder and half-saddle cast in one piece. Each cylinder/half-saddle "interchangeable," and "bolted to smokebox and to each other at center, and bolted and keyed to frame." Cylinders lagged (in asbestos), covered in No. 16 sheet iron, and jacketed.
- Pistons: Cast iron. Piston rings of cast iron, made in one piece and turned.
- Piston rods: Cold-rolled iron.
- Valve gear; crosshead guides: Hammered iron. Wearing surfaces case-hardened.
- Lift shaft and lift-shaft brackets: Wrought iron.
- Valves: Of "close-grained hard cast iron."
- Crossheads: Cast steel. Crosshead pin "cast in one piece with crosshead." (Here, "cast" refers to a one-piece, steel casting, the only such application on the engine.) Brass "gibs" (wearing surfaces) held in place with brass rivets.
- Main and side rods: Of "best hammered iron, finished all over." Rods of "I-section." Side rods have lubricant cups "forged solid with rod." Brass bushings, cast of "four parts copper to one of Ajax metal."
- Crank pins: Hammered iron, case hardened.
- All axles: Hammered iron.
- Driving wheels: Wheel centers "cast of the best charcoal iron." Tires of "Midvale steel."
- Engine truck and tender wheels: Cast iron centers with steel tires, without other specification.
- Engine truck: Wrought iron frame, wrought iron pedestals bolted on, cast iron center plate.
- Tender trucks: Wrought iron side frames. Iron bolster of "channel" section, with cast iron end caps and cast iron top and bottom bolster plates. Cast iron journal boxes with malleable iron covers, and brass journal bearings. Cast iron center plates.
- Tender: Frame made of angle iron, "riveted and braced." Two-inch-thick pine flooring over whole top of frame, with one-inch-thick oak flooring in coal space. Top of oak flooring covered in sheet iron. Water tank of ¼-inch sheet iron.
- Bell: Cast of "four parts copper to one of tin."
- Pilot (termed "cowcatcher" by the uninformed): Oak, painted and striped.
- Cab: Black walnut, "substantially built." "Ceiling of alternate ash and black walnut strips." Plate glass in sashes. "Woodwork to be well-rubbed, oiled, and varnished." (Railroads throughout this period employed many carpenters and fine woodworkers for cabs, passenger cars, freight cars, buildings, and bridges.)

No. 999 was elaborately finished and painted. Liberal use was made of Russia iron as a decorative jacketing. (The correct usage here is "Russia," not "Russian.") As historian John H. White Jr. has found, the formulation for this corrosion- and stain-resistant material is lost. The alloy is unknown to modern metallurgy. Apparently, from contemporary descriptions, it was soft gray in color and took a high polish, but with a low, slightly metallic luster. Throughout the 19th century and into the early 20th, it was used by many railroads to mark their finest passenger locomotives. Buchanan specified Russia iron for No. 999's boiler jacketing and the bands holding the jacket in place (it was a New York Central standard to lag and jacket the smokebox as well), the boiler jacketing inside the cab, jacketing around cylinders, around the stack, for the middle of cab handles, for cab brackets, and even for a casing on the boiler check valves.

Both engine and tender were "painted black [where there was no Russia iron jacketing] and varnished, each coat of paint to be well-rubbed before the next one is put on. All stamping and lettering to be done in aluminum leaf."

The locomotive carried an air-brake system for engine and tender, "Westinghouse ... schedule A1, with 9½-in. air pump (dimension referring to the size of the pump, which is located on the right side of the engine) ... and improved equalizing engineer's valve with feed-valve attachment." These terms refer to some of the improvements Westinghouse had made after the 1887 Burlington tests. The engine also has two injectors ("Monitor No. 10 on right-hand side, and No. 9 on left"). In the photograph on page 31, the left-side feedwater delivery pipe, its check valve, and an injector can be seen.

Except for a few features, the New York Central Class I was not significantly advanced in its engineering over the Pennsylvania Railroad's decade-older Class K. The similarities in these two classes reflected a cautious design philosophy, shared by nearly every American railroad locomotive official in the period. The empirical approach that was central to contemporary engineering, in all fields, was of little help in suggesting new approaches. To many designers, making engines bigger in incrementally small steps seemed to be the only reliable avenue toward better. For railroaders in 1893, however, a new approach did seem in the offing. Compound steam expansion in multiple cylinders was beginning to make inroads in locomotive design and production, and that is the subject of a following chapter.

No. 999 was a standard Class I, except in three respects: its degree of finish, its boiler pressure set 10 psi higher than its sisters, and its driving-wheel diameter. That last item raised eyebrows. At 86 inches, No. 999's wheels towered over anything seen in the U.S. for some time, not since the eight-foot drivers of the so-called Crampton engines conceived by Robert Stevens and Isaac Dripps in 1848-49 for the Camden & Amboy and Walter McQueen's seven-foot wheels for a few engines on the Hudson River Railroad in the 1850s. The drivers on No. 999 were only a few inches shy of the 90-inch-diameter drivers on Englishman John Ramsbottom's *Lady of the Lake* class, engines built in the 1860s with a single driving axle, one of which class was shown at the 1893 fair. The wheels on No. 999 were for one purpose: propelling a train for the first time to100 mph.

The fastest regular trains of the day customarily reached speeds between stops of 60-80 mph. But in a steam locomotive running still faster, the ride can

John Ramsbottom's British 2-2-2 engines, such as *Lady of the Lake*, were notable for their 90-inch-diameter driving wheels.

Author's Collection

be rather unsettling for those aboard, even on well-groomed track.[57] Forces do not just rise with speed, they rise geometrically, and stability is a major design concern. Before treating speed, *per se*, we should first consider: How could a 62-ton machine such as No. 999 achieve the necessary vehicular stability?

The secret lies in a trait shared by many 4-4-0 locomotives since Andrew Eastwick's *Hercules* of 1837: their "three-point" suspension. Eastwick's associate George Harrison materially improved on the idea a year later with his equalizer, which White calls "possibly the most important American contribution to locomotive design."[58] The equalizer has been well-appreciated for its function of distributing static loads evenly to all driving wheels, thus ensuring good traction. Less well understood is its essential role at high speed. The 4-4-0 plan, with equalized drivers and a proper truck, may be the ideal form for a steam locomotive to run at extreme velocities.

Many American steam locomotives in the mid-19th century had a three-point suspension, but not all. The comparison to an inherently stable three-legged stool is frequently invoked in the literature, with the lead truck as one leg and the suspended drivers on either side as the other two legs. That image needs critical examination. An early 4-2-0 engine of the 1830s, with the front of the locomotive frame supported on the truck by widely placed side bearings, does not have such a suspension. The truck can swivel, but the truck also provides strong lateral support, either by rollers or by springs suspended to the locomotive frame. Therefore the suspension carries the engine frame on four points: two points on either side at the front, and two points at either side at the back, on the driver springs.

On later 4-2-0s without such strong side support at the truck, the true three-point arrangement began haltingly to emerge. On many 4-4-0s of the

John B. Jervis designed *Brother Jonathan* (1833), the first locomotive with a lead truck, to provide better tracking on poorly built American railroads. The truck's side bearings resulted in four-point suspension.

Author's Collection

1840s and 50s, the four-wheel lead truck still had side bearings. The truck could take vertical irregularities imposed by uneven rails, by either pitching slightly or by means of springs that equalized the truck wheels fore and aft. But as long as there are side bearings or side springs on the truck directly carrying the locomotive frame, the suspension is four-point.[59]

The earliest 4-4-0, patented by Henry R. Campbell in 1836, did not have a three-point suspension; the front truck apparently could not even swivel and the four drivers were separately sprung. With Harrison's equalizer and the later advent of the centerplate truck, that all changed. By the 1870s, a fully developed 4-4-0 had a front truck with freedom to swivel. In trucks with a large centerplate, side bearings were eliminated. In trucks such as those used on No. 10 and No. 999, the truck wheels are equalized, but entirely within the truck frame, and without involving the locomotive frame.

As to the equalizer, one placed between an adjacent pair of driving wheels creates a simple two-wheel bogie, in which the total weight carried by the two drivers is always shared. If the equalizer's fulcrum is in the middle, the two wheels share their total burden equally, no matter whether one wheel is higher or lower in the frame.[60] In fact, in static situations, one wheel will always be higher and the other lower in the frame, if the rail underneath is uneven vertically. Each wheel will still carry the identical load as the other. In a mature 4-4-0, the two drivers on one side are fully equalized in a simple system with one fulcrum, and so are the other two drivers.

The three-legged stool is a static image. An engine at high speed is dynamic. Slight variations in the track become sharp bumps and sideward slams. There is no rubber or pneumatic cushion – the action of the wheels is steel-on-steel. The engine surges, jounces, and leans in the curves. Every wheel is working up and down, just a few inches in each excursion but at a furious rate. Obviously, if the locomotive is not to meet disaster, each wheel and its small flange must follow its rail with near-perfect fidelity. But more: in modern terms, the "L/V ratio" must never exceed a value of one. That is, the lateral force can never exceed the vertical force. Otherwise, even with the wheel in contact, the flange will climb the rail.

We cannot run the No. 999 again and study its behavior. It survived its dash in good order, however, so we can point out a number of interesting aspects of its design. For example, the equalizer between each pair of drivers is long. Therefore the equalizer has a long radius of movement at each end, which helps keeps spring-hanger geometry and axle-box motion straight and true as springs deflect. (No. 10 is also suspended this way. Eddy's equalizer arrangement, on the other hand, is not as direct, since on each side it combines two distinct equalizers, one long and one short. The friction in the system is therefore higher.) No. 999's truck is sprung and equalized fore and aft. The well of its centerplate is 23½ inches in diameter, making for a large bearing surface; there are no side supports at the truck for our 9½-foot-wide, top-heavy vehicle. The rigid-center form of truck has firm side-to-side

In 1836, Henry Campbell designed the first 4-4-0. Three-point suspension would later emerge with the invention of the centerplate lead truck and an equalizer bar to allow the drivers to move up and down independently.
Author's Collection

stability. So might a swing-hanger or centering-rocker form, but in 1893 there was no way to analyze the latter forms to be sure that sideward oscillations did not occur in the centering device at high speed. Intriguingly, No. 999 bears its engine weight almost equally on its three suspension points: 20 tons on the truck and 21 tons on each interconnected driver pair. It's a classic formula for superb weight distribution. Our three-point vehicle also puts one point forward and two aft, like a tricycle. It is no coincidence that modern aircraft use the "tricycle" form of landing gear exclusively; disposing the wheels that way helps ensure longitudinal stability after landing and during roll-out, when aerodynamic stability is reduced.

This analysis is not to suggest that a non-4-4-0 layout cannot provide an excellent high-speed platform. In 1905, when the Pennsylvania Railroad inaugurated an 18-hour schedule between New York and Chicago with its *Pennsylvania Special*, a 4-4-2 Atlantic-type was said to have hit 127 mph on instructions to the locomotive engineer to make up lost time.[61] In 1938, the British 4-6-2 locomotive *Mallard* set the only internationally recognized, fully documented speed record for steam: 126 mph.[62] And there is evidence that the PRR T1 4-4-4-4 of 1942 may have exceeded 130 mph fairly often. The argument is not that only a 4-4-0 can provide stability at speed; rather, that a 4-4-0 configuration has the least complexity, inertia, and friction in its equalization system, so response times for the unsprung weight (*i.e.*, wheels, axle boxes, axles) involved in staying tightly on the rail are minimal, and the locomotive's mass is more evenly divided over its three suspension points than other engine layouts. What is clear enough is that the 4-4-0 type was always noted, with few exceptions, for its fine-riding qualities at any speed.[63]

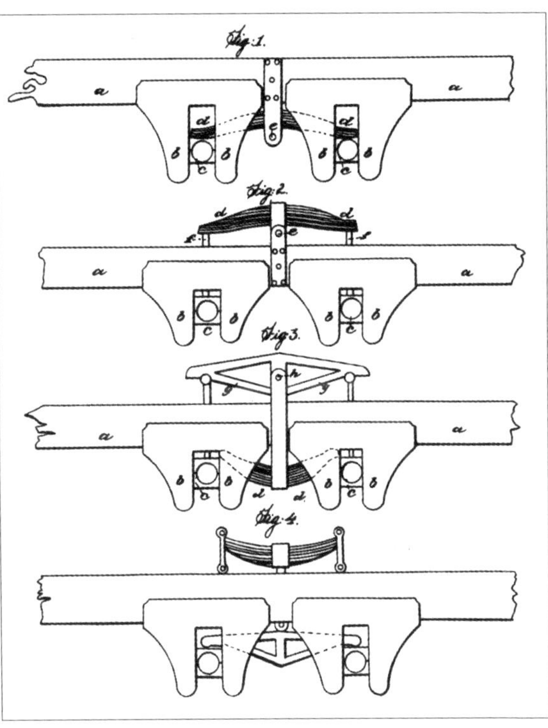

Joseph Harrison patented four designs for driving-wheel equalization in 1838.

Author's Collection

So what is the authenticity of the claim on behalf of No. 999 that is reached 112.5 mph on May 10, 1893, on the straight track west of Batavia, N.Y? Contemporary accounts paint an exciting, dramatic picture.[64] The railroad's officer in charge of passenger sales, George H. Daniels, was a promoter who led the creation in 1891 of the *Empire State Express*, an extra-fast and extra-luxurious train between New York and Buffalo. He was also the creative force behind the *Exposition Flyer* of 1893, inaugurated especially for the World's Columbian Exposition, with a 20-hour New York-Chicago schedule operated in conjunction with the Vanderbilt-controlled Lake Shore & Michigan Southern. The record run was explicitly a high-level publicity stunt for the fair, worked out by Daniels with the full approval of Cornelius Vanderbilt II, head of the Central. Buchanan responded to the idea by overseeing the construction of a special Class I locomotive at the West Albany Shops. One writer says the in-house construction cost was $13,000. Daniels gave the engine its subsequently famous number.

The selection of May 10th was no accident either. That was the well-known date, just 24 years previously, of the Golden Spike ceremony, completing the country's first transcontinental line. Daniels wanted that auspicious day, but he also did not want any early press leaks, so the locomotive was delivered, broken-in, and tested in some secrecy to be certain of its speed. Vice President H. Walter Webb selected senior locomotive engineer Charles H. Hogan and fireman Albert Elliott as crew. They began running their engine on the *Empire State Express* in late April or early May, on the portion of the route west of Syracuse. With the train at its original four cars – diner-coach, two coaches, and a parlor car – Hogan and Elliott are reported to have exceeded 100 mph on May 9. They must have had few doubts, because on May 10, the run was made on a regular train.

A number of railroad officers joined the train, including Webb, who oversaw timing. Other fare-paying passengers apparently joined in. No one considered the notion that ordinary patrons were being put in harm's way for the sake of publicity.

Time measurement is crucial to this story. There was no such thing as a speedometer on a locomotive, calibrated or otherwise. There were no provisions for any external timing for the run: no trip wires or photo-finish cameras set up on measured miles. It was just Webb and a few others with watches, looking out for mileposts. Timing by stopwatch from a moving train is fairly accurate up to 70 mph or so. But after that, mileposts rocket by in a hectic blur. Over a sustained run of several miles, the fact that one may miss a milepost or two is not important; speed calculated over a three- or four-mile interval is more reliable anyway. And if people with different watches take timings on overlapping intervals and compare results, the confidence in the timings is high. Unfortunately for No. 999's speed claim, there is no record that any of this was even intended, let alone done.

The flat, straight trackage selected for the dash to the record was just 14 miles long, which the train covered in less than nine minutes. In that time, people aboard said that the train was doing 90 mph on entering the stretch, accelerated to its top speed, did a mile in 31½ seconds, and immediately decelerated to 80 or so to safely take the curve at the end of the straight. The critical timing was for just a single mile. There was no opportunity to verify timings. As the train accelerated, people shouted out readings. Doubtless several watches caught the fastest mile. How many, if any, were actual stopwatches? That is not documented. How many were simply good pocket watches? How many had sweep second hands, necessary for good timing estimation? High-grade, 21-jewel railroad watches had no stop-second provision and had a tiny second hand on a separate dial. It is very easy to misread a watch by a few seconds on a vibrating railroad car, let alone catch a blurry milepost accurately, over just one mile. A mile at 106 mph is 34 seconds; at 109 mph, 33 seconds; at 112.5 mph, 32 seconds. A two-second error, easy enough to contemplate, is an error of six and a half miles per hour. Webb triumphantly declared the speed to be 112.5 mph. He generously rounded up the "31½ seconds." He was hardly a disinterested observer.

There is a less obvious but more profound basis for doubt. That is the thermal and horsepower capacity of the locomotive itself. It has been argued that No. 999, with the resistance of the train taken into account, simply could

New York Central 4-4-0 No. 999, at Syracuse, N.Y., during its celebrated speed-record attempt on May 10, 1893.

Library of Congress

not have reached speeds much over 100 mph.[65] The assertion is easy to critique. First, the locomotive's cylinder horsepower rating can be calculated from the ratios of heat released at different boiler pressures from tubes and firebox, developed in 1914 by Francis J. Cole, engineer for the American Locomotive Co. These "Cole ratios" became a reliable, standard method to estimate engine performance. Better yet, the methods for calculating locomotive capacity and train resistance, treated in the 1942 text of Ralph Johnson, head of engineering for the Baldwin Locomotive Works, can be applied.[66]

The calculations are thus straighforward. The basis is the evaporative surface of No. 999's boiler, its boiler pressure, and conversion factors for cylinder performance. Resistances of the locomotive and train are based on weights and numbers of axles, and assume level, straight track. We know the cars that it pulled and their weights.[67] Taking into account that No. 999 is a "saturated" (that is, non-superheated) engine, and generously estimating valve and cylinder performance based on the engine's big port openings, it seems clear: Even 100 mph is near the limit of its capacity. The claim of 112.5 is probably out of the question. Available tractive power falls far too rapidly after 85 or 90 mph, and train resistance, which can be accurately computed, steeply climbs.

Knowledgeable commentators on locomotive horsepower computation in later years frequently asserted that the methodology was too conservative. Engines on dynamometer test, it was said, outperformed their estimates, and engines in regular service sometimes seemed to haul tonnages or reach speeds unpredicted by formula. The cylinder horsepower predicted by the Cole ratios was sometimes included on locomotive specification cards and, in a couple of cases known to the author involving late-model 4-8-4 locomotives on the Santa Fe Railway, there is indeed a discrepancy with horsepower found in test. Alfred Bruce, on the other hand, chief steam designer at the American Locomotive Co. in the 1940s, shows that by using the methodology of the time, horsepower estimates and actual test results highly corresponded.[68]

Johnson cautions designers not to trust calculated horsepowers for high rpm. Estimating horsepower at low rpm is reliable, but when an engine "attains speeds exceeding 300 rpm, at which there is considerable throttling of the steam due to restricted cylinder passages, further complicated by the action of the valve, it becomes more difficult."[69] By "throttling," Johnson does not include the locomotive engineer's throttle, which is assumed to be wide open. He is referring to flow restrictions imposed by an engine's steam passages and ports, what designers in Buchanan's time called "wire-drawing" of the steam. Bruce would include all of the sources of drag and restriction at every point downstream of the boiler. No. 999, at an assumed 112.5 mph, would be travelling at 438 rpm. At each piston stroke, exhausting of each cylinder took about .07 seconds or less. At the short cutoff required for such a speed, inlet of steam took about .03 seconds or less. To reliably predict the results of all that was as hard in the 1940s as it was in the 1890s. The only difference in method was the "correction factor" applied, based on accumulated test results.

No. 999 almost surely attained 100 mph. Daniels and Webb had sound basis for believing the attempt would succeed, or otherwise they would never have gone ahead with the engine's special construction, nor with their elaborate plans, with such apparent confidence. In 1892, a train on the Central Railroad of New Jersey had reached 97 mph.[70] Writers have asserted that Buchanan's 78-inch-drivered engines occasionally topped 100 on their regular trains, presumably when engineers had to make up lost time or face the wrath of managers. Perhaps Daniels and Buchanan went forward on such information.

No. 999 lost its special wheels in 1899 and was given 70-inchers. Its boiler pressure was dropped back to 180 psi like the others of its class, and the engine then pulled milk trains and locals in Upstate New York. Today it is exhibited at the Museum of Science & Industry in Chicago, after a careful restoration by J. David Conrad, a leading modern-day steam locomotive mechanic. With the smaller drivers and other changes made over the years by the railroad, its appearance is much different than it was in 1893. An example of an "Eddy Clock" is in St. Louis, at the Museum of Transportation. No Class-K locomotive survives, though a descendent, D16sb-Class 4-4-0 No. 1223, resides at the Railroad Museum of Pennsylvania in Strasburg.

The steam locomotive, a machine that looks so antique today, was once the fleetest human contrivance on the planet. In the late 1930s and through the 1940s, the Milwaukee Road in the Midwest ran steam-powered trains whose daily schedules permitted 120 mph. It is sobering to reflect that, a century after No. 999's claimed speed, the fastest trains in North America were regularly operating at just a few miles an hour faster.

Chapter 1 Notes

1. BLW annual production in *History of the Baldwin Locomotive Works, 1831-1923*, BLW 1923, pp. 181-82. See also Jack Brown, *History of BLW*. For freight traffic growth, 1870s-1900, see John H. White Jr., *The American Railroad Freight Car* (hereafter, *Freight Car*), chapter 1.
2. James Lauder, President's Address to MMA, *Report of Proceedings of the ... American Railway Master Mechanics' Association* (hereafter, *Master Mechanics' Proceedings* or *MM Proceedings*), XIV (1881), pp. 8-9.
3. See *Railroad Gazette*, Jan. 26, 1877, p. 35: performance of BLW 2-8-0 for PRR (exhibited at the 1876 Centennial Exhibition), subsequently used on Philadelphia & Columbia Division with 20 tons per car on 1:132 (.76%) grade. See *MM Proceedings*, IX (1876),

pp. 121, 131, for PRR tests with 2-8-0 on "practically a level division," with 14 tons per car. See discussion of train speeds in White, *Freight Car* (Note 1), pp. 117-20; and in White, *A History of the American Locomotive: Its Development, 1830-1880*, pp. 73-74.

4. White, *Freight Car*, pp. 13-17.
5. Dates of iron-to-steel transition for rails; cf. Sinclair, *Development of the Locomotive Engine* (1907), p. 354. See also *MM Proceedings*, XIV (1881), p. 8, "... steel rails."
6. *MM Proceedings*, XIV (1881), p. 76.
7. White, *The American Railroad Passenger Car*, Table B.1, p. 658.
8. Eddy's career in White, *American Locomotives* (Note 11), pp. 451-52 and pp. 26, 57, 172, 205, and other places; *Locomotive Engineer*, 4:3, March 1891, pp. 41-42; Angus Sinclair (1907, White ed.), pp. 205-09; *Railroad Gazette*, 1888, p. 145; *MM Proceedings*, XVIII, p. 158; *MM Proceedings*, XXXII, p. 304; Railway & Locomotive Historical Society *Bulletin* (R&LHS) No. 22, pp. 9-39.
9. See Jan 26, 1877 *Railroad Gazette*, p. 35; 1881 *Railroad Gazette*, p. 603; 1886 *Railroad Gazette*, p. 220 and p. 549 (appointed ME in Aug 1886); 1889 *Railroad Gazette* p. 169 (Ely then Gen'l Supt of MP, elected to Institution of Civil Engineers, England); 1892 *Railroad Gazette*, pp. 422-23, 445, 849-50; 1893 *Railroad Gazette*, p. 230 (appt'd to "newly created pos'n" of Chief of Motive Power); Alvin F. Staufer, *Pennsy Power*, p. 6: Vogt to ME in 1887, and p. 7: Gibbs to GSMP (Lines East) in 1903; Fry American Society of Mechanical Engineers, Trans. v. 47 (1925), p. 1272: Wallis to GSMP in Jan. 1912 and to Chief of Motive Power in March 1920 ("The greater part of the activity of the Altoona [test] plant has been carried out under J.T. Wallis. ..."); Sinclair (1907, White ed. 1970), pp. 354-55 (called CMP).
10. See Alvin F. Staufer, *NYC's Early Power, v. II, 1831-1916*, pp. 58-63; 1889 *Railroad Gazette*, p. 737: SMP&RS, NYC&HRRR, gold watch for "40 years with the RR, 1849-1889;" 1889 *Railroad Gazette* pp. 528-29, Buchanan firebox to reduce smoke "below 125th St." in dispute with N.Y. Board of Health; 1880 *Railroad Gazette*, p. 261: from SMP, Hudson Div. to SMP Hudson and Harlem Divs.; 1883 *Railroad Gazette*, p. 254, leaves as Cons. Engr to Mexican Nat'l Construction Co.; 1884 *Railroad Gazette*: appt'd SMP of NYC, "eff. 1/1/85" and also in charge of car dep't.
11. For the definitive story of locomotive development in the U.S. before 1880 – design of locomotives and their component parts, as well as production and use – see John H. White, Jr., *American Locomotives: An Engineering History 1830-1880* (Baltimore: Johns Hopkins, 1968); reprinted in 1979 and 1998 as *A History of the American Locomotive: Its Development, 1830-1880* (N.Y.: Dover).
12. Drawing from *Locomotive Engineer*, March 1891, p. 41 (Note 9). (See R&LHS vol. 22; also see White, *American Locomotives*, p. 26, on weights.).
13. White, *American Locomotives*, p. 172.
14. *Locomotive Engineer* (Note 11), pp. 41-42. Also see White, pp. 106, 161, 163.
15. See White, *American Locomotives*, pp. 95-96, for a full discussion of the relative merits of wagon-top vs. straight boilers.
16. *Locomotive Engineer*, p. 41, describes the drypipe "perforated along the top" only. White, pp. 96-97, for history of this idea.
17. See White, *American Locomotives*, p. 184, for discussion of locomotive brakes before 1880.
18. For Eddy's preferences, *MM Proceedings* VII (1874), p. 195; *Locomotive Engineer*, pp. 41-42. For example of an extended discussion by many practitioners of valves, port sizes, etc., see *MM Proceedings* VII (1874), pp. 184-207.
19. For Eddy's views on air vs. vacuum brakes, see *MM Proceedings* V (1872), pp. 124-26, and VII (1874), pp. 267-78. For his views on the superiority of the 4-4-0, see *MM Proceedings* IX (1876), pp. 129-32, 152-54, and see White, *American Locomotives*, pp. 57, 451-52. The test between an Eddy engine and a Rhode Island Locomotive Works Mogul to which White refers on p. 57 appears in *MM Proceedings* IX "Appendix," pp. 177-80. (White's footnotes 19 and 20 on p. 57 refer to the 1876 MMA report, not 1872 as given.) For Eddy's views on steel or iron in fireboxes, see below.
20. The *MM Proceedings* throughout the period are full of reports and extensive recorded discussion on every aspect of locomotive design.
21. *MM Proceedings* V (1872), pp. 28-29. In English practice, copper was favored for fireboxes through the 1930s.
22. Ibid., p. 29.
23. Quotations in Ibid., various places, pp. 28-36, with report and extensive discussion on firebox materials, pp. 17-36.
24. *MM Proceedings* XII (1879), pp. 65-66. See White, *American Locomotives*, pp. 104-05; the PRR had many locomotives with steel fireboxes ten years before this master mechanics' report.

25. *MM Proceedings* XVIII (1885), p. 158. See also 50th wedding anniversary notice in *Railroad Gazette*, 1888, p. 145.
26. *Railroad Gazette*, 1889, p. 169.
27. Sinclair, *Development of the Locomotive Engine* (1907, White ed. 1970), p. 354.
28. *Railroad Gazette*, 1881, pp. 603 (engraving), pp. 616-17 (fold-out section elevation), p. 620 (specs.), p. 625 (performance), pp. 626-29 (half cross-sections), pp. 644-45 (steam reversing gear). PRR Consolidation data and sections in *Railroad Gazette*, Jan. 19, 1877, p. 29 (section elevation) and Jan. 26, 1877, pp. 35-37 (discussion, data, and cross sections).
29. Vogt was made Mechanical Engineer in March 1887 (Staufer, p. 6); Ely was made ME in August 1886 (*Railroad Gazette*, 1886, p. 549).
30. See sectioned views of No. 10. For discussion of the cylinder saddle, as connection between cylinders and front frame (Eddy did not use a saddle), see White, p. 207.
31. For water-bar grates, see White, pp. 108-10, and *MM Proceedings* XXX (1897), pp. 132-33.
32. See White, pp. 173-74. Alba Smith patented the four-wheel, swing-link truck for locomotives in 1862.
33. See *MM Proceedings* VII (1874), "Report of Committee on Continuous Train Brakes," pp. 244-65, esp. 258-61. Also, *Journal of the Franklin Institute*, April 1874. White, *Passenger Car*, pp. 548-57; White, *Freight Car*, pp. 539-46.
34. To understand why this point is true, the following may be helpful:

    In applying the automatic air brake, using the types of engineer's valves found in locomotive cabs from 1873 through the 1950s, the engineer manipulated this valve to vent some pressure from the train's air-line. This action was called "making a reduction," which initiated a brake application throughout the train. Next, to hold his application, the engineer moved his valve to "lap," which sealed off the train air-line at the reduced pressure.

    The triple-valves in the cars in the train were so reliable in operation because they worked exclusively by differential pressure, and that basic feature of their operation is true on the most advanced types used today. Reducing the air-line pressure to less than the pressure in each car's reservoir opened a passage within the triple-valve that let air flow from the car reservoir to the car's brake cylinders. Any further reduction in the train line, followed by lap, let more air flow from the reservoirs to the brake cylinders and resulted in a stronger application throughout the train.

    To release brakes, the engineer moved the engineer's valve to "release," which reconnected the locomotive reservoir to the train air-line, bringing line pressure back up to normal.

    In "release," as soon as the rising air pressure in the line became greater than that in each car's reservoir, the triple-valve let air begin to flow back into the car reservoir. As part of the same action, the triple-valve closed off the connection between car reservoir and brake cylinder and vented the cylinder, fully releasing the brake shoes.

    Even though the Burlington tests focused on brakes for freight trains, Westingthouse developed his graduated-release feature when the only widespread application of his brakes was to passenger trains. The engineer could put his valve to "release" for just a brief time and then return to "lap." The partly restored pressure in the train-line caused a new equilibrium in a modified triple-valve, such that only part of the air in brake cylinders was vented. But the most sophisticated Westinghouse system was never, even in the 20th century, as smooth in operation as a vacuum brake.

    Early applications of Westinghouse brakes to freight trains had graduated release, but in a long string of freight cars, air pressure changes in the train line took time to propagate from car to car. Westinghouse's quick-action system vastly improved the speed with which brakes throughout a long train would come on. But if an engineer used graduated-release ineptly while handling a long train (more than about 50 cars), he could set up a dangerous situation: As car brakes eased off toward the front of the train, cars toward the rear, being delayed in that action and their brakes still on more strongly, could break the train in two. After 1924, graduated-release was dropped from freight-car triple valves but was retained in passenger-car triple valves.
35. White, *Passenger Car*, p. 550.
36. *History of Technology Annual 11*, 1986. Also Ellis, *Railway Carriages in the British Isles.*
37. *MM Proceedings* VII (1874), p. 255.
38. *Railroad Gazette*, 1881, pp. 644-45 (Note 30).
39. Forney; Grimshaw. See also Bruce, p. 204, for hazard of Johnson bar with dry valves, apparently meaning valves that were poorly lubricated and therefore offered high resistance to the valve gear. With slide valves, the balanced valve was much easier to move and therefore took less horsepower to run. The author had two years' experi-

ence running engines (PRR 1223 and "7002") equipped with manual reverse lever, occasionally with mild kick-back.

40. *MM Proceedings* XV (1882), pp. 109, 137-38 on steam reverse gear. For an 1895 photo of No. 10, see Staufer, p. 106. No. 10 was then renumbered to 1066 and given class D6 in the 1895 PRR reclassification (Staufer, p. 103). Note that Staufer's 1883 date for No. 10 is in error.
41. Bruce, p. 205.
42. *MM Proceedings* VII (1874), p. 263. White, p. 184.
43. *Railroad Gazette*, Nov. 11, 1881, p. 625. The figure of 27 pounds of coal per passenger was calculated by assuming a ratio of four coaches to one baggage, mail, express, diner, or other car without sold-seating per train; assuming about 35 passengers per 52-seat coach (PD Class car, 1878-79). Distance of 90 miles x 8.32 lbs. per car-mile x 5 = 3744 lbs. for every five cars. 3744 / 140 pax = 26.7 pounds per traveler.
44. *Railroad Gazette*; *Leslie's Weekly*; New York City, Buffalo, and Chicago newspaper clips on the May 10, 1893 run; Exposition articles.
45. Data from Edson, Staufer, NYC roster. No. 999 data, drawings, and specs from James Dredge, *Record of the Transportation Exhibits at the World's Columbian Exposition of 1893* (London and New York: *Engineering*, and Wiley, 1894), pp. 211-27.
46. See *MM Proceedings* XXI (1888).
47. George Henderson, *Locomotive Operation*; Ralph Johnson, *The Steam Locomotive*; F.F. Bruce, *The Steam Locomotive in America.*
48. Train lengths from NYC public timetables and study of contemporary photographs of NYC trains. There certainly must be exceptions, but no evidence could be found of the 78-inch engines hauling more than six cars on a "name" train of the period.
49. *MM Proceedings* III (1870), p. 46.
50. White, *Locomotive*, pp. 107-08.
51. Staufer, pp. 60, 74.
52. Higher boiler pressure requires stronger boilerplate to contain it. No. 999's steam pressure was set 10 psi higher than all its Class I sisters, but boiler construction, plate thickness, etc., was the same.
53. *Trains* magazine articles on the NYC-PRR rivalry; *Leslie's Weekly* on luxury trains.
54. Comparative heating value, anthracite and Eastern bituminous, in BTU/lb. Heat release from 35 or 31 sq. ft., for total BTU release.
55. For examples of discussion, see *MM Proceedings* reports, extensive discussion, and illustrations of "Draft," "Exhaust Appliances," and/or "Exhaust Nozzles," for nearly every year from 1869 to 1900.
56. Specifications from Dredge, 1894.
57. Canadian National No. 6060, a 4-8-2 built in 1944, sustained 80-85 mph for more than an hour with the author aboard. On good track, the ride was not smooth.
58. White, *American Locomotive*, p. 48.
59. From the literature on suspensions, the swiveling truck, etc., this interpretation of early engine trucks may seem controversial. But the point here is indisputably valid from elementary analysis.
60. White, *American Locomotive*, p. 153.
61. See also Burgess & Kennedy, *Centennial History of the Pennsylvania Railroad Company* (Philadelphia: Pennsylvania Railroad), p. 650.
62. Andrew Dow, "201 km/hr: Mallard Takes the Laurels for Steam," *Railroad History* issue 200; 2009.
63. *Railroad Man's Magazine*; J.J. Thomas, *Fifty Years on the Rail* (New York: 1912).
64. Note 47.
65. New York Central System Historical Society, *Central Headlight*. 1980, vol. 4.
66. F.J. Cole, *Locomotive Ratios*, Alco *Bulletin* 1017, 1914. See also White, in Sinclair (1907, 1970 ed.), p. 669. Ralph P. Johnson, M.E., *The Steam Locomotive in America: Its Theory, Operation and Economics* (N.Y.: Simmons-Boardman), 1942, 2nd ed., 1945, chapters 10 ("Tractive Force"), 11 ("Horsepower"), and 12 ("Resistance.")
67. White, *Passenger Car*, pp. 107, 111; *Engineering News*, Dec. 14, 1893.
68. Alfred Bruce, *The Steam Locomotive in America* (N.Y.: Norton, 1952), pp. 141-44.
69. Johnson, p. 173.
70. Johnson, p. 405.

446
236
446
446
SOUTHERN PACIFIC LINES

Chapter 2

More Wheels and Bigger Fireboxes:

Ten-Wheelers, Moguls, Consolidations, Decapods, Mastodons, and Other Animals in the Bestiary

In 1886, the Northern Pacific Railroad and the Baldwin Locomotive Works announced new title-holders for the "largest locomotives in the United States." NP Nos. 500 and 501 each weighed more than 70 tons. In each, Baldwin design chief William P. Henszey and assistant William L. Austin included ten driving wheels, laid out on a 2-10-0 plan.

Not the first 2-10-0s nor the first by Baldwin, the two new "Decapods" essentially duplicated an engine the firm had produced for Brazil's five-foot-gauge Dom Pedro Segundo Railway the previous year.[1] The design of all three was intended to produce high drawbar-pull on steep grades while spreading weight over five driving axles. Other locomotives would exceed the size of these engines within a few years, yet they illustrate the challenges designers faced in the 1880s in providing locomotives with high tractive power.

Until the 1890s, the 2-10-0 type was extremely rare. The long wheelbase made the Decapods ungainly on railroads with curves of ordinary radii. The 1886 engines were specialized, tailored to a particular situation the Northern Pacific faced. Only completed from St. Paul, Minn., to Tacoma, Wash., in 1883, the NP three years later was building a more direct route across Washington State and over the Cascades. NP's 2-10-0s carried both freight and passenger trains over a series of switchbacks on a temporary line that ascended Washington's Stampede Pass while laborers, including Chinese, dug a nearly two-mile-long tunnel and laid its approaches. The switchback line included a 5.6 percent grade – twice that tolerable on a main route.[2]

A heavy 2-8-0 might have provided the needed drawbar pull, but on NP's temporary track the axle loading would have been high. In addition, ordinarily sized driving wheels – even the smallest diameter that designers normally put on heavy freight engines – would not have given sufficient rpm to maximize power at speeds down to five mph up the grade. Extra-low 45-inch driving wheels allowed a fifth driving axle to be inserted within a reasonable wheelbase, while keeping driver rpm and working piston velocity up to customary minimums at low speed.[3]

The conception of specialized locomotive designs for separate duty in freight, passenger, helper, or switcher service was a relatively new thing in

Southern Pacific Lines 2-6-0 Mogul-type engine No. 446 leads train 236 under a plume of black smoke, probably produced for the benefit of the photographer.
Bruce Wilson, Courtesy Kalmbach Media

ABOVE Northern Pacific 2-10-0 Decapod-type No. 2, illustrating the type's characteristic small-diameter driving wheels, was delivered by Baldwin in 1886 as NP No. 501.
R.V. Nixon, Courtesy Kalmbach Media

RIGHT The Decapod engine built by Baldwin in 1885 for export to Brazil's five-foot-gauge Dom Pedro Segundo Railway.
Railroad Gazette

1870. By 1880, however, design for specific duty was the rule. As the NP 2-10-0 exemplifies, key design parameters of a locomotive – weight per axle, number of driving wheels, diameter of those wheels, rpm, piston speed – were inextricably linked to each other. Matching the boiler to the machinery was also involved. Total weight on the driving wheels determined the adhesive limit for tractive pull, since maximum locomotive pull could not exceed about one-fourth of the weight on drivers, or else the engine simply slipped. Thus, piston size was governed by the maximum usable tractive pull at the adhesive limit and by boiler pressure. Sustainable steam consumption – and thus sustainable power output at working speeds – was determined by piston bore, stroke, driver diameter, working rpm, valve timing, and the boiler's steam generating capacity. Before 1870, most railway traffic could be well handled by a few locomotive types, predominantly the 4-4-0. But as trains became heavier, especially freight trains, different speeds and locomotive outputs became optimal for passengers and freight. As a result, new types emerged.

The Ten-Wheeler

Among the important design departures from the 4-4-0 in American practice were the 4-6-0, the 2-6-0, and the 2-8-0. All three appeared in significant numbers in the 1860s. John H. White Jr. gives their early engineering history in detail. Fitted with a bigger boiler, the 4-6-0 was a rather straightforward extension of its predecessor. The other designs, with two leading wheels instead of four, were distinguished by a different and more complex suspension system. The history of the three types is basic to understanding any of the engineering developments that affected steam locomotion after 1880.

The 4-6-0 "Ten-Wheeler" began as a freight locomotive. The first of its kind in the U.S., made by the Norris Locomotive Works in 1847, pulled coal trains for the Philadelphia & Reading Railroad. The *Chesapeake* could pull trains considerably heavier than was possible with a 4-4-0, with "ease to the rail and bridges."[4] Although its weight on drivers and therefore drawbar pull were greater than a heavy 4-4-0, its driving-axle load was less. The 4-6-0 was rare until after the Civil War period, when traffic growth made the type increasingly popular for freight. As the type grew in size, a primary design difficulty was providing a larger firebox, while also equalizing and springing the two rear-most pairs of driving wheels: Firebox and wheels both competed for the same space at the back of the engine.

The odd spacing of the driving axles – usually more space between the second and third axles than between first and second – allowed for a big enough grate area and, as important, a big enough ashpan. A long equalizer connected the second and third driving wheels on each side. The complete equalization system provided a tripod suspension, on the identical principle as the 4-4-0, as described in Chapter 1. Equalized drivers on one side were one point of suspension, equalized drivers on the other side were the second point, and the lead truck provided the third.[5]

The long distance between first and last drivers relative to the total length of the engine, however, sometimes made it difficult to put adequate weight on the lead truck. As boilers grew larger in the 1880s (especially at the front as forward courses and smokeboxes became larger and hence heavier relative to the rest of the boiler), the weight-distribution problem eventually became moot.

Ten-Wheelers became favored for passenger trains in mountain districts. For level terrain, the type was often used where passenger train length

LEFT Indianapolis & St. Louis Railroad 4-6-0 Ten-Wheeler No. 56 illustrates the type's typically staggered driving-wheel spacing.
Courtesy Kalmbach Media

BELOW Boston & Maine Railroad 4-6-0 Ten-Wheeler No. 175 charges through Salem, Mass., with train 21 in 1900.
Collection of Fred D. Hager, Courtesy Kalmbach Media

exceeded seven or eight cars. By the 1880s, driver diameter became a good indicator of the kind of service for which a particular Ten-Wheeler was intended. For slower speeds, or where grades prevailed, driver diameters for the type in the mid- and late-1880s generally ranged around 52 to 57 inches; for faster speeds in level territory, around 62 to 73 inches. The point is not the diameters, *per se*. The point is that available power output at the speeds a locomotive was designed for was acutely sensitive to driver size. Hence, size was a visible index, well understood in the trade, indicating the usable speed/power range of the engine. The smaller the driver, the higher the torque (tractive effort) at starting and at low speed. More important to the economic capacity of the locomotive was this critical relationship: For locomotives with small drivers, more of a boiler's potential horsepower was available at slower speeds, and conversely, less horsepower was available at higher speeds.

Tied to driver size were cylinder dimensions – piston diameter and stroke. In earlier decades, designers talked often, and sometimes heatedly, about the esoterica of these dimensions. The heat was gone by the 1880s, replaced by the light of straightforward calculation. Other things being equal (*i.e.*, driver size and piston diameter), a longer stroke gave more torque at lower rpm. On a freight engine, a practical location of the crank on the driver was the limiting factor on longer stroke. On a low driving wheel, the crank could be only so close to the rim and still have enough metal around the pin to provide a firm seat so the pin could not work loose. On a passenger engine with large-diameter wheels, locating the crankpin was not an issue. At higher rpm, however, a stroke that was too long reduced torque where a passenger engine needed it – at medium and high speed. In a given engine some designers and railroad officers might prefer a couple of inches more, some might prefer less. As for piston diameter, that was a simple determination made in relation to the other two dimensions (wheel diameter and stroke) and the boiler pressure to give an initial tractive force that did not exceed the adhesion limit of the locomotive – *i.e.*, a tractive effort not much exceeding one-fourth the weight on drivers.

Some locomotives had tractive-effort values that exceeded the normal adhesion limit. Such values were entirely theoretical and designers knew it. Some locomotives were "slippery" – hard to start without spinning the drivers or, far worse, prone to "lose their feet" while climbing a grade – even if they had tractive-effort numbers calculated well within the one-fourth rule. To exceed the rule was risky business.[6]

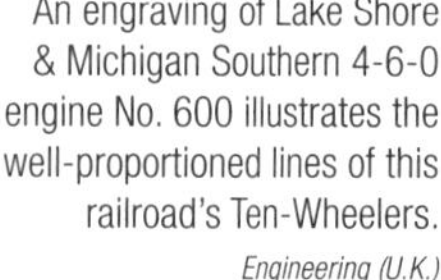
An engraving of Lake Shore & Michigan Southern 4-6-0 engine No. 600 illustrates the well-proportioned lines of this railroad's Ten-Wheelers. *Engineering (U.K.)*

Illinois Central Ten-Wheeler No. 377, on the turntable at Memphis, Tenn., in November 1897, was an identical sister of IC No. 382, made famous in 1900 by its role in the Casey Jones tragedy. Note the unusual clerestory cab roof.
C.W. Witbeck, Courtesy Kalmbach Media

With tall drivers (up to 80 inches in diameter by 1900), the wheels could be evenly spaced, still leaving room for a long firebox and adequate ashpan. The spacing consideration was mostly aesthetic. Surely some of the handsomest passenger locomotives ever to run were the large 4-6-0s of the Lake Shore & Michigan Southern at the turn of the century. A long, clean, and gently curved boiler, gracefully grand and lacy wheels, rakish pilot, and carefully proportioned cab combined to produce an archetypal image that was reproduced or copied many times in children's books and in wide-circulation magazines such as *Harper's* and *Leslie's*.

Perhaps the most famous Ten-Wheeler was associated with John Luther "Casey" Jones, Illinois Central No. 382. Jones lost his life in 1900 when No. 382 and its speeding passenger train ran into the rear of a freight at Vaughan, Miss., that had not cleared a siding. Fireman Sim Webb survived. A few years later, a Tin Pan Alley song with a lilting beat became popular. Had it not been for the song, Casey would have been remembered by few, and only for ignoring prudence and speed limits that night. In the 1920s, Webb related his perspective on the tale into a wire recorder; his recording and the official report on the accident survive. The song lyric got the type of engine wrong, however. It was not a "six-eight wheeler." Writers T. Lawrence Siebert and Eddie Newton needed more syllables, apparently.

The Mogul

If the Ten-Wheeler was a 4-4-0 with an added driving axle, then the 2-6-0 "Mogul," in its general proportion, was a 4-4-0 with a pair of lead-truck wheels changed to drivers. In its total weight, a 2-6-0 with the same axle-load limits could differ from a 4-4-0 only to the extent that the load limit on a driving axle normally exceeded that on a lead axle by several tons. The chief benefit was that a greater percentage of the engine's total weight could be applied to adhesive weight, permitting greater tractive pull from a similarly sized boiler. The 2-6-0 seemed extraordinarily powerful to contemporary observers – hence the name Mogul – but the name was not commonly associated with the specific type until the early 1870s.

The first Moguls could actually be regarded as 0-8-0s with the first axle not driven. In each of these locomotives, originated by designer James Millholland in 1852 for slow freight, the four axles were held in one frame; there was no swiveling front truck. As White describes, this wheel arrangement "overloaded" the first axle.[7] No wonder: The equalization interconnected all four axles. Thus there was no tripod, and hence the first pair of wheels carried about the same load as the other pairs. That, combined with the long wheelbase, meant that the leading wheels, despite any lateral play provided, had to withstand flange-loadings much higher than the other wheels in curves. Wear on the iron rails of the period and on the lead wheels' iron flanges must have been rapid.[8]

The success of the 2-6-0 depended on controlling the weight on the lead truck. Just letting it swivel was not enough. The whole point of a lead truck, either four-wheel or two-wheel, was to guide a locomotive into curves and to ease flange-loading on the first pair of drivers. If the lead truck remained independent of the rest of the suspension, enough weight could never be placed on it, relative to the rest of the locomotive, for the truck to function properly. The tripod principle was the key. Levi Bissell invented a two-wheel truck in 1857. His early form of truck, however, which was not equalized with any of the rest of the wheels, derailed often enough to discourage its wide use. Designers John Laird and John Whetstone worked on better forms, attempting to equalize the truck with the first driver pair.[9]

In 1863-1864, William S. Hudson made the essential improvement: a direct equalization of the lead truck with the first drivers, using a longitudinal beam on a fulcrum with a transverse equalizer connecting the front driver springs.[10] The longitudinal beam distributed weight fore-and-aft between the front truck and the first driver springs; the location of the fulcrum determined the distribution. The transverse (or "cross") equalizer is a crucial element. The cross-equalizer pivoted on a floating fulcrum connected to the rear end of the longitudinal beam, distributing its share of the weight equally to the right driver and to the left driver. Note that if the engine rocked slightly from side to side, the weight carried on the forward end of each front driver spring stayed the same. Another crucial feature was the *separation* of the equalization of the front drivers and truck from the rest of the drivers' equalization. The truck was no longer independent; the weight upon it and the weight upon the first pair of drivers was now distributed by an interconnected set of equalizers. But that system was independent of the equalization of the other drivers. Thus, the familiar tripod was again created. The front truck and driver pair, with equalizers connecting them both longitudinally and transversely, formed one point of suspension. The other equalized drivers on each side (with no transverse equalization) provided the other two points.[11]

Swing links, adapted in 1862 by Alba Smith from similar devices for car trucks patented two decades before, could be incorporated into either four-wheel or two-wheel lead trucks. The principle was simple: In traditional truck

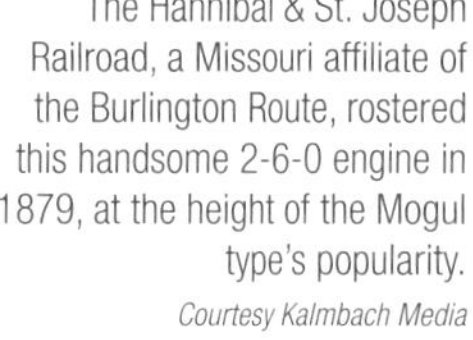
The Hannibal & St. Joseph Railroad, a Missouri affiliate of the Burlington Route, rostered this handsome 2-6-0 engine in 1879, at the height of the Mogul type's popularity.
Courtesy Kalmbach Media

designs, a transverse bolster was bolted to the truck sideframes, a design that magnified shocks from switches and rough trackwork, owing to its lateral rigidity. Swing links were a simple solution: The bolster was attached to a new component called the swing plank, on which springs were mounted to dampen the lateral motion. Swing links or similar centering devices caused a lead truck to resist lateral deflection and continually to seek its position at the centerline of the engine. This action greatly increased the stability of a locomotive running on straight track. In curves, the truck's resistance to lateral deflection pulled the rest of the locomotive around. On curves, centering devices increased flange forces on lead-truck wheels. The *radial* deflection of either a four-wheel or well-designed two-wheel truck, which kept the truck axles at right angles to the rail on curves, as well as the lower axle loading of trucks compared to drivers, kept actual flange wear low. Although Bissell is credited with an early two-wheel truck and with the self-centering idea, his name became associated with the mature form of equalized two-wheel truck actually perfected by Hudson. The truck's center-post – which moves vertically but not laterally and makes the connection between the swing links or centering rockers, the bolster, and the longitudinal equalizer – was commonly called the "Bissell post," or sometimes "bissell."[12]

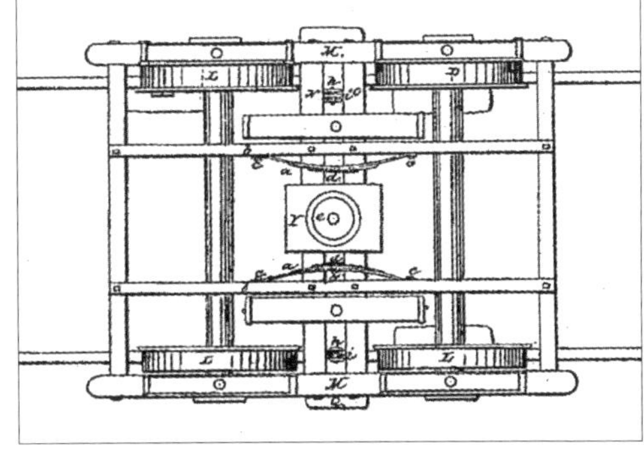

This drawing of a four-wheel truck from United States Patent No. 2071 illustrates how swing planks and their springs provided the bolster with a degree of cushioning from lateral shocks.
United States Patent Office

With Hudson's equalized truck, Moguls gained a better reputation, and by the 1870s various manufacturers were turning them out in greater numbers, though fewer than either 4-4-0s or 4-6-0s. Moguls hauled freight in the 1860s and '70s, and in the latter decade were tried in passenger service. Compared to a 4-4-0, a Mogul could start a train up to 50 percent heavier and keep it moving at lower speeds. But since a Mogul could weigh only several tons more than a comparable heavy 4-4-0, the Mogul's boiler could be only marginally larger. Therefore, at higher speed, the steam production needed to keep the heavier train rolling could exceed boiler capacity.[13] The 4-6-0, which had the same number of axles for tractive effort as a 2-6-0 and another axle by which to spread the weight of a substantially bigger boiler than a 4-4-0, proved to be more successful as a passenger engine than the Mogul. In freight duty, the 2-8-0 eventually eclipsed the 2-6-0. Built in declining numbers by the 1880s, Moguls pulled freight trains in territory without major grades or served as principal freight engines on smaller railroads or shortlines. After the turn of the century, Moguls became rare except on a few secondary lines.

The Consolidation

The first 2-8-0 may have been John Laird's adaptation of an old flexible-beam locomotive about 1864. The true progenitor was Alexander Mitchell's justly famous *Consolidation* of 1866. Incorporating the equalized lead truck, three-point suspension, a generous boiler with a proportionally large firebox (to burn anthracite coal), including a 26¼-square-foot grate and a modest combustion chamber to provide good furnace volume, Mitchell's design was precedent-setting in many ways. The locomotive went into service just as the Lehigh Valley and the Lehigh & Mahanoy railroads merged. The name, *Consolidation*, referred to the merger.

That name stayed with the type, the first to be used almost exclusively in freight duty throughout its history. Produced into the 1940s, more than 33,000 were constructed in the U.S., out of a total of some 180,000 steam locomotives made in this country from the 1830s through the 1950s. The Consolidation, or "Consolidated," or "Consol," became the most numerous type of all.[14] As with the Ten-Wheeler and the Mogul, the main design problem of the Consolidation-type was providing a larger firebox as total weight and boiler size of locomotives increased. In 1900, the limit of the relatively narrow firebox for bituminous coal, with the firebox's foundation ring and grate placed above the locomotive frame but between the driving wheels, was reached in the Bessemer & Lake Erie 2-8-0s. Compared to *Consolidation's* 43 tons, B&LE C3A-class 2-8-0s weighed 125 tons, not counting tenders. At starting, they exerted 63,829 lbs. of tractive effort. These locomotives were the latest "world's largest" when built by the Pittsburgh Locomotive and Car Works – just before that company's participation in the Alco merger of 1901.[15] It was the height of the "drag freight" era, and in service each of the engines plodded at an average of 8-10 mph, pulling 25-car iron-ore trains from Conneaut, Ohio, on Lake Erie, to U.S. Steel plants in Pittsburgh, then returning north with coal trains. The enormous boiler, with 3,800 square feet of evaporative surface, was supported by only 37 square feet of grate. Without the hottest, freely burning bituminous coal thickly spread in the firebox, the drag speed, and a skillful fireman, the steam consumption rate of the cylinders would have far outstripped the ability of the maximum combustion rate to stay in balance with power demand.

American designers tried to enlarge fireboxes in creative ways at least as early as 1847, when Ross Winans began devising boiler configurations that led to his amazing coal-burning "Camels," so named because the engineer's cab sat astride the boiler. Many of his contemporaries and later practitioners struggled within the limits imposed by frame and wheel widths, wheel locations, and weight distribution of boiler and engine in stretching the size of fireboxes. It is important to understand that the context for these efforts was anthracite coal. Before 1860, anthracite was much more popular for coal-burners in the East than bituminous, due to anthracite's ready availability. Wood was the most common fuel. In the Midwest, bituminous coal made important inroads during and after the Civil War as mines increased output. Many Northeastern railroads adopted anthracite, based primarily on close proximity to supply.

In the period after 1880, the most influential designer of enlarged fireboxes was John E. Wootten of the Philadelphia & Reading. He had been an assistant

Alexander Mitchell.

Mitchell's *Consolidation* of 1866 gave its name to the 2-8-0 wheel arrangement.
Courtesy Kalmbach Media

A Baldwin product of 1882, Burlington Route 2-8-0 engine No. 1420 was photographed at Galesburg, Ill., in 1900.

L.E. Griffith, Courtesy Kalmbach Media

Representing a later generation of 2-8-0 designs, Union Pacific Consolidation No. 619, a 1908 graduate of Alco's Brooks Works, simmers at Banks, Idaho, in 1941.

Henry R. Griffiths, Courtesy Kalmbach Media

to James Millholland, succeeding the latter as superintendent of locomotives in 1866. Wootten absorbed his mentor's views on the importance of bigger fireboxes as essential to greater locomotive power. By the mid-1870s it was apparent to Wootten and others that if ever-larger locomotives were to continue to use slow-burning anthracite, firebox sizes had to expand dramatically in order to produce the needed heat.

Contrary to many secondary assertions, anthracite does not have a much lower heating value than bituminous. In BTUs per pound, Eastern bituminous ranges from 12,500 to 14,500, depending on the mine. Anthracite burns more slowly, more cleanly (it is low in "volatile matter"), and it is comparatively high in ash. Most importantly for successful burning, as all designers recognized, anthracite requires a low stoking rate per square-foot of grate. That is, for the same total heat release in a given time, about the same amount of coal must be added to the firebox, but spread out over a bigger area. And a big ashpan needs to be included.

The far smokier but quicker-burning bituminous became, in the 1870s, increasingly competitive in price per BTU as the nation's appetite for energy soared in all sectors of the economy. In the meantime, vast amounts of culm – a fine-screened waste product left over from coal that was sized for home heating – surrounded every anthracite mine. These commercially undesirable leavings might be had cheaply for locomotive fuel if anyone could figure out how to burn them. The culm heaps represented a cost-saving opportunity for the railroads that directly served these mines, including the Central Railroad of New Jersey; the Delaware & Hudson; the Delaware, Lackawanna & Western; the Lehigh Valley; and the Reading. Wootten's long-term contribution was to design locomotives with markedly bigger furnaces in proportion to the rest of the boiler. As engineers only later discovered, the path to improved combustion efficiency in locomotive boilers – with any fuel – lay in making that *proportional* change. Wootten's invention preceded better science.

As usual, the inventor had help from prior art. Millholland, long before, had designed a locomotive with a firebox above the frame, increasing its width. Zerah Colburn, while consulting engineer for the New Jersey Locomotive & Machine Co., participated in designing and building a locomotive for the Lackawanna with a 90-inch wide firebox (much wider than the distance between the wheels on a standard-gauge engine) and 45 square feet of grate area, in 1856.[16] Wootten, trying to burn fuel of the consistency of rough sand and fine particles which could clump on the grate and choke off all air, had to experiment also with grate design, the percentage of air opening through the grate (which needed to be quite small, commensurate with the slow burning), and draft. He found that a practical stoking rate per square foot of grate had to be even lower than with lump anthracite. His final firebox arrangement used a level grate spanning over the locomotive frame with a total furnace width externally of almost nine feet, close to the clearance limit. In application, that width meant placing the grate in a new location: high, above the driving wheels.

After 1877, the year of Wootten's patent, his firebox was adapted for both passenger and freight engines, with most use on the latter. In the 1870s and

RIGHT Winans *Louisiana* was a "Camel"-configuration 0-8-0 designed to burn culm coal. *Courtesy Kalmbach Media*

BELOW Central of New Jersey 2-8-0 No. 680's distinctive "camelback" configuration, with its cab straddling the boiler ahead of the Wootten firebox, was dictated by the vast grate area needed for combustion of slow-burning anthracite coal. *Edward H. Weber, Courtesy Kalmbach Media*

Delaware & Hudson 2-8-0 engine No. 1119 exhibits the characteristic flared sides of the Wootten firebox, designed for optimum combustion of the anthracite coal favored by D&H and some neighboring railroads.
Jim Shaughnessy, Courtesy Kalmbach Media

through the 1880s, a favorite driving-wheel diameter for freighters that operated where there were any sustained grades was around 50 inches; such a low driver height facilitated putting a Wootten firebox entirely over the drivers. On passenger engines, with tall drivers, there was less vertical room and so less combustion space above the firebed. On a 4-4-0 or 4-6-0, however, the firebox was immense in relation to the remainder of the boiler. With adjustments to grates and draft, such engines could burn culm or regular anthracite. A more pressing problem was created, though. Now there was no room at the back of the boiler for a cab. The primary difficulty was not the width of the firebox but the extreme rear-end overhang.

No matter. Put the engineer's cab in front of the firebox, astride the boiler. As in Winan's old Camels, the fireman could shovel from a position at the front of the tender.

The 2-8-0 type was well suited to the Wootten firebox. A 2-8-0 on any fuel needed a big boiler. A culm-burner just needed a proportionally larger furnace and a lot of combustion space. (Not only the big firebox marked culm as the fuel. The big canopy over the tender coal space was not so much to shelter the fireman as to shelter the coal. Any significant amount of rain turned culm into a black mud incapable of being fired.) The anthracite roads ordered 2-8-0 camelbacks for heavy freight from various builders that were virtual copies of one another's designs. Elsewhere, on every major railroad throughout the country, the conventional end-cab Consolidation became a standard freight locomotive.

Wootten's firebox was later adapted to burn standard-grade anthracite instead of culm. Wootten's furnace design could provide the much greater total heat release needed for ample steam supply and even more-powerful boilers in new locomotives. By the 1890s, larger freighters and passenger engines fueled on anthracite incorporated Wootten fireboxes. On bigger passenger locomotives, the tall drivers reduced furnace volume, which (not appreciated at the time) reduced potential power.[17] For premier trains catering to upscale riders, the nearly smokeless anthracite was preferred. In dense urban areas on the East Coast, for all passenger trains, smoke abatement was already a political issue and railroads were threatened with smoke ordinances, either real or proposed. (To cite perhaps the most noted example, steam engines were outlawed on Manhattan's Park Avenue approaches to Grand Central Station, effective in 1908.) Wootten's firebox would be forever associated with anthracite burning. Yet, later in the 20th century, it would show the way to better furnace efficiency and greater capacity with any kind of fuel.

The Decapod and variants

Alexander Mitchell did not stop with *Consolidation* in 1866. The next year, Pennsylvania's Lancaster Locomotive Works built the *Ant* and the *Bee* to Mitchell's ideas, the first 2-10-0s, or "Decapods," in the U.S. With rails and tires of the time made of iron, flange wear on the first and last driving wheels must have been rapid, given the 2-10-0s' relatively long wheelbase. Reverse movement was also a problem on sharp curves. Sixteen years after its introduction, the *Bee* had its last driver pair removed, and trailing wheels were substituted, apparently in the form of a truck.[18]

Quite independent of Mitchell and of each other, the Philadelphia & Reading and the Jefferson, Madison & Indianapolis developed an 0-12-0 and an 0-10-0 in 1863 and 1868, respectively, for pusher duty; they were not reproduced. Baldwin's Henszey and Austin worked out an 0-10-0 for the St. Clair Tunnel Co. (part of the Grand Trunk Railway) in 1891. It was 23 tons heavier than one of the Northern Pacific Decapods, and four of them were delivered.[19] All these engines, without lead trucks, were intended for special use at extremely slow speed. Engines for road use without lead trucks were never popular in the U.S. after the 1850s because of alleged poor tracking and high driver flange wear at any speed over 10 mph. The 2-10-0-type became a preferred pusher locomotive in the 1890s, until the Mallet came to the U.S. in 1904-1906.

A type that had a brief tenure in the 1880s and 1890s for pulling the heaviest freight trains on main lines was the 4-8-0 "Twelve-Wheeler" or "Mastodon." The truck's primary contribution to the type was to permit a locomotive that was three to five tons heavier than a Consolidation. The Lehigh Valley tried one of the first Twelve-Wheelers in 1869-1870. The Rhode Island Locomotive Works made some for the Atlantic & Pacific in 1881. More were built the following year by Lehigh Valley and by Central Pacific under the direction of Master Mechanic Andrew Stevens. At CP's Sacramento (Calif.) Shops a short time later, Stevens made a 4-10-0 called *El Gobernador*. The CP 4-8-0s were successful; the 4-10-0 was not repeated. When compound-expansion locomotives began appearing in the late 1880s and early 1890s the 4-8-0 layout turned out to be ideal for accommodating the greater weight of Vauclain or cross-compound cylinders. As compounding in single-unit locomotives went out of fashion between 1905 and 1910, 4-8-0 production ended.[20]

With locomotives of every wheel arrangement growing larger, designers other than Wootten worked on ideas for different firebox arrangements. Baldwin introduced a modification of the wagon-top boiler, a variation the firm called an "extended crown," in 1887. What was actually extended was the roof sheet. The dome was now ahead of the crown sheet instead of over it. Moving the dome forward made sense in a long boiler, created more steam space near the dome and, most importantly, allowed the abandonment of the "crown bar" form of firebox construction. (Refer to illustrations of Ely's No. 10 and Buchanan's No. 999 in Chapter 1.) With the dome out of the way, direct radial stays could connect roof and crown, dispensing with the intermediate crown bars.[21] As well as providing less complicated crown sheet support, routine inspection by boilermakers and roundhouse inspectors was facilitated: hammer tests of all the crown stays could be made from inside the firebox, without having to remove the dome cap to inspect the crown bars (which, like every waterside surface around the firebox, were usually covered by boiler scale).

George Strong was master mechanic for the Lehigh Valley Railroad in 1886. He adapted the large-flue design of the Scottish marine boiler, thus making one of the rare attempts after 1830 to borrow marine practice for use in a locomotive. Rolling sheet steel into corrugated shapes for strength was becoming more common, and Strong thought he could take advantage of such shapes to eliminate staybolts altogether. His boiler incorporated two large cylindrical flues as fireboxes for anthracite, a generous combustion chamber, and a section with standard, small-diameter tubes. Ash clean-out was a definite problem. Before a locomotive's departure, lump anthracite was built up into a deep, thick fire within the twin flues-fireboxes. On the road, draft was gentle, and the fireman added coal to maintain the thick firebed.

Strong claimed that the contraction of the large flues and combustion chamber when the boiler was cooled down for the customary regular boiler washes would loosen boiler scale (a sort of self-cleaning action) and that the firebox-flues, because of their shape, would be far more resistant to failure in a low-water situation that would normally cause a boiler to explode. According to contemporary accounts, three such locomotives worked (at least part of the time) more or less well for a couple of years.[22] The lack of anything close to the needed amount of grate area to burn sufficient coal for the power output typical of a locomotive, and the restricted passages for air under the twin fires, doomed the design to eventual failure, regardless of any other attributes. Scottish marine boilers were fired at much lower combustion rates. The prestigious engineer and writer Angus Sinclair later derided Strong's idea as "a good illustration of what an amateur will do when he undertakes to design a locomotive."[23]

One thing worth marking for subsequent history came out of Strong's experiments. The first locomotive with his boiler design, Lehigh Valley No. 444, called the *Duplex* for its twin fireboxes, was built to a new wheel arrangement. Though about the size of a large Ten-Wheeler, it needed another axle to support the extended rear end. Thus the 444 of 1886 was built as a genuine 4-6-2; the trailing axle was no afterthought. Baldwin's later claim in 1901 notwithstanding, the failed Lehigh Valley

TOP Philadelphia & Reading's 0-12-0 engine of 1863 was built for pusher service.
Railroad Gazette

MIDDLE Jefferson, Madison & Indianapolis 0-10-0 engine *Reuben Wells*, built in 1868.
Engineering

BOTTOM Designed by Andrew Stevens, Central Pacific 4-8-0 engine No. 229 was built at the railroad's Sacramento Shops.
Railroad Gazette

locomotive was the first of the "Pacific" type – the most important steam locomotive type for passenger trains in the 20th century.[24]

The Belpaire firebox

A firebox development of long-lasting influence throughout the railroad engineering community came before Wootten or Strong, and it came from Europe. Alfred Belpaire worked for the state railway of his native Belgium after earning a degree at one of France's outstanding technical schools, Arts et Métiers. In 1860, he had been with the railway 20 years and was engineering head of locomotives and cars.

As Wootten did later, Belpaire considered how to burn cheaper fuel. In Belpaire's case, the cheaper fuel was the lower-BTU coal available within Belgium, as opposed to the better coal that had to be imported. Belpaire found that he needed an enlarged grate area to burn the poorer coal effectively. His first successful firebox arrangement combined a clever grate design to control air flow, a greater firebox width, and a revised system of staybolting to hold firebox and boiler sheets together. From 1861, new locomotives for the Belgian railway came with these changes, cutting fuel bills significantly. Three years later, Belpaire changed the design to create his hallmark.[25]

The new, "square" shape of the firebox hid insights into both boiler maintenance and stress. The straight connection of staybolts to inner and outer sheets was the most important feature. A flat crown and roof, together with fully parallel alignment of large portions of inner and outer side sheets, meant that most stays could be installed at a true 90 degrees to the sheet areas being supported against boiler pressure. Accurate calculation of stress was therefore easier; there was no angularity to alter a straight-line pull on each stay.[26] A minor consideration was that most of the stays – especially the long crown stays – could be made in a few standard lengths instead of cut in a welter of lengths. More important perhaps to long-term maintenance was that, according to engineers who believed in Belpaire's ideas, mechanical stresses were more consistent throughout the firebox as it withstood temperature and pressure variations in normal service, with little or no flexing of the stays.[27]

In the 1860s, there was nothing to separate Belpaire's firebox from standard forms as to thermal performance. His design succeeded in burning the poorer coal simply because he made the grate area bigger and the box wider, not because he shaped it differently. Compared to standard fireboxes in the 1870s and 1880s of similar grate width and area, Belpaire's shape gave a little more furnace volume and significantly more steam space above the crownsheet. Some railroads, attracted by the claims of better distribution of

Great Northern acquired Belpaire-equipped locomotives, such as 2-8-2 No. 3391, until the 1930s. By that time, the Pennsylvania Railroad was the only other American adherent of the Belpaire firebox.
Collection of N.F. Priebe, Courtesy Kalmbach Media

With its characteristic squared shoulders, Alfred Belpaire's firebox design was widely adopted in Great Britain, as in these examples of London, Midland & Scottish Railway 4-6-2 Pacific-type No. 6252, *City of Leicester*, and Southern Railway 4-6-0 engine No. 864, *Martin Frobisher*.

Both, Courtesy Kalmbach Media

thermal/mechanical stress, tried the design on their own coal, which was usually better than the Belgian, and found combustion performance to be excellent. To some locomotive designers, the slightly bigger furnace volume and bigger steam space seemed to boost the evaporative power of the boiler somewhat. Because there were always so many other variables affecting any comparisons (*e.g.*, size and types of locomotives, weight and speed of trains), no definitive conclusion could be drawn.

By the 1880s a few railroads in Europe had adopted the Belpaire firebox as their own standard, attracted by claims of slightly cheaper long-term maintenance and reinforced by their own satisfactory experience. In the U.S., the earliest major convert was the Pennsylvania Railroad. Superintendent of motive power Theodore Ely, who followed developments in engineering internationally and who had introduced the Class K in 1881, was apparently convinced of the virtues of the square firebox. In 1885 he approved a design made under the supervision of the railroad's mechanical engineer, John B. Collin, for a new 2-8-0 Consolidation incorporating the Belpaire.[28] The rationale for its adoption is unclear. Compared to earlier PRR 2-8-0s, mainstays of the railroad's freight operations, the new R-class enlarged the grate from 23 square feet to 31, raised boiler pressure 15 psi to 140, and increased engine weight 25 percent to 57 tons – all unremarkable and cautious changes. The engine was about average for new Consolidations then being made for principal railroads.

After extensive shakedown of a prototype, Ely must have been pleased. Altoona shopmen constructed a few more in 1886 and, from 1888, produced 161 with an additional 10 psi in boiler pressure and minor revisions to the firebox's shape. The R-class became the railroad's standard freighter. The Belpaire subsequently became a recognized trademark of Pennsylvania Railroad engineering practice from the late 1880s until Altoona stopped building steam engines in 1946.[29]

Elsewhere on U.S. railroads, the "foreign" firebox sparked endless contention among engineers. They were more expensive in initial price compared to normal construction, some said, which was true. Others said that claims of maintenance advantages or better thermal performance remained unproven, which was also true. The argument was never resolved. With capital goods as expensive as locomotives, no one could ever afford a controlled field test. For railroads that bought their engines from commercial manufacturers, and therefore paid the builders' overheads, the initial-cost disadvantage was likely persuasive, especially when other economic claims were controversial. A comparative handful of PRR locomotives, notably some passenger-engine classes designed in 1899-1901, reverted to radial-stayed fireboxes – again, for reasons that are unclear. But two of those classes were redesigned in 1902, when their production resumed, to include the Belpaire. Clearly, PRR management was convinced.

Throughout the 1890s and into the new century, the Pennsylvania continued in its reputation as having the most "scientific" locomotive engineering department of any railroad in America. Ely and supervising mechanical engineer Axel Vogt were universally admired. Yet the PRR's embrace of the Belpaire furnace was duplicated by few other U.S. railroads. The Great Northern, which was also a pioneer in compound-expansion locomotives, became the second-largest U.S. railroad to make the Belpaire a standard. GN managers showed off locomotives with such fireboxes in four wheel-types at the World's Columbian Exposition in 1893. The Burlington, the Norfolk & Western, and the Lake Shore also displayed Belpaire-equipped engines. Illinois Central purchased several such classes. Other than the PRR, however, only Great Northern persisted with the design, building or buying such engines into the 1930s.

Alfred Belpaire became president of the Belgian State Railways in 1893. He saw his invention used extensively in France, Great Britain, and several other countries. George Churchward of England's Great Western Railway, other British designers, Alfred de Glehn of the Société Alsacienne locomotive works in France, Vatslav Lopushinskii of the Soviet Railway, and André Chapelon of the Paris-Orleans and French National Railways, among other leading engineers, became strong proponents. Belpaire's innovation serves, however, to illustrate yet again that some engineering ideas can never be sorted out objectively, even something so seemingly straightforward as the shape of a boiler.

Coal vs. oil

The Pennsylvania Railroad's science made another contribution to railroad economics in the late 1880s – but it was a contribution that would affect railroads on the other side of the country, in the Southwest. Charles B. Dudley, the PRR's chief chemist, conducted experiments in 1887 burning light crude oil as locomotive fuel. Dudley's work gave the rough heating equivalence of crude oil to good coal (1 pound of oil equaled 1¾ pounds of coal) and demonstrated that oil could be a practical fuel without alteration of boiler and firebox proportions.[30]

Ten years before, PRR and John D. Rockefeller's Standard Oil Co. had waged a battle over carriage of petroleum from Pennsylvania fields, involving a company associated with the PRR, the Empire Transportation Co. Empire owned cars and oil-field facilities; the railroad used Empire's cars. When Empire acquired two refineries, thus threatening Rockefeller's business, he diverted all his oil traffic off the PRR. Standard Oil won the war when the railroad, to get its traffic back, was forced to buy out Empire and sell its refineries and pipelines to Standard. Rockefeller ended up with a monopoly on all of the infrastructure that brought petroleum out of the western Pennsylvania fields to transshipping points. (In those days, all long-distance movement of crude oil to refineries and refined products to market was dependent on rail.) Thereafter, Rockefeller enforced a "pool," which guaranteed PRR its traffic in return for exclusive "commissions" (*i.e.*, private kickbacks) to Standard.[31] The railroad and Standard Oil did not have an arms-length relationship: The PRR might keep in Rockefeller's better graces by becoming a customer itself, and thus, the experiments in oil as a locomotive fuel. Dudley's work was not done, as is sometimes assumed by railway historians, for scientific reasons.

In the East, light crude or "bunker" oil from refineries was much too expensive per BTU compared to coal.[32] In the far West and Southwest, however, there was greater potential for oil to compete with coal as Western oil fields began opening in the 1890s. The Southern Pacific was dependent on mines near Coalinga, Calif. The Santa Fe had access to good Midwestern coal in the eastern part of its system, but in the Southwest its bituminous coal supplies came from northwestern New Mexico and northeastern Arizona, with near-lignite – a low-BTU fuel – from mines near Gallup.[33] SP and Santa Fe both began experimenting with oil as a steam locomotive fuel in the late 1890s.

Developing a workable burner was tricky. Light crude oil could be light indeed, but it also tended to thicken below 70 degrees Fahrenheit, becoming molasses-like below 45 degrees. In response, engineering staff put steam-heat lines into locomotive oil bunkers. Spraying the fuel into fireboxes depended on atomization by some means, and the most dependable source for the needed atomizing pressure was steam from the boiler. If air were the source, a far greater continuous volume of air would be needed than any practical compressor could supply. Engineers tried many different burner designs.

Thomas Urquhart, an engineer supervising locomotives for a Russian railway that ran through oil fields in the Caucasus region, converted many engines to oil in the early 1880s.[34] A system developed by James Holden in the 1890s for Britain's Great Eastern Railway combined two burners, each spraying a thick grade of oil by means of a steam jet into a firebox that was also fired occasionally on coal. The objective of this dual-fuel system was smoke abatement, and the locomotive could continue to function if the burners clogged.[35] Neither of the burner designs worked reliably on crude or bunker oil available in the U.S.

On the Santa Fe and on the SP, the best designs atomized the oil by mixing the fuel into a steam jet. The advantage of this idea was much-reduced susceptibility of the burner to clogging from foreign matter or uneven oil-viscosity. With either set-up, though, a final pre-heating of the oil was advantageous, just before the oil entered the burner, to keep viscosity within a narrow range. None of these arrangements was perfected until after 1900.

Meanwhile, locomotive designers quickly perceived that conventional grates were no longer needed with oil as fuel. In fact, no grate was needed at all, just one or more air dampers. The Southern Pacific, after communicating with Cornelius Vanderbilt II of the New York Central, elected to try Vanderbilt's new boiler concept. His plan was based on Strong's failed furnace idea of 1886. In the new design, one large cylindrical firebox was supported inside the boiler proper, behind a bank of conventional tubes.[36] Good proportionate ratios among furnace volume, evaporative surfaces of firebox and tubes, and boiler size seemed to be observed, except that furnace volume was actually far less than normal.

SP tried several Vanderbilt-boilered locomotives in 1900-1901. They quickly developed insurmountable problems. The firebox, expanding under heat, worked against the tubes, causing innumerable leaks. Despite claims about the "Morrison suspension tube" form of corrugations (different in form from Strong's), the corrugations cracked. As designers soon found, heat from an oil burner could be intense locally against firebox sheets, and average heat within the box could vary much more quickly with oil than with coal, since a fireman – even a careful one – regulated the fuel rate in response to power demand. Expansion-induced leakage problems also doomed Vanderbilt-boilered coal burners on the New York Central and the Baltimore & Ohio.

John Player.
Kansas State Historical Society

John Player, superintendent of machinery on the Santa Fe from 1890 through 1901, tried another sort of tubular firebox. Baldwin delivered a Vauclain compound-expansion 2-8-0 to Santa Fe in 1901 with this radically different furnace. Player's boiler included three separate tubular chambers as fireboxes, each refractory-lined. Each chamber had a burner and a "bridge wall" – a deflector – to take the brunt of the heat from the burner. A combustion chamber made the transition between the three large firebox tubes and a bank of conventional, small-diameter tubes. No. 824 actually ran in service many years, until 1937, when it was rebuilt to an 0-8-0 switcher with a boiler from another engine. The firebox apparently was retained when San Bernardino Shop machinists rebuilt the cylinders in 1909. Crews in the 1920s and '30s called the engine "Mt. Pelee," after a Martinique volcano that erupted in 1902, for its burner's idiosyncracies. It was never duplicated, and a severe shortage of furnace volume surely hampered its performance. Player retired in 1902 but kept active as a consultant and in affairs of the railroad Master Mechanics' Association.

The three decades leading up to the end of the 19th century were remarkably inventive times for American railroads. Some inventions survived the crucible – sustained, demanding service at maximum thermal and mechanical load, in conditions of incredible dirt and grit, compounded by indifferent maintenance. Others inventions fell short. More innovation and more testing in the crucible were to come.

Chapter 2 Notes

1. *Railway Age Gazette*; *History of the Baldwin Locomotive Works, 1831-1923*, pp. 79-80; Inspection of photos shows the identical design of the Dom Pedro Segundo engine and the NP engines; all had 45-inch-diameter drivers and 22x26-inch cylinders. In 1881, BLW built two three-foot-gauge 2-10-0s for the Nacionales Mexicanos, according to BLW Construction Lists.
2. Charles R. Wood, *The Northern Pacific: Main Street of the Northwest* (Seattle: Superior, 1968), pp. 71-81. (Note drawing on p. 80 showing the 2-10-0s and a train on a switchback.)
3. Discussion in George R. Henderson, *Locomotive Operation* (1904, 1907), a popular engineering text by a well-known Baldwin engineer.
4. White, p. 58
5. Discussions on weight distribution in *Report of the Proceedings of the American Railway Master Mechanics' Association*. (The number of driving-wheel equalizing levers on each side does not affect the "tripod" principle; cf. White, top of p. 62.)
6. Henderson, *Locomotive Operation*, chapters 4 ("Slipping") and 7 ("Hauling Capacity"). On the adhesion limit, p. 276.

7. White, pp. 62-63.
8. The Pennsylvania Railroad's 1855 alteration of the design to a 4-6-0 (White, p. 63) not only provided some radial freedom to the leading wheels, it spread flange-loading over four wheels instead of two.
9. White, pp. 62, 174.
10. Ibid., plus. pp. 434-35.
11. Johnson, chapter 19, "Distribution of Locomotive Weight," has a full discussion.
12. As White notes (pp. 174-75), the use of both four-wheel and two-wheel trucks with centering devices increased after 1880, when the attempts of the Locomotive Engine Safety Truck Co. to claim infringement of its patents by any variation on the ideas of Hudson, Bissell, and Smith were resolved in court.
13. These comparisons are valid, of course, if axle-load limits for drivers and for truck axles are kept constant. If axle loadings increase, all locomotive types can be larger, heavier, and have bigger boilers.
14. White, pp. 65-66, 427-36. Locomotive production figures from Bruce, pp. 46-47, 287. The "180,000" total is corrected from Bruce's total (p. 47), because of an undercount of approximately 11,000 in Baldwin's production, as annotated by White from BLW Construction Lists, plus 20th century plant numbers through 1950.
15. Alco was the result of a 1901 merger of eight builders: Brooks Locomotive Works (Dunkirk, N.Y.), Cooke Locomotive & Machine Works (Paterson, N.J.), Dickson Manufacturing Co. (Scranton, Pa.), Manchester Locomotive Works (Manchester, N.H.), Pittsburgh Locomotive & Car Works (Pittsburg, Pa.), Rhode Island Locomotive Works (Providence, R.I.), Richmond Locomotive & Machine Works (Richmond, Va.), and Schenectady Locomotive Works (Schenectady, N.Y.). The resulting company had sufficient scale to take on the Baldwin Locomotive Works, and Baldwin and Alco would dominate U.S. locomotive production until the end of steam.
16. Sinclair, *Development of the Locomotive Engine* (1907, 1970), pp. 303-04; White, pp. 106, 110, 451.
17. Bruce, pp. 143, 175. See also E.L. Diamond, *Horsepower of Locomotives*, and C.A. Brandt, *Design and Proportion of Locomotive Boilers and Superheaters.*
18. Sinclair, pp. 316, 322. White, p. 456.
19. BLW 1923 *History*, p. 83. The St. Clair engines were bi-directional tank engines, used up heavy grades and through a 6,000-ft tunnel.
20. Bruce, pp. 288-89; and E.D. Worley, "Iron Horses of the Santa Fe Trail," pp. 154-155.
21. See Bruce, pp. 145, 148 on crown bars.
22. J.N. Westwood, *Locomotive Designers in the Age of Steam* (London: Sedgwick & Jackson, 1977), p. 253; *The Engineer*, Sept 13, 1889; R&LHS *Bulletin* 97.
23. Sinclair, p. 322. Cf. Bruce, pp. 149, 151; "firebox volume" was not the problem but, as Bruce says, "sufficient grate area."
24. Sinclair, p. 320, Fig. 142. Despite all the later debate by historians about which locomotive was the first Pacific, it is clear that the Lehigh Valley engine fulfills the definitional attribute: a separate trailing axle, behind the drivers, supporting an enlarged firebox. Cf. *Early American Locomotives*, plates 62 and 82; Bruce, p. 295; BLW 1923 *History*, p. 96: 1901.
25. Westwood, pp. 50-52, 184. *Locomotive Carriage & Wagon Review* (United Kingdom), Sept. 1932, Nov. 1939.
26. Bruce, p. 145.
27. Bruce, p. 125.
28. Paul T. Warner, *Motive Power Development on the Pennsylvania Railroad System 1831-1924* (Philadelphia: The Pennsylvania Railroad, 1924), pp. 33, 39.
29. Staufer. The "R" designation was later changed to H3. An example of an H3, PRR No. 1187, is on display at the Railroad Museum of Pennsylvania in Strasburg.
30. Warner, pp. 40-41. Fry (*Study of Locomotive Boiler*, 1924, p. 6) says that Thomas Urquhardt, an Englishman who supervised locomotives on Russia's Tsaritsyn-Gryaz Railway, fired locomotives on oil in 1889.
31. Burgess and Kennedy, *Centennial History of the Pennsylvania Railroad Corporation*, pp. 362-64.
32. Warner, p. 41.
33. Worley, p. 181.
34. Westwood, p. 259; *Engineering*, June 22, 1883; *The Engineer*, Feb. 8, 1889 and July 26, 1889.
35. H.C. Reagan, *Locomotives: Simple, Compound, and Electric* (New York: John Wiley, 1907), 5th ed., pp. 554-57.
36. Bruce, pp. 149, 151; Reagan, pp. 557-59 on oil-burning version for SP, pp. 575-83 on coal-burning version for Baltimore & Ohio.

OR SCHOOLS
ARDEEN
HOT WATER HEATING
EDW

Chapter 3

Vehicular Design for Horsepower:

The ongoing quest for speed and strength

As a new century dawned, locomotive designers found their goal-posts shifting yet again. Locomotives had become enormous compared to prior years, pulling heavier trains and doing more work. Infrastructure had grown in capacity at the same time. Meanwhile the national economy showed little sign of long-term slackening, so the incentives to build ever-bigger engines seemed unlikely to let up.

A result was an increasing stress on *time* in a designer's thinking about a locomotive's economic performance. The conceptual problem is captured in the imprecision of ordinary language. A locomotive may pull a given load a given distance, and that is a definition of work: pull times distance. But another word is popularly used: power. In this usage, however, power is a different concept altogether. Work *per unit of time* is what power actually means: How long does it take to do a given amount of work? A locomotive that pulled the same load the same distance, yet did so in less time, would have more power – more horsepower, in fact.

Time becomes an economic imperative when the interval taken by goods-in-transit measurably erodes economic value for shippers. Manufacturers have to pay back borrowed capital, like bonds and bank loans, on locked-in terms of amount and schedule. Paying back the cost of capital and earning a net profit must come from goods sold – and transit time in distribution delays a seller's stream of revenue. For large manufacturing concerns, potential revenue lost to time can be huge. As the American economy expanded in the first decades of the 20th century, large sectors became more sophisticated in their economic calculus, balancing the value of slow, cheap transport against the value of faster distribution.

Freight trains – *i.e.*, goods in transit – lumbered slowly at the turn of the century. Locomotives hauled bigger loads the same distances in the same amounts of time, which also took more horsepower. The definition is indifferent as to whether work is increased or time decreased. And, up to a point, shippers were indifferent as well: If more goods move, even at the same speed, the rate of distribution is increased. But during the first two decades of the century, designers had to reevaluate the horsepower equation. Raw pull

New York Central's *Empire State Express* is drawn by 4-4-2 Atlantic-type No. 3847 through Syracuse, N.Y., circa 1910.
Detroit Photographic Co., Library of Congress

per locomotive would reach its limit. To keep up with demands made on railroads, both load capacity and speed would have to increase.

There is a persistent idea in the literature on locomotive development that horsepower, as a concept relating work to speed, was somehow discovered in the mid-1920s.[1] Countering this notion, a reader can find an extended discussion of horsepower related to locomotive capacity in a leading text of 1904, which had a second edition in 1907.[2] Horsepower was regularly measured in tests, both at the Purdue University test plant established in 1891 and at the plant built by the Pennsylvania Railroad at Altoona, Pa., in 1904. Engineers understood the relationships. High horsepower can be generated at low speed, which is actually the most economical way to do it. Maintaining high average speed on a railroad requires multiple accelerations, together with overcoming higher frictional resistance. Thus total fuel consumption is higher for the same load carried the same distance. Speed costs extra.[3]

Reaching ever-higher values of tractive pull per driving axle at low speed made perfect economic sense. However, once a limit on that value was reached (as we have seen, from a limit determined by weight on the axle), then the only way to increase horsepower was through higher speed. Pull, however, does not leave the picture. Horsepower is work per unit of time. But a fully equivalent definition is: Horsepower equals pull times speed. To increase locomotive horsepower, pull at lower working speeds would have to increase, and sustained pull at higher speeds would also need to increase.[4] It was far from being an easy problem.

In a new cycle of change, designers created new locomotive types for both freight and passengers. At the same time that the distribution of goods was accelerating, passenger trains were adding more cars and speeding up schedules. New engine types incorporated a chassis feature that became the mark of higher horsepower: the trailing truck. In locomotive design, chassis arrangement and power production were always inseparable.

Trailing wheels at the back of the engine were themselves nothing new. Idle wheels behind the drivers can be found in some of the earliest locomotives. Robert Stephenson's 1829 *Rocket* had such an axle. Also in England, George Forrester and David Joy, in 1836 and 1847, respectively, built engines with idle axles behind the firebox; 2-2-2s were not uncommon in Britain and in Canada during the 1840s. In Germany, locomotives of three different wheel arrangements built between 1838 and 1841 included trailing axles. In the U.S., Ross Winans built a 4-2-4 in 1849, with a four-wheel truck underneath

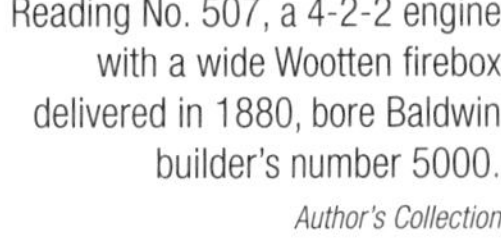

Reading No. 507, a 4-2-2 engine with a wide Wootten firebox delivered in 1880, bore Baldwin builder's number 5000.
Author's Collection

the firebox.[5] By the late 1860s, so-called "tank" engines (that is, locomotives having their boilers, fuel bunkers, and water tanks all on one frame), often had two- or four-wheel trucks under the rear of the locomotive, with the trailing truck equalized with the drivers.

In 1880, something of a precursor came to the Reading, a little 4-2-2 with a Wootten firebox. The engine carried Baldwin Works Number 5000. It was originally intended for fast commuter service with a light train. Soon after delivery the Reading altered plans and the engine went instead to the Eames Vacuum Brake Co. for use as a demonstrator of that braking device in England. Eames sold the engine for scrap four or five years later, after the company was done with it. Thus BLW No. 5000 was just a minor blip in the historical record. Odd, however, was the placement of the firebox and trailing axle: The firebox was entirely behind the drivers and over the trailing wheels, with those wheels equalized with the drivers. It was exactly the pattern that much bigger locomotives would pick up more than a decade later.

A landmark locomotive in the story of chassis and trailing wheels was the Baldwin Works' *Columbia* of 1893, a featured attraction at the 1893 World's Columbian Exposition in Chicago. This was an engine designed by Baldwin's William Henszey and William Austin with a 2-4-2 wheel arrangement, and it was exhibited at the fair, not far from New York Central's No. 999. Compared to No. 999, *Columbia* was lighter, had a smaller firebox, had less heating surface, and had compound cylinders.[6] The latter engine's innovation, based on rearranging its eight wheels and its suspension, was a deeper firebox. The narrow firebox was placed lower, giving a bit more combustion volume above the fire and allowing the centerline of the boiler (presuming equal driving-wheel diameters) to be slightly lower. Ease of access to the firebox externally for repairs, such as changing broken staybolts, was improved since the drivers were no longer in the way.

After the fair, *Columbia* proved sufficiently interesting as a high-speed passenger engine to the Chicago, Burlington & Quincy that it ordered many similar locomotives from Baldwin, beginning in 1895. For its specific design, the Burlington wanted simple-expansion cylinders and a bigger grate area, about 80 percent larger. So, for the first time, a wide firebox for bituminous coal was set entirely behind the drivers, over trailing wheels. Hardly a momentous change in itself, the same firebox-over-trailing-wheels arrangement, albeit for an anthracite-burning firebox, appeared the same year on a 4-2-2 for Wootten's Philadelphia & Reading.

Chicago, Burlington & Quincy 2-4-2 engine No. 590, shown at Galesburg, Ill., ca. 1895. Compared with a 4-4-0, it traded one leading axle for a trailing one to support a bigger grate, but it was unstable at high speed.
Harold K. Vollrath Collection

Philadelphia & Reading 4-2-2 No. 385, another attempt to re-arrange the 4-4-0. With only one driving axle, this wheel arrangement had poor traction. *Author's Collection*

In both the Burlington and Reading designs, the rear wheels were not carried in a truck but simply added as another wheel-pair in the engine frame, equalized with the drivers. Both wheel-types, 2-4-2 and 4-2-2, proved distinctly defective. The former had a tendency to sway disconcertingly at high speed; the two-wheel truck, at least in this design, gave poor lateral stability.[7] Although the Reading's 4-2-2s pulled five-car trains, the type had woefully inadequate traction. For enginemen, these locomotives must have been a slippery handful; the weight-on-drivers was only a little more than three times the theoretical tractive force.[8] The 4-2-2 type disappeared quickly, as did all locomotives with only one driving axle.

The Atlantic

A few months before delivering the initial Burlington and Reading engines, Baldwin also built the first of a new class for the Atlantic Coast Line. This was the 4-4-2, which came to be called the Atlantic-type. Henszey, Austin, and ACL locomotive officers agreed on a layout taken directly from the *Columbia*, but with a slightly longer boiler to make room for a four-wheel lead truck. In high-speed use, this well-tried form of lead truck provided better stability.[9] The next year, 1896, the Atlantic City Railroad got its first Atlantic, a racy looking compound-expansion locomotive intended for the beach trade between Camden, N.J., opposite Philadelphia on the Delaware River, and the South Jersey shore. This locomotive, once regarded as the world's fastest, is discussed more fully in Chapter 5. The 4-4-2 in various sizes became immensely popular with railroads in every part of the country, pulling their premier passenger trains and often bumping 4-4-0s or 4-6-0s into less-than-top-rank passenger duty.

Another celebrated speed-record claim is associated with an Atlantic: the supposed 127.1 mph dash of Pennsylvania Railroad E2 No. 7002 on June 11,

Although not the first engines with a 4-4-2 wheel arrangement, those built by Baldwin in 1895 for the Atlantic Coast Line gave the type its name: Atlantic. *Author's Collection*

1905. Engineman Jerry McCarthy was called at Crestline, Ohio, to take the westbound *Pennsylvania Special*. The newly minted flagship train was running late on its first Jersey City-to-Chicago run, to the acute embarrassment of railroad officials. According to oft-repeated accounts, McCarthy received orders to recover as much time on the schedule as he could. On a three-mile downgrade between AY Tower at Lima, Ohio, and the neighboring village of Elida, the daring Irishman was clocked at a speed that would stand as the fastest ever claimed for a steam locomotive anywhere in the world.[10]

There are two rather serious questions about the claim, however. First, the clocking was done late at night and consisted only of a towerman and a station operator comparing their respective timings, which they recorded in their logs, or timesheets. Station and tower clocks were set once a day against a telegraphed signal, and employees set their watches against the clocks to the nearest minute. Yet there was no recorded advance arrangement to exactly synchronize clocks. Logged times were those at which a passing train "cleared," that is, when the last car of the train, as shown by rear marker lamps, passed safely by a given waypoint. The *Special* presumably covered the three miles in less than a minute and a half. Timings to the second were never made in regular train operations. Even given accurate watches and good intentions, there were numerous chances for error by either or both of the operators. A few seconds' difference in clocks, a few seconds' difference in the manner in which the operators logged the train "by," and minor compounded differences (e.g., one timing a bit late and the other a bit early, or vice versa) could easily change the speed by 20 to 30 mph. The original timesheets no longer exist, unless they are in the hands of an unknown collector. Even if they did, no modern certifying organization would credit the speed claim. The aura of accuracy implicit in the figure of 127.1 has no merit.

Equally serious for the claim is the thermal capacity of the locomotive. Just as we have seen for New York Central's No. 999, the tractive pull and horsepower of a non-superheated locomotive is severely limited at high rpm, especially above 90-100 mph. The Pennsylvania's No. 7002 was a substantially bigger locomotive than No. 999, with larger furnace and boiler. But curves of tractive effort for any non-superheated steam locomotive fall rapidly after about 80 mph, as discussed later in this chapter, while the rolling resistance of cars continues to rise with increasing speed, even on a downgrade. On level track with a four- or five-car train, a speed of 110 mph for No. 7002 is at the outer bound of credibility. Casting even greater doubt on the claimed 127.1-

A record-holder of dubious veracity, PRR Class E2 4-4-2 No. 7002 is reputed to have achieved the fastest speed ever claimed for a steam locomotive – 127.1 miles per hour – in Ohio on June 11, 1905.

Author's Collection

For its *Hiawatha* fleet of 1935, the Milwaukee Road acquired A-class Atlantics from Alco, their 84-inch drivers partially hidden by a streamlined shroud styled by industrial designer Otto Kuhler.
Courtesy Kalmbach Media

mph speed are the unknowns introduced by grade and acceleration. The slight downgrade to the Ottawa River at Elida is preceded by a slight upgrade out of Lima. It is not known how fast McCarthy's train passed through the city of Lima and past AY Tower. If it was as slow as 60-70 mph, reaching even 110 by Elida would have been difficult. The only substantiated steam speed record remains that of Sir Nigel Gresley's *Mallard* on the London & North Eastern Ry. in 1938 – 126 mph on a slight downgrade by a far more potent locomotive.

As designers later enlarged the Atlantic type, two remarkable examples of the form came out in 1914 and 1935. Both were as advanced in concept as any steam locomotives of their weight ever built for everyday service in the U.S. The Pennsylvania Railroad Class E6, designed by Motive Power Superintendent Alfred Gibbs, produced more than 2,200 hp at the Altoona Test Plant from 56 square feet of grate; 80-inch-diameter drivers allowed for passenger-train speeds over 90 mph.[11] Two decades later, Milwaukee Road and Alco engineers conceived a steam locomotive to compete with diesels in heading up the new, lightweight, extra-fast passenger trains then appearing. This was the A Class, with 300 psi boiler pressure, 69 square feet of grate, and 84-inch drivers. Sporting a streamlined casing styled in light gray, yellow, and orange by industrial designer Otto Kuhler, these 3,000-hp engines regularly topped 100 mph pulling the *Hiawatha* between Chicago and the Twin Cities.

Although the Atlantic Coast Line locomotives of 1895 constituted the first big order for 4-4-2s, these were not the first of the type. George Strong of the Lehigh Valley Railroad designed the first engine with his unique firebox as a 4-4-2, which the Hinkley Locomotive Works constructed in 1887 as the *A.G. Darwin*, or "Strong Patent No. 1."[12] Two years later, the Santa Fe asked the Schenectady Works to build a near-duplicate, 4-4-2 No. 738. Having no luck in getting the Strong furnace to work reliably, shopmen of the Atchison, Topeka & Santa Fe Railroad lopped it off and rebuilt No. 738 with a conventional firebox as a 4-4-0 in 1892.[13] Strong, however, laid out the wheels of the *Darwin* and the No. 738 with the identical rationale applicable to later Atlantics: The trailing axle supported a larger combustion section.

The Prairie

Freight locomotives, too, were soon affected by the trend to bigger fireboxes. In 1897, Baldwin engineers responded to a specification from the Nippon Railway. The Japanese needed 3-foot, 6-inch-gauge locomotives of two types, one with two driving axles for passenger trains and another with four driving axles for freight. Both types would burn low-BTU coal with high ash content. Baldwin proposed a 4-4-2 for the passenger design and a 2-8-2 – a new wheel arrangement – for the freight. Baldwin first called the latter a "modified" Consolidation. Each design provided a generous grate area and large furnace volume in relation to boiler capacity, in order to accommodate the poor coal. In the 2-8-2, the trailing truck was not simply an idle axle suspended in the engine frame. The long wheelbase of the 2-8-2 layout required that the trailing wheels have more lateral motion than the minimal amount provided in early Atlantics. Though not yet a fully developed truck, a subframe carried the rear axle of the Japanese freighter under the engine's main frame, permitting the required degree of lateral motion and still allowing equalization of the rear wheels with the drivers. The full suspension of the locomotive followed the tripod principle.[14] Named "Mikado" for its Japanese roots – although Henszey and Austin supervised its conception – the 2-8-2 in standard gauge became a favorite for heavy freight in North America after 1910.

Before then, however, the 2-6-2 had a brief heyday. In 1900 the Chicago, Burlington & Quincy, having acquired a 2-4-2 fleet, tried a modification of that layout with an added driving axle, aiming to haul freight on faster schedules than 2-8-0s could handle. For the railroad's operations west of Burlington, Iowa, the nearest coal was semi-bituminous, lower in BTUs than coal available in Illinois. With a trailing truck, a 2-6-2 could equal the tractive pull of either a Mogul or Ten-Wheeler, yet could carry the larger furnace needed to burn the poorer fuel. To add volume, the CB&Q design used a Belpaire firebox. In 1901, the Santa Fe and the Lake Shore & Michigan Southern introduced tall-drivered 2-6-2s for high-speed passenger use. (The Lake Shore's elegant engines were designed by its superintendent of motive power, Waldo H. Marshall, who later became Alco's third president.) Other railroads later bought 2-6-2s for freight, with fireboxes sized for various grades of coal. The type gained a reputation for "free steaming," meaning that boiler capacity was generous in relation to the ability of the running gear to transmit power to the rail – something that could not be said of many large 2-6-0s and 4-6-0s. Burlington and the Santa Fe both called the type "Prairie" for its geographic association, and the name stuck.

LEFT CB&Q No. 1702, the second locomotive in Burlington's pioneering R-1 2-6-2 class of 1900.

L.E. Griffith, Courtesy Kalmbach Media

BELOW Great Northern 2-6-2 No. 1520. With its trailing truck, the so-called Prairie-type offered a bigger firebox than contemporary 2-6-0s and 4-6-0s.

Courtesy Kalmbach Media

According to Alco engineer and writer Alfred Bruce, however, larger 2-6-2s displayed unexpected instabilities, both laterally and vertically. The 2-4-2-type was not noted for riding stability at speed, and the 2-6-2 apparently was worse. Bruce attributed the Prairie's problems partly to its symmetry of weight distribution and piston thrust around the middle driver-pair. Since the center of gravity of the whole locomotive was very close to the main crankpins, piston thrust exerted maximum leverage around the engine's vertical axis. This action could produce a side-to-side yawing. A partial solution was to move the main crankpins to the third driver-pair, which was practical for drivers up to about 69 inches in diameter without having an excessively long main rod.

Bruce hints that a contributing source of lateral instability may have been the lack in early trailing trucks of any self-centering action. Thus there was no damping of yaw at the back of the locomotive, as would occur with later forms of trailing trucks incorporating self-centering. And apart from the lateral yaw, Prairies sometimes pitched like a hobby horse and derailed: The longitudinal symmetry of engine mass and wheels, combined with a relatively short wheelbase, made for vertical instability fore-and-aft.[15]

Prairies in high-speed use were short-lived. Somewhat contravening Bruce's litany of defects, the Santa Fe amassed a huge fleet of 69-inch-drivered 2-6-2s for medium-speed freight, 231 in all from 1901 through 1907. Fourteen of these machines were rebuilt from passenger engines that originally had 79-inch wheels. All AT&SF Prairies had their main crankpins on the middle drivers, and the engines built in 1906 and 1907 had trailing trucks with centering devices. Almost all of Santa Fe's Prairies ran until the late 1940s and early 1950s, albeit in low-speed local service for most of their careers.[16]

The Mikado

The 2-8-2 Mikado showed none of the Prairie's flaws. Bismarck, Washburn & Great Falls Railway, a small North Dakota line, ordered one in 1902. According to Baldwin's official 1923 history, it was the first U.S. locomotive built to burn lignite, so its firebox was comparatively huge in order to handle the low-BTU fuel. The Northern Pacific, which also burned North Dakota lignite, in 1904 fielded the first large 2-8-2 for mainline use, designed in cooperation with Alco's Brooks Works. NP's W-class, numbered 1500-1659, took full advantage of the wide and deep combustion space inherent in the 2-8-2 plan, resulting in a locomotive with all the low-speed pull of a

Northern Pacific Mikado-type No. 1529, at Gardiner, Mont. A trailing truck and a bigger grate meant better steaming than a 2-8-0 Consolidation-type.
R.V. Nixon, Courtesy Kalmbach Media

Louisville & Nashville 2-8-2 Mikado No. 1729.
Robert A. Hadley, Courtesy Kalmbach Media

Consolidation but more: Now there was a boiler capable of supplying the steam for greater pull throughout the speed range. Based on success with a firebox combustion chamber in a class of 2-6-2s built a year later, NP added combustion chambers to the boilers of most locomotives it bought thereafter, including 2-8-2s.[17] Combustion chambers added to boiler power, especially with poorer coal, by raising the furnace volume. Their use was controversial, though, since the additional staybolts meant an increased chance of bolts cracking or breaking.

NP's W-class Mikados weighed almost 132 tons and had grates of about 44 square feet. Within ten years, "Mikes" on NP and on other railroads throughout the country weighed nearly 150 tons, with grates to 70 square feet. Typical driver diameter was 63 inches. An outstanding example was the 1914 L1-class of the Pennsylvania, developed with the help of several years' prior research on the Altoona Test Plant. Every trunk line railroad adopted the 2-8-2 as a standard heavy freight locomotive. Smaller railroads ordered modestly sized 2-8-2s (and 2-6-2s) for logging and industrial use.

The Pacific

The 4-6-2 became the successful passenger counterpart to the 2-8-2 freighter. As we have seen in Chapter 2, George Strong designed the first legitimate 4-6-2 in 1886, but it was not until 1902-1903 that the type began to fill a genuine need for greater power in pulling premier passenger trains. As with the 2-8-2, the 4-6-2's concerted development was instigated by a foreign order. In 1901, Baldwin designed thirteen 3-foot-6-inch gauge locomotives for the New Zealand Government Railway. Intended to burn lignite, the boilers of these engines, though small by North American standards, required large grates. The type was dubbed "Pacific," in recognition of the New Zealand connection. Within two years, U.S. railroads were ordering standard-gauge Pacifics in mounting numbers.[18]

ABOVE Missouri Pacific No. 6501, at Monroe, La., in 1950. Built in 1902, it was the first of an eventual 106 4-6-2s for MP.
Harold K. Vollrath Collection

RIGHT Milwaukee Road 4-6-2 No. 155, at the railroad's Milwaukee shops in the 1940s. The 1910-built workhorse outlived Milwaukee's famous streamlined 4-6-4s of 1938.
Linn H. Westcott, Courtesy Kalmbach Media

One of the first railroads to try a large 4-6-2 was the Missouri Pacific, from the Brooks Works in 1902. The engine was only marginally heavier than, for example, one of Lake Shore's Brooks-built Ten-Wheelers, and despite the MoPac engine's wide grate, it had only a few square feet more grate area. Nonetheless, MoPac locomotive officers must have been pleased since they ordered more engines immediately. The 69-inch-diameter drivers were well suited to the line's rolling topography, with many short but demanding grades, and the boiler could supply the steam needed to keep average speed up. Additionally, one thing was clear to any knowledgeable observer: the 4-6-2 configuration had plenty of room to grow in firebox and boiler size, wheel diameter, and total weight within reasonable axle loadings, while the 4-6-0 and 2-6-2 types were already reaching their size limits. Just eight years later, a Pacific existed weighing 134½ tons – 46 percent heavier than the 1902 engine – with 39 percent more grate area, 38 percent more evaporative surface, and superheating. This was Alco's experimental No. 50000, designed by a team that adopted many ideas of Schenectady engineer Francis J. Cole. Tested under contract at the Altoona Test Plant, No. 50000 produced 2,600 horsepower in the cylinders.[19] No horsepower data exist on the MoPac engine, but it is likely that the big Alco very nearly doubled the output of its smaller, non-superheated predecessor. The story of Alco No. 50000 is treated in Chapter 7, and other benchmark Pacifics are covered in Chapters 9 and 10. For now, suffice to say that the experimental Pacific's weight and power were exceeded in a few years by locomotives used in daily fleet service on major railroads. No better example can be adduced of American railroads' response to an expanding national economy than such rapid, dramatic leaps in locomotive size and performance.

Horsepower and trailing trucks

Tractive effort is always included in published specifications; horsepower is rarely included. That's because rated tractive effort – which holds with little erosion from 0 mph up to 5-10 mph – is the basis of tonnage ratings. Such ratings for freight locomotives are for maximum pull at low speed to haul a maximum-tonnage train over the steepest grade (the "ruling" grade) on a given route. Average speed on the route may be high; speed on the ruling grade can be slow. It is the latter speed, and highest pull, which set the limit on how much weight the train can wrestle over the grade. For passenger locomotives, tonnage ratings on ruling grades were usually based on available pull – tractive effort – at a somewhat higher speed, usually 20-25 mph. Assigning helper locomotives to freight or passenger trains can raise the tonnage rating. Heavy passenger trains commonly got helpers on sustained grades. Heading west from Altoona up to the Gallitzin Tunnels, for example, even the crack *Broadway Limited* got a helper.

After 1913, the calculated cylinder horsepower, based on the methodology worked out by Cole, was usually included in the key information provided by builders to locomotive purchasers. Comparative horsepower figures were indeed useful. "Cole-rated horsepower" indicated the relative ability of a locomotive to generate ton-miles per train hour, the agreed industry measure of productivity related to time. Subsequent testing on the road with dynamometer cars and in the Altoona plant showed the Cole horsepowers to be generally conservative. Their comparative value, however (whether one locomotive was more or less capable than another), stood the test of time. The Cole ratios are discussed in more detail in Chapter 7.

The practical basis for the jump in locomotive horsepower was good trailing-truck design. Adding another axle with provision for adequate side-to-side movement was just the beginning. In locomotives of any size, the trailing wheels had to be equalized with the drivers in order to maintain a tripod suspension. In larger engines, the truck needed to stabilize the extended back end of the locomotive, giving lateral support at the main frame's rear corners, and the truck also needed to hold the locomotive steady against oscillations.

One of the earliest truck designs to go beyond simply suspending the trailing axle-boxes in the main engine frame was that of John Player, superintendent of the Brooks Works and consulting engineer to Alco after its 1901 merger. Player's inside-bearing truck had radial movement, meaning that the truck's axle was kept approximately at right angles to curved track as the axle moved side-to-side. Player did this by mounting the axle-boxes in a machined housing, curved to fit in correspondingly shaped frame pedestal jaws.[20]

Francis Cole's trailing-truck design, as applied to Alco 4-6-2 Pacific No. 50000.
Courtesy Kalmbach Media

Though the Player truck was applied only during the first decade of the century, Canadian Pacific's Motive Power Superintendent Henry Vaughan and Chief Mechanical Engineer William Winterrowd used a geometrically similar design with outside axle bearings from 1910 into the early 1920s. The Vaughan-Winterrowd truck, which succeeding CPR master mechanics employed into the 1940s, also used curved axle boxes shaped to move radially within the main locomotive frame. The boxes provided self-centering by being shaped at the top to slide against inclined planes.[21]

Baldwin's Kenneth Rushton and the Rogers Works' Reuben Wells invented trucks early in the century. The Rushton used a "radius bar" to guide a small amount of radial movement and used swing links to carry the axle-boxes. The links in early forms of the truck did not provide self-centering; in all variants the range of lateral motion was extremely limited. Wells' truck had swing links arranged to give self-centering, but lateral movement was restricted, and it wasn't radial.

All the early, inside-bearing trucks gave no particular stabilization laterally to the main engine frame. A locomotive with all its top-heavy mass was about ten feet wide; the axle-boxes and spring seats of inside-bearing trucks were spaced little more than four feet apart. Early outside-bearing trucks were arranged similar to the Wells truck, with self-centering but non-radial movement. Lateral support was markedly improved. But flange wear was certainly high, as such an axle – not keeping at right angle to the rails – "slewed" its wheels through curves and turnouts.

Alco's Francis Cole came up with the first truly elegant solution to all the conflicting requirements. He introduced an early form about 1903 but did not develop its final design until 1909-1910. The mature form incorporated outside-bearing axle-boxes with widely set lateral support, radial movement with a considerable degree of freedom to accommodate sharp curves, a direct equalizer connection from the last driver's spring hanger on each side to long-leaf truck springs, and self-centering via a transverse coil spring. The truck gave high stability with a well-cushioned ride. The long, C-shaped yoke running above the bearing-box is an easy way to identify the mature Cole truck; the yoke holds a sliding pad in position on top of the box, between the box and the spring saddle. These pads isolated the springs from lateral movement of the truck. The pads were lubricated with oil or grease and were easily replaceable when worn.

The trailing truck on B&O 2-8-2 Mikado No. 4500 features a Hodges truck, Baldwin's answer to the Cole design.
Courtesy Kalmbach Media

The Cole truck became an immediate favorite, showing up on most Alco locomotives and on others made by competing builders. The Cole shows up on Baldwin locomotives as early as 1911. Baldwin, no doubt smarting from having to pay royalties on the Cole patent assigned to Alco, came up with a roughly equivalent truck by 1909. Baldwin's W. Sterling Hodges devised a truck similar to the Cole but without the sliding pad. The truck's spring hangers were shaped in an attempt to accommodate sideward truck movement. Bruce, however, points out that the springs still twisted slightly as the truck swung to the side. Since locomotive springs, when they cracked or broke, did so in the hangers where stress was concentrated, the Hodges design must have required somewhat higher maintenance. The Hodges truck may not have been as well regarded as the Cole but nevertheless shows up on various Baldwin-built engines until at least 1936.

Materials and techniques used in locomotive construction began to change in the 1890s. Steel replaced wrought iron in axles and frames as more-powerful and heavier locomotives imposed higher stresses. Cylinders and half-saddles were still of cast iron but made in one piece. In 1898, Baldwin used its first cast-steel frames on some 2-8-0s built for the Santa Fe.[22]

Early in the first decade of the new century, foundries were turning out cast-steel driving wheel centers, first for tall-wheeled passenger engines. By 1910, engineers considered which alloy of cast steel was best for wheels or frames. Steel casting of large, intricate pieces became a high art. New or reorganized firms entered this new market, such as Commonwealth Steel Castings and General Steel Castings. Builders contracted with such specialty firms for driving wheels, frames, cast parts for trucks, cast-steel cylinders, and other high-strength pieces.

Valve gear

The Stephenson valve gear, in its developed form nearly universal throughout the world since the 1850s, began to pass from the scene after 1905.[23] John Muhlfeld of the Baltimore & Ohio reintroduced the outside-connected, crank-driven "Walschaerts" valve gear to the U.S. on his compound-expansion No. 2400 the previous year.[24] Aside from other innovative aspects of this locomotive treated in Chapter 5, Muhlfeld used a valve-gear form that William Mason, among others, had tried years before but which most European and American designers regarded as a bit inferior in its timing of valve motion.

Egide Walschaerts was an associate of Alfred Belpaire in the Belgian State Railways. While Belpaire advanced to chief mechanical engineer, Walschaerts was foreman at the Brussels-Midi engine terminal from 1844. Apparently because he was not a graduate of a technical school, he remained in that position until he retired in 1885. His valve-gear invention made him famous in the years before he died in 1901, yet his employer forbade him from patenting the device, and he never benefited financially. Walschaerts found a sponsor, a Mr. F. Fischer, to file a patent in 1844. In 1848, Walschaerts worked out a mature form that became the basis for a limited number of applications in Europe. There was confusion for many years as to credit for the gear, and some called it the Fischer valve gear. In 1849, the head mechanical engineer for the Taunus Railway in Prussia, Edmund Heusinger, patented a similar arrangement that he had independently developed; thus, in parts of Europe it was the Heusinger gear. Nonetheless, Walschaerts was without question the original inventor, as the international railway community and Heusinger later agreed.[25]

ABOVE Walschaerts valve gear on a Milwaukee Road class-F7 4-6-4 Hudson, showing the piston rod (1); crosshead (2); crosshead guide (3); reverse link (4); main rod (5); side rod (6); eccentric rod (7); and eccentric crank (8).
Courtesy Kalmbach Media

RIGHT CB&Q 2-4-2 No. 590 was equipped with Stephenson valve gear, which were located between the locomotive's sideframes and are thus largely invisible in most photos.
Courtesy Kalmbach Media

Relative effectiveness in valve timing was not the main issue among U.S. designers after 1905, or among European designers in the decades following. Rather, driving axles became so big in diameter and engine frames so heavy that there was little room left for mounting or adjusting axle-mounted eccentrics. For Stephenson gear, every pair of cylinders and steam-distribution valves required four eccentrics. Relative inaccessibility of the eccentrics also made their proper lubrication difficult in large locomotives.

Both valve-gear types share some fundamental characteristics. These characteristics are key to understanding the central role of valve gear in locomotive machine design to the end of steam development. First of all, steam-distribution valves (the formal name for the valves actuated by the "gear," and usually just called "the valves" when context is clear) are quite different from valves found in internal combustion engines. The valve gear continuously moves a valve that slides back and forth from a center position, sliding first in one direction and then in the other.[26] The valve is therefore near its middle position when the piston is at either end of its stroke, and the valve is near its middle position when it starts admission of steam to the proper side of the piston for each power stroke and opens the exhaust on the opposite side. Each end of the valve opens and closes a single set of ports, through which flow both inlet and exhaust. These ports are spoken of as having inlet (or steam) edges and exhaust edges, since it is at these edges that the timing events occur.

Since the valve is controlling steam flow to a one-cycle engine (every piston stroke is a power stroke on one side and an exhaust stroke on the other), the valve's motion is controlling admission and exhaust for both sides of the piston. As designers well recognized, requiring one valve to time both inlet and exhaust for both sides of the piston put some limits on cylinder efficiency. The mechanical simplicity of having one valve per cylinder, however, was a persuasive virtue.

One of the most prized skills in a locomotive backshop was that of the valve setter. Once the setter completed his work, the relationship of valve events was fixed. But the length of the valve's excursion – its travel – could be altered while the locomotive was underway. When an engineman adjusted his reverse lever to adjust cutoff, as discussed in Chapter 1, he was actually altering valve travel. The length of the valve's travel determines how long the inlet and exhaust ports are open and closed during a stroke. At full valve travel, the inlet is open for nearly the full length of piston stroke, and cutoff, as a percentage of piston stroke at which steam admission ends, is at maximum. At less than full valve travel, the inlet is open for a lesser portion of piston stroke, and cutoff is reduced.

In the shop, valves were set with a necessary adjustment called "lead." The inlet edges of the ports are therefore opened slightly in advance of the piston reaching end-of-stroke. Both Stephenson and Walschaerts valve gears provide for lead, but somewhat differently. In the Stephenson, each cylinder's valve has an eccentric for forward movement of the locomotive and another eccentric for backup movement. Thus the valve setter could arrange for optimal timing in both directions. At full cutoff, there is a small amount of lead, which the valve setter arranged by advancing the eccentric (the "angle of advance"). Also, since both eccentrics participate in moving the link that moves the valve, a result of this geometry is that lead is "variable." When an engineman shortens cutoff as speed increases, lead slightly increases. Variable lead is a desirable property. At higher rpm, the lead helps get the maximum amount of steam into the cylinders during steam admission and has the added effect of cushioning the reversal of piston and rods.

Walschaerts gear, on the other hand, has but one eccentric (the eccentric crank) per valve. The angle of the eccentric crank is set in relation to the link, which rocks on a fixed pivot. When the piston is at end-of-stroke, the link is at the mid-point of its arc, in either direction of locomotive movement. There could be no lead without some other source of motion added to the valve. To provide for lead, a "combination lever," taking its motion from the crosshead, is included. As the crosshead moves and as the valve approaches its mid-position, the combination lever moves the valve farther forward. The added distance ahead, opening the inlet port edges sooner, is the lead. In the Walschaerts, lead is fixed, not variable.

The main rod and drivers play a subtle role in valve timing. The angularity of the main rod means that, during a driver revolution, the piston moves faster through half of its stroke than through the other half. This geometric reality is why separate eccentrics in the Stephenson gear for forward and backup movement were valued. With the Walschaerts, the valve setter could set the best timing for one direction of locomotive movement but had to compromise timing somewhat in the other direction. The designer of the locomotive, by predetermining the geometry of the Walschaerts combination lever, set the desired amount of lead for the locomotive's average working speed. The valve setter ensured that the desired geometry was maintained.[27]

The Walschaerts' great virtue was external mounting of all valve gear components. No longer did valve setters and mechanics have to struggle in a shop pit, within the tight dimensions of an engine's frame to make the needed mechanical adjustments; in management's view, that saved labor hours. And since locomotives produced their economic output within a narrow range of average speed (and in one direction of movement), the niceties of the Stephenson gear were not that important in the overall scheme.

With either valve gear, designer and valve setter included "steam lap" in the arrangement of the valve itself. Taking one side of the piston at a time, lead advances the time of inlet opening as the valve moves in one direction; steam lap advances the time of inlet closure (cutoff) as the valve moves in the other direction. The machined portion of the valve that actually covers the ports is somewhat longer than the ports. This provision means that, even with full valve travel, the valve will stop steam admission before the piston reaches its end-of-stroke, and before lead has its maximum effect on valve position. The amount of steam lap was usually set to give a cutoff of 75 to 90 percent of piston stroke with the valve moving back and forth at full travel. When valve travel is decreased (*i.e.*, when the engineman moves his reverse lever out of the corner of its quadrant), cutoff is decreased still further in percentage.

Conversely, "exhaust lap" was also a consideration. If, at the point where the valve is exactly on its center, the valve faces overlap the exhaust edges at both sets of ports, that is the amount of exhaust lap. If there is no exhaust lap, the valve is said to be "line-on-line" at exhaust. Exhaust lap affects the point of exhaust release and closure. If there is an amount of positive exhaust lap, exhaust release is delayed, which allows more steam expansion within the cylinder before release. However, exhaust closure is advanced, which adds to cylinder compression. "Negative" exhaust lap (also called "exhaust clearance"), where the exhaust edges of both sets of ports are slightly open with the valve at mid-point, has an effect opposite from positive exhaust lap: release is advanced and compression is delayed. Advancing release may seem nonsensical because steam expansion is ended prematurely. But for high-speed locomotives, exhaust clearance often improved performance; the duration of exhaust opening is longer and the amount of exhaust port opening is increased. This wider exhaust opening lowered cylinder backpressure and therefore could increase power at high rpm. Low-speed locomotives usually had valves line-on-line at exhaust or had a slight amount of positive exhaust lap.

The reader can appreciate how complex valve design and setting was – and still is for those who restore historic steam locomotives today. Since one valve is controlling both inlet and exhaust functions for both ends of the cylinder, inlet and exhaust timing are inextricably tied together. For the valve setter, timing and duration of steam inlet cannot be altered without affecting timing and duration of steam exhaust. The same holds true for the engineman out on the road. As he shortens cutoff to save steam, two things inevitably happen: With any of the valve gears treated in this chapter, exhaust release occurs sooner on the power side of the piston, *and* exhaust closure occurs sooner on the exhaust side of the piston. Except in high-speed engines, early release prevents full expansion and erodes economy. Early exhaust closure causes excessive compression. Some compression is desirable, since it adds to the effect of lead in cushioning the reversal of the rods, but too much causes the piston literally to work against itself near the ends of its stroke. For high-speed engines – running at the shortest cutoff possible – excess compression put a severe limit on just how short the cutoff could be shortened.

The trick for the valve setter in the shop was to balance – for as much of the working cutoff range as possible – the pressure of compression with the pressure of early admission at just the right point ahead of the end of piston stroke, while delaying exhaust release and exhaust closure. If achieved, the result was a smooth-running, economical engine. If not achieved, the result was a rough-running, steam- hungry engine.

A hallmark of a well-timed locomotive was four exhaust beats of equal loudness and crispness from the stack per driving-wheel revolution, at either long or short cutoffs. A poorly timed locomotive betrayed itself by pronounced inequality in either the rhythm or the sound of the beats, especially as cutoff was reduced. As crews would say, the engine was "lame" or "out of square." Tonnage rating could be affected and economy certainly was. One authority estimated that valves out of adjustment from wear, or badly set in the shop, consumed eight to 20 percent more fuel per ton-mile.[28] No wonder, then, that valve setters were paid at premium rates – and that designers spent so much time trying to perfect the imperfectible.

Large steam passages, large ports, and long maximum valve travel seemed to engineers to be the most reliable road to good cylinder performance. Large passages and ports presumably allowed steam to flow with less restriction. Long valve travel meant that ports, while open, were open wider and also that the speed of the valve was faster at the various valve events, reducing the time of relatively restricted opening and thus reducing the time when unpredictable pressure variations might occur. By the geometry of the links, maximum valve travel for either Stephenson- or Walschaerts-actuated valves was about eight inches.[29] This was because the link, at its greatest angle forward or back, and the link block all the way up or down, could not move the radius rod (connected to the valve) any farther.

Around 1903, Abner D. Baker, an independent innovator and sometime entrepreneur, was trying to improve valve gears for steam traction engines – the big steam-powered tractors that, on large farms, had replaced horse teams for plowing and provided portable power for threshing and other operations. Traction engines had valve gears, just like locomotives. Many parts of Stephenson or Walschaerts valve gears wore, especially the links and link blocks, requiring adjustment every few months to keep valve events tolerably symmetrical. Baker's solution eliminated the link and link block. His design put all the moving parts of the gear on axial bearings. Maintenance frequency and thus maintenance cost were reduced.[30]

In Baker's layout, the reverse lever to alter cutoff is suitably connected to a carrier yoke in the gear for each valve. The yoke carries a lever that imparts

Baker valve gear on New York Central class-J1 4-6-4 Hudson No. 5298, showing piston rod (1); crosshead (2); crosshead guides (3); union link (4); combination lever (5); valve rod (6); valve gear frame (7); valve gear connecting rod (8); main rod (9); side rod (10); eccentric rod (11); eccentric crank (12); reverse yoke (13); and reach rod (14).
Courtesy Kalmbach Media

motion from the eccentric rod to a bell crank; the bell crank, in turn, moves the valve. By setting the carrier yoke forward or back, motion to the bell crank is altered. If the operator adjusts the yoke in one direction, the bell crank runs the valve for forward movement of the engine. If the operator adjusts the yoke fully in the other direction, this reverses the action of the bell crank and runs the valve for backup movement. Intermediate positions of the carrier yoke give various cutoffs. A combination lever provides a fixed amount of lead. Baker tinkered with his valve gear and patented a mature version in 1911.

After about 1913, Baker gear became a direct competitor to the Walschaerts gear. Baker sold his rights to the newly formed Pilliod Co., which aggressively marketed his invention. Steam designers saw the virtues of a gear whose overall geometry might vary minimally over time. The Erie, the Rock Island, and the Delaware & Hudson were among early users of the Baker. In service, mechanics found that lost motion in the gear from even a little wear in the bearings could cause bad angles in the bell crank that overstressed the gear at long cutoffs. In later models of the Baker, roller or needle bearings were used instead of plain bearings; wear was virtually eliminated as a factor that degraded the valve setter's work.[31]

Nothing came free, of course. Initially setting the Baker gear was difficult. Small variations in the parts could seriously affect timing; realigning the parts could mean re-machining bearing mounts. For modern locomotive restorers, lacking daily experience with such precise adjustments, resetting a badly aligned Baker valve gear properly can be a major headache.

The Baker's performance advantage was longer valve travel. Up to nine inches was practical – and even 9½ inches with a long eccentric crank, without serious geometric distortion at the extreme ends of valve movement.[32] The proportionately longer travel gave wider port openings at any given cutoff setting, and quicker action of the valve, so that valve events were more sharply defined. By 1918, Baker valve gear was so well-accepted among designers and mechanics that it was included on many of the standard locomotive designs prepared for the U.S. Railroad Administration. On the great majority of American railroads, though, master mechanics preferred the Walschaerts, most likely because it was far easier to set accurately.

Many other valve-gear forms occasionally competed. Mechanics and inventors tried perhaps 200 valve-gear designs throughout the course of steam engineering history. Only a few of these proved workable. For locomotives in the 20th century, the Southern valve gear was favored briefly in the 1910s on the Southern Railway and on a few other lines. Invented by William S. Brown, an engineman on the Southern, this gear used a shifting fulcrum, similar in principle to the Baker. There were two connections to the forward end of the eccentric rod. One connection held the forward end of the eccentric rod at an adjustable radius; the other connection moved a bell crank. There was no combination lever, since lead was provided by the difference in motion of the two connections to the eccentric rod. Bruce points out that these long connections could vibrate laterally, eventually causing mechanical failure.[33]

Otis W. Young took the old idea of running the valve on one side of the locomotive from the crosshead motion of the opposite side, which gave the needed 90-degree primary motion to the valve. Hence there was no eccentric crank. The link on one side ran the valve on the opposite side. Lead was given by a long combination rod to the link on the same side. The Young gear was rarely used, and generally only between about 1915 and 1925.[34] It was practical on switchers and in other low-speed operation. Unfortunately, torsion could not be eliminated in carrying motion transversely from one side of the engine to the other, so valve events became distorted at high rpm.

BELOW Southern valve gear on a 2-8-0 of its namesake railroad. Valve travel and event timing was satisfactory, but lateral stability was a recurring problem.

Courtesy Kalmbach Media

BOTTOM Young valve gear, seen here on a Union Pacific 2-10-2 engine, was not widely used. Valve events easily became distorted at high rpm.

Lima Locomotive Works

Apart from valve gears, the design of the valves themselves changed during the century. Slide valves were rapidly replaced by piston valves in new construction, and there were bolt-on kits to convert older, slide-valve locomotives to piston valves. Designers experimented with different kinds of sealing rings and tried double-ported valves. The different types of valves are discussed more fully in Chapter 7. Cam-operated valves ("poppet" valves), which appeared experimentally early in the century but were not tried seriously in Europe or the U.S. until the 1920s, are treated in Chapter 19.

Valve gears always fascinated. Since the greatest loss of thermal efficiency of a steam locomotive came after the steam left the boiler, valve action was crucial to any improvement in fuel and steam economy. Given the small amount of steam expansion that actually could occur within the volume of a cylinder, the relative improvements in valving made in the century were remarkable. In the next chapter, another essentially intractable problem of engine and vehicular design is covered: driving-wheel counterbalancing.

Chapter 3 Notes

1. David P. Morgan, "Lima's Finest in Twilight," *Trains,* July 1956.
2. Henderson, *Locomotive Operation*, 2nd ed. (Chicago: Wilson Co., 1907), chapters 6-7, sections on "Maximum Horsepower," pp. 357-63, "Horsepower Characteristics," pp. 416-21. (Henderson was a consulting engineer for Baldwin.)
3. Thus, during the fuel shortages of the 1970s and early 1980s, freight train speeds were reduced as a fuel-saving strategy. Commercial aircraft cruising speeds were likewise reduced, and a 55-mph speed limit was imposed on the nation's highways.
4. Plain language is often a good way to express simple mathematical relations. If "power is work per unit of time," then:

$$\text{power} = \frac{\text{work}}{\text{time}} \qquad \text{and that is,} \quad \text{power} = \frac{\text{pull x distance}}{\text{time}}$$

If "power is pull times speed," then $\text{power} = \text{pull x } \frac{\text{distance}}{\text{time}}$, which is the same.

Horsepower is defined as 33,000 foot-lbs. per minute. The definition includes a unit of work (the foot-lbs.) and a rate of time (minutes). It can be converted into any unit of power, such as watts (1 hp = 745.7 watts). For locomotives, a convenient equation for horsepower is:

$$\text{hp} = \frac{\text{(pull or tractive effort in lbs., for a given speed) (the speed in mph)}}{(375)}$$

(The "375" is simply a constant to convert different units – such as pounds, miles, or hours – into multiples of 33,000 foot-lbs. per minute.)

Note that horsepower is a function of both pull and speed, taken together. Example: A locomotive exerting 30,000 lbs. of pull at 20 mph is generating 1,600 hp. (If the pull is measured at the tender rear coupler, then it's called "drawbar horsepower.") See R. Johnson, *The Steam Locomotive* (1944), Ch. 11, "Horsepower." (Johnson was chief engineer for Baldwin.)
5. Sinclair (1907; White ed., 1970), pp. 34-35, 98, 613. Examples of early locomotives with a trailing axle include Forrester's 2-2-0 of 1834, rebuilt as 2-2-2 in 1836 (see White's note, p. 34); Joy's *Jenny Lind*-class 2-2-2; Kinmond (Scottish builder) 2-2-2s of 1847 for Montreal & Lachine Ry; Germany's *Saxonia* 0-4-2 (1838); *Der Münchner* 2-2-2 (1841); and *Borsig* 4-2-2 (1841).
6. Dredge, 1893 *Exhibits*; A.W. Bruce, *The Steam Locomotive in America* (1952), p. 291.
7. Bruce, plate 2 following p. 276; p. 291.
8. Bruce, plate 99. *History of the Baldwin Locomotive Works, 1831-1923*, pp. 86-87.
9. BLW 1923 *History*, pp. 85-86.
10. Trade journals *Railway Gazette* and *Railway & Locomotive Engineering* covered the claim. However, Sinclair's comprehensive 1907 history, sent to press 24 months after No. 7002's purported world record, makes no mention of the event. Sinclair does discuss the Atlantic type in his last chapter, "The Locomotive of Today," and he includes the E2-class in a table of proportions of noted locomotives. If he had given the claim credence, one would suppose that such an authority as Sinclair would have mentioned it in passing.

11. Fred Westing, *Apex of the Atlantics* (Milwaukee: Kalmbach Publishing Co.); PRR Test Plant Reports on the E6.
12. Paul T. Warner, in R&LHS *Bulletin* 92; see also Worley, p. 234.
13. Worley, pp. 233, 240. No. 738 became 4-4-0 No. 40.
14. BLW 1923 *History*, p. 89.
15. Bruce, pp. 293-95. The author has experienced the pronounced yawing action that can occur, even under light power, in an 0-6-0 with drive on the middle axle, co-located with the engine's center of gravity – in this case, Strasburg Rail Road No. 31, a 1908 Baldwin product.
16. Worley, pp. 156-72. This count excludes two engines of the 564-class and the four 1200-class Pacifics that were rebuilt to 2-6-2s in 1929-1932. The count includes the 1000-class as rebuilt.
17. Bruce, pp. 296-98.
18. BLW 1923 *History*, p. 96; Bruce, pp. 295-96.
19. Bruce, p. 295. As the term suggests, cylinder horsepower is measured in the cylinders, using a device called an indicator. Cylinder horsepower does not include frictional resistance of the locomotive itself, which can amount to several hundred horsepower at 50 to 60 mph; and operation of the valve gear, which can range between 25 and 50 horsepower. The usual term for cylinder horsepower is indicated horsepower, abbreviated as "ihp." Horsepower measured at the tender coupler, and hence the net of all deductions taken by the locomotive itself, is called drawbar horsepower, abbreviated as "dbhp." Dbhp at a given speed is thus always less than ihp. For both indicated and drawbar horsepower, what is physically measured is pounds of pull. For indicated horsepower, it is the pull averaged over a full stroke of either piston, and the combined pull when the pistons overlap; for drawbar horsepower, it is the actual pull on the coupler averaged over seconds or minutes of time.
20. Bruce, pp. 250-55.
21. Omer Lavallée, *Canadian Pacific Steam Locomotives*, chapters 7, 9-12. G3-class 4-6-2s were built at least through 1943 with the Vaughan-Winterrowd truck. One could reasonably argue that the Vaughan-Winterrowd truck (and the Player before it) was not even a truck, but simply a transversely sliding axle held within the locomotive's main frame.
22. BLW 1923 *History*, p. 90.
23. See White, pp. 187-204. The so-called Stephenson form with double eccentrics and changing cutoff, used so extensively from 1855, was not attributable to either George or Robert Stephenson. The firm, Robt. Stephenson & Co., favored a single eccentric per valve and cylinder in the early 1830s. Double eccentrics (one for forward travel and one for reverse, per valve and cylinder) were tried by William T. James in 1829 and patented by Stephen H. Long, an associate of Philadelphia's Norris Locomotive Works, in 1833. James claimed to have invented the mature Stephenson form – the link motion – in 1832, but without notice by the wider engineering community. In 1842, Williams and Howe, two workers at Robt. Stephenson & Co., independently devised a link motion. Stephenson and other builders rapidly adopted it. The "hook motion," using double eccentrics and favored by most American builders to about 1855, did not have any provision for changing cutoff underway.
24. See Chapter 5 for further discussion of Muhlfeld's No. 2400. William Mason had used Walschaerts valve gear in 1874 on a Mason-Fairlie engine (White, p. 201), and the gear was in use on a number of locomotives in Europe, though the Stephenson form was favored.
25. *Locomotive Carriage & Wagon Review*, (United Kingdom), Sept. 1932, Feb. 1933.
26. The valve's motion is in contrast to that of a cam-driven valve. Such a valve opens (goes "up") and closes (goes "down"), as determined by its cam. The valve's motion is not back-and-forth from a center position. A cam-actuated valve is timed by the position of the crankshaft – as is a steam-distribution valve. But a cam-actuated valve's motion (e.g., duration and lift) is also determined, wholly apart from crankshaft/camshaft rotation, by the shape of the cam.
27. This and the following discussion of valve gears are from Bruce, pp. 196-209; Johnson (1944), pp. 239-51; Henderson (1907), pp. 81-164; C.H. Peabody, *Valve Gears for Steam Engines* (1900); and White (1979), pp. 187-202.
28. Johnson, p. 239.
29. Bruce, p. 200, says 8 inches. Johnson, p. 245. says 8½ inches. Johnson, who worked for Baldwin, was evidently partial to the Walschaerts gear as opposed to the Baker, and Bruce, who worked for Alco, was partial to the Baker.
30. *Locomotive Carriage & Wagon Review*, March 1937.
31. See Johnson, p. 245; Bruce, p. 201.
32. Bruce, p. 201.
33. Bruce, p. 201; E.W. King, Jr., *Trains*, May 1984, pp. 34-41.
34. Bruce, p. 201.

Chapter 4

Big Wheels Turning:

A History of Counterbalancing, or, Science and Snake Oil

THE PRECEDING CHAPTER DEALS WITH improvements in vehicular design up to the turn of the century, improvements largely forced by the increasing weight, speed, and power of American locomotives after 1880. That forcing, in turn, was driven by the rapidly accelerating economic growth of the country in the 1880s and 1890s, leading to huge increases in rail traffic. As John H. White Jr. has pointed out in *The American Railroad Freight Car*, locomotive sizes, rail cross-sections and alloys, track structure, bridges, cars, freight-train lengths, and passenger-train speeds all grew or developed together in interlocked fashion.

As we have seen in previous chapters, however, the ways in which locomotive designers chose to respond to new engineering challenges had only partly to do with economics. A fine case in point is locomotive driving-wheel counterbalancing. A seemingly trivial story – balancing rather large masses of iron or steel with other large masses – turns out to be filled with various measures of science, pseudoscience, and black art.

A driving-wheel counterweight is the sector- or crescent-shaped part of the wheel directly opposite the crankpin. As seems intuitively clear enough, this part of the wheel contains extra weight to balance the mass of the rods attached to the pin. As the rods revolve on their pins, so revolve the counterweights. The opposite masses of rods and weights allow the locomotive to speed down the line without unbalanced centrifugal forces in the wheels putting big kinks into the rails.

These basic physical principles were known at least as far back as the time of the classical Greeks or Mesopotamians. Most of the science is no more involved than the physics of a balance scale or a teeter-totter. Two equal weights directly opposite one another, each disposed an equal distance from a central pivot, will balance. The weights are in balance whether at rest or spinning around the pivot. If, however, one of the weights is closer to the central pivot than the other, balance is achieved only if the weights are changed in proportion to the difference in their distances. Put one weight at half the distance from the pivot, for example, and one must double that weight to maintain the balance. Any other balanced relationship of weights and distances around the pivot

More than meets the eye: How to balance the revolving mass of the connecting rod and drivers with the reciprocating mass of the piston and crosshead? And what about the main rod, which revolves on one end and reciprocates on the other? It was a complex problem that engaged the best locomotive designers.
Philip R. Hastings, Courtesy Kalmbach Media

is a matter of simple proportion and arithmetic. Kids today learn the math by the sixth grade.

The earliest known locomotive counterweights are those seen on the only contemporary drawing of the English-built *Stourbridge Lion* of 1829, the first locomotive in America.[1] Why counterweights were applied to the *Lion* is puzzling, however, since that engine otherwise followed British design of the time for colliery locomotives, which did not use such weights. These locomotives, with their vertical cylinders and walking beams, moved along slowly; they simply did not reach speeds at which counterbalancing was necessary. Even with the widespread adoption of direct-connected drive – following Robert Stephenson's *Rocket* locomotive of 1829 – many British designers ignored counterbalancing into the 1840s, or only balanced for the revolving, or "dead," weight of cranks and back-ends of main rods. (Balancing for the revolving dead weights was common in stationary-engine practice.) In some early locomotives, the balance weights, if present at all, were hidden inside the wheel rims or, if tubular wrought iron spokes were used, hidden inside the spokes.[2]

Counterweights became increasingly common practice on American locomotives by the late 1840s, but again, only for the revolving masses. Some designers tried to minimize the aesthetic intrusion of the counterweight by blending it artfully into the wheel, between and below the plane of the spokes.[3] If, in the early 19th century a well-made carriage wheel was a symbol of graceful motion and an aesthetic ideal, then the appearance of any asymmetry in a wheel must have offended designers' sensibilities.

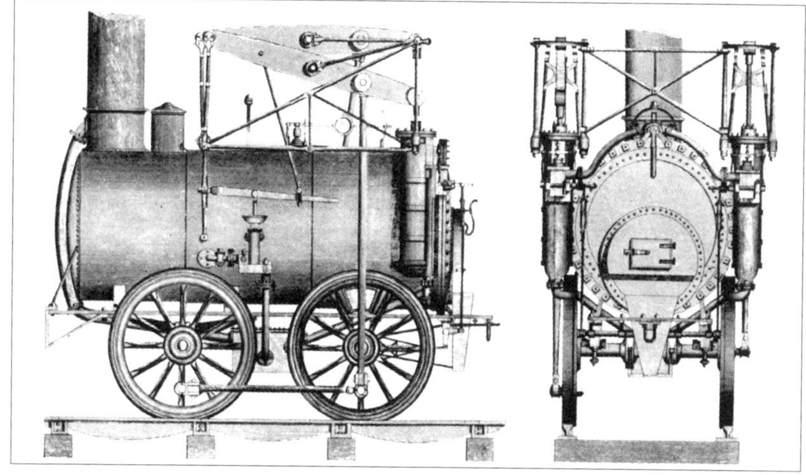

The *Stourbridge Lion* had counterweights, visible here behind the main rod. This is the only contemporary illustration of the *Lion*; it was prepared by James Renwick, a Columbia College professor who advised Delaware & Hudson's engineers.
James Renwick, Treatise on the Steam Engine, 1830

America, an 1867 product of the Grant Locomotive Works of Paterson, N.J., had counterweights between the spokes. The riveted-on design allowed for easy change-out and experimentation.
Author's Collection

In American practice in the 1850s, the weight itself was sometimes cast into the wheel center near the rim or, more often, made in the form of separate, cast weights secured by well-fitted iron plates riveted or bolted between the spokes.[4] In the latter case, aesthetic considerations were subordinated. The riveted-on form allowed change to the weight used, since – as will be seen below – the amount of weight required for the best riding quality included more than that needed to balance revolving masses; exactly how much to use was problematic.

Related to the amount of weight was the weight's shape. Before long, designers realized that a weight that filled a whole sector of the wheel was rather inelegant. The center of gravity of such a weight was well inward from the wheel's rim. If that center of gravity were moved closer to the rim, a given weight of side rods could be balanced with less mass in the counterweight. (The situation is exactly the same as a lighter-weight child being able to balance a heavier child on a seesaw by sitting farther from the fulcrum.) Hence, beginning in the 1860s, a common shape for a counterweight became a broad arc, with the arc's outer edge as close as possible against the rim. A weight in such a shape was cast integrally with its wheel and with one or more cavities; the precise amount of counterweighting in the wheel could be adjusted by lead poured into the cavities and then sealed off. By the 1870s, it was common for a given locomotive to have counterweights that all appeared to be the same size. But the counterweights had different amounts of lead within – and significantly more for the main driver, which unlike the other drivers had the heavy main rod attached.

The problem in determining the actual amount of counterweighting to use lay in the fact that the counterweights actually had to balance two different sets of motions by the rods against the engine's crankpins: revolving motions and reciprocating motions. This difference became generally appreciated only after the mid-1850s. Balancing the revolving masses was in fact trivial. The so-called "side" rods – those rods that connected adjacent driving wheels and thus stayed always parallel to the ground – revolved in perfectly circular fashion and thus could be perfectly balanced by revolving counterweights. The rub lay with the reciprocating masses: the pistons, piston rods, crossheads, and some indeterminate portion of the main rods. A piston and a crosshead only reciprocated; a main rod reciprocated at one end and revolved at the other. Somehow, these complex motions had to be dynamically offset by counterweights that only revolved. When locomotives were relatively light and their power machinery light as well (*Phantom*, for example), the inertial forces

Charleston & Savannah 4-6-0 engine No. 100 had arc-shaped weights. The weights were divided into hollow sectors that could be filled with variable amounts of lead.

James Dredge, A Record of the Transportation Exhibits at the World's Columbian Exposition of 1893

Phantom, built by William Mason of Taunton, Mass., in 1857, required no counterweights.
Artizan, February 1, 1859

involved were small. As locomotives grew more powerful, counterweighting for both revolving and reciprocating forces became necessary and an arena of hot debate for designers.

If left uncompensated, the reciprocating masses – alternately accelerating back and forth on each side of the engine – caused a locomotive to surge fore-and-aft and to twist and yaw around its vertical axis. Since the pistons and cranks in any two-cylinder steam engine must be set at 90 degrees from one another (see Chapter 1), the surging and lateral yawing in a locomotive could take on a highly disconcerting "galloping" quality. The yawing, usually called "hunting" or "nosing," could get severe at speed, spreading rail or worse.

It was not a question of steam thrust. It was entirely a question of the inertial forces of masses in motion. How those masses were moved was not the physical issue, nor the source of the longitudinal and vertical forces disturbing the locomotive at running speeds; it was only the motions of these masses that were the culprit.[5]

So, how did designers balance, or attempt to balance, the reciprocating masses? In every formula, the first step was to add the weights of the asymmetric revolving parts affecting each wheel, including side rod, rod bearing, and asymmetric wheel weight due to the presence of the crankpin and the wheel's reinforcement around the pin. Based on the distance of these masses from axle-center or rim, a preliminary counterweight mass and its distance from axle-center or rim could be easily determined for each wheel.

The next step was to add the weights of all the reciprocating parts on each side of the engine together. Piston, rings, piston rod, crosshead and crosshead slippers, crosshead key, wristpin, associated wristpin bearing, and retaining nuts could be directly weighed. But what of the main rod, which both reciprocates and rotates? Lacking any real theory in the matter, designers simply had the main rod weighed at each end. Main rods were often tapered, with the "fatter" end toward the crankpin at the wheel. The weight on the crankpin end was taken as revolving and hence added to the preliminary, revolving counterweight on the main driver. The weight on the wrist-pin end was taken as reciprocating. The latter weight was added to the other reciprocating weights to determine the total reciprocating mass per side.

Then – and this was perhaps more art than science – a percentage of the reciprocating mass was taken and the result was added to the counterweights. The percentage varied with the designer, but through the mid-1860s it was generally 75 to 100 percent. This extra counterweight mass per side was called the "excess balance," or, later on, the "overbalance." One of the pioneering British engineers in counterweighting, Daniel K. Clark, noted the work of Louis Le Chatelier in balancing some locomotives in France in 1849. Clark referred to "the disturbing forces" upsetting the balance, and he understood that more than the revolving masses needed to be compensated for. After several experiments, he was given permission to revise the balance on the locomotives Canute and Norman on the London & South Western Railway in 1856. By adding more weight – in fact nearly doubling the mass of the counterweights over and above the amount needed for the revolving masses – Clark greatly improved riding quality and, as Le Chatelier had also done, fuel economy. (Less energy was required in the cylinders to propel a better-balanced locomotive at a given net power output.) Clark recommended for outside-connected locomotives (those with cranks on the outside of the driving wheels), that 100 percent, and "not less than seven-eights," of the reciprocating mass be added to the balance weights in the wheels per side.[6]

A few designers in the early years placed the excess balance only in the main driver. More commonly, the excess balance per side was divided and distributed equally in the main and adjacent drivers. The excess balance in the driving wheels partly offset the motions of the reciprocating masses on each side and thereby reduced yawing or hunting. But there was a severe penalty: The excess balance naturally upset the driving wheels' revolving balance.[7]

The whole proposition was an inherent compromise. A locomotive could have a lot of excess balance in the counterweights and have little or no yaw. But the wheels, imbalanced in rotation, then produced a cyclic vertical oscillation of up-and-down pressure on the rails. Or a locomotive could have less excess balance in the counterweights, to minimize vertical imbalance, but then yawing might be excessive.

The vertical part of the oscillation was usually called "rail pounding," but there were many misconceptions, and still are today, among working railroaders about such pounding. Seeing daylight under the drivers was sometimes reported. Nevertheless, a badly out-of-balance locomotive, once it reached even a moderate speed, would surely scare the daylights out of an engine crew, due to a lot of surging in the engine frame. An all-steel driving wheel-and-tire, however, can't act like a rubber tire. As long as the oscillation force upward was less than the weight of the engine carried on that wheel, then the wheel itself, in theory, couldn't move upward and thus would stay in firm contact with the rail. If the wheel couldn't move up off the rail, there was no pounding. Imbalance was nevertheless a very serious issue: The change in vertical pressure on the rail, upward and downward, with each rotation, could indeed kink the rail. And that condition was not subjective. A spinning driving wheel carrying, say, 30,000 pounds of static load would stay fully in contact with the rail even when the upward force from imbalance reached, say, 25,000 pounds. In that case, of course, 25,000 pounds was added to the static load by the force of imbalance every time it came back down.

Designers argued about what percentage of reciprocating weight to use for counterbalancing, and whether the percentage to choose was affected by either the weight of the locomotive, its speed, or both. There was no single answer. Riding characteristics of some engines were wonderfully smooth. Other locomotives rode harshly in one way or another at certain speeds

A crescent shape allowed the counterbalancing weight to be close to the driving-wheel rim, minimizing the weight needed for effective balance.
Courtesy Kalmbach Media

no matter how much mechanics adjusted the weights; evil traded for evil. Unknown were dynamic effects while a locomotive was underway at high speed, such as lateral rocking of the whole locomotive, which would clearly change the load carried by the drivers, or elastic properties of a steel wheel on a steel rail, especially when the rail was not firmly supported by ties and trackbed. Engineers certainly appreciated the fact that a rail could bend, and the reader can watch today how track, even if heavily built, moves slightly up and down in the ballast as a train rolls by.

By the late 1880s, and apart from the debate on the percentage of reciprocating weight to balance, designers were again trying differently shaped weights. Although the arc-shaped counterweight predominated, chord- and especially crescent-shaped weights began to proliferate. The justification was simple: the geometry of the new shapes allowed the center of gravity of a given counterweight to be located as close as possible to a driving wheel's

Small driving wheels sometimes didn't have enough space for arc-shaped weights. Even on this passenger engine with relatively large 69-inch drivers, space was at a premium.
Harold K. Vollrath Collection

rim, thus minimizing the weight required for a given amount of balancing. Even if the percentage of reciprocating weight to balance was the same, large and heavier pistons and rods demanded more counterweight mass. But the heavier spokes on heavier wheels left little available room for the needed weights, especially on freight locomotives. A crescent-shaped counterweight allowed an effective balance to be made where, in many cases, an arc-shaped counterweight having a center of gravity close enough to the rim could not be physically fitted in the wheel.

Two factors contributed to reducing the percentage of reciprocating weight that had to be balanced in the driving wheels. The first was the ever-increasing size and weight of the new locomotives, which tended to reduce the proportion of total engine weight (*i.e.*, exclusive of tender) accounted for by the heavier pistons and driving gear. Designers found that the excess balance, or overbalance, could be reduced to 60 to 70 percent (or sometimes less) in heavy locomotives and still result in acceptable riding qualities. Around 1900, the idea that a certain proportion of the total weight of the engine could be left out of the overbalance took hold. The Master Mechanics Association recommended that the unbalanced reciprocating weight per side could be 1/400 of the total engine weight.[8]

The second factor to help cut the overbalance was longer engine wheelbases. With a wheelbase extended over three or more driving axles, a lead truck, and a trailing truck, the lateral stability of a locomotive was significantly improved. With greater lateral stability less overbalance was needed to provide adequate damping of the yawing or hunting forces. In heavy 4-6-2s for passenger-train speeds, designers found that the overbalance could be reduced to 60 percent, and sometimes less. This lower amount of overbalance meant that the rotational balance of the driving wheels was improved, allowing higher rpm.

Reducing overbalance even a few percent was beneficial. The inertial forces on the rail and on the locomotive caused by machinery imbalance increase with the square of the locomotive's speed. A locomotive going twice as fast as another identical one, for example, has four times the forces from a given amount of unbalanced mass. Considering the cyclic forces imposed on the rail by the drivers, designers coined a term for the vertical component of rotational imbalance in the drivers: "dynamic augment." (Since dynamic augment increases with the square of the speed, the common belief among today's rail enthusiasts that a steam locomotive is "balanced for" a given speed can be seen to be quite mistaken; a two-cylinder locomotive is never in balance at any rpm, and the imbalance gets worse the faster it goes.)

Engineers calculated dynamic augment (DA) in pounds at various rpm. Upward, the DA value subtracts from a driving wheel's load on the rail; downward, DA adds to the wheel's load. At the highest speed the locomotive might reach, the upward DA obviously could not exceed the static wheel load – if it did, the driving wheel would certainly lift off the rail. Engineers knew it was wise to limit the DA to a value far less than the static load. But what limit?

One leading designer analyzed a typical, high-speed passenger locomotive of 1900, a 4-4-2 with 80-inch diameter drivers. Being a rather lightweight locomotive, the 1/400 rule gave the overbalance of 80 percent: The reciprocating mass per side added up to 600 lbs., so 480 lbs. of overbalance (80 percent) was added to the counterweights per side, or 240 lbs. per driving wheel, over and above the revolving balance. At 80 mph, the overbalance of 240 lbs. per wheel produced a DA of nearly 10,000 lbs. – five tons up and five tons down, with every revolution at that speed.[9] This DA value was well below the static driving-wheel load of 24,000 lbs., but it also meant a total vertical oscillation of 10 tons on the rail per wheel with every revolution. Rather than "dynamic augment," many railroaders – including civil engineers responsible for track – went beyond calling it "pounding" to assail it (erroneously) as "hammer blow."[10]

Sometimes the imbalance did not seem to play by the physical rules as then understood. Despite the use of accepted counterbalancing practice, locomotives of various classes differed markedly in both vertical and lateral oscillations at speed. In 1904, Prof. W.F.M. Goss of Purdue University used a test plant erected by the Pennsylvania Railroad at the the St. Louis world's fair to investigate such alleged "hammer blow." While a locomotive ran at various rpm on the plant, Goss ran lengths of annealed steel wire between a driving wheel and its supporting roller. Index marks allowed the squashed wires to be interpreted in relation to rotational positions of the driving wheel.[11]

W.F.M. Goss.
Purdue University

Writing in 1908, Vaughn Pendred, editor of *The Engineer*, the journal of the Society of Engineers in Great Britain, summarized Goss's findings:

> Where a wheel is lifted through the action of its balance weight, its rise is comparatively slow and its descent rapid. The maximum lift occurs after the counterbalance has passed its highest point. [In this description, the wheel is not leaving the rail, but is varying its vertical load on the rail.] The rocking of the engine on its springs may assist or oppose the action of the counterbalance in lifting the wheel. It [the spring action] therefore constitutes a serious obstacle in the way of any study of the precise movements of the wheel. The contact of the moving wheel with the rail is not continuous, even for those portions of the revolution where the pressure is greatest, but is a rapid succession of impacts. There is a reason, however, to believe that the [effect described] is the result of the metals concerned, namely, the surface of the tire and the rail.

Pendred then offered the punchline:

> These experiments go to show that the received theory that a driving wheel rolls quietly on a rail with an insistent pressure varying rhythmically throughout each revolution is not quite consistent with the facts, the phenomena of the relations of wheel and rail being complex instead of simple."[12]

At no time throughout the history of the steam locomotive could designers analyze the dynamics of wheel or rail elasticity, nor could they predict the compound interactions of wheel imbalance, rail elasticity, wheel elasticity, and the driver springs. It was a conundrum beyond solution then – and one that would challenge even today's analytical modeling techniques. So designers ignored the conundrum and continued using their empirical rules.

From about 1900 to 1910, as the debates about counterbalancing went on, a number of railroads bought some real snake oil. The bogus prescription was alleged to lessen "hammer blow." In this method, two counterweights were placed on each driving wheel, the weights arranged at 120 degrees from the crankpin, as seen on the Missouri Pacific engine on the facing page. This so-called three-point balancing was supposed to direct the unbalanced forces in three directions instead of two, thereby alleviating the imbalance in any one direction.[13]

It was, to borrow a metaphor from another kind of transportation, bilgewater. In any unbalanced system around a pivot – or around an axle – with any number of fixed weights, a simple resolution of vectors will show a single vector (*i.e.*, a single amount of weight at a single direction and distance) that is equivalent to the sum of the others. All that was accomplished by putting two counterweights on one wheel was to increase the total mass in the wheel required to balance the various masses working on the crankpin.

Leading railroad mechanical departments were not fooled, and no builder, save perhaps Dickson,[14] pushed the idea. Still, a number of mechanical officers bought in. The Cleveland, Cincinnati, Chicago & St. Louis (the "Big Four Route"), for example, ordered many locomotives with the three-point balancing during a period of several years. A few other railroads did likewise. Perhaps some difference in riding quality was noted. But there were, as seen above, many complicating variables. After some dozen years, the technique died out. The wonder is that it persisted for so long.

By 1900, in fact, the techniques of locomotive counterbalancing began to incorporate some new principles borrowed from physics. In the 19th century, balancing techniques were based on principles that engineers would describe today as *statics* – forces in fixed structures, including static balancing. After 1900, principles from the study of *dynamics* – how to resolve forces that result from complex motions and accelerations – began to play a bigger role.

For example, engineers reconsidered the motions of the main rod, which rotates at one end and reciprocates at the other. Using some basic dynamics, the main rod could be studied as a pendulum. By measuring a main rod's natural period of oscillation (recall that "period" is the time of swing of a free pendulum), better calculations could be made of the rod's net centrifugal force at the crankpin end and of its accelerations and inertial force at the wristpin end, at various rpm.[15]

In practice, therefore, counterbalancing for a particular class of locomotives began, as before, with weighing all the purely reciprocating parts per side, weighing the side rods, and weighing the main rod. But a new step was added: Shop men actually hoisted up a main rod, swinging it at the wristpin end to find its period as a pendulum, and then swinging it from the other end as well. From there, the designer could calculate the main rod's own inertia at its various angles throughout a stroke. Rather than simply considering one end of the rod as revolving and one end as reciprocating, the actual longitudinal

Round counterweights, set at a 120-degree angle, enjoyed brief popularity on a few roads in the early 20th century.

Harold K. Vollrath

and vertical forces at each end of the rod could be resolved for a given rpm and a reciprocating balance better determined.[16]

The overbalance, in pounds added per wheel, thus became a percentage of the best available calculation of the reciprocating force, instead of a percentage of a reciprocating force when just using the static weight of the forward end of the main rod. Unfortunately, however, that extra refinement did not give any answer to the question of what percentage to use. Whether the overbalance should be 80 percent or 50 percent of the calculation above, or based on the 1/400th-of-the-engine-weight rule, was just as elusive as ever.

Another, more advanced, technique entered the lexicon at about the same time: "cross-counterbalancing." This refinement actually improved a locomotive's rotational balance considerably. In this method, the other principles of statics and dynamics still applied. But instead of the designer balancing driving wheels on each side of the engine, he balanced each driving-wheel pair, taking two wheels and their axle, together, as the unit to be balanced.

Railroad master mechanics had frequently gotten reports that, for heavy locomotives with large counterbalances, their driving wheels and axles sometimes wobbled laterally at moderate and high speed, the axles rocking transversely in the engine frame. The insight here was to see that, in any given driving wheel, the counterweight and the rods attached to the crankpin necessarily revolve in two different planes. With thick rods, the lateral separation of the plane of the counterweight's rotation and the plane of rotation of the rod or rods (main rod and side rod at the main crankpin) could be significant. Hence, the rotating driving wheel was not balanced at all, side to side.

Using the rules of vectors, it was a simple matter for designers to see that the imbalance in any one wheel caused by its counterweight and rods revolving in different planes could be offset by a small weight placed in the other wheel of the same axle. Consider one driving wheel "near" to you and the other wheel on the same axle "far" from you. On the far wheel of that axle, a new weight was placed exactly opposite the crankpin of the near wheel. Likewise, a new weight was placed on the near wheel exactly opposite the crankpin of the far wheel.

On each wheel, the new weight was therefore set at 90 degrees from the main counterweight. The result was that both driving wheels on the axle – as a pair – were in much better rotary balance. The new cross-counterbalance weights balanced the revolving masses around and across the axle in all planes and on all axes.

In a cross-balanced axle, each wheel now had two weights, one very large (the main counterweight) and one comparatively small (the cross-balance weight). If desired, the two weights in each wheel could be geometrically summed. The resultant single weight was slightly "tilted" – away from the 180-degree line from the wheel's crankpin. This tilt is quite easily seen and is a visible trademark of cross-balanced locomotives. The tilt is always in the direction of the crankpin of the "far" wheel on the same axle.[17]

Principles of cross-balancing and other advanced methods were worked out by William Dalby, a professor of engineering at London's Imperial Institute (now Imperial College London) in a 1902 paper and in his classic

1907 work, *The Balancing of Engines*. Dalby used small brass models held in the air on springs, to test his vector calculations and to verify the dynamic stability of various arrangements of wheels, axles, balance weights, and attached connecting rods and reciprocating parts. A mathematical treatment especially for locomotive designers appeared in *Locomotive Operation* by George Henderson, a Baldwin Locomotive Works engineer who went on to a lucrative consulting practice.

Railroads pretty well ignored the new analyses of main-rod action and of cross-balancing for more than a decade. The problem with applying the sophisticated new rules seemed to be their use in the field. Even if the original manufacturer used the new rules, locomotives required machinery overhauls every few years, and it was essential that balancing rules be understood and applied by railroad field engineers and shop staff.

Recurring balancing problems in large locomotives kept the debate pot boiling, however. By the mid-1920s, cross-balancing of main driving wheels – since those wheels had the most massive counterweights, due to the attachment of the main rods to those wheels – became more frequent in high-speed passenger engines. Cross-balancing of drivers other than the mains, and of slower-speed locomotives altogether, remained rare.

The ever-more-massive counterweights needed in high-speed freight engines pushed the art along. By the late 1920s, locomotives for high-speed freight duty ordinarily ran at 50 mph or better on driving wheels of only moderate diameter. Freight locomotives needed smaller-diameter drivers than passenger engines, so that piston speed and rpm could be matched to give the highest torque at moderate speed. In the 1920s, it was difficult to find enough physical room on a freight engine's main drivers to accommodate the needed counterweight. Cross-balancing (sometimes called "dynamic balancing" in the trade literature) offered a partial solution because cross-balancing had an effect on the calculations of reciprocating overbalance. Without cross-balancing, the previously standard calculations gave too little balancing weight for the revolving parts. With that deficiency corrected, the amount of reciprocating overbalance mass in the counterweights could actually be reduced for a given amount of reciprocating mass attached to the wheel.[18]

Committees of the Master Mechanics Association and of the American Railway Association (ARA, predecessor to the modern Association of American Railroads) tried to codify recommendations. In 1915, the master mechanics had ruled that overbalance should be 50 percent of reciprocating weight per side, and this rule stood for many years.

Since there was still no theoretical basis for this percentage, and since empirical results still varied widely in terms of locomotive riding, the debates recurred. Committees of railroad mechanical officers tried to reconcile old balancing rules derived from statics with the new rules from dynamics, which only added to the general confusion for railroad shopmen and frontline supervisors not conversant with advanced physics.

In 1931, an ARA committee recommended (1) that at least the main drivers be cross-balanced; (2) that the overbalance be about 32 percent of total reciprocating weight per side, with that weight equally distributed in all the drivers; and (3), in a move that seemed shockingly regressive, that the reciprocating and revolving masses of the main rod be found simply by weighing each end. Forget all the "pendulum" business; just weigh each end, as was done in 1880.

The new recommendation was smarter than it appeared. The ARA committee found that if the main drivers were cross-balanced, just weighing each end of the main rod and using an overbalance of about 32 percent was, in most locomotives, virtually equivalent to apportioning the weight of the main rod with a lot of involved math and then using a 50 percent overbalance. In the average railroad's mechanical department, the "gravity" or "scale" method for apportioning the weight of the main rod was certainly more understandable. After feedback from the field, the ARA revisited the balancing issue in 1934 and revised the overbalance percentage to 40, "on the basis that this would improve riding of the locomotive without raising the track stresses to any appreciable degree."[19]

As to the perennial question of the main rod's inertia, designers at the major builders did not accept the ARA's simplified method. By 1930, leading designers dealt with the main rod as a "compound pendulum," an improvement over the original pendulum method described in 1904 by Henderson. In the more modern method, the main rod was hoisted up and swung from the wristpin end, the rod's natural period was found, and a calculation was made to find the rod's "center of percussion."[20] The reciprocating portion of the main rod thus found was added to find the total reciprocating weight, and 30 to 40 percent was generally added as overbalance to the counterweights. There was a lot of variation, however. A sampling of high-speed passenger locomotives built between 1935 and 1940 shows overbalance values from 26 percent to 37 percent.[21]

Ralph Johnson, chief engineer at Baldwin, echoed in 1942 the same notion put forward by Henderson in 1904 when he wrote that "… the proper fraction of reciprocating balance is not correctly expressed as a per cent of total reciprocating weights. [The best approach is to determine] the portion of the reciprocating weight which may be *left unbalanced in proportion to the total weight of the locomotive*…."[22] (Emphasis added.)

Based on his comparative study, Johnson felt that "a ratio of unbalanced reciprocating weights on each side to the total weight of the locomotive of 1/285" would give results in riding quality as good as the best locomotives of the 1930s. Compared to the old Master Mechanics' recommendation of 1/400th of the engine weight left unbalanced, Johnson was recommending a considerable increase in proportion of reciprocating mass to leave unbalanced.

Counterbalancing theory never advanced any further. European high-speed steam locomotives from 1900 to the end of their development – especially locomotives of French and German design and some of British – continued to rely on multiple cylinders to give superb balance, as described more fully in the next chapter. Passenger locomotives with three or four driving axles powered by four balanced cylinders, with either compound or simple steam expansion, were common in continental Europe. In the U.S., with its high comparative labor costs, just two cylinders were the rule for both freight and passenger locomotives, with from two to five driving axles.

In the 1920s, a few American railroads – New York Central, Lackawanna, Union Pacific, Southern Pacific, and some others – ordered three-cylinder engines. They came in 4-8-2, 4-10-2, and, finally, 4-12-2 configurations. These were simple-expansion locomotives, and the advantage of three cylinders lay in the increased traction they provided compared with two cylinders; three pistons cranking on the driving wheels gave smoother torque and greater tractive effort for the same weight on drivers. Balancing issues, though, were little affected. That was because, with the Gresley conjugating valve gear that was always used on these U.S. locomotives, the outer crankpins were necessarily set at 90 degrees from each other. Thus, the two outside cylinders' valve motion was combined (by the small, lateral valve-actuating rod seen at the front of any Gresley-geared locomotive) to produce the middle valve's motion. That valve motion was proper for the middle cylinder, provided that the crank-axle was set at an angle precisely between the two outside crankpins (*i.e.*, at 135 degrees from both outside pins).[23]

In such an engine, balancing the middle reciprocating and revolving masses was realized by twin counterweights surrounding the crank webs of the crank-axle; balancing the outer reciprocating and revolving parts was done in the usual manner in the wheels. Overbalance percentages per side and in the crank axle were calculated according to the usual rules. Three-cylinder locomotives ran smoothly and delivered high traction, but most railroad master mechanics objected to the extra labor costs of maintaining internal driving gear, just as they had objected to internal driving gear in other, multi-cylinder engines. Three-cylinder locomotives remained rare in the U.S.

In two-cylinder engines, meanwhile, the only path to better balance was lighter-weight moving parts. Starting in the mid-1920s, designers made a concerted effort to reduce the weight of pistons, crossheads, and rods. If these parts were made lighter, any given balancing-percentage rule would mean lighter counterbalances and therefore less dynamic augment, oscillating vertically on the rails.

Better design of cast-steel pistons and crossheads reduced weight; improved alloys for the rods did the same. Vanadium steel became common in rods. New, multiple-bearing crossheads were much lighter than older forms. By the mid-1930s, rods and reciprocating parts generally weighed ten to fifteen percent less than they did in the early 1920s.

Next came the design of the driving wheels themselves. Again, it was a search for light weight, more room for the counterweight mass, and equal or improved wheel strength. In the early 1930s, Commonwealth Steel Castings introduced its "Boxpok" driving wheel design (pronounced "box-spoke;" the company made that clear in its ads). Instead of using spokes, the new wheel was a hollow casting that derived its strength from its inner and outer plates joined by box-girder like sections. In the depth of the Depression, it was a gutsy move by a wheel supplier to introduce a new product; locomotive orders were a trickle and most erecting halls closed for at least some part

Disc drivers saved weight while increasing strength. This is the Boxpok design from Commonwealth Steel Castings. *Courtesy Kalmbach Media*

of 1931-33. But as locomotive orders picked up after 1933, Commonwealth found a somewhat growing market. Other suppliers introduced competitive hollow-cast, "disc" designs, or offered wheels with lighter, reinforced spokes ("web spokes") to cut wheel weight.

The hollow, so-called disc driving wheels – which many rail buffs today erroneously assume were somehow cast solid – achieved a functional yet sculptured look that bordered on art. Possibly the most elegant looking were the Scullin "double disc" wheels, which were used on very few locomotives. Industrial designer Henry Dreyfuss wanted these wheels in 1938 for the locomotives he had streamlined for New York Central's restyled *20th Century Limited* and for 1941's *Empire State Express*. Although two different wheel designs were eventually used on the J3a-class Hudson-type locomotives for the *Century*, those engines with the Scullins became the virtual trademarks of the restyled train. For *Fortune* magazine in 1938, artist Charles Sheeler painted a celebrated, super-realist picture whose composition was simply a portrait of

RIGHT Baldwin disc drivers on Santa Fe 4-8-4 Northern No. 3780.
Courtesy Kalmbach Media

BELOW Scullin "double-disc" drivers of NYC J-3a Hudson No. 5429, streamlined in 1941 for *Empire State Express* service.
Courtesy Kalmbach Media

a J3a's three huge disc drivers about to move; Sheeler called it "Rolling Power." Critics commented that the picture embodied the energy of a brave new streamlined era, as the nation pulled out of economic and spiritual Depression.

There was another, subdued aesthetic twist in Sheeler's faithful depiction: Any appearance of counterweights was gone. Just as designers in the 1850s sometimes hid away those asymmetric inconveniences inside hollow spokes, so did the designers of the Scullin wheels mask their counterweights behind smooth discs. There's something about a wheel – or its observers – that does not like asymmetry.

There was another element in Sheeler's painting that was adopted by a number of railroads in the late-1930s and 1940s. This was the design of thin-section, lightweight, special alloy side- and main-rods originated by the Timken Roller Bearing Co. Roller bearings on locomotive axles, introduced by Timken in the early 1930s, had spread rapidly, radically reducing axle-bearing failures and improving locomotive reliability. Roller bearings on crankpins and rods never became as popular. In some high-speed passenger engines, where locomotive designers wanted ultra-light weight in the rods to help with counterbalancing and thereby reduce dynamic augment, roller-bearing rods were tried. New York Central, Norfolk & Western, Chesapeake & Ohio, Santa Fe, and the Pennsylvania Railroad applied Timken rods on new passenger locomotives. Results were mixed. Santa Fe liked the new rods. In Norfolk & Western's experience with its powerful class-J 4-8-4, however, the Timken rod's thin section of steel immediately surrounding a roller-bearing race tended to distort under high thrust loads. With only slight distortion in the steel supporting a rod bearing race, the roller bearing failed.[24]

On railroads across the country, practical problems of counterbalancing persisted. Despite all the years of improvement, dynamic augment values in new locomotives were still ordinarily 4,500 to 7,000 lbs. per wheel at driver-diameter speed. And in older locomotives, lead sometimes disappeared from counterbalance cavities, since the soft metal was pulverized by vibration. Locomotives thus could become underbalanced; one such locomotive, underbalanced by some 1,000 lbs. of missing mass in each main driver, kinked more than 700 39-foot rails in a distance of 100 miles. Other locomotives were found with too much overbalance; rebalancing with updated methods improved rotational balance and therefore speed. A difference of only 100 lbs. in counterweight mass could make a substantial difference.[25] Even new locomotives were not immune to difficulties. The twelve class R-1 4-8-4s for the Atlantic Coast Line, built by Baldwin in 1938, were designed with an overbalance of just 26 percent per side. This low percentage of overbalance improved the driving wheels' rotational balance and gave a low dynamic augment, but these engines quickly gained a reputation for very rough riding.[26]

The apogee in balancing for high rpm came with the Norfolk & Western J-class 4-8-4s, built in the railroad's own shops at Roanoke, Va., from 1941 to 1950, and used in passenger service. Chief Engineer Robert Pilcher and the N&W design staff rethought the balancing problem. The driving-wheel diameter of the J needed to be about 70 inches – small for a passenger engine – in order to develop optimal rpm and horsepower for an average of 40 to 60 mph on N&W's mountainous profile. But smooth riding at 80 mph was also required on the tidewater flats south of Norfolk.

The right-side main 70-inch driving wheel of Norfolk & Western Class J 4-8-4 No. 611, showing the "big end" of the main rod (at top), the eccentric crank (at center), and the big-end concentric rod (at bottom). *Historic American Engineering Record, Library of Congress*

Pilcher and his team reasoned that if the lateral stability of the locomotive could be improved, then the overbalance could be reduced below the figure called for by the conventional rules. The only reason for the overbalance, after all, was to prevent the locomotive from laterally yawing or hunting. The bad experience of the Atlantic Coast Line R-1, however, was a cautionary tale. So the N&W designers greatly stiffened the lateral resistance built into the centering devices of the J's lead truck and of its trailing truck. This greater stiffness at both ends of the engine, together with the long 4-8-4 wheelbase, led designers to try an overbalance value that was unheard of: 20 percent. Calculations of lateral stability based on total mass of the locomotive and resistance imposed by the trucks gave confidence in the choice.[27]

The J, as built, developed it highest drawbar horsepower at 45 to 50 mph, as planned – and it could run with the wind. In a test that was much remarked upon in the trade, a J with a 1,025-ton train hit 110 mph across Tidewater Virginia's Great Dismal Swamp. At that speed, its 70-inch drivers and attached roller-bearing rods were turning at an amazing 528 rpm. Railroaders were shocked: 80-inch diameter wheels were considered the minimum size for such a speed, even though such tall drivers sacrificed low-end pulling power. The Association of American Railroads' pre-war locomotive performance goal of 100 mph with a 1,000-ton passenger train had been shattered by an engine that was actually intended for more-modest speeds.

There was, ultimately, an unavoidable penalty for the J to pay. When diesels finally came to the N&W and the Js were bumped to duty on curvy branch lines, the J's lateral stiffness made them totally unsuitable. The big locomotives could not cope with sharp curves: either the engines promptly derailed or they flopped rails right over.

In the end, the new diesel locomotives from General Motors, the American Locomotive Co., and others rendered all the counterbalancing business moot. Diesel-electrics did not have main or side rods. A diesel's tractive torque was perfectly smooth and its dynamic augment was nil. A wonderful story of creative address to an insoluble problem, carried on for more than a century and vital to the transportation of an ascendant industrial age, was utterly swept away.

Chapter 4 Notes

1. James Renwick, *Treatise on the Steam Engine*, 1830.
2. See Vaughn Pendred, *The Railway Locomotive: What It Is and Why It Is What It Is* (1908); Zerah Colburn, *Locomotive Engineering and the Mechanism of Railways* (1871); and Angus Sinclair, *Development of the Locomotive Engine* (1907). At the date of publication of the present volume, all of these books were available on the internet.
3. See White, pp. 320 ff. For examples of aesthetics, see *Croton*, p. 333; *Columbia*, p. 338; *Superior*, p. 343; and *Phantom*, p. 387, the last of which had no counterweights. See also *Champlain*, p. 325; and *Talisman*, p. 361, both of which had sector-style counterweights. Engines not originally built with counterweights often had them added later.
4. Remember that the term "wheel center" refers to the entire wheel inside the tire. For the riveted-on form of counterweight, see White, pp. 361 and 393; both engines were built in 1857.
5. The counterbalancing problem involves inertia, mass, and accelerations of mass; steam thrust has nothing to do with it. In a locomotive at any speed, the forces of steam thrust more-or-less balance themselves: the steam's force against the piston is equal and opposite to the force against the cylinder head, and the force against the cylinder head is equal and opposite to the force against the rail. Because a cylinder's centerline and its associated driving wheels are in somewhat different planes, there is an asymmetry of thrust between piston and rail, but not nearly the degree of asymmetry that exists between the locomotive's center of gravity and the inertial forces of the reciprocating masses of pistons, crossheads, etc., slinging back and forth at the engine's sides. High steam thrust in a short-wheelbase locomotive will produce a yawing or hunting at low speed, but imbalanced reciprocating masses produce increased yawing forces the higher the speed.
6. Colburn, Chs. 20-21, pp. 252-56. Also see Pendred, pp. 76-78.
7. Daniel Kinnear Clark, *Railway Machinery* (1855); Alexander W. Makinson, "On Some of the Internal Disturbing Forces of Locomotive Engines," an 1862 paper delivered to the Institution of Civil Engineers (U.K.); Colburn, *Locomotive Engineering and the Mechanism of Railways* (1871); Forney, *Catechism*, Ch. 19 (1873, 1889); J.G.A. Meyer, *Modern Locomotive Construction* (1892), pp. 221-59; G.R. Henderson, *Locomotive Operation* (1907), pp. 41-74; Pendred, *The Railway Locomotive* (1908), Ch. 9; A.J. Wood, *Principles of Locomotive Operation* (1915), Ch. 14; see also Ralph P. Johnson, *The Steam Locomotive: Its Theory, Operation, and Economics* (1942) Ch. 16, and Alfred W. Bruce, *The American Steam Locomotive* (1952) pp. 222-24.
8. Henderson (1907 ed.), pp. 45-46.
9. Henderson (1907 ed.), pp. 64-69.
10. Pendred, p. 79.
11. *Locomotive Testing Plant at the Louisiana Purchase Exposition, St. Louis, Missouri, U.S.A.*, Pennsylvania Railroad, 1904.
12. Pendred, p. 82.
13. The originator of this bogus method is yet to be determined. The author was unable to find any discussion of it in the professional journals of the day.
14. *Railroad History*, issue 197 (Fall-Winter 2007), p. 26.
15. Henderson (1907), pp. 50-64.
16. Henderson (1907), pp. 50-64.
17. Henderson (1907), pp. 70-74.
18. Johnson (1942), pp. 256, 262-65.
19. Johnson, p. 265.
20. Johnson, pp. 255-58.
21. Johnson, Table 16, p. 268.
22. Johnson, p. 267.
23. This permitted the middle cylinder's valve to be actuated by a simple "conjugated valve gear," *i.e.*, a valve motion derived from the two outer valve gear, thus precluding the need for a third eccentric and its associated valve gear. The conjugated motion was developed by Nigel Gresley in Britain.
24. Based on the author's discussions with Scott Lindsay, formerly of the Norfolk & Western steam crew.
25. Johnson, pp. 256, 278.
26. Johnson, p. 268; David P. Morgan, *Steam's Finest Hour*, (1975), p. 71.
27. Based on the author's discussions with Ed King, Jr., Norfolk & Western steam historian, who interviewed Robert Pilcher.

Section II: 1900-1920

"Science and Empiricism in Conflict"

From Compound Cylinders to Superheating

During the 1890s, designers became increasingly anxious to improve locomotive efficiency, as measured in fuel and water consumption per ton-mile hauled. That meant thermal efficiency – a locomotive's net power output per unit of fuel consumed and steam produced. For railroad managers, costs and efficiency were measured more simply – on accounting and tonnage sheets.

More than the direct bills for fuel and water were involved. If a locomotive of a given size and weight could be made more thermally efficient, its maximum power could be greater because a higher percentage of the fuel burned became horsepower in the cylinders at working speeds. Another result was labor efficiency, since the ton-mileage produced per locomotive crew increased. Between runs, maintenance also had complex cost consequences. Servicing and maintenance simplicity was key to reduced labor hours in the roundhouse and backshop. In turn, this resulted in better asset utilization of the locomotives, as they spent a greater percentage of their time on the road, generating revenue.

Designers understood these issues. Among engineers in any field, improved efficiency had always been a universal objective, and one that translated into prestige among peers and employers. But better thermal efficiency came most often at the price of more complex boiler and engine systems. Hence, designers knew an all-important caution: What was gained in fuel and labor savings out on the road could be eaten up in shop costs and reduced productivity. Nonetheless, the pressure on designers to make performance improvements was unrelenting and capital-driven, and not merely limited to theoretical concerns.

In the 1880s and after, that pressure stemmed from the increasingly competitive nature of railroading as an investment. In prior decades, the overwhelming economic advantage of railroads over other forms of transport such as wagon roads and canals – in transit time, in cost, or in the combination of the two – ensured generous capital inflow to almost any railroad that could throw tracks down between viable shipping points.[1] By the mid-1880s, however, the maturing railroad network was characterized by several companies competing for trade between almost any pair of large cities or major industrial centers. Bankers and stockholders unrelentingly pushed the railroads, always capital-dependent, to maximize return. Put another way, higher-profit railroads attracted needed capital; lower-profit lines did not. As price competition (and, later, regulation) pushed down shipping prices, the only avenue left was reducing unit costs.[2] Locomotive fleet managers and therefore designers lived squarely in the middle of this food chain.

In that setting, designers paid close attention both to science, as they understood it, and to locomotive engineering practice on railroads throughout the industrial world. Two highly significant innovations – two of the most important in steam locomotion's 150-year history – were essentially of European origin and were developed by a combination of thermal science and Edison-style "try-it-and-see." These innovations were, first, cylinder compounding and, a few years later, steam superheating. In North America, the first became the focus of intense development and use from the late 1880s through about 1910. Then, except for limited application on a very few U.S. lines, its use quickly disappeared in new locomotives on this continent. The second, superheating, was first adopted in fleet use in this hemisphere by the Canadian Pacific in 1904. After 1910 and through all the remaining years of steam power, nearly every new U.S. and Canadian road locomotive, and many older engines by retrofit, were superheater-equipped.

Evidence suggests that the two innovations could provide roughly equal improvement in thermal performance. In many countries in Europe, both were developed to a high degree through the 1940s. But on this side of the Atlantic, one had a brief heyday and collapsed in popularity. The other spread like wildfire and became a permanent feature. The story is a fascinating one of the limits to the science of the day, applied economics, and personal risk-taking in an engineering context.

1170

Chapter 5

Compounding:

A Burst of Engineering Creativity

In October 1889, the Baldwin Locomotive Works delivered an ordinary looking 4-4-0 American-type locomotive to the Baltimore & Ohio Railroad. B&O No. 848 included, however, a new design element. Instead of the two usual cylinders at the front of the engine there were four, with two of unequal size on each side of the engine. Each pair of cylinders, on each side, was arranged for "compound expansion." Baldwin's noted general superintendent, Samuel Vauclain, was especially pleased: the new locomotive was designed according to his patents.[3] B&O officials, whose readiness to try out new engineering ideas had encouraged Vauclain, found that their new locomotive significantly cut fuel charges. Suddenly, compounding became the talk of the American railroad community. In 1890, Baldwin geared up to respond to orders from carriers throughout the country, orders that surged through the decade.

As a method of increasing the thermal efficiency of steam cylinders in producing power, compound expansion was hardly a new idea. Compounding was standard practice in marine and stationary steam engine design in the late 1880s. The first such locomotive in the world was tried on the Erie Railroad 20 years before, but it was not a success.[4]

To appreciate the history of compounding, the reader needs to understand some of its basic principles. Cylinder function is relatively simple: Boiler steam, once fed to a single cylinder, volumetrically expands to produce power. When the cylinder's inlet port is closed ("admission cutoff"), the steam pressure in the cylinder is about the same as in the steam chest, which is some ten to fifteen percent below boiler pressure, due primarily to dynamic losses on the pathway from boiler to steam chest. After cutoff, the steam expands on its own, dropping in pressure and temperature until the exhaust port opens ("exhaust release"). Unfortunately for the cylinder's efficiency in converting steam to work, there is a great deal of pressure remaining – and energy wasted – at release.

For example, in a typical locomotive of the 1880s, boiler pressure might be 160 psi. Entering the cylinders, pressure would be about 140. Expansion occurs and work is produced, but at the point of exhaust release, the cylinder

The Santa Fe Railway had an intense but troubled love affair with compounding during the early 20th century; Mallet compound No. 1170 was a 2-6-6-2. Ultimately souring on the technology, Santa Fe would push the boundaries of simple expansion instead.
Courtesy Kalmbach Media

Baltimore & Ohio 4-4-0 No. 859, *Director General*, was a Baldwin-built Vauclain compound. It was exhibited at the 1893 World's Columbian Exposition. *James Dredge, A Record of the Transportation Exhibits at the World's Columbian Exposition of 1893*

pressure is still perhaps 70 psi, with considerable energy remaining in the steam. In a conventional locomotive, the exhausted steam provides draft, but no other benefit. However, if a second cylinder could be installed which took its inlet steam from the first (*i.e.*, the two cylinders to work in "compound"), more energy could be extracted. Expansion in the second cylinder could proceed from about 60 psi – allowing for pressure loss in passing between cylinders – down to about 30 psi. The area of the piston in the second, low-pressure cylinder would need to be about two to two-and-a-half times larger than the piston in the first, so that the two pistons generated equal thrust. In the example, energy is released from 140 psi down to 30 psi, rather than just from 140 to 70.

But, as we see so frequently in steam locomotive design, there were a number of unavoidable tradeoffs. Whenever a designer improved one aspect of locomotive performance, usually another aspect was harmed. With compounding, the first complication was the much-reduced exhaust steam pressure to the smokestack. (In our example, instead of 70 psi directed to the stack, now it was 30.) The resulting problem was less draft on the fire. The lower final exhaust pressure meant that the steam exhaust nozzle in the smokebox had to be restricted – made much smaller in diameter – in order to generate enough jet pressure in the stack to induce adequate draft in the firebox. The restricted nozzle increased backpressure against the cylinders, destroying some of the economy from the enhanced expansion ratio.[5]

Compounding made the problem of condensation in the cylinders, endemic to locomotives of the time, even more troublesome. Steam taken from the boiler was at the saturation point for its pressure and temperature. Any subsequent expansion of the steam below boiler pressure inevitably resulted in condensation, which was further exacerbated in the low-pressure cylinders of a compound engine. More condensation created more pressure loss, and too much water could do mechanical damage to valves and cylinders because of the water's incompressibility.

Another issue was simply the greater number of cylinders. In marine and stationary plant design, with generous physical limits on installation size, triple expansion was common. Steam was sent through three successively larger cylinders and then into a condenser at below-atmospheric pressure before completing an expansion cycle. On a locomotive, however, with its tight dimensional limitations on overall width and height, adding cylinders was difficult to do, and a condenser was out of the question. Additional cylinders also incurred added maintenance cost, primarily labor cost in the backshop whenever machinery overhaul or major adjustment such as setting of valve timing was needed. Two-thirds of total locomotive maintenance time went into the running machinery.

The challenge in taking a fundamental idea – any engineer familiar with Nicholas Carnot's classical thermodynamics or with William Rankine's basic principles of heat exchange knew perfectly well the benefits of greater expansion – and then dealing with all its practical consequences was daunting.

In the 1870s, American and European locomotive designers tried various compounding schemes. In 1870 and 1873, respectively, William Baxter, working with the Remington Arms Co., and William S. Hudson, working with the Rogers Locomotive and Machine Works, proposed compound locomotives.[6] Baxter built a few engines, and Hudson – one of the leading designers of his time – drew up a plan for a steam reheater. Steam exhausted from a high-pressure cylinder would pass through a chamber in the smokebox before being passed to the inlet of the low-pressure cylinder. Though he never built his device, Hudson was addressing the vexing problems of condensation and low exhaust-nozzle pressure. Locomotive boiler pressures practical in the 1870s were seldom above 125 or 130 psi. Such initial pressures, when used in cylinders of sufficient size to produce the tractive power that U.S. lines were then accustomed to, made the design of a workable compound locomotive nearly impossible. Final exhaust pressure would be so low that adequate drafting of the fire would be uncertain, and so much water would remain in the low-pressure cylinder that a cylinder head might blow out after exhaust-port closure, which trapped the incompressible water.

Anatole Mallet

Swiss-born Anatole Mallet was an engineer practicing in France. His name would later become associated with the most long-lived application of compounding on U.S. railroads. He built three diminutive compounds in 1876 for the Bayonne-Anglet-Biarritz Railway, a short line for tourists on the Bay of Biscay near the Spanish border. Mallet had taken out a patent for a compound locomotive two years before, and he was a promoter by temperament. Evidence suggests that he persuaded the owners of the resort line to let him try his idea. The tiny size of his engines likely made for tolerable conditions of heat and pressure in the low-pressure cylinders, and the engines performed well.[7]

By the late 1880s, boiler construction allowed for pressures of 150 psi or better, and compound designs proliferated. In 1888, Mallet conceived a layout for compounding that would make him famous in railroad circles around the world: the four-cylinder, "articulated" arrangement. First applied to a small fleet of engines used on a light railway of 24-inch gauge at the Paris Exposition of 1889, Mallet's new layout put two separate "engines" – *i.e.*, two separate sets of drivers and cylinders – under a single boiler. Two higher-pressure cylinders were rigidly attached to the main locomotive frame at the rear of the boiler, and these cylinders propelled the four rearmost driving wheels. Two low-pressure cylinders were attached to a subframe that swiveled under

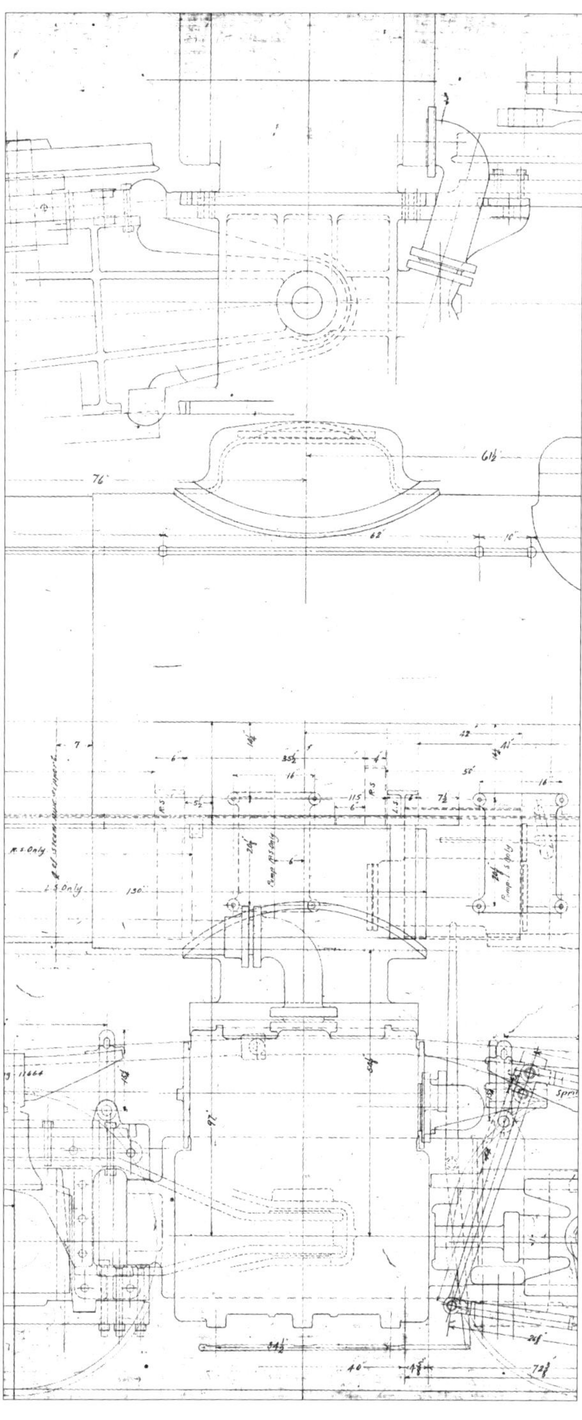

Detail from Baldwin Locomotive Works erecting-card drawing, circa 1912, showing the articulation hinge of Pennsylvania Railroad Class CC1 0-8-8-0 locomotive No. 3397 in plan view (TOP) and left side elevation. *MG-286 Penn Central Railroad Collection/ Pennsylvania State Archives (PHMC)*

the forward end of the boiler. This subframe, hinged to the main frame, carried another set of drivers. (The swiveling action of this set of running gear was the source of the term "articulated," which has remained in the railroading lexicon ever since.) Under the Whyte System of locomotive classification, these machines were 0-4-4-0T types, with the "T" denoting a water tank aboard the locomotive, instead of on a separate tender. Boiler steam fed the rear engine, and piping with flexible couplings led the exhausting steam of the rear cylinders to the inlet chamber of the front cylinders. Flexible couplings then directed the front cylinders' exhaust steam to the smokebox and stack.[8]

Mallet's layout distributed the extra weight of multiple cylinders over a relatively long wheelbase, and the articulated frames made for easy movement of four or more pairs of driving wheels around sharp curves. Mallet chose the size ratio of his cylinders so that all four produced roughly equal thrust. Each of the two engine-units had its own cylinders and valve gear arranged in a straightforward manner without extra mechanical complication. A great virtue was that cylinders, steam chests with valves, and valve gear were all readily accessible for servicing and maintenance, in contrast to other three- and four-cylinder compound designs which placed one or more cylinders and their valves within the engine frame or in otherwise inaccessible locations, which added to maintenance time. Although Mallet's steam path between high- and low-pressure cylinders was long, temperature loss along the piping was minor and did not, of itself, interfere with good performance. In fact, the long pipe carrying a high-pressure cylinder's exhaust (known as a "receiver pipe" or just "receiver") acted as a buffer. As later appreciated by designers, a receiver of generous volume tended to even out pressure variations, which in turn made for more predictable conditions at the low-pressure inlet.[9]

In Europe, the "Mallet articulated" (or simply "Mallet") type became popular on narrow-gauge lines with steep grades and tight curves. Such locomotives were built with four and six driving axles, giving high traction.

In the U.S., the Mallet form came later, first to the Baltimore & Ohio in 1904. Before then, however, Vauclain's layout of 1889 found more favor here.

Samuel Vauclain

In this country, nearly all compound locomotives built in the 1890s were, like the Vauclain, locomotives with one engine. The several cylinders to work in compound expansion were all set at the front; there was just one set of driving wheels, and one main frame carried cylinders and drivers. The Vauclain was by far the most popular. The Baldwin Works built it in many variations, for high-speed passenger trains and for low-speed freight.

Samuel M. Vauclain had an enormous ego. After apprenticeship as a machinist and serving as a locomotive purchasing inspector for the Pennsylvania Railroad, he started with Baldwin in the tender shop in 1883. He soon rose to foreman and then superintendent of the entire shop. "Most men welcome good leadership," he wrote later, with no touch of modesty. He could also be ruthless. When he became manager of tender production, he wrote, "The next day I laid off four hundred men. ... We worked ten hours that day and in the next twenty-four hours I laid off two hundred more. I kept all the good men and gave them a chance to do efficient work."[10]

In each of the ever-larger sections of the Philadelphia plant that he was given to run, Baldwin's speed and quality of production rose. When the firm was reorganized in 1886 with the death of partner Edward Longstreth, Vauclain became general superintendent at the ripe age of 30. Ten years later he was made a full partner. More an aggressive manager than an engineer, he nevertheless understood the basic thermal science of his day. ("... I'd given up hope of a college education though I had put in many nights studying the elements of engineering."[11]) His compound design created a big part of his reputation, and the boost it gave to Baldwin's sales no doubt impressed those he worked for.

In the Vauclain plan, each side of the engine had a pair of cylinders. The high-pressure cylinders were usually set on top, with the larger low-pressure cylinders underneath.[12] On each side, two unequally sized pistons drove a single crosshead. Steam exhausting from the high-pressure cylinder was fed to the opposite end of its low-pressure mate. It was a direct and simple system, and only one steam-distribution valve was needed per side to control steam flow to each cylinder pair. Operating experience, however, revealed two flaws. Neither was fatal, but maintenance costs were somewhat higher as a result.

Milwaukee Road Class A2 4-4-2 engine No. 915, built by Baldwin in 1901, showing the Vauclain compound arrangement of small high-pressure cylinders and large low-pressure cylinders.
Courtesy Kalmbach Media

The first problem had to do with the "starting valve." Any compound engine, in order to start from a standstill, must provide for boiler steam to be fed directly to the low-pressure cylinders until a flow of steam from the high-pressure cylinders can begin. In the Mallet, the engineman would set a valve in the cab that, linked to the throttle, sent boiler steam through a reducing valve straight to the receiver pipes. After a few revolutions of the driving wheels, the starting valve could be closed, since high-pressure exhaust now filled the receivers, supplying the low-pressure cylinders. For the first few turns of the drivers, piston thrusts of high- and low-pressure pistons were rarely equal. In the Mallet, the unequal thrust at starting was not a major issue. If one engine-unit slipped (usually the low-pressure unit in front), the engineer simply cut back the throttle and recovered as he would do in any other locomotive. The reducing valve between boiler and receiver kept thrust differences tolerable.

Samuel Vauclain in 1929.
G.G. Bain, Library of Congress

But in the Vauclain, the starting valve allowed boiler steam to pass directly from one end of the high-pressure cylinder to the other and then, through the exhaust ports, to the low-pressure cylinder. The locomotive started smoothly, but with highly unequal work by the two pistons in each pair. In fact, the larger piston provided nearly all the thrust, since the starting valve when open effectively neutralized pressure on either side of the high-pressure piston. The greatly unequal thrust wracked the crosshead with every stroke, until the starting valve was closed.[13] Baldwin beefed up the crosshead design, and enginemen who made gentle starts and closed the starting valve as soon as possible could obviate most of the problem. But excessive wear on crosshead shoes and leaks in piston-rod packing became common on Vauclain compounds.[14]

The other flaw had to do with the location of the steam-distribution valve for each pair of cylinders, which in the Vauclain layout was always a piston valve. The valve needed to be directly adjacent to the high-pressure cylinder. With the high-pressure cylinder on top, the valve was fairly accessible for repair, adjustment, or changing its rings. On low-drivered locomotives, where clearances required the high-pressure cylinder to be on the bottom, access to the piston valve was blocked by the lead truck. Hence the truck had to be disconnected and pulled out whenever mechanics needed to reach the valve.

Fuel economy for Vauclain compounds could be startlingly good. In 1890, the Northern Pacific Railroad ran about a week of tests comparing two 2-6-0s in freight duty on 109-mile runs between Staples, Minn., and Fargo, N.D. The engines were nearly identical in all respects except that one was built as a four-cylinder Vauclain compound, and the other as a conventional, two-cylinder single-expansion (also called simple expansion) locomotive. Both were given equal-weight trains. On average, the Vauclain saved 28 percent on coal.[15]

Baldwin sold about 2,500 Vauclain coumpounds through 1909, which indicates that many railroads found them to be good performers. The variations ranged from slow 2-8-0 freighters to 4-4-2 speedsters. Baldwin also built such oddities as an 0-6-6-0 double-Vauclain, with a total of eight cylinders. It was designed in 1892 for Pennsylvania's Sinnemahoning Valley Railroad, which used the locomotive in low-speed duty on a 1.2 percent grade.[16] The high-speed capability of the Vauclain was spectacularly demonstrated by the Atlantic City Railroad's 4-4-2 No. 1027. This celebrated engine pulled the *Atlantic City Flyer* daily across New Jersey in 1897 at a scheduled average speed of 69 mph. In

Sinnemahoning Valley Railroad 0-6-6-0 double-Vauclain engine No. 3, built by Baldwin in 1892.
Harold K. Vollrath Collection

this demanding service, carrying hordes of beachgoers from spring to fall that year, the train was late not even once.[17]

Among compounds intended strictly for slow freight, the two-cylinder compound was more numerous than the Vauclain in the 1890s. Indeed, Baxter's short-lived engines of 1870, noted earlier in this chapter, had been two-cylinder compounds. Such a layout placed its cylinders in the usual, outside-front position, but one cylinder was much larger than the other in order to provide the right volumetric ratio. As in any compound, there was only one cutoff setting of the reverse lever at any particular throttle setting (or, only one throttle position for any given cutoff setting) at which piston thrust of the two cylinders was actually equal. In all compound layouts but the two-cylinder form, some thrust inequality between high- and low-pressure did no harm to the engine or track at most working speeds. But as the reader might imagine, a large amount of unequal thrust across the engine in a two-cylinder compound caused a noticeable "surging" action in the locomotive if cutoff and throttle were not adjusted properly for a given speed.

The attractiveness of the two-cylinder (or "cross-compound") arrangement was its utter simplicity, akin to that of a conventional locomotive. The limitation was speed. A less-than-skilled engineman, changing throttle or reverse at speeds of more than 15 or 20 mph, could cause a big imbalance of lateral forces. Below those speeds, most enginemen could get acceptable riding and excellent fuel economy. Helping economy was the inclusion, on most two-cylinder compounds, of the idea suggested by William S. Hudson: The receiver carrying steam between the high- and low-pressure cylinders ran through the smokebox, acting as a reheater.

The starting valve for a cross-compound incorporated a reducing valve, and the locomotive could be worked in simple expansion (*i.e.*, with boiler steam going to both cylinders), at high tractive effort, both in start-up and at speeds below about 10 mph. The reducing valve affected steam pressure to the low-pressure cylinder only partially, so the larger cylinder did more work in simple than the other, smaller cylinder. (It helps here to realize that, in a full driving-wheel rotation of a conventional two-cylinder engine, even without compounding, the maximum thrust of one piston occurs during zero thrust of the other, and vice versa. This is because the drivers are "quartered" – set at 90 degrees from each other – on each axle. Hence, a cross-compound at low speed rode little worse than a normal locomotive.) Starting valves, called

Two-cylinder compound locomotives, such as New Haven 4-4-0 No. 255, employed cylinders of different sizes, with one much larger than the other.
J.W. Swanberg Collection

"intercepting valves" if their design was advanced, came in several patented forms, some manual and some featuring automatic changeover from simple to compound after receiver pressure rose high enough. The latter forms had a manual override for switching back to simple when needed. The ability to work "simple" was an operational advantage on steep grades. An engineman could get a boost in tractive effort if a stall seemed imminent.

Many U.S. and Canadian lines purchased cross-compounds. For the Richmond Locomotive & Machine Works and the Pittsburgh Locomotive Works, such engines became a modest staple and were called "Richmond compounds" and "Pittsburgh compounds" by many railroaders. Baldwin, Schenectady, and other major builders offered them. Most railroaders agreed that cross-compounds were suitable only for freight trains, which averaged only about ten mph anyway.

The Pennsylvania Railroad, ever the experimentalist, tried to achieve a high-speed cross-compound in 1892, with an 84-inch drivered 4-4-0 erected at Altoona. It incorporated a "Lindner" valve, after its inventor in Germany, which improved on the usual intercepting valve. When the engineman set the cutoff at maximum, boiler steam through a reducer fed the low-pressure cylinder, but as soon as the engineman brought the cutoff lever back any amount, the locomotive ran in compound. The PRR, on another locomotive, also tried an idea from Austria. Here, no starting or intercepting valve was needed. When running at maximum cutoff (full back-and-forth travel by the standard steam-distribution valves), "starting ports" cut into the valve faces let boiler steam into the low-pressure cylinder at the beginning of each piston stroke. When cutoff was shortened (less than full travel), the valve no longer opened these ports and so the engine worked compound. Balance both of steam thrust and of reciprocating masses was poor, and the Pennsylvania did not duplicate either of these locomotives. They illustrate, however, the high degree of attention U.S. designers paid to innovations from Europe.

Another type of compound competed for freight locomotive sales in the 1890s. This was the ungainly looking "tandem compound" (a type first tried by H.O. Perry on the Erie). In this four-cylinder arrangement, the

Santa Fe "tandem compound" 2-10-2 engine No. 977. Note the large counterweights on the drivers, which were needed to counteract the large reciprocating mass of the pistons.
Courtesy Kalmbach Media

Great Northern tandem-compound 2-8-0 No. 515, built by Brooks, was displayed at the Columbian Exposition of 1893.

James Dredge, A Record of the Transportation Exhibits at the World's Columbian Exposition of 1893

high-pressure and low-pressure cylinders on each side of the locomotive were set on a common centerline. Each cylinder had its own steam-distribution valve, again on a common centerline. Because of the large piston diameters required for the high drawbar pull of freighters, this layout made for very heavy reciprocating weights moving in unison on each side of the engine. On the low driving wheels of such engines, large counterweights were needed. Still, with the same percentage of reciprocating mass balanced as in other locomotives, the total unbalanced reciprocating mass was high. Despite this concern, a few railroads took to the "tandems." Whereas the Vauclain layout for freight engines had the same problem of high unbalanced reciprocating masses, the tandem layout eliminated any wracking action on the crosshead.

The Great Northern, with its mountain grades in Montana, Idaho, and Washington state, acquired some of the first tandem-compounds in the U.S. since Perry's. The railroad displayed one of its new engines proudly at the Columbian Exposition of 1893. Representative of the pursuit of high efficiency, it was a 2-8-0 made by the Brooks Works to a design worked out by its engineer and superintendent, John Player (who coincidentally had the same name as the well-known superintendent of machinery for the Santa Fe Railway, who was introduced in Chapter 2).

Santa Fe's John Player, head of locomotive design on that railroad from 1890 through 1901, became a leading tandem-compounding enthusiast. In 1899 and 1900, Santa Fe's Topeka, Kan., shops built five 2-8-0s and two 4-6-0s to a configuration that staff referred to as the "Player system." In 1901-02,

Santa Fe 2-10-2 No. 939 was part of the largest class of tandem compounds on any railroad. Note the crane attached to the smokebox, which was used to facilitate removal of the high-pressure cylinder during frequent re-packings of piston rods – a common complaint on tandem compounds.

Harold K. Vollrath Collection

Baldwin and the American Locomotive Co. at Schenectady built three huge 2-10-0 tandem-compound Decapod types to Santa Fe specification. These were followed by a couple of 2-6-2s and 40 2-8-0s and, beginning in 1903, by the largest fleet of tandems ever: 159 2-10-2s, the heaviest locomotives in the world when introduced. Called the "Santa Fe" type, their fat boilers were 88 inches in maximum diameter; steam pressure was 225 psi, the highest to that date in a production locomotive. The railroad exhibited one, the No. 984, at the Louisiana Purchase Exposition in St. Louis the following year. Santa Fe found their economy satisfactory, though as with the cross-compound, the low average speed of freight trains on all railroads was a fundamental part of the context. Alfred Lovell, Santa Fe's superintendent of motive power, presided over the development of a whole variety of compound-expansion engines, in a welter of sizes and types. The New York Central and the Northern Pacific, among others, also used tandems in freight service.[18]

Alfred de Glehn

The issue of counterbalancing came to the fore with the de Glehn compound. Between 1886 and 1891, Alfred de Glehn of French locomotive builder Société Alsacienne de Constructions Mécaniques and Gaston du Bousquet of the Nord Railway worked out a new compounding layout. In burgeoning numbers, Glehn's design was running on several railways in France by 1900. Noted for superb mechanical balance of driving wheels and reciprocating parts, the new design could accelerate quickly and run as fast as track allowed and engine crews dared.

The Glehn type used four cylinders with four main connecting rods. Pistons on each side of the engine moved not together (as in the Vauclain and tandem compounds), but in dynamic opposition to one another. The high-pressure cylinders, mounted outside at the front of the engine, drove the second pair of drivers. The low-pressure cylinders, placed within the locomotive frame, drove cranks set into the first driving axle. High- and low-pressure pistons on each side reciprocated 180 degrees apart. With a little adjustment to the actual weights of pistons, and allowing for the different lateral distance of each piston in a pair from the centerline of the engine, any reciprocating mass in the drive was now dynamically offset by an opposing mass. This reciprocating balance entirely eliminated the need for any excess rotating mass in the driving wheel counterweights. Hence, in the Glehn – and unlike any other competing layout – the driving wheels were in near-perfect rotational balance.

A Glehn had essentially the same torque characteristics as a conventional locomotive, since the two piston-pairs had to be set 90 degrees apart. Thus, the impulses of piston thrust to driving wheels were no different than the usual two-cylinder engine. But compared to a Vauclain or a tandem, with their heavy reciprocating parts and therefore poor balance in the drivers, a Glehn rode like a dream. Important to track-maintenance officers especially, the Glehn's driving wheels did not pound the rail, as did the drivers of any other simple- or compound-expansion locomotive at high rpm. So-called "track pound" – inherent in any two-cylinder locomotive as well as in the Vauclains and tandems – was a controversial issue among railroaders; the effect it actually had on track was debatable. There was no doubt, however, as to quantifying driving-wheel imbalance; it was called "dynamic augment" in the trade, and was worse at higher rpm. After a number of American railroad officials journeyed overseas to inspect and ride in the cabs of the new locomotives, there was no doubt as to their remarkable stability and amazingly good ride at any speed.[19] The French design was discussed at great length among American railroad mechanical engineers.[20]

Feeling a potential market threat, Vauclain suggested to his Baldwin engineers that they come up with a competitive answer to the Glehn design. The result rolled forth in January 1902: the Baldwin Works' engine No. 20,000. Billed as simply a "modification" of the Vauclain compound (no one dared suggest that the original Vauclain format had any defects), the locomotive was in fact a new design altogether. Four cylinders, in opposed pairs, were arranged at the front of the engine. Unlike the Glehn, the low-pressure cylinders were placed outside and the high-pressure inside. Balance characteristics were similar to the French engine.[21]

Significantly for potential maintenance costs, the balanced-compound design used one pair of steam-distribution valves and one pair of valve gear for the four cylinders; the Glehn used a separate valve gear for each cylinder. On a Glehn, an engineman could adjust the cutoffs separately on the high- and low-pressure cylinders, an option which could improve both fuel economy and power. Whether the extra complication was worthwhile in terms of total economy was the question. Baldwin staff felt that the simpler arrangement of their design would be seen as a virtue by railroads' locomotive officers. In 1904, Baldwin received its first big order for balanced compounds, 53 4-4-2 passenger locomotives for the Santa Fe – the same railroad, in the same year, that began receiving its large fleet of tandem-compound 2-10-2 freight engines. In following years Baldwin delivered balanced compounds to various railroads in four different sizes and wheel arrangements.

The American Locomotive Co. also offered a balanced compound, designed by its well-known engineer Francis J. Cole. Cole's engine put the inside, high-pressure cylinders out front above the pilot beam, for easier accessibility in maintenance. As in the Baldwin, there were just two sets of valve gear, but unlike the Baldwin there was a separate steam chest for each cylinder. New York Central tried one. Cross bracing at the front of the frame was weak, however, and the engine had to be rebuilt with outside valve gear to make room for more bracing. The type was never popular.[22]

PRR 4-4-2 No. 2512 was a Glehn-designed engine, built in France in 1904 and displayed at the St. Louis Exposition.
Courtesy Kalmbach Media

In 1904 the Pennsylvania Railroad, under president (and civil engineer) Alexander Cassatt, brought a genuine Glehn to the U.S. Constructed by the Société Alsacienne as a modification of a Glehn type then running on the Paris-Orleans Railway, the engine was shipped to Philadelphia. After some shakedown, PRR engineers installed it on their treadmill testing plant at the St. Louis exposition. The railroad's test report cited the marvelous balance and improved fuel economy obtained.[23]

But unlike the Santa Fe and other lines, the Pennsylvania did not bite much further into the compound apple. Cassatt strongly encouraged experimentation, but decisions on designs for serial production were another matter. Since the early 1870s, PRR managers had put unique stress on design standardization and, from about 1900, on a high degree of mechanical simplicity for engines to be manufactured in volume. Judging from the PRR's subsequent decision making, the projected fuel savings of compounds were considered unlikely to cover the added maintenance expected from multiple cylinders.

In the same year that the Pennsylvania Railroad's Glehn came to St. Louis, so did the first Mallet-type to appear in North America. It also went on display at the Exposition. John E. Muhlfeld, 32 years old and the recently promoted head of motive power for the Baltimore & Ohio, believed in the compound gospel. He developed a plan for a locomotive based on Mallet's patents, but of unprecedented size. B&O No. 2400, domestically constructed and weighing 167 tons without its tender, was the new "world's largest" of 1904 – and it became one of the most popular attractions at the fair. The big Schenectady-built engine carried four cylinders on an articulated frame and had six pairs of driving wheels. The low-pressure pistons were a table-top size 32 inches in diameter; the 235-psi boiler incorporated more evaporative surface area than ever, nearly 5,600 square feet.[24]

Later named for its designer, the *J.E. Muhlfeld* began daily service on the B&O after the fair closed. In pusher duty on the long and difficult Sand Patch grade west of Cumberland, Md. – so named for all the sand left on the right-of-way by struggling locomotives – No. 2400 proved to be a sound investment. Admiring crews nicknamed it "Old Maud."

The secret to No. 2400's success was only partly due to its relative fuel economy. More important was its labor-cost saving for the work performed: With 12 driving wheels and good traction it could pull or shove almost twice as much tonnage as any other freight engine the B&O had.[25] One engine crew could produce almost twice the work. The bigger boiler, though more costly to build than a smaller one, was only a bit more expensive in monthly labor hours to repair and maintain. The two sets of running gear doubled the machinery maintenance, but given the doubling of work out on the railroad, the machine maintenance per ton-mile was the same. In the net calculation of unit costs, "Old Maud" amounted to a huge jump in productivity.

Embracing the Mallet

In 1906, with the 2400's reliability and economy well established, other U.S. railroads began ordering Mallets. The Great Northern Railway, an early experimenter with compounds, needed helper locomotives to assist heavy trains up a steep, 2.2 percent grade in the Cascade Mountains. Five 2-6-6-2 Mallets from Baldwin, slightly less powerful than B&O's prototype, came

Santa Fe 4-6-2 No. 1235 was a balanced compound.

Harold K. Vollrath Collection

with an important addition: lead and trailing trucks. Being too big for GN's turntables at the time, the new locomotives had to run bi-directionally. The trucks laterally stabilized the Mallet's two engine units and let an engineman run at speeds up to 30 mph or so. Finding that these Mallets rode well enough for both low- and moderate-speed use, the GN bought a second batch in 1907 built to a slightly revised design – not for pusher duty but as road locomotives for regular freight trains. Freight train length, and productivity, took a leap.[26]

Builders responded to a flurry of orders from railroads across the country. Mallet designs quickly grew larger. At first the most popular type was the 2-6-6-2, similar to the GN engines, but without the Belpaire firebox. The Erie bought some pusher engines from Alco with, for the first time, eight driving axles under a single boiler. Other railroads put enormous 2-8-8-2s into regular freight service in mountain districts. Beginning in 1909, the Southern Pacific had Baldwin build oil-burning 2-8-8-2s and 2-6-6-2s to a "cab forward" design, which, by flipping the boiler to put the firebox to the fore and the stack to the rear, kept smoke from asphyxiating engine crews in the Sierra snowsheds. Elsewhere there were 2-8-8-0s and even a few 2-6-8-0s. In 1909, Santa Fe and Baldwin engineers designed two 4-4-6-2s for passenger use.

Two years later, Santa Fe constructed ten 2-10-10-2s at its Topeka Shops. For each, the back of the boiler and the rear running gear came from a previously built 2-10-2. This "half" was then grafted to a boiler front-section and front engine-unit, shipped new from Baldwin. These new "world's largest" champions hauled long freights on the Santa Fe's heaviest California grades, between Bakersfield and Barstow and between Barstow and San Bernardino.

The Santa Fe deserves special mention here – not for engineering success but for failure. In the end, it was a failure so spectacular that Santa Fe top management replaced or demoted its top mechanical engineers. Thereafter, the railroad's staff redesigned and rebuilt some 200 locomotives, at great expense to the company.

BELOW Baltimore & Ohio 0-6-6-0 No. 2400 – known to crews as "Old Maud" and renumbered 7000 by the time of this 1934 view – was the first Mallet-type locomotive in North America.

Harold K. Vollrath Collection

After acquiring its first four Mallet compounds in 1909, railroad and Baldwin engineers designed seven more such classes in 1910 and 1911, for a total of 83 locomotives. Except for five from Topeka, Baldwin made them all (or, in the case of the 2-10-10-2s, made the front halves). Most were 2-6-6-2s, and of those, seven had jointed boilers. Whether with jointed or rigid boilers, all the Santa Fe Mallets were designed to a boiler concept that originated with Baldwin in 1909, the "separable boiler." The goal was to increase boiler efficiency, to transfer more of the boiler's heat to steam production.[27] The Mallet cylinder layout, meanwhile, was relatively non-controversial, at least at first.

The jointed boiler, unique to Santa Fe, caused the biggest stir in the locomotive design community. Nothing quite like it had been seen before. The purpose of the joint – in two locomotives a kind of huge ball-and-socket connection, in five locomotives a bellows made of mild steel plates – had nothing to do with the boiler's steam-making function. The purpose had to do with a Mallet's traction. In early Mallets, the drivers of the front engine-unit slipped on the track much more often than the drivers of the back engine-unit. To Santa Fe designers, putting more weight directly on the front engine-unit seemed a possible solution. In a normally configured Mallet, the front of its rigid boiler was carried by the front engine-unit on a sliding plate, but with the hinge that was used between front and back frames, weight could vary on the front engine-unit as the locomotive rolled down uneven track. The jointed boiler, in which the front engine-unit and the front of the boiler were now a single mass, put a steadier and more predictable weight on the front drivers.[28]

The central flaw in this idea lay with the basic proportions of the boiler, not with the jointed connection. The jointed (or "flexible") boiler was simply a variation on Baldwin's "separable" idea. In such a boiler the front half, more or less, of the barrel was not really part of the boiler. The front half was a feedwater pre-heater and, in many applications, also contained a re-heater for steam passing from the high- to the low-pressure cylinders. Baldwin manufactured a number of Mallets with separable boilers for several railroads after 1909. At a point near the high-pressure cylinders, the boiler barrel ended at an internal bulkhead. All steam evaporation took place in the rear

RIGHT Southern Pacific 2-8-8-2 "cab-forward" Mallet No. 4004.
Courtesy Kalmbach Media

BELOW Santa Fe 4-4-6-2 Mallet No. 1398 was designed for passenger-train service, but failed to meet expectations.
Courtesy Kalmbach Media

Santa Fe's 2-10-10-2s of 1911 were the product of the railway's Topeka, Kan., shops, where portions of existing 2-10-2 locomotives were grafted behind forward sections newly built by Baldwin.

Courtesy Kalmbach Media

section. The barrel to the front, with its own internal bulkheads, contained the pre-heater (in modern power plant terms, an "economizer") and, if used, the re-heater. Longitudinal bolts at the joint rings held the whole assembly together. (In neither the rigid nor jointed form of the separable boiler was the joint itself subject to boiler pressure.) Flue gases from the firebox passed through tubes in the boiler proper, through the tubes in the re-heater, and then through tubes in the economizer to the smokebox. Feedwater, first filling the economizer, was carried by internal or external connections to the boiler section. These connections also kept both boiler and economizer at equal pressure. The Santa Fe was not alone in using separable boilers: Great Northern, Southern Pacific, Virginian, Norfolk & Western, and other companies also tried them.[29]

The idea – basically sound – was that most of the boiler's flue-gas heat would support evaporation in the usual way, yet more total heat would be recovered after the gases left the evaporative section. Thanks to the Pennsylvania Railroad's test plant, engineers knew that combustion gases in a locomotive boiler give up 80 to 90 percent of their heat in the first 15 to 18 feet of flue travel. Furthermore, water circulation, which affects total evaporative efficiency, was impossible to predict within a very long boiler. Given the great jump in total length of the new Mallets, why not functionally divide their boilers to get better heat recovery?

Rather than heat recovery, the fundamental problem in retrospect was heat *production*: The fireboxes of all the Santa Fe Mallets were far too small to support the intended mechanical work of four cylinders, at any achievable efficiency of boiler heat transfer and cylinder expansion. The first of the Santa Fe Mallets to prove unsatisfactory were the two 4-4-6-2 passenger locomotives. After numerous "road failures" – *i.e.*, engines running out of steam or unable to keep schedule – they were withdrawn from service in 1915, taken apart, and rebuilt as ordinary 4-6-2s, *sans* the separable front boiler sections. The freight locomotives were apparently a bit more successful, provided that speed or trailing load or the combination of the two did not exceed unforgiving limits far below original expectations. Above ten mph with a decent load, they rapidly ran out of steam. Most of the 2-6-6-2s operated until the mid- and late-1920s, even those with flexible boilers. The ten 2-10-10-2s, though, were taken apart and reconstructed as 20 simple-expansion 2-10-2s, starting in 1915.

The redirection of the Santa Fe mechanical department occurred sooner than that. In May 1912, John Purcell, formerly an assistant to the Santa Fe's

TOP Santa Fe 2-6-6-2 Mallet No. 1157. The boiler rode atop the rear engine unit; the front unit housed a feedwater pre-heater and a re-heater for steam exhausted from the high-pressure (rear) cylinders. *Courtesy Kalmbach Media*

ABOVE Close-up of the jointed boiler on Santa Fe 2-6-6-2 Mallet No. 3322. *Courtesy Kalmbach Media*

president, was put in charge of locomotive design and fleet management. (He also maintained the title of assistant to the president for several years, which perhaps indicated his unusual degree of authority.) A capable engineer, he viewed economy not in terms of thermal performance but in per-mile total cost. Much of that was maintenance. The performance debacle of the big and expensive Mallets surely precipitated Purcell's ascent, but he immediately took draconian steps to reduce locomotive maintenance costs.[30]

Given the Mallets' deficient hauling capacity, the two engine-units of each locomotive certainly could not produce work proportionate to the doubled machine maintenance. The elaborately complex, multi-section boilers were far more difficult to clean internally during monthly boiler washouts, and repairing tubes required much more extensive disassembly than conventional boilers. All this added to downtime. Meanwhile, the tandem-compound 2-10-2s of 1903-07 had become, by 1912, notorious for high maintenance. On these engines, the packing glands between high-pressure and low-pressure cylinders were totally inaccessible yet needed frequent renewal; leaks through the gland destroyed the pressure difference on which compound expansion depended. It took a full shift to remove the high-pressure cylinders of one of these locomotives and replace the packing of valve and piston rods, a one-hour job on most engines. (The 2-10-2s had little jib cranes permanently attached to their smokeboxes to help mechanics remove the high-pressure cylinders.)[31]

Where he could not cut labor time, Purcell cut wage costs. He brought in Japanese immigrant machinists to the major repair shops in Southern California – people who would turn out high-quality work at $1.80 per day instead of the customary $3.50 paid to a white machinist. A few small strikes ensued, to little effect.

New locomotives – simple-expansion, not compound – began arriving. About 1916, Purcell started a full-scale program of rebuilding compounds into simple-expansion form. By 1923 nearly all the 2-10-2s were so converted.[32]

Santa Fe's belief in compounding, initiated by John Player and carried on by Alfred Lovell, was over. That belief was not irrational, as many secondary accounts have implied. Throughout much of its territory, Santa Fe had to deal with long desert hauls, bad water quality from its wells, and (before oil became cheap) poor coal. The search for water- and fuel-saving economy made sense.

For 20 years, from 1890 to 1910, compounding was an accepted and vital part of the engineering canon for locomotive designers. Unfortunately for

Player's successors, the empirically based techniques available to predict boiler and cylinder performance, generally reliable for average-sized locomotives, were inadequate for boilers and engines that greatly exceeded the norm in size and complexity. In particular, the critical dependence of combustion rate and initial heat transfer on firebox volume, the vagaries of back pressure in long pipes and between multiple cylinders, and the relationships of draft and heat release in long boilers to exhaust steam pressure and volume, were unknowns.

What may seem unconscionable is that Baldwin was happy to sell 78 badly performing locomotives to Santa Fe during three years. Performance warranty by a builder was sometimes done, but there is no evidence that any applied in these cases. Among the railroad and builder's engineers jointly involved, who blamed whom is not recorded. Ordinarily, if a railroad's engineers approved a design, they carried the final responsibility. It's worth noting that all of Santa Fe's subsequent purchases of steam locomotives, right up to the final class of 4-8-4s in 1944, came from Baldwin, suggesting that the railroad bore no grudges related to its treatment at the hands of the builder.

Another compounding disappointment began in 1914, at the other end of the country. This was the much remarked-upon *Matt H. Shay* of the Erie Railroad, designed by Baldwin consulting engineer George R. Henderson. Also referred to as a "triplex," this locomotive was a colossus with three groups of driving wheels and six cylinders. Despite its nickname, the locomotive was not triple-expansion. High-pressure steam went first to the middle pair of cylinders, from which it was exhausted to a receiver that fed the front and rear cylinders; all cylinders were of the same dimensions. Only the front low-pressure cylinders' exhaust was used for draft. The rear low-pressure cylinders exhausted directly to atmosphere, probably to reduce backpressure. Tractive effort working in compound was calculated at 160,000 lbs., three times that of a heavy 2-8-0 or a large 2-8-2.

The Erie intended the *Matt H. Shay* for pusher duty on the steep Susquehanna grade in southern New York State and extreme northeastern Pennsylvania, over Starucca Viaduct, the same service in which the earlier 0-8-8-0s were used. The triplex must have done fairly well, because two years later the Erie ordered two more. Also in 1916, the Virginian Railway bought one. This variant used a four-wheel trailing truck at the rear and had slightly more tractive effort. The Virginian's locomotive failed miserably on sustained runs pulling heavy coal trains; the boiler could not keep up with steam demand if speed was more than dead slow. The locomotive is said to have stalled with a train on its acceptance run. This time the railroad's managers, certainly cognizant of the Santa Fe's experience, had a warranty. Baldwin had to take the locomotive back and rebuild it – into a 2-8-8-0 and a 2-8-2. The Erie's trio fared reasonably well, lasting in service until as late as 1933.[33]

The Erie Railroad's *Matt H. Shay*, a 2-8-8-8-2, was built by Baldwin for pusher service.
Courtesy Kalmbach Media

Other railroads did not throw out the babies with the bathwater. The separable boiler and the triplex idea were failed experiments but useful in extending knowledge. With their relevant design relationships better understood, Mallet compounds with large, conventionally designed boilers became staple power for freight trains in mountain territory. A dozen major railroads bought heavy 2-8-8-2s; more railroads bought 2-6-6-2s. In 1918, the Virginian got some 2-10-10-2s that worked. Between 1912 and 1918, designers had learned a great deal about compound performance in large locomotives. Used in slow "drag" coal-train service, Virginian's immense Mallets performed admirably for 40 years. They had fireboxes and boilers sized to provide all the steam the cylinders could consume (the rear boiler course was 119 inches in diameter, by far the largest ever), and the cylinders were enormous – the low-pressure pistons were 48 inches in diameter, again the largest ever.[34]

Important to ultimate success, for all the Mallet forms, were a few seemingly small details. C.J. Mellin, formerly chief mechanical engineer at the Richmond Works and a consulting engineer to Alco after 1901, perfected an intercepting valve that was widely used, even in competitors' locomotives. The "Mellin" valve, developed in the early 1890s for use in cross-compounds, solved the problem of excessive backpressure between high- and low-pressure cylinders when starting in simple-expansion. It also permitted an engineman, when underway in compound, to switch quickly and smoothly back to simple-expansion when needed. As did other starting valves, Mellin's device sent boiler steam through a reducer to the receiver. His device combined starting and reducing valves in one unit and, at startup in simple-expansion, automatically switched to compound as receiver pressure rose. If an engineman switched back to simple, high-pressure cylinder exhaust was "intercepted" and sent either to the atmosphere or to the stack. Thus, when in simple-expansion operation, the high-pressure cylinders ran against greatly reduced backpressure. The idea was hardly original to Mellin. His was a practical device that functioned reliably, kept thrust more equal among all four cylinders in simple-expansion operation, and maintained generous passageways for free flow of the steam.[35]

Another vital contributor to a Mallet's traction was the hinge between the main locomotive frame and the subframe carrying the front engine-unit. The hinge had to take a tremendous load but not bind. It also had to resist torquing around the longitudinal axis, and participate in keeping a steady load on the front drivers to minimize slipping. Many designs were tried. Some, with too much play, contributed to poor traction of the front drivers. This was the problem the Santa Fe's flexible boiler was intended to address, before designers realized that the hinge, itself, was a contributor to dependable traction. Spring centering devices were sometimes used. Weight transfer to the front subframe at the hinge turned out to be crucial, along with the weight carried by the subframe at the front. By the 1920s, Baldwin's flexible radius-bar design, with two pins, and Alco's single-pin design were the dominant forms.[36]

For engineers in the railway field, the period covered in this chapter was an exciting time. The fuse was lit by simple economics. The result was an explosion of creativity. Except for the Mallets, though, compounding as a technology faded quickly in American railroad practice after 1910. Thus writers have tended to assume it was some sort of foolish mistake. The mistake is to simplify the issues with which designers contended.

Chapter 5 Notes

1. Data in George Rogers Taylor's *The Transportation Revolution, 1815-1860* supports a roughly ten-fold drop in long-distance shipping prices between rail and wagon from the 1840s to the 1860s, not counting the five- to ten-fold drop in time en route. Canals remained competitively cheap per ton, but the penalty in time increased severely for canals as the time value of manufactured goods in transit became a major concern in an increasingly industrial economy. Transit time means lost value and lost economic return in the cycle of goods from manufacturer to purchaser.
2. F.W. Powell, *Railroad Promotion and Capitalization in the United States*, 1909.
3. U.S. patents 406011 and 406012. Vauclain became Baldwin's general superintendent in Feb. 1886, having joined the firm in 1883. See *History of the Baldwin Locomotive Works, 1830-1923*, p. 80. Vauclain's autobiography, *Steaming Up!*, is curiously silent about the invention. Perhaps, in 1930 when the book was written, Vauclain didn't want to dwell on an invention that the railroad industry had discarded as obsolete.
4. White, *A History of the American Steam Locomotive, Its Development: 1830-1880*, (1979 ed.), p. 210.
5. Arthur Tanatt Woods, *Compound Locomotives*, revised edition by David L.Barnes, 1907.
6. P.M. Kalla-Bishop, *Tandem Compound Locomotives* (1949); Fred Herbert Colvin, *American Compound Locomotives*, 1903.
7. Angus Sinclair, *Development of the Locomotive Engine* (1907), p. 194.
8. *The Engineer*, (U.K.), May 3, 1889.
9. William Ernest Dalby, *Steam Power*, (1915).
10. Samuel M. Vauclain, *Steaming Up!*, (1930) pp. 99, 112.
11. Ibid., p. 111. See also *History of the Baldwin Locomotive Works, 1830-1923*, pp. 4, 80.
12. On locomotives with small drivers – and therefore less ground clearance – the large, low-pressure cylinders were sometimes placed on top.
13. Vauclain and others surely realized the problem. But with one steam-distribution valve per cylinder pair – otherwise a virtue, since two valves per cylinder pair would add enormously to mechanical complexity – no other starting valve arrangement apparently was feasible. The two-way flow of steam through the starting valve prevented use of a reducing valve to control pressure. However, the crosshead "wracking" problem was not as severe an issue in service as most secondary accounts have claimed. A conventional crosshead is also subject to a similar asymmetry of force, just to a lesser degree. Large crosshead bearing surfaces helped.
14. *Report of the Proceedings of the American Railway Master Mechanics' Association* (ARMMA), 1892-1898.
15. Fred Westing, *The Locomotives That Baldwin Built*, (1966), p. 38.
16. Sinclair (1907), pp. 195-96.
17. *Railway Age*, December 1897.
18. E.D. Worley, *Iron Horses of the Santa Fe Trail*, (1965), includes chapters on each of Santa Fe's wheel arrangements; see especially pp. 104, 127, 159, and 202-11.
19. Dalby, *The Balancing of Engines*, (1906). See also ARMMA *Proceedings*, 1900 and 1901.
20. *Railway Age*, various issues, 1899-1900.
21. Frank M. Swengel, *The American Steam Locomotive*, vol. 1, (1967).
22. Sinclair (1907), pp. 652, 658-59.
23. *The Pennsylvania Railroad System at the Louisiana Purchase Exposition: Locomotive Tests and Exhibits*, 1904.
24. Sinclair, 1907, pp. 194-97, 329-30; *Railway Age*, 1904.
25. Compare B&O 2-8-0 Vauclain compound of 1900, with 36,600 lbs. of tractive effort, with No. 2400's 71,500 lbs. (Swengel, p. 63). A typical single-expansion 2-8-0 of the time had about 40,000 lbs.
26. Competing Northern Pacific in 1907 ordered similar 2-6-6-2s, the railroad's first of many Z classes, for helper service in the Cascades.
27. Lionel Wiener, *Articulated Locomotives*, (1930).
28. See Worley, *Iron Horses of the Santa Fe Trail*, (1965).
29. Wiener, p. 326-29.
30. Worley comments on the draconian changes brought about by Purcell.
31. Worley, p. 203.
32. Worley, p. 205.
33. George H. Drury, *Guide to North American Steam Locomotives*, (2015), p. 175.
34. Swengel, pp. 180-81.
35. Wiener, pp. 335-36; Woods, pp. 205-06.
36. Wiener, pp. 318-23.

"Without question, the superheater was one of the most important contributions made in the development of the steam locomotive during the period 1900 to 1950." *– Alfred W. Bruce, 1952, Former chief steam locomotive designer, American Locomotive Co.*[1]

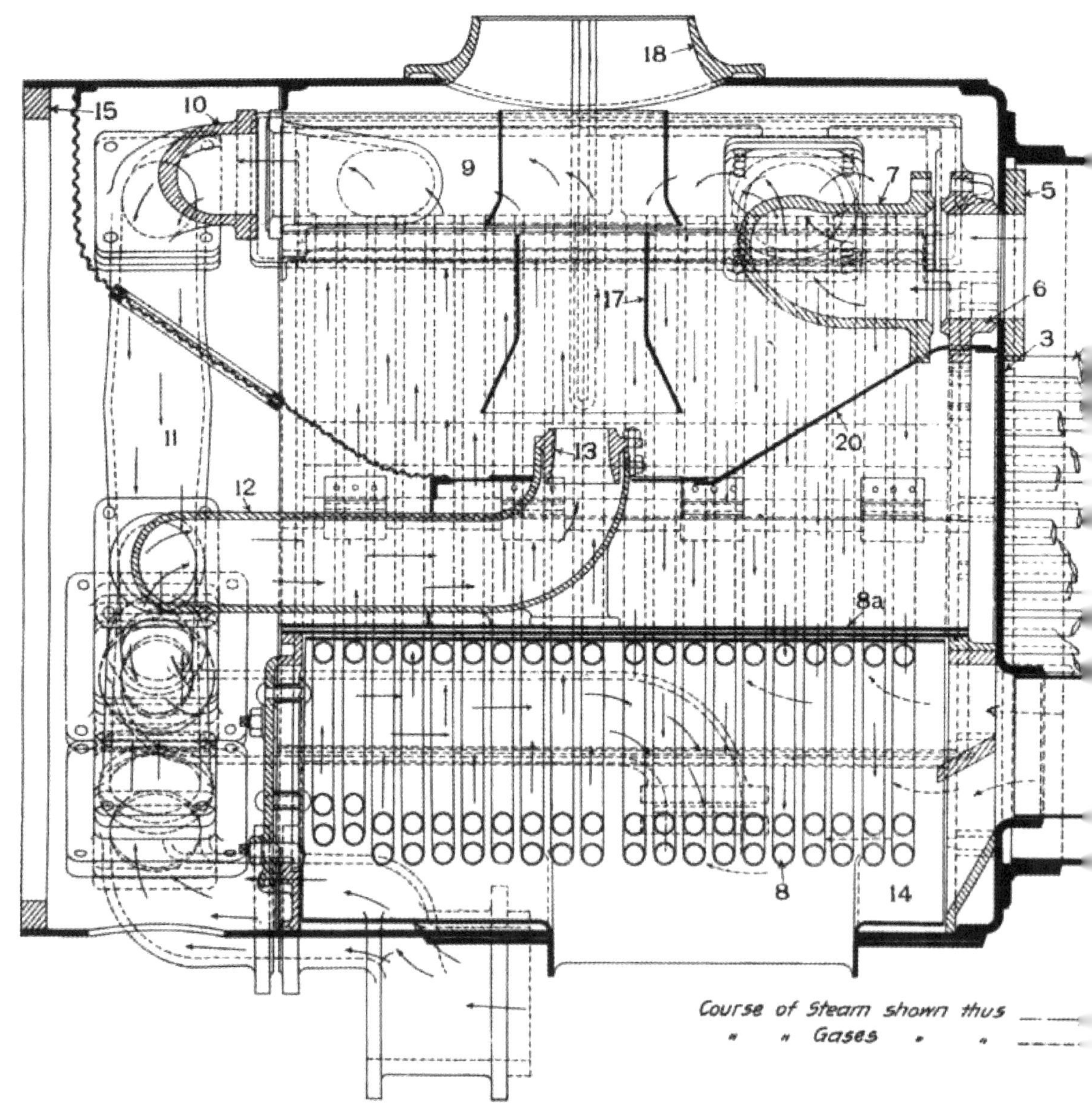

Chapter 6

Superheating:

Design and Risk

RELATIVELY FEW COMPOUND LOCOMOTIVES were made after 1910. Orders for Vauclains dropped precipitously from 1903. Cross-compound orders stopped around 1905. Santa Fe had the biggest fleet of tandem-compounds; Northern Pacific, Great Northern, and New York Central ordered them as late as 1904. Balanced compounds continued to attract attention through 1914. Showing that Santa Fe's motive power chief John Purcell had not written off compounds altogether, that same year he approved the purchase of 35 balanced-compound 4-6-2s for passenger trains. At the time, his railroad already had 121 such 4-6-2s, in three classes dating from 1905, as well as 205 other balanced compounds; the company certainly did not lack for experience with such engines.[2] Several other railroads liked the type, notably the Rock Island and the Nashville, Chattanooga & St. Louis.

The myth persists that the superheater "slew" the compound, as one well-known writer put it in an oft-repeated phrase.[3] The economy of the former swiftly rendered the latter redundant. The implication is that history in this case was decided with brutal objectivity, based on total operating costs. One technology was so clearly superior, the reasoning goes, that it simply replaced the other.

In fact, the "replacement" model works only partially in this case. Both technologies – compounding and superheating – could be applied quite well to the same locomotive. Economy was indeed a driving force, whether one considers thermal efficiency or relative maintenance costs. But the designers and engineers need to be brought back into the story.

Superheating was an old idea. American and European engineers tried to invent practical devices to accomplish it from the time the first stationary steam engines came into use in the late 18th century. The objective was understood: Take steam already produced and add still more heat, raising the steam's temperature above the boiling point. The resulting superheated steam has the desirable characteristic of increased cubic volume at any given boiler pressure. A pound of saturated steam at 200 psi, a typical boiler pressure for 1900-era locomotives, has a volume of 2.13 cubic feet, but a pound of steam that's been heated by 300°F has a volume of 3.10 cubic feet – almost 50 percent more.[4]

The Schmidt superheater used by Canadian Pacific was one of several designs that revolutionized the steam locomotive. The steel cars and heavier trains of the 20th century wouldn't have been possible without them.

Locomotive Dictionary, 1916

350°F, before any superheating. A smokebox superheater might add 30 to 50 degrees, still a feasible working temperature for the lubricants.[7]

Attempts to work out an effective superheater were more energetic in Europe. In the early 1890s, a young German who trained at a technical school in Dresden, Wilhelm Schmidt, studied a half-century of prior efforts. A key factor was that lubricating oils had improved by his time. In 1894 he developed a superheater for a stationary engine that caught the attention of many fellow engineers. Four years later he persuaded the Royal Prussian State Railways to test his smokebox-type superheater for locomotives. Two new locomotives, of different overall design to provide a better comparative evaluation, were so equipped. Railroad officials were skeptical and insisted that Schmidt's device be modified so that it could be bypassed – that is, the locomotive readily switched to saturated operation – if there was difficulty on the road. There were difficulties, but after a reasonable trial period the engines ran well, with somewhat reduced fuel consumption. A state railways director who was also chief mechanical engineer of the Berlin Division, Dr. Robert Garbe, saw enough promise that he became the principal supporter of Schmidt within the railway bureaucracy.[8]

Thus encouraged, Schmidt began work on a firetube superheater. In this, as one of his contemporaries pointed out, Schmidt benefitted from work done long before in France. A firetube superheater arrangement much like Schmidt's final design was tried on the Montereau-Troyes Railway in 1850. In the locomotive tested, total steam temperature is said to have reached 650-700 degrees. Since such temperatures were entirely impractical, further development was dropped. When Schmidt patented his firetube superheater of 1901-02, his layout duplicated many features of patents issued to French railway officer Jean de Montcheuil in 1849-50.[9]

Schmidt first applied his firetube superheater to a Belgian locomotive in 1901. The Prussian railways agreed to another trial, this time of the new, firetube form. Managers and engineers were impressed at the results, and from 1902, the Prussians ordered all of their new locomotives with Schmidt superheaters and gave enthusiastic backing to further work of the inventor.[10]

The Schmidt firetube (or sometimes called smoketube) superheater is a simple affair, deceptively so. From the boiler's dome, saturated steam flows down the

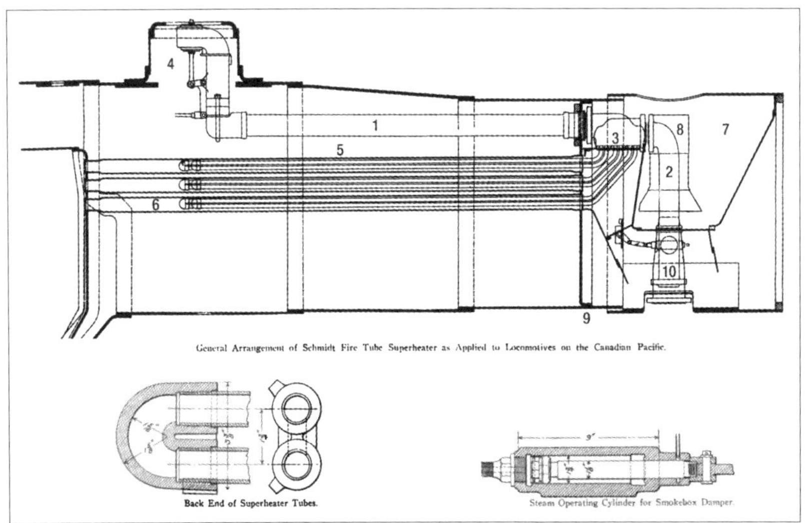

Components of a locomotive equipped with a Schmidt superheater include: 1) Dry pipe; 2) Steam pipe; 3) Superheater headers; 4) Steam dome; 5) Superheater tubes (inside the firetubes); 6) Fire tubes (flues); 7) Smokebox; 8) Petticoat; 9) Front tube sheet; 10) Exhaust pipe.

Adapted from Locomotive Dictionary, 1906

dry pipe to a header, a cored-out casting mounted on the boiler's front flue sheet. From the header's receiving chamber, steam is routed through multiple tubes of approximately one to one-and-a-half inch diameter. Each superheater tube, nested inside a five-inch diameter flue, makes two loops before passing its steam to the header's discharge chamber. From there, the now superheated steam is passed to the branch pipes feeding the locomotive cylinders' valve chests. Early tests confirmed that Schmidt's arrangement added 150-200 degrees to the steam. Thus, for example, if boiler pressure was 200 psi, saturated steam temperature was 388°F. Adding, say, 200 degrees results in a total steam temperature of 588 degrees – within the tolerable range of steam-cylinder oils then available.[11]

If the devil is in the details, then three details were fundamental to success: type of connection of the superheater tubes to the header; ability of the whole assembly to withstand vibration without leaks; and ability of the superheater tube material, at the bend closest to the firebox or back flue sheet, to withstand the pummeling of cinders flying through the flues at 200 mph or more. As to the last factor, cinders are not just carbon but contain incombustible impurities, often heavy in silicates, that can cut into steel. Cinder guards, made of a harder steel alloy than the tube itself (the tube material must be capable of being formed into sharp bends without cracking), became standard for the return bends facing the firebox. The type of connection of the tubes at the header, after a few trials, became a robust compression fitting, able to stay steam-tight despite any warping of the tubes, and relatively easy for mechanics to loosen despite buildup of caked, hardened soot and prior exposure to great heat. In available metallurgy and in such details, Schmidt's design was much advanced over that of de Montcheuill five decades before. Also, Schmidt paid great attention to all of the mechanical context: lubrication, engine performance, and, as his ideas gained wider acceptance, overall locomotive design to take best advantage of the higher steam temperatures.

The payoff was a claimed 15 to 20 percent reduction in steam consumption per horsepower-hour, with a similar percentage boost in net power output, compared to a similar two-cylinder, simple-expansion locomotive running at the same fuel rate. The improvement, with little variation, held true over the power range of boiler and engine, from low to high output, and over the complete rpm range of the engine. Moreover (actually part of the thermal performance), at around 200 degrees of superheat, condensation was eliminated – steam temperature was still a bit above saturation after expansion and at the point of exhaust release.[12]

Canadian Pacific 4-6-0 No. 548 ushered in the widespread adoption of locomotive superheaters in North America, following the success of the ten-year-old engine's 1901 retrofit with a Schmidt smokebox superheater.
Author's Collection

The news spread quickly and internationally. Such results were, in the railroad trade, dramatic. The Prussian railway management was happy to help proselytize. Other European and British railroad officials expressed keen interest and agreed to tests supervised by Schmidt. The first North American railroad to set up a trial was the Canadian Pacific.[13]

Canadian Pacific's chief locomotive officer, Edward A. Williams, had already been in touch with Schmidt and Garbe. When Williams took office as the CPR's superintendent of rolling stock in January 1901, he had heard of Schmidt's work. Williams sent one of CPR's mechanical engineers, A.W. Horsey, to Germany to witness superheater tests on the Prussian railway. That summer, 1901, Williams had a CPR locomotive retrofitted with a Schmidt smokebox superheater – 4-6-0 No. 548.

Two years later, with confidence built by No. 548's performance and by Horsey's further reports of the tests and experience with firetube superheaters in Germany, Williams ordered one engine from each of two new groups of cross-compound 4-6-0s to be built with Schmidt's firetube superheater. The first such locomotive – No. 1300, delivered to CPR in November 1903 by the American Locomotive Co. of Schenectady, N.Y. – was the harbinger of a change that would affect every railroad in the U.S. and Canada.[14]

Williams left CPR in December 1903 to join the management of the Erie. His successor, Henry H. Vaughan, picked up on the superheating agenda. In mid-1904, with No. 1300 and the other cross-compound engine with a Schmidt firetube superheater performing well, Vaughan had a simple-expansion locomotive refitted with a Cole-Field firetube superheater.[15] The American Locomotive Co.'s Francis Cole and a colleague had devised a firetube superheater that Alco promoted. Later in 1904, Vaughan approved the design and purchase of CPR's first group of locomotives to have superheaters as part of their original specification: 41 single-expansion 2-8-0s, 20 with the Schmidt and 21 with the Cole-Field. Based on remarks he made later, it is apparent that Vaughan was already convinced of the superheater's value and intended a massive adoption in the years to follow, but he wanted a good field test of competing styles.[16]

At the same time, he and Horsey set about designing a superheater of their own. In the first six months of 1905, the Vaughan-Horsey firetube superheater was patented, the first installation was made and tested, and manufacture was begun on 10 more engines at CPR's Angus Shops in Montreal with the new superheater design as original equipment. More than developmental questions were at issue. There was little real difference in the heat-transfer efficiency of the leading firetube types. But just as Alco sought to get around Schmidt's patents, Vaughan could do the same and save CPR a lot of royalty payments.

While this activity was going on in Canada, there was little in the U.S. Cole designed an improved version of his device, Baldwin offered a smokebox arrangement, and, in 1904, a German locomotive ran on the Pennsylvania Railroad's test plant at the St. Louis fair with an alternative form called the Pielock type, after its inventor.[17] In the Pielock design, the superheater is a steam chamber that's placed in the middle of the boiler barrel, with the boiler's firetubes running through it. The design was adopted principally in Germany, Italy, and Hungary, but was never popular in the U.S., due mostly to the chamber's inaccessibility relative to other types of superheaters.[18] Baldwin did use the Pielock design in some of its separable boilers, however. Many

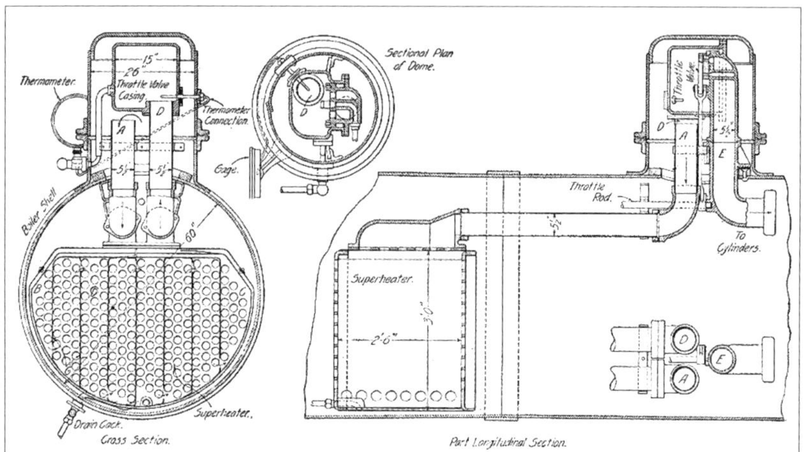

In the Pielock design, the superheater is a steam chamber that's placed in the middle of the boiler barrel, with the boiler's firetubes running through it.
A Practical Treatise on Locomotive Boiler and Engine Design, Construction, and Operation, 1920

of the Santa Fe's ill-fated Mallets of 1910-11 had reheaters, and its 2-10-10-2 design included a superheater and a reheater, both of the steam-chamber type.

Through December 1906, according to a tally made by Vaughan, only 15 locomotives in the U.S. had superheaters. The Chicago, Rock Island & Pacific had six and the Chicago, Burlington & Quincy (which had briefly experimented with a smokebox superheater in 1870) had three. Five other lines accounted for the rest. It was not exactly a groundswell. Meanwhile, CPR owned 197 and would buy or build 175 more in 1907.[19] Although the Vaughan-Horsey type became the favorite in new construction and refitting, the Schmidt and the Cole were also used.

Vaughan kept track of fuel costs for the superheated locomotives, but not in any controlled fashion. Most of his data came from the field, as the new engines ran on regular trains. A service test in 1906 compared the newest 4-6-0 saturated-steam cross-compounds with superheated, simple-expansion 4-6-0s running in freight duty over three divisions between Fort William, Ontario and Winnipeg, Manitoba. On two of the three divisions, no significant difference was found in fuel costs. Compared to the saturated compounds, on only one division (Fort William to Ignace) did the Vaughan-Horsey and Cole-equipped engines show any marked superiority. The Schmidt-equipped engines actually consumed a bit more coal than the saturated compounds on that division. On another division, the Schmidt did better and the Cole did worse. On the third division, the superheated engines consumed a bit more coal than the compounds, but the result was a virtual dead heat.[20]

Six months of records kept for the short but mountainous run between Revelstoke and Field in British Columbia indicated an average 11 percent reduction in coal use by superheated, simple-expansion engines, compared to saturated compounds of similar size. Vaughan described himself as "exceedingly" pleased with the overall results. Oddly, at no time was there any test of an important potential comparison: between either of the two Schmidt superheated compounds built in 1903 and the new superheated single-expansion engines.

Tests before 1910 on U.S. railroads comparing just single-expansion locomotives – superheated with the latest Schmidt or Cole variants vs. comparable unsuperheated engines – invariably showed good improvement. Fuel savings as high as 20 or 30 percent were claimed, but usually for newer engines in comparison to relatively elderly locomotives with lower boiler pressures and in far-from-controlled conditions. Prof. William Goss, probably the most respected locomotive theoretician in the U.S., conducted a careful series of tests at the Purdue University test plant between November 1906 and July 1907. Goss tested a Cole-equipped engine, in which superheat temperatures were about 150 degrees above saturation, at various boiler pressures. The engine gave a fuel saving of 13 to 17 percent compared to the same locomotive running saturated as originally built. The higher the boiler pressure, the less the saving; the 13 percent was obtained at 200 psi.[21] These results and data from Europe were widely shared and discussed within the trade. The amount of superheat was important. At 200 degrees of superheat in larger locomotives, fuel savings of 10 to 15 percent (comparing single-expansion engines) seemed to be reliable. Few tests of compound, superheated engines were made in the U.S. The German locomotive run at St. Louis was one of the few. Its fuel rates seemed little different from those reported in Germany for superheated simple engines, but its superheat temperatures were only around 170 degrees.[22] Garbe strongly argued, in a 1907 series of articles in *The Engineer*, that superheating rendered compounding superfluous. Though he describes it as his opinion,

> The use of highly superheated steam in a simple two-cylinder locomotive ... increases the power of the engine to such an extent that the demand for increased hauling power ... can be met without recourse to four-cylinder compounds, which are both complicated in construction and costly in maintenance.[23]

Garbe, in effect, set the terms of the debate. Not everyone agreed. Designers in France, such as Glehn, and other German engineers continued working on compound designs that included superheaters. American designers applied superheaters to Mallet compounds starting in 1909, and not just on the Santa Fe. A historian has suggested that the Prussian State Railways' undemanding, level territory and access to cheap coal had already created a bias in that organization against the complexity of compounding, long before Schmidt came on the scene.[24]

Santa Fe Railway's unhappy experience with compounding, reported in the trade press and discussed at mechanical officers' conventions, was a splash of cold water not only for that railroad's engineers but for railroad managements throughout the country. By 1911 the trade well knew of Santa Fe's Mallet problems, and the maintenance headaches of tandem compounds were obvious long before that. Spring 1912 – when Santa Fe's management installed John Purcell as head of the mechanical department – showed the personal risks involved in engineering failure.[25]

Much has been written on the role of failure in advancing engineering insight. What is less clear is the role of risk – what happens in decision-making before the failures. It is often stated that human beings, especially in bureaucracies, are risk-averse. But people are also creative, when there is reward for that.[26]

Laying out the design for a locomotive was an extraordinarily complex task, involving thousands of explicit decisions. There were many potential sources of failure that could not be known until the machine was built or in service for some months. Drafting rooms used "standard practice sheets" – for

Southern Pacific 2-8-8-2 No. 4000 – built by Baldwin in 1909, first in a class of two – had both a superheater and a reheater. Here, it works at Gold Run, Nev., in 1909.
Author's Collection

frame layout details, for boiler details, for driving wheels and running gear – to reduce risk. Codes developed by the American Society of Mechanical Engineers (ASME) covered boiler construction, including standards for tensile stress, plate thicknesses, and safety factors for different boiler pressures. But major problematic decisions determining performance – decisions about boiler and firebox proportions, rpm related to the work to be done in service, and use of devices claimed to increase operating efficiency – were supported mostly by accumulated empirical wisdom in the trade. Making decisions about any of these things involved personal risk for the engineer. Controlled tests were exceedingly rare and far between and, because the few locomotives actually tested under controlled conditions were so different in important parameters from any locomotive in the design stage, the accumulated test record was of limited helpfulness.

Predictability is desirable in engineering decision-making. If a design includes elements that are unlike any previous design, engineers need a basis for predicting the performance effects of the new elements. The difficulty in designing larger compound locomotives in the 1900-1915 time period was that their thermal performance was not reliably predictable. Without the analytic tools available today, estimating the cylinder performance of a compound engine was difficult at best. Engineers grappled with dynamic temperature and pressure variations; with different lengths and dimensions of steam passageways that affected drag in unknown ways; and with valve timing changes – all of which introduced variables far more complex than those allowed for in the straightforward expansion/heat exchange rules from standard texts.[27] The relationship of cylinder economy to boiler steam-generating efficiency and capacity was incompletely understood; it was not uncommon, at high output in a given locomotive, to have good cylinder economy (*i.e.*, low steam consumption) but still have poor net fuel economy, even with a simple engine. The only fully trustworthy guide to all these variables was empirical data. Unfortunately, any design for a compound engine that did not simply duplicate an earlier one differed from any of its predecessors in hundreds of ways that affected net performance.

In the first decade of the 20th century, railroad officials who operated compounds claimed good economy numbers. Vauclain compounds and balanced compounds seemed generally to be about ten percent better in fuel economy than comparable simple engines, especially if most of their duty was at moderate rpm. Cross-compounds were similarly thrifty of coal, were no more expensive to maintain than a simple engine, but were severely limited in speed. Tandems were done in by speed limitations and maintenance: If anything, they were more costly to maintain than any other four-cylinder form. (Even in the four-cylinder balanced type, mechanics did not have to take apart the engine in order to perform running maintenance on cylinders and valves, as they did on tandems.) Most Mallets – if equipped with large and conventionally designed boilers – were solid investments from the beginning, given the doubling of haulage capacity with one boiler and one road crew; thermal performance was a secondary consideration. But in the rare instances when compounds were actually tested, such as the Glehn or the German superheated compound in 1904, fuel efficiency numbers were disappointing at best. At higher rpm, efficiencies were mediocre, in a few instances worse than a simple, saturated engine. The upshot was that, despite all the claims and counterclaims, there was no reliable guide to compound thermal performance in terms of power output per pound of fuel. "Good" performance numbers were questionable. The few controlled and published tests, in Europe and the U.S., showed wide variations in economy. Designing and building a compound was a shot in the dark.

Into this context came the superheater, a device that could be adapted easily to fit any locomotive, with no changes to running machinery and with only minor alteration to boiler flue arrangement. Another advantage in an age of unreliable performance data was that superheaters could be removed easily if they didn't work. That never proved necessary, of course, though many railroads changed superheater makes and models – CPR being the obvious example. But superheaters worked – reliably and predictably. Simply adding a superheater to an existing saturated locomotive gave an immediate and entirely obvious 10 to15 percent boost in top power and hauling capacity, with a similar reduction in coal consumed at a given output. This was in fact the most persuasive, controlled, and unambiguous test one could ever have: Just bolt the device in and see the result in the same locomotive. On every railroad that tried superheating, that test occurred.

The only unknowns, then, were cylinder-oil reliability and maintenance of the superheater itself. Mechanical officers were especially concerned that superheater tubes might burn out in service. After a few years the verdict was again obvious: Cylinder maintenance was virtually unaffected; superheaters were reliable and had minor impact on boiler repair costs. At the same time, the improved locomotive performance records simply accumulated. Only one machinery change was required: Steam-distribution valves had to be of the piston form. As was understood in 1900, locomotives with boiler pressures in excess of about 210 psi ran better with piston valves; high pressures made it difficult to keep slide valves on their seats. And if steam was entirely dry (i.e., superheated), valve lubrication was more reliable with piston valves.[28]

If railroad managements wanted economy, here was a surefire solution. Aside from reliably predictable fuel economy, a designer who suggested the adoption of superheating could depend on no increase in maintenance charges. Compared to a two-cylinder superheated locomotive doing identical work on the road, any manager could also appreciate that a four-cylinder compound, no matter how reliable its operation, required more machine

Superheated steam can do more work before it condenses, and it reduces or eliminates condensation within the locomotive's cylinders, which can damage cylinder heads and pistons. Condensation was a particular problem for locomotives, due to the distance from the boiler to the smokebox.[5] As long as locomotives used saturated steam, their power would be limited by rapid condensation.

Richard Trevithick, the Cornish mining engineer who's generally regarded as the father of the steam locomotive, devised a successful firetube superheater in 1828. In his design, a superheater tube was installed within the boiler tube, heating the steam past its boiling point, thanks to its proximity to hot gasses in the firetube. It was the forerunner of the superheaters that were installed on almost all 20th century American steam locomotives.

Other engineers designed superheaters that used heat in the smokebox or stack. John H. White Jr. describes and discusses locomotive superheaters up to 1880. In North America, James Millholland of the Philadelphia & Reading, A.F. Smith of the Hudson River Railroad, Henry Tyson of the B&O, James Martin of Grand Trunk Railway of Canada, and William S. Hudson of the Rogers Locomotive and Machine Works did important work on superheating from the 1850s through the 1870s.[6]

In the smokebox form of superheater, steam generated by the boiler passed through a chamber or set of tubes exposed to flue gases within the smokebox, thus adding heat to the steam right before it reached the cylinders. In the firetube form, the idea was to pass boiler steam through tubes exposed to flue gases *before* these gases reached the smokebox. In the latter form a much higher degree of superheat could be achieved. Of all the possible variations, one that was impractical was passing steam tubes right into the firebox; the intense heat would lead quickly to failure of the tubes.

Truly high superheat temperatures were not usable anyway. Excessive heat broke down the primitive lubricants of the late 19th century, which were still mostly based on animal fats. Until late in the century, no cylinder oil available could perform reliably if total steam temperatures exceeded 400-425°F. Given the limitations of early lubricants, inventors initially focused their efforts on the smokebox form of superheater. For example, at a boiler pressure of 120-125 psi, typical in the mid-1870s, saturated steam temperature is about

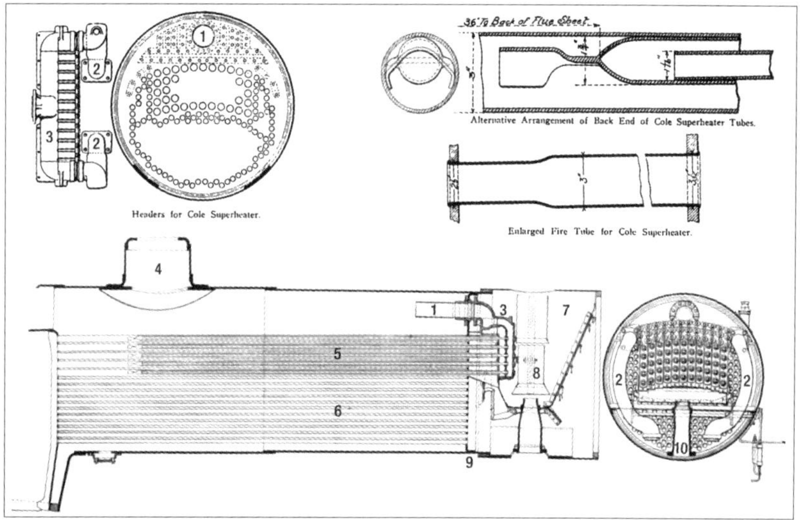

Components of a locomotive equipped with a Cole superheater include: 1) Dry pipe; 2) Steam pipes; 3) Superheater headers; 4) Steam dome; 5) Superheater tubes; 6) Boiler tubes; 7) Smokebox; 8) Petticoat; 9) Front tube sheet; 10) Exhaust pipe.
Adapted from Locomotive Dictionary, 1906

time in the backshops – and therefore more machinists. Recommending superheating was free of risk. Compounding entailed the opposite.

By 1910 few new locomotives, for any railroad in the industrialized world, were delivered without superheaters of some kind. Firetube superheaters became universal in the U.S. and Canada for new road-locomotive orders after 1911. Compounding was a separate issue. Mallets ran well and pulled enough additional tonnage to more than justify their expense. When Santa Fe, however, pushed the Mallet art beyond the boundaries of empirical understanding and – along with Baldwin engineers – relied on boiler and cylinder heat-transfer theory of the day, the risks to railroad investors, managers, and locomotive-department heads were made real for all in the industry to see.

Even given the state of theory, sophisticated designers knew also that superheating economies and compounding economies could never be additive. That is, one could never have an engine in which a 10 percent improvement in fuel efficiency from compounding alone would add to a 10 percent improvement from superheating alone for a total of 20 percent. That's because both technologies affected expansion efficiency by affecting heat loss from condensation.[29]

Most of the heat loss within cylinders running on saturated steam, whether simple or compound, is from condensation. (Most of the total cylinder heat loss is simply out the stack.) As anyone knows who has boiled steam in a kettle and used a suitable thermometer, it takes heat to bring the water up to boiling temperature. Once at that temperature, however, it takes still more heat to initiate boiling and a lot more heat to convert all the water to steam. The change from liquid phase to gas phase stores considerable heat energy, apart from the temperature change. If boiling takes place at well above atmospheric pressure, stored energy can be released by expansion. It is the stored energy in the phase change from liquid to gas, however, that allows a great deal of expansion and pressure reduction to take place without all the steam (gas) turning to vapor (liquid). Fundamentally, without the energy difference stored in the gas phase, a steam engine could not work at all. The fact is, then, if superheating is enough to prevent condensation altogether, most of the heat loss in the cylinders amenable to practical reduction has been prevented. That's true whether the engine is a simple or a compound.

In his famous book of 1908, Dr. Garbe declared:

> Any noticeable saving in steam consumption by the use of superheated steam in compound engines, as against its use in simple engines, could only be effected by avoiding condensation in the low-pressure cylinder as well, but this would involve superheating to 570° [or more; about 200 degrees of superheat]. It should be borne in mind that it is a matter of indifference whether the steam is expanded in one or two cylinders.[30]

Given the boiler pressures and superheat levels achievable in practice at the time, Garbe was right. He articulated the view that both boiler pressures and superheat temperatures could be moderate, the highest practical thermal efficiency could be achieved, and the extra mechanical complexity of compound cylinders could be eliminated. Just eliminate condensation.

An early supporter of this view was the internationally influential designer George Churchward of the Britain's Great Western Railway. He had designed compounds and was often an advocate for them. However, he had run two extended field trials, one in 1903 of a Glehn and another, in 1905, of two larger Glehns. Fuel economy was only marginally better than comparable simple engines then in fleet use on the GWR. Thereafter Churchward designed a balanced, four-cylinder compound for high-speed service (the "Star" class), but to achieve smooth riding quality, not economy. As superheating took hold in Britain, Churchward turned his attention to simple-engine design, kept superheat temperatures moderate in his locomotives, and stated that higher temperature beyond what was needed to eliminate condensation would not improve fuel efficiency.[31]

Garbe's and Churchward's views could not take into account boiler pressures of 300 psi, or superheat temperatures of 300 to 400 degrees, or lubricants able to take up to 800 degrees – all of which were common by the late 1930s. Garbe's assertions neglected the additional boiler efficiencies that would eventually result from big superheaters and higher boiler pressures working together to help fuel economy, prior to steam entering the cylinders. Nor did theory, at the time, account for key properties of fully superheated steam affecting cylinder performance. Even after all heat loss to condensation is prevented, the percentage heat loss to walls of passages and cylinders is somewhat reduced as superheat temperature increases still further. And, most important, as superheated steam – a true gas and not a gas-vapor mixture – takes on additional heat at the same pressure, it expands in volume. Each increment of heat means that less steam, by weight, does the same work in the cylinder. Nor did theory or experience in Garbe's time dispel the widespread – and as it turned out, entirely false – notion that compound economy depended on running at low rpm. Within the confines of the practical locomotive art of 1908-1915, Garbe and Churchward were persuasive. Starting in 1909, designers added superheaters to compound Mallets, but with the aim only of reducing or eliminating condensation – which would nonetheless improve their fuel economy.

Thus, between the guideposts of limited theory and actual experience, designers could substantially reduce risk in new designs by sticking to simple-expansion locomotives for anything other than the slowest, heaviest freight service. Moreover, with superheating one could actually reduce boiler pressures and achieve better economy than with saturated engines. Whereas many saturated locomotives in 1900 had boiler pressures of 200 psi or better, a lot of new road engines after 1910 went back to 180 or even 175.[32] To do so also reduced design risk. This was not risk of boiler explosions; designers by then knew how to construct a boiler so that, unless there was blatant human error on the part of crews and/or mechanics, it would not blow up. The reduced design risk lay in the fact that the higher the boiler pressure, the more firebox repair could ensue.[33]

Many railroads, such as CPR and Santa Fe, began rebuilding their huge rosters of compounds into simple-expansion engines (CPR beginning in 1911; Santa Fe in 1915, though it kept many balanced compounds in unaltered use until the mid-1920s). This was expensive major surgery, involving the redesign of running gear, the casting of new cylinder saddles, making new cylinders, and rerouting large steam pipes. The lesson for designers of compounds was clear: Making a poorly performing engine was not a good career move.

Schmidt's reaction to all of these issues was happily to sell more superheaters. He licensed an American firm, the Superheater Co., to manufacture and market his designs. Competition from all his imitators did not seem to bother him. His royalties made him rich, he relished working in the field to see that his devices were installed properly, and he was a true believer – to him the main point was to spread the superheater gospel, Most superheaters installed were of his design; competing models like the Vaughan-Horsey or the Cole soon proved to have slightly higher maintenance, mostly because they were harder to remove and service. When Schmidt died in 1924 at the age of 66, he was known to many in the trade as "*Heißdampf* Willy" – "hot steam Willy."[34]

And what of H.H. Vaughan, who truly launched "the superheating movement" in North America? He left the Canadian Pacific in 1915, by mutual agreement between himself and CPR vice president George Bury. Bury wrote that Vaughan was "... a superior engineer and most capable designer ... [but] not an administrator or a shop man."[35] Those who have wrestled a Vaughan-Horsey superheater header and tubes out of a smokebox may agree with the last piece of that statement.[36] Nevertheless, Vaughan went on to a fine career as a consulting engineer. He died in 1942, in Philadelphia, and is buried in Montreal, not far from his beloved Angus Shops.

Chapter 6 Notes

1. A.W. Bruce, *The Steam Locomotive in America: Its Development in the Twentieth Century*, 1952, p. 153.
2. Purcell had been chief of locomotive design and maintenance for at least a year and a half when the order for the new compounds was approved. In addition to the 4-6-2s and the Mallets, Santa Fe had 117 4-4-2 and 88 2-6-2 balanced-compounds (the latter for freight). The 2-6-2s were not rebuilt to simple-expansion until the late 1920s; the 4-4-2s were scrapped as compounds at about the same time. Despite their early promise, however, the superheated, balanced-compound 4-6-2s of 1914 apparently did not show enough fuel economy – compared to superheated, simple-expansion engines – to warrant Santa Fe's further interest in any type of compound. The 4-6-2s were rebuilt with simple cylinders starting in the early 1920s; Purcell must have concluded by 1920 that the big investment in rebuilding them would be cost-effective.
3. S.R. Wood and David P. Morgan, "The Thrifty Compound," *Trains*, September 1951, pp. 44-48.
4. Bruce, *The Steam Locomotive in America*, p. 153.
5. John H. White, Jr., *A History of the American Locomotive, Its Design: 1830-1880*, (Dover, 1979), p. 143.
6. White, pp. 142-44.
7. C.D. Young, "Locomotive Superheaters," *Journal of the Franklin Institute*, (July 1914).
8. J.N. Westwood, *Locomotive Designers in the Age of Steam*, (1977), pp. 132-36. Several authors describe the 1898 superheater as Schmidt's first, but confuse it with his first firetube type, which didn't come until 1901 (See White, p. 144).
9. Montcheuill, in turn, based his design on an earlier patent for a firetube superheater for stationary boilers, developed by M. Quillacq – the first name is uncertain, since "M" probably stands for "monsieur." Schmidt's debt to Montcheuill in C.D. Young, in *Bulletin of the International Railway Congress*, April 1908; *Railroad Gazette*, Nov. 1, 1907.
10. Robert Garbe, *The Application of Highly Superheated Steam to Locomotives*, 1908. See also Westwood, p. 136.
11. W.F.M. Goss, *Superheated Steam in Locomotive Service*, (1910), Chapter 3.
12. Bruce, pp. 151-55.
13. Omer Lavallée, *Canadian Pacific Steam Locomotives*, (1985), pp. 106-26, 259, 295, 435-36.
14. CPR No. 548 is generally credited as the pioneering superheater application in North America, but CPR No. 1300 was the first to have a firetube superheater, and that's the type that revolutionized steam locomotives on this continent. Besides, even CPR No. 548 wasn't the pioneer: James Millholland applied a small smokebox superheater to his 1859 4-4-0 *Hiawatha*, and Hudson River Railroad's A.F. Smith applied his own

smokebox superheater that same year. In Canada, Grand Trunk Master Mechanic James Martin applied smokebox devices to several locomotives in the 1860s. (See White, pp. 143-44.)

15. CPR 4-6-0 No. 552, originally built (like the 548) in 1891.
16. H.H. Vaughan, *Transactions of the American Society of Mechanical Engineeers*, 1907.
17. *The Pennsylvania Railroad System at the Louisiana Purchase Exposition: Locomotive Tests and Exhibits*, 1904.
18. Llewelyn V. Ludy, *Locomotive Boilers and Engines: A Practical Treatise on Locomotive Boiler and Engine Design, Construction, and Operation*, (1920), p. 63. See also Bruce, p. 154.
19. H.H. Vaughan, *Transactions of the American Society of Mechanical Engineeers*, (1907).
20. Ibid.
21. W.F.M. Goss, *Superheated Steam in Locomotive Service*, (1910), Chapter 3.
22. *The Pennsylvania Railroad System at the Louisiana Purchase Exposition: Locomotive Tests and Exhibits*, 1904.
23. Robert Garbe, *The Application of Highly Superheated Steam to Locomotives*, (1908), p. 21. The whole chapter, "Compounding and Superheating," is an argument that, both theoretically and practically, the fuel economy of a compound, superheated locomotive compared to a simple, superheated engine, "would only be small, and would in no way make up for" the higher costs of construction and maintenance. Garbe also alleges a compound's "difficulty in starting" and "general want of adaptability" (p. 25).
24. Westwood, p. 212.
25. Changes in Santa Fe's motive power department were reflected in the *Pocket List of Railroad Officials*, 1911-1913.
26. Henry Petroski, *To Engineer is Human: The Role of Failure in Successful Design*, (1992); Walter G.Vincenti, *What Engineers Know and How They Know It: Analytical Studies from Aeronautical History* (1993). See also the extensive writings by Herbert A. Simon on organizational behavior, especially *Administrative Behavior* (1947), *Models of Man: Social and Rational*, (1957), and *Organizations* (1957, with James G. March.
27. Ralph P. Johnson, *The Steam Locomotive: Its Theory, Operation, and Economics* (1942), comments on the unknowns in estimating cylinder performance at higher rpm, noting that they were little changed from 30 years earlier. Johnson's book was written only six years before the last steam locomotive was produced by a U.S. commercial builder.
28. Slide valves relied on a little condensation for good total lubrication. In a saturated engine, the pressure drop between boiler and steam chest provided just enough moisture.
29. In an engine, simple or compound, condensation came from two inherent sources: from the expansion itself and from the heating, cooling, and reheating of cylinder walls that occurred with every stroke. Superheating, if high enough, could prevent condensation altogether, even with the unavoidable cylinder-wall heat loss. Compounding improved the expansion ratio (a greater volumetric expansion of steam in a driving-wheel revolution, since steam could expand twice instead of once), but a good deal of the efficiency gain derived from keeping the total condensation tolerable.
30. Garbe, p. 22. What Garbe neglects to point out, however, is that no simple locomotive could run at much less than 20 to 25 percent cutoff, at which point premature exhaust-port closure begins, with any known radial valve gear. Therefore, the expansion ratio in a simple could never be large, compared to a compound. The compound could run smoothly at 30 to 40 percent cutoff and achieve a higher total expansion ratio than a simple, within the fundamental expansion limits imposed by condensation. A high-speed superheated compound, running at 30 percent cutoff in both cylinders, could have a 50 percent better expansion ratio and could run without condensation.
31. Westwood, pp. 128-30, 135. W.A. Tuplin, *Great Western Steam*, 1958. H.C.B. Rogers, *G.J. Churchward: A Locomotive Biography*, 1975.
32. Frank M. Swengel, *The American Steam Locomotive*, vol. 1, (1967).
33. In the early decades of the 20th century, chemical treatment of boiler feedwater by railroads to control scale was spotty or nonexistent. Boiler scale deposits inevitably built up on the water side of fireboxes. Scale interfered with heat transfer, so with higher boiler pressure, mechanical stress caused firebox staybolts, or sheets near the affected bolts, to crack. Boilermakers and locomotive maintenance chiefs knew that. Superheating let the designer both improve fuel economy and reduce the chances of his design having excessive downtime from firebox repairs.
34. Westwood, p. 132.
35. Lavallée, p. 136.
36. The author recalls such a conversation with Linn Moedinger of Pennsylvania's Strasburg Rail Road. Moedinger is one of the most highly regarded steam locomotive mechanics of the present day, and he was relating the story of CPR 4-6-0 No. 972.

"Words can hardly express the thrill of a 19-year-old tallowpot, confronted for the first time by this image of mechanical perfection." *– Fireman Andrew Goobeck, recalling his impressions in 1911 of Alco locomotive 50000*[1]

Chapter 7

Francis Cole:

The Triumph of Empirical Science

IN THE SUMMER OF 1910, A SLENDER, MUSTACHIOED gentleman with thinning hair watched as skilled machinists, boilermakers, and pipefitters assembled a new locomotive in the vast erecting hall of the American Locomotive Co. plant at Schenectady, N.Y. The gentleman took more than a casual interest. The new engine was special, unique in many respects, built to his designs, and constructed at his company's sole expense. The company had assigned its builder (*i.e.*, serial) number 50000[2] to the engine, a number that took into account all of Alco's predecessors, which merged into one company in 1901. With No. 50000, Alco sought to make a splash in a sluggish locomotive market.[3] For Francis J. Cole, this was risky business, for both him and his employer.

Cole had been born in England in 1856 and, as a youngster, had emigrated to the U.S. with his family, led by his Episcopal-priest father. The farm life his father chose in Virginia was apparently not to young Francis's liking, so at 18, he went to Baltimore and signed on as an apprentice machinist in the Northern Central Railroad's Mount Royal Locomotive Shop. Cole was attracted to design work. For him, in the mid-1870s, there was little opportunity for formal training. A degree in mechanical engineering was rare and, with Cole's resources, quite beyond reach. When his apprenticeship concluded, he did the normal thing at the time for someone particularly interested in the conception of machines: He accepted a position as a draftsman, in his case at the Newark, Ohio, shop of the Baltimore & Ohio Railroad. In rather quick succession, he went to another railroad for a somewhat better position, returned to Newark as chief draftsman, and then was invited to become chief draftsman at the B&O's home shops and central mechanical engineering department at Mount Clare, Baltimore. Along the way, Cole was supervised by or worked with others who later made important careers in locomotive engineering, including John Player, J.E. Sague, and W.F. Dixon, all at the West Shore Railroad, and G.B. Hazlehurst at the B&O.[4]

Well into the 20th century, the title "draftsman" implied a great deal of thoughtful work, often creative, on engineering details. In the mid-1870s, when Cole went into railroading, most engineering degrees were for civil engineering,

The "backhead" of a steam locomotive cab was where the expertise of both designer and builder was put to the test of daily operation. This is the cab interior of Santa Fe 4-8-2 Mountain-type No. 3710.
Courtesy Kalmbach Media

and the U.S. Military Academy was still the leading source. A chief draftsman carried considerable responsibility for engineering problem-solving.

So it was for Cole. By 1890, he was B&O's mechanical engineer in charge of the design of equipment, cars, and locomotives. He led an effort to standardize cars and locomotives on the B&O and published widely-read articles on locomotive design, proportion, and construction. In 1896, at the age of 40, he made his transition to the locomotive suppliers' side of railroading, going to the Rogers Locomotive Works in Paterson, N.J., as mechanical engineer (*i.e.*, as the head such engineer). His old friend Dixon, who had held that position, recommended Cole to legendary works superintendent Reuben Wells when Dixon sailed off to Russia to build a locomotive plant for the czar. In 1899, Cole landed where he would remain: the Schenectady Locomotive Works, at the behest of friend Sague, head of engineering at the Upstate New York firm.

Alco 50000

The road to the 50000 began in June 1901. In that month, eight locomotive-building firms merged, including Schenectady.[5] Their respective fortunes had been deeply eroded by the competitive onslaught of the Baldwin Works in Philadelphia. Baldwin, so much larger than the other firms, used its economies of scale to keep its bids low and its quality high – and gradually to drive competitors out. Were it not for regional loyalties between railroad motive power officers and certain builders (*e.g.*, Richmond Works with Southern railroads, Brooks and Pittsburgh with some of the Northeastern and Midwestern lines), several of the weaker firms would have expired. With the merger, Cole became assistant to Sague, and then Alco's chief mechanical engineer after Sague's elevation to an assistant vice-presidency. Clearly, Cole advanced both on talent and on the associations he had made with contemporaries.

Motivations for building the 50000 are not clear-cut. By 1910, however, Alco was gaining a reputation as an innovator. Cole was an able leader in seeking better component design, in trying newer materials like cast steel, and in sizing and proportioning boilers for optimum performance, especially for the newer classes of locomotives coming into use with trailing trucks, large fireboxes, and longer boilers. He worked with foundries on casting methods and looked at new alloys, and he assiduously studied the locomotive boiler and horsepower test reports that had recently begun flowing from the Pennsylvania Railroad's elaborate test facility at Altoona, Pa. Meanwhile, production accelerated in 1906 and 1907 at some U.S. locomotive plants, until a severe recession reduced 1908 orders to about one-third of the average annual locomotive output since 1900. A modest recovery began

Today it would be called a test bed. Alco wanted to make a splash with its innovative 50,000th locomotive, and it succeeded.
Courtesy Kalmbach Media

in 1909, with continued improvement the following year. So perhaps Alco president Samuel Callaway thought the timing looked right to respond to the engineering progressivism espoused by his design chief and to steal a march on archrival Baldwin.

In conceiving the 50000, Cole worked toward a goal well-recognized in many engineering circles but, as a practical matter, rather new at the time for locomotives: increasing the power-to-weight ratio. Such a goal is not as esoteric as it may seem. To build a more powerful locomotive (and thus, a more economic one, since bigger loads could be hauled), a larger boiler was called for. But a larger boiler is necessarily heavier, and dealing with the increased weight is not so easy. To add a significantly more powerful boiler to a locomotive of a given wheel arrangement, without exceeding most railroads' wheel- and axle-loading limits, weight would need to be pared ruthlessly from every other part of the machine.

Francis Cole.
Author's Collection

In the first decade of the 20th century, big locomotives with weights nearing 30 tons per driving axle often strained existing track structure. Cole wanted his design not just to set new power records, but to do so with a maximum axle load well below that 30-ton mark. If he could succeed, many railroad operating and civil engineering officers would be interested, especially on the vast majority of railroads with lighter-weight rail than that laid by a few leading companies. Better power-to-weight ratios would mean the broadest possible customer base for Alco.

In considering its initiative to build a prototype, Alco's leaders must have felt that a locomotive design for heavy passenger service would have widest appeal. On railroads around the country, the recently accelerating conversion from wood to steel in passenger-car construction and ever-growing numbers of travelers were straining the capacity of locomotives purchased just a few years before. Cole was well experienced in the increasingly popular Pacific (4-6-2) type. He had designed, among others, the noted K28 of 1907, a single experimental engine that Alco constructed for the Pennsylvania Railroad, and which had led to the PRR's first production fleet of Pacifics. The K28 had not been superheated, however, and by 1910, the ascendance of the superheater was so far advanced that railroad officers regarded the device as essential in new construction.

The 50000 emerged in July. In keeping with its hoped-for celebrity, the lagging shop gave it an unpainted, burnished jacket of light-gray Russia iron that gleamed in the sun – a decorative touch not often seen since the 1890s. Underneath and below the shiny jacket, innovations bristled.[6]

Cast steel was used to an unprecedented extent. Its cylinders – including the integral valve chests and saddle halves, with cast-iron bushings in the cylinder and valve bores – were the first in the U.S. to use cast steel. Cast steel was likewise used in high-stress parts like driving- and truck-wheel centers, crossheads, trailing-truck components, frame cross-ties, link supports, link yokes and yoke brackets, and equalizer fulcrums. Vanadium-alloy steel – giving greater strength with lighter weight – was specified for the rolled-steel engine frames and springs, for the cast cylinders, and for forged parts such as piston rods, main rods, side rods, crankpins, and all of the valve-motion rods. As a result, these parts could be made smaller in cross-section and still provide the necessary strength. The saving in weight on the cylinders alone,

The weight-saving "Cole truck" and the self-centering valve-stem guide, as installed on Alco 4-6-2 locomotive No. 50000. *American Engineer, January 1912*

compared to the usual hard cast iron, was 4,000 pounds. A revised design of trailing truck – the "Cole truck," conceived earlier but thereafter to become virtually standard on Alco engines – cut 3,000 pounds. Various cast steel parts saved another 3,000 pounds; the use of vanadium steel thousands more. Even the seemingly inconsequential trick of making the pilot and front bumper beam out of pressed steel cut 1,532 pounds.

The boiler was impressive, with an 87-inch maximum diameter that was an inch greater than that of the first Mallet. Aside from the large grate (60 square feet) and high boiler pressure (185 psi), thermal performance and horsepower were enhanced principally by the largest superheater yet installed on a passenger engine in the U.S.: a Schmidt Type A with a surface of 897 square feet. In road tests with a dynamometer car, and with boiler instrumentation connected to various points in the steam flow, pyrometers

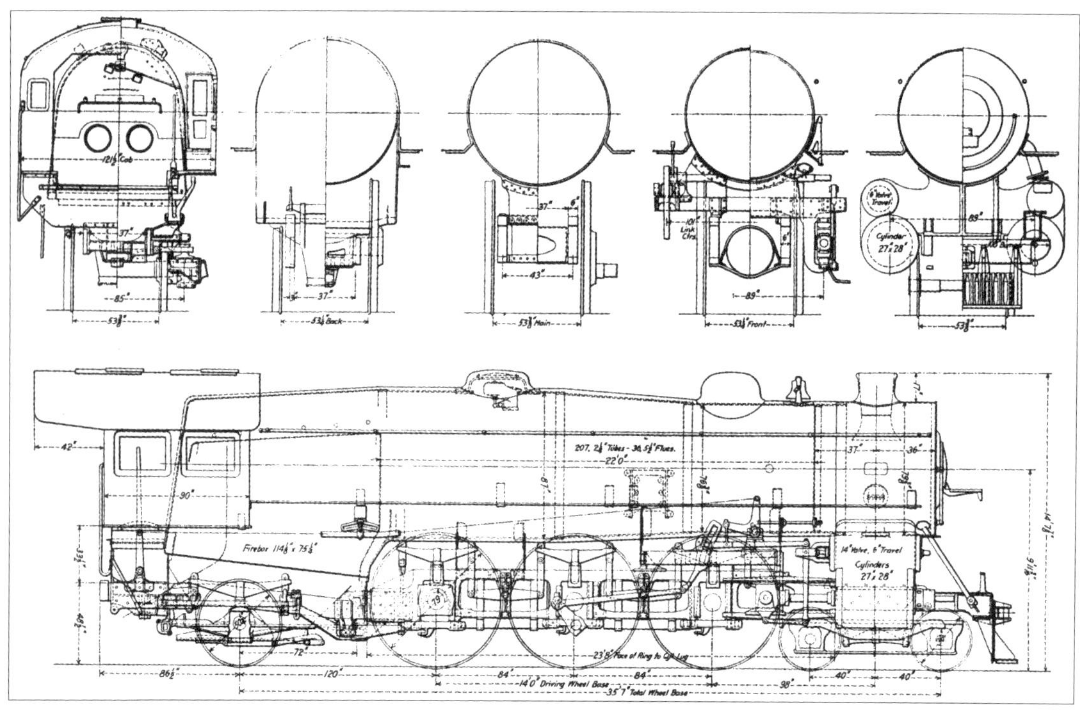

Alco No. 50000. *Railway Age Gazette, December 29, 1911*

A construction view of Alco No. 50000's outside steam pipes, and the "screw-type" reversing gear in the cab.

American Engineer, January 1912

showed a maximum superheat of some 340°F, with an average of 276 degrees.[7] Added to the saturated steam temperature, the total temperature thus ranged from about 650 to 720 degrees – hot indeed, and above 700 degrees,[8] not far below the limit tolerated by the cylinder/valve lubricant.

Another performance boost came from a surprising source: the outside steam pipes, the first such U.S. application on a two-cylinder engine.[9] The previously standard routing of boiler steam from drypipe to smokebox header to valve chests was via live steam passages through the cast iron cylinder saddle. Foundrymen advised Cole that, if such passages were incorporated in the usual way, the difficult coring involved was impractical for successful casting of the cylinders in steel. Simplification was needed. So Cole removed the inlet-steam passages from the saddle altogether. Performance tests later showed markedly better draft, since considerable obstruction to draft had been taken out of the smokebox interior.[10] The arrangement was quickly copied in subsequent production by every builder.

For the engineman, there was something to make control easier and more effective: a "screw-type" reversing gear, used to set cutoff. For the value of this device, it is worth quoting from contemporary trade sources:

> "... [I]t is becoming very difficult to handle the ordinary reverse lever, and ... it is often dangerous to alter the point of cut-off when operating at high speed."[11]

And,

> "In the large locomotives of the day ... considerable loss in economy and efficiency in operation ensues from the fact that steam is not used expansively with the full throttle and the cut-off [set] at the most economical point. This is due to the fact that when any speed is attained it is *often a risk to change the reverse lever because of the liability of the lever getting out of the hands of the engineer.* ... [Emphasis added; see Chapter 8, on safety hazards in the engine cab.]
>
> Also, in reversing direction from a stop ... time [is] consumed by the engineer in getting into position and *well braced before he can exert sufficient muscular force* to throw the reverse lever."[12] [Emphasis added.]

The new form of reverse and cutoff control was adapted from types popular in Britain and in Europe. Alco's variant accommodated the heavier weight of valve-actuating gear used in larger North American engines. It gave the engineman about 11 times more leverage than an ordinary lever without power-assist, and fine adjustments to cutoff were easy and safe to make, since there was no danger that a lever would fly out of the engineman's hands from kick-back in poorly balanced or insufficiently lubricated valves. After the 50000, a few railroads, notably the New York Central, adopted the screw-reverse in some locomotives; most railroads grudgingly adopted a different form, the air-assisted power-reverse lever, but only in later years. Either form obviated the hazards of the traditional and notoriously hazardous "Johnson bar."

Cole's trailing truck, used on several Alco-built locomotives before the 50000, was an improvement that lasted in new production well into the 1930s. Its virtues were light weight, radial movement laterally of plus or minus five inches without twisting the spring carriers, equalization of spring deflection as the engine rose and fell underway, and lateral centering action from a combination of a transverse coil spring and inclined-plane friction plates. The U-shaped, lateral yoke on each side of the truck – a virtual trademark of the Cole type – was hinged to the locomotive's rigid rear frame. Each yoke carried a self-aligning friction plate, which bore the weight imposed by the truck spring. The truck's journal box carried a corresponding bottom plate. The sliding plates, which took grease lubrication, allowed lateral movement of the trailer wheels and their journal boxes, independent of the yoke. This clever arrangement solved a critical problem for radial trucks. All such trucks needed to be equalized with the locomotive drivers. But in the Cole, when the truck wheels and axle moved laterally, the truck springs were not pulled out of vertical.[13]

Other Alco niceties included a self-centering valve-stem guide, made so that the guide could be removed or replaced without additional lining up; its design ensured that valve stem and valve chamber stayed in concentric alignment. Also, an "extended piston rod" – with the piston rod carried through the piston and out the front cylinder head – was thought desirable for maintaining better alignment of the piston within the cylinder bore. An extended piston-rod guide in front carried the piston's weight, in concert with the conventional crosshead that held the rear of the piston rod. Superheated steam, designers thought at the time, would eventually destroy and blow past piston rings if the conventional piston arrangement was used – with the moving piston and its weight simply left to slide, unsupported otherwise, on the bottom of the cylinder bore. Inevitably in this usual arrangement, with normal wear concentrated on the bottom of piston and bore, the piston was often in very imperfect concentricity with its cylinder, adding to stress on rings.

A number of superheated locomotives introduced between about 1910 and 1915 included extended piston rods, but in time designers found them unnecessary. After a few years of service on the Erie Railroad, mechanics removed the 50000's rod extensions and fitted normal cylinder heads. In fact, the extended rods turned out to be a maintenance headache on all railroads that tried them. Another packing seal to each cylinder (sealing the piston rod passing through its front cylinder head) had been added, along with the packing for the piston rod already through the back cylinder head. Worn packings were always troublesome sources of steam leaks out of cylinders, destroying steam economy and adding to maintenance downtime. One packing per piston rod was bad enough.

Alco arranged for road tests of the new engine in 1911 and 1912 on the Erie Railroad. The results were widely touted, with accounts published in the trade press. Cylinder horsepower was said to reach 2,216, the best ever posted by a Pacific. Better yet, that power translated into one horsepower per 121.4 pounds of total engine weight. One might have quibbled about the false degree of claimed accuracy.[14] Nevertheless it was a triumph for Cole and for Alco, which claimed that the horsepower-per-ton was 25 percent better than any previous Pacific. His record-setting locomotive weighed 134.5 tons (in working order, coal in the firebox and water in the boiler, less tender), but was "light on its feet," with an agreeable load of 28¾ tons per driving axle.

Bigger and more powerful Pacifics would soon appear – including from Cole's own drafting office. Nevertheless, the 50000 established the high reputation Cole would keep until his death in 1923, and afterward as well.

By fall of 1911, the 50000 was in a daily grind of hauling regular passenger trains on the Erie as part of an extended service trial. Its light-looking running gear caused comment. According to fireman Goobeck's account, a senior Erie engineman – one of the "old heads" whom every fireman worshipped – looked over the engine and declared that it had "nice legs and ought to run like a deer, but they'd better not hook anything heavier than a handcar on behind her."[15]

He needn't have worried. In service beginning November 17, 1911, and ending February 25, 1912, the 50000 made 170 runs. Trains averaged nine cars and often up to 12. At first the engine made a 178-mile round trip each day between Jersey City, N.J., and Port Jervis, N.Y. For the second half of the test period, the regular round trip was 386 miles – Jersey City to Susquehanna, Pa., and back on Erie train Nos. 5 and 6.

Grades characterized the entire trip, especially over the Susquehanna ridge, where the slope measured from one percent to a heavy 1.4 percent. Overall speed had to average, with dozens of station stops, 35 mph; top track speed anywhere on the run was 60 mph, so it was difficult to make up lost time. To meet schedule, turning the engine at Susquehanna was limited to 1½ hours, including ash disposal, lubrication, full inspection, taking fuel, and taking water. (Fuel was also taken at Port Jervis, with water there and at two other intermediate stops, each way.) To compound matters, the winter of 1911-1912 was one of the worst in memory according to contemporary writers, with record snows and unusually low temperatures. (Steam locomotives lose power and tonnage-rating the lower the temperature, more than ten percent at 0°F. Aside from lost power, injectors freeze, oil congeals, and conditions in the drafty cab can be abominable.) Incredibly, the 50000 ran 96 percent on-time, with only seven of the 170 trips even a minute late at the western or eastern terminals.[16] Modern railroads have trouble equaling such reliability.

"Because of the severity of the past winter, more than ordinary interest attaches to the performance of [50000]," said a lead editorial in *Railway Age Gazette*, noting that "[i]n the coldest weather in February, from the 5th to the 10th, the schedule time was bettered by an average of 10 minutes for each of 12 runs."[17] More than the quoted horsepower data, the reality of such sustained, real-world dependability impressed the trade.

Fireman Goobeck's run came on a morning in late January. Being a youngster at the bottom of the seniority list (unable, therefore, to hold a regular run, let alone one on a prestigious passenger assignment), his trip was a fluke. The regular fireman for Train No. 6 was sick. Goobeck was at the Susquehanna roundhouse awaiting another job, and so he got the call.

> I can still conjure up a vivid picture of the 50000's unfamiliar cab, as I saw it when I climbed in. The hoghead [locomotive engineeer] told me that everything was ready, except for taking water. [I did that job quickly] and, swinging clear the crane, I lost no time in tending my fire for the mountain climb.

The 50000 was hand-fired, which was the norm on most coal-burning engines of any size in 1912, and keeping boiler pressure up while distributing fuel evenly to its expansive grate would have been a challenge for any fireman. Unusual were 50000's two circular firedoors, an installation apparently intended to make firing easier but having just the opposite result.

> Once out on the hill, I began to have trouble. The pressure fell steadily because I was totally unacquainted with the engine's vertical-type pneumatic firedoors. The pedal on the left side was installed in a position that made it very difficult to fire the back left leg of the firebox, and not until we were half way to Gulf Summit did I get the knack of it.

Recovering boiler pressure on a working steam locomotive is hard enough; doing so while the engine is working at full capacity up a long grade is doubly difficult. Steam must be created at a maximum rate, yet falling boiler pressure subtracts from the steam's ability to do work in the cylinders. Thus even more steam must be created. The fireman cannot simply fire to excess, however. It is critical that the firebed be kept level and built up carefully, otherwise combustion will be choked off and firebox temperature will drop, causing boiler pressure to drop still further. Fireman Goobeck's account conceals a well-practiced skill and a sophisticated knowledge of firing conditions. He recovered boiler pressure to just below 50000's nominal 185 psi – enough to make a "preliminary lift" of the first safety valve, but not enough to fully lift the valve and waste precious steam.

> Then we went over the crest with a nice tail [of steam] flowing at the pop valves. The rest of the trip was certainly the shortest, as far as time sense went, that I ever made over the division. So wrapped up was I in the performance of the 50000 that we were slowing for Port Jervis before I had time to realize my day's work was done.[18] [Another engine crew would take Train 6 to Jersey City.]

Through the spring and summer of 1912, 50000 worked in regular duty on the Erie. In comparison to another superheated Pacific of similar weight built earlier, the Alco's fuel and water economy was 13 percent better.[19] In June 1912, Erie ordered five near-duplicates of 50000 – but, in a surprising move, from the little Lima Locomotive Works of Lima, Ohio, heretofore best known for specialized, geared-drive logging engines.[20] The Erie purchased the 50000 itself in the fall of 1912, a little over two years after its roll-out at Schenectady, giving it the unglamorous road number 2509 to fit in with its earlier class of Pacifics.

Cole did not wait for all these developments. In 1911 Alco constructed three more precedent-breakers: the Pennsylvania Railroad's special K29 Pacific and two 4-8-2 locomotives for the Chesapeake & Ohio. The latter two engines, to which C&O gave its class J-1, were the first 4-8-2s on this side of the Atlantic.

On both the K29 and the J-1, Cole no doubt cooperated with PRR and C&O engineers. Both railroads had outstanding mechanical engineering departments, and the C&O locomotives were constructed at Alco's Richmond Works, a plant which often supplied that railroad's eclectic fleet.

Altoona might have built the developmental K29 by itself. With his leadership on the earlier K28 and his achievement with 50000, however, Cole had earned enormous respect. Alco was awarded the contract and thus the primary responsibility. Given the PRR's unusually heavy rail and the inapplicability of the weight restrictions governing 50000's conception, the Pennsy asked for a blockbuster Pacific, almost 20 percent heavier and with a load on each driving axle of nearly 34 tons. All the features of the earlier engine were included nevertheless: extensive use of cast steel, a screw-type reverse, the Cole truck, and the same-size cylinders, together with a new type of cylinder-relief or "drifting" valves to aid in maintaining lubrication on cylinder walls on long descents.[21] The extra permitted engine weight went into a still bigger boiler. A steam-driven mechanical stoker, one of the first on the PRR, helped the fireman feed a firebox that was ten percent bigger than 50000's. The superheater was also ten percent bigger in surface. In contrast to the 50000's 2,200 cylinder horsepower, the K29 could reliably put out 2,800 – an amazing 27 percent increase – for a better power-to-weight ratio than its predecessor, according to PRR's test report.[22] Never before had such singular locomotives as Cole's two record-shattering Pacifics appeared within just a year of one another.

The C&O J-1 stemmed from an operational need rather than a desire to experiment. For its best passenger train, which traversed a long succession of steep West Virginia hills, the C&O needed more low-speed pulling power than a heavy Pacific could provide, yet more speed than its existing, large 2-8-2s could sustain. The latter were freighters and unsuited to everyday

TOP The Pennsylvania Railroad's K29-class 4-6-2, also built by Alco, improved on the principles that were pioneered by No. 50000.
Harold K. Vollrath Collection

BELOW Chesapeake & Ohio's J-1 class, the first American 4-8-2. It was essentially a stretched Cole Pacific, providing more low-speed power and lighter axle loadings than the PRR K29.
Courtesy Kalmbach Media

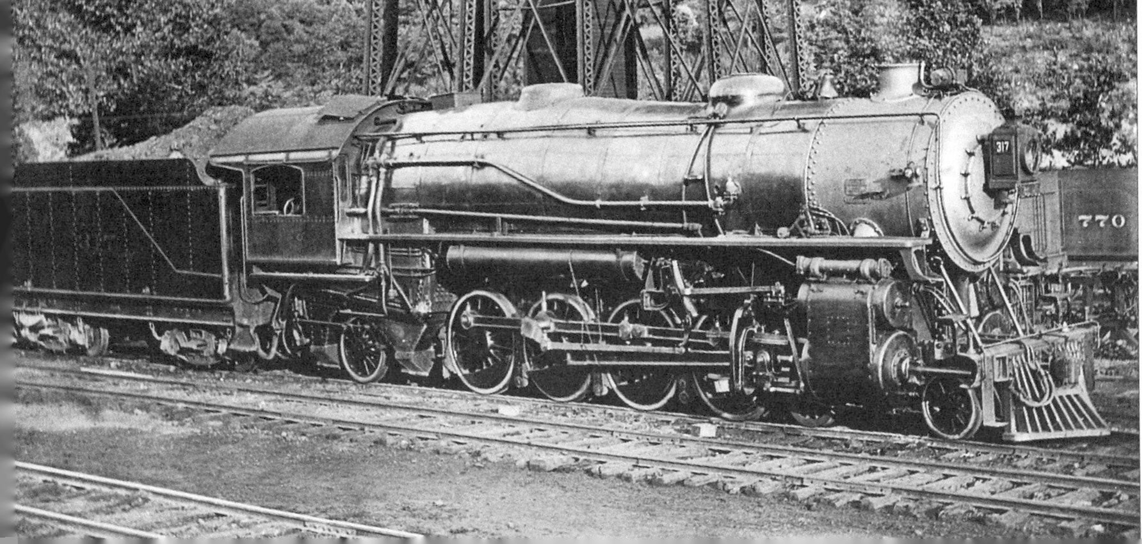

speeds much over 40 mph. The C&O train needed a locomotive that could sprint to 60 mph, pull hard and steadily at 25, and not exceed the benchmark axle load of 30 tons. Cole's staff and the railroad's engineers at Huntington, W.Va., added a fourth pair of appropriately-sized drivers to achieve the required low-speed pull and to lighten the loadings on each driving axle, retained the four-wheel lead truck typical of passenger designs for high-speed stability, and put on the fattest boiler possible within the weight restriction. An early form of mechanical stoker was included. The cylinders were a bit unusual, with the diameter slightly more than the stroke – but the stroke was limited by the locomotive's 62-inch drivers, which were relatively small for a passenger engine. Alco installed the same drifting valves as Pennsy's K29. For an advanced locomotive, the J-1's inboard-bearing trailing truck looked retrograde, but it accommodated clearances for an enlarged ashpan with supplemental, outboard ash hoppers. The first two engines of 1911, which C&O named the Mountain type, succeeded in many respects, but their drivers were incapable of the higher-speed operation required for the road's best passenger trains.[23] Subsequent 4-8-2s had bigger drivers, and the Mountain-type became a standard heavy passenger engine on C&O and many other roads.

Cole ratios revolutionize design

Was there some sort of secret to Cole's successes in locomotive performance in so short a time? Simply scaling boiler-and-engine design proportions – *e.g.*, scaling key indicators such as firebox size, evaporative heating surface, superheating surface, boiler diameter, cylinder dimensions, and/or locomotive weight – does not explain the power differences, either between the 1910-1911 Alco designs and earlier ones, nor between locomotives like the K29 and the 50000. Some other explanatory factors must have been at work.

Cole disclosed those factors, in their fully developed form, to the trade as a whole in late 1913. He had a wealth of data at hand by early 1910 to work out his basic approach, as exemplified in his two pioneering Pacifics. In his "Locomotive Ratios," Cole upended decades of tradition in the sizing of boiler and machinery components, and in the estimating of locomotive performance during design. In January 1914, Alco published its *Bulletin* No. 1017, in which Cole detailed his method. Probably the most widely read of any technical paper ever circulated in the locomotive engineering profession, an Alco writer in 1923 called it "a radical departure from former methods and today ... universally used."[24]

The 50000 and PRR's K29 follow Cole's 1914-published principles quite closely. It seems clear that he used his new approach in designing these engines. He could not have risked Alco's reputation and his own without high confidence in his predictive methods.

Essentially, Cole replaced former principles based on static measures with a dynamic model. One example is the proportions of boiler parameters such as grate area and evaporative surface to cylinder size. Former methods, in order to match boiler size to cylinder size – Cole cites the standards recommended by the American Railway Master Mechanics' Association in 1897 – took the volume of one or both of a locomotive's cylinders and then prescribed the sizes of grate area and boiler heating surfaces in proportion to that cylinder volume. Thus, the steam to be provided from the boiler would be greater as cylinders were made larger. The ARMMA standards added a separate proportion between heating surface and grate area. The recommended ratios varied according to whether the coal was bituminous, anthracite, or anthracite-and-culm in order to take account of the differences in heating value as measured in BTU per pound.

For example, for bituminous coal, the recommended ratio of grate area in square feet to the volume of two cylinders in cubic feet "should not be less than" 3:1, according to the old standard. Likewise, the ratio of evaporative heating surface in square feet to the volume of two cylinders in cubic feet was to be 200:1 or more. And the ratio of evaporative heating surface in square feet to grate area in square feet, without considering the cylinders, was to be not be less than 60:1. Such ratios were deemed to work more-or-less equally well for designing passenger and freight engines. The various differences among such engines in piston stroke, piston diameter, and driver diameter presumably equaled out, since most locomotives were designed for a fairly tight range of piston speed for their average working speed out on the road.

These minimum ratios reflected decades of experience. But as locomotive sizes continued to escalate, some designers found that the ratios could be boosted significantly if a given locomotive was subject to extraordinarily heavy passenger or freight duty. Cole noted that in recent locomotive types with trailing trucks, fireboxes behind the drivers, and thus longer tubes compared to non-trailing-truck engines, ratios of heating surface to cylinder volume as high as 300:1 or 325:1 were being successfully used. Cole pointed out that with the advent of superheating, higher boiler pressures, and other "radical changes" in locomotive construction, it was becoming "difficult to obtain even rough approximations, using the cylinder volume as a base, unless a number of corrections are introduced for each condition." Such attempted corrections to the recommended ratios to account for boiler pressure, superheating, heavy service, and numerous other factors "often became confused, with consequent unsatisfactory results."[25] The usefulness of the old methods – based on accumulated experience under conditions that had now shifted – had collapsed.

Oddly, the situation was reminiscent of many points in the history of steam technology going all the way back to the late 1700s. Once again, theory

TABLE No. 26—CYLINDER HORSE POWER OF SATURATED LOCOMOTIVES FOR VARYING PRESSURES AND DIAMETERS OF CYLINDERS

Piston speed 700-1000 feet per minute.

H. P. = .0212 x P x A. A = Area of 1 cyl. sq. inches. P = Boiler Pressure.

Diam. of Cylin.	Area	Boiler Pressure													
		150	160	165	170	175	180	185	190	195	200	205	210	215	220
16 "	201.0	638	680	701	723	744	765	787	808	829	850	871	893	914	935
16½"	213.8	681	726	748	771	794	816	839	861	884	907	929	952	975	998
17 "	227.0	722	769	794	818	842	866	890	914	938	962	986	1010	1035	1059
17½"	240.5	764	815	840	866	891	917	941	967	993	1018	1043	1069	1095	1121
18 "	254.5	809	863	889	917	944	971	998	1024	1052	1078	1106	1131	1159	1186
18½"	268.8	855	912	940	969	997	1026	1055	1083	1112	1140	1168	1197	1225	1255
19 "	283.5	902	962	992	1022	1052	1082	1112	1142	1172	1202	1232	1262	1292	1322
19½"	298.6	948	1010	1043	1074	1106	1138	1170	1201	1233	1264	1296	1327	1359	1391
20 "	314.0	999	1067	1099	1132	1165	1199	1232	1265	1299	1332	1365	1398	1432	1465
20½"	330.0	1050	1120	1155	1190	1225	1260	1295	1330	1365	1400	1435	1470	1505	1540
21 "	346.3	1103	1176	1213	1250	1286	1323	1360	1397	1434	1470	1506	1543	1580	1617
21½"	363.0	1157	1236	1273	1311	1350	1388	1427	1465	1504	1542	1581	1620	1650	1695
22 "	380.0	1211	1291	1332	1371	1412	1452	1493	1533	1574	1614	1655	1695	1735	1766
22½"	397.6	1264	1348	1390	1433	1475	1517	1560	1601	1645	1686	1727	1770	1812	1856
23 "	415.5	1323	1410	1455	1500	1543	1587	1631	1675	1720	1764	1807	1853	1896	1940
23½"	433.7	1380	1472	1518	1564	1610	1656	1703	1748	1795	1840	1886	1932	1978	2025
24 "	452.4	1440	1536	1584	1632	1680	1728	1776	1824	1872	1920	1967	2015	2063	2110
24½"	471.4	1500	1600	1650	1700	1750	1800	1850	1900	1950	2000	2050	2100	2150	2200
25 "	490.9	1562	1665	1718	1770	1822	1874	1926	1978	2030	2082	2134	2187	2238	2290
25½"	510.7	1627	1734	1788	1842	1896	1950	2005	2059	2112	2168	2222	2275	2330	2386
26 "	530.9	1689	1803	1858	1915	1971	2027	2084	2140	2197	2252	2310	2365	2421	2478
26½"	551.5	1754	1870	1928	1986	2045	2104	2151	2220	2280	2338	2397	2455	2512	2572
27 "	572.5	1821	1942	2002	2063	2125	2185	2247	2308	2368	2428	2489	2550	2610	2671
27½"	594.0	1888	2012	2075	2139	2201	2265	2327	2390	2453	2516	2580	2642	2703	2766
28 "	615.8	1957	2088	2152	2218	2283	2348	2415	2480	2545	2610	2674	2740	2805	2871
28½"	637.9	2025	2160	2228	2295	2362	2430	2498	2565	2632	2700	2768	2836	2901	2970
29 "	660.5	2100	2240	2310	2380	2450	2520	2590	2660	2730	2800	2870	2940	3010	3080

Cole's ratios provided a reliable means of predicting performance before the locomotive left the drawing board.

Alco Locomotive Hand-Book, 1917

had utterly failed to keep up with applied advances. As to the advances themselves – in this case superheating, higher pressures, bigger fireboxes – every practitioner could see that great performance improvements had resulted. But if available theory couldn't handle the variables and make reliable predictions of the extent of the improvement, design was once again full of risk. In fact, the 1897 "standards" look incredibly crude, even if applied to the small-fireboxed, unsuperheated locomotives of that time.

Cole could not escape the essentially empirical nature of his work, but his genius was in escaping the thrall of previous approaches altogether and beginning with a new analysis of the variables. His paper partly shows how he did it. First, he pored over data concerning on-the-grate combustion rates (pounds of coal per square-foot of grate per hour), reports on tube and flue lengths and their varying evaporation rates over different lengths, and – crucially – tests showing cylinder horsepower related to piston speed. His data could be duplicated by any designer. The University of Illinois had verified steam evaporation rates in its test facility during the 1890s, and similar rates were found in other tests in Europe and the U.S. The Pennsylvania Railroad's test plant at the St. Louis world's fair of 1904 (which was moved to Altoona in 1906), verified Cole's results in evaporation and cylinder performance.

To Cole, "the idea of using the cylinder horse-power suggested itself as forming a very desirable basis for the heating surface, grate area, and tube area." The essential clue may have been Cole's understanding of the maximum horsepower a steam cylinder could generate as a function of piston speed – a point of research in locomotive engineering for some time. The best data available showed that saturated steam produced peak cylinder horsepower at a piston speed of 700 to 1,000 feet per minute, with less horesepower capacity above or below that speed. A cylinder on superheated steam, however, reached peak horsepower at about 1,000 feet per minute and retained full horsepower capacity beyond 1,700. Irrespective of the precise values, Cole's insight was that the flow of steam through the cylinders, rather than any ratios of static dimensions to each other, was the best basis for sizing the boiler and its components.

Any time horsepower is introduced as a measure, or as the basis for other measures, the notion of time is also introduced. In ratios of cylinder volume to evaporative area, or measures of locomotive pull or tractive effort, time is left out. Measures of work, such as foot-pounds or train tonnage hauled over a given number of miles, also ignore time. Horsepower, however, is work per unit of time. Thus, Cole's method relates to the amount of work a locomotive could do per hour – or, in terms of generating profit for its owners, the work a locomotive could do in any other unit of time, such as per month or per year.

As in previous methods, Cole sought a basis for predicting a locomotive's top sustainable output – that is, *one point on the curve* of output rather than the full curve. This focus on only one point on a curve may look odd to engineers schooled in modern methods. Cole and his contemporaries knew very well that heat-transfer rates, cylinder efficiencies, etc., may not follow straight-line relations with other known variables. To railroad managers, though, an engine's peak performance entirely determined the engine's usefulness. For a freight locomotive, tonnage rating depended solely on its top output; for a passenger locomotive, its ability to pull so many cars on a given schedule depended on top power. Other points on output curves were of mostly academic interest but were indeed researched, especially in tests at the Altoona plant.

Understanding Cole ratios

At this place in the chapter, readers uninterested in the details of Cole's method can skip ahead to page 152. For others, the few pages to follow will equip even the mathematically challenged to easily determine the "Cole rated horsepower" of almost any single-expansion steam locomotive built – and to better understand a great deal about the engineering trade-offs, design successes, and design failures treated later in this book.

Early on, Cole verified an old assumption: "Because the horsepower [of cylinders] is based on piston speeds, the stroke and the diameter of wheels are omitted ... making this method of proportioning apply equally both to passenger and freight service." Cole saw that, by including just two other variables and a "speed factor" derived from cylinder-horsepower tests, piston speed could be directly converted to horsepower.[26] A little algebra, based on the definitional formula of one hp = 33,000 foot-lbs./minute, gave the correct coefficient to calculate the maximum cylinder horsepower an engine could generate if one knew just the piston speed, boiler pressure (assumed at 85 percent of nominal boiler psi), and piston area. The calculation was simplified still further if one used 1,000 ft./minute as the piston speed, for either freight or passenger engines. Everything else in Cole's method followed from there.

His great insight, and his method *per se*, were not dependent on particular values used to calculate cylinder horsepower, nor were they dependent on particular values of boiler steam evaporation and consumption. If his method were to be useful and reliably predictive, however, he needed to determine such values accurately and present them in such a way that engineers could easily use them. A key rate was the amount of steam consumed to produce one horsepower. The horsepower capacity of the cylinders – as the basis for sizing the boiler – came directly from piston speed, boiler pressure, and piston area; the amount of steam needed to realize that horsepower in the cylinders had to be known.

Numerous tests – at the University of Illinois, at the small test plant at Purdue University, and at Altoona – had established that one horsepower for one hour in conventional, single-expansion locomotive cylinders running at peak-horsepower piston speed took approximately 27 pounds of saturated steam and between 20 and 21 pounds of superheated steam, net of all the thermodynamic and other energy losses characteristic of such cylinders. Each of these values, for either saturated or superheated steam, held within a very close range; Cole chose his numbers, above, toward the higher end of the applicable range in order to be conservative. The maximum steam consumption rate per hour was thus known for an engine of a given indicated horsepower.

Cole's method then moved to the evaporative values in the boiler. With the steam consumption known, evaporative rates in the boiler for the heating surfaces of firebox, of combustion chamber (if present), and of tubes and flues were determined, so that the total evaporation (in pounds of steam per square foot of heating surface) could supply that consumption. In this method, a boiler capable of supplying the maximum consumption rate in the cylinders was thus termed a "100 percent boiler."

Tube and flue evaporation rates had been investigated by many researchers since the late 19th century. It was well appreciated that the heat within a tube, and therefore the heat transfer rate to the surrounding water, fell off rapidly from the back of the tube (by the firebox) to the front (where the flue gas emptied into the smokebox). The great temperature difference between firebox and smokebox – say, 2,000°F and 700°F, respectively –demonstrated the fall-off in heat transfer rate with length of tube. Therefore an average evaporation rate per square-foot of tube surface had to take account of huge variation in heat transfer from front to back.

About the time Cole started work on his method, the available data suggested that evaporation from a tube varied inversely to the square-root of its length – a classic "inverse-square law." This assumption worked fairly well. Engineers created simplified tables that allowed a designer to pick off an average evaporation per square-foot of tube surface, according to length and diameter of the tube. Shorter, smaller-diameter tubes were "hotter" per square-foot, but a longer tube transferred more total heat simply because it was longer. Many tests at Altoona with pyrometers at various points on the tubes of different locomotives provided accurate empirical data. Although the inverse-square assumption was a good approximation, it proved somewhat off.

In his paper, Cole used the Altoona data, which also included evaporation differences according to spacing of the tubes among each other. Cole produced a convenient table giving evaporation for standard configurations: for 2 and 2¼-inch-diameter tubes, for 5½ and 5⅜-inch-diameter flues, for lengths of 10 to 25 feet, and for a variety of inter-tube spacings from ⅝ to one inch. Tighter tube spacing allowed more tubes to be stuffed into a boiler of a given diameter, nominally increasing total tube surface, but Cole cautioned that tight spacing interfered with water circulation. His table factored in a correction that deducted half the gain in surface as tubes were packed closer than ¾-inch apart. "Tube spacing depends principally on the quality of feed water." Accretion of scale was the problem. Cole recommended a spacing of ⅞ of an inch to one inch in hard-water regions, but as little as ⅝ of an inch could be used "in good water districts and for short flues."

Next was the evaporation rate for firebox surfaces – the so-called "direct heating surface" of the firebox sheets. These surfaces, exposed directly to the furnace flames, transferred a great deal more heat to the surrounding boiler water per square-foot of surface than did tubes. For his paper, Cole took the firebox evaporation found in the "Coatesville boiler tests."

Prof. William F.M. Goss, by then at the University of Illinois, conducted these boiler tests, famous in railroad circles, at Coatesville, Pa., in 1912 for the Jacobs-Schupert Boiler Co. This firm was primarily interested in demonstrating that its patented form of firebox construction was safer than the usual staybolted form. Tests to destruction did indeed show that the Jacobs-Schupert design, compared to a similar boiler conventionally constructed, could tolerate operating with a dangerously low water level for a longer time before the firebox blew up. Goss apparently persuaded the firm that, before the destructive tests were done, he be allowed to run an elaborate series of evaporation and capacity tests to establish heat-transfer rates for tubes and firebox surfaces at various steam output levels. The Jacobs-Schupert design did not affect heat transfer rates of sheets and tubes, and perhaps the firm was also interested in showing that its boiler was the equal of any in evaporation. One of the unique opportunities presented was to divide a boiler into two separate "compartments," with the firebox and its surrounding water isolated from the tubes and their surrounding water. Thus the steam output of each section could be directly measured and their relative evaporation determined, per square-foot of surface, for different total outputs.

For his purposes, Cole was interested in firebox evaporation at maximum boiler output. A little extrapolation from the Coatesville "dual-compartment" tests showed that, at highest output, the firebox sheets evaporated 55 pounds of steam per square-foot per hour. For 18-foot long, 2¼-inch-diameter tubes (spaced 15/16 inches apart), the corresponding evaporation was 10 pounds of steam per square foot per hour.

With the following set – maximum cylinder horsepower, cylinder steam consumption for that power, and maximum evaporation from the tubes/flues and from the firebox sheets so as to supply the total steam required – the remaining task was to determine grate area. Cole observed that firing rates of 200 pounds of coal or more per square-foot of grate per hour had sometimes been attained, but that such high rates were "wasteful of fuel and ... that the evaporation per pound of coal under these conditions is very low." However, figuring a firing rate per square-foot of grate that was too low for a given total heat release could lead to a grate area that was too large. An excessively large grate was also wasteful,

> ... owing to the fact that at least 20 per cent of the coal burned produces no useful work in hauling trains, but is consumed in firing up, waiting at roundhouses or terminals, on side tracks, or to the fact that the greater portion of the time locomotives are used at considerably less than their maximum power.[27]

For the total heat release needed – heat actually liberated from the fuel and released into the firebox, net of unburned fuel and all other heat losses – Cole recommended using a rate of one pound of coal to evaporate 6¾ pounds of water per hour "as a fair average value." In his paper he does not give his source, but corroborative data was available from many tests at the University of Illinois and from the 1904 and subsequent reports of the PRR test plant.

Cole assumed 14,000 BTU per pound of bituminous coal, and so his "6¾" pounds of water per pound of coal could be scaled according to actual BTU content of different coals. For saturated locomotives, the figure above of 27 pounds of steam to produce one horsepower-hour, equated to the coal rate, worked out to 4 pounds of coal per horsepower-hour in the cylinders. For superheated locomotives, the rate of 21 pounds of steam per horsepower-hour in the cylinders, combined with 6¾ pounds of water evaporated per pound of coal, equated to about 3.1 pounds of coal per horsepower-hour. Cole made a correction based on heat absorbed in the superheating of evaporated steam and therefore recommended 3.25 pounds of coal per horsepower in the cylinders per hour.

To reduce combustion losses (unburned fuel carried out the stack, and heat lost out the stack), Cole used a maximum firing rate of 120 pounds of coal per square foot of grate per hour. Therefore, his recommended grate area was the total coal required per hour divided by 120. For anthracite, the firing rate could be only 55 to 70 pounds per square foot of grate per hour, but about the same total amount of coal would have to be burned per hour, depending on BTU per pound. Anthracite often has comparable BTU/pound as bituminous, but just burns slower. Another point to note is that "firing rate" or coal "burned" on the grate, in the usual terminology of steam locomotive designers, actually meant the coal *delivered* to the grate. Whether combustion of the carbon was actually complete was not implied. "Firing rate" meant coal stoked and thereby consumed, inclusive of losses such as fuel lost unburned out the stack (which was considerable at high firing rates). Such losses, at rates common at high boiler outputs, were incorporated in the coal consumption data Cole relied on.

To illustrate how simple Cole's method was in application, he provided a direct conversion of horsepower to grate area. Using the above coal rates, another bit of elementary algebra could set the grate area for bituminous coal from the previously found cylinder horsepower: The grate area for a saturated engine was simply the horsepower divided by 30; the grate area for a superheated locomotive was the horsepower divided by 36.9.[28]

Thus Cole's use of cylinder horsepower as the basis for sizing all parts of the boiler carried through all the way from tube and firebox surfaces to grate area. And, with the simplified tables and easy conversions Cole provided in his paper, the method could be used by any motive power officer. In fact, with the information provided above, the reader can readily determine what designers called "Cole horsepower" for any steam locomotive.

Cole commented, too, on oil-burners, from the roughly two decades of experience accumulated by oil-burning railroads. "Locomotives for burning oil should be designed with the same proportions of heating surfaces, grate, etc., as for bituminous coal." Not mentioned were four-cylinder locomotives, such as Mallets. To use the Cole method, one had only to use steam rates appropriate to compounded cylinders. The appropriate rates were approximations garnered from road tests, since no Mallet could fit on an existing test plant. As for the boiler, its sizing could be done as for any locomotive once the total steam consumption rate was known, or assumed.

It is important to realize that Cole intended to be conservative. His steam rates in the cylinders erred slightly on the high side of the known data, and his evaporation per pound of coal and his evaporation rates per square foot of

Alco's celebrated No. 50000 was sold to the Erie Railroad in 1912 and, as Erie No. 2509, hauled passenger trains until 1950. The most obvious alteration during its Erie career was the replacement of its original tender with a Vanderbilt design, with its characteristic cylindrical tank. *Pierre M. Ditto, Courtesy Kalmbach Media*

surface erred slightly on the low side. All such actual rates varied somewhat in particular locomotives whose test records were available, depending on the conditions tested (high and/or moderate output, high and/or moderate piston speed). Cole's stated intention was that his method be a reliable guide, slightly underestimating actual maximum engine performance so that estimated performance could be assured, up to the limit he set on stoking rate.

That firing rate, however, could be fairly easily exceeded. Any locomotive boiler could be "forced" for either short or long periods; *i.e.*, worked on the road with heavy draft so that coal was consumed at rates up to 150 or 175 or more pounds per square foot of grate per hour. A locomotive could not thereby gain horsepower in proportion. Escalating combustion losses meant that the horsepower increase was less than the increase in fuel consumed. Most superheated engines, when forced, could probably achieve cylinder horsepowers at least ten or 15 percent higher than calculated, albeit with loss of fuel economy.

Cole's method implies that he knew these things very well indeed. In a prescient paragraph, he wrote:

> It must be remembered, however, that the boiler capacity for a locomotive *cannot generally be made too large* within the permissible limits of weight [emphasis added], and it can be shown by numerous tests, especially by Dr. Goss' investigations, that such increase in boiler capacity makes for considerable economy in the use of fuel and steam. For passenger service, the boilers may often be made with advantage over 100 per cent.

As the future would show, boilers would continue to get larger and heavier, and become not only more powerful but more economical. And as railroads sought locomotives for faster freight trains, Cole's last sentence above would apply to freight engines as well as passenger. One of the engineers at Schenectady from 1900 was William E. Woodard, who became Cole's direct assistant in 1907 and was chief engineer in 1916 when a reorganized Lima Locomotive Works hired him away.[29] Woodard would enlarge fireboxes far beyond what his old boss might have thought prudent.

And what of the locomotives that proved the wisdom of Cole's insights? All three original C&O Mountains, with some running gear modifications, lasted in service for 40 years. The K29 helped lead the way to the Pennsylvania Railroad's superb K4s of 1914, replicated later in 424 copies. The K29 itself was never significantly altered and served in daily mainline duty on the PRR's Pittsburgh Division until 1929.

The wonderful 50000 of 1910 hauled passenger trains on the Erie until 1950, as that road's No. 2509. Over the years, parts of its trailing truck were slightly changed, various fixtures such as the headlight were relocated, and it got a Vanderbilt-style tender in common with other Erie engines. Its scrapping in 1950 was a thoughtless act of historical vandalism. Diesels were coming, and few people took much thought for 40-year-old steamers. A locomotive that had set such a crucial array of precedents, precedents that so benefited the art and science of transportation, should have found a place in a museum collection. But the Erie in 1950 was a poor railroad and couldn't consider gestures irrelevant to its corporate fate. Locomotives of far less significance populate museums today.

Chapter 7 Notes

1. Andrew Goobeck, "I Fired The 50000," *Railroad Magazine*, January 1974, p. 26. "Tallowpot" was a slang term for fireman, one of whose duties in the mid-19th century was to keep a good supply of tallow for cylinder lubrication. High fat content kept the oil effective in the hot, chemically active environment of steam, which caused ordinary petroleum oils to lose effectiveness. High animal-fat content characterized steam cylinder or valve oils into the mid-20th century.
2. The editors have chosen to render the locomotive's number as 50000 – without a comma – since that was how Alco referred to it.
3. The number 50000 – intended to get the trade's attention – was a bit of a fudge. It was supposed to represent not just Schenectady's production to date, but the total locomotive production of all the firms that had come together between 1901 and 1905 to form the Alco of 1910. The giant Baldwin Works always celebrated in the trade whenever its production passed another 10,000. Alco apparently sought to gain similar notoriety. If the precision of the arithmetic involved was open to some question, 50000 was certainly close, and Alco made its point thereby: The merger that was Alco was now a competitive, sizeable, and aggressive firm with sufficient size to rival Baldwin.
4. Cole obituaries in *Railway Age*, January 20, 1923, pp. 253-54; *Railway & Locomotive Engineering*, February 1923, pp. 61-62; *Railway Mechanical Engineer*, February 1923, p. 82. Player, later to go to the Pittsburgh Locomotive Works (Chapter 5), was Cole's supervisor in the motive-power department of the West Shore Railroad at Frankfort, N.Y. Sague was a fellow draftsman and Dixon a special apprentice in the same department.
5. The eight firms were Brooks Locomotive Works (Dunkirk, N.Y.), Cooke Locomotive & Machine Works (Paterson, N.J.), Dickson Manufacturing Co. (Scranton, Pa.), Manchester Locomotive Works (Manchester, N.H.), Pittsburgh Locomotive & Car Works (Pittsburgh, Pa.), Rhode Island Locomotive Works (Providence, R.I.), Richmond Locomotive & Machine Works (Richmond, Va.), and Schenectady, which was in the best health of the lot and led the merger effort. Montreal Locomotive Works was created as an Alco subsidiary in 1904 and Rogers (Paterson) joined in 1905. The Rhode Island and Dickson plants soon closed, in 1907 and 1909, respectively. Manchester closed in 1913, Rogers in 1915, and Pittsburgh in 1919. With the closure of Cooke (1926), Richmond (1927), and Brooks (1928), only the Schenectady and Montreal plants were left. Despite the closures – indeed, because of them – the rationalized Alco was a formidable competitor to Baldwin, matching the Philadelphia builder order-for-order until the end of steam. See *Railroad History* issue 197, Fall-Winter 2007.
6. *Railway Age Gazette*, December 29, 1911, pp. 1322-27; *American Engineer & Railroad Journal*, January 1912, pp. 5-12; *Railway and Locomotive Engineering*, February 1912, pp. 50-51; *Railway Age Gazette*, March 29, 1912, p. 739; *Railway Age Gazette*, October 4, 1912, p. 645; *Railway and Locomotive Engineering*, April 1912, p. 145; *Railway and Locomotive Engineering*, November 1921, pp. 285-87.
7. *Railway Age Gazette*, December 29, 1911, p. 1324.
8. Boiler pressure was 185 psi, giving a saturated steam temperature of about 382°F. Total steam temperature is the sum of saturated steam temperature and superheat temperature.
9. Alco claimed that the outside steam path on 50000 was a first. This isn't quite correct: Early Mallets used outside steam pipes to supply the rear, high-pressure cylinders. The first North American Mallet, B&O No. 2400, built by Alco in 1904, is one example. No. 50000 was the first such design for a non-Mallet.
10. *Railway Age Gazette*, Dec, 29, 1911, p. 1324. The removal of obstruction within the smokebox by relocating the steam pipes was especially advantageous at the bottom of the smokebox interior. In most locomotive front-ends, cinder-filtering arrangements and an even distribution of draft force on the tubes required an arrangement of deflectors. In the most effective arrangements, flue gases passed under a horizontal plate placed below the exhaust nozzle. Removing the steam pipes from the vicinity of this passage alleviated unnecessary restriction to high-speed flue-gas flow under the plate.
11. *American Engineer and Railroad Journal*, January 1912, p. 9.
12. *Railway Age Gazette*, December 29, 1911, p. 1324-25.
13. *American Engineer and Railroad Journal*, January 1912, pp. 5-12.
14. With all the variables, road tests were never capable of determining performance to a mathematical accuracy of more than three significant figures. Thus quoting 2,210-2,220 indicated horsepower and a power-to-weight of 1:121-122 would be more

credible. Even those figures would include a lot of variables, such as: How long did the engine sustain 2,200 ihp; *i.e.*, over what time period were horesepower indicator readings averaged? Or was 2,200 a fairly rare peak figure? Cole was quite conservative in his pronouncements – see following main text on his "Locomotive Ratios." One would expect him to have quoted a top horsepower that had been averaged over at least a few minutes, but, since indicator cards could not be taken second-by-second, the horsepower may have been calculated from just one indicator card. There is no clue one way or the other in the trade articles referenced here. Questions about implied accuracy are implicit in all road-testing claims, through to the end of steam locomotive production in the early 1950s.

15. Goobeck, p. 28.
16. Ibid.
17. *Railway Age Gazette*, March 29, 1912, p. 739.
18. Goobeck, p. 28.
19. *Railway Age Gazette*, Oct. 4, 1912, p. 645.
20. *Railway Age Gazette*, July 1912. Perhaps Alco plants, because of orders already accepted, could not deliver the five engines that Erie desired fast enough. Or perhaps Lima offered a lower price. Nevertheless, it was a strategically important order for Lima – its first big engines for a major railroad. Erie went back to Alco and Baldwin for the rest of its numerous Pacifics.
21. Running a steam locomotive downhill, especially on long descents, requires a high degree of skill. Closing the throttle altogether can cause "carbonization," whereby hot smokebox gas – drawn into the cylinders via the exhaust ports by the under-pressure within the cylinders – overheats and hardens the dwindling lubricant on cylinder walls. Lubrication failure and cylinder-wall damage can quickly result. To avoid this, the engineman must use just enough throttle going downhill to keep a bit of steam flowing into the cylinders, both to maintain lubrication (which is carried into and distributed to the valve and cylinder walls and rings by the inlet steam), and to maintain a slight positive pressure. The positive cylinder pressure, however, adds to the potential rolling momentum, which thereby adds to the braking force needed to control train speed. "Drifting valves" or "snifters," mounted to the valve chests and which open when inlet steam pressure falls near zero, break the partial vacuum in cylinders by admitting a small amount of air. Thus, air is pulled into the cylinders instead of smokebox gas, and oil on cylinder walls is much less likely to carbonize. On extended descents, however, the engineman must still "work a little steam" frequently in order to keep up the lubrication. Drifting valves were therefore only a partial solution. They were most commonly found on locomotives operating in mountainous territory.
22. See also F.M. Swengel, *The American Steam Locomotive*, pp. 142-43.
23. Alfred W. Bruce, *The Steam Locomotive in America*, 1952, p. 298.
24. F.J. Cole, "Locomotive Ratios," American Locomotive Co., *Bulletin* No. 1017, Jan. 1914.
25. Cole, pp. 1-2. All later quotations are from the paper.
26. The "speed factor" was the percentage of initial tractive effort available in typical steam locomotive cylinders as piston speed increased. As speed increases, tractive effort falls. Cole stated that his speed factors were deliberately conservative. "The maximum [cylinder] horse-power can sometimes be increased to a greater amount than [the tabulated speed factor would predict]." He says this increase could occur when the locomotive was operated under "most favorable conditions" – presumably if the engineman set throttle and cutoff accurately for the prevailing speed. Not mentioned is that further improvement in design of valves and steam passages would improve cylinder performance in future years.
27. Cole's caveat was well understood by contemporary locomotive designers but is generally unknown to latter-day rail enthusiasts who regard grate area as the primary index of a steam locomotive's maximum capacity. The trade called it "standby loss" – the large quantities of burned fuel that produced "no useful work in hauling trains." Fuel burned just to maintain an idling fire or to keep the boiler hot was a loss endemic to external combustion.
28. For saturated engines, one horsepower per hour took four pounds of bituminous coal. At a firing rate of 120 pounds per square foot per hour, the grate area is the horsepower divided by 120/4 – or the horsepower divided by 30. For superheated engines, the grate area is the horsepower divided by 120/3.25 – or the horsepower divided by 36.9.
29. Letter from Lima Locomotive Works President Samuel G. Allen to the Franklin Institute's Henderson Medal Committee, August 5, 1938; Franklin Institute Awards files, Philadelphia. Unlike Cole, who had no university training, Woodard was a Cornell mechanical engineering graduate, class of 1896.

"Thank you for that fine forensic analysis, Mr. Bodine.
Of course, the experience of it was somewhat different." *– The character Rose in the film* Titanic, *1997*

Chapter 8

Locomotive Safety Regulation:

The Locomotive Inspection Act of 1911 and the Nationwide Shopmen's Strike of 1922

TO A MODERN SENSIBILITY, AND TO A MODERN regulatory eye, the working conditions inside a steam locomotive cab would appear absolutely appalling: ambient temperatures up to 130°F, constant vibration, noise levels frequently exceeding 90 decibels, sometimes noxious gases laden with particulates and sulfur, tripping and head-bumping hazards everywhere, and utterly no sign of contemporary safety concerns, ergonomics, or crashworthiness. Crews regularly worked in such conditions up to 16 hours at a stretch, taking it all for granted.

> You par-broiled in the summer and froze in the winter. It was just part of the job. We loved that job. ... Sure, we had a union. That was to get us better pay. Safety? I always thought the job had its dangers. But it was as safe as any other.[1]

There were other serious safety issues for engine crews besides their normal working conditions. Boilers occasionally blew up, flues ruptured, injector valves suddenly failed, water glasses burst; there were many ways to get scalded or killed. In severe collisions and in high-speed derailments, it was not unusual for an engine crew to be buried in tons of coal flying forward from the tender into the cab. Hazards to an engine crewman when outside the cab, such as being struck by a train on an adjacent track while walking around one's locomotive during an inspection, or falling into a servicing pit in the roundhouse, were everyday concerns. By comparison, incidents involving failure of the boiler or of its associated systems were less frequent. When railroads began to stress employee safety in training programs and in official handbooks after about 1900, the emphasis was on notoriously common hazards, such as brakemen falling off car tops or getting hands or bodies crushed during coupling, yard crewmen tripping on rails or getting hit by moving trains, or conductors and engineers mistaking hand and lantern signals and thus causing unsafe movement of cars or trains. For the most part, "Safety First" on the railroads throughout the 20th century meant that employees, either individually or together on a crew, had to watch out for themselves.[2]

With respect to locomotives, however, cab crews vehemently disagreed that they could do much about boilers that were in unsafe condition. Railroad

Make no mistake: The cab of a steam locomotive was a dangerous place, with little margin for error on the part of engineer or fireman.

Frank Clodfelter, Courtesy Kalmbach Media

One day after this photograph was taken at Helena, Ark., on April 26, 1865, three of four boilers aboard the Mississippi River steamboat *Sultana* exploded near Memphis, killing an estimated 1,800 – mostly recently released Union prisoners of war – in what remains the United States' worst maritime disaster. The vessel's normal passenger capacity was fewer than 400.
Library of Congress

union writers noted that steamboat boilers had come under stringent federal inspection by 1852. But exploding steamboat boilers had killed hundreds of passengers, sometimes 50 or more in single incidents, and there had been intense public anger. In contrast, exploding locomotives in nearly all cases killed only a few crewmen at a time; members of the public and most other employees were little affected. One of the most influential rail unions, the Brotherhood of Locomotive Engineers, took matters into its own hands. In 1904, in a show of progressive-era politics, the BLE overwhelmingly passed a resolution at its annual convention to lobby for federal legislation to regulate railroad boiler safety.[3]

The salient context for this resolution was the 1893 passage of the Railway Safety Appliance Act, which led to universal adoption of standard couplers and brake systems. The safety consequences of this law became readily apparent to employees over the next ten years, even though the railroads and supplier firms themselves kept full control of developing the applicable technologies: Crew casualties due to defective or ineffective couplers and braking systems dropped.

There was a complication to the debate about the leading causes of locomotive boiler explosions. On board a running locomotive, the fireman and engineer manually controlled the flow of boiler feedwater and visually monitored its level; if the crew let the water level fall too low, a boiler in even the soundest condition would explode due to catastrophic structural failure of the firebox from overheating. Without adequate water surrounding all parts of the firebox, steel in its walls failed from softening by the 2,000-degree fire, the pressure containment of the boiler then ruptured, a couple of thousand gallons of superheated water flashed more or less instantly to steam, and the consequent explosion generally ripped the locomotive boiler off its frame and sent it flying a hundred feet or more into the air and several hundred feet down the track. The ensuing damage could make it unclear whether crew error, faulty water-monitoring devices, or some prior flaw in the boiler was the underlying cause.

By 1900, locomotive boiler explosions due to original design flaws were rare. Railroad mechanical engineers and managers blamed explosions on the crews. Crews blamed defective repairs, lack of adequate inspections, "bad water" that could foam in the boiler and give faulty readings of water level, and unreliable water-level indicating devices. Union writers demanded to know how it might be that crewmen would purposely let the boiler water level drop too low, given the lethal consequences to themselves.

But crews were loath to admit that common practices of firemen and engineers on board their locomotives when underway were sometimes causal. In situations where an engine was being worked hard, a fireman often "traded water for steam." That is, if the fireman saw his boiler pressure falling – from poor coal, inexpert firing, or poor running technique by the engineer – he could often rescue the situation by aggressively firing while he cut back temporarily on water supply. Feedwater cooled the boiler, lowering boiler pressure, which was the last thing a fireman wanted when pressure was already down. Cutting back on water rate let the boiler pressure recover, preventing a loss of locomotive power. In cases where the locomotive was working at full power on a steep hill, cutting back on water could prevent a possible stall, the worst professional embarrassment for both fireman and engineer. Once water level was down, however, it could be very hard to regain a normal water level with an engine continuing to run at high output.

Union Pacific 4-12-2 No. 9018 after its boiler exploded near Marysville, Kan., in 1948. Boiler and cab have been violently detached, leaving the smokebox, running gear, and a mass of tubing, along with the tender.
Courtesy Kalmbach Media

On the other hand, for well-experienced and highly competent crews, a continual strategy of trading-off the firing rate and the water-supply rate against each other in a sequence of careful adjustments to keep boiler pressure steady, while anticipating in advance the ever-changing power demands on the boiler due to changing grades and train speeds, was simply good boiler management. Trading water for steam was not something that could be regarded as bad practice in absolute terms; it was a description of a continuum of technique that could be bad or good, depending on the skill of the fireman and the tolerance of the engineer. Moreover, a locomotive ran at peak power with the boiler water somewhat below normal, making steam drier and more potent. Thus, a few engineers required their firemen to carry the boiler water at a minimum level, leaving little margin. A key reality in all this is that firing and running practices in the cab were entirely controlled by the professionalism and discretion of the crew; front-line supervisors (in an engine crew's case, a road foreman) were aboard only a few times per year.

> I hate to tell you how many times I had to trade water for steam to get out of a pinch. ... Once with a K4 [locomotive], I got behind on the fire and was down on the water to where you couldn't see anything in the bottom of the glass except when the engine bounced. The engineer knew what I was doing but kept right on going. He was going to make schedule. I was bailing away on that coal scoop and the pressure came back to 170 [psi; still 30 psi below that desired]. Then I got my gun [the injector] back on. I sweated there for a while. It was a big relief to see that water come back in the glass. My engineer just shook his head and didn't say anything.[4]

Sen. Elmer J. Burkett.
Library of Congress

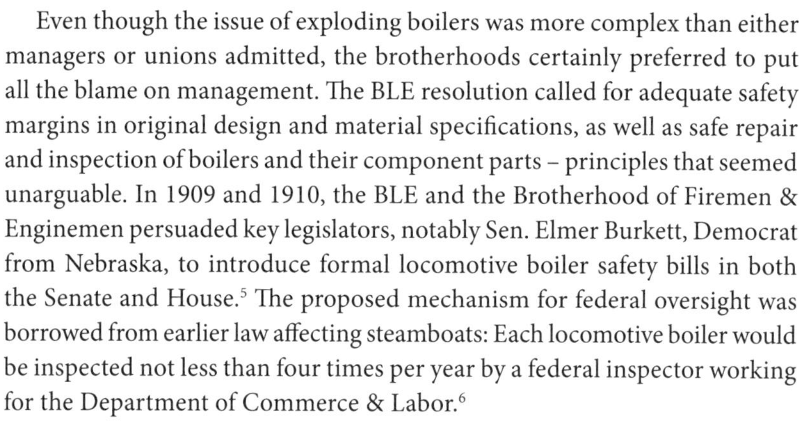

Even though the issue of exploding boilers was more complex than either managers or unions admitted, the brotherhoods certainly preferred to put all the blame on management. The BLE resolution called for adequate safety margins in original design and material specifications, as well as safe repair and inspection of boilers and their component parts – principles that seemed unarguable. In 1909 and 1910, the BLE and the Brotherhood of Firemen & Enginemen persuaded key legislators, notably Sen. Elmer Burkett, Democrat from Nebraska, to introduce formal locomotive boiler safety bills in both the Senate and House.[5] The proposed mechanism for federal oversight was borrowed from earlier law affecting steamboats: Each locomotive boiler would be inspected not less than four times per year by a federal inspector working for the Department of Commerce & Labor.[6]

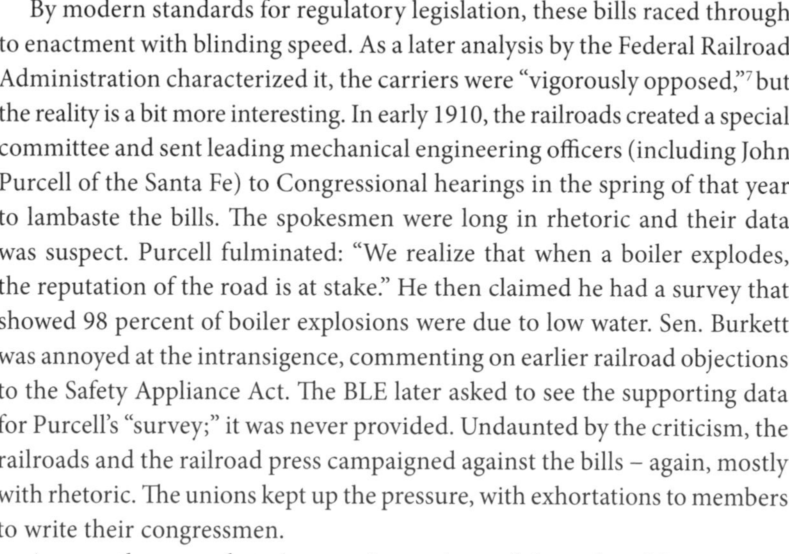

By modern standards for regulatory legislation, these bills raced through to enactment with blinding speed. As a later analysis by the Federal Railroad Administration characterized it, the carriers were "vigorously opposed,"[7] but the reality is a bit more interesting. In early 1910, the railroads created a special committee and sent leading mechanical engineering officers (including John Purcell of the Santa Fe) to Congressional hearings in the spring of that year to lambaste the bills. The spokesmen were long in rhetoric and their data was suspect. Purcell fulminated: "We realize that when a boiler explodes, the reputation of the road is at stake." He then claimed he had a survey that showed 98 percent of boiler explosions were due to low water. Sen. Burkett was annoyed at the intransigence, commenting on earlier railroad objections to the Safety Appliance Act. The BLE later asked to see the supporting data for Purcell's "survey;" it was never provided. Undaunted by the criticism, the railroads and the railroad press campaigned against the bills – again, mostly with rhetoric. The unions kept up the pressure, with exhortations to members to write their congressmen.

Apparently somewhat chastened, members of the railroads' committee agreed to a series of meetings with brotherhood representatives beginning that summer. In the meantime, the committee had put together a set of "guidelines" to which it might agree. If there was to be legislation, the railroads insisted that it should be general in nature and deal with the structure of administering any program. Specific details of design or specific safety devices should not be locked into a law that would take Congress to change or later amend. Specific inspection criteria should also not be legislated but left to subsequent agreement as to inspection rules.[8] And since railroad mechanics would still have to inspect their own locomotives regularly anyway, the committee strongly objected to federal inspectors duplicating this work and inevitably adding to downtime, raising locomotive operating cost. Anticipating a heavily technical discussion and not wanting to be outfoxed, the unions sent representatives who were particularly expert in the details of locomotive construction, inspection, and repair.[9]

With plenty of prodding by Sen. Burkett, his aides, and powerful congressmen of both parties, a compromise bill emerged. Late in the game, even President William Howard Taft put the prestige of his office behind federal regulation. In his December message to Congress, he stated:

> The protection of railroad employees from personal injury is a subject of highest importance. ... It seems to me that with respect to boilers, a bill might well be drawn requiring and enforcing by penalty a proper system of inspection.[10]

But Taft's advisers were simply putting the President's imprimatur on a deal that had already been cut.

Union negotiators agreed to the railroad committee's principal guidelines, but in exchange, the unions insisted on clear and unequivocal enforcement power for federal inspectors. The final structure, paralleled to this day by current railroad and aviation safety-inspection law, placed the primary responsibility for inspection where it already was: on the carriers and their mechanical officers. To cement that, the bill made it illegal to operate a defective locomotive or to falsify its records. Federal inspectors would have authority to visit engine terminals unannounced, to examine any locomotive and its records, and to require engines found defective to be withdrawn on the spot until properly repaired and re-inspected. However, with the number of inspectors agreed at 50, and with some 62,000 locomotives nationwide, the federal role was not primarily to inspect engines but to monitor the validity of each railroad's own inspection system. Bureau inspectors would also be empowered to directly supervise and conduct accident investigations. Each carrier was to draw up its rules, inspection criteria, and procedures for the regular inspections of its locomotives, and to submit the plan for approval to a new Bureau of Locomotive Inspection of the Interstate Commerce Commission. The ICC's role in the discussions is unclear, as it offered no testimony on the bills. But since the ICC already oversaw all other railroad regulation, perhaps the agency did not want any of its authority over rail matters shared with the Department of Commerce & Labor (which didn't become separate departments until 1913).

In early 1911, editorials on the boiler-regulation issue in the trade journals switched from vituperation to cautious praise for the proposed law. Union spokesmen were exultant. The compromise bill passed with big majorities in both houses of Congress in February 1911, to take effect that July. To the editor of the fireman's brotherhood journal, it was "a signal victory" for the union.

Federal inspection

In modern regulatory terminology, the agreed structure reflected a remarkable case of "negotiated rule-making," a term coined in the mid-1990s by the U.S. Department of Transportation to describe a new approach to revising safety regulations. Under this plan, representatives of federal safety offices and affected carriers developed new draft regulations jointly. In 1910, however, there was an added wrinkle. Since the unions had agreed to nearly all the railroad committee's demands as to the structure of the proposed law, the railroads did not subsequently object when the first chief inspector to head the new bureau was a BLE member, appointed by the President from a list prepared by the BLE.[11]

Part of any railroad's inspection plan was to include regular, notarized locomotive condition reports, of a form and frequency to be determined after passage of the act. The federal inspectors responsible for each of the 50 local ICC inspection districts were to scrutinize and file the reports and, in addition, visit the roundhouses and engine terminals in their districts to look for unsafe locomotives. With an average of 1,250 locomotives per district, that was a tall order. Under the leadership of Chief Inspector John Ensign and one of his assistants, Frank McManamy – both former BLE members and individually expert in the subtleties of locomotive design and construction – the system as implemented worked effectively, but not for reasons specified by Congress.

McManamy, who succeeded Ensign in 1913, put a lasting stamp on the routine of federal safety regulators and on their overall relationship with railroad mechanical superintendents. Section 6 of the law conferred upon inspectors their enforcement and visitation rights. In theory, the frequent site visits would allow an inspector to become familiar on a first-hand basis with conditions in the roundhouses and shops, with the maintenance and repair practices actually being used, and with the condition of locomotives themselves over time. By law each inspector was to be a civil servant, yet a person experienced and qualified in locomotive mechanics. In practice, this meant that inspectors were former railroad employees, which gave opportunity for corrupting the system. Under chiefs Ensign and McManamy, the contrary occurred. McManamy, especially, insisted on a non-confrontational style on the part of inspectors, in which their working relationship with railroad mechanical superintendents was based on the inspectors' establishing credibility through expertise. At the same time, McManamy insisted on full use of the authorities in Section 6 and gave full backing from the Washington office on technical issues and on interpretation of the law. Ensign and McManamy proved to be articulate and talented leaders, and established their bureau as an organization with an extraordinary degree of independence and integrity.

Their tough yet cooperative approach with carriers, based on a deep knowledge of locomotive engineering, quickly earned the respect of railroad officials at all levels. A formative example was the conference held in 1912 to formulate precise inspection rules for district inspectors to oversee. By early that year, months after the act's effective date, only a minority of the country's 50 dominant railroads and few of the more than 2,000 other railroads had submitted their inspection rules, as required by the law. On the other hand, the law empowered the ICC to unilaterally impose rules of its own on noncomplying carriers. Rather than take that precipitous approach, Ensign called a meeting of leading railroad mechanical officers and union representatives; the sessions were chaired by McManamy. Noting that most railroads already used inspection procedures that closely followed those recommended by the railroads' Master Mechanics Association, Ensign suggested the group establish a set of common rules – something the law did not require.

Ensign's suggestion, coupled with McManamy's negotiating skill, was a brilliant stroke. The resulting inspection procedures, codified as "Rules and Instructions for Inspection and Testing of Locomotive Boilers and their Appurtenances," were thorough, objective, and consistent with good practice throughout the industry. In barely 15 pages as published, the rules established responsibilities and inspection criteria for:

Frank McManamy.
Library of Congress

- safe working pressure and its calculation for both new and repaired boilers;
- daily, monthly, annual, and other periodic inspection intervals and procedures for boiler interiors and exteriors;
- hydrostatic pressure testing;
- staybolt testing;
- steam pressure gauges;
- safety valves;
- water glasses, gauge cocks, and injectors;
- boiler washing;
- steam leaks;
- regularity and format of related reports and the legal witnessing of the foregoing;
- accident reports.

The conferees agreed to make the rules binding from the law's original effective date. Commenting publicly a few years later on this and subsequent joint meetings called by the Bureau of Locomotive Inspection, H.T. Bentley, Superintendent of Motive Power for the Chicago & North Western, noted that he had been to these meetings, worked with McManamy on the rules, and "so that if there is any criticism about them, I am as much responsible for them as [he is]."[12]

There was little outcry when the bureau inspectors went to work. This was despite an alarming rate at which the ICC inspectors found defective locomotives during their site visits. During such a visit, an inspector looked over the available engines at a given roundhouse or servicing terminal and focused on those that appeared in need of closer examination. With permission from the railroad superintendent involved (and there are no records extant that such permission was ever refused), the "federal man" personally inspected suspect locomotives. Defects explicitly covered in the rules but judged by the inspector as marginal or not likely to cause an immediate failure were noted and a list given to the superintendent on the understanding that these would be remedied before the engine was placed back in service. If defects were deemed to pose imminent danger, the ICC inspector "red-tagged" the locomotive, meaning that it would be illegal to dispatch the engine until it was properly repaired and a copy of the railroad's report of these repairs provided to the inspector. With the size of the ICC inspection force, an inspector could examine a particular engine in his district once in about ten to 14 months; he attempted to see every engine at that rate.

In 1912, the first full year the law was in effect, two-thirds of locomotives examined had clear safety violations, with varying degrees of severity. The percentage of engines found defective gradually declined, although by 1920 it was still more than 50 percent. Slapdash maintenance was all too common.

Nevertheless, an editorial in a leading railroad journal praised McManamy's "fair-mindedness" and the bureau's "idea of co-operation," and railroad officials remarked on the results of the law upon the effectiveness and timeliness of locomotive operators' inspections. To use a modern term of the negotiating art, the carriers had become invested in the law and its rules, since they had suggested the structure of the former and had participated closely in formulating the latter. McManamy and other bureau inspectors spoke frequently at railroad officers' professional meetings, deemphasizing the politics of labor-management relations, stressing the objective nature of their work, and calling on carriers and federal inspectors to work together.

The relationship thus effected between railroads and the bureau soon had an effect on standards of original design for locomotive boilers. It was another consequence not written in the law. As part of the common inspection rules adopted in 1912, railroads filed a "specification card" for each new and existing locomotive. Such a card was a form (the ICC "Form 4") that listed tensile strength and thickness of all boiler plate and sheets, gave construction details (such as rivet seams, staybolt size and spacing in the firebox, and strength of interior braces), and thus permitted a knowledgeable mechanical engineer to calculate the safe working pressure of the boiler. A knowledgeable inspector at the bureau's Washington office would then recalculate and verify the calculations.

The inspectors found that many boilers were operating at low and dangerous "factors of safety," in comparison to good contemporary practice. A safety factor of 4.0, for example, meant that a boiler, while carrying a safe level of water, would not burst from mechanical failure unless boiler pressure reached four times the working pressure. (A locomotive boiler's safety valves are set to its working pressure.) Steel's strength at rupture is its tensile strength, but as engineers had known for many years, steel begins to stretch, or reach "elasticity," at about half its tensile strength. Good engineering design practice in 1912, therefore, called for a safety factor of 4.0, with 3.5 as a minimum in new locomotives. By 1913, McManamy and his assistants were finding that more than 15 percent of locomotives had boiler safety factors of less than four, and many older locomotives had factors down to 3.0 or even less. Because of the obvious hazard, the bureau convened another meeting in 1914 of railroad mechanical and union representatives and addressed issues of tensile strength for boiler steel, shearing strength of rivets, and design safety factors. The group agreed to an absolute minimum safety factor of 3.25 for engines built before 1912, with the minimum factor increasing in steps to 4.0 over the following ten years for every engine in service. Almost immediately, however, locomotive manufacturers adopted 4.0 as the minimum in new locomotives, and railroads began withdrawing older, substandard locomotives.

There was a bump on the cooperative road in 1915. Two years before then, the bureau had proposed that the law be amended to include inspections of locomotive running gear and wheels, brakes, draw gear, tenders, and other parts, since federal inspectors were finding thousands of such defects, unrelated to the boiler. Railroad officers objected to any enlargement of the law. In 1915, however, the Senate held hearings, persuaded by the credibility that the new ICC bureau had established. Railroad spokesmen at the hearings were divided on the issue; the C&NW's Bentley testified that under the law as applied to boilers, his railroad had significantly improved the reliability of engines used in service. Interestingly, while the locomotive brotherhoods and the Brotherhood of Railroad Trainmen (brakemen, conductors) supported a revised law based on their safety concerns, the Boilermakers' Union was opposed, based on concern that an extended law would dilute attention to boilers. In March 1915, President Woodrow Wilson signed a revised law, after passage with big majorities in both Houses.

Thereafter, McManamy, now as Chief Inspector, convened another joint conference to establish "Rules and Instructions for Inspection and Testing of Locomotives and Tenders," just as he had done for boiler inspection rules and safety factors, but this time for all the mechanical parts of the engine. Railroad officers and union spokesmen again praised the process and, after a few years of living under the rules, the results. In 1919, for example, Union Pacific mechanical officer John Mohun wrote an extended article in *Railway Mechanical Engineer*, the most widely read railroad mechanical engineering journal, on "Injuries from Locomotive Failure." In it he commented that the "beneficial results [of the inspection rules] are fully recognized."

So how effective were the law and its rules? In the years up through 1916, the bureau, the unions, and railroads congratulated themselves on how much locomotive safety had been improved by federal enforcement of rules adopted by consensus. In 1915, McManamy referred to his raw data and declared that, compared to 1912, injury- or death-producing boiler accidents had been cut 50 percent and fatalities 85 percent. After 1916, however, the trend reversed. In an econometric analysis published in 1994, Mark Aldrich analyzed boiler explosion rates and locomotive fatality rates, relating these to the number of inspections per locomotive made by federal inspectors, miles run per locomotive, and other factors, for the years 1912-1945.[13] Aldrich's graph of annual fatalities due to steam locomotive boilers and systems is reproduced at right. In order to highlight statistical trends, the number of fatalities graphed for each year are not numbers taken directly from historic data but are three-year moving averages. (Each plotted point is a 3-year moving average, computed from data in *Annual Reports of the Chief Inspector*, Bureau of Locomotive Inspection, ICC.)

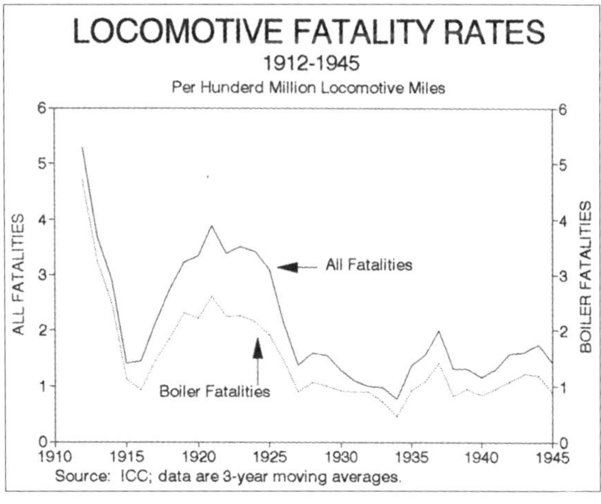

Mark Aldrich, Railroad History 171

The abrupt drop in fatality rates from 1912 to 1915 is dramatic. The climb in rates after 1916 is equally noteworthy and seems to indicate resumption of unsafe repair practices by railroads. After 1925, however, the rates drop sharply again, climb back up somewhat in the mid-Depression years, drop a bit before World War II, and then climb slightly during 1941-44. After 1945, the diesel revolution was well underway, with drastic reduction in railroads' use of steam. What would explain this mixed experience?

Aldrich points out a number of historic factors. One is that 1912 was an atypical and horrendous year. A Southern Pacific engine blew up in San Antonio on March 18 while parked near a shop building. A defective safety valve was found to be the culprit, allowing steam pressure to far exceed the locomotive's working pressure. Twenty-six employees were killed and 32 others injured in the worst locomotive boiler explosion ever. Fifty-five more people died in locomotive boiler explosions that year, for a total that exceeded by about 60 percent the average fatalities from that cause in immediately prior years. Another factor was that, between 1912 and 1916, annual locomotive miles declined as a result of the recession caused by World War I, starting in 1914. Aldrich found, throughout the period of his analysis, that boiler explosion rates were strongly associated with locomotive usage rates. As locomotives were used more intensively in a given year, explosion rates per locomotive mile rose also, and vice versa.

The reversal in fatality rates shown in the graph after 1916 is thus partly associated with U.S. entry into World War I. American involvement in the war caused rail traffic levels to soar, which raised locomotive usage rates. In addition, thousands of older locomotives in storage – 6,000 in 1917 alone – were pulled off "dead lines" and hastily returned to service. In the press of war traffic, inspections were often slighted. Railroad superintendents for the first time argued with bureau inspectors when the latter, as the result of their site visits, pulled unsafe engines out of service. With the federalizing of the railroads in late 1917, some bureau inspectors were diverted from their primary duties to help manage the unclogging of yards and terminals, which severely reduced their rate of visits to engine shops and roundhouses.

In the five years after 1923, federal inspection activity increased significantly. In 1924, Congress authorized fifteen more inspectors, and by 1928, site visits per locomotive were up more than 70 percent. Instrumental was a reduction in the number of locomotives – 69,400 in 1923, down to 63,100 in 1928. As the average size and power of new locomotives grew, a smaller fleet was needed, even though rail traffic steadily increased through 1929. Older locomotives were retired. By 1940, the fleet nationwide numbered just over 44,000. Explosion and boiler-related fatalities remained between 0.5 and 1.5 per hundred-million engine-miles through 1945, with increases during the depths of the Depression and during the early years of World War II. Maintenance degraded somewhat in the mid-1930s and, in the early 1940s, engine utilization shot up to record levels.

The 1922 Shopmen's Strike

But hidden in the graph of moving averages is one of the most important events in all of American labor history: the nationwide Railroad Shopmen's Strike of 1922. Yale University labor historian David Montgomery called it "by any measure ... the largest strike in the history of the United States." In discussing the years surrounding the peak locomotive/boiler fatality rate, Aldrich mentions the strike in half a sentence. The raw data in ICC reports, coupled with an understanding of the strike, reveal a deeper story.

The year 1921 was a fairly typical year, with casualties only slightly higher than in previous years; 1922 was below the average for prior years. The next year, however, fatalities reached a new record level – and, more indicative

The 1922 Shopmen's Strike led to violence and the hiring of replacement workers. They were often protected by National Guard troops, as seen in this photo from the Chicago & Alton shops in Bloomington, Ill.

Dan Cupper Collection

that something was terribly wrong, injuries shot up to almost double the number of any previous year. Total locomotive-related casualties were 1,429, the highest number in the 20th century and 360 more than the next-worst year. That year is 1924, which is also the peak year for deaths.

The 1922 Shopmen's Strike, which affected all of the nation's largest railroads, began on July 22, three weeks after the beginning of fiscal year 1923. (The federal fiscal year began on July 1 until 1976, when it was changed to October 1.) Thus, FY 1923 fully captures the strike's first 11 months. The strike continued on many large railroads through September 1923, two months after the close of FY 1923, and, except for two railroads, was not fully broken until early 1925. The two companies holding out the longest, the Pennsylvania and the Long Island (a PRR subsidiary), held until the unions called off those strikes in September 1928. With none of the legal protections for union organizing that are taken for granted today, the Shopmen's Strike was one of the most bitter of the 20th century. More than 400,000 shop craftsmen walked out, from a railroad work force of over two million. At that time, railroad workers outnumbered the combined workforce of the iron and steel, construction, and textile industries. Railroads were the principal industrial employer and were the vital link among every other industry. The strikers walked away from more than 1,750 shop complexes, directly affecting 1,500 of the country's largest cities and leading industrial towns. The railroad companies responded by hiring legions of replacement workers and armed guards – the PRR hired an armed guard for every 1.5 strikers. Governors called out state militias. There were shootings on the picket lines, stoppage of trains by force, kidnappings, riots, numerous murders, killing of children by stray bullets, and infiltration of union meetings by railroad spies. In its nationwide impact, there has never been a strike like it since, in any industry.

From the summer of 1921 until early 1922, there was a short but sharp recession in the U.S. economy, leading to a drop in rail traffic, revenues, and locomotive utilization. A government wage board, held over from the December 1917-March 1920 federal takeover of railroads, approved company petitions for two wage cuts for their employees, the first in mid-1921. As the economy recovered in early 1922, union employees expected a restitution of at least some of the cuts, but management persuaded the wage board to approve yet another reduction. The shopcraft unions – boilermakers, machinists, steamfitters, carmen, carpenters, sheet-metal workers, electrical workers, blacksmiths, and foundrymen – were particularly incensed. For them, an additional issue was the growing railroad practice of contracting out, with attendant loss of shop jobs. Unions had been accustomed to encouragement and protection of labor interests under the Wilson administration, and now they were smarting from the reactionary turnaround of President Harding and his rabidly anti-union, blatantly red-baiting attorney general, Harry Daugherty. The shop crafts voted to strike. These unions were part of the American Federation of Labor, and its chief, Samuel Gompers, supported the action. The operating brotherhoods, which were not part of the AFL – the engineers, firemen, conductors, and brakemen – voiced general agreement with the action of the shopmen but did not strike; their wages were not reduced by the 1922 cut, nor were their jobs threatened.

Harry Daugherty.
Library of Congress

The result of the strike in locomotive shops was a rapid and marked deterioration in quality of work, as less-than-skilled replacement workers made repairs while under the protection of armed guards, with picketers taunting them from outside the shop gates. The percentage of engines found by federal inspectors to be defective hit 65 percent. Chief Inspector Alonzo Pack (McManamy had been elevated to Interstate Commerce Commissioner in 1918) made the remarkable statement in his FY 1923 report that "[m]any of the carriers have apparently lost sight of the principal requirement of the law" making it illegal to operate any locomotive unless it was "in proper condition and safe to operate ... ." Further, he wrote:

> Soon after July 1, 1922, it was brought to our attention that inspections, tests, and repairs were not being made by many of the carriers as required. ... it was necessary for our inspectors to issue special notices for repairs, withholding 7,075 locomotives from service until proper inspections and repairs were made, and to obtain information to show that locomotives were being used while in violation of the law, so that court proceedings might be instituted.[14]

That is, more than ten percent of the fleet nationwide was illegally operated at some time during the year – and this was only the ten percent that 50 harried inspectors happened to catch. Clearly, the era of good feeling between mechanical superintendents and ICC inspectors was over.

The condition of locomotives declined so obviously that the operating brotherhoods on several large railroads conducted a wildcat strike for ten days in August 1922. To get the trains running again on some railroads, including the Pennsylvania, managers made formal agreements with the operating brotherhoods that engine and train crews could refuse to run unsafe locomotives and cars.

The strike eventually disintegrated. After a few months, railroad operating schedules had almost fully resumed. Railroad revenues rose steadily in the

In a 1950 mishap, thrown main and side rods sheared away boiler jacketing and cosmetic sheet metal from streamlined Milwaukee Road F7-class 4-6-4 No. 102. Fortunately, the cab and its occupants were spared.
Jim Scribbins, Courtesy Kalmbach Media

eight years after 1922. The context for the huge increase in locomotive-related casualties in fiscal years 1923 and 1924, however, is apparent. "Moving averages," at least in this case, obscure such context.

Danger beyond boilers

Another reality can be seen in the ICC reports, in particular in the data from accident investigations. Annually listed are the locomotive systems and sub-systems that failed and caused the casualties. Not only did whole boilers blow up, but pressurized air reservoirs burst, firebox arch tubes ripped open, axles broke, blow-off cocks flew out, crank pins failed, side rods flew off, flues collapsed, foot boards fell off, grate shakers broke, injectors failed, steam pipes cracked, water glasses shattered – the failures of more than 50 separate components were tracked each year in the reports.

Boiler explosions caused the most deaths, but, as discussed earlier, it was often unclear whether engine defect or crew error was the cause in a particular case. ICC investigators, however, sorted boiler explosions into categories: those due to low water where "no contributory cause" could be found (*i.e.*, explosions likely due to crew negligence); those due to low water where a "contributory cause" could indeed be found (defective water glass or gauge cocks, foaming in the boiler, or some other problem that probably misled the crew as to water level); firebox ruptures due to broken staybolts or cracked sheets; firebox ruptures with adequate water level but where foaming caused local overheating of sheets; and boiler shell failures. The latter two types of failure were rare. Only in the first years of the Inspection Act did a few such failures occur. The cause of about 97 percent of explosions was low water. There was no closure, however, on "contributory" causes: in the early years of the Act, about 60 percent of explosions were judged as due to crew error. After 1925, as repair practices improved and the number of explosions per locomotive-mile fell, the proportion of explosions attributed wholly to the crew rose to around 85 percent by the 1940s. In his analysis, Aldrich found that federal inspection activity was strongly associated with maintenance-related boiler explosions: *i.e.*, as the rate of ICC inspectors' site visits increased in a given year, the number of boiler explosions with contributory causes went down, and vice versa. Interestingly, there was no association between rate of site visits and explosions due to the crew. Federal oversight affected quality of maintenance but apparently not crew behavior.

In addition to safety factors, federal inspectors became involved in boiler design in two other ways. As welding became a common form of repair for fireboxes in the 1910s, investigations of torn firebox seams and of boiler explosions disclosed that welded seams frequently failed catastrophically, either before or during an explosion. Spotty quality of welds (*i.e.*, welds made with less than "full penetration"), compounded with the inability to test welds after a repair, were a disastrous mix in too many cases. The ICC therefore objected strenuously when locomotive builders proposed to manufacture whole boilers with welded seams instead of riveted ones. Bureau reports strongly argued against welding in either fireboxes or boiler shells. For the much thicker steel of boiler shells, the American Society of Mechanical Engineers (ASME), which set codes for original boiler construction, agreed with the ICC and refused to approve welded boiler shells. Given the welding techniques of the time, full-penetration welds were difficult to make reliably in the inch- to inch-and-a-half thick steel of shells. In the cases of fireboxes, however, with thinner steel of about half an inch thick, and therefore easier to weld, the argument was a standoff for several years, with railroads arguing that welding be permitted. As welding technique rapidly improved in the 1920s, ASME standards committees agreed to the welding of firebox seams in new construction, and the bureau acceded to firebox welding for repair. Welding of boiler shells, except for a few experimental locomotives, was never formally approved during the period covered by this book.

The other contentious design issue was that of boiler gauge cocks – a series of three test cocks mounted vertically on the backhead, near the water line, so that the cab crew could check boiler water level. Open the top cock, and steam only should come out; the middle cock should emit steam and water if the boiler were properly filled, and the bottom cock should pass water only. Valid reading of boiler water level was fundamental, yet the issue set the ICC against railroad mechanical officers for years. Through the 1870s, gauge cocks were the only way to check boiler water level on most locomotives; water glasses in theory would show water level at a glance, but early designs, able to reliably withstand the vibration of locomotives, did not exist. Even in the 1920s, when both a glass and the cocks were universal, many senior locomotive engineers did not trust a water glass, feeling its visual indication was indirect and that the glass was subject to plugging. Better to trust the cocks, they thought.

Chief Inspector Pack proposed a thorough test, one of the few formal tests of a safety device ever conducted by the ICC. In 1920, Pack's staff determined that, on a boiler under power, gauge cocks were often wrong, indicating the water level as being several inches higher than it was. This effect was dubbed the "false head" phenomenon. Water circulating up the back of the boiler's interior and past the cocks gave a false reading at the cocks. A crew running with low water could thus be lulled into thinking the level was adequate, which may have been a factor in some of the boiler explosions for which bureau investigators could find no sign of a "contributory cause." Wrote Pack in 1921, "Investigations have clearly established that gauge cocks when screwed directly into the boiler do not correctly register the proper water level over the crown sheet ... ."[15]

The problem could be solved partly by mounting the cocks so that they were not "screwed directly into" the boiler, but mounted with extended interior nipples to help counteract the false-head effect. Unfortunately, railroad boilermakers and roundhouse crews often failed to reinstall the proper nipples when removing and cleaning the cocks, a procedure that occurred every month on every engine, during boiler washout. The ICC prevailed in its recommendation for both a glass and cocks on all locomotives, but its proposal for a much better but slightly more expensive solution – the water column, which obviated the false-head phenomenon altogether by virtue of the column's inherent design – was ignored by most railroads. Pack, still relying on consensus in seeking new additions to the inspection rules, was not successful getting the more reliable water column into regulation. Pack's thinking was sound, however: His recommendation turned up 75 years later, in an investigation and report in 1996 by the National Transportation Safety Board of a steam locomotive boiler explosion in 1995. Again, the water column was not subsequently mandated by federal rules, but another of Pack's proposals, the installation of a second water glass on every locomotive, was made a federal requirement as of January 2001.[16]

The human toll

With respect to design items affecting crew safety, there is another story buried in the ICC's raw data on casualties. Between 1917 and 1925, a significantly greater number of firemen were killed and injured than engineers. From the time the extended locomotive inspection rules were effective until 1925, an average of 14 engineers were reported killed annually due to locomotive component failures, and an average of 271 were injured. For firemen, the equivalent figures are 18 and 361. The firemen's injury rate is one-third higher. Then there is a striking break in the annual, uncorrected statistics after 1925-1926. From those years through 1938-1940, annual deaths and injuries of engineers and firemen drop noticeably and become virtually identical, averaging five deaths and slightly over 100 injuries for each craft.

Some important factors reducing total yearly casualties are apparent. The number of locomotives in the fleet dropped from a peak of 70,000 in 1920 to 45,000 in 1940. This reduction affected injury rates *per locomotive-mile* in two ways: Many older, less-safe engines were retired, and newer engines with more power meant fewer crews and man-hours were needed to handle a given tonnage over the road. Certainly maintenance procedures improved, as the federal inspection/site visit rate more than doubled from less than one federally conducted inspection per locomotive per year from 1916 to 1924, to 2.4 per locomotive per year by 1940. The percentage of engines found defective by bureau inspectors drops to ten percent in 1931 and hovers around that percentage through 1940.[17]

But what could explain the pre-1926 engineer/fireman differential? Or explain the post-1926 elimination of that differential? When a boiler blows up, statistics show that the engineer and the fireman are equally likely to be killed; it is unusual for either to escape death, along with any other crew who may be in the cab at the time, such as a head-end brakeman. Something about the nature of the engineer's and fireman's work before and after 1926 must be in play.

Boiler explosions were not the only hazard. The fifty-odd other sources of harm listed in ICC reports could kill and maim as well. In a locomotive cab or during a typical engine crew's workday, a number of these hazards were more likely to afflict the fireman.

In the ICC data, one of the more surprising sources of injury was the squirt hose – a rubber extension hose for use in the mundane tasks of periodically cleaning spilled coal off the engine deck and suppressing dust by lightly wetting down the coal in the tender. The squirt hose was plumbed off an injector, which supplied the hose's water. The hose water was under pressure and hot – scalding, in fact. Bursting squirt hoses injured far more people than any other single component, sometimes scalding more than 80 people a year. In an engine cab it was usually the fireman – as engineer's apprentice – who washed off the deck or wetted the coal. The poor quality of hose material compared to the post-1945 era added to the risk.

Table 1
Locomotives and Locomotive Inspection

Year	Locomotives in Service	Inspection Rate	Percent Defective	Percent Retired
1912	62,262	1.19	66	3.15
1913	63,378	1.43	60	3.82
1914	64,760	1.43	53	2.98
1915	66,502	1.11	44	2.44
1916	65,595	.79	47	4.22
1917	66,070	.72	55	2.33
1918	67,936	.62	53	1.54
1919	68,877	.87	58	1.55
1920	68,942	.72	52	1.95
1921	69,122	.89	50	1.75
1922	68,515	.94	48	2.62
1923	69,414	.92	65	5.77
1924	69,486	.98	53	3.89
1925	68,082	1.07	46	4.52
1926	66,816	1.36	40	4.97
1927	65,348	1.50	31	4.89
1928	63,311	1.61	24	5.18
1929	61,257	1.60	21	5.50
1930	60,189	1.70	16	3.94
1931	58,652	1.75	10	3.31
1932	56,732	1.74	8	4.41
1933	54,228	1.65	10	5.36
1934	51,423	1.78	12	6.14
1935	49,541	1.94	12	4.71
1936	48,009	2.07	12	4.07
1937	47,555	2.16	12	3.03
1938	46,544	2.33	11	2.90
1939	45,172	2.42	9	4.04
1940	44,333	2.40	10	3.41

Sources: Column 1 is for classes I-III railroads from ICC, *Statistics on Railways*, various years. Retirements are also from that source but are for class I carriers only and so are expressed as a percent of locomotives owned by those carriers. Locomotives inspected and percent defective are from ICC, *Annual Report of the Chief Inspector of Locomotives*, various years. The inspection rate is inspected locomotives expressed as a proportion of column 1.

Mark Aldrich, Railroad History 171

The second most common cause of injury to the fireman were the grate shakers. The fireman used them in the essential task of cleaning his fire. The problem, pointed out repeatedly in annual reports of the bureau, was due to non-standard and ill-fitting shaker bars. To use the grate shakers, the fireman took his shaker bar from its place of stowage, attached it to one of several shaker levers on the floor of the cab, and pulled the bar back and forth to "rock" the grates and clean the fire of ash and clinkers. A fireman had to pull the bar back and forth with considerable force, and if the bar was not well fitted to the grate operating lever, it could come loose. When it came loose unexpectedly, a fireman could be thrown severely. As ICC inspectors found, many engines did not have shaker bars that came anywhere close to fitting properly; non-standard bars were mixed among non-standard shaker arrangements. Again, as with the squirt hose, engineers rarely did the dirty task of cleaning the fire.

Slightly less frequent but far more hazardous were bursting flues and arch tubes inside the firebox. When these items failed, steam pressure and boiler water was released instantly into the firebox. If, at that instant, a fireman was hand-firing with the scoop and thus standing back of an open firedoor, the suddenly released steam usually tore a large quantity of burning coals from the firebed and blew them right into the fireman's face and body. In that event, few escaped death or, at the least, serious burns.

The firedoor itself was an issue. A poorly designed door could be blown open by a rupturing flue or arch tube, exposing the fireman to the full force of the rupture. The bureau urged adoption of "mechanically operated" firedoors, which could not be blown open when closed, as a crew-protection measure. A fireman on a hand-fired engine needed to have the door open only as each shovelful of coal was pitched in. In between scoops, the firedoor should remain securely closed. For the fireman to open the door only when needed, a foot treadle was required, since he needed two hands on his scoop to throw the coal in. Such self-closing, mechanically operated doors were used by only a few railroads. Wrote Chief Inspector Pack in 1921 and again in 1922:

> This recommendation [for mechanically operated doors] is based on the results of many investigations of boiler failures ... where steam and water contained in the boiler at the time of the accident [were] discharged into the firebox, many times being directed toward the fire door. The old swing-type door, which is largely used at present, is almost invariably blown open in case of such accidents. ... Such accidents frequently occur while coal is being put into the fire box, and with the fire door necessarily open, under such circumstances it is impossible for it to be closed. The automatic fire door would remain closed if closed when the accidents occur. If open, it would automatically close the moment the [fireman's] foot was removed from the operating device, thus preventing the direct discharge of the scalding water and fire into the cab of the locomotive ... .

Rule 118, as eventually adopted by Bureau and railroad consensus, required such doors universally. The precise design of the door was not specified, but the favored type was a "scissors" or "butterfly" form that could not be forced open by a firebox explosion. It is perhaps sobering to a modern eye to see so much attention devoted to a seemingly unsophisticated thing like a small, cast steel door on a boiler.

In the pre-1925 era, the fireman's job was the second most dangerous job in railroading, after the brakeman's. Where was the engineer when potential hazards to his fireman suddenly became real? Usually, the engineer was where he properly needed to be, seated on the right-hand seatbox, at the controls of the locomotive. For all the risks detailed above, the engineer was generally out of harm's way. But what could have happened after 1926 to so dramatically equalize the firemen's and engineers' casualty rates?

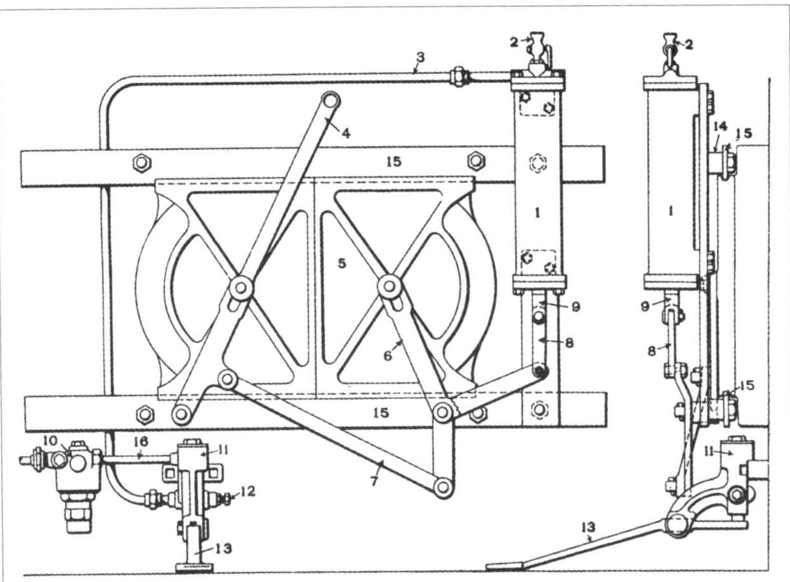

Mechanically operated firedoors, like this 1906 Franklin Railway Supply Co. design with a foot treadle, made the fireman's job safer. Such firedoors would not become mandatory until the 1920s.

Locomotive Dictionary, 1906

Prior to the debut of mechanical stokers, coal-hungry locomotives such as Erie 0-8-8-0 Mallet No. 2602 – with its large Wootten firebox – required two firedoors and two firemen.
Courtesy Kalmbach Media

The secret is the advent of the "automatic stoker," a steam-powered mechanical device that used an auger running from the coal bunker in the tender to the firebox to convey fuel to the fire. The stoker was not really "automatic." Instead of shoveling, the fireman could now manipulate a valve to control stoker speed (*i.e.*, fuel delivery rate). He could also control the final distribution of coal onto the firebed; on most stokers, this was accomplished by an array of steam jets controlled by valves in the cab. Just as much manual skill and careful attention were required to fire with a stoker as with a shovel. The big difference, insofar as safety was concerned, was that the fireman could spend most of his trip on his own seatbox, on the left side of the cab, much like the engineer on the right side. Except for preparing the fire before starting out on a segment of a trip, and except for very occasional dressing of the fire by hand when underway, the fireman no longer needed to spend the bulk of his time at the firedoor. Moreover, a stoker-maintained fire required much less cleaning; *i.e.*, much less use of the shaker bar during stops. With its continuous delivery of coal, a stoker permitted a thin fire, one that was only a few inches thick upon the grates. Such a fire required little or no shaking at intermediate stops during a run.

Various designs of locomotive stokers had been proposed and many were marketed from the first decade of the 20th century, but there ensued a vociferous debate among railroad managers as to whether they were really needed. As boilers grew larger, many railroads adopted them in the 1910s for the biggest locomotives – those that strained the ability of a human shoveler (or shovelers; a few Mallet-type engines had two firedoors and two firemen) to satisfy their voracious appetites for coal. The fireman's union (BLF&E) eagerly pressed for automatic stokers by writing editorials, circulating petitions at meetings, and writing to congressmen. Some railroads fought hard against the idea. The Pennsylvania Railroad went so far as to run a series of tests at the Altoona Test Plant on two otherwise-identical locomotives that showed "conclusively" that a skilled fireman shoveling was more "efficient" than a stoker. The stoker-fired engine burned about five percent more coal throughout its power range, due to the fact that a stoker ground up the coal, injecting more of the coal as powder that was lost out the stack.

The ICC stayed out of the stoker wars, seeing the issue as an economic one for the railroads and their employees to sort out, rather than a safety issue. By the mid-1920s, nearly all major railroads were specifying stokers on new orders for big road locomotives anyway, and retrofitting stokers to larger existing locomotives. It was becoming clear enough that an unaided fireman, no matter how skilled, could not reliably sustain the fuel rates required by locomotives that generated 2,500 or 3,000 hp. According to accounts in the fireman's union journal, there were far fewer "road failures for steam" on stoker-equipped engines. That is, such locomotives had far fewer occasions of stalling due to loss of steam pressure from poor firing – or from exhaustion on the part of the fireman.

Only in 1939 was ICC inspection rule 118 modified to require stokers on heavier locomotives, under duress from both the firemen's and engineers' unions and with little objection by then from the railroads. Bureau chief John M. "Monty" Hall, who had succeeded Pack in 1936, oversaw the agreement, which required stokers on all new engines over a specified weight in "fast or heavy" service and provided a five-year period to equip older engines. By then, however, the regulatory requirement was largely academic. Stokers were the norm by the mid-1920s on heavy road locomotives above the weights specified (80 tons or more on drivers for passenger engines, about the same as a USRA light 4-6-2; 87½ tons or more on drivers for freight engines, smaller than a USRA light 2-8-2). Although switching engines and the relatively few light road locomotives for smaller railroads were customarily built without stokers, there were in 1939 many older engines above these weights in largely secondary service. Railroads frequently sought exemption for such locomotives, based on their use in other than "fast or heavy" duty. ICC inspectors did not budge if that assertion was unfounded. Exempt engines, because of weight or service, shouldered a relatively small proportion of ton-miles. Even the recalcitrant Pennsylvania Railroad finally had to convert some of its older passenger and freight engines.[18]

Stokers themselves were not trouble-free. They jammed from bits of steel, rocks, or wet hardwood that had mixed in with run-of-mine coal. Auger shafts sometimes broke, and there were other hazards, such as the danger of getting a foot taken off if a careless fireman left the auger turning when venturing back into the coal bunker to clear a jam. When the stoker failed, the fireman had to go back "on the scoop."

But with the wide adoption of stokers by the late 1920s, the fireman's job had changed from that of skilled manual artisan, accurately sending his shots of coal to various regions of the firebed while standing exposed before an open firedoor, to that of a skilled operator of mechanical controls. The fireman thus occupied a safer position in the cab. At the same time, there were other, unanticipated consequences. As mentioned, the stoker reduced the need to use the shaker bar. And a stoker also meant a cleaner cab. In contrast to hand

Although great strides in improving locomotive safety, and reducing crew injuries and deaths, were made during the 1920s and 1930s, the risks to engine crews remained. In the aftermath of its 1948 explosion near Marysville, Kan. (see p. 155), the massive boiler of Union Pacific 4-12-2 No. 9018 came to rest several hundred feet away from the balance of the locomotive.
Courtesy Kalmbach Media

firing, a stoker when running spilled little coal on the deck, and thus the need for the fireman to hose off the deck was less frequent.

Overall, the casualties for locomotive crews dropped by a startling degree after 1925. For engineers, annual locomotive-caused injuries dropped 62 percent between the two time periods compared in the table; the firemen's average annual injuries from the same causes by 71 percent.[19] These marked improvements reflect many factors in addition to better locomotive inspections. The end of the Shopmen's Strike was clearly a turning point. Later, railroads began seriously to adopt safety campaigns as a permanent part of employee and supervisor training, and the rather careless ethos among employees of previous decades was replaced in the late 1920s and 1930s by a widespread consensus among workers and managers that safe operations were a hallmark of good, professional railroading.[20] After 1930, the combined effects of the Depression-era loss of traffic and the reduction in the national locomotive fleet meant far fewer hours in the cabs – and simply far less opportunity for injuries per year. Nonetheless, the ICC played a key role in the ascent of safety as an accepted goal in railroading, and what had been the most dangerous industry after coal mining became a much improved place to work.

The ICC's Bureau of Locomotive Inspection went through a passage from respected consensus builder, to adversary in the eyes of many mechanical superintendents during the mid-1920s, and back to respected consensus builder once again in the 1930s and '40s. The integrity of the bureau was maintained throughout by Chief Inspectors Ensign, McManamy, Pack, and Hall. The principle of federal spot inspections to verify regular and thorough cycles of daily, monthly, and annual inspection by operators themselves became well established. No amount of second-party inspection could prevent willful mediocrity or negligence. The most effective role the bureau played was that of honest broker in safety-related engineering issues, helping to raise professional standards among front-line supervisors and their mechanics. Receiving a clean bill of health from an ICC inspector became something of a badge of honor among shop forces.

Chapter 8 Notes

1. Words of Lloyd Arkinstall, a retired Pennsylvania Railroad fireman, as told to the author in 1972.
2. Mark Aldrich, "Safety-First Comes to the Railroads, 1910-1939," *Railroad History*, Spring-Summer 1992.
3. *Locomotive Engineers' Monthly Journal* (BLE), Convention Issue, 1904. *Locomotive Fireman & Engineman's Magazine*, February 1910, p. 231. See also, Angus Sinclair, "Boiler Inspection" in *Railway and Locomotive Engineering*, November 1912, p. 406. For steamboat boilers and their regulation, see John Burke, "Bursting Boilers and the Federal Power," *Technology & Culture*, Winter 1966.
4. Arkinstall interview, 1972.
5. Hearings, S236 and S6702, bills to *Promote the Safety of Employees and Travelers Upon Railroads by Compelling Common Carriers to Equip their Locomotives with Safe and Suitable Boilers and Appurtenances Thereon*, 61st Congress, 2d Session, SD 446, March 2, 1910. The companion House of Representatives bill was HR 1974, *Locomotive Boiler Inspection*.
6. For pre-1900 history of locomotive boiler explosions and analysis of the legislative history leading to the 1911 Act, see Mark Aldrich, "Safe and Suitable Boilers: The Railroads, the Interstate Commerce Commission, and Locomotive Safety, 1900-1945," *Railroad History*, Fall 1994.
7. U.S. Department of Transportation, Federal Railroad Administration, Advance Notice of Proposed Rule Making, Docket RSSL-96-1, Notice 1, January 27, 1998, pp. 4-5.
8. The distinction, in modern terms, is that between an authorizing law on the one hand and a subsequent set of regulatory rules determined administratively (and amended administratively as technology changes) on the other.
9. Various issues, Brotherhood of Locomotive Engineers *Journal* and Brotherhood of Locomotive Firemen and Enginemen *Magazine*, 1910.
10. *Congressional Record*, December 6, 1910, p. 33.
11. Aldrich (Note 6) says that the list of proposed chief inspectors was drawn up by the BLE. Given the lack of controversy over the resulting appointments, it is likely that railroad and union negotiators agreed to this arrangement in advance. One can interpret the legislative record as a case where union negotiators may have trumped the railroads' committee. The unions agreed to the railroads' inspection structure, but by insisting on unequivocal enforcement power for the new bureau and on strong union influence over initial staff appointments, BLE and BLF&E negotiators kept considerable control on how that structure would be implemented.
12. Frank McManamy, "Locomotive Inspection Laws," Western Railway Club *Proceedings*, March 21, 1916.
13. Aldrich, *Railroad History*, Fall 1994, pp. 23-44.
14. Interstate Commerce Commission, *Annual Report of the Chief Inspector of Boilers* 12, 1923.
15. Interstate Commerce Commission, *Annual Report of the Chief Inspector of Boilers* 10, 1921.
16. Federal Railroad Administration rule, 49 CFR, Parts 209 and 230.
17. Aldrich, *Railroad History*, Fall 1994, p. 38.
18. After World War II, about half the total coal-burning fleet did not have stokers. This proportion may seem low, but these were locomotives below the weight cutoff, in secondary use, or held in reserve as diesels rapidly made their inroads. Nearly all the coal-fired steamers in heavy service had stokers. [ICC Reports, 1946, 1947]. See John H. White, Jr., in the 1970 reprint of Angus Sinclair's *Development of the Locomotive Engine*, p. 673.
19. For engineers' injuries, from an annual average of 270.6 for the 1917-1925 period to 102.5 in the 1926-1938 period, a decrease of 62 percent. Firemen's injuries went from 360.8 to 105.1 in the same period, for a decrease of 71 percent.
20. The degree to which working-level railroaders took safety to be a part of "good railroading" is unappreciated by many historians. The opposite – unsafe practices that jeopardized fellow crewmembers – came to be despised as a matter of collective survival, in a work environment in which one 50-ton car moving unexpectedly can kill in an instant. In Lloyd Arkinstall's understated put-down, such events were just the result of "loose railroadin'."

5341

Chapter 9

Leadership in Industrial Research:

The Altoona Test Plant and the K4s Locomotive

Of all American locomotives designed up to 1925, probably the most praised by contemporary mechanical engineers, and by writers then and now, was the K4s-class 4-6-2 of the Pennsylvania Railroad. Universally regarded as a landmark design by engineers in both the U.S. and Europe, the first K4s locomotive came in 1914. By 1928 the class numbered 425, the third most prolific locomotive class in North America.[1] In its time, the K4s class headed the Pennsy's fastest passenger trains – the *Broadway Limited*, the *Congressional*, and the *Red Arrow*, among many – and continued in heavy use until replacement by diesels in the mid-1950s.

Reams have been written about the K4s type, and aspects of its history have been treated in dozens of books and in literally hundreds of articles. Yet despite this vast coverage, primary engineering documents that still exist from the time of the locomotive's genesis have gone unread. Myths abound in secondary literature.[2]

The necessary context for understanding the design and international influence of the K4s is the work of the Pennsylvania Railroad's Research & Test Department, and particularly that department's Locomotive Testing Plant at Altoona, Pa., which began operations there in 1906. The work of the PRR's test plant constitutes a remarkable record of American industrial research. Although other testing facilities operated elsewhere in the U.S. and in England, Germany, and Russia, no other plant in the world came close in scale and scope to that of Altoona. The K4s design was the first full fruit of the test plant, and as such, may be regarded as the first scientifically-designed locomotive.

Altoona's test plant, too, has a context. The first attempt to test dynamically a locomotive held stationary was that of chief engineer Alexander Borodin of the Russian Southwestern Railway in 1881-1882. In order to assess practical theories related to compound-expansion and thermal losses, Borodin rigged a locomotive up on blocks at Kiev so that the driving wheels could turn freely; he then connected a belt to the driving wheels and used their rotation to power the railroad's machine shop. In this way, he could vary the load against the locomotive and test it under different speeds and outputs. Borodin ran tests with several locomotives at Kiev until 1886. In 1906, a more permanent test

Pennsylvania Railroad Class K4s 4-6-2 engine No. 5341, under evaluation in the railroad's Altoona Test Plant.

PRR; Dan Cupper Collection

plant, designed by Prof. M.V. Gololoboff, was built in St. Petersburg. Russian engineers drew up plans in 1913 for another, larger facility nearby, but the October Revolution intervened; this test plant, at the Proletarian Locomotive Works, was eventually built, beginning operations in 1924.[3]

Apparently unaware of Borodin's work, Purdue University's Prof. W.F.M. Goss, a leader in developing the thermodynamic theory of locomotives, designed and built a plant at West Lafayette, Ind., in 1891 (which is often referred to, erroneously, as the world's first). This plant was conceived around a single locomotive of modest size held stationary on rollers. Goss installed a braking system for the rollers and a dynamometer to measure power output from the running locomotive, and he attached instrumentation to record temperatures and rates of steam evaporation. The plant was used for research in boiler performance and for teaching. The building burned in 1894 and was then redesigned for somewhat larger locomotives.[4] Other test plants arose in Chicago (1895, for the Chicago & North Western Railway, under engineer Robert Quayle); in New York City (1899, at Columbia University, under Prof. F.R. Hutton); at Swindon, England (1904, for the Great Western Railway, by designer G.J. Churchward); at the University of Illinois (1914, for the Department of Railway Engineering under Prof. E.W. Schmidt, with Goss, formerly of Purdue, as head of the College of Engineering at Illinois); and in Esslingen, Germany (1923-1924, as part of a project to build two diesel-electric locomotives for the Soviet Railway, with both plant and locomotives designed by Prof. George Lomonossoff; this plant was moved to Dusseldorf in 1925.[5]) The protocols and results of the work at these plants, especially of the university-based laboratories, were published and widely discussed in the U.S., Britain, and Europe.

Alexander J. Cassatt.
Library of Congress

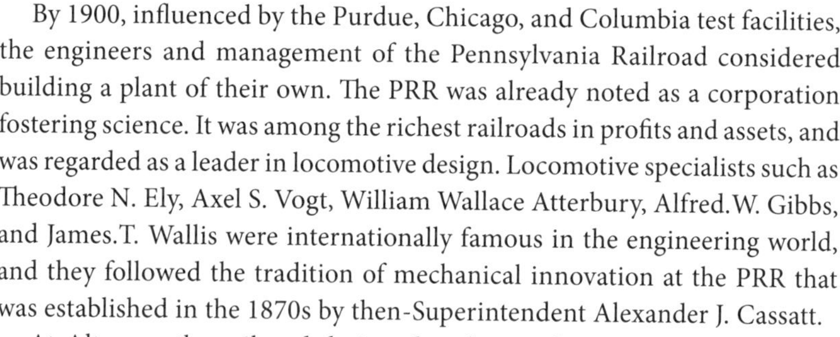

By 1900, influenced by the Purdue, Chicago, and Columbia test facilities, the engineers and management of the Pennsylvania Railroad considered building a plant of their own. The PRR was already noted as a corporation fostering science. It was among the richest railroads in profits and assets, and was regarded as a leader in locomotive design. Locomotive specialists such as Theodore N. Ely, Axel S. Vogt, William Wallace Atterbury, Alfred.W. Gibbs, and James.T. Wallis were internationally famous in the engineering world, and they followed the tradition of mechanical innovation at the PRR that was established in the 1870s by then-Superintendent Alexander J. Cassatt.

At Altoona, the railroad designed and manufactured most of its own locomotives and many of its cars, had its largest repair shops, and had a small laboratory that studied hundreds of products and materials. These included the chemical treatment of wood against rot (a railroad had up to 3,000 wooden crossties in every mile of track, together with thousands of wooden cars, bridges, buildings, and other structures); the strength of steels and iron used in locomotive and car construction; and the durability of purchased components for track and vehicles. Altoona would be the logical site for a locomotive testing complex.

Cassatt, president of the railroad from 1899, took an active role in engineering affairs. He had long before established a reputation as one of America's foremost railway engineers and managers. Brought up in a prominent and close-knit Pittsburgh family (his younger sister was Mary Cassatt, the famous impressionist painter), Alexander traveled in Europe, attended engineering courses at Darmstadt University, and graduated at age 20 from Rensselaer Polytechnic Institute in New York State, with a degree in civil engineering. Between 1861, when he first joined the PRR, and 1870, when he became a general superintendent, Cassatt brought German notions of engineering and applied research to his employer. In the early 1870s, Cassatt helped lead the development of the first series of standardized locomotives on any American railroad. In 1882 he was first vice-president of the company but left the PRR to head the building of another line – the New York, Philadelphia & Norfolk. He was also said to be miffed at being passed over for the PRR's presidency. Seventeen years later, the PRR's directors brought him back as president and chief executive. He immediately embarked on a strategic agenda that would make his railroad preeminent in U.S. transportation, including its engineering, both mechanical and civil.[6] (His sister later persuaded him to have his official portrait painted not by some hack but by the outstanding American portraitist of the day, John Singer Sargent, who also did a celebrated portrait of Theodore Roosevelt.[7]

In civil works, Cassatt is remembered best for his daring tunnel approach into Manhattan and the construction of Pennsylvania Station there. In addition, he led the complete rebuilding and realigning of the main line to high standards capable of handling burgeoning traffic, which demanded bigger, faster, and more powerful locomotives.

The record is unclear as to motives, but Cassatt evidently decided that a highly visible way to launch the PRR's test-plant project was to build such an installation – to be open for public view – as part of its exhibition at the Louisiana Purchase Exposition at St. Louis in 1904. There, after months of construction, the Pennsy began in June to test locomotives on a giant treadmill, with instrumentation to study temperatures, pressures, boiler and machine efficiency, and horsepower. There was also, according to the PRR organizers, something of a sense of mission:

> It was expected originally that such a plant would serve merely as an exhibit which, after the close of the Exposition, would be given a permanent location on the company's property and utilized in the study of locomotive design. Further development of this idea, however, led to the determination to carry on at St. Louis a series of tests and endeavor to enlist the interest of the engineering profession and railroad companies in making them as comprehensive as possible.[8]

In this proselytizing spirit, PRR tested not only its own locomotives but those of other railroads, including rival New York Central, the Santa Fe, and engines of advanced design from France and Germany. In all, eight locomotives (four freight and four passenger) of various sizes ran, one at a time, before an amazed public between June and December 1904 – pistons driving, wheels spinning at speeds up to an equivalent 60 mph, fireboxes roaring, exhaust howling up a large vent, dials and graphs recording, and the floor shaking. PRR engineer of tests E.D. Nelson managed the show and the detailed, published analyses. It was a splendid, dramatic display of engineering science and one of the most popular events of the Exposition.[9]

After the fair's close, railroad staff dug up and crated the whole lot and shipped it to Altoona. Reconstruction began in July 1905. By December 1906, associated buildings had been erected, the plant reinstalled, testing gear

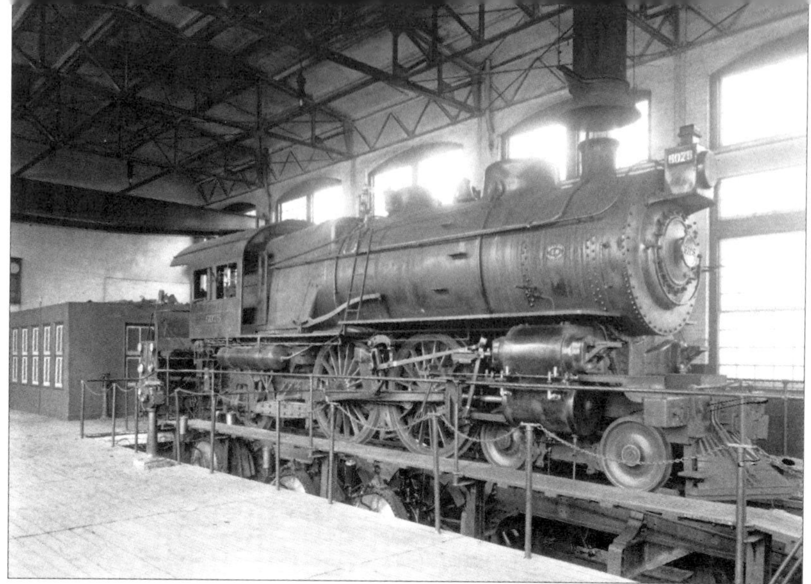

PRR class E6 4-4-2 No. 5075 under evaluation at the railroad's Altoona Test Plant. The E6 was one of the earliest classes of PRR locomotives to benefit from the railroad's test plant regimen. *PRR; Dan Cupper Collection*

calibrated, laboratory staff augmented and trained, and a locomotive – a Class E3d 4-4-2 passenger engine, No. 3001 – selected and made ready for tests.

It is important to understand the basic operation of such a plant and the nature of the data it recorded. Large rollers, whose location could be adjusted fore-and-aft to accommodate different-sized locomotives, were arranged in a pit. Removable sections of rail flush with the top of the rollers permitted a locomotive to be moved into position, the weight of the driving wheels taken by the rollers, and the drawbar of the locomotive secured to the head of a dynamometer. The sole purpose of the dynamometer was to register the locomotive's pull in pounds or kilograms. Rpm, or equivalent speed, was measured mechanically. Then, a simple relation provided a horsepower figure:

$$HP = (T \times V) / K$$

where T is pull, V is rpm or speed, and K is a constant (If T is in pounds and V is in mph, then K is 375; other units for T and V entail a different constant, but the algebraic relation is the same: 1 hp = 33,000 foot/lbs. per minute, which is also 2,545 Btu per hour).

Horsepower, at the drawbar, then provides the standard measure with which to compare every other measure. Fuel consumed and water evaporated by the boiler, per unit of time, could be measured and equated to power output. Boiler efficiency at different power outputs was therefore expressed as heat energy in the steam produced, as a percentage of the heat energy in the unburned fuel. Various parameters of valving, cylinder, and machine design could be varied methodically and equated to power; mechanical efficiency at different power outputs was therefore expressed as the energy realized at the drawbar as a percentage of the heat energy in the steam produced.[10] Testing conditions could be controlled tightly as individual parameters were varied, and results were reproducible.

Practical issues of plant design included a suitable braking system for the rollers (to place variable loads on the working locomotive) and a venting system to carry off the exhausted smoke and steam from the engine's stack. The energy dissipated in the braking system did not have to be measured, since the energy calculated from dynamometer pull at a constant speed is exactly the same (Newton's third law: For every action there is an equal and opposite reaction). The trick was to provide precise and smooth control of the braking. The Altoona plant used a system of "water braking," pumping water through patented Alden hydraulic disc brakes.

Stack venting was less a problem, since few people worried about noise and smoke pollution in the early part of that century. For boiler studies, heat lost in the stack gases could not be measured directly, but furnace and smokebox temperatures could be measured, other sources of heat losses analyzed, and stack loss inferred.[11] Sampling of smokebox gas could be made to analyze chemistry, particularly the proportions of carbon dioxide and carbon monoxide, which indicate combustion efficiency.

As to the effluvia and noise from testing, neither railroad managers nor city politicians cared much about any effects on the residents of Altoona. The city was, after all, a large company town, beholden to the railroad for its very existence. The test plant occupied prime space on railroad property directly adjacent to the business district on one side and a central residential area on the other. The principal thought on locating the test plant was, apparently, that it be next to the engineering and research offices and thus convenient to the engineers. Altoona residents who remember the test plant running in the 1930s and 1940s recall the roaring din, overlain on the general noise and smoke of the railroad yards and shops. The plant occasionally ran on Sundays and could be heard inside the nearby Roman Catholic cathedral, a half-mile away.[12]

Mechanical studies included the taking of cylinder indicator cards at constant output, and at varying valve cutoff and throttle settings, in order to study energy losses in the valves and cylinders under different conditions. The simultaneous difference between cylinder hp, calculated from the indicator cards, and drawbar hp, calculated from the dynamometer, revealed the extent of mechanical losses between cylinders and drawbar.

Axel Vogt and his assistant William F. Kiesel, Jr. supervised the plant installations at St. Louis and Altoona, working under the leadership of PRR motive power chief Theodore Ely. With improvements made for the reinstallation, the PRR now had a plant with the largest capacity in the world by far, able to handle the most powerful locomotives. Cassatt also expanded the associated laboratories for physical testing and chemistry, and enlarged the development staff in all specialties. It was an engineering research complex that rivaled the industrial research center of any American corporation, of any type. In a sad coincidence, A.J. Cassatt died on December 28, 1906, the very day on which the first locomotive test commenced.

By the time the K4s was designed in 1913-1914, the PRR plant had run more than 52 test series, each series comprising up to 48 separate runs, involving 33 different locomotives. Among the studies conducted: steam evaporation, combustion, compound expansion, effect of throttle control on boiler and mechanical efficiency, firebox grate design, briquetted coal, grease vs. oil lubrication, firebox configuration, exhaust nozzles and drafting efficiency, cinder filtering in the smokebox, burning and ash characteristics of different coals, firing techniques, steam action in cylinders and valves, types of superheaters and their efficiency, types of mechanical stokers, alternate forms of valve gear (including, in 1910, the Baker type), types and sizes of piston valves, smoke abatement, and specific performance of both existing and prototype locomotives.[13]

After the PRR plant went into business, the much smaller plants in Chicago and at Columbia University closed. Purdue's modest plant primarily served teaching needs, and the University of Illinois plant of 1914, also incapable of handling the largest locomotives, worked in the service of both teaching and research.[14] Although the Altoona plant was a private facility, and most of its work by modern standards would be considered proprietary, nearly all its tests were covered in detailed, analytical reports that were widely circulated to the trade. It was a case of corporate *noblesse oblige* in sharing cutting-edge engineering research, and it's hard to imagine such a thing today. The PRR plant became the fount of theoretical and practical studies in locomotive design for engineers in the U.S. and in Europe – and for all commercial locomotive manufacturers around the world. There was simply no other adequate source for the developmental data and analyses required to improve the art.

The test reports, taken together, are an untapped source of insight into the K4s design.[15] The locomotive's consistency with, and remarkable departures from, past design are made clear. The K4s was not the first all-new PRR engine to emerge after the start of testing on the Altoona plant; these were the Class K2 4-6-2 and E6 4-4-2 locomotives, both initially constructed in 1910 and subsequently altered with plant-derived improvements. Both were saturated-steam, non-superheated designs.[16] The E6, developed at Altoona, needed only minor tweaking to become a success. The K2 turned out to be a disappointing performer despite all attempts at correction. It took time to collect a solid body of empirical information about all the fundamental design variables, tested under a sufficiently wide range of conditions. The K2 was designed by the engineering staff at PRR's shops in Fort Wayne, Ind., and built in large numbers at the Juniata Shops in Altoona.

Thermodynamic understanding before 1906 was based on limited theory and on severely limited or haphazard data. The PRR test reports, accumulating from 1905, do not include comprehensive analysis, nor do they reflect improved understanding of several key boiler and mechanical variables until the fall of 1913. In that year, they began to include the results of comparative tests begun in 1910 on two significant parameters of locomotive design, valve size and superheater arrangement.

In particular, the advent of superheating, initiated in Germany and first adopted in North America on the Canadian Pacific between 1903 and 1905, was one of the most profound changes ever in boiler design. Superheating did not become standard for PRR engines system-wide until 1913, following road trials of a superheated K2s in 1911 and trials of three different superheated locomotives at the test plant in 1912.

Thus the stage was set for the K4s in late 1913. Design studies began under J.T. Wallis, then general superintendent of motive power and successor to Ely as head of locomotive engineering at Altoona. Locomotive design had always been done mainly by extrapolation from successful, existing designs, and it was no different for the K4s: No set of empirical tests, no matter how sophisticated or complete, can directly produce invention. By definition, invention involves something new – not subject to test until after some alchemy of the creative effort has made the thing itself.

The design team included Wallis, Vogt, Gibbs, and as a junior member, Kiesel.[17] Which of these men had what parts in the creative leaps expressed in the K4s design is not recoverable today. Nor is the contribution of many holding the title of draftsman, who today would be credited for the problem-solving engineering work they often performed. Gibbs and Vogt were noted for their innovative approach and had vital roles in developing several engineering features that would become trademarks of PRR design, such as the large Belpaire-style firebox, a cantilevered trailing truck first seen on the E6, and lightweight valve gear. Professional colleagues viewed Wallis and Gibbs as "progressive" engineers and managers. Vogt was the meticulous European-trained engineer, noted for work "of unusual beauty and perfection of details."[18]

Preceding locomotives that deeply affected the K4s were the problematic K2, the K3s (a superheated revision of the K2, only 30 of which were built), and the E6. Most important, however, was K29 experimental 4-6-2 No. 3395, mentioned in Chapter 8 – a single engine designed and built for the PRR by the American Locomotive Co. of Schenectady, N.Y., in late 1911. Alco had persuaded PRR managers to buy a large, superheated Pacific-type engine to face off with the K2. Earlier, in 1907, Alco's Pittsburgh Works had built the PRR's first Pacific, the one-off K28 No. 7067, which was not superheated. It quickly gained the nickname "Fat Annie" among crews. With both engines, Alco was clearly trying to break into the large potential market the PRR fleet represented. Alco's Francis J. Cole, one of the most respected mechanical engineers in the U.S., supervised both designs and pulled out all the stops on the K29. The trade press viewed Cole's 1911 engine as a big step forward. PRR gave it a few shake-down runs and put it on the test plant within a few weeks of delivery.[19]

Altoona's team, with C.D. Young as engineer of tests, wrung out the K29 for a couple of months and extracted its secrets. By prior agreement, the PRR published the results and analysis but did not order any engines from Alco, preferring the long-standing policy of designing and building its own, or farming out production of its designs to its favored on-line builder, Baldwin. The report, however, reveals a precedent-breaking locomotive:

> These tests are unique in presenting a complete series of results at very high speed and power, with the largest passenger locomotive of its type, and one fully equipped with the devices which are known to add to the power of the locomotive and the convenience of its operation. (p. 3)
>
> Furnishing the steam cylinders of this locomotive with highly superheated steam at 200 pounds boiler pressure resulted in an economy in water approximating 30 per cent ... and an economy of coal of between 20 and 30 per cent may be expected [compared to the best non-superheated engines]. (p. 144)

Dozens of aspects of boiler and machine design were studied comparatively at speeds up to 77 mph and were duly tabulated, charted, graphed, and discussed. Drawbar horsepower peaked at nearly 2,300, cylinder horsepower at 2,580, and net thermal efficiency at 6½ percent. That net efficiency was startlingly high – almost twice as high as the non-superheated E2 tested in 1906. Perhaps even more impressive, its efficiency was higher at all speeds between 28 and 48 mph than the exotic, four-cylinder balanced compound German locomotive that was tested at St. Louis in 1904.

Versions of the K2 and E6 locomotives had been tested in 1910-1911, and after the K29 test, improved and superheated versions of both classes –

PRR class K4s 4-6-2 No. 1737, a 1914 product of the railroad's Juniata shops and the first of the class to be built. Designers' expectations of superior performance were confirmed by the test plant. The K4s class served PRR until the end of the steam era.
PRR; Dan Cupper Collection

the K2s and E6s – were tested in numerous separate trials through March 1914. The K29 was tested again in October and November 1913, and again in January 1914. In these and runs with other locomotive types, the plant examined coal combustion, boiler proportions, valves, and exhaust systems. From December 1906 through 1918, the plant was in virtually continuous operation, except for a few months each in 1908 and 1911 when it was closed for substantial upgrading.[20]

Five crucial test series, held between 1910 and 1913, dealt with an all-important aspect of machine design: the valves regulating steam input to, and exhaust from, the cylinders.[21] The most precipitous drop in net locomotive efficiency occurred not in the boiler but at the valves and cylinders. No good theory guided engineers in approaching efficient performance in the valves. Only past practice and vague practical rules about smooth steam flow and generous port openings prevailed. At Altoona, engineers for the first time could study valve-dimension parameters methodically and see the effects in relation to valve timing. The final series of valve tests, to determine optimal valve diameter in relation to steam flow, ran in August 1913.

With this body of knowledge, the K4s designers could apply rules of size and proportion based on sound data. More than that, the range of tested data for key variables did not have to be extrapolated in most cases; the available data included the size ranges applicable to the new engine. Such reliable guidance had never existed before. Always in the past, a good deal of extrapolation beyond available data from any of the world's test facilities had to be used. And extrapolation meant risk. Time and again, poorly understood thermal relationships got designers in trouble; locomotives (such as the K2) that were larger than before failed to perform as expected. Rules of thumb that predicted good results with smaller engines failed embarrassingly for larger ones.

In fact, the sophistication of theory was little improved through the 1920s. Altoona's test plant was essentially a factory for empirical information. But as the sizes of locomotives grew to satisfy the ever-increasing traffic needs of the carriers, size and testing – both developmental testing for new design and "proof testing" once a design was initially set – went hand in hand for the first time.

By early spring, 1914, Wallis's engineers had drawn up a locomotive with design features that, just a few years prior, would never have been attempted due to their radical extension beyond past practice. The risk would have been far too great – personal risk to professional careers and corporate risk in the potential for squandered resources.

A table from the test report on the new K4s, No. 1737, is powerfully indicative:[22]

			Increase of K4s Over K2sa
	Class K4s	Class K2sa	K4s Over K2sa,%
Total weight in working order, lb.	309,140	293,200	5.4
Weight on drivers in working order, lb.	202,880	179,900	12.8
Cylinders (simple), inches	27 x 28	24 x 26	36.3
Diameter of driving wheels, inches	80	80	0
Heating surface in tubes (water side) sq. in.	3728.64	3436.37	8.5
Firebox heating surface. sq. ft., including arch tubes	306.77	208.02	47.5
Heating surface of superheater, fire side	1171.85	989.32	18.5
Total heating surface (based on water side of tubes), including superheater, sq ft.	5207.26	4633.71	12.4
Total heating surface (based on fire side of tubes), including superheater, sq. ft.	4863.96	4312.40	12.8
Grate area, sq. ft.	69.26	53.72	28.9
Boiler pressure, lbs. per sq. in.	205	205	0
Valve, type	12 in. Piston	16 in. Piston	
Valve motion	Walschaerts	Walschaerts	
Firebox	Wide Belpaire	Wide Belpaire	
Number of tubes	237	202	17.3
Number of flues (superheater)	40	32	25.0
Outside diameter of tubes, inches	2.25	2.25	0
Outside diameter of flues, inches	5.5	5.5	0
Length of tubes, inches	227.23	250.08	-9.1

The comparison was between the K4s and the fully modified and superheated K2 of 1911 (the K2sa). Just three years separated these engines, both of which were heavy 4-6-2 Pacifics. The K4s had the same boiler pressure, but its cylinders were 36 percent larger, its firebox heating surface was almost 48 percent larger, its firebox grate area was 29 percent larger, and its superheating surface was 19 percent larger, thanks to 25 percent more superheater flues.

In the rigorously conservative milieu of American railroading, no engineering staff would have made such huge, non-incremental changes without great predictive confidence, especially for the boiler proportions. At the same time, the staff shaved weight by close attention to mechanical design. The two engines have the same driving-wheel diameter and general layout, yet the K4s is just five percent heavier. In March, the drawings went from the drafting rooms to the Juniata Shops nearby, and on May 29, the new engine appeared. The trade was respectful, but skeptical.

The PRR engineers actually designed two new locomotive classes at once. The K4s boiler and the boiler for the new L1s 2-8-2 freight engine were made to be identical in every respect, the first time such a thing had occurred under the PRR's policy of attempted standardization. Although the drawings for the K4s and L1s were completed at the same time, the first L1s, No. 1752, came out of Juniata in April and went on the test plant in July. The railroad had a greater need at the time for more freight locomotives, so the L1s was given its proof runs on the plant first, prior to full production.[23]

In fact, the Pennsy almost immediately placed orders for 160 production L1s engines, starting in September 1914, but waited three years before ordering mass-production K4s engines.

The K4s, No. 1737, went to the plant in September for two months. By early 1915, word was getting out on both the L1s and K4s tests. The first test plant data on the K4s officially appeared first in the fall of 1915, when a PRR report entitled "Comparison of Passenger Locomotives" was published. Then, in early 1916, the PRR published the full test-plant report on the 1737 K4s to enormous interest and subsequent professional discussion that went on for years.[24]

The K4s outperformed every other locomotive tested before on the plant, in power output and thermal efficiency. In most cases, the superiority was by a generous margin. The K4s was four tons lighter than the K29 but produced much more drawbar horsepower, more than 3,000, versus the K29's 2,300. K4s cylinder horsepower reached almost 3,200. Thermal efficiency at high speed was unheard of: well over eight percent on one test, registered in a 90-minute plant run at 75 mph at moderate power. Steam production per pound of fuel at all speeds was dramatically higher than ever before, as were power in the cylinders and net power at the drawbar per pound of coal.

The K4s's greatly enlarged combustion volume (427 cubic feet in firebox and combustion chamber), the vast firebox heating surface (half-again more than the K2), the larger grate area, and the optimization of tube length, superheater surface, valve diameter, and cylinder size were the sources of the performance improvement. The secret inherent in the greater furnace volume is "residence time," the average time that any given particle of fuel can stay in the furnace, combine with oxygen, and release its heat. With a draft up to 300 mph in the flues, such time is brief. Once in the tubes, any given fuel particle ceases burning, as the tubes conduct heat rapidly to the surrounding boiler water. The added firebox volume – provided by pushing the firebox walls out wider and higher, together with the inclusion of a combustion chamber – extends residence time and increases heat release. (In the 1920s, designer Kiesel would expand the combustion chamber in a later engine class, the M1 4-8-2, to a size bigger than the firebox itself.)

But optimization is the real secret. For example, the length of tubes in the K4s boiler was substantially less than those of either the K2 or the K29, but lengthening the tubes on the standard, superheated E6s improved that engine's efficiency and power.[25] Given the strict clearance limits within which any locomotive must fit, no increase in any desirable design parameter could be made without cost to another. This is especially true for combustion-chamber length vs. tube length, superheater layout, and valve and cylinder design. Only the test plant could have provided the basis for the proportional relations found in the K4s. For an engineer, finding such optimality is more than economics; it creates an aesthetic – like that remarked about Vogt – of "unusual beauty."

Of all the results, one of the most interesting to mechanical designers was the unprecedented rise in average locomotive thermal efficiency throughout the speed range, up to 85 mph. The K4s gained in average efficiency at different outputs as speed rose; every other previous engine, superheated or not, showed a sharp drop in efficiency as speed increased. In a rare departure from the usual deadpan narrative style of its engineering reports, the authors of the K4s report described its efficiency characteristics as "a distinct advance in the art of locomotive design."[26]

It is often asserted that the K4s derived from the earlier E6/E6s, with which it shares a superficial appearance.[27] The boiler of the E6, however, was first designed in 1910 without superheating and, more significantly, was of a size and output comfortably within known boiler performance data. It was the K29 testing that led to confidence in the K4s/L1s boiler proportions.

The K4s design did, however, draw directly from the E6/E6s suspension and running gear layout. This included a four-wheel pilot truck equalized with the first pair of drivers, and a trailing truck with one-piece, cantilevered side frames. Running experience with the E6s engines on the fastest schedules between New York and Philadelphia showed better stability at high speed compared to earlier engines with four-wheel lead trucks, so the E6/E6s equalization was carried over to the larger engine.[28] In later years, however, the K4s suspension was simplified as engines were cycled to Juniata for major repair, and the equalization between lead truck and first driver-pair was removed. Designers had no adequate theory for the dynamic behavior of suspension systems that could reliably predict riding stability at speed. Probably the longer wheelbase of the K4s rendered the E6/E6s-style equalization unnecessary.

The K4s began series production at Juniata in 1917. Start of production was delayed due to the priority on building L1s 2-8-2 and I1s 2-10-0 freight engines – not, as often repeated, because of any need to test the 1737 K4 further. A K4s did not go back on the plant until 1931, and that was for trying out particular grate arrangements.

The legacy of the K4s was pervasive. The standardized locomotives developed by U.S. engineers in 1918 for the United States Railroad Administration in several classes – designs which became popular on a number of railroads even after the war – were influenced by the K4s's proportions. Every class of heavy passenger engine developed later in the U.S. was affected, especially in the ratios of boiler output to cylinder and machinery dimensions. Nigel Gresley, one of the leading designers in Britain, developed a Pacific-type in the early 1920s with boiler proportions closely following those of the K4s. This was Gresley's *Great Northern*, built at Doncaster, South Yorkshire, in 1922. Later British engines followed a similar pattern.

Pennsy considered the design to be so good that it continued to build and order K4s engines until 1928, 14 years after the prototype was built. In 1929, two experimental and larger K5 4-6-2s did not significantly improve on the K4s's performance. Thus, it was left to the 52 four-cylinder Class T1 streamlined 4-4-4-4 engines, built by Juniata and Baldwin in 1942 and 1945-1946, to replace the K4s's.

Today, two K4s locomotives survive, one at the Railroaders Memorial Museum in Altoona (this engine, No. 1361, a Juniata-built engine from 1918, was restored to operation in 1985-1987 and ran occasionally through the fall of 1988), and another at the Railroad Museum of Pennsylvania at Strasburg. This is No. 3750, a Juniata-built engine of 1920, which PRR preserved in its historical collection but gave it a fake identity as No. 1737, because the original

PRR K4s No. 5341, inside the Altoona Test Plant.
PRR; Dan Cupper Collection

K4s had deteriorated too far, and was scrapped. The 3750 was given its correct number after it was moved to the museum in Strasburg. Fittingly, perhaps, that museum's collection also includes the statue of Alexander Cassatt, twice life-size, that once stood in New York's Pennsylvania Station. The statue had honored Cassatt's role in beginning the Hudson River Tunnels and in laying out Penn Station, but it was Cassatt also who brought the Altoona test plant into being. The test plant, which had evaluated locomotives as small as an 0-6-0 switcher of 1911 and as large as a Class Q2 4-4-6-4 freight design of 1944-1945, last saw use with the construction of the Class T1 4-4-4-4 engines in Altoona in 1945-1946. The test plant buildings were demolished soon after PRR merged with New York Central in 1968 to create Penn Central.

Chapter 9 Notes

1. The most numerous class, the I1s 2-10-0 heavy freighter of 1916, which eventually numbered 598 engines, was also a PRR design; the second most populous class was the PRR L1s 2-8-2, at 574 engines. The other five were Class L2s, light USRA Mikados built for a subsidiary line, the Grand Rapids & Indiana, and subsumed into the PRR class system. Of the 425 K4s engines, 350 were home-built by PRR at Altoona and 75 were built by Baldwin.
2. Lawford H. Fry, David P. Morgan, Bert Pennypacker, Alvin F. Stauffer, and Fred Westing have all written excellent articles about the K4s's. By far the best mechanical description is in Brian Reed, "Pennsylvania Pacifics," in *Locomotive Profiles* (London: Profile Publishing Co., 1968), vol. 2, pp. 25-48.
3. A. Borodin, "Experiments on Steam-Jacketing and Compounding of Locomotives in Russia," in *Proceedings of the Institution of Mechanical Engineers* (U.K.), 1886, p. 317. See Lawford H. Fry, "The Locomotive Testing Plant and Its Influence on Steam-Locomotive Design," American Society of Mechanical Engineers *Transactions*. vol. 47, 1925, pp. 1267-93; see pp. 1286, 1291.
4. W.F.M. Goss, ASME *Transactions*, vol. 14, 1893, and vol. 25, 1904.
5. See Fry, 1925 (Note 3). Also, British locomotive engineers, starting in 1937, planned a new locomotive testing facility at Rugby. Because of World War II, this plant did not start operations until ten years later.
6. Albert J. Churella, *The Pennsylvania Railroad: Building an Empire, 1846-1917*, pp. 627-29.
7. Sargent's portrait of Cassatt is now in the Railroad Museum of Pennsylvania collection at Strasburg, Pa.
8. *The Pennsylvania Railroad System at the Louisiana Purchase Exposition: Locomotive Tests and Exhibits*, 1904, p. 1.
9. *Locomotive Tests and Exhibits*, pp. 112-16. The engines were, in order, PRR-built Class H6a simple 2-8-0 No. 1499; Lake Shore & Michigan Southern (New York Central) Brooks-built (Alco) simple 2-8-0 No. 734; Michigan Central (NYC) Alco-built

compound 2-8-0 No. 585; Santa Fe Baldwin-built compound 2-10-2 No. 929; PRR deGlehn compound 4-4-2 No. 2512, built by the Société Alsacienne de Constructions Mechaniques in Belfort, France; Santa Fe Baldwin-built compound 4-4-2 No. 535; four-cylinder compound 4-4-2 No. 628, built by Hannoversche Maschinenbau-Actien-Gesellschaft for the Royal Prussian Railway and delivered at the close of the Exposition; and New York Central & Hudson River (NYC) Alco-built compound 4-4-2 No. 3000.

10. Net or total locomotive efficiency, therefore, was a combination of boiler and mechanical efficiency, and defined as the actual power finally produced at the drawbar as a percentage of the heat energy in the unburned fuel.
11. There was, however, a flaw in this reasoning, pointed out later in Fry's seminal book, *A Study of the Locomotive Boiler*, 1924.
12. Interview with Fred E. Long, May 20, 1987.
13. A listing of all locomotive tests performed on the Altoona Test Plant between 1904 and February 1938 survives at the Naional Railway Museum archive at York, England. I am indebted to librarian Philip Atkins for its discovery.
14. University of Illinois, *Engineering Experiment Station Bulletin* No. 82, 1915.
15. Surviving copies of these reports are rare. The Smithsonian Institution's National Museum of American History has many of the reports published through 1929. Others are in the collections of the Railroad Museum of Pennsylvania at Strasburg, the Barriger Collection at the Mercantile Library in St. Louis, and at the Hagley Library in Wilmington, Del.
16. A word on PRR classification nomenclature: When superheating was introduced, locomotives that were either built with or retrofitted with that feature gained a letter "s" behind their class designation. Thus, A K2 4-6-2 became a K2s and with additional modifications, a K2sa or K2sb; the initial saturated-steam E6 4-4-2 of 1910 was retrofitted and became class E6s, like the 82 E6s's that followed. In 1924, PRR discontinued adding the suffix "s" to new steam design classes, as by then, superheating was universally applied to all new engines. As a result, the class names for C1 0-8-0s, J1/J1a 2-10-4s; K5 4-6-2s, Q1 4-6-4-4, Q2 4-4-6-4s, S1 6-4-4-6, S2 6-8-6, and T1 4-4-4-4s omitted that suffix, as did a proposed but never-built V1 steam-electric turbine.
17. Atterbury, active in locomotive matters through 1902, had been elevated to a general manager by Cassatt in 1903. By 1913, Atterbury was system vice president of operations. In 1925, he became president.
18. Goss and others, in *Locomotive Tests* (note 8), p. iv.
19. PRR Test Department, "Tests of a Class K29 Locomotive," *Bulletin* No. 19, 1912.
20. See listing of tests (Note 13), and "Tests of a Class K2sa Locomotive" *Bulletin* No. 18, 1914, and "Tests of a Class E6s Passenger Locomotive," *Bulletin* No. 21, 1913.
21. Results appear in two reports from the PRR Test Department, "Piston Valves," *Bulletin* No. 7, 1912; and "Piston Valve Diameter and Valve Stem Stress," *Bulletin* No. 23, 1914.
22. PRR Test Department, "Tests of a Class K4s Locomotive," *Bulletin* No. 29, 1915, p. 4.
23. A case could be made, therefore, that the L1s, not the K4s, was the "first scientifically designed locomotive." However, the discussions and test data in the reports for the K4s and L1s suggest strongly that the K4s was the primary focus of the K4s/L1s design project, which was in fact a simultaneous project for both types. The L1s report, "Tests of a Class L1s Locomotive," *Bulletin* No. 28, 1915, indicates that the common boiler for both types was better suited to the K4s, not to the L1s. Top drawbar horsepower achieved by the L1s was 2,600 at 30 mph, vs. 3,000 for the K4s at 47 mph, showing that the boiler could deliver superheated steam more efficiently at the piston speeds and cutoffs characteristic of a passenger locomotive. The L1s report throughout compares the new engine with the H9s 2-8-0; the new L1s, being much larger than the H9s, naturally outperforms the older locomotive in every respect. The H9s, although limited to about 1,600 drawbar horsepower, could deliver that power at better efficiency than the L1s, up to the H9s's maximum output. The L1s was a superior freight locomotive to anything the PRR had ever had before, but it was not the "barn-burner" the K4s was. The K4s raised eyebrows because it was so superior to the best previous locomotives of similar type and size.
24. K4s test report (Note 22), and "Comparison of Passenger Locomotives," *Bulletin* No. 22, 1915.
25. Ibid.
26. K4s test report, p. 79.
27. Brian Reed, "Pennsylvania Pacifics," in *Locomotive Profiles* (London: Profile Publishing Co., 1968), vol. 2, p. 27.
28. Fred Westing, *Apex of the Atlantics: Story of the PRR E6*, Kalmbach Publishing, 1963.

Chapter 10

Federal Takeover:

Engineering and Politics - The U.S. Railroad Administration, 1917-1920

In December 1917, some eight months after American entry into World War I, President Wilson signed an order federalizing the nation's railroads. There was no congressional mandate for the move. Wilson claimed authority from the April 6, 1917, congressional declaration of war, and from sections of the mobilization acts of April and August that year, but the essential ground was an executive order. Forthwith, a United States Railroad Administration came into being, and Treasury Secretary William G. McAdoo took on the added title of director general of railroads. He also took on sweeping powers to manage directly the day-to-day operations of all the large railroads in the country. For one of the nation's biggest private-sector industries, it was a stunning blow both to owners' presumed rights and to management pride.[1]

Newspaper editorial writers, legislators, and rail-employee unions enthusiastically supported the action. Most of the traveling and shipping public, locked in a dependency/hate relationship with railroads dating from the "robber baron" era of the late 19th century, seemed to approve as well.[2] Precipitating Wilson's order was a colossal breakdown of the interconnected rail freight system. Despite the companies' creation of an industry-sponsored Railroad War Board on April 11 to coordinate military shipments, launched with patriotic statements supporting the war effort, the rail system headed rapidly to gridlock. As wave after wave of war matériel and troop trains converged on East Coast seaports, yards jammed. Congress had devised a system by which shipments could be prioritized by presidential order, but at one point, nearly 85 percent of shipments bore priority tags.[3] Switching crews couldn't sort the freight cars fast enough or deliver them to docks on schedule. Ships couldn't sail on time. Making matters worse, thousands of railroad employees had enlisted in the Army. In cascading order, freight yards in the Midwest backed up. Soon there was a shortage of available empty freight cars to load the burgeoning traffic, compounded by inability to offload cars delayed en route. In the growing glut, blocked troop trains waited in sidings, sometimes for a day or more.[4]

By mid-summer of 1917, General John J. Pershing, commander of the American Expeditionary Force in France, was calling on the president to take

William G. McAdoo.
Harris & Ewing, Library of Congress

drastic measures. Bernard Baruch, head of the government's War Industries Board in Washington, did the same. Repeated assurances from railroad presidents that the situation would be reversed quickly began to ring hollow. Congressmen called the railroads' patriotism into question.

Treasury Secretary McAdoo fancied himself a railroad expert. He had formerly managed the transit company in Knoxville, Tenn., and had led the Hudson & Manhattan Railroad when it built the first tunnels under the Hudson River. (H&M is now known as the Port Authority Trans-Hudson, or PATH.) As one of Wilson's key campaign supporters and closest domestic-affairs advisers (he was also married to Wilson's daughter, Eleanor), McAdoo argued that half-measures should be bypassed and that only a complete takeover of the railroads would have timely results. Wilson signed a proclamation creating the USRA and describing its powers on December 26.[5]

By mid-January 1918 the new agency was a work in progress, but it was up and running and issuing directives. Director General McAdoo appointed a civilian "federal manager" as chief executive for each railroad, to whom the company's sitting president, management, and directors had to answer. McAdoo sought outside advice on these appointments, but relied heavily on Henry Walters, chairman of the Atlantic Coast Line and Louisville & Nashville railroads.[6] The federal manager appointed to each of the big Eastern and Midwestern roads was a respected executive, sometimes a former rail or other industry leader called out of recent retirement, with few if any former ties to the line. In several cases in the Far West, where railroad service had not deteriorated, the company president was named federal manager for his line, but under orders to operate strictly according to federal policies.[7]

With railroad assets now under government control, politically potent issues immediately arose. Committees of the USRA and the Interstate Commerce Commission began to consider questions arising from the federal takeover, including formulas for the government's rental of private property during the war and compensation after the war, and changes in assessed value (from wear and tear, for example, net of accrued interest). A parallel federal entity, the War Labor Board, already had jurisdiction over rail wages, as it did for wages in other industries; McAdoo created a subordinate USRA Board of Wages and Working Conditions to back up the Labor Board.

The main business was to get the trains moving. Standing groups within USRA, consisting of government administrators and selected managers from the railroads, addressed logistics, joint routing, and scheduling issues. Because the traffic crunch was mostly in the Midwest and East, the main focus was on those regions. Before the takeover, top managements' exhortations to expedite joint routings had fallen on mostly deaf ears, even within their own companies. Connecting carriers were now required to speed interchange at junctions. Freight cars delivered to an industrial shipping dock now had to be either on- or off-loaded within strict time limits, under sanction of federally imposed fines to the shipper or consignee. The many boxcars accommodating less-than-carload (LCL) shipments for smaller industries and forwarders had to be loaded to capacity rather than run partially loaded. Federal inspectors from the ICC enforced the new regulations.[8]

In 1917, hard on the heels of the war declaration, Wilson had brought industrial leaders together in a Council of National Defense to advise on war production efforts throughout American industry. That summer, the council appointed a pair of committees to look into the standardization of freight car and locomotive designs, and to help speed their production. Both were manufacturers' committees – one for locomotives and one for cars – and both were chaired by the widely respected Samuel Vauclain, engineering vice president of the Baldwin Locomotive Works. The three-member locomotive committee, with senior representation from Baldwin's rival, the American Locomotive Co., and from H.K. Porter, a much smaller builder that specialized in light industrial locomotives, was ineffectual. Locomotive design standardization had been a perennial topic of theoretical discussion from the mid-19th century, with next to no result. (The Pennsylvania Railroad, which built many of its own engines, had embraced the idea, and Union Pacific and Southern Pacific, managed under E.H. Harriman, had instituted "Common Standard" designs beginning in about 1905.) Railroad managers and motive power officers universally supported the notion of increased wartime locomotive production and the idea that government might help finance it – but with railroads free to order according to their own specifications and designs.

The car committee made somewhat greater progress, since the participating car makers stood to gain a much greater percentage boost in new production than the engine builders. The Council of National Defense had proposed that the federal government might buy up to 150,000 cars and put them out on the rails as soon as possible. Members of the car committee consisted of the president or vice president of the four largest freight-car producers: Pullman, American Car & Foundry, Standard Steel Car Co., and Pressed Steel Car Co. Vauclain, as chair, was clearly an interloper in the car business. Normally, locomotive and car people interacted rarely, either in the corporate field of railway supply or within railroad managements below the top level. For the car manufacturers, Vauclain's prestige and "disinterested" neutral status in their trade probably helped guide a touchy process among four normally bitter competitors. The committee reached the stage of some trial specifications, but there was no consensus, since any standard might favor the construction methods of one firm over another.[9]

Immediately after USRA's creation, McAdoo assigned Henry Walters the task of re-studying the question of car and engine standardization. Walters got the National Defense Council's car committee delegated to USRA and, backed by McAdoo, redirected it to move rapidly from studies to real designs, promising that government car orders would be divided equitably among the makers. The railroads' trade group, the American Railway Association (predecessor of the modern Association of American Railroads) had already investigated standardizing boxcar design. Car builders might squabble over exact specifications for cars, but the railroads themselves voiced no opposition to standardized freight cars. Under Walters' prodding, the car committee made rapid progress. Then, in early February 1918, McAdoo announced that he was going to form what *Railway Age* called a "new committee on locomotive standards," presumably within USRA.[10]

The month before, the forceful and outspoken McAdoo had made several pronouncements that indicated his impatience with industry resistance to standardization. Considerable maneuvering among Walters, USRA staff, builders, and railroad representatives took place in the two weeks after McAdoo's proposal for a new committee on engines. In mid-February, the earlier locomotive manufacturers' committee (with uncharacteristic speed) rendered a brief report to Walters, "recommending several standard types of locomotives," based on popular general types for either freight or passenger service.[11] In the meantime, Walters had formed a panel of railroad locomotive officers under H.T. Bentley, head of motive power and machinery for the Chicago & North Western. With the sketchy recommendations from Vauclain's committee, Bentley's railroad group began working on February 22 in Room 1009 of the ICC Building at 12th Street and Constitution Avenue in Washington.[12]

There were nine appointed members besides Bentley: three members designated by each of the three USRA regional directors who now administered the country's rail lines. The politics behind the selection of the nine members are unrecorded. The Chicago & North Western, a major but not dominant line, had two representatives, both the chairman and Robert Quayle, the company's well-known general superintendent of motive power. Oddly, the mighty Pennsylvania was not represented initially, but archrival New York Central was. For the USRA's Western District, Santa Fe's John Purcell participated, but competing Southern Pacific was unrepresented. Major roads such as the Baltimore & Ohio and Union Pacific were left out. Hardball was the order of the day, however, and representation quickly became more equitable. J.T. Wallis, motive power superintendent for the western lines of the Pennsylvania Railroad (and a leading architect of the K4s design), simply showed up at the initial meetings and stayed. By the first week of March, locomotive officers from the B&O and the Milwaukee Road were participating, plus additional engineers from the Erie, Illinois Central, Norfolk & Western, and the Pennsylvania. The Southern Pacific sent its director of purchasing, a man well versed in locomotive engineering issues. There was only limited, and entirely unofficial, input from the builders. Railroad mechanical engineering staffs knew just as much about the empirical theory and practical issues of locomotive design as did the builders' engineers.[13]

While the panel worked in all-day, back-to-back sessions through March, the vocal McAdoo let his own views be known. He declared that a kind of locomotive "flying squadron" or "circulating reserve" would be assembled, with these government-owned engines sent as needed to railroads experiencing motive-power shortages. That these engines needed to be of standard design was part and parcel of McAdoo's concept, to facilitate both rapid production and "interchangeability" from road to road.

There was more than a purely engineering or operational agenda here, however – far more. McAdoo was a Democratic Party progressive and a spokesman for the view that an activist government should intervene forcefully to correct capitalist abuses. He foresaw his new locomotives – with a big "U. S." emblazoned on each of their tenders – as symbols of government-to-the-rescue, bailing out a failed private industrial empire and thus helping reassert citizen control over that industry's former oppressions. With the USRA's mandate solidified by the federal Railroad Control Act of March 21,[14] McAdoo gave a flamboyant talk in April to Southern Pacific railroad employees in El Paso, Texas:

By one stroke of the pen, the president of the United States has transformed all these railroad systems, these separate competitive systems, into one great unified transportation system. ... The railroads of the United States have for a long time been the football of finance, of politics, and of all sorts of things. I am frank to say that I think it has been very hurtful to the country. ... So long as the railroads of the United States were used primarily for private and selfish ends, so long as they were made a political question, the difficulties of reconciling contending and competitive interests with the public interest have been insuperable."[15]

For McAdoo, the word "competitive" was a pejorative. He was no friend of business. Progressive writer Frank Norris, who had 17 years earlier described the venerable Southern Pacific (and all other big rail companies by implication) as "The Octopus," would have been pleased. Railroad executives must have been horrified.

The locomotive committee finished most of its work by the first week of April. As a panel of locomotive users rather than builders, the members grappled directly with their own and other companies' operational issues, and with their prejudices. The collective attitude seems to have been one of making the best result possible under tremendous external pressure to produce consensus quickly. Under Bentley's leadership, the members worked through their divisions.

The group decided at first on three basic wheel arrangements for the road locomotives. There would be "light" and "heavy" versions of each. For freight, the consensus choice was the 2-8-2 configuration; for passengers, the 4-6-2; and for fast freight and heavy passenger use, the 4-8-2. The light and heavy versions would differ primarily in boiler size (and hence, power) and in axle loading (the heavy versions were to be limited to 30 tons per driving axle, with the light versions 2½ tons per axle less). Heavy versions could serve the leading carriers, with their heavier rail; light versions could operate on the lighter-section rail typical of smaller railroads and of the big companies' secondary lines. Two switchers, an 0-6-0 and an 0-8-0, were also specified. During March, the proposed array was expanded to include a light and a heavy 2-10-2, as well as two compound-expansion, four-cylinder Mallet designs, a 2-6-6-2 and a 2-8-8-2; all these were for heavy freight.[16]

With "U.S." initials painted on its tender, Southern Railway Class Ss-1 2-10-2 engine No. 5222, at Alexandria, Va., in May 1919, was built to a USRA "light" design. As was the case with locomotives throughout the nation, it continued to work under USRA oversight even after the 1918 Armistice.

Harold K. Vollrath Collection

General specifications for the initial three USRA wheel arrangements, in their original "light" and "heavy" configurations, were:[17]

Wheel arrangement and type name	Cylinder dimensions	Weight on drivers (lb.)	Tractive power (lb.)
2-8-2 Mikado (Light)	26" x 30"	220,000	54,600
2-8-2 Mikado (Heavy)	27" x 32"	240,000	60,000
4-6-2 Pacific (Light)	25" x 28"	165,000	40,700
4-6-2 Pacific (Heavy)	27" x 28"	180,000	43,800
4-8-2 Mountain (Light)	27" x 30"	220,000	53,900
4-8-2 Mountain (Heavy)	27" x 30"	240,000	57,000

Robert Quayle, one of the participants, spoke to railroad executives in Chicago on April 15:

> I was a member of the committee of nine that was called on to prepare these designs. It was a big job, to reconcile every member of the committee to each particular thing that was adopted. All the roads represented had their own standards, and they were all different. Many had to give up the fancy notions they cherished and had to take up the notions of someone else, in order that the committee might agree. ... We saw that we could not bring in localism or sectionalism; what we did had to be for the good of the nation. It was essential that we get together and do what we could to help out.[18]

BELOW Louisville & Nashville USRA light 4-6-2 No. 242, at East St. Louis, Ill., in 1949.
Harold K. Vollrath Collection

BOTTOM Erie Railroad 4-6-2 No. 2918, at Chicago in 1922, was a USRA heavy Pacific.
Harold K. Vollrath Collection

In counterpoint to this task-focused assessment of the committee's work, C.A. Greenough, a vice president of the Baldwin Locomotive Works, offered at the same gathering his views on the pros and cons of standardization. He summarized the advantages as "interchangeability between railroads, the possibility of some rapidity of construction, interchangeability of repairs and a somewhat lower cost." However:

> The capacities of the locomotives are based upon average conditions; hence there is no provision for the extreme requirements which these locomotives do not cover. Where even the light locomotives are too heavy ... and where the heavy locomotives are not of sufficient capacity [then] special locomotives will have to be provided. ... [T]hose requiring the heavier locomotives [must] change their system of operation so as to use the heavy standard government locomotive. In such instances where railroads have been equipped from one end to the other to use power of maximum capacity for the purpose of reducing train movements, such action would prove a negative economy."[19]

The code language here involves both capital and, more importantly, labor costs. It's a waste of capital when crews operate locomotives that are bigger than the need. But when crews operate locomotives that are even slightly too small, more crews have to be paid for the same total traffic. Note that Greenough dwells longer on the labor-cost dimension: Changing "their system of operation" or arranging an operation "for the purpose of reducing train movements" is code for labor cost implications.

LEFT Rock Island 2-8-2 No. 2318, at Ruston, La., in 1950, was a USRA light Mikado.

Harold K. Vollrath Collection

BELOW Great Northern 2-8-2 No. 3208, at Minneapolis in 1932, illustrates the heavy variant of the USRA Mikado design.

Harold K. Vollrath Collection

Greenough then makes an appeal that should resonate for a modern reader used to the rapid technological changes of the 21st century:

> ... [I]mprovements in the permanent way [track and bridges] have invited and made possible increases in the size and capacity of locomotives which have thrown to the winds any idea of standardization of locomotives which would extend over any appreciable period of time. ... [We can] not permit a system of standardization which is so inflexible as to choke further improvements.

And then, in surprisingly modern language:

> The ideal standardization provides for the elimination of unnecessary diversity, and progress invites and necessitates diversity.[20]

So resistance was not intransigence. The subtleties articulated by Greenough were certainly on the minds of committee members. All of them were held to account by their employers for the economic results of their decisions. Belying vague assumptions about railroads' engineering conservatism, the committee decided early to incorporate the best current

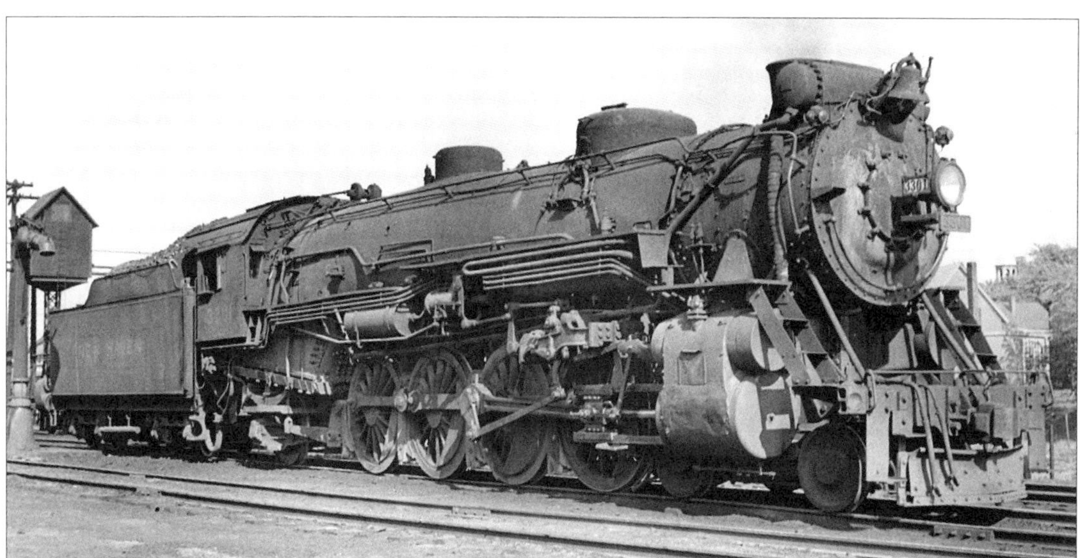

BELOW New Haven 4-8-2 No. 3301, at Lowell, Mass., in 1937, was a USRA light Mountain type. *Harold K. Vollrath Collection*

BOTTOM A USRA heavy Mountain type, Chesapeake & Ohio 4-8-2 No. 547 was photographed at Charlottesville, Va., in 1948, by which time it had come to resemble its owner's other locomotives, a common occurrence on many roads as the USRA engines aged. *Harold K. Vollrath Collection*

technology for thermal performance, safety, and crew comfort. (As a trade writer put it at the time, "modern devices of proved merit will be approved, but those in the experimental stage will not be included."[21]) The designs included combustion chambers, firebox arches, superheaters, mechanical stokers for all the large road engines, mechanical grate shakers, mechanical coal pushers for the smaller engines without stokers, air-operated power reverse gear, and – following safety recommendations of the ICC's Bureau of Locomotive Inspection – mechanically operated firedoors, two water glasses, gauge cocks mounted on a water column, and better in-cab lighting.[22]

As to the subtleties of boiler proportions, the engines were quite advanced. Although conventional in construction details, the boilers were generous, with large fireboxes. In its own published specifications, the committee pointed to its advanced thinking about boiler proportions by specifically including the ratio of grate area to total evaporative surface. Engines to operate mostly at higher rpm (and hence put out high boiler horsepower in relation to boiler size) had ratios of 1:50 to about 1:55, while engines for slower rpm (and high continuous tractive effort but at slow speeds, below peak boiler horsepower) had ratios of 1:58 to 1:61. The two Mallets – designed for the slowest-speed work – had still-higher ratios.[23]

The firebox combustion chambers, used on all but the switcher designs, gave big combustion volumes. In 1918, the combustion chamber was still highly controversial: Unless it was well-designed for thermal stresses, all the additional staybolts such a chamber required increased the boiler's susceptibility to staybolt breakage in service, risking higher maintenance costs. The committee apparently felt that such potential problems could be minimized by subsequent, detailed engineering of the staybolt layout pattern for boiler construction. The recent

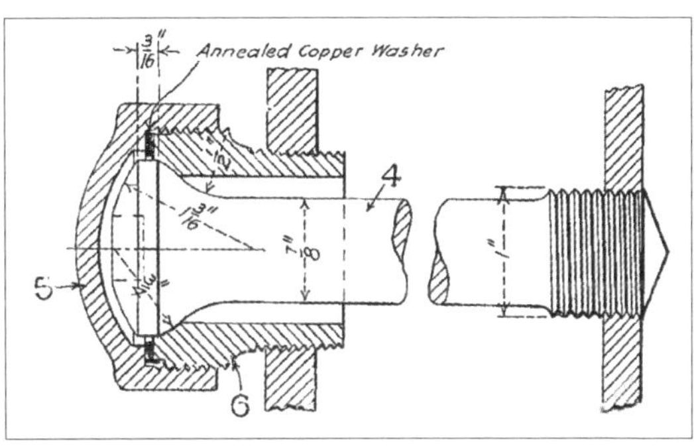

ABOVE The inner and outer sheets of the firebox are subject to dramatic differences in temperature, and flexible staybolts were installed at the places of maximum stress. This 1911 Pennsylvania Railroad design had a ball (5) on the outside end of the firebox and a thread on the inside end. The ball sat in a plug (6), unthreaded, allowing the inner firebox sheet to flex, relative to the outer sheet, thus minimizing stress on the bolt.

Locomotive Dictionary, 1916

LEFT Rows of staybolts are visible on the firebox of Missouri Pacific 4-6-2 No. 6001. The prominent extra plumbing is an exhaust steam injector.

Courtesy Kalmbach Media

invention and wide adoption of the "flexible staybolt" for use in high-stress regions of the firebox no doubt increased the committee's confidence. Because of the combination of a big firebox plus a combustion chamber, each road-engine design, freight or passenger, included a trailing truck to carry the enlarged rear end. Although common by 1918 in new construction of large engines, the trailing truck was far from universal. Its inclusion was a visible symbol of the USRA committee's desire to create high-efficiency designs and not simply lowest-common-denominator compromises.

The committee came up with various ways of standardizing major components. The light 2-8-2 and the light 4-6-2 shared the same firebox foundation ring and grate; the heavy 2-8-2, the light 4-8-2, and the heavy 4-6-2 also shared a common foundation ring. The light 2-8-2, heavy 4-6-2, and light 4-8-2 shared the same first boiler ring and diameter of the largest boiler course. Various boilers shared the same course diameters or the same tube length or the same numbers of tubes, in different combinations. The twelve separate designs shared six driver diameters and (other than the Mallets) six piston diameters. The shared structural components in boiler and machinery affected design considerations for performance; the size of the components could not be "ideal" for a given locomotive. As discussed later in this chapter, however, the trade-offs between performance considerations

BELOW USRA also produced designs for two switcher wheel arrangements. Illinois Central No. 321 was a USRA 0-6-0. *Harold K. Vollrath Collection*

BOTTOM Kansas City Terminal Railway No. 38 was a USRA 0-8-0 switcher. *Harold K. Vollrath Collection*

and commonality in structure proved remarkably successful. As to differences between initial parameters and final outcomes for driver axle-loads and cylinder sizes, only one engine departed an inch in cylinder size; the light 4-6-2 and 4-8-2 both ended up a bit lighter; and the heavy 4-6-2 ended up with 32.8 tons per driving axle. (The latter figure was almost ten percent more than first planned, and thus on the hefty side for most railroads.)

The knottiest problem was that of the "specialties" to be included. A short list of such parts and designs includes valve gear, reverse gear, stokers, fire doors, injectors, boiler safety valves, lubricators, air-brake pumps and air-brake systems, draft gear, sanders, cab gauges, generators, lights, tubes, flues, metallic packing, and arch brick. The railroads wanted freedom to specify these items according to their own design practices (which were often proprietary), and the vendors wanted as big a share of the potential market as they could get.

In early March, USRA staff stated a flexible policy for such parts, "sufficiently elastic to admit of all types that can conform to standard dimensions."[24] The problem became so divisive, however, that USRA senior staff, backed by McAdoo, declared a policy requiring that any proprietary devices had to be interchangeable in installation on the locomotives. That is, for example, a Westinghouse or a New York Air Brake compressor, or a Nathan or Hancock injector, or a Ragonnet or Lewis reverse gear, or a Duplex or Standard stoker had to be mountable on the locomotive without significant alteration. Neither the vendors nor railroads were satisfied: Which devices, *exactly*, were going to be included in the *actual* orders?

Locomotive builders Baldwin and Alco did detailed engineering work in April, refining boiler, frame, and machinery specifications for production, and recalculating weight estimates. USRA staff conferred with the three regional USRA offices as to locomotive needs, and with the builders as to production capacity. McAdoo approved USRA's issuance of an order for 1,025 locomotives on April 30, with 555 to Alco and 470 to Baldwin. The Lima Locomotive Works, then a smaller builder, received none of the first order since its plant was then producing at capacity. Total value of the order was $60 million. About the same time, the agency ordered 100,000 freight cars, including boxcars, gondolas, and coal hoppers, at an estimated cost of more than $250 million, distributed over 17 manufacturers.[25]

Meanwhile, as vendors and railroad motive-power superintendents clamored, the argument over the locomotive "specialties" dragged on. Beginning April 1, the USRA's central purchasing committee met with representatives of the component makers. Bids were requested by May 1. The following week, Bentley's locomotive committee, in camera, advised on the bids. But it was not until early June that the purchasing committee issued orders for most of the critical devices. For every item, from brakes to gauges, the purchasing committee played Solomon, allocating among the competing interests. On June 14, in publishing a summary of the orders, a trade writer wryly noted that "some of the orders for the specialties have not yet been definitely settled."[26]

Trade press coverage and editorials had been guarded in tone through March. The advent of the USRA was clearly one of the most important turns-of-events in the whole history of railroads, and every rapidly evolving legal, operational, and purchasing development was reported in extensive detail.

In mid-April, a lead editorial in the weekly *Railway Age* averred that

> ... the Railroad Administration has been in danger of making a serious mistake in the matter of locomotive standardization .... It is hoped ... that the standardized locomotives will be treated as what they are actually, *viz.*: an experiment; that the number of them ordered will not be excessive; and that the individual lines which require other types will be given an early opportunity to obtain them.[27]

In the principal journal reflecting its constituency, this broadside was sending a clear signal to McAdoo, one that its readers – senior railroad managers – could not send personally for fear of ruining future relations. Since early March, USRA had prevented railroads from ordering engines of their own design, at least until the standardization committee's work was done, to free up locomotive manufacturing plant capacity. Meanwhile the locomotive shortage in the field was acute. Now the question was whether USRA intended only that the "flying squadron" of standard engines become a supplement to the existing fleet, or whether the agency was going to force

BELOW Two versions of 2-10-2 locomotives were also produced to USRA designs. Duluth, Missabe & Iron Range No. 510, at Proctor, Minn., in 1951, was a USRA light 2-10-2.
Harold K. Vollrath Collection

BOTTOM Pennsylvania Railroad Class N2s engine No. 8903, at Chicago in 1948, was a USRA heavy 2-10-2. Built with a radial-stay firebox, PRR retrofitted its preferred Belpaire design, seen here.
Harold K. Vollrath Collection

the railroads to accept only the government-owned designs for the duration. Railroad locomotive officers loathed the prospect of having to blend too many of these "orphans" into their rosters after the war. And what if they turned out to be ill-performing designs?

USRA responded by calling a meeting of its regional directors, its head of the transportation division (a direct report of McAdoo's), Walters, railroad representatives, and Vauclain. As a result, USRA attempted to placate the railroads by sending out a memo saying that the agency "appreciated that there are special conditions" affecting locomotive service and promising that any railroad could "make representations to the director general as to its individual necessity for a departure from the standard type."[28]

The memo only poured gasoline on a fire. In late April, the magazine fulminated that "the question of standardization is by no means settled," that the program now underway "was entered upon somewhat hastily," and that all consideration of its practical effect was done after the program had already been decided upon.[29] Then came USRA's April 30 order for the first 1,025 engines, accompanied by an official press release hailing the order as "the first time that any real forward steps" toward engine standardization had ever been made, that the new standard types "are expected eventually to supersede the many miscellaneous types and varieties of locomotives in service" (a tall order, given the 60,000 engines nationwide), and implying strongly that the agency was "looking to the wide standardization" of locomotives.[30]

The next lead editorial howled betrayal. Though unclear in its wording, the USRA's press release had seemed to signal a major shift. Evidently, said the editorial, "none but standard locomotives are to be ordered," a policy that would be contrary to the earlier agency memo that railroads "having peculiar conditions would be allowed to order suitable engines. ... In other words, those in favor of an extreme policy of standardization seem to have prevailed."[31] More discussion blasting the agency filled adjacent pages. McAdoo's inflammatory April 17 speech in El Paso was reprinted (without comment; none was needed). Obviously, a large segment of railroad management was upset.

In a sense they had a right to be. Despite the elliptical pronouncements of the agency over the following weeks, as a practical matter few non-USRA designs were ordered during the agency's tenure, mostly because USRA work, taking precedence, filled up the factories. The Pennsylvania, with its own production facility at Altoona and its unique designs, kept making a few of its own engines – but even that independent-minded company had ultimately to accept 135 government freighters and 30 switchers. The roads with anthracite-burning engines (Delaware & Hudson, Lackawanna, Reading, *et al.*) got some of their own designs, since the USRA types were incompatible with such fuel.

In June, USRA ordered 390 more engines: 245 from Alco, 100 from Baldwin, and 45 from Lima. (This order, however, included 30 non-USRA designed 2-8-0s – anthracite-burners for the Reading.) Alco's greater numbers in the first orders reflected available capacity in its five plants, compared to Baldwin's huge Philadelphia site. Eventually, still more standard engines were built, for a total of 1,856 by government order. The first, a light 2-8-2, rolled out of the Baldwin Works on July 1, with big American flags flying at

ABOVE Mallets in 2-6-6-2 and 2-8-8-2 wheel arrangements were also produced to USRA designs. Wheeling & Lake Erie 2-6-6-2 No. 8002 leads a coal train near Brewster, Ohio, in 1950.
Harold K. Vollrath Collection

RIGHT W&LE 2-6-6-2 No. 8003.
Harold K. Vollrath Collection

BELOW Virginian No. 703, at Page, W.Va., in 1952, was a USRA 2-8-8-2 engine.
Harold K. Vollrath Collection

the front. It went into service on the Baltimore & Ohio within a week. More of the light 2-8-2s, 625, were made than any other USRA type.[32] Derisive managers called the new engines "the McAdoos," a pun on "Mikado."

In late June, the director general approved another policy change: His "circulating reserve" idea was abandoned as impractical, and neither the cars nor engines were to be kept under federal ownership. Ownership of the cars and locomotives would go to the receiving railroads, like other property under federal procurement, with the engines subject to transfer to other lines if new shortages developed. Railroads would finance the purchases themselves, with loans as needed from the USRA's finance and purchases division.[33] McAdoo's heroic conception of the USRA's trust-busting role was fraying around the edges.

A figure instrumental in the advent of locomotive and boiler safety regulation in 1912, Frank McManamy, played a central support role throughout the standardization saga. While still chief inspector for the ICC's Bureau of Locomotive Inspection, McManamy headed the locomotive section within USRA's Division of Transportation, which was responsible for locomotive, car, engineering, and safety issues. McManamy's section concentrated on repair issues, persuading railroads to streamline maintenance procedures to put more engines through the shops. McAdoo had persuaded the shopmen's unions to agree to work longer hours. Railroads then put their shops on multiple shifts, and men worked 60 hours (and some, 72 hours) per week. McManamy also got railroads to cooperate in reducing repair backlogs by sending delayed engines to other railroads' shops with unused capacity; some 80 engines per week were then repaired in "foreign line" facilities. These strategies resulted in a 20 percent jump in the numbers of locomotives repaired per week, thus adding to the serviceable fleet. McManamy's staff developed a five-part classification scheme for locomotive repairs that continued through the 1950s, long after the USRA ceased to be.[34]

Despite all the doubts and criticism, the USRA engines succeeded brilliantly. Performance and power met all expectations, and repair costs proved normal. These engines affected all decisions about steam locomotive boiler and mechanical proportions afterward.

The two switch engines influenced every switcher design to follow. The light 4-6-2 and 2-8-2 were particularly successful and were replicated in whole or in overall proportion and mechanical design by many railroads well after the USRA mandates were gone. The heavy 2-8-2 also became popular and was reordered under USRA authority and afterwards. The heavy 4-6-2, similar in many ways to the largest Pacifics built up to that time (like Alco's experimental No. 50000 of 1911 and the K4s of 1914), was indeed heavy and was used only by the Erie Railroad. But it became the basis for later celebrated 4-6-2 designs, such as the Baltimore & Ohio P-7 and the Southern Railway Ps-4 classes – including No. 1401, which is enshrined in the Smithsonian Institution's National Museum of American History. The USRA heavy Pacific also led to the 4-6-4 Hudson-type of 1925. The USRA 4-8-2s and 2-10-2s were superseded in new construction by the "Super-Power" locomotives developed between 1922 and 1930 by Lima (Chapter 11), but they performed well in the meantime. The USRA 2-8-8-2 was refined by the Norfolk & Western Railway to become the most cost-efficient slow-speed steam freighter ever. The 2-6-6-2

Built by Baldwin in mid-1918, B&O 2-8-2 No. 4500 was the first USRA locomotive.
Courtesy Kalmbach Media

was never very popular on mainline freight, but Baldwin's last steamer for a U.S. road, built in 1949, was a duplicate. Besides the 1,856 locomotives procured by the government, American railroads later ordered, on their own, more than 3,200 additional locomotives through 1944 that were either identical to USRA designs or based substantially on them.[35]

And in overall esthetics, the USRA designs set a pattern for cabs, placement of fittings, domes, and general shape that was perpetuated until the end of steam production. What writer H. Stafford Bryant called "the Georgian locomotive" – a reference to the classical shape and architecture of the typical American steam locomotive of the 1920s through the 1950s – first found expression in the USRA pattern.[36]

Despite war's end in November 1918, the USRA continued to control American railroads until March 1, 1920, when it was formally dissolved. Throughout 1919, railroad managers chafed under the policies they thought would end with hostilities. Unfortunately for them, the USRA was viewed by the public as a great success in running the trains on time, and unions viewed the agency favorably, since their wages and influence had both risen under Wilson and McAdoo. There was serious public debate about whether to continue the USRA indefinitely, resulting in the "Plumb Plan," after an economist who proposed just that.[37] Eventually, railroad executives' pressure on Congress and the president, supported widely by business organizations, got USRA closed down. McAdoo himself remained highly popular among Democratic Party members, leading on several ballots for the 1920 and 1924 presidential nominations before ultimately falling short. He served in the U.S. Senate from 1933 to 1939, representing California.

McAdoo's rousing speech to the El Paso railroaders in April 1918 encapsulated his earlier dream:

> The old private control has been abolished. We have a competitive system of railroads in the United States no longer. When I look at a locomotive or a freight or passenger car passing me, I do not care what name is painted on it – I cannot see it. The only thing I can see on them is "U.S."... I see those great machines going by, pulsating with life and energy, representing the majesty of America, with Uncle Sam's engineers and firemen in the box and Uncle Sam's freight men and trainmen in control.[38]

A love/hate relationship, indeed. The dream died as railroads acquiringMcAdoo's engines quickly painted out the "U.S." and substituted the corporate names for which he did not care. The first USRA locomotive still exists. Baltimore & Ohio No. 4500, completed on July 1, 1918, resides today at the B&O Railroad Museum in Baltimore. The "U.S." is still painted out.

Chapter 10 Notes

1. *New York Times*, Dec. 27, 1917.
2. *New York Times*, *Chicago Tribune*, and *Emporia* (Kan.) *Gazette* editorials, December 28, 1917. (Legendary journalist William Allen White wrote the *Gazette's* editorial.)
3. *Encyclopedia of North American Railroads*, Indiana University Press, 2007, p. 1072.
4. *New York Times*, ongoing coverage during summer 1917.
5. Presidential Proclamation No. 1419, December 26, 1917.
6. *Railway Age*, February 22, 1918, p. 418
7. *The Official Guide of the Railways*, February-March 1918, lists the federal managers for each railroad.
8. John Westwood, *Railways at War*, 1980, Chapter 5. See also *Railway Age*, January-April 1918 for descriptions of USRA rules and restrictions.
9. *Railway Age*, March 8, 1918, p. 509.
10. *Railway Age*, February 22, 1918, p. 418.
11. *Railway Age*, March 1, 1918, p. 446.
12. *Railway Age*, May 10, 2018, p. 1182.
13. *Railway Age*, March 1, 2018, p. 446. See also March 8, 2018, pp. 509-10; and June 14, 1918, p. 1436.
14. *Railway Age*, April 26, 1918, pp. 1067-69.
15. *Railway Age*, May 10, 1918, pp. 1171-72.
16. *Standardized Locomotives Built for the U.S. Railroad Administration*, American Locomotive Co. pamphlet No. 10049, 1920.
17. Original table in *Railway Age*, March 8, 1918, p. 510.
18. *Official Proceedings of the Western Railway Club*, April 15, 1918.
19. Ibid.
20. Ibid.
21. *Railway Age*, March 8, 1918, p. 510.
22. Ibid.
23. *Railway & Locomotive Engineering*, May 1918, pp. 137-39.
24. *Railway Age*, March 8, 1918, p. 510.
25. *Railway Age*, May 3, 1918, p. 1145; May 10, 1918, p. 1169.
26. *Railway Age*, June 14, 1918, pp. 1448-49. For calendar of the purchasing committee and its bid solicitations, see *Railway Age*, May 10, 1918, p. 1170.
27. *Railway Age*, April 19, 1918, p. 1057.
28. *Railway Age*, April 26, 1918, p. 1085.
29. Ibid, p. 1086.
30. Quoted in *Railway Age*, May 3, 1918, p. 1145.
31. *Railway Age*, May 10, 1918, p. 1153. See also pp. 1162 and 1171.
32. George Drury, *Guide to North American Steam Locomotives*, 2015, p. 50.
33. *Railway Age*, June 28, 1918, p. 1558.
34. *Railway Age*, April 26, 1918, pp. 1072-73. Throughout the design standardization exercise, McManamy advised on maintenance and safety issues. In July 1918 he left the Bureau of Locomotive Inspection to join the USRA's reorganized operations division, heading all its engineering functions, and to chair a new committee on standards which replaced Bentley's design panel. The new committee, with some members carrying over from the old one, monitored the new engines' performance after production. In 1920, McManamy collated and published a booklet giving insight into the engineering issues of the standardization debate. See McManamy, *Comments and Criticisms on Standardized Locomotives and Cars*, USRA/Government Printing Office, 1920.
35. *Standardized Locomotives Built for the U.S. Railroad Administration*, American Locomotive Co. pamphlet No. 10049, 1920; William D. Edson, "U.S.R.A. Locomotives," Railway & Locomotive Historical Society *Bulletin*, Fall 1955, pp. 73-93.
36. H. Stafford Bryant, *The Georgian Locomotive*, 1962.
37. Colin Davis, *Power at Odds*, 1997.
38. *Railway Age*, May 10, 1918, pp. 1171-72.

Section III: 1920-1960

From Super-Power to What Might Have Been

Sir Isaac Newton famously wrote that he saw farther because he had stood on the shoulders of giants. Scientific knowledge, and the technology that flows from it, is like that: Understanding begets more understanding, and technology grows and accelerates like a snowball.

The American steam locomotive was no different. First through trial and error, and then with increasing reliance on newly understood principles, locomotives by the 1920s had reached the threshold of their final form. A key catalyst was an upstart builder, the Lima Locomotive Works, and a pair of aggressive new owners who wanted to enter the big time. They hired some of America's best designers from other builders, most notably luring William E. Woodard away from Alco. Together, they pioneered the epoch that became known (from a phrase by Lima's own publicists), as the Super-Power Era.

Within a remarkably short span of time – 1925 through 1927 – the North American two-cylinder steam locomotive reached its climax. Strongly influenced by the success of Woodard's 2-8-4, with its enlarged firebox carried over a four-wheel trailing truck, designers introduced three more new locomotive types between November 1925 and February 1927: the 2-10-4, the 4-6-4, and the 4-8-4, with the last two almost simultaneous in their initial development. The virtue of these locomotives was high horsepower at medium and high speed, rather than raw pull at low speed. The new types therefore extended the Woodard gospel of improved productivity by moving heavy traffic faster. These engines quickly demonstrated their prowess and became popular on many different railroads, with various models produced by all three major locomotive builders.

The 2-10-4 became a favorite of several railroads for fast, heavy mainline freight trains. The Chesapeake & Ohio and the Santa Fe, in particular, developed versions of the type that were truly extraordinary machines. The 4-6-4, well suited to pulling the fastest passenger trains on relatively level track, proliferated to 275 engines on the New York Central and to 212 more on other railroads. The Milwaukee Road's version ran daily schedules at 100-120 mph; the Central's version, the "Hudson," became probably the most famous single class of locomotive in America, due to its indelible association with the fabled *20th Century Limited* and to thousands of miniatures of the engine made by the Lionel Corporation. The 4-8-4, meanwhile, became the most popular type in new steam locomotive orders for mainline service from 1930 onward, for railroads across the country. Unlike the other two types, the 4-8-4 quickly evolved into a true dual-purpose engine, capable of handling both fast freight and heavy passenger trains.

Super-Power principles were also applied to articulated locomotives, most of them of the single-expansion variety by 1920, culminating in Lima's 2-6-6-6 Allegheny-type and in the 4-8-8-4 Big Boy, designed by Alco and Union Pacific. As internal combustion began to threaten steam power, designers sought to push steam technology to the next level with turbines, duplex-drives, poppet valves, and other advances. Given another 10 years or so, these technologies might have gained a beachhead, but they had come too late: The diesel-electric was relentless and its victory was total, leaving a host of "what-ifs" in its wake.

THE CU
IRTHM
ULTRY
1444

Chapter 11

The Formative Contest:

Horatio Allen, the Lima A-1, and Baldwin's No. 60000

DURING THE 1920S, THE QUANTITY OF RESEARCH to improve locomotives' economic performance reached its all-time zenith. A number of conditions supported this phenomenon. National economic conditions improved through most of the decade, except for a few sharp but brief downturns, and railroads became immensely profitable. Yet three things in particular shook railroad executives' confidence in continued long-term profitability: The increasingly strict regulation of freight rates and passenger fares by the Interstate Commerce Commission (stemming from the Hepburn Act of 1906 and subsequent legislation), the 1912 Supreme Court decision favoring injured employees in the Second Employers' Liability cases, and the complete federal takeover in 1918-1920 by the U.S. Railroad Administration.

Clearly, Progressive-era public and congressional sentiment favored tighter regulation to counteract the railroads' monopoly on long-distance travel and freight carriage. A serious strike – the nationwide Shopmen's Strike of 1922, even though broken quickly by the railroads – further rattled management complacency. The upshot was deep and vocal concern for lowering railroad operating costs – especially in running trains.

Out of this concern came strong corporate support for improved locomotive design. More than any other single factor – except fighting off higher wages — buying locomotives that were cheaper to run could add to profits, due to the enormous share of total costs entailed in locomotive fuel, servicing, and repair. The pages of the leading trade journal, *Railway Age* (in the 1920s this journal was no mere monthly, but a weekly magazine of 100 to 150 pages each issue), were filled with announcements and discussions of locomotive innovations, both real and proposed. Another widely circulated journal, *Railway Mechanical Engineer*, covered locomotive design in detail; numerous other publications, such as the *Proceedings of the American Society of Mechanical Engineers*, often featured papers on locomotive research. Major railroads with their own research departments, and builders flush with cash from strong sales, supported these efforts. Engineering faculty at universities – Purdue, Illinois, Northwestern, Columbia, Cornell, and Berkeley among them – eagerly participated.

Boston & Albany 2-8-4 Berkshire type No. 1444 charges through Chatham, N.Y. B&A's main line through the Berkshire mountains of Massachusetts gave this wheel arrangement its name, with B&A (a New York Central subsidiary) recipient of the first production examples.

Courtesy Kalmbach Media

Among railway mechanical engineers, competing philosophies of design solidified. One of the most respected practitioners and spokesmen for a school of design based on "science" was John E. Muhlfeld. He had led the design of the first Mallet compound-expansion locomotive in the United States, on the Baltimore & Ohio. He had also worked as consulting engineer to the Delaware & Hudson in the 1920s, reporting to company CEO Leonor F. Loree, a man of strong opinons when it came to motive-power design. Muhlfeld championed further improvement in design, based on fundamental thermodynamics. For Muhlfeld, innovation was, explicitly, a careful extrapolation of scientific principles. In the case of locomotives, those principles included the natural laws of thermodynamics for heat engines developed by Carnot, Rankine, Moliere, and many others.

Leonor F. Loree.
Cyclopaedia of American Biography, 1914

For Muhlfeld and those of like mind, the royal road to greater efficiency was through compound expansion and higher boiler pressure. The least efficient part of the steam-generating and -using cycle was expansion in the cylinders; in most locomotives, the cylinders converted only around ten percent of the heat energy in the delivered steam to mechanical work. Even to a theoretician, the steam cylinder has some important characteristics – such as stable efficiency over a wide range of rpm or load, and quick reaction to the frequent changes in output needed in railroad operations – that made it superbly suited to locomotives. But as an "expander," the cylinder was subject to inherent heat losses. The valves admitting and exhausting steam gave only an approximation of ideal valve timing; the inside surfaces of cylinders and ports, cooled in every stroke by the contained steam's expansion, wasted energy in reheating those surfaces at every injection of fresh steam; and mechanical limitations of cylinder size and stroke meant that most of the remaining energy went out the exhaust ports anyway. Compound cylinders, in which the exhausted steam of the high-pressure cylinder provided the inlet steam for the larger low-pressure cylinder, could reduce a significant portion of the waste, essentially by providing a better total expansion ratio (*i.e.*, a bigger pressure difference between initial steam inlet and final steam exhaust). As a practical matter, compounding had lost favor on railroads with the widespread adoption of superheating after 1910, but a fresh combination of compound expansion with superheating held out obvious potential for significant improvement in cylinder performance. "Aside from the increased economy," stated Muhlfeld, "the compound cylinder, properly proportioned, gives a much wider speed range for economical fuel consumption and low water rates."[1]

To Muhlfeld, higher boiler pressure was another principal part of the equation. Again, it was elementary thermodynamics: The higher the boiler pressure, the greater the heat energy stored in each cubic foot of steam. This meant improved boiler efficiency from a given amount of fuel burned and, in any arrangement of cylinders, a greater heat drop during expansion, thus extracting more energy. The catch, however, was that a different form of boiler was required to safely contain significantly higher steam pressures than the 200-225 psi customary by the early 1920s.

The conventional fire-tube boiler contains its pressure within the large, water-containing boiler barrel. This form gives an extremely strong and rugged construction. But at around eight feet or more in diameter, the boiler shell is limited as a pressure vessel; at even moderate pressure, the big diameter requires a shell up to an inch thick. At pressures above 300 psi on large locomotives, the boiler becomes impractically heavy. In the water-tube form of boiler, such as found commonly on ships, the pressure-containing parts (containing the boiling water or steam) can be arranged in a series of smaller-diameter drums and tubes. The reduced diameter of these parts permits greatly increased steam pressure for a given wall thickness. Adapted for the severe dimensional limits inherent for locomotives, a water-tube boiler becomes a hybrid form but can safely operate at much higher pressure without excessive overall weight.

In late 1923, Loree allowed Muhlfeld to try out these ideas in a brand-new, experimental locomotive. Since taking the presidency of the cash-rich D&H in 1907, Loree had established a personal style. He built a new, grand office building in downtown Albany, N.Y., a multistory confection of embellished Flemish Gothic that dominated the city's riverfront and commanded one end of State Street, even as the state capitol building dominated the other. He also spoke out vociferously and often on national railroad issues (under the federal regulation of the 1920s, he said railroading was "no longer a business," but a "calamity"), and he made his relatively small railroad an innovator. D&H had its own locomotive-design department and locomotive erecting shops at Colonie, N.Y., which worked closely with Alco's design staff in nearby Schenectady. At the D&H in 1910, Loree and Muhlfeld had introduced a new class of enormous, Alco-built, 0-8-8-0 Mallet compounds (then the most powerful locomotives in the world) that greatly reduced costs for freight-train pusher service. Muhlfeld also helped launch a rebuilding program to upgrade many of the railroad's existing engines. Based on these successes, Loree enthusiastically supported Muhlfeld and the D&H designers.[2]

Constructed by Alco to D&H drawings, the new engine appeared in December 1924 to much comment in the trade press. Muhlfeld immodestly described it later as "an epochal event in steam locomotive development."[3] Named *Horatio Allen* (after the engineer who had run the D&H's *Stourbridge Lion*, the first locomotive in America), the new locomotive was a hefty and conventional 2-8-0 in wheel arrangement, and unconventional in every other aspect. A water-tube boiler permitted a 350-psi boiler pressure, and the two cylinders operated in compound fashion, with high-pressure on the right and low-pressure on the left. The boiler also incorporated Muhlfeld's ideas for improving combustion and heat-transfer efficiency. He significantly enlarged the firebox in proportion to the boiler as a whole and radically increased the ratio of firebox heating surface to total evaporative surface.

Delaware & Hudson 2-8-0 No.1400, *Horatio Allen*, at Colonie, N.Y., in 1924.
Harold K. Vollrath Collection

Over one railroad district, the *Horatio Allen* could substitute for two heavy 2-8-0s and burn one-third less coal hauling the same tonnage, thus slashing both crew and fuel costs. On a test run upgrade with 3,200 gross tons and averaging 16 mph, the *Allen* topped 8.7 percent thermal efficiency at the drawbar, the highest ever achieved to that point, and substantially higher than any previous engine in a test on the road.[4] The *Allen* vividly demonstrated the stakes in seemingly small, incremental improvements in overall efficiency numbers: Running at eight percent efficiency, instead of the typical six percent of a well-designed but normal locomotive, meant a gain of one-third – and thus a one-third reduction in fuel consumption.

Loree wanted the *Allen* thoroughly tested in pool service, covering all seasons. After two years, Alco built the *John B. Jervis*, similar to the *Allen* but with 400 psi in the boiler. Two more D&H *tours de force* appeared, designed by a team led by George Edmonds, chief mechanical officer of the D&H, and

TOP D&H 2-8-0 No. 1401, *John B. Jervis*, at Saratoga, N.Y., in July 1930.
Harold K. Vollrath Collection

MIDDLE D&H 2-8-0 No. 1402, *James Archbald*, at Colonie, N.Y., in 1930.
Harold K. Vollrath Collection

BELOW D&H 4-8-0 No. 1403, *L.F. Loree*, at Colonie, N.Y., in 1935.
Harold K. Vollrath Collection

Muhlfeld: The *James Archbald* appeared in 1930 and the *L.F. Loree* in 1933. Both of these carried 500 psi, and the last was a wondrous triple-expansion 4-8-0 with four longitudinally-opposed cylinders: one high-pressure cylinder, one intermediate-pressure, and two low-pressure. Instead of valves in the usual piston form, it used double-ported poppet valves actuated by a rotary-cam drive. A young Austrian, Julius Kirchhof, employee of Dabeg Industries (a French firm that owned rights to the most successful form of poppet valve), supervised the installation of the valves under Edmonds. The *Loree's* net thermal efficiency in regular service was 10.5 to 12.5 percent, cutting fuel consumption in half for the same work.[5] By 1930, however, the Depression was underway, effectively ending hope of any mass duplication of these engines. Their mechanical complexity was another drawback – particularly on the *Loree* – as was their low-speed operation in an age when increased truck competition was spelling an end to the drag-freight era.

William E. Woodard

William E. Woodard.
Author's Collection

At about the same time that Muhlfeld was contemplating the *Allen*, another engineer was thinking along different lines on the definition of "efficiency." This was William E. Woodard, chief of design at the Lima Locomotive Works. Muhlfeld focused on the locomotive as a heat engine to produce work; Woodard thought about the locomotive as part of a larger system for moving traffic in a given unit of time, with the locomotive generating both revenues and costs in a subtle economic relationship.

Woodard first made headlines in the trade in 1922. That summer, a large 2-8-2 freighter he designed, and which his employer built at its own expense on a contingent agreement with New York Central subsidiary Michigan Central, performed so well that NYC ordered 190 more after only a month of road testing. Altogether, NYC would amass a fleet of 301 similar Mikados, split between Lima and Alco. It was an unprecedented success for Lima, which was an upstart firm in the view of the two established major builders, Alco and Baldwin.

Lima had been building locomotives in its namesake Ohio city since 1879, initially as a mere supplement to its primary businesses of making powered saws for the timber industry and building agricultural implements. The firm's locomotives were relatively small "Shay" types, specially designed for logging railroads after a patent by Ephraim Shay. These engines featured two or three cylinders mounted vertically, driving a jointed gearshaft that powered wheels mounted in two or three swiveling trucks. The gear drive allowed the cylinders to run briskly at low speeds, giving high torque for terrific grade-climbing ability, while the swiveling trucks allowed negotiation of the sharpest

New York Central 2-8-2 No. 8000 was Woodard's first big success at Lima. There would be many others.
Harold K. Vollrath Collection

Shay geared locomotives were a successful niche for Lima, but new owners of the builder in 1916 aspired to bigger things.
Lima Locomotive Works

curves. Both characteristics endeared the Shay to backwoods loggers, and Lima prospered. In 1912, with lumbering in decline and Shay orders waning, the company invested in an expanded plant and went after orders for large, standard engines. In the big leagues, Lima locomotives earned a reputation for excellent craftsmanship but poor design.

Woodard came to the firm in 1916, when new owners bought control. Wall Street financiers Samuel Allen and Joel Coffin had previously organized a couple of companies with interlocked directorates, the Franklin Railway Supply Co. and the American Arch Co., which supplied major locomotive components to builders and railroads. Eventually, the same interests controlled the Superheater Co., which made the superheaters installed in nearly every locomotive in the United States. Sensing that the recently improved but underutilized Lima plant was ripe for takeover, Coffin engaged his friend William H. Winterrowd, then assistant chief mechanical engineer at the Canadian Pacific, to look over the facility. Based on Winterrowd's advice, the Coffin-Allen group negotiated a bargain price. Then, to staff their new acquisition, the group authorized Allen to make premium offers to attract some of the best engineers from Alco, Baldwin, and elsewhere. Woodard came from Alco with a couple of stated conditions: He would have final say on all engineering decisions, and he would need an engineering office in New York – his wife Phebe [*sic*] simply would not move "out west" to Ohio. To Woodard's surprise, Coffin and Allen agreed and offered him the position of vice president of engineering.[6] Most of the engineering staff worked at Lima, while Woodard divided his time between Ohio and New York. To colleagues, his forte was a cerebral but warm leadership style, effective in pulling a diverse and talented team together. He had graduated from Cornell University's Sibley School of Engineering in 1898 and worked for Baldwin and Alco, at the latter company under Francis J. Cole. He had also made a reputation for tackling difficult problems creatively. For an analysis of the instability of certain railcar and tender trucks, he studied them on the road at speed — by putting his head through a hole he had ordered to be cut in the car's floor. Two years into the new regime at Lima, the USRA takeover occurred; Woodard used it as an opportunity to further develop his staff by leading Lima's delegation to the committee that designed the standardized USRA locomotives.[7]

As Woodard assessed opportunities for locomotive performance improvement in the early 1920s, it occurred to him that performance contributed to both cost and revenue for the railroads. Costs were a complex combination of fuel, watering, share of infrastructure (roundhouse stall, wear and tear on track, etc.), maintenance supplies, parts, amortization of purchase price, and, above all, labor. Labor was involved in every aspect of ownership:

fueling, servicing, hostling, repairing, operating. Under the traditional ICC accounting rules, cost accounting in the modern sense was not regularly done in the 1920s, but labor for servicing, maintenance, and repair accounted for one-third to one-half of all locomotive expenses. Crew wages came to about 15 percent. Fuel was about one-third.[8]

Revenue, on the other hand, was something mechanical engineers rarely talked about. Yet surely, locomotives generated revenue by pulling trains. Operating managers did not have a measure for revenue contribution, but they did have a standard measure for aggregate train pulling: ton-miles per train-hour. Clearly, if a locomotive produced more ton-miles per train-hour (TMTH), it generated more revenue in a given unit of time — per hour, per week, per year. A locomotive might be more costly to operate per mile, but if it produced significantly more TMTH, it could handle more traffic, generate more revenue, or handle the same traffic with fewer engines. To boost the TMTH equation, the engine could either pull more cars, or pull faster, or both.

The 2-8-2 freighter that Woodard's team had designed in 1922 had done just that. Weighing only two percent more than the New York Central's then-best 2-8-2 and having only marginally more starting tractive force in its cylinders, the Lima engine gave 17 percent more horsepower at road speeds of 30-40 mph. It thus could pull more cars on a faster schedule, generating about 15 to 20 percent more TMTH. But although it was a simple-expansion engine with a conventional boiler, the Lima performed with improved fuel and water economy compared to other such engines. Incorporated in its design was a larger firebox, hotter superheating, and a waste-heat recovery device (a feedwater heater, which recovered some of the heat otherwise lost in the cylinders' exhaust). To help start the heavier train that it could pull at speed, the locomotive used a "booster," a small, two-cylinder auxiliary steam engine mounted on the trailing truck. Designed by Franklin Railway Supply (part of the Coffin-Allen group), the booster could be used for starting and up to about 15 mph.[9]

A comparison with Muhlfeld's similar-size *Horatio Allen* was striking. While it was far more economical on fuel, the *Allen* was also slower; its two-cylinder compound design (with high-pressure cylinder on one side and low-pressure on the other) was suited to working speeds no higher than about 20 mph – just right for D&H's plodding coal trains. Imbalanced forces in the two cylinders became problematic at higher speed, however. As to the *Allen's* 350-psi, water-tube boiler, it involved a host of unknowns as to maintenance costs; Woodard's 210-psi boiler, though re-proportioned a bit, was thoroughly conventional in construction and fully compatible with skills in existing boiler shops. Engineers could debate the merits, but Lima and Alco built more than 300 copies of its 2-8-2 in two years, while Muhlfeld continued experimenting.

Speed was the thing: not the dramatic, 60-80 mph speeds customary for passenger trains, but 30-40 mph for freights. It was freight that earned the railroads' keep, generating 80 percent of revenues and (in the opinion of most managers) all of the profit. Not that average freight train speed could be raised that much: That average resulted from a host of variables, including the necessarily-slow ascending and descending of long grades, the stop-and-go of myriad local freight trains that set out and picked up cars at industrial sidings alongside main track, and the slow pace of coal and ore trains (which were a major share of all freight but earned a low revenue per ton). But if a fast freight locomotive could pull longer freight trains of manufactures, food, and other high-revenue cargo at significantly higher speed, the economics of locomotive ownership would be powerfully altered for a sizeable portion of the nationwide fleet.

In 1923, Woodard set out to improve on his 2-8-2. He studied all the published or well-known boiler tests (including the Coatesville, Pa., and Gardenville, N.Y. tests, as well as the analyses of his former mentor, Francis Cole), studied the Pennsylvania Railroad's Altoona Test Plant reports, and asked the New York Central to run some tests of locomotive starting and acceleration.

Horsepower would be the principal criterion. At the time, locomotives were rated solely in terms of their initial pull – their "starting tractive effort." Two locomotives might have the same tractive effort, ultimately limited by the number of driving wheels and the axle loading. (Regardless of piston thrust, starting tractive effort is limited to about one-fourth of the weight on drivers; more effort would necessarily entail more weight, which in turn requires more wheels.) But those two locomotives might differ in their pull at speed. In any locomotive, tractive effort falls as speed builds; tractive effort at 40 or 50 mph might be half of the tractive effort at 10. Horsepower is simply the relation of tractive effort and speed. Of two locomotives at the same speed, the one with the greater tractive effort at that speed has the higher horsepower.

Horsepower is also work per unit of time, since a locomotive at 0 mph isn't performing any work. Here Woodard had his most compelling insight: Horsepower is a perfect surrogate for TMTH, which is also a measure of work per unit of time.[10] Engineering and overall operating economics – revenue-generating capacity per unit of time as well as costs – could be correlated.

The first requirement for more horsepower is to burn more fuel. In a steam locomotive, the efficiency of burning coal is limited by the stoking rate per square foot of grate. At high stoking rates (up to 200 pounds per square foot per hour), a great amount of fuel is wasted, sailing unburned out the stack. Keeping the rate down (to 100-150 pounds at high boiler output) is critical to good combustion. A companion requirement is a chassis and running gear capable of high speed. In the case of a freight engine, this meant 30 to 50 mph. Thus, boiler and running gear had to be designed together.

The firebox had to be bigger, that was clear. To meet the horsepower target, 100 square feet of grate would be needed, a size never tried before on an eight-drivered locomotive. Such a grate, however, would be a challenge to locate on the engine. A grate over the rear driving wheels, such as Muhlfeld used for the Allen, would not give enough room for an adequate ashpan under the grate, nor permit the grate size needed in any case. The grate would therefore need to be located behind the drivers. That, however, meant something else never tried before: a four-wheel trailing truck.

Woodard gave the task of designing the truck to one of his young engineers, James Smith. Smith later described the interaction with Woodard:

> Will – everyone called him Will – laid out the problem. We discussed it in detail, every aspect. Later, he was there whenever I had a question. At several points, he made suggestions. But I felt he really put me in charge. He expressed a lot of confidence in how I approached it. He was the best engineering boss I ever had, before or since.[11]

The practical issues were formidable. The long overhang of the engine and cab behind the drivers meant a wicked set of angles between engine mainframe, trailing truck, and tender when on sharp curves. In particular, the angle and lateral displacement between the buffer plates at the rear of the engine and at the front of the tender might become too great on curves in yards, especially through switches at tight crossovers in which a right-hand curve is followed immediately by a left-hand one, or vice versa. Also, truck swing could interfere with installation of the ashpan. To add to the challenge, a booster engine on the second trailing axle, together with the booster's flexibly jointed steam and exhaust connections, had to be accommodated.

Smith worked out the complicated geometry and then suggested an articulated truck, in which the truck frame actually became a hinged extension of the main frame, which ended behind the last driving axle. In his design, the truck transmitted the pulling forces to the tender, and the ashpan was mounted directly to the truck and moved with it. In this way, the angles between mainframe, truck, and tender buffer became acceptable, and ashpan capacity was kept generous. An ancillary benefit of the ashpan design is that it increased draft in the firebox. Woodard called other members of the staff together in several open critiques. Smith's ingenious solution was accepted. It was an important decision, because if the new engine had any tendency to derail on difficult curves, it would be an Achilles heel affecting the practicality of the whole locomotive.

Woodard was as cognizant of thermodynamic laws as Muhlfeld. To boost heat efficiency, he specified a larger feedwater heater and an improved set of superheater units. To improve cylinder efficiency, a long-stroke, Baker valve gear was incorporated, also from the 2-8-2, plus a "limited cutoff" feature. The latter prevented the engine from running at a valve cutoff of more than 60 percent, even at starting, meaning that steam expansion in the cylinders (the "expansion ratio") was improved at all speeds. Limited cutoff was controversial among operating people; such an engine had more uneven torque at 10 mph and below, which made for a slippery engine at lugging speeds. Woodard reasoned, however, that the new engine would be sold based on its performance at 15 to 40 mph; it was not intended as lugger.

The Lima team excelled at "the painstaking refinement of subordinate parts," as David P. Morgan put it. Cutting unneeded weight was a strategy throughout: Cylinders would be cast steel in an integral unit rather than bolted together, saving two tons and holding the cylinders in alignment more permanently; axles would be hollow; main and side rods would be lighter, made of stronger alloy and more carefully designed to shave unnecessary material; lighter rods meant that driving wheel counterweights could be lighter, giving a better-balanced engine with less track pound at speed (see Chapter 4). Part of the machinery weight-saving came from Woodard's new invention of "tandem" rods. At the main driving-wheel crankpin, the main rod had a large clevis, into which the rear side rod fitted. The main rod and rear side rod thus aligned in the same plane, allowing the thrust on the main crankpin to be partly borne by the pin behind. The load on pins was more evenly shared, and the total width of the engine over the cylinders could be reduced by up to five inches, further reducing main pin load for the same piston thrust.

The team designed the boiler for a pressure of 240 psi, 30 pounds more than the 2-8-2. Certainly a higher boiler pressure was desirable. In any boiler, conventional or otherwise, a practical consideration is the build-up of boiler scale. In the 1920s, chemical treatment of boiler water to alleviate scale was spotty and imperfect at best. The rub is not only that scale interferes with heat transfer. When the scale accumulates around a boiler staybolt on the inside of a conventional boiler, or around a structural joint on the inside of a watertube boiler, the upset in local heat transfer puts an extra mechanical stress on the bolt or joint. The scale is thus an insulator, where insulation is not wanted. That extra stress leads to cracking at the bolt or joint. A local thermal imbalance from any given quantity of scale is more severe the higher the boiler pressure, since a higher boiler temperature goes along with a higher pressure. Federal rules then – and still in effect today – required a steam locomotive boiler to be washed out at least every month. In many regions of the country, where mineral content in water is high, railroads had to wash out boilers more frequently to keep ahead of scale. At each washing-out, a day of engine service was usually lost, and several roundhouse men labored to drop the fire, vent off the remaining boiler pressure, remove all the wash-out plugs, flush and examine the boiler, carefully reinstall the plugs, refill the boiler, and lay a new fire. At the conclusion of the process, the boiler was brought back up to pressure, but very slowly, in order to prevent undue mechanical strain from overall thermal change. (A large boiler expands up to two inches

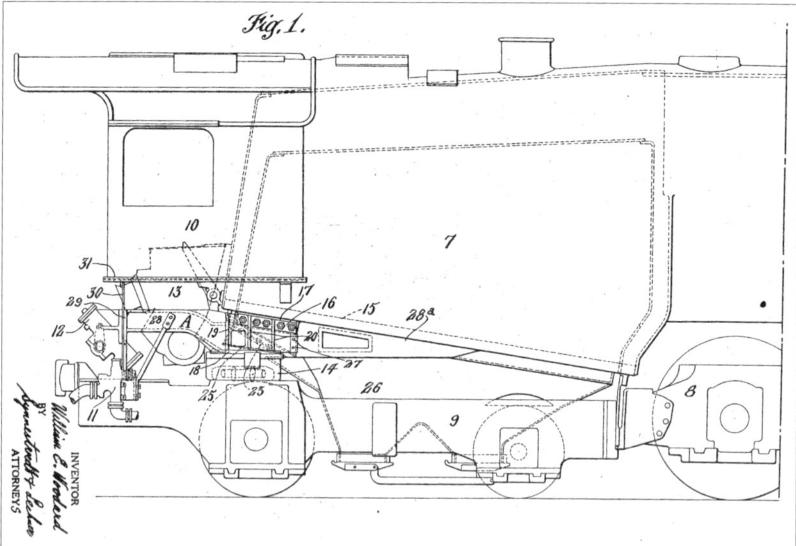

RIGHT Lima engineer James Smith was an unsung hero: Without his articulated trailing truck, shown here in a patent drawing, Super Power might have remained only a theory. *United States Patent Office*

BELOW The articulated truck transmitted the pulling forces from locomotive to tender, thus shortening the locomotive frame and allowing the bigger grate area essential to Super Power. *Courtesy Kalmbach Media*

in length from cool to hot.) Woodard's team pushed up boiler pressure as far as it dared, given the widespread caution of maintenance officials concerning boiler servicing and repair costs.[12]

The Berkshire

The new locomotive appeared in January 1925. A clever publicist for Lima, George Basford, had it named the "A-1" to symbolize this new departure for both Lima and locomotive design. Weight on drivers and starting tractive effort was virtually the same as the 2-8-2. The larger boiler was some 27 tons heavier, with the extra weight carried by Jim Smith's four-wheel truck, and so the engine was a 2-8-4, a new wheel arrangement. In February, Lima employees took the engine from Ohio to Selkirk, N.Y., for an exhaustive battery of road tests on the Boston & Albany, another New York Central subsidiary. With an awkward-looking, wooden wind deflector on the front to shield technicians taking indicator cards, and with a dynamometer car spliced in behind the tender to record drawbar pull and speed, the A-1 hauled trains back and forth across the Berkshire Mountains for almost two months.

The results were astonishing. Generally, the A-1 consumed 12 to 20 percent less fuel per horsepower-hour than the Lima 2-8-2, while putting out about 3,400 to 3,600 horsepower at the tender drawbar, 900 more on average than the 2-8-2. A comparative test in April was particularly revealing. After a thorough inspection in the roundhouse to be sure it was in top condition, one of NYC's Lima 2-8-2s left Selkirk for a planned nonstop run to North Adams Junction, Mass., with a train of about 1,700 tons. Forty-seven minutes later, the A-1 followed with about 2,300 tons, switching to a parallel track some distance east. An hour and fifteen minutes after its departure from Selkirk, the A-1 and its train pulled even with the 2-8-2 and passed it. An hour later, the 2-8-4 arrived in North Adams, ten minutes ahead of the other train. Such a performance, in comparison with an engine just two years old and until then considered one of the best general-freight locomotives anywhere, challenged the trade to rethink the economic measures of engine performance.

The A-1 and dynamometer car then departed on a tour across the Northeast and Midwest, hauling freight trains on seven railroads. Everywhere it went, the A-1 earned accolades. In October, it sped a well-known passenger train, the Milwaukee Road's *Pioneer Limited*, on its 421-mile route between Chicago and Minneapolis – its 63-inch drivers notwithstanding. The Boston & Albany

Lima A-1 2-8-4 during evaluation on the Boston & Albany. Tests showed that the new locomotive produced about one-third more horsepower than the 2-8-2 depicted on page 213, with a fuel saving of up to 20 percent.
Courtesy Kalmbach Media

ABOVE Texas & Pacific's early adoption of the 2-10-4 wheel arrangement gave the type its most common name: Texas. *Harold K. Vollrath Collection*

RIGHT Building on the success of the A-1's evaluation, Boston & Albany 2-8-4 Berkshire engines are under construction at Lima. *Courtesy Kalmbach Media*

ordered the first batch of production 2-8-4s and took the privilege of naming the type, calling it the Berkshire.

At the same time the A-1 was on its first trials, Woodard's team made drawings for an even more-powerful machine, a 2-10-4, after the Texas & Pacific Railroad expressed interest. Dubbed the Texas type, the elongated locomotive shared all the features of the A-1 except the external dry pipe and, although the 100 square-foot grate area was the same, a modest combustion chamber was added, which the A-1 did not have. (Woodard had not included a combustion chamber in the A-1 in order to minimize the number of staybolts, to hold down boiler repairs. The power of the bigger 2-10-4, about 4,100 drawbar hp, necessitated greater firebox volume.) T&P bought the first ten 2-10-4s before the first production 2-8-4s went to the Boston & Albany.[13]

In the mid- and late-1920s, Woodard gave several lectures to professional audiences, describing and explaining his horsepower gospel in persuasive economic terms: Individually, high-horsepower engines could handle heavier trains at less expense and, in fleet use, such engines could handle the same or greater traffic with fewer locomotives. The controlling economics, explained Woodard, lay in "increasing the usefulness of each mile of main line track." And by 1929 he could fairly state,

> Locomotives embodying [the A-1's design] characteristics have made such pronounced reductions in fuel consumption and increases in gross ton-mile-per-hour output, along with lower maintenance, that these principles of construction are now very generally accepted by the leading railroads as essential to locomotives designed for producing maximum tonnage output with minimum operating costs.[14]

Publicist Basford coined the term "Super Power," which Lima used in a blitz of ads in the trade journals starting in 1925. Lima produced a short movie to explain the economics, and Woodard and other Lima officers used it on the lecture circuit. The competing steam builders had never been so aggressive in marketing. Coffin and Allen no doubt delighted in the strong sales that resulted. Lima was now on the map as a major player in the locomotive trade.

Baldwin 60000

Alco and Baldwin took note. For several years prior to 1925, they, too, had been promoting ideas for advanced locomotives. Baldwin especially, under president Samuel Vauclain, pushed the notion of higher steam pressures and multi-cylinder, compound drive. As a designer at Baldwin in the 1890s, Vauclain had come up with a form of four-cylinder compounding that was somewhat popular for a brief time. In the early 1920s it seemed clear to Vauclain and those on his design staff, as it was clear to Muhlfeld, that after superheating, the next step was a revival of compounding together with better boilers.

In mid-1925, with the A-1 trials catching everyone's attention, Vauclain determined that Baldwin would build its own demonstrator locomotive and retake the company's accustomed leadership. The designers, including Paul T. Warner and Lawford H. Fry, knew that part of the Lima formula was undeniably sound: speed and horsepower. The question was whether Baldwin might best Lima at its own game with a design of greater boiler and machine efficiency.[15]

To achieve a significantly higher boiler pressure, a water-tube type boiler was laid out, of a somewhat different configuration from Muhlfeld's. The Baldwin boiler would be much larger, with fewer steam drums in the water-tube firebox but, as in the D&H boilers, also without staybolts. Pressure was set at 350 psi, with high superheat. Grate area, at 82.5 square feet, was smaller than the A-1; the higher boiler efficiency would mean less coal fired per unit of time.

Instead of an eight-drivered locomotive, No. 60000[16] would be ten-drivered, giving the potential of 25 percent more pull at any given speed. Instead of a two-cylinder, simple-expansion engine with limited cutoff, the 60000 would be a two-stage, three-cylinder compound, with the three cylinders grouped at the front. The middle cylinder (the high-pressure one) would crank on the centerline of the engine, connected to a crank-axle on the second pair of drivers. The two outside cylinders, both low-pressure and with pistons connected to the third driving axle, would take their steam from the middle cylinder's exhaust. This arrangement gave an excellent expansion ratio and much smoother torque than any two-cylinder locomotive. With the smoother torque, actual tractive effort at speed could be higher per axle without slipping. On the road, the working pull would be the equivalent of many twelve-drivered engines of equal axle loading.[17]

To much fanfare, the new locomotive rolled out of Baldwin's Eddystone, Pa., plant in March 1926. The final configuration was a 4-10-2, with a four-wheel lead truck required to carry the extra front-end weight of the three cylinders and associated machinery. After steam tests and break-in runs, Baldwin sent the engine to the Pennsylvania Railroad's Altoona Test Plant in August and September. Results were impressive. The Altoona engineers ran the engine at equivalent speeds of 15 to 40 mph, exceeding 4,500 horsepower in the cylinders at 37 mph, the highest horsepower the plant had ever recorded. Drawbar horsepower was somewhat less, as expected, and a bit better than the Lima 2-10-4. Fuel rates per horsepower-hour were less than the A-1, but surprisingly, not by much: 2.7 to 2.8 pounds of coal per horsepower-hour for the 60000, versus 2.9 to 3.0 for the A-l – a seven percent improvement for the Baldwin.[18] The rotational balance of the engine on Altoona's treadmill was remarkable; its smooth torque greatly reduced "the usual vibrations" at higher rpm.[19]

Starting in October, Baldwin sent the 60000 on a nationwide sales tour. The Pennsylvania Railroad, the Baltimore & Ohio, the Erie, the Burlington, the Santa Fe, the Southern Pacific, and the Great Northern tested the engine extensively on heavy freight and a few passenger trains. On the Southern Pacific, which had successfully introduced three-cylinder, simple-expansion locomotives in California's Sierra Nevada, the 60000 burned oil for its road tests and was given minor machinery repairs after an accumulated 75,000 miles. In ceremonies at SP's Sacramento Shops, the 60000 stood before an admiring throng, clad in fresh, dark purple paint with gold-leaf trim. An ICC inspector, however, became the skunk at the garden party and refused to let the locomotive operate further once he saw the 350-psi boiler pressure. It took a couple of frantic calls to the ICC's locomotive safety office in Washington to call off the conscientious local inspector.[20]

In February 1928, the 60000 returned to Eddystone, having failed to attract a single order. Railroad officers' objections, although tactfully voiced, concerned the three-cylinder drive and the boiler. Maintenance access to the middle cylinder was difficult, increasing labor cost for adjustments and repairs. But mostly, it was the boiler that gave pause. Washing the boiler monthly and removing scale was far more time- and labor-consuming. There were more than 100 washout plugs to remove and replace in order to clean the insides of the firebox tubes and the hollow mudring, and there were heavy, bolted plates to remove in order to clean the twin drums at the top of the firebox. This compared to approximately 12 to 20 plugs in a conventional boiler.[21]

Baldwin demonstrator 4-10-2 No. 60000 was built in response to Lima's engineering and marketing. Its water-tube boiler was expensive to maintain, and it failed to attract a single order. It was sold by Baldwin in 1933 to Philadelphia's Franklin Institute for one dollar. Museum officials Dr. Henry Butler Allen (at left) and Richard Lloyd formally accept the locomotive from BLW President Charles Brinley (at right) in 1939, after a new exhibit hall had been opened to accommodate it. *Dan Cupper Collection*

The 60000 might have been able to duplicate the horsepower of the Lima A-l or a 2-10-4, but its downtime for boiler service would have been much worse, its machinery repair more costly, and its fuel economy insufficient to make up the difference. Its rejection in the marketplace must have been a blow to Baldwin's pride as well as its sales.

In the fall of 1933, with the Depression at high tide, Baldwin sold the 60000 for $1 to Philadelphia's Franklin Institute, a science museum, where it remains one of the most popular exhibits. The 60000 wasn't the game-changer that Baldwin hoped, but at least Philadelphia has an impressive souvenir of its one-time biggest employer.

And what of the A-1? Sold to the Illinois Central and eventually numbered 8049, it ran regularly as just another pool engine into the early 1950s. Without reflection on the part of its owner, it was scrapped soon after, thus completing its life-cycle economics.

Chapter 11 Notes

1. John E. Muhlfeld, quoted in *Encyclopaedia Britannica*, "Locomotive," 1949 edition, volume 14, p. 280b.
2. David P. Morgan, "Loree's Locomotives," *Trains*, July 1952, pp. 20-25.
3. John E. Muhlfeld, quoted in *Encyclopaedia Britannica*, "Locomotive," 1949 edition, volume 14, p. 281c.
4. Ibid., p. 281d.
5. Ibid.
6. Author's 1972 interview George H. Woodard (W.E. Woodard's son), at Bryn Athyn, Pa. According to the younger Woodard, Winterrowd, a 1907 Purdue graduate, came to Lima in 1923 as assistant to the president, after serving as chief mechanical officer on CP in 1918. He became a Lima vice president in 1927, vice president of Franklin Railway Supply in 1934, and vice president of operations at Baldwin in 1939. He died on December 7, 1941 (*New York Times* obituary, appeared the following day).
7. Ibid.
8. Extrapolated to the 1920s from Paul Kiefer, *A Practical Evaluation of Railroad Motive Power*, 1948, p. 48.
9. Alfred W. Bruce, *The Steam Locomotive in America*, 1952, pp. 261-62.
10. HP = (T x V) / 375, where T is tractive effort, V is speed, and 375 is a conversion factor to make measurements consistent.
11. Author's 1972 interview with James Smith, via telephone and at Orleans, Mass.
12. Neither D&H nor Muhlfeld revealed specific boiler maintenance costs for the four experimental engines, and how these engines might have fared in true fleet use is unknown. Water quality in the area served by the D&H was good.
13. William L. Withuhn, "The Great Dynamometer Test of Locomotive 610," *Trains*, February 1978, pp. 33-37.
14. "Super-Power Versus Reassigned Locomotives for Secondary Service," *Proceedings of the New England Railroad Club*, April 9, 1929, p. 86.
15. Fry was the author of a seminal book, *A Study of the Locomotive Boiler* (1924); Warner and Fry co-authored Baldwin's trade book, *Locomotive Number 60000: Description and Results of Plant and Road Tests* (1928).
16. The editors have chosen to render the locomotive's number as 60000 – without a comma – since that was how Baldwin referred to it. Like Alco's earlier 4-6-2 No. 50000, Baldwin's machine bore the builder's serial number, nominally the 60,000th locomotive built by the firm.
17. Warner and Fry, *Locomotive No. 60000: Description and Results of Plant and Road Tests* (1928).
18. Ibid., p. 23. See also "Modern Locomotive Design," a paper by William E. Woodard in *Official Proceedings of the New York Railroad Club*, January 1927, pp. 8234-55.
19. Fred Westing, "Baldwin's Barnstorming Behemoth," *Trains*, April 1954, pp. 50-56.
20. Ibid., p. 56.
21. The number of boiler washout plugs is based on the author's personal inspection at Philadelphia's Franklin Institute, where No. 60000 is a permanent exhibit.

Chapter 12

The Steam Locomotive's Final Form:

The Texas Type

THE 2-10-4, 4-6-4, AND 4-8-4 WHEEL ARRANGEMENTS were closely related to each other, shared common roots, and sprang from common understandings by engineers of the design issues involved. This chapter treats the first of these types.

The first 2-10-4s, intended for freight duty, followed hard on the heels of the original Lima A-1 2-8-4. Even as the A-1 began its initial road trials in February 1925 on the Boston & Albany, mechanical officers of the Texas & Pacific Railroad in Dallas began discussions with Lima staff for an enlargement of the 2-8-4. Setting the context for the T&P were the ongoing efforts of president John L. Lancaster in the 1920s to substantially upgrade his railroad, which connected New Orleans, Shreveport, and Texarkana with El Paso. The Texas economy was booming. As rail freight traffic grew, T&P managers sought commensurate increases in capacity – and competitive advantages against rival Southern Pacific. Lancaster oversaw the development of the first modern hump yard in Texas (near Fort Worth), the installation of heavier rail on T&P's entire main line, and, later, the commissioning of one of the first centralized traffic control (CTC) systems in the region, all to reduce net transit time.[1]

Locomotives that could move freight faster dovetailed with Lancaster's strategy. By early 1925, T&P mechanical engineering staff under Mechanical Superintendent R.Q. Prendergast had examined designs for Mallet articulateds and Alco proposals for three-cylinder locomotives. Prendergast's staff paid close attention to the A-1 tests back East. The performance comparison (as described in Chapter 11) between the A-1 and the almost-new Boston & Albany 2-8-2 in April with freight trains between Selkirk, N.Y., and North Adams, Mass., certainly was noted, as it was throughout the railroad trade. By the time the A-1 was on its nationwide demonstration tour, which included runs on T&P parent Missouri Pacific, Lima and T&P designers had already agreed to a specification. The new engines would each have ten driving wheels rather than eight, since T&P wanted tractive force at least as great as one of its large 2-10-2s. In July, T&P formally contracted for ten of the Lima design. They were to be the first commercially ordered Super Power locomotives (a term coined by Lima to describe the principles pioneered by William Woodard).

Pennsylvania Railroad 2-10-4 engine No. 6439 climbs Horseshoe Curve, west of Altoona, Pa., with a westbound freight train in 1939.
Courtesy Kalmbach Media

TOP Texas & Pacific 2-10-4 No. 635, delivered in 1928, was part of T&P's third order of 2-10-4s.
Gerald M. Best, Courtesy Kalmbach Media

ABOVE Lima builder's photo of T&P 2-10-4 No. 650.
Courtesy Kalmbach Media

Classed as I-1 on the T&P, the first of the new locomotives arrived at Lancaster Shops, Fort Worth, in November 1925. Looking like an elongated A-1, the I-1 incorporated all the features that became Super Power hallmarks:

- A four-wheel trailing truck supporting the added weight of an enlarged and more efficient firebox.
- A "Type E" superheater, with greatly increased heating surface compared to earlier forms, as developed by Elesco, a Lima-associated firm.
- A closed-type feedwater heater, as developed also by Elesco, boosting net evaporative power.
- A front-end throttle (meaning that it was mounted in the smokebox instead of the then-conventional location in the steam dome, putting the throttle closer to the cylinders, where the steam would be used, thus improving responsiveness).
- Baker valve gear, giving long, 8¾-inch valve travel.
- "Limited compensated cut-off," with a maximum cutoff of 60 percent, to economize on steam while working hard at low and medium speeds.
- Woodard's tandem-rod drive, with main-rod thrust divided over the third and fourth driving axles.
- A locomotive "booster" engine mounted on the trailing truck for extra low-speed pull, as developed by another Lima-associated firm, Franklin Railway Supply.

The I-1 class also incorporated two features not found on the A-1: a combustion chamber, extending the furnace 42 inches farther forward into the boiler, and a pair of Nicholson thermic syphons, to increase direct evaporative heating surface and to improve water circulation in the boiler around the firebox. All this innovation cost money. At an average of $104,000 each, the I-1 was one of the first two-cylinder locomotives to be priced at more than $100,000.[2]

Since the I-1 class burned oil, a common fuel for steam locomotives in the Southwest, a burner and a firepan with damper replaced the grate and ashpan. Grate area (measured the same way for both coal- and oil-burners) was a huge 100 square feet, the same as the A-1, and so the two designs shared the same firebox "foundation ring," the one-piece, rectangular casting that joins the base of the firebox to the boiler. Diameter of the boiler courses and the number of flues and tubes varied slightly from the A-1, to accommodate a boiler evaporation sufficient to power ten drivers instead of eight. The most significant change was the addition of a short combustion chamber to the I-1 firebox.

The furnace (*i.e.*, firebox) design displayed Woodard's sagacity in the eternal trade-offs between power capacity on the one hand and maintenance expense and downtime on the other. The A-1 did not have a combustion chamber, which was surprising to some in the trade, since locomotive designers by then appreciated that higher boiler output at good efficiency requires proportional increases not only in grate area, to burn more coal, but also in furnace volume, to permit proper combustion of the fuel being burned. In the early 1920s, however, added furnace volume in the form of a combustion chamber meant possible maintenance trouble in two ways: more staybolts, and longer, riveted firebox seams.

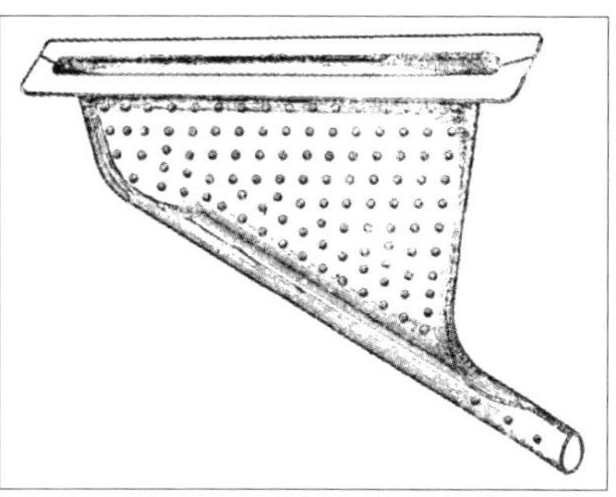

Mounted with its syphon tube at the front of the the firebox, the thermic syphon conducted relatively cold water from the bottom of the boiler to the crown sheet of the firebox, thus improving heat transfer and efficiency. This is a Nicholson design of the same basic type installed on the T&P I-1 class.
Author's Collection

A firebox is made of relatively thin sheets – usually about one-quarter of an inch thick – to provide maximum thermal transfer. A firebox and the hundreds of threaded staybolts that support it within the boiler flex under normal temperature changes. A poorly designed firebox, or a well-designed one abused in service, can break several staybolts per month. At the same time, long, riveted seams knitting firebox sheets together are prone to springing leaks in such a flexible structure. Replacing staybolts was routine but meant downtime for the engine; a good boilermaker could change a staybolt in about 30 minutes. Repairing a leaky riveted seam in a firebox, on the other hand, could be something of a nightmare and could involve far more downtime. If rivets had worked loose such that recaulking the seam from inside the firebox with an air hammer didn't work, there were two choices: welding the leaky seam, or if welded repairs failed and leaks became severe, removing the entire firebox for re-riveting or replacement.

In the A-1, requisite design ratios among coal firing rate, BTU input, grate area, and firebox volume were achieved without a combustion chamber. As can be seen in comparison to later, more advanced coal-burners of similar or greater power, the A-1's grate is actually overgenerous in proportion to maximum boiler evaporation. More than achieving a low firing rate per square foot of grate – clearly a principal goal – Woodard also achieved an adequate furnace volume in the A-1 by means of an enormous grate size. Given the controversies that had raged for years at Master Mechanics' Association conventions over the problems encountered in keeping ever-bigger fireboxes and combustion chambers in repair, the Lima designers surely knew the value of minimizing such maintenance headaches.

In the more powerful I-1, however, greater furnace volume over the A-1 was unavoidable. And with oil as fuel, designers knew that the I-1's firebox grate area could have been smaller provided the added total volume was there.

Woodard's trick in using the same foundation ring as the A-1 meant that the I-1's combustion chamber size was a minimum for the needed volume. Secondarily, the common ring avoided the expense of yet another big mold in the foundry.

In contrasting the performance of the new I-1 to the largest engines on the T&P up to that time, the results were dramatic. When the A-1 had competed with the Boston & Albany 2-8-2, the older locomotive was no slouch, being one of the most advanced of its type. But the T&P's largest engines before the Limas arrived were an embodiment of conservative design from the preceding era. The T&P's 44 G-1 class 2-10-2s, Baldwin-built between 1916 and 1919, had the same size and number of driving wheels as the I-1, had a booster, had superheating, and were only about three tons lighter per driving axle. The new I-1, though, had 50 pounds more steam pressure, 50 percent more firebox heating surface (including the syphons), and nearly 2.4 times the superheater heating surface. Predicted pull at 40 mph was 50 percent greater.

From January through March of 1926, T&P operating staff compiled the numbers: Comparing the I-1 class to G-1s, train tonnage per locomotive jumped 44 percent, average train speed shot up 33 percent, and fuel burned per ton-mile dropped 42 percent. Fireboxes and combustion chambers performed reliably. Repair costs were comparable: 27.3 cents per mile for the G-1s, which were relatively young at six to ten years old; 19.4 cents per mile for the brand-new I-1s. The trade press buzzed: Such a combination of simultaneous tonnage increase, speed increase, and fuel-consumption decrease had never before been recorded.

Texas & Pacific took the prerogative of naming the new type: "Texas," of course. President Lancaster approved orders for 70 I-1s in five batches from Lima through 1928, out of a total T&P locomotive fleet of 370 in that year.[3]

One serious problem immediately arose, which affected all I-1s until they were later rebuilt: counterbalancing. Prendergast assigned Hugh D. Hollis, then mechanical engineer and later chief mechanical officer for T&P, to the case. At 65 mph or better, the imbalance became severe. In a few observed but apparently isolated cases, the main drivers lifted up and, part of a revolution later, slammed back down in a horrendous oscillation. "You could actually see daylight under the drivers," said Hollis.[4]

This experience was scary, as well as an engineering puzzle. The I-1 and the A-1 shared similar running machinery, including drivers of identical size: 63 inches in diameter, which was then typical for fast freighters. But the main and side rods of the more-powerful I-1 were heavier. In consultation with Lima, it became apparent that there was insufficient room in the main driving wheels for the proper weights to balance an I-1's heavier rods, especially the main rods. Not enough lead could be added to the main drivers opposite their crankpins to achieve the amount of "overbalance" called for by the accepted formulas. Lima engineers assured T&P, however, that rotational balance was well within accepted tolerances. Only if some lead were actually missing should there be any excessive imbalance at high rpm. In the latter event, the heavy main and side rods would actually be underbalanced.[5]

Based on his field observations, Hollis suspected that T&P's 110-pound (per-yard) rail and associated track structure might have something to do with it. Could it be that, at unique combinations of wheel rpm and rail

ABOVE Chicago Great Western's Texas-types were substantially identical to T&P's: Coal fuel, a second sand dome, and Coffin or Worthington feedwater heaters were the biggest differences.
Collection of Ernest Sevde, Courtesy Kalmbach Media

LEFT Central Vermont's 2-10-4s were atypical, since small grates and 60-inch drivers precluded speeds faster than 35 mph.
Jim Shaughnessy, Courtesy Kalmbach Media

stiffness affected by temperature, a vertical harmonic vibration was set up between an I-1's imbalanced main driver and the rail, perhaps amplified by the driver springs, thus causing wheel lift to occur at a speed much lower than calculated?[6] Hollis had no working theory to predict when or if such a harmonic vibration could occur, but traditional wheel-balancing calculations ignored this possibility altogether. The high piston thrust of the I-1 was perhaps another factor; it was well known that the angle of a main rod at its point of maximum thrust, combined with sufficient piston force at high rpm, tended to lift a main driver. But, in terms of classical analysis, such forces were far outweighed by the static load on the wheel. Lima and T&P engineers could not agree on a solution.[7]

The result was that the T&P operating department imposed a 45-mph speed limit on the I-1 class. Although this limit flew in the face of the professed objective of higher freight-train speed, the productivity of the I-1s was little affected. They could still maintain a much higher average speed than the G-1s, and that is what counted in the statistics. Beginning in 1937, and using expertise from Baldwin, T&P rebuilt all the I-1s with hollow cast main driving wheels and lighter-weight rods. After that, the I-1s were good for 70 mph, although they were normally limited to 60. The higher speed limit helped them to handle record levels of traffic during World War II, although average running speed was still 40-45 mph.[8]

ABOVE Canadian Pacific was one of the few roads to use 2-10-4s – which it called Selkirks, after one of the mountain ranges they traversed – in passenger service. Here, CPR Class T1b No. 5927 leads the transcontinental *Dominion* west of Banff, Alberta.
Canadian Pacific

RIGHT Bessemer & Lake Erie 2-10-4 No. 647 hauls hopper cars near Conneaut, Ohio.
Courtesy Kalmbach Media

BELOW Builder's photo of Kansas City Southern 2-10-4 No. 900. The KCS engines, resplendent in green boiler jackets, were Lima's last 2-10-4s, and thus, arguably, the type's ultimate expression.
Courtesy Kalmbach Media

North American railroads bought a total of 429 2-10-4s through the 1940s. Buyers included Santa Fe, Chicago Great Western, Chesapeake & Ohio, Burlington, Bessemer & Lake Erie, Central Vermont, Pennsylvania (which acquired the largest 2-10-4 fleet of all, 125), Canadian Pacific, and Kansas City Southern – all lines suited to the 2-10-4's characteristic of extraordinary power at medium to high speed, 30 mph or better.

C&O's T-1 design

The 2-10-4 reached maturity in 1930, with the Chesapeake & Ohio's T-1 class. As the number of 2-10-4s increased after 1925, the number of 2-8-4s increased even faster, mostly on Eastern and Midwestern roads, since the smaller type was well matched to the topography and typical freight train sizes in those regions. Between 1927 and 1929, the Erie Railroad bought 105 2-8-4s, the largest such fleet on a single railroad. These Erie locomotives led directly to the C&O 2-10-4.

Both the Erie and the C&O were controlled by the Van Sweringen brothers of Cleveland, who in 1929 also controlled the Nickel Plate Road and the Pere Marquette. In 1929, an "Advisory Mechanical Committee" (AMC) was formed for the Van Sweringens' railroads, headed by Erie's chief mechanical officer, William G. Black. The committee's role was more than advisory; its mandate was to approve new locomotive designs for any of the lines and to standardize where possible.

In 1926-1927, Black directly supervised the design of the Erie 2-8-4s. Known as the S class, they were a considerable enlargement on the A-1. Black's staff consulted with all three commercial locomotive manufacturers, not just with Lima. While the A-1 and the T&P I-1 were entirely Lima designs, the Erie took back the engineering lead, reflecting the traditional builder-customer relationship.[9]

Black wanted the basic layout of the A-1, but with a host of changes:

- A bigger boiler for even more horsepower, achieved with larger-diameter boiler courses, allowing more heating and superheating surface.
- Larger-diameter driving wheels in order to avoid counterbalancing difficulties at speeds above 45 mph, as experienced by the I-1.
- An open-type feedwater heater, which Black regarded as less prone to internal buildup of scale, as compared to the closed-type preferred by Lima.
- A front-end throttle of the multiple-valve type rather than the single-valve form on the A-1 and first I-1s.
- A simplified form of trailing truck – a "Delta"-type truck rather than the Lima "articulated back-end" truck used on the A-1 and I-1 – thus permitting a deeper firebox and more furnace volume than the A-1.

The larger boiler and heavier frame cost weight: An S-class came in at 69,000 pounds on each driving axle, close to the maximum tolerable on most railroads. Since the A-1 was initially a manufacturer's demonstrator locomotive, intended to motivate sales from many different railroads with different track standards, Lima's staff had purposefully kept weight down to 62,000 pounds per driving axle, regarded by railroad civil engineers as moderate. T&P, for its part, had specified an even lighter axle load of 60,000 pounds.[10]

"Advances are always initiated as a result of comparisons," said Will Woodard the year after the Erie's S-class began to appear.[11] Black had a railroad

Erie S-class 2-8-4 Berkshire No. 3303, at Marion, Ohio, in 1949. The Van Sweringen roads wanted a heavier 2-8-4 than Lima's A-1 (compare with the photo on p. 219), and their Advisory Mechanical Committee design became the basis for the 2-10-4s on sister-road Chesapeake & Ohio.
Harold K. Vollrath Collection

capable of taking a heavy axle load and he made his own comparisons. Then he rubbed a bit of salt into the wound of a lost sale for Lima by ordering his first 2-8-4s from rival builder Alco. Eventually, though, all three manufacturers shared in the total run of 105 engines, in four sub-classes.

In 1929, the AMC considered what might be needed to augment the Chesapeake & Ohio's five-year-old 2-8-8-2 articulated locomotives on the heavy coal trains that ran between northeastern Kentucky and the Lake Erie shore at Toledo, a distance of about 250 miles. As later described in the trade press, the operational goal was to "handle the entire train in a continuous movement from Russell [Ky.] through Columbus to Toledo, eliminating the re-handling of the train and a locomotive change at Columbus."[12] It was a goal that exemplified the notion of reducing transit time (and thus increasing revenue per unit of time) by thinking not just of locomotive performance, but by thinking of performance in a system context.

The AMC borrowed an S-3 class 2-8-4 from the Erie, jacked up its boiler pressure a bit, and ran an extended series of tests between Russell and Toledo. The larger, 70-inch-diameter drivers on the S-3 proved their worth, giving a smoother ride and allowing the engine to build up speed rapidly on flatter sections of track in order to carry train momentum up steeper sections. At speeds of 25 mph or below, however, the S-3 simply lacked enough driving wheels to maintain sufficient pull for the heavy trains the C&O intended. Chessie's big H-7a 2-8-8-2s, in contrast, had more boiler capacity and plenty of low-speed pull. But their 57-inch drivers, though not plagued with the severe balance problems of the T&P I-1, hindered acceleration.

The AMC's conclusion was that a new design for the Russell-Toledo coal trains should have the 70-inch drivers of the S-3 and at least the boiler power of the H-7a. The committee also concluded that drivers larger than 63 inches could not be combined successfully with an adequate boiler design on an articulated. The rearmost pair of drivers, at 70 inches, would unduly obstruct the grate and ashpan, compromising combustion capacity. And an articulated's long boiler above 70-inch drivers would have to be reduced in maximum diameter, to keep either the total height or the total weight of the locomotive within acceptable limits. In all events, AMC's report on the matter stated that boiler capacity would be inadequate.[13] Rather than a four-cylinder articulated, therefore, the AMC investigated the practicality of a two-cylinder, enlarged S-3.

The result was a 2-10-4, but one far surpassing anything imagined in the Lima-T&P design of 1925. The AMC and C&O designers took no prisoners: Compared to the I-1, they expanded the grate by 22 percent, increased maximum boiler diameter by 10 percent, and then stuffed in more tubes and flues, thereby adding 1,500 more square feet of evaporative heating surface and 1,000 more square feet of superheating surface. The driving-axle load was a whopping 74,600 pounds. At 69 inches, the drivers were just a shade under the targeted 70 inches, probably to give a little more clearance under the massive boiler.

As in the S-3, the four-wheel trailing truck allowed the firebox to be set over the truck and entirely behind the driving wheels, which in turn allowed the grate to be placed as low on the frame as possible, with no interference by the tall drivers. This grate placement added furnace volume. The new 2-10-4's boiler also included a 66-inch long combustion chamber (the S-3, like the A-1, had avoided one), which added more volume. The H-7's boiler included a combustion chamber of about the same size, and hence the AMC had that maintenance experience with which to predict boiler repair time for the new engine. How the C&O's civil engineers felt about the high axle loading is unrecorded – the loading was fully 6½ tons heavier than that on each H-7 driving axle.

In late 1929, Lima got the order – and immediately billed it in trade ads as an apex of Super Power. Forty of the new T-1 class 2-10-4s began entering service in 1930, soon replacing the 2-8-8-2s on the Russell–Toledo run, and freeing the H-7s for use on C&O's main line through West Virginia, where the mountain topography better suited the articulateds' high power at low speed. After some bridges were reinforced, the T-1s did the work they were planned to do, hauling gargantuan trains of 160 cars and 13,500 gross tons all the way across Ohio at average running speeds of 40-50 mph. Only on

A Chesapeake & Ohio 2-10-4 under construction at Lima Locomotive Works in 1930.
Courtesy Kalmbach Media

Chesapeake & Ohio T-1 2-10-4 No. 3032 hauls coal through Ohio in 1950.
W.G. Fancher, Courtesy Kalmbach Media

16-mile Powell Hill, just north of Columbus, were helpers needed. Despite having considerably less starting tractive effort than an H-7, a T-1 could haul 3,000 tons more over the road and move it 20 percent faster. The T-1's massive tender (carrying 23,500 gallons of water, almost 10,000 gallons more than an I-1's tender) allowed a "run-through" operation, with additional water taken only at Columbus. Among railroad managers, the C&O's trans-Ohio coal movement became one of the most celebrated freight runs in the U.S.

During World War II, the Pennsylvania Railroad needed a major infusion of freight locomotives to handle burgeoning wartime traffic. Between 1942 and 1944, the PRR built 125 near-duplicates of the C&O T-1, with the only differences being cab design, different tenders, and arrangement of pumps and plumbing. Common lore was that the War Production Board had denied permission to PRR to build its own 2-10-4 design, but recent scholarship indicates that there was no such WPB restriction. Rather, the Board had

Pennsylvania Railroad 2-10-4 No. 6170 at Altoona, Pa., in 1956. Based closely on C&O's T-1s, Pennsy's 2-10-4s were a ready answer to the World War II motive-power crunch.
Don Wood, Courtesy Kalmbach Media

already decided that the Lima plant would produce Sherman tanks and locomotives for the U.S. Army, and it ordered that all production of the PRR 2-10-4s be shifted the railroad's Juniata Shops. There was no WPB mandate for PRR to replicate the C&O engines: PRR engineers and managers made that decision themselves in order to save a year or more of design and testing.[14] Especially given the keen rivalries among railroad motive power departments, not to mention the PRR's leading role in American locomotive engineering, its choice of the C&O T-1 was a tribute to the AMC's design decisions.

Developments on the Santa Fe

In 1930, the Atchison, Topeka & Santa Fe's motive power officers paid close attention to the introduction and subsequent operational success of the T-1s. After experimenting with numerous Mallet and other articulated locomotive designs in the first two decades of the 20th century – in fact, trying out some of the most bizarre and remarkably unsuccessful multiple-cylinder engines ever seen – the Santa Fe had sworn off articulateds of any type by 1920. Also plagued throughout its dry, desert territory in the Southwest with bad water – *i.e.*, water with high mineral content that caused excessive scale deposits in boilers and led to high maintenance costs – the Santa Fe after 1920 bought only two-cylinder locomotives of straightforward design, evidently reasoning that they would require the lowest overall maintenance to boilers and running gear.

In that context, the idea that a two-cylinder locomotive with just five driving axles could not only replace but outperform a modern, four-cylinder articulated with eight driving axles, and do so on such an extended run, must have had particular appeal to Santa Fe. By 1930, though, the Great Depression was beginning, and railroads everywhere were seeing traffic fall. Nonetheless, Santa Fe management authorized the purchase of an experimental locomotive from Baldwin, the railroad's traditional supplier.

Three years before, the railroad had purchased 15 2-8-4s but had not repeated the order, preferring to stick with its large, existing fleet of 2-8-2s and 2-10-2s for mainline freight. Additional engines of both these types had been added to the roster in 1926 and 1927. In 1929, John Purcell, top motive power official and assistant to the company's vice president of operations, A.G. Wells, studied Santa Fe's future freight locomotive needs. Purcell and his staff began discussions with Baldwin engineers, and in early 1930, Baldwin draftsmen completed drawings to Purcell's specification for a 2-10-4.[15]

More than a decade before, Purcell had experimented with a four-wheel trailing truck. In 1919, one of an order of heavy 2-10-2s for Santa Fe was altered to include a four-wheel truck that was specially made by Commonwealth Steel Castings Co. Whether Commonwealth or Purcell initiated the idea is unclear. The Santa Fe 2-10-2s of 1919 were significantly bigger engines than previous such types on that railroad, and axle loadings were probably a concern. Though technically a 2-10-4, it is not to be confused with the Lima efforts of just six years later; this was still a drag-freight engine at heart, and there was no attempt to apply Super-Power principles. In the early 1920s, Commonwealth perfected a two-wheel version of its truck with cast side frames and a three-point suspension (the "Delta" type) that became popular. The Santa Fe locomotive, meantime, kept its odd four-wheel truck until scrapped in 1955,

ABOVE Santa Fe 4-8-4 No. 3751 was built in 1927 with a short-wheelbase Commonwealth/Purcell "Delta" trailing truck.
Courtesy Kalmbach Media

RIGHT Santa Fe 2-10-4 No. 5000, known to the railway's engine crews as "Madame Queen."
Courtesy Kalmbach Media

but no other engines of its class were so modified.[16] However, when Santa Fe acquired its 15 2-8-4s and a sole 4-8-4 in 1927, the Commonwealth/Purcell truck (with short wheelbase and a three-point suspension was included. Also, in late 1926 and again in 1927, similar trailing trucks from Commonwealth but with longer wheelbases appeared under the back end of the first 4-8-4 (on the Northern Pacific), and under some of William Black's S-class 2-8-4s for the Erie. Apparently, the concerns that Will Woodard had expressed to his design staff in 1924 about excessive drawbar angles between engine and tender on curves, which led to the Lima hinged-frame truck on the A-1 and T&P I-1, had proven unfounded. Furthermore, in 1925-1926, the Lima truck showed an occasional tendency to derail while backing up on yard tracks that were less than perfectly aligned[17] – a fact no doubt noted by Commonwealth salesmen. The Commonwealth trailing truck quickly became standard on locomotives with four-wheel trailing trucks after 1927.

Santa Fe's coal-fired No. 5000 of 1930, immediately named "Madame Queen" by crews, was highly comparable to the C&O T-1. Key boiler parameters were similar (grate area, for example, was virtually identical; a combustion chamber six inches longer was included; total heating surface was less); driver diameter was the same; and overall weight was considerably less, largely because boiler diameter was four inches smaller. Driving axle load was just under 70,000 pounds. Most significant from a developmental standpoint were a 300 psi boiler pressure – which from a structural standpoint was very nearly the top limit for working pressure in a fire-tube type boiler for locomotive use – and a one-piece locomotive frame with cylinders cast integrally.

Just coming into favor at the end of the 1920s, the one-piece locomotive frame with integral cylinders had been introduced by the General Steel

Castings Corp. Such a precision steel casting, more 50 feet long with bearing pedestals, cylinders, cradle, and all major brackets incorporated, was a major advance in the pursuit of reduced maintenance. Piston thrusts in large locomotives had become so punishing that cylinder saddles often worked loose after a few years of service. In that event, a major tear-down and rebuilding of the locomotive frame and cylinder attachments was required, which first necessitated removal of the boiler from the frame. The upshot, of course, was great expense coupled with lost availability of the engine. The one-piece casting of frame and cylinders eliminated the problem and, in fact, became essential in making the very large steam locomotives of 1930-1950 practical.[18]

Extensive road testing on trains between the terminals of Clovis and Belen, N.M., in 1930 and 1931 showed that, in comparison to the biggest 2-10-2s, No. 5000 could save 17 percent on fuel while pulling 15 percent more gross tonnage, and cover the run in nine percent less time.[19] But with the Depression intervening and rail traffic falling off precipitously, that fine performance was pretty academic in 1931.

It was not until 1937 and 1938 that Santa Fe bought more 2-10-4s, which the company called the 5001 class. The design had been significantly refined. Firebox seams were now welded, since the Interstate Commerce Commission's Safety Office now permitted welding in fireboxes not only for repairs but also for original construction, eliminating troublesome rivets in the firebox and combustion chamber. The feedwater heater was now of the open-type. Boiler pressure was raised to 310 psi, the highest ever used in a fire-tube boiler. (Kansas City Southern's 2-10-4s were also built to operate at 310 psi, but the resulting thrust knocked the drivers out of quarter, and pressure was soon reduced to 300 psi.) And, most dramatically insofar as railroaders were concerned, the driving-wheel diameter was increased to 74 inches, a size normally associated only with high-speed passenger engines. With ten such tall drivers in a single frame, these engines had the longest driving wheelbase ever used in a two-cylinder locomotive. As on the C&O T-1, lateral-motion devices – permitting up to 1½ inches of sideward movement on either side of centerline for some of the driver pairs, cushioned by lateral springs – were essential to navigating curves.

On the lonely desert stretches of the Santa Fe in West Texas and New Mexico, long freight trains moved at 45-60 mph between helper districts. Thus, a heavy freight engine that could move even faster than the No. 5000 made sense, if total running times were to be reduced further than promised by the 1931 tests. The helper districts could not be eliminated; the grades involved were too steep and too long. And so Santa Fe designers opted, in the 5001-class, to make no compromise at all between low-speed pull and high-speed power. Helpers would continue to help long freights slog uphill; the job of the new 2-10-4s was to move over the flatter districts as fast as possible.

The larger-diameter wheels, reducing piston speed at any given rpm, meant that the locomotive's speed for its highest horsepower was pushed up. As

Cast one-piece locomotive frames, with integral cylinders, bearing pedestals, cradle, and brackets gained acceptance in the late 1920s. This later example is from a Pennsylvania Railroad T1 4-4-4-4 locomotive.
Courtesy Kalmbach Media

With a 1936 Dodge automobile providing a sense of proportion, Santa Fe 2-10-4 No. 5004 shows off its gargantuan size, including its 74-inch driving wheels.
Courtesy Kalmbach Media

Woodard had seen, maximum locomotive productivity depends on matching the speed of top drawbar horsepower with average running speed. A steam locomotive has one speed of highest horsepower, with lower power below and above that speed. The T&P I-1 reached the top of its drawbar-horsepower curve at 30 mph, and the C&O T-1 put out its top power at about 40 mph, but the Santa Fe's new 5001-class reached peak power at about 50.[20]

The pioneering T&P I-1 was actually hampered in its productivity, since average running speed often exceeded its speed of top power. And so, as much for better productivity as for better counterbalancing, the standard driving-wheel size on most fast freight locomotives constructed after 1925 went quickly from 63 inches (as on the A-1 2-8-4 and the T&P I-1 2-10-4) to a more optimal 69 or 70 inches (as on the Erie S-class and C&O T-1). Santa Fe's 5001-class engines were a special case; they were matched to higher average freight train speeds than most railroads would have found useful.

Ten locomotives of the new class came to Santa Fe in 1938, plus 25 more in 1944 to help shoulder record traffic levels. One test produced 5,600 drawbar horsepower – over 1,500 more than the T&P I-1 of 1925 and the highest ever recorded by a two-cylinder locomotive. Such remarkable power was explained by the big increases in boiler dimensions and hence, greater weight, compared to the 1925 design. Nonetheless, given the severely restrictive "envelope" – height, width, length, weight, gauge of track – within which designers had to work, it was an impressive accomplishment.

For Santa Fe there is a wrinkle in the weight story. To cut weight by about six tons, the railroad specified nickel alloy steel for the boilers of the 1938 engines. So-called "nickel steel" has a higher tensile strength than the standard carbon steel alloy usually used in boilers, and so boilerplate thickness could be slightly less for a given theoretical bursting strength. It turned out to be

Santa Fe 2-10-4 No. 5010. One member of this class produced 5,600 drawbar horsepower in a dynamometer test.
Courtesy Kalmbach Media

a costly choice. By the late 1940s, some of the nickel-steel boilers on the 5001-class (and on two classes of 4-8-4s purchased in 1938 and 1941) were showing serious embrittlement, indicated by tiny cracks appearing in the boiler shells. The situation was alarming and unexpected.

Like several other railroads with bad-water problems, Santa Fe had spent a lot of money installing a system-wide program of chemical conditioning of the water supplied to engine tenders, to reduce boiler scaling. Could the chemical water treatment be playing some unforeseen role? Metallurgical examination suggested not; the stress cracks were the result of temperature changes in the steel that accompanied the normal duty cycle of locomotive boilers. The higher-tensile material was unsuited for use in a big locomotive boiler, which in normal use changed its length by two or more inches from cold to hot.

Between 1949 and 1953, six of the ten 5001-class boilers, and 14 of the 21 boilers in the two affected series of 4-8-4s had to be entirely replaced. The 25 2-10-4s ordered in 1944, as well as other steam locomotives built during the war, experienced no such difficulty. Because of War Production Board restrictions on the use of critical steel alloys, locomotives after 1941 all used the customary, and lower-tensile, carbon steel. As a result, the wartime 2-10-4s and 4-8-4s were heavier than their prewar counterparts. And Santa Fe, which had been buying diesels since the mid-1930s, had one more reason to like internal combustion.

A few of the 2-10-4s survive today. Museums and private individuals have preserved an example from the Texas & Pacific, three from the Santa Fe, one from the Bessemer & Lake Erie, and two from Canadian Pacific. The T&P engine ran on exhibition for several years in the late 1970s and was the subject of a published dynamometer test conducted by the author.[21]

Chapter 12 Notes

1. Charles M. Mizell Jr., "T is for Texas, Texas & Pacific, and Two-Ten-Four," *Trains*, February 1978, pp. 22-32.
2. Ibid.
3. Ibid.
4. Author's interview with Hugh Hollis, July 1977. See also Mizell, p. 28.
5. Mizell.
6. Ibid, p. 29. See also G.R. Henderson, *Locomotive Operation* (1907), pp. 45-46.
7. Mizell, p. 29.
8. Author's interview with Hollis, July 1977.
9. Author's 1972 interviews with former Lima engineer and William Woodard protégé James Smith, via telephone and at Orleans, Mass.
10. Ibid.
11. Quoted by David P. Morgan in "Blueprint Locomotives," *Trains*, March 1952, pp. 18-23.
12. *Railway Age*, January 17, 1931.
13. As seen in several later designs, however – including Seaboard Air Line's 2-6-6-4s, the Alco 4-6-6-4s for several roads, Norfolk & Western's A-class, and even the AMC's own 2-6-6-6 of 1941 – AMC's 1929 conclusion was simply incorrect.
14. Eugene L. Huddleston, *Uncle Sam's Locomotives: The USRA and the Nation's Railroads*, pp. 97-99.
15. E.D. Worley, *Iron Horses of the Santa Fe Trail*, 1965.
16. Ibid., p. 333.
17. Author's interview with Hugh Hollis.
18. Robert L. Frey, "The Biography of a Heavy Pacific," *Railroad History*, Fall 1976, pp. 59-78.
19. *Railway Mechanical Engineer*, December 1931.
20. William L. Withuhn, "The Great Dynamometer Test," *Trains*, February 1978, p. 37.
21. Ibid.

NEW YORK
CENTRAL
SYSTEM

Chapter 13

The Steam Locomotive's Final Form:

The Hudson

IT IS, EVEN NOW, A MAGICAL NAME: The *20th Century Limited.* Publicists for the New York Central System called it "the Most Famous Train in the World," and "a National Institution." It was both. The *Century's* long red carpet was rolled out at New York's Grand Central Terminal for statesmen and stars, for politicians and promoters, for executives and entrepreneurs – a distinctly upscale set of travelers. This was an all-first-class, all-room train: Pullman compartment sleepers (no open-section sleepers with only curtains for privacy), parlor cars, and fine dining. Those who wanted cheaper accommodations could take other trains.

To New York Central management, the *Century* was the highest priority movement on the line. Every choreographed step of its overnight passage between Grand Central and Chicago's LaSalle Street Station was tightly scheduled. The train often ran in multiple "sections" – identical trains, separated by only minutes, as many as seven sections per night. The first item on the daily agenda for the morning meeting of the Central's president and senior staff was, how close to time did the *Century* run last night? The attention stemmed not from the train's profitability. The *Century's* explicit role was to project to its predominantly business clientele – a clientele that influenced freight routings – the punctuality and service quality of its parent railroad.

The locomotive type most closely identified with the *20th Century Limited* over the course of the train's 65-year tenure was the J-class 4-6-4 Hudson type. The train was in its third decade when this new locomotive first appeared in 1927. The Central's Hudsons established new benchmarks for high-speed passenger engine performance, significantly improved the *Century's* schedule, and eventually handled all of the railroad's principal passenger trains. And, in an era of public dependence on railroads for most long-distance travel, the Hudsons became probably the most famous locomotives in America, the subject of countless ads and newspaper stories.

By 1925, operations and motive-power officers of the New York Central faced a number of issues system-wide. Ridership on all passenger trains was up. More important, the distribution of that traffic had changed. According to one internal analysis, total train miles on the main parts of the system rose 26

Destined to become an icon of 1930s Moderne design, Henry Dreyfuss's J-3a Hudson, streamlined for New York Central's 1938 *20th Century Limited* (shown here departing Chicago's La Salle St. Station), concealed a proven greyhound.

NYC, Kevin J. Holland Collection

percent between 1919 and 1924. But while chair-car and coach miles in the period had increased only 3½ percent, Pullman sleeping-car miles had grown 33 percent. This greater Pullman mileage meant that typical train weights had risen substantially. The 4-6-2 Pacific types assigned to the *Century* were increasingly unequal to their task.

Not only the *Century*, but many other popular trains ran in sections or were double-headed, because a single Pacific could not handle more than 14 or 15 heavy cars – even on New York Central's famously flat "Water Level Route".

In January 1926, Paul W. Kiefer became NYC's chief engineer of motive power and rolling stock. Educated at Cleveland's Central Institute, Kiefer had begun his career in 1912 as a machinist apprentice at railroad shops in that city. After several years' service as a machinist, a construction inspector, and in other related jobs, he moved to the motive power office, where he advanced rapidly through positions of draftsman, dynamometer engineer, locomotive designer, chief draftsman, and assistant engineer. When he took charge of locomotive design, Kiefer was already immersed in a detailed evaluation of his company's motive-power needs that had been initiated by his noted predecessor, F.H. Hardin, the previous year.[1]

Standard NYC passenger locomotives then were the company's numerous K-3 Pacifics, 281 of which had been acquired since 1911. In 1924, Hardin's staff and Alco engineers jointly developed a substantially bigger Pacific, the K-5. Larger grate area, feedwater heater, mechanical stoker, and better superheating yielded a marked improvement: The K-5 put out 50 percent more horsepower than a K-3. Through 1927, 36 K-5s came to NYC subsidiary lines Michigan Central; Pittsburgh & Lake Erie; and Cleveland, Cincinnati, Chicago & St. Louis (the "Big Four") – routes where motive-power shortages were acute. Ten more Pacifics, class K-6, went to NYC subsidiary Boston & Albany; the only significant difference from the K-5 was a four-inch smaller driving-wheel diameter, to give somewhat better torque at lower speeds for the B&A's hilly terrain.

But, Kiefer judged in 1926, the K-5 and K-6 designs were not powerful enough, and their axle loadings – particularly at the trailing truck – were too high for significant parts of the NYC system. In the words of NYC engineering staffer G.T. Wilson:

> The single-axle trailing truck presented a rather serious problem as the weight of the Pacifics was increased. This isolated load [at the rear truck] may develop an unusually high rail stress, due to the fact that the rail, when considered as a continuous beam, tends to deflect in an upward direction at a point between the position of the back driver and the trailing wheel.[2]

New York Central Class K-3 4-6-2 Pacific-type No. 4810. By the mid-1920s, heavier trains and faster schedules led NYC to develop a replacement for the 4-6-2: the 4-6-4 Hudson-type. *Courtesy Kalmbach Media*

In the midst of all these considerations, the first of 45 brand new 2-8-4 Berkshire-type locomotives for freight service were on their way from the Lima Locomotive Works to the Boston & Albany; the initial 25 arrived in February and March of 1926. B&A had seen the initial road test in 1925 of Lima's prototype 2-8-4, and Kiefer had participated in those tests. Hardin and Kiefer had recommended the purchase of B&A's new Super-Power freighters.

Hence the notion took hold a year later that a new passenger locomotive would need a four-wheel trailing truck. In fact, a 4-6-4 wheel arrangement was hardly original to the New York Central. Milwaukee Road Chief Mechanical Engineer C.H. Bilty conceived such a design in 1925, but his railroad's bankruptcy that year put off Bilty's plans.[3]

The best design of trailing truck for such new locomotives was unclear, however. The Lima truck, carried over from the A-1 protoype to the T&P 2-10-4s and B&A 2-8-4s, was constructed as a hinged extension of the main engine frame, with the locomotive drawbar attached to the back of the truck. By 1926, Alco and Commonwealth Steel Castings were pushing the "Delta" truck as an alternative to Lima's design.

The Delta trailing truck – its name derived from the design's three-point suspension – provided improved lateral stability in high-speed operation.

Courtesy Kalmbach Media

In the design of both leading and trailing trucks, an important consideration was the incorporation of self-centering. On straight track, a locomotive's riding stability depends on the trucks' suspensions having a self-centering action, so that the trucks progressively resist side-to-side motions of the locomotive, or yawing. On curved track, the trucks' centering action may provide for a degree of controlled weight transfer off the drivers, reducing lateral pressure on the flanges of the driving wheels in curves.

Prior to the Delta form, trailing-truck centering devices relied on laterally mounted springs (which usually did not provide the weight-transfer feature) or on pairs of inclined planes in contact; either device gave a forceful action to push the truck back to the locomotive centerline when the truck was displaced laterally. The weight-bearing, inclined planes, such as used on the Lima truck, required heavy lubrication for reliable functioning. The Delta dispensed with both springs and planes in favor of rockers, which required little lubrication and which could be altered easily to provide differing amounts of centering resistance and weight transfer.

Better yet, whereas inclined-plane centering devices gave a *constant increase* in centering force as the truck was displaced laterally, the rockers could be shaped to give a *variable increase* in centering force as the truck moved laterally. A relatively heavy and progressive centering force could be incorporated for slight or moderate side-to-side excursions of the truck, to give high stability on mainline track, but with a constant centering force for moderate-to-wide swings of the truck, to better accommodate the sharp curves of yard track.[4]

In a locomotive designed for stable riding at high speed, performance of the trucks would be especially critical. Alco engineering staff apparently persuaded Kiefer that the Delta truck would be the superior form for high-speed use. But by the late fall of 1926, when detail design of the 4-6-4 was well advanced at Alco, no four-wheel Delta-type truck had ever been used on any production locomotive. So in November 1926, Kiefer had a K-3q-class heavy Pacific No. 3284 fitted with a four-wheel trailing truck, presumably as an in-service test before unalterable commitment to the Delta truck for the new locomotive.

In the meantime, by mid-summer of 1926, Kiefer's staff was well along in producing the 4-6-4's comprehensive design specification, prior to hand-off to Alco for detailed engineering. Kiefer later wrote about the performance goals he had in mind. For 20th-century locomotive designers, it is rare to have such first-hand commentary. The following is extracted from an address Kiefer gave to the Kiwanis Club of Brookline, Mass., in 1929.[5]

In his "story of the conception of the Hudson," Kiefer stresses the limitations in power and weight of the K-3, K-5, and K-6 Pacific designs. For the J-class Hudson, he said, the "seemingly insignificant difference" between a two-wheel and a four-wheel trailing truck "make it possible for us to change the entire character of the locomotive." He went on to summarize the design goals for the J:

> Greater starting tractive force; a substantial increase in cylinder horsepower capacity with the maximum output delivered at much higher speeds; a boiler of ample capacity to satisfy the cylinder requirements at all times and under adverse conditions; weight distribution of such character as to keep rail stresses and rail impact loads within much lower limits than heretofore had been observed, regardless of the increase in power; increased thermal efficiency; overall clearance limitations which would permit operation without restrictions over all lines comprising the system; and in addition, a symmetrical appearance as free from miscellaneous appliances, piping and other details as possible.[6]

Some analysis is in order. "Greater starting tractive force" is, *per se*, an unremarkable item, being a rather universal performance quality to be desired in a new design. However, to get more starting tractive force with the same number and diameter of driving wheels as the up-to-date, heavy K-5 and K-6 – which also sported a NYC-developed booster on the trailing truck to add about 10,000 additional pounds of force – would be unexpected.

The "increase in cylinder horsepower" with a simultaneous increase in the speed of peak power can be understood in context with Kiefer's following statement on boiler capacity. What he is describing is another rewriting of the accustomed, pre-1925 design ratio of boiler power to cylinder output begun by Lima's William Woodard. What Woodard began for freight engines – substantially increasing steam-generating capacity in relation to cylinder steam-consumption – Kiefer brought to passenger engines and escalated further. Described another way, Kiefer sought not only to raise the entire curve of cylinder horsepower at all speeds but to raise it the most at the highest speeds, flattening an otherwise-sagging horsepower curve at speeds above 50 to 60 mph.

Satisfying cylinder demand "at all times and under adverse conditions" refers, in the railroad context, specifically to speed with excess tonnage in tow. Elsewhere in the paper, Kiefer states that he wanted a "performance margin." Thus, in its contemplated service, the J was intended to have boiler power in reserve. In older terms, Kiefer expressly wanted his engine "over-boilered." The trick was to do it within weight and clearance limits. To do it within lower "rail stresses and rail impact loads" was unheard of.

As to clearances – the extreme permissible dimensions of overall height and width, overhang in curves, and special clearances at platforms – New

ABOVE Boston & Albany Class A-1 2-8-4 Berkshire-type No. 1409 clearly shows that aesthetics weren't uppermost in designer Will Woodard's mind.

Harold K. Vollrath Collection

LEFT New York Central Class J-1 4-6-4 Hudson No. 5200. Even in its later years, the first New York Central Hudson exhibits cleaner lines than the A-1. See p. 248 for a builder photo of the brand-new 5200, the lines of which are cleaner still.

Harold K. Vollrath Collection

York Central was known as having the most restrictive such limits of any major railroad in North America. In everyday usage by rail traffic planners and shippers, "New York Central limits" meant the tightest clearances – a key consideration when routing even slightly oversize railcars or other equipment. Hence Kiefer's reference to "operation without restrictions" is not a toss-away line.

Kiefer's reference to "increased thermal efficiency" *is* a toss-away. Designers had observed since the 1910s in many dynamometer tests of new locomotives on the Altoona test plant that if boiler capacity were raised in proportion to cylinder capacity, better thermal efficiency at a given power output would result, since thermal efficiency inherently degrades as boiler output reaches maximum. Thus, a boiler customarily operating at a lower percentage of its top output – *i.e.*, a boiler having reserve capacity – is more efficient. The problem here was always that better meant bigger and heavier. And in the 1920s, nobody had any real idea how to predict thermal efficiency precisely; there was too big a gap between the thermodynamics of Carnot and Rankine and accurate predictive theory. So, as a vague goal, improving efficiency was fine. The result, however, could only be found by test, *post hoc.*

Highly unusual are Kiefer's direct comments on aesthetics – that he wanted from the outset "a symmetrical appearance" and a design "free from miscellaneous appliances" or haphazard plumbing. To have a leading 20th-century engineer and designer comment contemporaneously that he actually valued appearance is practically unknown. By contrast, for example,

ABOVE New York Central's K-5a class of 1925 shows a more cluttered mass of plumbing compared with the Hudsons. *Harold K. Vollrath Collection*

RIGHT Debuting in the same year as the Hudson, NYC's K-5b class of 1927 reflects Kiefer's evolving emphasis on aesthetics, with concealed injector pipes and hidden sanding pipes. The clean lines had nonetheless been marred by the time of this 1949 view at Bellefonte, Ohio. *Harold K. Vollrath Collection*

Woodard's plumbing-infested designs of the 1920s made it clear that aesthetic considerations played no role whatever, and he seems never to have spoken publicly on the matter. To a present-day reader, however, accustomed to smooth, post-1950s aerodynamics, the kind of styling at issue here may seem obscure.

The aesthetic taste expressed in the J was hinted at in the K-5b of 1926. The original K-5's design in 1924 had been supervised by Hardin; Kiefer added his own touches to the K-5b. Note in the K-5b, for example, the casing just ahead of the cab (which conceals injector piping and blends the lines of the cab into those of the boiler), the hidden sanding pipes, and the arrangement of visible piping into straighter runs precisely parallel to the boiler. The effect is a less cluttered look. The injector's casing, in fact, has no "objective" justification; it actually interfered with ready maintenance access to the devices beneath.

For the J class, Kiefer used similar touches, and then paid special attention to the locomotive's front end. As he told the Kiwanis,

> During the detail engineering work ... numerous improvements in the application of appliances and details were worked out. Foremost among these were an improved application of feedwater heating equipment and a unique design of cast-steel pilot and drop coupler.[7]

Surprisingly, Kiefer is here not talking about layout engineering in the modern sense, but solely about appearance.

Compare the feedwater heater installations on the K-5a and K-5b, models with the J. On the Pacifics, the cylindrical heater juts out awkwardly across the top of the smokebox, ahead of the smokestack. In the J, the heater is "buried" in the smokebox, faired into the boiler. Again, this installation made major repair or replacement of the heater more difficult than on the K-5. The J's cast-steel pilot adds a very noticeable aesthetic element, one that blends the progressively angled, vertical lines of classic 19th-century locomotive pilots into a modern, one-piece casting. The pilot's drop coupler, although justified as a safety device to keep autos from being impaled at grade crossings, certainly gives a cleaner line to the locomotive's front end. (This pilot was later retrofitted to many of the K-5s.)

Kiefer goes on to describe more specifically the core of the J's realization: its boiler. His comparisons with earlier NYC designs are easier to follow in tabular form, as below, summarizing the differences Kiefer stresses among the boilers of the K3, K5, and J1:

	Heating Surface (Firebox, Tubes, and Flues) sq. ft.	Superheater Heating Surface sq. ft.	Boiler Pressure psi	Grate Area sq. ft.
K-3	3769	839	200	56.5
K-5	3952	1150	200	67.8
J-1	4484	1951	225	81.5

Most noteworthy are the significant jumps in superheater surface and grate area. The former represents a 70 percent increase on the basis of greatly elevated total steam temperature. The latter, a 20 percent increase, results from greater heat-generating power. Compared to the K-5, the J also had 28 percent more furnace volume.[8] These increases came with the following axle loadings:[9]

	Weight per Driving Axle, Pounds	Weight on Trailing Axles: First Axle	Second Axle
K-3q	64,833	57,000	—
K-5b	61,667	58,500	—
J-1	60,667	44,000	53,500

The NYC and Alco staffs engineered a much bigger, more powerful boiler despite lighter axle loadings. Clearly, the extra weight of the boiler had to go somewhere; the extra trailing axle and a bit more weight on the lead truck provided the basis for the boiler's growth.

With evident pride, Kiefer emphasized the effect of these axle-load reductions on rail stresses at speed. All three designs shared the same number and size of driving wheels. Yet, at 79-80 mph,

> ... the combined rail stress imposed by the Hudson locomotive is 5 per cent less than for the K-5 and 20 per cent less than for the much less powerful K-3, although the figure for the last-mentioned class does not exceed the limits of good practice.[10]

Kiefer discusses the extensive road testing done by his staff on the first Hudson with the company's dynamometer car. Among U.S. railroads in the

1920s and '30s, the NYC did probably the most detailed and extensive road testing of its new locomotives. Kiefer lists the extraordinary comparative results:[11]

	K-5	J-1	Percent Improvement
Actual Max. Starting TF, w/ booster, lbs.	48,750	56,500	16
Max. Cylinder HP	3,200 at 54 mph	4,075 at 66 mph	27
Lbs. Dry Coal per Cylinder HP-Hour, incl. auxiliaries	2.43	2.28	6
Overall Thermal Efficiency (at Drawbar)	5.17%	6.32%	22
Locomotive Weight per Cylinder HP (not incl. Tender)	94	84	11

Given the weight and clearance limitations affecting the J's design, these are more than incremental changes. According to the NYC company magazine in October 1927, the average thermal efficiency was, to that time, the highest ever recorded for a non-compound locomotive.[12]

The road tests were not completed until several months after the first J-1's roll-out in February 1927. Nonetheless, when that roll-out took place on Valentine's Day at the American Locomotive Co.'s main plant in Schenectady, N.Y., New York Central management already sensed that they had a world-beater. The press was called, and Miss Marguerite Davey, a NYC freight

RIGHT Roll-out of NYC Class J-1 4-6-4 No. 5200 at Alco's Schenectady, N.Y., plant on February 14, 1927.
Courtesy Kalmbach Media

BELOW Alco builder's photo of New York Central Class J-1 4-6-4 No. 5200. The white outline around the locomotive is the first step in the "opaquing" process, used to mask the often-cluttered backgrounds of such images by hand-brushing the original negative or a master print with an opaque paint.
Courtesy Kalmbach Media

clerk, whacked a "bottle of sparkling beverage" over the pilot according to the *Schenectady Gazette*. (Actually, it was a bottle of water from the Mohawk River, adjacent to the Alco plant; Prohibition was still in effect.) Officials made speeches, and J-1 No. 5200 was turned over to a beaming NYC crew, including H.J. Miller, engineer; John Grant, fireman; a road foreman; and a trio of inspectors.[13] The *Albany Times-Union* called the 5200 a "far chug from the *De Witt Clinton*" (the 1831 locomotive of NYC's predecessor Mohawk & Hudson) and a "new 'supergreyhound of the rails.'"[14]

In the New York Central's company magazine in March, the lead article discussed the 5200's various engineering features and then offered this notable paragraph:

> One of the striking features of the new locomotive is its appearance, its design calling for 'stream lines' with all the many pipes and other pieces of machinery necessary which customarily show on an engine completely hidden. This simplicity of design will tend, it is believed, to convey a striking impression on the public of its power and efficiency, sometimes lacking in locomotives of past years.[15]

The engine went the same day to the Rensselaer, N.Y., enginehouse. After break-in on a few passenger and freight runs, the 5200 began its test program, which did not end until mid-April. More than a dozen NYC technicians, augmented by representatives from Alco and equipment suppliers, used NYC dynamometer car X8000 to run four test series. Tests included locomotive performance; coal and steam consumption; capacity tests to establish the engine's speed, pull, and horsepower curves; acceleration tests on level track and on grades, and from both standing starts and various initial speeds; and "division time calibration" and train loading tests, to establish tonnage ratings applicable to the various railroad operating divisions and their particular limits of curvature, trackbed, and speed. For a six-drivered locomotive, the weight of the test train was enormous: 25 steel coaches plus the X8000, aggregating about 1,800 trailing tons. (For some acceleration tests, the number of coaches was reduced to 20).[16]

In contrast to the Pennsylvania Railroad's reliance on its Altoona test plant for generation of performance data, and the American and European locomotive engineering community's general belief in and preference for the controlled nature of such data, New York Central had a different philosophy:

> Road tests can be made under road conditions that are surprisingly constant and with such degree of accuracy that the percentage of error will be sufficiently small for practical purposes, and it is just this information of the locomotives under variable conditions that are encountered in practice that the railroad man needs most to know.[17]

The Central's approach to testing was unusually meticulous and exhaustive. An indirect indication of this care is the company's selection and training of test observers, the staff who actually took the coal, water, and temperature or pressure readings.

> Accurate tests depend very largely upon the care and faithfulness of the observers .... Weighing coal or measuring the height of water in the tender, though simple enough, requires care ... as any blunder will spoil the tests. Every observer recommended by the Supervisor of Apprentices is so selected because of his reputation in the shops of being careful, systematic and methodical.[18]

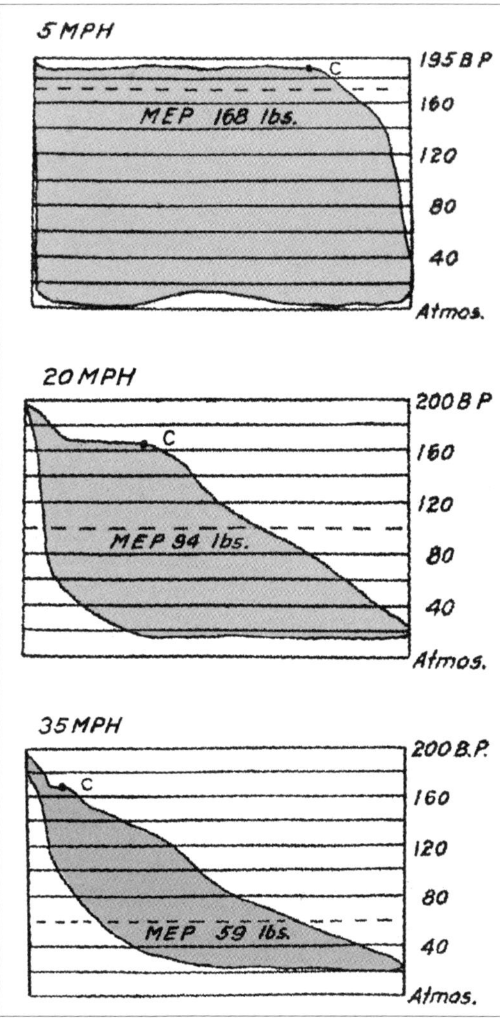

Indicator cards show the actual work (shaded area), relative to the maximum work possible for a piston, assuming constant boiler pressure during each stroke. The top card reflects a long cutoff, while the others reflect shorter cutoffs, with resulting decrease in mean effective pressure, or MEP. These cards came from 1909 tests on a Southern Pacific 2-8-0 Consolidation-type engine. *J. Parker Lamb Collection*

The 5200 was fitted temporarily with a wooden deck and windbreak on the engine's pilot, enabling a test engineer and observer within this rather fragile-looking box to take indicator cards while the locomotive ran at speeds up to 70 mph. Each card recorded the varying pressure in a cylinder over a full piston stroke and thus allowed calculation of a cylinder horsepower figure, valid for the locomotive's speed when the card was taken. To produce a full curve of the cylinder horsepower over the locomotive's entire speed range, cards were taken at a sufficient number of speeds, and at several cutoff and throttle settings for each speed, to plot a valid curve.

To provide data to analyze evaporation and steam consumption, two banks of dial instruments were mounted, one atop the engine's boiler, to be read while underway by an observer braving wind and flying cinders on the running board, with another bank forward, in the pilot box. The gauges on the boiler read pressure of feedwater into the boiler and pressures of steam in the dry pipe, in the superheater, in the steam branch pipe after the throttle and in the steam chest, and at the exhaust. Pyrometers and thermometers in the pilot box and in the cab gave temperatures of feedwater before and after the feedwater heater; of steam leaving the superheater, at the steam chests, and at the exhaust; and of smokebox temperature. Periodically, the pilot-box crew took smokebox gas samples for later analysis of combustion efficiency – primarily by CO/CO_2 ratios. Observers in the tender weighed all coal in a scale above the stoker trough before delivery to the firebox and kept track of water consumption. Another observer with the engine crew recorded the calibrated throttle and cutoff settings, boiler pressure, and boiler-water level.

The dynamometer car itself took measurements that would allow accurate calculation of drawbar horsepower (the reading was actually done at the tender's rear coupler). Horsepower is defined as pull times speed, so combining the pull readings from the dynamometer head with precise reading of train speeds by a calibrated speedometer gave the needed information. To allow calculated horsepower corrections for grade, acceleration, and curves, an observer in the X8000 continuously recorded the train's location on its route, noting mileposts and the clock time at which these were passed. (The X8000's caboose-like cupola was for the milepost observer.) These horsepower corrections yielded calculations of drawbar horsepower that were valid for level, straight track at constant speed. By superimposing the civil engineering department's route profile on the raw pull/speed data, exact grades and curves at any point could be extrapolated for the proper horsepower determinations.

Plotting of a drawbar horsepower curve over the engine's speed range required numerous runs, with throttle and cutoff set correctly for the locomotive to reach maximum output at each given speed. Skill and experience of the test engineman controlling the locomotive came into play here: His throttle and cutoff settings for maximum power at, say, 25 mph were not the same as the settings for maximum power at 60 or 70.

Comparing the cylinder horsepower curve (calculated and plotted from the indicator cards) with the drawbar horsepower curve (calculated and plotted from the dynamometer car's pull and speed readings) produced a measurement of mechanical efficiency. To study cylinder efficiency *per se*, the X8000 crew ran tests of the 5200 at 85 percent maximum cutoff and 225 psi boiler pressure, and at 65 percent maximum cutoff and 250 psi. (See Chapters 5-7 for discussions of the importance of cutoff in cylinder performance).[19]

The test results in and analyzed, Kiefer passed his recommendations to NYC Vice President R.D. Starbuck and President Patrick Crowley. On May 10, 1927, the company placed an order with Alco for 59 more Hudsons, classed J-1b but virtually identical to J-1a No. 5200. Alco's hometown *Schenectady Gazette* crowed that these engines were "destined to revolutionize railroad locomotive power."[20] A less tepid characterization appeared later in the Central's in-house magazine, by guest journalist Charles Frederick Carter:

> It is all so like a railroad man's dream of paradise that it is to be hoped that the lucky men assigned to those sixty Hudson types will bear themselves with becoming humility and so not aggravate the heartburnings and envy of their less fortunate fellow workers.[21]

By late summer, the first production Hudsons were hauling the *20th Century Limited* and the Michigan Central's *Detroiter*. In September and October, NYC management showed off the 5205 in the daily locomotive parade at the Baltimore & Ohio's Centenary Exposition, "The Fair of the Iron Horse," at Halethorpe, Md., near Baltimore.

Operating results lived up to expectations. A J-1 could handle 12 heavy Pullmans up Albany Hill between the Hudson Valley and Schenectady – the steepest grade on the NYC – without a helper, and 17 to 18 Pullmans on level

NYC Class J-1 4-6-4 No. 5200 leads an 18-coach train in July 1927.

Courtesy Kalmbach Media

track at speeds in excess of 75 mph in daily service. These were trains 25 to 30 percent heavier than those a K-5 could handle on the same routes. The J maintained faster average speeds in so doing, burning about 7,000 lbs. of coal per hour in regular service.[22]

The railroad continued its acquisitions, ultimately amassing a fleet of 275 Hudsons in several sub-classes from 1927 to 1938. Alco built them all, except 10 that were built by Lima for the Boston & Albany in 1931-1932. The latter group was part of an agreement between NYC and Lima to keep the Ohio plant open in the teeth of the Depression, but the builder received no orders from anyone else until 1934.

Capable of assignment to much longer runs without engine changes, together with higher average speed, the J-1s posted monthly and annual mileage statistics far in excess of the K-5s; the average was about 50 percent more. The combination of greater train weights and higher monthly mileage was another expression of the high-productivity philosophy first articulated by Lima's Woodard. Engine performance, by itself, was not the point: The important thing was to consider the engine as a part of a traffic-moving system in which more tonnage moved per unit of time. This translated not only into lower costs, but into more revenue generated per locomotive.

The J-1 classes, all with 79-inch-diameter drivers, differed only in minor details. The J-2 class had smaller drivers (75 inches, later increased slightly to 76), higher boiler pressure (240 psi instead of 225), and a feature limiting maximum cutoff to 65 percent. These changes somewhat improved the locomotive's drawbar horsepower and steam economy at lower speeds, making performance better suited to the hilly profile of the B&A through the Berkshire Mountains of Massachusetts.

The Hudson type became the very symbol of the New York Central, its image on public timetables and in ads in popular magazines. In 1937, the Lionel Corporation, the maker of the most popular electric trains in the U.S., brought out its "Model 700E," a scale model of NYC J-1e No. 5344, the most elegant model ever made by the pre-1970 incarnation of that toy producer. Other public notoriety was frequent. For example, in a popular 1937 book for the general market, *Portraits of the Iron Horse*, industrial designer Otto Kuhler and writer Robert Selph Henry extolled the NYC Hudson as "a harmonious design, of rare grace and balance ... ."[23]

Despite the ongoing Depression and dismal passenger traffic (passengers carried by U.S. railroads would not increase until 1939, and then only slightly from the low reached the preceding year), NYC president Fred Williamson anticipated recovery and in 1936 and 1937 approved orders for 50 more Hudsons. A financing guarantee from the Reconstruction Finance Corporation, however, was essential. For these new engines, classed J-3, Kiefer and staff had come up with some further improvements, based on design work done since 1931.

Most important, there was a combustion chamber (the J-1s and J-2s did not have them), which added 60 percent to the furnace volume, and a 50-psi boost in boiler pressure to 275 psi. The firebox was fully welded. To accommodate the 43-inch combustion chamber, the tubes and flues were shortened 18 inches and the front tube sheet pushed about two feet forward – which shortened the smokebox accordingly. The final specification for the changed boiler

New York Central's first Class J-3 "Super Hudson," No. 5405, leads the *Southwestern Limited* at Garrison, N.Y., in May 1939.
J.P. Ahrens, Courtesy Kalmbach Media

proportions was based on a 1933 improvement in the calculation of predicted boiler evaporation, which used heat release per unit of firebox volume to find boiler efficiency, and thus quantified the benefits of greater furnace volume.[24] Then, a few years later, the Interstate Commerce Commission's Safety Bureau granted permission to weld inner firebox sheets, including combustion-chamber sheets, eliminating troublesome riveted seams.

To save weight, boilers were of nickel steel, rods were made of lighter alloy steel, and cabs and running boards were made of aluminum – one of the first extensive uses of aluminum in a production steam locomotive. Benefitting from NYC tests of roller bearings on several J-1's, all axles on each J-3 were equipped with roller bearings. Each J-3 also came with a one-piece, cast-steel engine frame. The technology for precision-casting of such large and intricate structures did not exist when the first J-1s were built, but Kiefer had tried out such frames in later models and had documented their maintenance savings.

Always interested in rail stresses, Kiefer had seen the report of the Bridge Stress Committee circulated in Britain about 1929. The J-3 thus incorporated full cross-balancing on all drivers, which helped reduce track stress still further from the low values posted by the J-1. From about 1930, Kiefer had had full cross-balancing added to J-1s then in production.

Performance results on the first J-3, delivered in September 1937 and tested that fall, seemed to improve on perfection. From a maximum cylinder horsepower of 4,075 for the J-1, that of the J-3 jumped to 4,725, a 16 percent increase. From the J-1's 3,490 drawbar horsepower at 55 mph, the J-3's drawbar hp hit 3,880 at 65 mph. At the same time, efficiency improved: From 2.28 pounds of coal per cylinder horsepower-hour for the J-1, the corresponding coal rate dropped to 2.03, an 11 percent improvement. The J-3 quickly picked up the nickname, "Super Hudson."

Also that fall, NYC management decided on a stem-to-stern facelift for the now-venerable *20th Century Limited*. The context for this facelift was the fresh style in art, architecture, fashion, and design that had spread since the late 1920s: Art Deco, or Art Moderne. The Central had been the first railroad to try full-scale streamlining on a steam locomotive, with its Case School-conceived, upside-down-bathtub shrouding of J1e 5344 in late 1934 as the *Commodore Vanderbilt* (see Chapter 14). By 1935, new diesel trains such as the Burlington's *Pioneer Zephyr* and others were stealing a lot of press. Industrial designer Henry Dreyfuss had restyled two K-5 Pacifics for the Central in 1936, for the new Cleveland-Detroit *Mercury*, and so the railroad turned to him again.

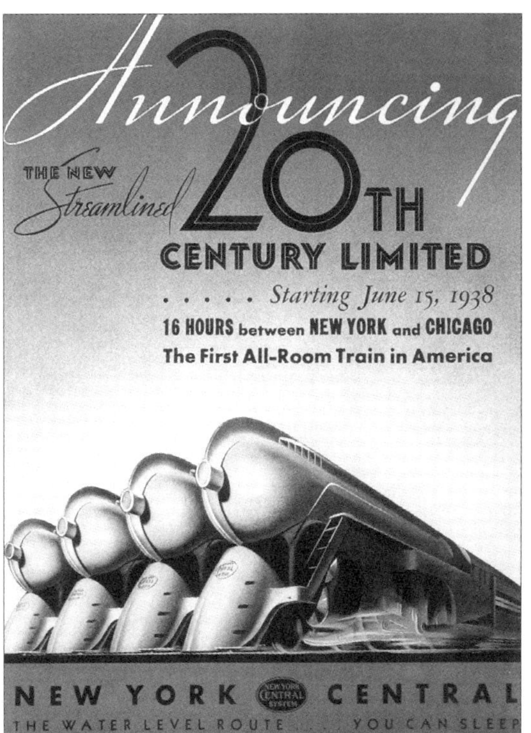

ABOVE The future arrived with the *Century's* 1938 makeover – and it looked like a Dreyfuss-styled Hudson.
Author's Collection

Just 33 years old in 1937, Dreyfuss was already famous as a Broadway set designer, with a growing reputation in the new field of industrial design that was being pioneered by Norman Bel Geddes, Raymond Loewy, Otto Kuhler, and Dreyfuss himself. Turning an everyday home appliance or a large industrial machine into a piece of sculpture was Dreyfuss's *forte*. New shapes for Royal typewriters, "Big Ben" alarm clocks, Hoover vacuum cleaners, General Electric washing machines, and later, Princess telephones and Honeywell thermostats, were among his best-known commissions.

A startlingly reborn J-3 emerged in June 1938. It had streamlining radically different from the J-1's comparatively tentative "stream lines" praised by company publicists back in 1927. Each of the final ten J-3s got a new Dreyfuss nose, side skirts, and boiler shrouding. Some got Timken roller-bearing rods and special Scullin disc driving wheels. Meanwhile, new *20th Century Limited* train sets came from Pullman, also styled inside and out by Dreyfuss. With much fanfare the new 13-car, all-room *Century* began running on a 16-hour schedule between New

RIGHT NYC Class J-3 4-6-4. Flash Gordon would have felt at home.
Courtesy Kalmbach Media

York and Chicago that lopped 30 minutes off the 1936 schedule and was two hours less than the 1932 timing. Judging from press and newsreel coverage, no train ever captured the imagination of the American public like the revamped *20th Century*. Here was a rolling, 1,200-foot Art Deco sculpture in its own right, one that stood not only for a new look, but for a reinvigorated approach to passenger travel. 'This is the future,' shouted this design, 'and the future is now.' Even *Fortune* magazine was impressed, commissioning a super-realist painting of a new Hudson's shining, disc-wheeled running gear by Charles Sheeler.

The Dreyfuss Hudson and its stylish train became an immediate hit; even though most other rail-travel patronage statistics stayed flat, the *Century's* popularity surged. By 1942, the train's consist was increased to 17 cars to satisfy wartime demand. The fin-nosed locomotive symbolized an era and became an American icon.

From 1938 through 1945, the J-3s ran off an average of 110,000 to120,000 miles per year per locomotive; the 10 Dreyfuss engines accumulated more than 130,000 miles each annually, with some logging 16,000 to 20,000 miles in some months, due to their longer 700- to 925-mile through runs each way on the *Century*. In terms of ton-miles hauled per year per locomotive, this was an amazing, six-fold increase in productivity over the K-3 fleet of the mid-1920s. Part of this high utilization rate was attributable to decreased downtime for repair. Each J-3 rolled up to 200,000 miles between major shoppings.[25]

Several other railroads designed and acquired their own Hudsons. A total of 437 ran on U.S. and Canadian lines in 1940. Owners included Nickel Plate (four came off the Alco floor right after the first NYC J-1), Santa Fe (ten oil-burners from Baldwin in 1927, with six more having 84-inch drivers in 1937), Lackawanna, Milwaukee Road, Chicago & North Western, Burlington, New

LEFT Nickel Plate Road's first four Hudsons, Class L-1a, were contemporaries of NYC's earliest examples. Alco-built L-1a No. 172 was at Euclid, Ohio, in July 1939. Four more were built by Lima in 1929 as Class L-1b.
Courtesy Kalmbach Media

BELOW Santa Fe 4-6-4 No. 3462. This class, with 84-inch drivers, pulled Santa Fe's finest trains from Chicago to La Junta, Colo., a daily run even longer than NYC's *20th Century Limited.*
Courtesy Kalmbach Media

ABOVE Milwaukee Road Class F-6 4-6-4 No. 6414. Milwaukee had the first 4-6-4, but bankruptcy prevented large deliveries until 1930. By then, the "Hudson" moniker had stuck.
Courtesy Kalmbach Media

RIGHT In 1937, Burlington Route 4-6-4 No. 4000 became *Aeolus* – Keeper of the Winds – the first stainless-steel streamlined steam locomotive. The shroud came off during World War II.
Harold K. Vollrath Collection

RIGHT Delaware, Lackawanna & Western's five 4-6-4s were designed for 80 mph. Built in 1937, they were Lackawanna's last steam passenger engines.
Courtesy Kalmbach Media

BELOW Canadian Pacific No. 2850, specially decorated for service leading the cross-Canada 1939 royal train of King George VI and Queen Elizabeth. Following that tour, CPR's semi-streamlined 4-6-4s officially were known as "Royal Hudsons."
Courtesy Kalmbach Media

Haven, Canadian Pacific, and Chesapeake & Ohio, which rebuilt some from big Pacifics and later acquired the last 4-6-4s, five L-2 class in 1948.

Few Hudsons survive. Two remain from Canadian National (along with three former Grand Trunk Railway 4-6-4T engines). Five Hudsons survive from Canadian Pacific – one is operable at this writing. A Chesapeake & Ohio L-1, which is also the only remaining locomotive with Type A poppet valves, is preserved at the Baltimore & Ohio Museum. Five of the Burlington's distinguished Hudsons survive, and one from the Nickel Plate Road. Two of Santa Fe's Hudsons remain; they routinely pulled the road's fastest trains 990 miles from Chicago to La Junta, Colo., without a change of power.

And New York Central's Hudsons, the legendary design that started it all? A tender from No. 5313 survives at Steamtown National Historic Site in Scranton, Pa., having been rebuilt as a steam generator car by NYC subsidiary Toronto, Hamilton & Buffalo. Beyond that one meager remnant, the Central's Hudsons remain only in memory and in pictures.

Chapter 13 Notes

1. *New York Central Lines Magazine*, August 1927, p. 77.
2. G.T. Wilson, quoted from an internal New York Central report, 1930.
3. George H. Drury, *Guide to North American Steam Locomotives*, 1996, p. 272.
4. Alfred E. Bruce, *The Steam Locomotive in America*, 1952, pp. 255-57.
5. Paul W. Kiefer, "The Hudson Type Passenger Locomotive," a paper to the Kiwanis Club, Brookline, Mass., reprinted by Franklin Railway Supply Co., a Lima Locomotive Works affiliate. Internal references make clear that the year is 1929. I am indebted to Richard Bartlett and Francis Hartigan for finding this paper at the DeGolyer Library, Southern Methodist University.
6. Ibid., pp. 4-5.
7. Ibid., p. 5.
8. Bruce, p. 305.
9. Weight and other data from *The Locomotive Cyclopedia*, 1927 and 1938 editions.
10. Kiefer, p. 6.
11. Ibid., p. 7.
12. C.F. Carter, "Concerning Those New Hudson Locomotives," *New York Central Lines Magazine*, October 1927, p. 12.
13. *Schenectady Gazette*, February 15, 1927, p. 1.
14. *Albany Times-Union*, February 15, 1927, section 2, p. 1.
15. "'Hudson Type,' Passenger Locomotive of New and Improved Design, in Service," *New York Central Lines Magazine*, March 1927, p. 12.
16. "New York Central Conducting Road Tests on Locomotive No. 5200," *New York Central Lines Magazine*, August 1927, pp. 71-78.
17. Ibid., p. 71.
18. Ibid., p. 72.
19. Ibid., pp. 72-76. Also see "Dynamometer Car Tests Promote Development of Locomotive," *Central Headlight*, Dec. 1942, p. 4; P.W. Kiefer, "Tells How N.Y.C. Cars and Engines are Designed and Maintained," in *Central Headlight*, June 1942, pp. 4-5; Peter P. Sloss, "Testing a New York Central Mohawk," *Railroad History*, Spring 1977, pp. 49-54; J. Parker Lamb, "Dissecting the Indicator Card," *Railroad History*, Spring-Summer 2010, pp. 70-76; and Ralph P. Johnson, *The Steam Locomotive: Its Theory, Operations and Economics*, 1944, chapters 21-22.
20. "Will Build 59 New Engines," *Schenectady Gazette*, May 11, 1927, p. 1.
21. C.F. Carter, "Concerning Those New Hudson Locomotives," *New York Central Lines Magazine*, October 1927, p. 12.
22. Kiefer, p. 5.
23. Kuhler and Henry, 1938 edition, p. 63.
24. Bruce, pp. 143-44. For furnace-volume increment of the J-3 over the J-1, see Bruce, p. 306.
25. C.M. Smith, "The Final 40 Years of Steam Locomotive Development on the New York Central," Railway & Locomotive Historical Society *Bulletin*, Spring 1970, pp. 43-51.

Chapter 14

Streamlining

THE STREAMLINED STYLING OF STEAM LOCOMOTIVES was a subject of hot debate among railroaders. After all, lurking underneath the new, external skin was still a conventional locomotive. Was the added façade worth the trouble?

When an engine was subjected to this treatment, either during its original construction or as a subsequent makeover, shopmen fabricated the designer's curved or "bullet" nose and side skirts in the sheet metal shop and then applied them to a supporting armature secured to the boiler. The final result was a locomotive looking quite new, but deceptively so.

Whether the fresh look was functional depended on one's definition of that term. To locomotive maintenance crews, the new sheet-metal panels interfered with ready access to lubricators, pumps, and other components that required daily attention, thus adding to servicing time. The addition of servicing doors or hatches helped somewhat, but the otherwise simple troubleshooting of a run of plumbing, for example, still required removal of entire panels. To some designers, the new external shape promised a reduction in air resistance. Wind-tunnel tests were part of the development of several early steam streamliners. To traffic department officers, however, the "functional" role of the streamlining was to attract more paying passengers and thus to rejuvenate Depression-decimated rail ridership. According to a contemporary journalist, one railroad officer stated that "the whole point of streamlining is not to lower air resistance but to lower passenger resistance."[1]

Railroad mechanical engineers in the U.S. sought to handle aerodynamic questions scientifically, within their own professional context. Engineers ran several series of tests of a moving train's air resistance, beginning as early as 1906. An "Electric Railway Test Commission" made tests that year near St. Louis and found different values for the air resistance of cars with variously shaped front-ends, by taking pressure measurements from a variety of points on the cars' outer surfaces. A front-end shaped as a parabolic wedge reduced air resistance at 60 mph by two-thirds, compared to a flat front. The actual values at that speed, however, were small: 835 pounds of resistance for the flat front and 245 for the parabolic.[2] Investigators found the air resistance

One of the New Haven Railroad's ten bullet-nosed I-5 class streamlined 4-6-4 Hudson locomotives, built by Baldwin in 1937, powers the *Bay State* in February 1948.
J.P. Ahrens, Courtesy Kalmbach Media

Built new by Alco in 1937 for Milwaukee Road's *Hiawatha* streamliners, the road's Class A 4-4-2 Atlantic locomotives were styled by industrial designer Otto Kuhler. Concealment of plumbing and hardware behind streamlined shrouding (as on the later Milwaukee Road Class F-7 4-6-4 Hudson engine shown at lower right) impeded troubleshooting and maintenance.
Courtesy Kalmbach Media

generated by the carbody's sides and top to be a relatively modest factor, but air resistance caused by the undercarriage was neglected. Later tests, of increasing sophistication, were done in the 1920s and '30s by the University of Illinois, by the New York Central, by Canada's National Research Laboratories in Ottawa, by the Massachusetts Institute of Technology for the Burlington Railroad, and by the American Locomotive Co. using New York University's small wind tunnel.[3]

By the early 1930s, it was understood that although air resistance increased with the square of a train's velocity, the reducible amount of air resistance below 100 mph was tiny in comparison to mechanical resistance from bearings or the interaction of flanges and rails. The greatest resistance factor, however, overwhelmingly, was the train's weight on even the smallest grades. Computations made from formulas established in the 1930s and still used today show that, for an unstreamlined locomotive moving at 70 mph, about 280 horsepower is absorbed by air resistance. An achievable amount of streamlining on a steam locomotive – smooth casing over front and sides with rolling machinery left uncovered – could reduce air resistance by 35 percent. Meanwhile, the locomotive might have to put out 3,500 horsepower to keep a heavy passenger train moving at 70 mph on level track, and more than 5,000 horsepower to keep the same train rolling at just 40 mph up a one-percent grade.[4]

Researchers in the 1930s found that in a passenger train with multiple cars, the locomotive accounted for about one-third of the air resistance. Most was due to the open gaps between the trailing cars and, unavoidably, to the turbulence caused by the cars' trucks and underbodies. Underbodies were cluttered with battery boxes, mechanical gear, brake rigging, and air conditioning components, all of which had to be readily accessible for daily inspections and servicing, thus making enclosure impractical. What really threw all the aerodynamic theory into a cocked hat was that, at speeds below 100 mph, a train rarely encountered the air straight-on. In nearly all cases, the "relative wind" (incident air from the prevailing wind combined with the motion of the train) impacted the train at various angles off the front quarter, thereby negating much of the effect of a streamlined nose and other aerodynamic measures, and greatly increasing total air resistance compared to that of an ideal, head-on wind.

The real story of streamlining was written by the industrial designers who understood "function" as including unquantifiable factors of psychology and fashion. Artist and designer Otto Kuhler articulated a concept of "improved railroad design as a means of getting more people to ride trains."[5]

> For tradition-bound railroad men, some of [their] innovations might look quite radical. Not so to the public. It takes dramatic changes to hit the public between the eyes, to catch the public's attention and imagination, and ultimately the public's patronage. ... Speed alone is not enough. ... You run a fast train. Then let me design a much slower train. Let me paint it in ... colors, offer the public interior beauty and comfort suggested by the exterior color scheme, and put an exciting new streamlined engine on the front. I am willing to bet that my train will be packed and make money.[6]

Kuhler was one of the first to suggest streamlining a steam locomotive, publishing watercolor drawings of a streamlined New York Central Hudson-type in 1928 – six years before J-1e No. 5344 was stylized by the Case School for NYC as the *Commodore Vanderbilt*.[7] His earliest sketches showed an influence

New York Central J-1e Hudson No. 5344, named *Commodore Vanderbilt*, was streamlined in 1934 with what came to be known by critics as an "inverted bathtub" shroud.

Courtesy Kalmbach Media

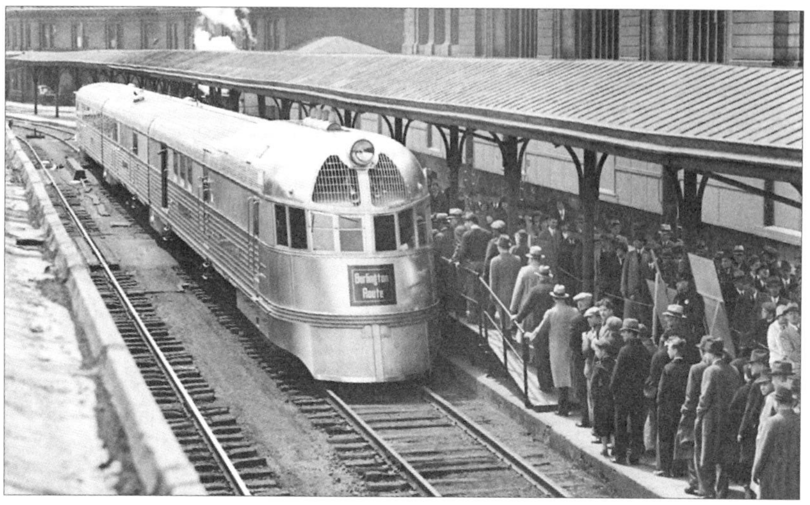

Burlington Route's stainless-steel *Zephyr* 9900 (known in later years as the *Pioneer Zephyr*, and preserved in retirement at Chicago's Museum of Science and Industry), on exhibit at New York Central's Albany, N.Y., station during an April 1934 barnstorming tour.
Courtesy Kalmbach Media

from French and German locomotives which, although unstreamlined in the Art Deco sense, often incorporated "wind-splitter" designs and rakish lines; Kuhler had grown up in Germany and came to the U.S. in 1923. Retained as a consultant by the American Locomotive Co., Kuhler won acclaim for his design of the Milwaukee Road *Hiawatha* of 1935, a streamlined, steam-hauled train in the highly competitive Chicago-Twin Cities market. His design was an immediate hit with the public.

At about the same time, streamliners with internal-combustion power were already making a splash. Union Pacific's M-10000, featuring a distillate engine and aluminum carbodies, arrived first, in February 1934. The Burlington's *Pioneer Zephyr* debuted in May, with a diesel engine and stainless-steel

Kuhler combined his artistic and design talents for the American Locomotive Co., designing the builder's advertisements as well as streamlined steam locomotives. This 1936 ad commemorated the 200th anniversary of James Watt's birth.
Author's Collection

ABOVE Otto Kuhler's final streamlined steam locomotive design was this 4-6-2 Pacific, restyled in 1941 for the Southern Railway.

Courtesy Kalmbach Media

LEFT In his streamlined steam repertoire, Kuhler reused favorite design elements from one client to another. Baltimore & Ohio's *Royal Blue* P-7 class Pacific of 1937 predated Southern No. 1380 by four years, but both shared a bulbous "torpedo" nose, narrow skyline casing, and concentric headlight trim.

B&O, Kevin J. Holland Collection

construction that would become more typical of the streamlined era. It set a new long-distance railroad speed record, dashing nonstop from Denver to Chicago's Century of Progress world's fair in 13 hours, an incredible average of 78 mph, with sprints to 112 mph. These clean, lightweight trains immediately gave steam a bad image: Diesels were the wave of the future; steam was on the way out.

So another agenda became apparent. Steam-locomotive builders saw streamlining as a way to protect their passenger-engine market. Alco Vice President Joseph Ennis was instrumental in getting Kuhler hired. Ennis's notion was that Kuhler could help Alco convince railroads to stick with steam. A streamlined steam locomotive was about half the purchase price per unit of horsepower as a diesel, yet would project to the public, Alco argued, an equally progressive image.

Kuhler turned out to be right, for a while. Steam-propelled streamliners, with fresh car interiors to match their sleek external looks, became co-stars with the diesels in an otherwise bleak passenger trade. Between 1935 and 1940, American railroads introduced more steam streamliners than diesel ones. Whether internal- or external-combustion, these trains made good money for their sponsors, while conventional train patronage kept in the doldrums.[8] Kuhler designed a greater number of streamlined steam trains, together with the outer casings for their locomotives, than anyone else. He liked bold shapes, overlaid with multiple stripes, multiple colors, and added decorative elements.

Virtually identical locomotives at their mechanical core, Pennsylvania Railroad K-4s 4-6-2 Pacifics 3847 and 3768 (the latter restyled by Raymond Loewy) illustrate the extent to which streamlining could convey a sense of modernism, but could also restrict maintenance access to newly concealed appliances.
Courtesy Kalmbach Media

Shown here leading the *Broadway Limited*, PRR No. 1120 was one of four K-4s Pacifics streamlined by Loewy's firm in 1940. Nos. 2665, 3678, and 5338 were similarly restyled.
Harold K. Vollrath Collection

Raymond Loewy was equally taken by the challenge of styling locomotives. While Kuhler was almost unknown outside the railroad industry, Loewy was a leading industrial designer by the mid-1930s. The Pennsylvania Railroad was a major patron, giving him numerous makeover projects, from wastebaskets to entire trains. Despite his later notoriety as the designer of Studebaker automobiles, the livery for Air Force One, and a host of other iconic images, Loewy stated near the end of his life that the locomotive commissions were his most fulfilling.

Loewy illustrated his approach in a popular little art-photo book published in 1937, *The Locomotive (its esthetics)*.[9] To Loewy, the effect on potential passengers was rather secondary. He was through-and-through a modernist, interested in smooth, clean lines with only an accent of decoration. While not mentioning Kuhler by name, Loewy takes a swipe at his rival. Below a photo of Kuhler's *Hiawatha*, Loewy writes that, "Its orange and aluminum colour scheme is rather irritating."[10]

Loewy was interested in heroic image, "romance" and "glamour." Railroad trains were, for him, the ultimate symbol of power and speed. In his preface to *Locomotive* he gushes:

My youth was charmed by the glamour of the locomotive. ... Never did I dream that my career as an artist-engineer would lead me some day to that glorious adventure, the designing of a steam engine.[11]

Consciously or not, his style through the 1930s embodied a great deal from the Futurism movement that arose among some painters and sculptors in Italy, France, and Britain in the first decade of the 20th century. To Futurists, the machine was the focus, with humans often subservient to the machine, with shapes that gave a powerful musculature to mechanical elements.

Henry Dreyfuss was human-centered. His design approach is explicit in the title of his 1955 book *Designing for People*, which has autobiographical elements but is mostly an artistic manifesto.[12] To him,

Industrial design is a means of making sure the machine creates attractive commodities that work better because they are designed to work better. It is coincidental, but equally important, that they sell better. ... *What we are working on is going to be ridden in, sat upon, looked at, talked into, activated, operated, or in some way used by people. ...* [If] *people are made safer, more comfortable ... or just plain happier – the designer has succeeded.*"[13] [Emphasis in the original.]

When it came to trains, Dreyfuss only designed three, all for the New York Central: the *Mercury* of 1936, the *20th Century Limited* of 1938 (both steam-hauled), and the *20th Century Limited* of 1948 (a slight redesign from 1938 but incorporating General Motors diesel locomotives). Although Kuhler, Loewy, and Dreyfuss each redesigned exteriors and interiors, Dreyfuss was much more interested in the latter. "The ideal in train design is a car-to-car integration of all passenger comforts."[14] As for locomotives, diesel had entirely supplanted steam by the time he wrote his book:

Train exteriors acquired the new look they have today in the early thirties and haven't been changed much since. Railroad men found that ease of maintenance was more important than fancy skirts and pseudo streamlining, which had a brief flair, and settled on standardized cars.[15]

Henry Dreyfuss's first project for New York Central was the *Mercury* of 1936, comprising this streamlined 4-6-2 Pacific locomotive and a train of cosmetically modernized cars.
Courtesy Kalmbach Media

Dreyfuss's reference to "pseudo streamlining," though having the benefit of post-1930s hindsight, is indicative of his disdain for anything other than a thoroughgoing, inside-and-out, organic philosophy of design. Tacking on tinware over an unchanged mechanical device was inimical to him. Yet it is perhaps ironic that one of his best-remembered designs is the *20th Century Limited's* steam locomotive, an icon of 1930s industrial high-fashion. Its image reappears regularly, even today, in articles and books on the period.

If trains could be thought of as having an architecture, in which exterior design reflects an interior aesthetic as well, and in which exterior and interior are conceived together, then a Futurist façade applied to a traditional form confuses the meaning of either and lacks integrity. To modern semioticians, this might be, in Marshall Blonsky's acid phrase, "the sign of architecturalness. A thin veneer."[16]

If 1930s streamlining was intended in part to convey a dramatic sense of velocity (Kuhler sometimes called it "speedlining"), then present-day readers need to appreciate that the train as a socially understood symbol of speed long predates Art Deco. At the turn of the 20th century, a picture of a rushing locomotive – a steam locomotive with all its erect, vertical lines and conflation of circular and rectangular shapes – was an exemplar of the fastest vehicles on the planet. *Frank Leslie's Illustrated Newspaper* and other popular magazines frequently ran such images, usually in connection with some new world speed record (inevitably, a *rail* speed record) or a railroad company's introduction of some new express train.

Artists developed a set of techniques to accentuate the feeling of speed: smoke flowing back, streaks of steam around the wheels. Photographers, using vertical-shutter cameras, produced images with the locomotive appearing to lean forward in its pell-mell haste. By the 1910s, better cameras removed the lean, but photographers knew how to use low angles and dramatic light to convey speed. Steam locomotives for fast passenger trains, from the 1850s to the last 4-6-4 Hudson type, always had large-diameter driving wheels, and such tall wheels were themselves a symbol of speed. Dreyfuss, for his *Mercury* design, installed lights to illuminate the engine's driving wheels at night; Loewy wrote that the "new type of balanced disc" drivers of the 1930s "greatly contribut[ed] to modernized appearance."[17]

Santa Fe's only streamlined steam locomotive, 4-6-4 No. 3460 – dubbed the "Blue Goose" for its two-tone blue livery – was built by Baldwin in 1937. *Courtesy Kalmbach Media*

Olive Dennis was a designer hired by the Baltimore & Ohio in the 1940s to help spruce up a staid corporate image. She revamped car interiors, designed dining-car china and tableware, and, in at least one case, streamlined a steam locomotive and its train. This was the handsome, post-war *Cincinnatian*, which garnered the B&O considerable press.

B&O, Kevin J. Holland Collection

Streamlining of steam locomotives, therefore, is best understood as being embedded in the artistic vocabulary of the Art Deco or Art Moderne period. Streamlining of these engines was a brief symbolic phase, within a century-and-a-quarter of symbolic change from the 1820s through steam locomotion's final demise. Speed was always a key element in the meaning of trains, whether mechanical engineers or industrial designers controlled their outward shape. By the mid-1940s, nearly all the steam streamliners had had their skirts and casings removed. The clean-running diesels, whose shape related to their nature as internal-combustion vehicles, had brought with them a new set of symbols, derived from those of the 1930s but superseding them. In the meantime, new realizations of speed – including the airplane and the automobile – had begun to take the place of trains in the popular imagination.

Chapter 14 Notes

1. David P. Morgan, "He Sold Streamlining," *Trains*, July 1952.
2. R.P. Johnson, *The Steam Locomotive: Its Theory, Operation and Economics* (1944 ed.), pp. 186-87.
3. Ibid., pp. 184-93.
4. Ibid., p. 189. Other locomotive and train resistance formulas appear in Johnson, Chapter 12.
5. Otto Kuhler, *My Iron Journey*, National Railway Historical Society Intermountain Chapter, 1967, p. 223.
6. Ibid., p. 233.
7. Ibid., p. 158.
8. Mark Reutter, "The Lost Promise of the American Railroad," *Wilson Quarterly*, Winter 1994.
9. Raymond Loewy, *The Locomotive (its esthetics)*, 1937. Reprinted in 1988.
10. Ibid., figure 62.
11. Ibid., Preface.
12. Dreyfuss, *Designing for People*, 1955; reprinted in 1974.
13. Ibid., p. 112
14. Ibid.
15. Ibid., p. 122.
16. Marshall Blonsky, quoted in *The Washington Post*, July 9, 1992, p. C1.
17. Loewy, *Locomotive*, figure 57.

1635

Chapter 15

The Northern

IN ALL THE WEALTH OF LITERATURE on locomotive development, context rarely plays a part. Improvements seem to have followed an internally ordered genesis. In time, the story goes, larger engines replaced smaller ones, and better auxiliary gadgets replaced those of less efficiency. Leaders in locomotive design reinforced the idea. Frequent writer-to-the-trade Lawford Fry, prominent as a Baldwin Locomotive Works consulting engineer and author of a seminal 1924 analysis of boiler performance, made the point often in his own or quoted maxims. For example, "the changes made since 1830 in the size and shape of locomotive engines have been more matters of detail than of principle" and "designers may express their personalities in details such as trucks, but the logic of the engineering requirements is inescapable."[1]

Alfred Bruce, Alco's last chief steam designer and author of a comprehensive 1952 history of 20th century steam locomotive development, took that view regarding the first 4-8-4 Northern-type of 1926-1927: "This type was, of course, the logical successor to the 4-8-2 type" and "[t]he use of four-wheel trailer trucks instead of two-wheel trucks was the result of pure arithmetic and little else."[2] Of course.

The 4-8-4, "the standard modern American steam locomotive"[3] in the words of one authority, and produced for at least 36 North American railroads over a 24-year span, has a much more interesting history. Context, as well as pure arithmetic, is key.

As Bruce and many later writers have pointed out, the Northern ultimately incorporated a convergence of many engineering changes since World War I, in materials, fabrication techniques, frame and running gear design, boiler proportions, mechanical stoking, feedwater heating, and numerous other details. The availability of alloy steels, better casting techniques, improved reliability of welding, newer valve gears, better counterbalancing, advent of roller bearings, higher-temperature superheat, larger combustion chambers, bigger grate areas (beyond the size that could be manually stoked), waste-heat recovery devices, and even things like better en route signaling all provided the internal engineering context.

Not every railroad referred to its 4-8-4 locomotives as "Northerns." Delaware, Lackawanna & Western 4-8-4 No. 1635 was one of that company's "Pocono" types, named for the Pennsylvania mountains where DL&W trains faced challenging grades.

S. Botsko, Courtesy Kalmbach Media

A larger context was World War I itself. For railroad managers, the federal takeover from December 1917 to March 1920 was traumatic. After enthusiastically pledging in the spring of 1917 every resource to help the war effort and quickly creating a special board to coordinate war shipments, railroad leaders saw their traffic systems head toward collapse. War supplies and troops all rushed east, bound for Atlantic ports. A federally instituted system to prioritize shipments broke down because too many shipments received priority tags. More freight cars filled yards near ports of embarkation than switching crews could sort and get to the docks; ships couldn't sail on schedule and rail yards backed up throughout the Midwest. Troop movements were caught in the glut. Eastbound trains of soldiers waited in sidings, stuck behind other trains ahead. In a few celebrated cases, such delays ran to more than a day, and people in adjacent towns brought over hot meals. Meanwhile, thousands of skilled railroad employees jammed Army recruitment centers and signed up. Other men, some working 18-hour or longer shifts and sensing a bargaining opportunity, threatened strikes, and there were a number of wildcat walkouts.[4]

In 1930, a writer for the New York Central observed that

> The general public does not readily appreciate the progress made by the railroads of America since the late war. The World War, so far-reaching in its effects, brought about a revolution in the operation of our railroads. During the war there was a continual plea for speed in the transportation of supplies and troops. Under such pressure, railroad men handled equipment [*i.e.*, moved trains] in a far different manner than was ever tried before, or even considered practical.[5]

This is, to say the least, a rather incomplete gloss on the events of the war, but the pressure he describes for a more time-conscious operating style is real.

USRA's waning influence

The United States Railroad Administration (USRA), under William G. McAdoo, flatly took charge of all aspects of logistical planning and operations, with a federal manager in charge of each railroad. Until then comfortable in their monopoly on long-distance haulage, railroad executives were used to moving traffic at a leisurely pace. Except for the flagship "limiteds" and "flyers" for well-heeled patrons, most passenger trains only occasionally exceeded 50 mph, general freight trains plodded at 20 to 30 in between long stops at sidings, and "drag" freights might move for hours at 15. Such low-speed operation was entirely rational: It saved wear and tear on equipment, saved fuel, and did not tax either the air-brake equipment of the era or the dispatching system. Freight customers of the time were adapted to the pace; the idea of alacrity had no relevance for the great bulk of freight, since customers had no alternative. Being so utterly dependent on railroads, shippers could affect railroad schedules about as well as they might affect the weather.

While USRA officials concentrated on dispatching and coordination issues, another decision was the immediate expansion of locomotive production. McAdoo, however, had a twist. He wanted standardized locomotives, and designated a panel of engineering talent from the three major locomotive manufacturers and from selected railroad motive-power departments to design them. The panel's objectives were to cut the delays caused by the railroads' traditional system of custom design and to create an interchangeable fleet. But another important objective was to get new engines into use with the latest, most efficient design features in order to improve productivity. The engineering panel, which included Baldwin's Samuel Vauclain, Alco's Francis Cole, and Lima's William Woodard, ably responded with twelve excellent designs in eight wheel arrangements.

Many railroad managers, though subject to federal authority, at first expressed deep resentment, not only to the takeover but to the idea of locomotive standardization. The story of the USRA designs and the railroad community's reaction is told in Chapter 10, but there is an important connection to the genesis of the 4-8-4. Between 1918 and 1920, more than 1,000 new locomotives of conventional though advanced design came into the U.S. fleet. About 800 more engines, also of USRA design, eventually followed.

After the end of USRA control in 1920, new kinds of federal intervention, and new competition, only added to the pressure. Any return to prewar norms was stymied by the combination of economic recession in the early '20s, labor unrest, ICC delay (and outright refusal) to grant rate increase, and losses of short-haul carriage to trucks and autos. Railroad industry measures to accelerate speed included wider deployment of automatic block signals, streamlined procedures for delivery of telegraphic orders, improved yards, installation of heavier rail on mainline routes, and, in some cases, double-tracking of former single-track subdivisions prone to bottlenecks.[6]

Genesis of the Northern

The prelude to the 4-8-4 now becomes more specific. In March 1920, just released from federal control, management of the Northern Pacific Railroad in St. Paul, Minn., considered a specification for a new passenger locomotive, significantly larger and more powerful than any class then on NP. Assistant Mechanical Superintendent William J. Bohan, charged with evaluating alternatives, used the USRA 4-6-2 and 4-8-2 designs as his standards.[7] NP had not acquired any USRA engines of these types, since its existing passenger engine fleet handled war traffic acceptably and the locomotive needs of Eastern railroads had taken priority. Bohan's choices for comparison, however, reflected the high regard in the trade these designs had earned since they first appeared in 1918.

By 1920, NP's passenger traffic had seemed to stabilize, although the trains were getting heavier. All-steel passenger cars, bought since 1915, had replaced wooden cars on most mainline trains. Steel cars increased train weights some 15 percent, from about 70 tons per car to more than 80. These weight increases overtaxed NP's Q-class 4-6-2s on the NP's mountainous profile, resulting in unwanted double-heading or late trains.

Primary design criteria in Bohan's evaluation were axle loading, tractive effort, boiler capacity, and driving-wheel diameter. Loading was to be under 65,000 pounds per driving axle, tractive effort needed to be 25 to 30 percent greater than NP's then-newest 4-6-2 type (the Q-4 class), and driver diameter would permit higher speed. Bohan recommended a design based on the USRA light Pacific type but with slightly larger cylinders and a longer combustion chamber to give greater cylinder and boiler power. Because of the somewhat larger boiler, estimated overall weight of Bohan's design was about 10 tons

Northern Pacific Class Q-5 and Q-6 4-6-2 Pacific-types. NP's search for a new passenger engine started with the 4-6-2s and led ultimately to the 4-8-4. Labor troubles at NP's coal mines played a central role. *R.V. Nixon, Courtesy Kalmbach Media*

heavier than the USRA counterpart, but axle loading at 62,500 pounds was well within NP's limit. Advanced devices such as a stoker and a feedwater heater were to be fitted.[8]

The driver-diameter choice was significant. Bohan and other mechanical department staff definitely wanted the 73-inch diameter of the USRA light Pacific, four inches taller than that of the Q classes, to raise the speed of maximum power. The USRA heavy Pacific was definitely out, since it exceeded the 65,000-pound axle limit. The USRA light and heavy Mountain-type designs, while having ample power and lower axle loadings, had the same 69-inch driver diameter as the Q class, which the NP staff felt would entail speed restrictions. A 4-8-2 with 73-inch drivers was not specifically considered. The operating vice president, W.T. Tyler, expressed the view that, in all events, a 4-8-2 would be larger, and therefore more expensive, than needed. Under pressure from top management to keep equipment acquisition costs down, reserve capacity per locomotive was not a concern. The foremost economic factor to the mechanical and operating departments in this case was locomotive purchase price.[9]

The 20 Q-5s turned out to be a bit overweight, due to design changes requested by NP after the initial contract. The engines also came in at a higher price than originally estimated (together with labor inputs, total weight was traditionally a key factor in the builder's calculation of final price), leading to a flurry of complaints from NP officials to manufacturer Alco. Alco was a preferred supplier to NP, however, because it almost always underbid its competitors. Another 20 engines, class Q-6, were ordered in 1923. But NP managers were disappointed: The new Pacifics proved unable to keep schedules when their trains were longer than usual. In late 1922, mechanical department chief H.M. Curry observed that passenger operations were still plagued with late trains due to insufficient locomotive capacity, a problem the Q-6s did not solve.[10]

The 1921-1922 recession put off further passenger locomotive purchases. Then, a new factor fundamentally altered the picture: strikes in NP-owned coal mines in Montana.

Northern Pacific owned deep mines at Chestnut and Red Lodge, which produced a good grade of bituminous for locomotive fuel. Miners there began organizing during the war and unionized themselves in the early 1920s. Under labor law of the day, the railroad did not need to recognize the union or grant its wage demands, which caused more walkouts. In 1923, the railroad responded by building track toward new pits in Colstrip, Mont., in Rosebud County. These were to be strip operations, so workers would be fewer, non-union, and would earn lower wages. This fuel source had not been tapped previously because the heating value of Rosebud coal (a subbituminous, almost lignite mineral) was low: only about 8,000-8,500 BTU per pound, versus 12,000 BTU for Red Lodge coal, and up to 15,000 BTU for coal used by Eastern U.S. railroads. Moreover, the ash content and moisture of the new coal were both high, at about 10 and 20 percent respectively.[11] On all counts, this was exceedingly poor stuff for locomotives, but top management at NP was determined to use it. The Colstrip mines began production in September 1924.

Older and smaller engines on NP, such as the elderly 4-6-0 and 2-8-0 types used on branchline passenger trains and local freights, tolerated the Rosebud coal, since these locomotives seldom ran at maximum power and could empty their ashpans several times each day. For larger engines, working the main line on longer runs, the low-heat, high-ash coal was simply inadequate with existing firebox designs. As an experiment, the mechanical department modified a Class W-3 2-8-2 freighter with an expanded grate area, to permit more coal to be burned at one time. But there was apparently too much air coming up through the grates and not enough firebox volume for efficient burning, and engine performance suffered. Thus, for most of its traffic, NP was still dependent on the deep-mined fuel.[12]

In early 1926, NP General Mechanical Superintendent Silas Zwight directed his staff to begin working up specifications for a new passenger locomotive. The basic performance hurdle was that the new engine should keep schedule with the same train weight as a Q-5 or Q-6, but ascend grades twice as steep without a helper. At the same time, Zwight told E.L. Grimm (who had succeeded Bohan) and mechanical engineer E.R. Manor to set up a task force to solve the problem of burning Rosebud coal in large engines.[13]

George L. Ernstrom (who in the 1940s became Mechanical Superintendent) was part of the task force. He knew that locomotives running on western parts of the Burlington Route used coal from Sheridan, Wyo., which was low in heat and high in moisture, although not as poor as Rosebud. By comparing grate arrangements, Ernstrom found that Burlington used a ratio of air openings to grate area of about 25 percent, as compared to 43 percent on NP. The task force then arranged for another W-3, at Livingston, Mont., to run tests with grates having differently sized air passages. A surprisingly low nine percent air-to-opening ratio worked best for combustion. But the inflowing air, accelerating through the restricted grate passages, then tended to lift coal off the grates, tearing apart the firebed. This action allowed coal to drift in pileups toward the front of the firebox, preventing even burning. The solution was a larger grate area, a 12.5 percent air ratio, and a reduction in

The Delta trailing truck on Alco-built NP Class A 4-8-4 No. 2600 is partially obscured by the ashpan. All succeeding classes of NP 4-8-4 were Baldwin products, with a slightly different trailing-truck design.
R.V. Nixon, Courtesy Kalmbach Media

the normal slant of the firebox to practically flat (to prevent the coal pileups forward), together with modified drafting at the smokestack.[14]

Back at NP headquarters in St. Paul, analysis progressed on the new locomotive specification. For the needed speed and tractive effort, a 73-inch-drivered 4-8-2 seemed the most promising configuration – similar to the design rejected in 1920 as too big. Clearly, however, such an engine was entirely hypothetical: It could not burn Rosebud coal and sustain enough evaporation to power the cylinders, since a large enough grate could not be carried on a one-axle trailing truck. Then the task force's conclusions came in. It soon became apparent to the design team that a flat grate of 115 square feet, with Ernstrom's air ratio, would be needed. In a passenger locomotive, such a huge grate area would be unprecedented. The firebox would also need a big combustion chamber to allow an immense furnace volume, something on the order of 800 cubic feet.

Thus was born the 4-8-4 – in a direct line from a class of 4-6-2s. Alfred Bruce's characterization of the 4-8-4 as the product of "pure arithmetic and little else" ignores a rich, contextual history of engineering decision-making. In fact, the 4-8-4 is primarily an expression of reaction to labor trouble; miners are as important to its story as engineers. The 4-8-4 is also an expression of some management changes at NP and a consequent change in what was regarded as "economic" – away from favoring an engine with a lower price tag, and favoring one that could reduce the need for helper engines and crews. And the pressure toward higher average speeds and more reliable schedule-keeping for all trains, not just for the premier expresses, did not come from within the railroad industry. Only after such exogenous factors are understood does arithmetic, albeit logical, have any bearing.

After Alco engineers received the specification from NP and worked out the detailed engineering, the first of 12 new locomotives were towed out of the Schenectady, N.Y., finishing shop in December 1926. They received a designation symbolizing their departure from the past, NP Class A, and a name, the "Northern Pacific" type (later shortened to "Northern").

The chosen design of trailing truck was from an Alco-favored firm, Commonwealth Steel castings. The Class A employed the first four-wheel version of the popular "Delta" form in a production engine. In contrast to the experimental, short-wheelbase Commonwealth trucks applied earlier to an engine on the Santa Fe and to another on the New York Central, the truck on the NP's locomotive had an extra-long, 84-inch wheelbase.[15] This wheelbase spread weight over a longer rail length, which was important to a railroad that still had some 90-pounds-to-the-yard rail, regarded as a minimal weight for main lines. Axle loading, at 65,000 pounds on each driving axle and 60,000 pounds on the second, booster-equipped axle of the trailing truck, was a few hundred pounds less than a Q-5. To handle the greater total engine weight, NP strengthened bridges on affected routes – something the company did not want to do in 1920.

Overall engine length was a remarkable 63 feet, and so drawbar angles between engine and tender when on sharp curves had been an important concern. A lateral-motion device for the first driving axle not only cushioned the flanges of the wheels on that axle, it also kept drawbar angles within reason.

Boiler efficiency was aided by a relatively new device: an "exhaust-steam injector," mounted on the engineer's side. The Coffin-brand, closed-type feedwater heaters used on many NP locomotives gave trouble from deposits building up on the water side of the heater, such that heating effectiveness in service was greatly reduced.[16] Boiler power was then degraded by 5 to10 percent. NP designers were therefore willing to try an alternate way of recovering heat from exhausted steam that otherwise was wasted out the stack. The exhaust-steam injector used a two-stage combination of live steam and steam from the locomotive cylinders' exhaust to carry water into the boiler, with an action similar to a conventional injector. Unfortunately the waste-heat recovery rate, and the boiler-power increment, was only about half that of a feedwater heater,[17] and so NP did not put the devices on any additional engines. Eventually, the open-type Worthington feedwater heater proved superior. By the nature of its design, scale or deposits did not affect its efficiency, and it reduced dissolved oxygen in boiler water, which prolonged boiler life. NP applied the Worthington heater to later 4-8-4s and retrofitted other mainline engines, including the Q-5 and Q-6 classes.

In road tests using a dynamometer car, with the boiler operating at 225 psi, a Class-A engine reached 3,500 indicated horsepower (i.e., cylinder horsepower) between 43 and 50 mph, and topped at 3,100 drawbar horsepower at 43 to 45 mph. On another run, the same locomotive briefly

This elevated view of NP Class A-5 No. 2684 shows the Worthington feedwater heater, protruding from the top of the smokebox ahead of the smokestack, just behind the bell.

Courtesy Kalmbach Media

peaked at 4,000 cylinder horsepower at 44 mph. The road tests and analysis showed that, despite the large grate area, the boiler could only supply steam at a continual rate to sustain 3,200 cylinder horsepower, meaning 2,800-2,900 horsepower at the drawbar. (At least 200 horsepower was lost due to the presence of the exhaust-steam injector instead of a proper feedwater heater.)

The high tractive effort at lower speed – more than 61,000 pounds at starting, plus another 12,000 pounds from the booster – allowed the locomotive to meet its performance goal of hauling nine steel cars up a 1.9 percent grade. In fact, the new engine could move such a train on schedule up a 2.2 percent grade without a helper. But in horsepower, and hence in performance above 20 mph, the Class A was disappointing. Maximum output was less than the 4,075 horsepower of the smaller Hudson type, introduced by the New York Central two months after the first Northern. The NP mechanical department concluded that, given its fuel, the Class A was under-boilered.[18]

The necessary draft to burn Rosebud coal resulted in high back pressure in the cylinders, so NP engineers tried many different alternative designs of front-end exhaust nozzle, petticoat pipe, and stack to reduce the back pressure, yet adequately burn the fuel. With a larger-diameter exhaust nozzle that gave reduced back pressure, however, locomotive power dropped by 600-900 horsepower. As found by Ernstrom, a taller smokestack provided a better venturi effect and a net benefit. After 1926, most NP engines were built with stacks as tall as clearance limits would permit.[19]

A major operating improvement did come with the NP 4-8-4s. In 1923, there were 14 passenger districts between St. Paul and Seattle, meaning that 14 locomotives and 13 locomotive changes were involved in a one-way passenger run across the system. As the Q-6 Pacifics came into service, a few districts were consolidated. In 1927, the districts were reduced to just six, with Northerns handling the trains between Jamestown, N.D., and Glendive, Mont. (323 miles), and between Livingston and Missoula, Mont. (240 miles, including Bozeman Pass). Doubleheading of Q-5s and Q-6s was eliminated in these districts, thus cutting engine crew costs in half for the affected runs. Schedules were improved and annual cost savings, including fuel and labor as well as extended runs of through freight trains, amounted to about $260,000, or almost $4 million in 2019.[20]

Timken's "Four Aces"

In 1931, as the Depression was taking a firm grip and rail traffic was plummeting, NP got involved with another 4-8-4, but not one of its conception. Two years before, T.V. Buckwalter, vice president of the Timken Roller Bearing Co. in Akron, Ohio, had proposed an innovative sales tool. Paid for with $150,000 from Buckwalter's employer, Alco engineered and built a unique Northern-type, completed in March 1930. Sporting road number 1111, and christened "Four Aces," the locomotive began a nationwide, 100,000-mile promotional tour. With Timken boldly lettered in silver leaf on its tender, and with the pips of spade, heart, diamond, and club painted on its sand dome, Four Aces took to the road. And for the first time on any North American locomotive, it had roller bearings on all of its axles.

Timken had been trying, with high visibility but with little success, to break into the railroad market for several years. A few locomotive designers

Timken's "Four Aces," conceived as a promotional tool, was the first locomotive with roller bearings on every axle. Three women demonstrated the free-wheeling qualities of the 356-ton machine at Chicago Union Station.

Courtesy Kalmbach Media

tried roller bearings on trucks, mostly on lead trucks, where an overheated conventional bearing had the highest likelihood of causing a derailment. But motive-power officers were dubious about roller bearings for driving axles, which would take a lot of fore-and-aft pounding from piston thrust. Railroads had even declined the company's offer to equip an existing locomotive with roller bearings at Timken's expense. Inasmuch as the order for Four Aces came months after the October 1929 stock market crash, it is unclear why Timken went ahead with the project. Perhaps, as its mainstay orders declined for wheel and transmission bearings for automobiles (as automotive production dropped), the company increased its interest in penetrating the relatively stable railroad supply market. If the engine's nickname was any indication, Timken regarded its effort as a gamble, albeit a promising one.

The 1111 was an excellent locomotive. It embodied all the accepted performance-enhancing features. An unusual but savvy feature was a moderate overall weight combined with a variable axle loading. By the arrangement of its equalizing gear, more or less weight could be transferred on or off the drivers (with the difference taken by the trucks), thereby suiting the engine for different axle-load restrictions on the roads the locomotive toured. Driving axle load could be set for 61,000 or 66,000 pounds.[21]

Between March 1930 and early 1932, the 1111 operated on 14 railroads, mostly in the East and Midwest, pulling freight and passenger trains. For press photographers, a favorite ploy to demonstrate the engine's radically reduced rolling friction was to park it by itself on perfectly flat track at a station, release brakes, and then have three or four men (or women!) pull the locomotive several yards with a stout rope.

Far more important to railroaders was the demonstrated reliability of all its cool-running axle bearings. On hard runs in the winter of 1930-31, icicles hung from the bearing boxes. The driver bearings ran with no difficulty whatever, under all conditions. Such bearings were four or five times as expensive as conventional bearings, yet as Timken people pointed out, eliminating just a few bearing failures over the life of a locomotive would pay for the extra cost, not even considering the avoidance of train delays. Highly attractive to locomotive designers and maintenance officers was another benefit: Properly and regularly inspected, roller bearings might run 500,000 miles or more, at least ten times farther than ordinary bearings. Conventional bearings wore beyond tolerance in a few months of heavy service, thereby throwing extra stress on other running-gear parts.

The virtue of roller bearings lay entirely in reduced locomotive downtime and maintenance costs. The reduction in starting resistance was nice but rather unimportant, since both roller and conventional bearings had identical resistance at train speeds above 5 mph or so, according to Timken literature. Operationally, keeping a heavy train moving at adequate speed was the limiting factor in locomotive performance, not starting the train.

Timken achieved its ultimate aim. Although locomotive production numbers hit bottom in the early 1930s, new locomotive orders after those years commonly included roller bearings in the driving boxes. Increasingly, new locomotives had roller bearings on all axles, as maintenance savings became obvious. Also, from 1933, new cars for mainline passenger trains almost universally incorporated such bearings.

Four Aces became something of an orphan. NP was the last railroad to host the 1111. In March and April 1932, NP ran dynamometer tests on the engine. In the most valid tests, the 1111 at 3,700 peak horsepower compared favorably with an NP Class A. Firing the 1111 was more difficult, since it had a grate area (88 sq. ft.), air-opening ratio, and front-end drafting designed for average- to good-quality bituminous coal, rather than for NP's subbituminous. On the Chesapeake & Ohio, which used high-heat, West Virginia coal, the Timken engine had tested 800 horsepower – or 22 percent – higher. Given the low-heat fuel used by NP, the locomotive's performance was outstanding.[22]

NP 4-8-4 No. 2626 – the former Timken Four Aces, sold to NP in 1933 – at Seattle, ca. 1949.
R.V. Nixon, Courtesy Kalmbach Media

Its promotional tour concluded, Timken offered to sell its engine to NP. Since the firebox had been designed for much different coal than NP's, the railroad was reluctant. Finally, in February 1933, as much to settle a squabble between the NP and Timken over some serious damage done to the engine by a negligent NP fireman, the railroad took the 1111 for a bargain-basement $30,000.[23] Renumbered as NP 2626, the engine worked the 999-mile St. Paul-Livingston, Mont., passenger run, then one of the longest through runs anywhere. It later ran on other divisions until 1957, when it pulled one of the most publicized "last runs" to occur at the end of the steam era.[24]

NP's later Northerns

The performance of the 2626 served to highlight the rather poor horsepower capacity of the NP A-class engines. Thus in 1934, when NP developed its A-2, the railroad turned to a different builder: Baldwin. The biggest changes were increases in boiler diameter (from 94 inches maximum outside diameter to 99, primarily for more total cross-sectional gas area through the boiler's tubes and flues); longer combustion chamber (from 74 inches to 90); better drafting (with a stack-height extender that put the top of the stack more than 17 feet above the rails, about a foot higher than NP's normal clearance limit); and driver diameter (from 73 inches to 77, to raise the speed of top horsepower). Grate design remained the same. Boiler pressure rose to 260 psi. These changes increased the weight to an axle loading of almost 74,000 pounds. Impermissible in 1926, this loading was facilitated by NP's subsequent installation of heavier rail on all its main lines and controlled sidings.

The most significant construction feature on each A-2 was a one-piece, cast-steel frame, which by 1934 was almost standard on large locomotives. The A-1 class, built with frames and cylinder saddles made separately and assembled together, soon loosened their frame-cylinder attachments, causing constant maintenance headaches. The Q-5 and Q-6 Pacifics had done the same. On a few occasions, A-1 engines sheared off main driving axles, sending detached wheels and rods flying off into the woods. In such cases, the cylinder saddle had worked itself so loose that intolerable, cyclic stresses wracked the main crankpins and carried through to the axles.[25]

Similar to many other engines built from the late 1930s through 1941, the NP classes built in those years with alloy-steel boilers eventually suffered from insidious, small cracks at rivet holes. In NP's case, the material involved was not nickel steel, but carbon-silicon steel used in the A-2s built in 1934, and silico-manganese steel used in the A-3s and A-4s of 1938-1941. Like nickel steel, silico-manganese steel saved weight in ever-larger boilers.

According to a 1950 mechanical department report, more than 60 percent of the silico-manganese boilers and 70 percent of the carbon-silicon boilers

Baldwin builder's photo of NP Class A-4 Northern No. 2674.
Courtesy Kalmbach Media

developed cracks requiring patching. This work had to be done carefully, according to standards set by the American Society of Mechanical Engineers, usually with reports made to ICC inspectors. The culprit, in the case of silicon-containing steel, was different from those of nickel-steel boilers. With nickel-steel, the manufacturing process caused incipient cracks that spread with the physical expansion and contraction of the boiler. With silicon steel, the problem was chemical. Like most railroads by the 1930s, NP treated its boiler water to reduce buildup of scale. Ordinary sodium bicarbonate, used to control pH, also produced a certain amount of caustic soda, which caused embrittlement of steels containing silicon. The chemical remedy was to use sodium nitrate to reduce the amount of caustic soda, but that meant more sophisticated control of feedwater chemistry and, for NP, the cure came too late. Mechanical engineers argued that the true cause of the cracking was the practice of riveting itself, which locally overstressed the harder alloy steels. When some of the 4-8-4s' boilers had to be replaced, some circumferential riveting of boiler courses was eliminated by fusion welding, one of the first times the ICC permitted welding of the thick steel of boiler courses rather than just on the thin steel of fireboxes and combustion chambers.[26]

Through 1943, NP bought 36 Northerns, Classes A-2 through A-5, in addition to the original 12 and the Timken engine. Tested horsepower improved to 4,600 at 45 mph on the A-4, or 31 percent better than the originals.[27]

The numbers of engines constructed, however, tell a story in themselves. Forty-nine locomotives of a popular general type, added to a major railroad's roster over a 17-year period is comparatively few, based on the norms of the 1900-1925 years, when railroads customarily ordered as many as 50 engines at a time and owned 100 or more of just one subclass. For comparison, New York Central owned more than 200 K-3 Pacifics, while the Pennsylvania built and purchased more than 400 of just one design and more than 500 of another.

The 4-8-4 beyond NP

Northern Pacific was not unlike most of the railroads owning 4-8-4s, however: Acquisitions were not numerous. The Santa Fe, for example, owned one of the largest fleets, 65, built from 1927 through 1944. The Northern type, though sometimes praised as the "standard" large American steamer of the 20th century, never numbered more than 1,200 or so, or about three percent of the total North American fleet.

The number of railroads using the 4-8-4 type (about 36, including Canadian and Mexican lines) was considerable, and the type was usually put on the best passenger trains and on the most time-sensitive freights. The Depression and World War II, however, dramatically curtailed accustomed practices in replacing locomotives. Orders dried up in the early 1930s and only moderately recovered later in the decade, as railroads patched up older engines they normally would have retired. The Second World War caused a flurry of steam locomotive orders, but older engines still soldiered on, since every locomotive was needed to meet record-setting traffic levels. By 1946, it was obvious to all but the most nostalgic railroad executives that steam was done and that diesels were the only new engines sensibly to buy – not only for glamorous, new passenger trains but for the mainstay freights as well. Santa Fe's 1941-1944 record with its large group of General Motors FT models was

Santa Fe had one of the largest fleets of Northerns: 65 engines in four classes. No. 3751 was the first, in 1927; No. 3767 was in the second batch, arriving in 1938.

Courtesy Kalmbach Media

the unequivocal test. That experience, with its cost and performance records shared by both GM and Santa Fe throughout the trade, was the test that railroaders needed, demonstrating that diesels could haul heavy freight trains reliably. By 1947, 90 percent of new locomotive orders from U.S. railroads were for diesels, mostly for freight-train duty.

After NP, the next railroads to order 4-8-4s were Lackawanna (five 77-inch drivered engines in 1927 from Alco), Santa Fe (one in 1927 from Baldwin), and Canadian National (52 in 1928 from the Montreal Locomotive Works, the Canadian Locomotive Co., and Alco-Schenectady, with the 12 from Alco earmarked for Grand Trunk Western). It was Canadian National that introduced the "dual-service" concept for 4-8-4s, explicitly intending them for both passenger and freight trains. After that, Baldwin and Alco enjoyed incoming orders from many customers. Lima, meanwhile, concentrated on producing its Super Power 2-8-4s and 2-10-4s for freight.

Canadian National Class U-2-e 4-8-4 No. 6173 – a 1940 product of Montreal Locomotive Works – leads the southbound *Washingtonian* over subsidiary Central Vermont Railway at Essex Junction, Vt., in March 1956.

Jim Shaughnessy

Santa Fe's 2900 class were the heaviest Northerns ever built, thanks to World War II restrictions on lighter-weight alloys. They're widely regarded as one of the best 4-8-4 designs. An extendable stack boosted combustion efficiency where overhead clearance restrictions were not a concern. *Stan Kistler, Courtesy Kalmbach Media*

The argument has been perennial: Which of the 4-8-4s was the most powerful? The largest and heaviest 4-8-4s were Santa Fe's 2900 class, 30 of which were built by Baldwin in 1943 and 1944. Oil burners, the 2900s could make about 4,500 drawbar horsepower, according to reported road test results. From available records, only two designs exceeded 5,000 drawbar horsepower: the New York Central S-class (which the Central called Niagaras, evoking the power of an on-line natural wonder), 27 of which Alco produced in 1945 and 1946, and the Norfolk & Western Class J, 14 of which were constructed in its N&W's Roanoke Shops between 1941 and 1950. The three J-class engines of 1950 were among the last mainline steam locomotives made in North America.

The S-class was Paul Kiefer's final steam project, on which he and NYC staff collaborated with an Alco team led by Alfred Bruce. To get the largest boiler diameter they could (100 inches) within the NYC's tight clearance limits, the designers took the radical step of doing away with the steam dome. To avoid drawing water into the drypipe, the pipe was placed as high inside the boiler as possible; slots along the pipe's upper length provided for a plentiful intake of steam. This arrangement probably reduced turbulence in steam flow into the drypipe, which could reach 110,000 pounds of steam per hour. The rest of the design was as advanced in all its details as Kiefer and Bruce could manage. They even allowed for two different-size driving wheels (75 inches or 79) to be installed for tests. After New York Gov. Thomas E. Dewey

New York Central S-class 4-8-4 Niagara-type No. 5500. *Courtesy Kalmbach Media*

Norfolk & Western Class J 4-8-4 No. 600.
Courtesy Kalmbach Media

himself dedicated the first one at the Schenectady plant in March 1945, the engine embarked on the kind of thorough road tests for which the Central was famous. Performance was stellar: 6,600 horsepower at 85 mph, and 5,050 drawbar horsepower at 60-65 mph. A poppet-valved version produced about the same power, at reduced fuel and water consumption.[28]

The N&W J was designed by the railroad's own capable engineering staff, led by Mechanical Engineer H.W. Reynolds, who had succeeded John A. Pilcher in December 1938. The engineering office developed by Pilcher and Reynolds was noted throughout the railroad industry as one of the best. In the J, the designers pulled out all the stops. Every performance-determining parameter – grate area at 108 square feet, combustion chamber length of 102 inches, boiler diameter of 102 inches, boiler pressure at 300 psi, inclusion of

Rock Island 4-8-4 No. 5114.
Charles H. Kerrigan, Courtesy Kalmbach Media

Milwaukee Road Class S-3 4-8-4 No. 267, at West Milwaukee, Wis.
Courtesy Kalmbach Media

an open-type feedwater heater – was over the top, or nearly so. As discussed in an earlier chapter on counterbalancing, Reynolds and staff worked out an unusually low amount of "overbalance" or "excess balance" for the drivers, an amount that depended on having very stiff centering action in the trucks. The reduced overbalance allowed 70-inch-diameter drivers, which gave better power at the drawbar at 40 to 50 mph – a typical speed range on N&W's West Virginia grades. Yet as road tests proved, a J could still rocket up to 110 mph, despite its relatively small drivers. The lower driver diameter also gave room for the increased boiler diameter. No better example could be cited of the complex inter-relationships that affected locomotive running gear and boiler dimensions. In its tests, running on good-quality, high-heat Pocahontas coal from on-line sources, a J could easily reach 5,100 drawbar horsepower.

The last U.S. railroad to receive new, commercially built 4-8-4s was Western Maryland. Baldwin built 12 of the so-called Potomac class (WM eschewed the "Northern" designation) in 1947, and they were used in pool freight service with the Reading between Hagerstown, Md., and Allentown, Pa. Their small drivers (69 inches), big grates (107 square feet), generous combustion chambers (74 inches), and huge boiler diameters (106 inches) meant high power. According to crews, they were free steamers.[29] Unfortunately for the historical record, they were not tested. And perhaps the order date for the Potomacs was unintentionally symbolic. In 1947, Western Maryland also bought its first freight diesels, and within just seven years, the Potomacs were gone.

Western Maryland 4-8-4 Potomac-type No. 1408 at Hagerstown, Md., in 1951.
Russell L. Wilcox, Courtesy Kalmbach Media

Several 4-8-4s are preserved, and as of 2019, some can still operate at high speed with big trains. Milwaukee Road 261, Southern Pacific 4449, and Union Pacific 844 have all enjoyed decades-long careers as excursion engines. The 844 is the only one that's still working for its original owner, never having been retired. Other Northerns have cycled into or out of the ranks of active engines, including Santa Fe 2926 and 3751; Chesapeake & Ohio 614; Reading 2102; Spokane, Portland & Seattle 700; and Cotton Belt 819. Norfolk & Western's J-class 611 now belongs to the Virginia Museum of Transportation in Roanoke. It still operates occasionally, but generally resides quietly at the museum, about a mile from its birthplace.

Chapter 15 Notes

1. Howard Lawford Fry, *A Study of the Locomotive Boiler*, 1924, p. viii.
2. Alfred W. Bruce, *The Steam Locomotive in America*, 1952, p. 308.
3. George Drury, *Guide to North American Steam Locomotives*, 2015, p. 39.
4. John F. Stover, *The Routledge Historical Atlas of the American Railroads*, 1999, pp. 53-54.
5. New York Central, *The Development and Performance of the Hudson Type Locomotive*, 1930 (pamphlet). See also C.M. Smith, "The Final Forty Years of Steam Locomotive Development on the New York Central," Railway & Locomotive Historical Society *Bulletin*, April 1970, pp. 43-51.
6. Note the change in manual-block procedure, from Form 31 orders, which required signatures (and therefore often necessitated stopping of trains), to Form 19 orders, which could be "hooped up" to crews on passing trains, with no signature required. Louis T. Renz, *The History of the Northern Pacific Railroad*, 1980, pp. 244-45.
7. Robert Frey, "Biography of a Heavy Pacific," *Railroad History*, Fall 1976, pp. 59-78.
8. Ibid.
9. Tyler letter, quoted in Frey, p. 64.
10. Letter from Curry to NP General Mechanical Superintendent Silas Zwight, September 15, 1922, referenced in Frey, p. 64.
11. Renz (Note 6), pp. 240-242. See also Lorenz P. Schrenk and Robert L. Frey, *Northern Pacific Railway Supersteam Era, 1925-1945*, 1985, pp. 78-79.
12. Schrenk and Frey, p. 79.
13. Ibid., pp. 54 (on Zwight's role), 80.
14. Ibid., p. 79.
15. Ibid., p. 210.
16. Frey, pp. 67-68.
17. Bruce, pp. 157-59.
18. Schrenk and Frey, pp. 82-85.
19. Ibid., pp. 79-80, 84.
20. Renz, pp. 241-42; Schrenk and Frey, pp. 85-86.
21. Fred Westing, *Erie Power: Steam and Diesel Locomotives of the Erie Railroad from 1840 to 1970*, 1983, pp. 326-29.
22. *Railway Age*, February 13, 1932; T.V. Buckwalter in *Railway Age*, November 29, 1930.
23. A Seattle Division fireman had let the boiler water run low and had warped the crown sheet (which was replaced right after NP took the engine). This damage evidently dissuaded any other railroad, including those with more appropriate fuel, from taking it. See Schrenk and Frey, pp. 114-15.
24. R.V. Nixon, "The Four Aces 4-8-4," *Trains*, November 1957, pp. 16-20.
25. Schrenk and Frey, p. 87.
26. Ibid., pp. 144-49. What the authors do not discuss is that welding is problematic for thick steel plates, such as one- or two-inch boiler shell plate, due to problems in assuring full penetration. Present-day welding methods are much more sophisticated, and the needed quality-assurance methods for inspecting critical welds, such as by X-ray, were not then available.
27. Ibid., p. 138.
28. New York Central, "Capacity-Acceleration-Performance" (test report on S-class), July 3, 1948; P.W. Kiefer, *A Practical Evaluation of Railroad Motive Power*, 1948, pp. 49-56; Bruce, pp. 142-44; "1000 Cheer as Central's Biggest High Speed Engine is Accepted by President Metzman," *Central Headlight* (NYC employee publication), April 1945, p. 1.
29. David P. Morgan, *Steam's Finest Hour*, p. 38.

1523

Chapter 16

Giants Upon the Earth:

The Mallet Reconsidered

In late 1923, the Chesapeake & Ohio Railway began taking delivery of the first of a different breed of locomotive. Like Mallets, the lanky C&O freighter had two sets of running gear and four cylinders, and the front engine unit was hinged. But the front pair of cylinders was no larger than the rear pair – a sure sign that this was not a compound. Rather, all of the equal-sized cylinders received their steam from the boiler and exhausted their spent steam directly to twin stacks. To crews, management pointed out that without the compounding, the new engines weren't true Mallets, but were "simple-expansion articulateds." The term "articulated" referred to the hinged frame. C&O crews smiled at all the nomenclature and coined a nickname that stuck: Simple Simon.

The Simple Simons had their precedents. In 1911, Pennsylvania Railroad motive-power and operating officers wanted to try out the concept of four-cylindered, sixteen-drivered engines as helpers on freight trains up the Allegheny ridges. For both trial and comparison, the railroad bought an experimental, superheated 2-8-8-2 from Alco in 1911. Designed by Francis Cole and his staff at Alco, it used its steam directly in all cylinders and was the first four-cylinder, simple-expansion locomotive in the U.S. Piston valves rather than slide valves controlled steam flow to the front cylinders as well as the rear, since piston valves kept their lubrication more reliably under high temperature than did cheaper-to-build slide valves.

The first steaming of Cole's engine in 1911 followed by just a few days the delivery of an odd 0-6-6-0 "simple" built at Canadian Pacific's Angus Shops in Montreal that October. The Pennsylvania accumulated data on its locomotive for almost 18 years, while it shoved on the rear of freight trains climbing the steep grade from Altoona to Cresson, Pa., but the railroad did not change its motive-power policy and acquired no copies of them.

Still pursuing the simple-expansion idea, Pennsy erected a 2-8-8-0 in its Juniata Shops in 1919.[1] The beast was gargantuan by contemporary standards: 407 tons at working weight, including the tender, and more than 100 feet long. Designed for head-end road service on the Allegheny climb, No. 3700 tested several propositions. With one crew it might do the work of two eight-

Delaware & Hudson J-class 4-6-6-4 Challenger-type No. 1523 at Carbondale, Pa., in June 1951.

S. Botsko, Courtesy Kalmbach Media

ABOVE Chesapeake & Ohio Class H-7 2-8-8-2 No. 1119. C&O crews soon dubbed these simple-expansion articulated locomotives "Simple Simons."
Courtesy Kalmbach Media

RIGHT Chesapeake & Ohio Class H-7 2-8-8-2 No. 1541 and a second locomotive lead a coal train at Linworth, Ohio, ca. 1949.
Richard E. Dill, Courtesy Kalmbach Media

drivered locomotives, and from an engineering point of view it included two important and advanced ideas. Its cylinders were all simple-expansion but arranged with limited cutoff, and its boiler featured a radically large combustion chamber measuring more than 11½ feet from firebox throat to rear tube sheet. Boilermakers could have played two tables of poker in the 3700's furnace, one in the firebox proper and one in the forward chamber. Both the limited-cutoff feature and the voluminous combustion chamber affected the thinking of many designers about boilers and running gear for two-cylindered as well as articulated locomotives, and so it is appropriate to discuss these innovations here.

BELOW Designed by Alco's Francis Cole, PRR Class HH1s 2-8-8-2 No. 3396 posed for its builder's photo at Schenectady in 1911.
Courtesy Kalmbach Media

BOTTOM PRR Class HC1s 2-8-8-0 No. 3700 was built at the railroad's Juniata shops in 1919.
Courtesy Kalmbach Media

PRR evaluations

Limited cutoff could, in theory, achieve much of the economy of compounding. The PRR had tried the idea in a drag-freight locomotive, its two-cylinder (simple) I1s-class 2-10-0 of 1916. Two years later the railroad began building duplicates, eventually amassing a fleet of 598 engines by 1923 – the greatest number of a single locomotive class anywhere in the Americas. Based largely on this success, several other railroads included the limited-cutoff concept in some of their slower-speed road locomotives, and in the mid-1920s it became one of the ingredients of the Super Power philosophy.

The idea was to limit the cutoff to 50 percent at full tractive effort, so that even when the engineman worked the locomotive with the reverse lever all the way forward at low speed, steam admission ceased when each piston reached half stroke. Steam therefore worked expansively, cut off from the boiler, for a much greater percentage of stroke than a conventional engine at its maximum tractive effort.[2] The added expansion time could cut steam consumption in the cylinders at low rpm. Because of the reduced cutoff at full-reverse setting, limited-cutoff locomotives had larger-diameter pistons than conventional engines for the same tractive effort.

Only one modification had to be made: For the locomotive to start or accelerate from a dead stop, small "starting ports" were cut into the spool of the long-lap valve at each cylinder. Recall that in a portion of the crank circle on each side of any locomotive, the valve cannot admit steam to its cylinder because of valve lap (Chapter 3) or cutoff. At full reverse setting with limited cutoff, there were some positions of the driving wheels at which boiler steam could not get to either cylinder.[3] Underway, expansion of steam already in the cylinders obviated any difficulty. Starting ports allowed boiler steam to bypass a valve when the valve had already passed the cutoff point. As speed rose to about five mph and above, the starting ports, because of their carefully constricted size, admitted relatively little steam.

Tests at Altoona compared a couple of two-cylinder, simple-expansion freight engines, both running at a typical drag speed of seven mph and at top available power, with their reverse levers set all the way down in the corner. The comparison demonstrated that limited cutoff could halve the amount of steam consumed per horsepower-hour at single-digit speeds.[4] Later applications of limited cutoff on other railroads sometimes put the longest cutoff at 60 or 70 percent, at a loss in potential economy but giving smoother torque at low rpm.[5] The 3700 proved that limited cutoff could work effectively in a four-cylinder, simple-expansion locomotive.

The engine's monumental combustion chamber showed that increased furnace volume could improve combustion efficiency in a large boiler by reducing carbon loss when the boiler ran at high output. PRR's engineers had incorporated combustion chambers of modest sizes in their boiler designs since the first E6 passenger engine of 1910. Such chambers reduced smoke and boosted boiler output somewhat. The I1s, K4s, and L1s boilers included them. For the 3700's boiler, specified to have 112 square feet of grate, or 60 percent more grate area than the three other boilers mentioned, designers decided to test a chamber of even greater proportionate size.

The experiment must have been regarded favorably. A chamber of only slightly smaller dimensions, but similar in volume proportionate to grate, came four years later with the M1 4-8-2 of 1923, a class that quickly became the PRR's standard heavy passenger and fast-freight locomotive. The M1's principal creator was William F. Kiesel, Jr., who became the PRR's Mechanical Engineer in February 1919 (under Chief Mechanical Engineer, J.T. Wallis) when Axel Vogt retired. Kiesel therefore may have had a strong hand in the conception of the 3700's boiler. By 1923, Kiesel was in full charge of design and the M1 was very much his.[6] Even though the M1 boiler incorporated the same-size grate as the three standard classes previously mentioned, it could efficiently burn larger quantities of high-BTU coal and could produce almost one-third greater horsepower.[7]

Big combustion chambers like those on the M1 and the 3700 had two definite downsides. The first was the far greater number of high-maintenance staybolts needed – almost twice as many in the M1 as in the K4s and L1s boilers. Helpful were improved designs of flexible staybolts for areas of the firebox subject to particularly high stresses; "flexees" installed in the right places materially reduced the monthly rate of broken stays. The second problem was the riveted construction of fireboxes. Such construction prevailed until the ICC permitted, by stages, welded repairs and construction of fireboxes in the late 1920s and early 1930s. Riveted seams joining together the relatively thin-walled sheets of a firebox were prone to develop leaks resulting from the mechanical stress induced by changing temperatures.

Boilermakers tried to repair such leaks by air-hammering the edges of rivets to close up tiny gaps that had developed under the rivet heads, or by "caulking," *i.e.*, air-hammering a leaky seam along the sheet's edge that could be reached inside the box. Severe leaks that called for re-riveting a firebox seam necessitated removing the whole box, since replaced rivets could not be bucked with the firebox in place. Removing a firebox was an elaborate, time-consuming procedure. In order to get the box out, the boiler tubes had to come out, and all the staybolts – hundreds of them – had to be removed and new ones threaded-in and hammered over when the box was reinstalled. Until the advent of the welded firebox and flexible stays of reliable design, few railroads other than the PRR were willing to risk the higher maintenance usually involved with big combustion chambers. By the late 1920s, however, their clear performance advantage in both decreasing fuel consumption per horsepower-hour and boosting steam output was such that they became standard in newly designed large boilers.[8]

The 3700 also had a sophisticated exhaust arrangement, with two exhaust stands, one for each cylinder pair. Each stand had two exhaust jets, and thus there were four stacks. Therefore, for each stack, the proportion of diameter to height was increased (smaller diameter per unit of height). This installation improved draft efficiency and bears the mark of Kiesel's thought.

Kiesel made the study of better draft – effective draft force through the boiler tubes with reduced backpressure in the cylinders – one of his specialties. His later "star" nozzle, retrofitted to early K4s engines and used on other PRR locomotives (Chapter 9), added several hundred horsepower, about 10-12 percent, to a K4s in tests at Altoona, compared to the original exhaust geometry. The 3700's multi-jet arrangement, combined with a single casting for the four stacks, influenced exhaust design thereafter for the big boilers used with four-cylinder, simple-expansion locomotives on railroads across the country. Except that the PRR wasn't one of them.

PRR Class CC2s 0-8-8-0 No. 9357 at Columbus, Ohio.
Glenn Grabill, Jr., Courtesy Kalmbach Media

The one-off 3700 may have confirmed the potential of combustion chambers, but it did not persuade Pennsy managers that the locomotive's labor savings in over-the-road crew costs outweighed its other limitations. The locomotive's 135,000 pounds of starting tractive force (almost the same, incidentally, as that of the Union Pacific Big Boys of 1941) could yank out drawbars or break couplers on trains of sufficient weight to use the engine's capacity, unless the cars happened to have the sturdiest type couplers then available.[9] Thus the 3700 spent its comparatively short life of ten years as a pusher. Running shorter, more frequent freight trains up the mountains of western Pennsylvania with smaller I1s-class 2-10-0 engines, or double-heading these standardized engines as necessary, must have appeared less costly under analysis. The PRR was an industry leader in analyzing the economics of any of its ventures in full context, from acquisition cost to all operating costs and maintenance charges, including labor costs in the shop and on the road. The assertion in some sources regarding the 3700, that the railroad abandoned a good thing that was simply ahead of its time, is based only on post-hoc reasoning inapplicable to the railroad's economics at the time.

In 1919 the Pennsy did buy a small group of four-cylinder, articulated locomotives, but they were compounds: ten 0-8-8-0 Mallets having drivers of minimal diameter. These engines served as freight-train pushers up the Gallitzin grade from Altoona to Cresson, Pa., until the I1s-class replaced them. They then worked until the late 1940s, shoving long cuts of cars in hump yards west of Pittsburgh, such as at Conway, Pa., and Fort Wayne, Ind.

C&O's experience

When the so-called Simple Simons began coming to the Chesapeake & Ohio in 1923, that railroad possessed a remarkable fleet of 2-6-6-2 compounds, 241 of them, acquired in essentially five groups since 1910. They moved trains of high-grade bituminous coal out of southern West Virginia in immense, ever-gathering currents flowing east and west. Mallets hauled the coal eastward to the rail junction town of Clifton Forge, Va., for other engines to take toward Atlantic seaboard cities. Mallets worked the laden hopper cars west to the classification yards at Russell, Ky., where cars were regrouped into trains headed to Ohio and to Lake Erie coal docks. No less important were the counterflows of empty hoppers returning to mines that were dispersed in a web of branchline tracks into the mountain hollows.

As the mid-1920s boomed and the country's energy needs expanded, the C&O needed to increase its coal-moving ability yet again. A growing bottleneck was the route over the highest point on the C&O main line, which lay between Hinton, W.Va., and Clifton Forge. Eastbound coal loads had to be lifted upgrade some 50 miles to the summit; westward strings of empty hoppers had a steeper, 30-mile climb. Additional locomotives could increase the daily tonnage.

To increase system capacity without adding to the number of trains, managers must have reasoned, there needed to be more horsepower per engine than provided by the existing Mallets. Designers at Huntington, W.Va., and at Alco mutually developed a specification for the world's first fleet of four-cylinder, simple-expansion articulateds. Greater tractive power was included, but the compounding was eliminated.

Historians have made much of the higher speed that simple articulateds were capable of, compared to Mallets. Most of this discussion is based on the speed capabilities of simple articulateds that came after the C&O engines, such as the 2-6-6-4s and 4-6-6-4s of the mid-1930s, intended for high power at speeds of 50 mph and more. The 25 pioneering C&O locomotives were not, in fact, high-speed locomotives. Their driver diameter and piston stroke were tailored for working up the steepest grades under load at 10 mph or so, giving the same average piston speeds at which the Mallets ran uphill. Rather than speed, *per se*, the rationale for the first simple articulateds was based on other factors. Speed and rpm were indeed part of the equation, but in ways more subtle than is usually assumed.

One of the practical issues for the C&O and Alco engineers, in working out what would become the railroad's Class H-7, was the size of its front pistons. If the H-7 were a compound with the desired tractive effort, these pistons would need to be at least 39 inches in diameter. (Compare to the USRA heavy

BELOW Chesapeake & Ohio Class H-7A 2-8-8-2 No. 1572. *Courtesy Kalmbach Media*

BOTTOM Rio Grande Class L-107 2-8-8-2 No. 3506. The two locomotives have virtually identical tractive effort, but the simple-expansion C&O machine has much smaller cylinders than D&RGW's compound. *Courtesy Kalmbach Media*

Mallet or to the Denver & Rio Grande's 3500-class Mallet of 1923, engines of nearly identical low-speed power as the C&O 2-8-8-2.) As a "simple," all four pistons of the H-7 could be just 23 inches in diameter. Such a diameter cut the weight of the front pistons by more than half. This reduction made the balancing of the front engine much easier. Recall Chapter 4; Balancing the reciprocating mass of piston, crosshead, and front portion of the main rod was the eternal puzzle in balancing any steam engine's running gear.

Reciprocating balance was especially critical for a Mallet because of the relatively small mass of the front engine unit (front frame, low-pressure cylinders, and running gear) in relation to the front unit's reciprocating mass. In powerful Mallets with big front pistons, the running stability of the front unit, at high speed or low, was abhorrent. As a result, the front unit's driving wheels often lost traction and slipped, especially when power output was high or when rails were wet. As a percentage of reciprocating mass, the overbalance in the counterweights had to be quite high to prevent low-speed hunting and medium-speed shimmy in the front unit, and so rotary balance of the drivers was poor. For most Mallets, front engine stability and driver balance vertically were both problematic.

In early Mallets, there was sufficient looseness in the hinge between front and back engine units for the front unit to pitch slightly up and down as track alignment demanded. In other directions as well – side-to-side laterally, or twisting about the longitudinal axis – stabilization was also poor. The front unit was held in check fore-and-aft by the rest of the locomotive through the hinge pin. The weight of the forward end of the boiler pressed down on the front unit through one or more sliding carrier bearings at the front of the boiler.

While reciprocating imbalance was the primary culprit at slow speed, rotary imbalance could not be denied at medium speed. Designers tried adding more weight to the front unit at the expense of the back unit, by placing the boiler as far forward as possible. Trailing trucks on such Mallets became vestigial. The Southern Railway even tried out three 2-6-8-0s, built between 1909 and 1911, in an effort to cure front-unit slipping by resizing the four cylinders to reduce the proportion of total tractive effort exerted by the front pair.[10]

Because of its small pistons, the H-7 improved both reciprocating and rotary balance conditions. Front-engine stability and traction were better, especially when rail adhesion was poor, because the front unit rode better. The H-7 was less thermally efficient than an equivalent Mallet, but it was more dependable in hauling high tonnage when traction was difficult.

Note the comparison with the Rio Grande 3500-class. That engine's boiler could be smaller than the H-7's in nearly all respects, because with a higher steam expansion ratio in the cylinders, the Mallet used less steam per horsepower-hour. For the same total engine power, however, even its smaller, high-pressure pistons needed to be nine percent larger in diameter than the H-7's, since a Mallet's high-pressure pistons worked against higher backpressure than the pistons of a simple. A Mallet was nonetheless the better locomotive in fuel and steam economy. But when pistons and running gear were sized for sixteen drivers, practical limits on its running-gear weight were reached. Instability was the overriding cost.

C&O's operating department initially put a 35-mph speed limit on the H-7s. They could easily attain 35 on flatter sections of track, of which there were few between Hinton and Clifton Forge, or downhill. The older Mallets at 35 bounced around considerably. It turned out that H-7s, with their better balance, could hustle lighter trains up to 50 mph or so if the grade wasn't too steep, without risking machinery damage.[11] Importantly, they slogged well at 10-15 mph, where most of their fuel was burned.

In 1926 the C&O ordered 20 more 2-8-8-2s, classed H-7A, for the flatter runs from Russell to Columbus, Ohio, and return. There the H-7s' comparative speed could be utilized, up to 45 or so as the grade allowed with heavy trains, and a good deal slower on the several hills en route. Compared to the 2-6-6-2s, the H-7s raised productivity, moving almost 50 percent more tonnage per locomotive.[12] They did so for two basic reasons: Each engine, with about one-third more tractive effort, was able to pull more, and, importantly, the H-7s raised the average speed of trains by moving them uphill at 10-15 mph instead of at 10 or less.

Western developments

Other railroads took note, including two that were far removed from the Appalachian coal country, the Denver & Rio Grande Western and the Northern Pacific. In 1927 and 1928 respectively, these railroads fielded Alco-built, sixteen-drivered simples with boilers that stretched near the limits of size and power. Generous clearances prevailing in the Far West accommodated locomotives with the sort of overhang on curves characteristic of such massive articulateds. These engines also increased driving-wheel diameter by six inches over that of the H-7, raising their speed limit substantially while keeping rpm within reasonable bounds.

The Rio Grande locomotives – ten built in 1927 and ten in 1930 – briefly held the title of world's largest. Before then, Rio Grande crews had become

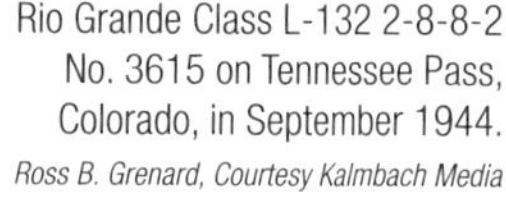
Rio Grande Class L-132 2-8-8-2 No. 3615 on Tennessee Pass, Colorado, in September 1944.
Ross B. Grenard, Courtesy Kalmbach Media

well acquainted with compound Mallets. Thirty-four such engines, acquired between 1909 and 1923, struggled up Rocky Mountain passes on grades that were three and four times steeper than those in West Virginia – 3.3 percent over Colorado's Tennessee Pass, near Minturn, and an incredible four percent on the original line over Soldier Summit, southeast of Salt Lake City.[13]

For such challenging topography, Rio Grande and Alco pushed all the indices – grate area, evaporative surface, and most interestingly, superheating surface. A 3600's superheater was bigger than an H-7's by fully 84 percent, and it elevated the temperature of boiler steam evaporated at 240 psi instead of at 205. Very likely, the total temperature of the steam produced was the hottest it could be without breaking down cylinder oils – around 800 degrees Fahrenheit. The Rio Grande used fairly good coal, most of it mined from the Utah counties of Duchesne and Carbon, and so the record-size grate undoubtedly produced high heat. The running gear – 26-inch-diameter pistons matched with 63-inch-diameter drivers – resulted in a remarkable combination of power and speed flexibility. The 3600s took over the heaviest freight trains between Grand Junction, Colo., and Denver, with the old compounds as helpers on the steepest sections.

Northern Pacific's operating staff wanted an engine that could serve on the high plains main line between Mandan, N.D. (a railroad center on the west bank of the Missouri River, across from Bismarck) and Glendive, Mont., on the Yellowstone River. Though not mountainous in the usual sense, this stretch extended more than 200 miles, crossed the Badlands straddling the North Dakota-Montana border, and included lengthy grades of 1.1 percent. Could a single locomotive replace two of NP's 2-8-2 Mikados on freight trains, yet keep average train speed up? The cargoes transiting NP included merchandise, manufactures, and agricultural produce that were far more time-sensitive than coal. Keeping an average westbound train speed of 35 mph or so, with 45 on the flats and 20-25 mph up the ruling grades, was essential.

Railroad mechanical engineers at St. Paul, Minn., and Alco designers at Schenectady, N.Y., came up with something superlative in 1928 – No. 5000, which NP classed Z-5 and called the Yellowstone type. The grate area, at 182 square feet the largest ever used on any locomotive, was designed to handle low-BTU, high-ash lignite coal from mines in Montana's Rosebud County. Following NP's success with the four-wheel trailing truck on the A-1 Northern design, the 5000 included such a truck to help support its back end.

Northern Pacific Class Z-5 "Yellowstone"-type 2-8-8-4 No. 5000.

Courtesy Kalmbach Media

After two years of shakedown, NP bought 11 more Z-5s – but from Baldwin, not Alco. Perhaps the NP motive-power staff was still leery of Alco after the spats over quality and price of the Q-class Pacifics and other engine orders. Until Union Pacific's 4000-class Big Boys and the Chesapeake & Ohio Alleghenies of 1941, the Yellowstones were the largest and heaviest locomotives in the world.

Rio Grande's L-132 class, however, ran on better fuel than NP's Rosebud coal, and exceeded the Yellowstones in boiler evaporative and superheater surfaces (7,673 and 3,219 square feet, respectively, for the Yellowstones, versus 8,015 and 3,505 for D&RGW's L-132 class). It is likely that the two classes were very similar in horsepower. Both types ran at peak horsepower at 25 to 30 mph, with their driving-wheel size readily permitting 50 to 55 on flats or on gentle grades, either up or downhill.

Through the 1940s, other outstanding simple-expansion articulateds with 16 driving wheels included:

- Great Northern 2000-series 2-8-8-0 rebuilds; R-class 2-8-8-2s, with Belpaire fireboxes.
- Western Pacific 250-series 2-8-8-2s.
- Southern Pacific AC-series 4-8-8-2 "Cab-forwards" (essentially backwards Yellowstones, with the four-wheel truck supporting the firebox).
- Duluth, Missabe & Iron Range M-3 2-8-8-4s.
- Baltimore & Ohio EM-1 2-8-8-4s.
- Union Pacific's 4-8-8-4 Big Boys (treated more thoroughly in Chapter 18).

As to speed capability, there is an additional, oft-mentioned point comparing Mallet compounds and simple-expansion locomotives. A Mallet with big front cylinders had to exhaust great quantities of low-density steam from its huge front-cylinder volume. As designers themselves observed, this exhaust flow impeded a Mallet's speed by creating undesirable backpressure

Two Great Northern Mallets: Class N-3 2-8-8-0 engine No. 2023 and R-class 2-8-8-2 engine No. 2049.
Right, R.D. Porter; Both, Courtesy Kalmbach Media

ABOVE Southern Pacific Class AC-7 4-8-8-2 "Cab-forward" No. 4159. This configuration was designed to improve air quality and visibility for crews operating through tunnels and snowsheds.
Courtesy Kalmbach Media

LEFT Western Pacific 2-8-8-2 No. 251 at Keddie, Calif.
Edward W. Bewley, Courtesy Kalmbach Media

LEFT Baltimore & Ohio Class EM-1 2-8-8-4 No. 7622.
Courtesy Kalmbach Media

BELOW Duluth, Missabe & Iron Range Class M-3 2-8-8-4 No. 227, with an iron-ore train at Two Harbors, Minn.
Philip R. Hastings, Courtesy Kalmbach Media

against the low-pressure pistons. However, it is also true that a simple articulated, running at the same speed and power, consumed and exhausted more steam per horsepower-hour. The Mallet's problem was not exhaust flow, *per se*. Once exhaust passages and valves for the low-pressure cylinders were adequately sized and drafting better understood, backpressure was reduced and was not an impediment. (See Chapter 20 for a more thorough discussion.)

The fact is that compound expansion was suitable for the highest rpm and the highest steam-flow rates per unit of volume in the cylinders. This truth is attested by the many high-speed compounds that ran in the U.S. near the turn of the 20th century. At that time, compounding was synonymous with speed. Multi-cylinder compounds were further developed in Europe for fast passenger duty, but they involved a degree of mechanical complexity unacceptable to American railroads. The inherent limit on speed for the Mallet lay not in its conditions of steam flow, but in the unbalanced reciprocating weight of its machinery.

As it turned out, the secret to building a four-cylinder, articulated locomotive capable of long runs at speeds of 50 mph or better was the design of a mundane part: the hinge joining the front unit to the engine's main frame. In fact, chassis design is the factor that fundamentally separates articulateds from other steam locomotives. Smooth riding over bumps and through curves at mile-a-minute speeds, with a machine weighing 350 tons and more (*sans* tender) was no small feat. It is appropriate to give such amazing capability its due.

Alco's articulation hinge reached its zenith with Union Pacific's 4-8-8-4 "Big Boys" in the 1940s. *Courtesy Kalmbach Media*

Weight and force transfer, back-to-front, and front-unit stability were the critical issues. The hinge should tie the two units together yet allow their suspensions to equalize weight on all drivers as the locomotive moved over rises and hollows in the track. Designers also recognized that the hinge must not interfere with proper lateral alignment of both engine units as the locomotive rolled around curves of varying sharpness. These were not trivial problems. Baldwin and Alco designers evolved different approaches.

By the 1920s, Alco was using the simplest hinge: a single, six-inch-diameter pin. The back of the front unit held a tongue, which fit into a pocket attached to the bottom rails of the main frame; the pin was dropped in from above. In relation to the two sets of drivers, the pin was not located at the midpoint, as one might expect. By locating the pin somewhat ahead of the midpoint, designers secured the best mutual alignment of the two units on curves, reducing flange wear on the first pair of drivers of the rear driving group.

Supplementing the hinge in early Alco Mallets, there were two long, adjustable bolts just behind the front unit's drivers, one bolt on each side. Each bolt vertically connected the rear, top corner of the front frame to the bottom corner of the main frame. These bolts, with flexible ball-and-socket connections at each end, tied the two units together vertically but allowed the front unit to swing laterally to either side. The bolts resisted twisting action of the front unit around its longitudinal axis. In practice, the bolts had to allow for some vertical play and so the anchorage for each (usually at the bottom) was via a coil spring.

In addition to the hinge, there were up to three sliding boiler supports. The forward sliding support(s) had laterally-placed, coil-spring centering devices to control lateral motion.[14] The supports were designed not only to place the weight of the forward end of the boiler on the front unit but, with slotted guides, to hold the boiler and front unit firmly together as the unit swung from side to side. Some vertical play in the sliding supports had to be provided, however, to prevent binding. Boiler supports also allowed for longitudinal expansion of the boiler from cold to hot.[15]

Baldwin, in its early Mallets, used two hinges – upper and lower, on a common centerline – to allow the receiver pipe carrying steam from rear cylinders to front cylinders to pass through a ball joint on the same centerline. The connection was supplemented by vertical bolts as in Alco's system. Usually, two sliding carrier bearings, one with a coil-spring centering device, supported the boiler.[16] By 1911, Baldwin had evolved a simpler system. A single tongue on the front unit fit into a socket in the high-pressure cylinders' saddle; a vertical hinge pin completed the connection. A small amount of vertical play at the back of the front unit was limited by physical contact between the front unit's frame rails and stops cast into the rear cylinder saddle. This arrangement replaced the spring-anchored vertical bolts.

In the 1920s, Baldwin modified the tongue: The vertical pin was made with a closer fit, and a horizontal pin was added. Baldwin called it the "flexible radius bar." The horizontal pin provided more up-and-down flexibility for the front unit; the hinge by itself did not resist pitching of the front unit in relation to the main frame. Frame-stops were eliminated; tightened clearance around the tongue closely controlled vertical play at the back of the front unit. The new radius bar effectively resisted any twisting action. Meanwhile, Alco stayed with its rigid tongue, enlarging it to resist both pitching and twisting, but keeping some vertical play, and disposed of the vertical connecting bolts as well.[17]

By 1930, both builders had reduced the forward boiler support to one sliding carrier bearing. Spring-centering had proved unnecessary. The sliding bearing, as before, was designed in such a way as to control vertical play between the front of the boiler and the forward engine unit as the locomotive rolled at speed along uneven track.

All this change and complication suggests that, into the 1930s, neither builder had come up with a truly satisfactory hinge. Baldwin and Alco had taken rather different approaches; where one was more rigid, the other was more flexible, and vice versa. Although the sources of play and lost motion were small, they were multiple and thus added up. The instabilities of the front unit could not be entirely contained.

The C&O H-7 of 1923 used Alco's then-current hinge. Springing and equalization followed an interesting scheme. (Recall Chapter 1 for the basics of the "tripod" principle of engine equalization.) Instead of equalizing the forward engine unit's wheels and leaf springs into a separate tripod (which Baldwin's flexible radius bar facilitated), Alco equalized the H-7's front-unit springs all the way from lead truck to the fourth driver on each side, with cross-equalization. The front unit wheels and springs therefore resolved into a single point of suspension for the whole locomotive. The drivers and trailing wheel of the rear engine unit, fully equalized on each side, but without cross-equalization, provided the other two points-of-suspension for the locomotive. The H-7s and other Alco Mallets suspended in this way rode more smoothly at working speed than most articulateds. The H-7's equalization, combined with the much-improved reciprocating balance possible with smaller pistons, had produced a locomotive more capable in handling trains than any sixteen-drivered locomotive built before.[18]

Throughout Mallet development, the flexible steam-pipe connections to the front cylinders were often a source of trouble. When a Mallet had a Schmidt-type superheater, steam fed to the rear cylinders could not go straight from the dome but had to run from the superheater header up front. Expansion joints were often required in long steam runs because, when fired up from cold to hot, the forward end of the boiler "grew" farther away from the back cylinders. Simple-expansion articulateds had one blessing: there was no receiver. Replacing it was the exhaust pipe or pipes from the rear cylinders to the smokebox exhaust stand. No jointed connection was needed, and space in line with the hinge usually occupied by the receiver's spherical joint could make room for a stronger hinge.

At the front, though, high-pressure instead of low-pressure steam continuously fed the forward cylinders. Designers had to allow for a lot of lateral movement at awkward angles between those cylinders and their source of steam supply. Various solutions tried to minimize strain on jointed connections and sliding sleeves. Even vertical movement was a factor. With the Baldwin hinge in particular, equalization over humps and hollows involved a limited amount of pitch change by the front-unit frame, as front and rear equalization systems adjusted within both frames, and even while the heavy front end of the boiler remained in undiminished contact with its sliding carrier bearing. Especially at higher boiler pressures, leakage at steam-pipe joints subject to all this motion kept many pipefitters employed.

C&O's H-7s introduced an important thermal improvement to articulated locomotives: an effective, easily maintained, and cost-efficient feedwater heater. From 1922 and William Woodard's use of an Elesco heater on Lima's successful H-10 2-8-2, the closed-type feedwater heater became increasingly popular on U.S. and Canadian lines. An old idea dating back at least to 1804, feedwater heating recovered otherwise-wasted heat from a portion of the cylinder exhaust. Such waste-heat recovery in a practical device increased boiler capacity and horsepower per pound of fuel by up to ten percent. This was a fairly dramatic jump in power and economy with minimal weight gain.

Baltimore & Ohio engineers at Baltimore's Mt. Clare Shops noted the higher-speed performance of single-expansion, articulated locomotives. B&O's management from the mid-1920s was in an experimentalist mood, initially in the context of flush economic times. Even as depression bore down in the early 1930s, the railroad's illustrious chief of motive power, George H. Emerson, persuaded B&O's top officers to fund new locomotive ideas.

Perhaps inspired by the Delaware & Hudson's John Muhlfeld and ideas from contemporary European engineers, Emerson's passion was the watertube firebox. He directed such installations on 14 locomotives between 1927 and 1937.[19] Reduced firebox maintenance and higher boiler pressures were the goals: The always-troublesome firebox staybolts were absent, and the watertubes and steam drums, because of their cylindrical form, could easily withstand far higher pressure than the flat, stayed surfaces of a conventional firebox.

Unfortunately, as in the Baldwin 60000 of 1926, in Muhlfeld's four high-pressure engines for the Delaware & Hudson of 1924-1933, and in two extraordinary multi-pressure engines constructed in 1931 – a New York Central 4-8-4 and a Canadian Pacific 2-10-4 – considerably higher maintenance cost was the consequence. The constant vibration and shocks typical of the railroad environment soon caused the vertical water tubes to leak at joints. Boiler-scale buildup resulted in more thermally-induced mechanical stress in tubes and joints than in a lower-pressure firebox,[20] and routine monthly boiler washouts (required by federal regulation) took twice as many man-hours.[21]

Emerson persisted. Baldwin built to B&O's order a pair of articulated 2-6-6-2s in 1930, along with a pair of 4-8-2s. One of each type had a watertube firebox, so that a comparative, in-service trial could be conducted. The articulateds were unique in another way. Both were intended for high speed on relatively flat track, pulling B&O's fastest merchandise trains. The 2-6-6-2s were single-expansion, had high boiler pressure for the day of 250 psi, and were fitted with tall, 70-inch-diameter drivers. These engines were the first attempt to turn a four-cylinder, hinged locomotive into a speedster.

The attempt was an embarrassment for both Emerson and his friend and former employee, Baldwin president Sam Vauclain. As designer-historian Alfred W. Bruce describes, the unexpected problem was "the riding instability of the front engine units at high speed."[22] As speed rose, the front unit bounced about both vertically and laterally, and traction was unsatisfactory at any speed. Engineers wondered if unequal weight on the units might be a factor. Statically, the front unit of one of the locomotives, No. 7400, had about three percent less weight-on-drivers than the back unit – an inconsequential amount in view of 7400's good adhesion ratio (driver-weight-to-tractive-force).[23] The difficulty wasn't statics but poorly understood dynamics.

In 1932, B&O's Mt. Clare shop staff rebuilt No. 7400 into a 4-4-6-2. Emerson hoped that, at the front, a ten-percent greater weight on each of the two remaining driving axles, combined with appropriately downsized cylinders (to keep the adhesion ratio favorable) and a four-wheel lead truck would make a good-riding performer out of the 7400. Despite the changes – all entirely reasonable in the practice of the time – the expensive rebuild was apparently worse than the original configuration. Again, expensively, the 7400 reverted to a 2-6-6-2 a year later. It pulled freights at reduced speeds for another 20 years, but at a capacity that one of B&O's many 2-10-2s could match. The railroad swore off any notion of high-speed articulateds.

The concept revived in 1935, when Seaboard Air Line bought five 2-6-6-4s from Baldwin with drivers just an inch smaller than those on the 7400.[24] SAL's management was encouraged by the fine performance of three heavier though slower 2-6-6-4s that Baldwin made the previous year for the Pittsburgh & West

Seaboard Air Line Class R-2 2-6-6-4 No. 2508.
Wiley M. Bryan, Courtesy Kalmbach Media

Virginia. These Belpaire-boilered engines had 63-inch drivers for pulling coal trains on a twisting main line. Baldwin engineers surely convinced Seaboard that the debacle on the B&O would not be repeated.

The adhesion ratio of the P&WV engines was nearly identical to that of B&O's 7400; the ratio for the SAL engines was actually less. Yet both designs ran beautifully, with excellent traction. Seaboard's articulateds were a few tons heavier than the 7400, yet placed just 27½ tons on each driver pair, so as not to strain lighter-weight mainline rail. Grate area was within a few square feet of the 7400. The first five SAL articulateds, Class R-1, could easily reach 60 mph while hauling manifest freight trains and occasional passenger trains between Hamlet, N.C., and Richmond, Va. P&WV bought three more of its heavier locomotives in 1937; Seaboard purchased five more 2-6-6-4s the same year, dubbed the R-2 class. In the winter tourist rush to Florida, an R-class engine could sometimes be found on second sections of the *Orange Blossom Special.*

Alfred Bruce, ever loyal to articulation pioneer Alco, wrote that a 2-6-6-4's "front engine unit is inclined to 'hunt,' although speeds of 50 to 60 miles per hour are reported for these engines."[25] Nevertheless, the P&WV, SAL, and (as described later) Norfolk & Western were well satisfied with the type. The intriguing question is: How did these locomotives solve the horrible instability of the B&O's Baldwins? What Bruce didn't mention was that, in the years after 1930, Baldwin had borrowed attributes of Alco's hinge design. Bruce frequently stresses his view that the best high-speed stability was ensured by the four-wheel lead truck, but that is only part of the story and obviously didn't help the 7400.[26]

An essential ingredient was tightening up the hinge and preventing pitch change in the front unit. Baldwin eventually abandoned the flexible radius bar, and both builders – gradually it appears, from design to design in the 1930s – tightened clearances at the hinge. Progress came fitfully, however, and the story is more complex than an overly simplified one of "steady improvements."

While designers reconsidered the hinge arrangement, they also considered equalization. On articulated locomotives with two-wheel lead trucks, equalization of the front unit was either as a tripod, with equalization divided

P&WV No. 1104, a 2-6-6-4 built by Baldwin in 1934.
Courtesy Kalmbach Media

on each side, or continuous. If the latter, as in the H-7, the front frame could more easily keep in-true vertically as the locomotive passed over humps and sags. The frame's alignment was held more or less in check at two points front and rear: the hinge in back and the boiler support(s) in front. The driver springs let wheels adjust vertically in both engine units.

Out of all these subtle changes came the Union Pacific's pace-setting 4-6-6-4s, introduced in 1936 and made by Alco. Union Pacific officers wanted a locomotive that could handle heavy passenger trains and fast freights. UP's and Alco's mechanical engineering staffs cooperated closely. For UP, Otto Jabelmann was chief of motive power and Arthur Fetters was one of the mechanical engineers; Alfred Bruce was by then Alco's leading designer. According to Fetters, he suggested a simple articulated that might outperform UP's massive 4-12-2s, but without the long, rigid, driver wheelbase, the better to take curves.

The Challenger's four-wheel lead truck promised the best lateral stability. Pistons and rods were as light as possible for excellent reciprocating and driving-wheel balance. Drivers were the same size as the SAL R-class. UP's design suspended the front unit as a tripod: The four-wheel truck was one point and the three equalized drivers on each side were the other two points. The rest of the locomotive was also a tripod: The forward end of the boiler rested on the front engine unit, while the three drivers and two trailing wheels on each side, all equalized continuously, formed the other two points. Contrary to conventional wisdom, the UP and Alco designers did not load the front unit more than the back. Bruce writes that "the weight on the front unit was ... about 90 per cent of the weight on the back unit."[27] Because the front unit was a tripod, Alco reverted to a vertically flexible hinge. By permitting a greater degree of vertical play at the hinge, the three-point "4-6-0" in front could find its own way over uneven track with less weight transfer from the back unit. But the engineering team applied a big friction snubber to dampen the up-and-down motions of the front unit.

The 15 new locomotives shone in freight service between the major terminals of Council Bluffs, Iowa, and Cheyenne, Wyo. Twenty-five more engines came in 1937. Alco fitted five as oil-burners. UP put these on its all-coach train, the *Challenger*, to keep a fast schedule on the mountainous western parts of the train's Los Angeles-to-Chicago route.[28] The articulated engines handled the train on the long, steep climb east out of San Bernardino and over Cajon Pass at 30-35 mph, could accelerate briskly, and rode smoothly at 60 mph on level track. The rest of the railroad trade was deeply impressed. UP gave the engine type the same name, "Challenger," as the railroad had used for the passenger train and for some of its scheduled hotshot freight trains.

Northern Pacific decided quickly to acquire the type, both for itself and for the Spokane, Portland & Seattle Ry., which NP jointly owned with the

Union Pacific Class CSA-2 4-6-6-4 Challenger-type No. 3915, built in 1937.

Courtesy Kalmbach Media

Northern Pacific Class Z-8 4-6-6-4 Challenger No. 5146, at Livingston, Mont., in 1953.
Courtesy Kalmbach Media

Great Northern. Twenty-one Z-6-class Challengers began arriving on NP in 1936 and six Z-6s on the SP&S in 1937. These engines all had enormous fireboxes for NP's low-BTU coal. The SP&S engines, however, burned oil. Other railroads – in 1938, the Rio Grande and the Western Pacific; in 1940, Western Maryland and Delaware & Hudson; and in 1942, the Clinchfield Railroad – ordered Challengers from Alco and Baldwin, the design details varying among the railroads. Three of these lines plus NP (with SP&S) put in repeat orders. The 4-6-6-4 was by far the most popular articulated type from 1936 onward: A total of 252 were built, 105 of which were Union Pacific's.

In the press of surging wartime traffic, Union Pacific and Alco improved on the Challenger in 1942. In an effort headed by Jabelmann and Bruce, the 4-6-6-4 was modified to gain significantly more horsepower, to tweak driver balance, and to improve chassis design still further. Grate area was increased 22 percent, boiler pressure went from 255 to 280 psi, cylinders were downsized one inch (thus making pistons lighter while keeping tractive effort the same) and the one-piece, cast-steel frames introduced on the second Challenger order in 1937 got an important change. This change was derived directly from the UP-Alco design work on the 4-8-8-4 of 1941.

The idea was to reduce vertical play of the front engine unit to an utter minimum. One-piece, cast-steel frames were entirely rigid, and in contrast to built-up frames, didn't degrade in alignment under punishing use. Earlier UP Challengers and other articulateds used a form of boiler support that accommodated their loose or flexible hinges as well as the various misalignments that could occur over the years in frames.

For the UP Challengers of 1942, the boiler supports on the cast front frame were increased in contact surface and machined absolutely flat. At the same time, the tongue of the front unit and the pocket in the rear unit had their horizontal mating surfaces machined for a minimum working clearance. The hinge-pin was given only the clearance to fit smoothly into its holes in the tongue and pocket. Experience showed that the fit of the pin had to be loosened slightly to prevent binding, but – crucially – the fit of the large horizontal mating surfaces of the tongue and pocket performed as advertised. Between the boiler support and the hinge, the front unit could move *only* laterally. Bruce later wrote:

> Now the front engine unit has only the vertical movement permitted by its spring deflections, as in the case of the rigid-chassis engine. The result is the most stable-riding articulated engine ever built, and one that is safely operated at speeds up to 60 or 70 miles per hour.[29]

Not to detract from the engineers at UP, Bruce then strongly implies that the revised boiler-support-and-hinge design was first applied by Alco to the Delaware & Hudson J-class 4-6-6-4s of 1940. He states that the chassis improvement in question originated "about 1940," and he includes the D&H engines when he says that the "flat bearing-plate surfaces required careful alignment on the erecting floor, but they were well worth the effort."[30] That he was involved in this engineering on a first-hand and intimate basis is unquestioned. Despite the modesty concerning his own role, his pride in the accomplishment is evident.

The story is complicated, however, by the A-class 2-6-6-4s of the Norfolk & Western. Designed by N&W engineers, the first two were built in the railroad's Roanoke, Va., shops in mid-1936. N&W Nos. 1200 and 1201 had one-piece, cast-steel frames, about a year before their use in the second group of Challengers for UP. The front boiler support for the A was similar to those used by that railroad in its articulateds for many years. The tightness of the single-pin hinge was is unclear, but it looks quite similar to what Alco used in 1940. The N&W locomotives were stable and fast. A close participant, senior N&W draftsman Voyce Glaze, stated:

> ... we had lots of experience with two-wheel engine trucks and knew how they could be designed to lead a locomotive safely around the curves. I believe that lateral resistance was about 30 percent of the center-plate load. I believe that an engine truck which moves smoothly through curves has enough stability to travel straight track without "hunting."[31]

N&W's locomotives are further treated in a later chapter, but suffice to say here that their riding characteristics were outstanding.[32]

Whatever the priority of invention, the simple-expansion articulated had been developed in just three decades from a ponderous and specialized beast into a fast, flexible, and potent machine. Only about 700 were ever built, but their contribution to railroad economics was disproportionate. Compared to most other freight engines, they let one engine crew handle twice the tonnage over the road, thus cutting labor costs. But that was just part of their value. Their combination of power and speed elevated productivity in another way – in railroad terms, by raising ton-mileage per train-hour. They raised system capacity by reducing the time taken by heavy loads in transit.

Chapter 16 Notes

1. See Robert A. LeMassena, *Articulated Steam Locomotives of North America*, 1979, for summary description of locomotives mentioned in this chapter. In some sources (not LeMassena), the boiler pressure of the 3700 is given as 250 psi, with the observation that such pressure was extremely high for its time – which it would have been, if true. The 250 is erroneous and is a typo in A.W. Bruce, *The Steam Locomotive in America*, 1952, p. 316 and picture 75. The correct pressure was PRR's then-standard 205.
2. Recall that in a normal locomotive, full forward (or back) on the reverse lever gives a maximum cutoff of about 85 to 90 percent; steam admission does not cease until 85 to 90 percent of stroke is reached.
3. Once in a while, an altogether conventional steam locomotive can be unable to start because it happens to stop at just the point where one piston is past the point of cutoff and the other piston, though receiving steam, can't move the train because its main rod doesn't have enough angular leverage on the crankpin. This is usually a problem only for a passenger engine with high drivers, short stroke, and valves with long lap; or, with a passenger or freight engine, when the train weight is at the

limit the locomotive can start. The engineman's solution is to reverse the valve gear. He first must take care to empty the cylinders of steam through the cylinder cocks in order to avoid giving the train a hard jolt as he moves the lever. If on a grade, the engine will roll back; if on flat track, there will be sufficient tractive force in the backward direction because of crankpin position. The engineman can bunch a little slack (very gently if it's a passenger train), and then start forward with the driving wheels at a different position. The author became very familiar with this maneuver on a former-PRR 4-4-2 of 1902, which then operated on Pennsylvania's Strasburg Rail Road, and is now at the Railroad Museum of Pennsylvania. With its 80-inch diameter drivers, long-lap valves, and short stroke, it was a likely engine to have the difficulty described.

4. It was always hard to draw strict comparisons between locomotives with and without limited cutoff. The magnitude of the saving described for the I1s class decreased considerably the higher the rpm, and disappeared when both engines in the test could run at the same cutoff. The other locomotive in the test was an L1s-class 2-8-2, a freight locomotive designed for higher average road speeds than the I1s. At 7 mph, and with each engine operating with all the power it could muster at that speed (1,740 indicated horsepower for the I1S and 1,230 for the L1s), the I1s ran at 50 percent cutoff and the L1s ran at a wasteful 85 percent. Their respective steam rates were 19½ and 31½ pounds per horsepower-hour, showing how crucial cutoff and long expansion were for economy. As to power available at the given speed, it is important to remember that steam locomotives have a pronounced curve of maximum available output. Both engines could exert much more horsepower at higher speeds. At its maximum output of almost 3,500 ihp at 25 mph – at the top of its ihp curve – the I1s's steam rate was lower still (about 17 pounds per horsepower-hour), but cutoff was set to about 40 percent because of the higher rpm than at 7 mph. See *PRR Test Plant Report, I1 Tests*, 1917. See also Paul T. Warner, *Motive Power Development on the Pennsylvania Railroad System, 1831-1924*, PRR, 1924, pp. 66-71 for similar figures and an excellent summary. Warner was a well-known technical writer and for a decade was an editor of *Baldwin Locomotives*, a quarterly for the trade published by Baldwin. (*Motive Power Development* first ran as a series of articles in the builder's magazine.)
5. Short cutoffs give a much less smooth turning effort to the driving wheels, since the steam thrust per piston stroke comes in impulses of shorter duration. The four impulses per driver revolution have sharper peaks in relation to the average turning force throughout the crank circle, and therefore a locomotive is more prone to slip on wet rail. Long cutoffs give longer steam impulses and smoother torque. To gain effective traction, an engineman will often lengthen cutoff when rails are slippery.
6. Wallis had led the design effort on the K4s and L1s (Chapter 9). In 1920, Wallis was elevated to system-wide chief of motive power, a mostly administrative rather than a design position, in a reorganization of the railroad. Another intellectual leader of PRR locomotive design, Alfred W. Gibbs, died in 1922. Gibbs had been general superintendent of motive power for PRR's Lines East from 1903 and had been chief mechanical engineer for several months in 1911 before Wallis's appointment.
7. With a grate thus smaller in proportion to the rest of the boiler, standby losses of fuel (see Chapter 7) would have been less than for a larger grate. And, certainly a factor in the PRR's locomotive policy, the firebox's foundation ring could be the same size for four dominant classes: I1s, L1s, K4s, and M1.
8. See Bruce, pp. 143, 175, 383 on changes to the Cole ratios with added factor for firebox volume.
9. Warner, p. 70; Alvin F. Staufer, *Pennsy Power: Steam and Electric Locomotives of the Pennsylvania Railroad, 1900-1957*, 1962, p. 19.
10. LeMassena (Note 1), pp. 151-52 on SR subsidiary Alabama Great Southern's No. 300; pp. 198 and 201 for the two such engines SR used on Saluda grade in North Carolina. Baldwin designed and built these three locomotives – perhaps to steal a march on Alco.
11. Bruce, p. 320, asserts that the H-7 "often made from 50 to 55 [mph]... ." On that locomotive's drag-speed-sized, 57-inch-diameter drivers, that would have been a bone-shaking experience. The H-7 was balanced conventionally and was capable of such speed only as an upper dynamic limit. Moreover, with its top cylinder horsepower produced at around 20, very little indicated horsepower was left at 55 (about 330 rpm). Both before and after the H-7s' introduction, railroads that wanted a new freight engine for service at speeds from 25 to 50 mph specified 63-inch-diameter drivers (see, e.g., the USRA designs, Chapter 10). The author has been on superbly maintained, mainline track at 55 mph in a well-maintained steam locomotive with 63-inch-diameter drivers, and one would not call it smooth. (One notes that Bruce's

book, although utterly invaluable as a first-hand source, sometimes misses important non-Alco locomotives and, in Bruce's modest and understated style, manages to praise most Alco designs.

12. Ibid.
13. Hence the name of the nearby town of Helper, Utah, where helper locomotives were added to both passenger and freight trains for the Soldier Summit climb. (At the date of this publication, Helper is still on the route of Amtrak's *California Zephyr*).
14. Lionel Wiener, *Articulated Locomotives*, 1930, pp. 320, and esp. 322. Location of hinge pin on pp. 318-19. The Erie and D&H 0-8-8-0s (1907 and 1911) also incorporated spring buffers between the front and back units on either side of the hinge (p. 321, Fig. 122).
15. For photos of the vertical-bolt-and-spring anchorage, see LeMassena (Note 1, above), pp. 240-41 (photo of D&H No. 1500, former P&WV, and photo of D&H 1601 of 1911 as rebuilt in 1924). For such bolts without the springs, see ibid., p. 242 (two photos of Alco-built Erie 0-8-8-0s of 1907).
16. Ibid., pp. 318 (Fig. 120), 319, 321-22 (Figs. 123, 124).
17. Ibid., pp. 319-20. Fig. 121 is explained on p. 320.
18. Further explanation of the tripod principle applied to articulateds appears in later chapters on Big Boys and Alleghenies, and Norfolk & Western's "Big Three."
19. George Drury in his *Guide to North American Steam Locomotives* (2015), p. 78, compiles from B&O rosters a nice summary of Emerson's water-tube firebox applications, either on new locomotives or on rebuilds: 1927, a 2-8-0 and a 2-8-2; 1928, a 2-8-0 and a 4-6-2; 1929, a 2-8-0; 1930, a 4-8-2 and a 2-6-6-2; 1931, a 4-8-2; 1933, a 4-6-4; 1934, a 4-4-4; 1935, two 4-6-4s; 1936, a 4-6-4; 1937, a rigid-frame 4-4-4-4.
20. Boiler scale – solid deposits on a boiler's interior surfaces – interferes with heat transfer between the fire-side and water-side of tubes and surfaces. The scale, in effect, acts like insulation. The same amount of scale, on the water-side of a surface at higher pressure and thus higher water-side temperature, causes a greater temperature difference between scaled and unscaled surfaces. It is that difference that unevenly stresses steel. In the 1920s through the 1940s, chemical water treatment to reduce scale formation was tried but was not very effective. In view of the prodigious quantities of water that steam locomotives consumed, chemical treatment of water supplies throughout a railroad's system was economical only in regions where water was unusually hard.
21. See Chapter 11 on the Baldwin 60000. The monthly boiler wash was the primary means of removing loose scale and inspecting the boiler interior for excessive buildup.
22. Bruce, p. 318.
23. For good traction, designers agreed that a ratio of weight-on-drivers divided by tractive effort of 4.0 or better was desirable. This "factor of adhesion" was 4.1 for the front unit of B&O 7400. I don't agree with LeMassena that the small weight discrepancy between the two units was a factor, given the failure of the 1932 rebuild.
24. The name Seaboard Air Line was a reference to SAL's relatively straight routes among its principal cities. The straight route was an "air line" – before companies operating propeller-driven machines appropriated the term. SAL was not unique in this usage.
25. Bruce, p. 323.
26. In Bruce, one can easily miss important aspects of design, especially if they were aspects well understood by his peers. In this regard, one observes that Bruce takes the three-point or tripod suspension principle pretty much for granted – which to Bruce's audience of fellow engineers needed no explanation – and he is equally obscure about articulated locomotive chassis design. Compare with the chapter on equalization in Ralph P. Johnson's 1942 text, *The Steam Locomotive: Its Theory, Operation and Economics*. Bruce's discussion of improved vertical stability of the front engine unit is brief, appearing in his section on the 4-6-6-4 (pp. 327-28). He doesn't discuss the related issues of equalization, and he mentions hinge design only obliquely. The modern reader can therefore miss their importance.
27. Bruce, p. 327.
28. Drury, p. 315, writes that six of this class were built for passenger service. LeMassena, pp. 116 and 119, writes that five engines, Nos. 3935-3939, were "delivered as oil burners ... for passenger service."
29. Bruce, p. 327.
30. Ibid.
31. Quoted in Ed King, *The A: Norfolk & Western's Mercedes of Steam*, 1990, p. 56. See also p. 61.
32. The author can testify to this first-hand. See William L. Withuhn, "1218: Home to Roanoke," *Trains*, September 1987, pp. 26-33.

"New epochs emerge with comparative suddenness." – *Alfred North Whitehead* [1]

Chapter 17

Counterpoint:

Why the Diesel?

THE END OF THE DINOSAURS CAME in the Cretaceous period, not the Jurassic. But as in Steven Spielberg's 1993 film, with its depiction of the variety of animal forms from that time, the late 1930s through the late 1940s were characterized by a wide array of locomotive forms. Steam, electric, and new diesel locomotive types fiercely competed in an unsettled motive power marketplace. In the end, of course, the diesel proved to be the Yucatan meteorite that swept the old order entirely away.

World War II both delayed and hastened dieselization. General Motors was the primary instigator of change in the 1930s. Despite GM's best marketing efforts and successful demonstrations of its internal-combustion prowess, American railroads only dabbled with diesels before Pearl Harbor. War brought a colossal surge in rail traffic that necessitated big orders for new locomotives, but war also brought governmental production restrictions that limited the number of diesel locomotives that could be built. War sold the diesel to conservative American railroads as no other demonstration could have.

Following the war, other profound changes in the national transport market only accelerated the quick displacement of steam. Motivations for the changeover, however, were not entirely the same as the results. Only after the diesel changeover was fully under way were the most important operational advantages discovered.

War's end came in the summer of 1945. The railroads had been indispensable, moving raw materials and coal to industrial centers, munitions and supplies from factories to ports, soldiers and sailors to embarkation, and all the while handling domestic freight and passengers on the home front. In a time of gasoline and tire rationing, railroads carried 83 percent of all travel and shipment from early 1942 through spring 1945. Freight went from 1.8 billion originated tons in 1940 to 3 billion in 1943. Passengers doubled to 900 million. Ninety-one percent of military goods and 98 percent of military travelers went by rail. Railroad employment, including a peak level of 115,000

An Electro-Motive model FT diesel-electric locomotive destined for the Atchison, Topeka & Santa Fe Railway is lowered onto its trucks at the builder's factory in La Grange, Ill., near Chicago in 1941.

Courtesy Kalmbach Media

This chapter is considerably revised, reinterpreted with new material, and annotated from Withuhn (ed.), *Rails Across America: A History of Railroads in North America* (New York: Smithmark, 1993), Chapter 8 (by Wiliam L. Withuhn). Adapted with permission of the publisher.

women, increased from about one million in 1940 to 1,420,000 at the war's end in 1945.[2]

In the public eye, the war reinforced the long-standing role of railroads as the backbone of transportation. Certainly, people knew that automobiles, trucks, and airplanes would compete with railroads in the postwar era – exciting images of modern technology were everywhere, including in auto showrooms by 1946. But railroads would remain the nation's basic means of overland transportation. Or so most people assumed, including railroaders; optimism regarding the postwar years was a common theme of industry advertising, even before the war ended. The nation's highway system at the end of 1945 was pretty much what it had been five years earlier, despite some construction to ease the way for military trucks. Air travel was negligible and not a serious competitor. The 15-year struggle of Depression and war now behind them, railroaders anticipated a prosperous peace.

It was not to be. It seemed that every GI came home dreaming of a family, a civilian job – and a car. Automobile sales soared.[3] The motoring public, in turn, clamored for better roads, so their legislators responded by underwriting a boom in highway construction. In an economic recovery unprecedented so soon after a major war, tax funds came plentifully. Truckers took to the improved highways, carrying more freight, particularly on hauls of short or medium distances where delivery by rail was customarily slow. Relishing their success, truckers began to encroach seriously on long hauls, especially for the carriage of light manufactured goods. Trucks could deliver high-value goods quickly and, more to the point for manufacturers and shippers, on highly predictable schedules. Railroads could not. The age of the true long-distance, semi-tractor-trailer was dawning.

At the same time, air traffic began gradually to increase. Before the war, flying had been strictly for the few, the rich, and the somewhat daring. The war had transformed the technology of aircraft design and production. With the lessons thus learned, builders such as Douglas and Lockheed unveiled planes such as the DC-7 and the Super Constellation. These were more commodious, more reliable, and much cheaper to operate per seat-mile than pre-war models. Air travel began to lose its rakish image.[4]

Cheap gasoline fueled and accelerated these changes on the highways and in the air. Refinery capacity had multiplied due to the war. With petroleum supplies flowing in from Texas, Oklahoma, Louisiana, California, and from newly tapped fields in the Middle East and North Africa, the glut of low-priced fuel was a fundamental factor in helping truckers and airlines post competitive freight rates and airfares. Motorists, too, relished the freedom and exhilaration supported by bargain gasoline.

For railroads, a crisis loomed. Along with absolute levels of traffic, railroads began rapidly to lose their proportionate share of tonnage and riders to other carriers. From the peak year of 1944, rail travel declined in both absolute and proportionate terms. Americans abandoned trains, first in their overwhelming support of taxes for roads, and then with their gas pedals. By 1950 railroads carried just 47 percent of all common-carrier passenger-miles. In 1960, the figure was just 29 percent. These figures include only rail, bus, and air carriers, but together, those three modes accounted for just 20 percent of intercity passenger miles; private automobiles accounted for fully 80 percent.[5]

The story was similar, though not as stark, for freight: from 69 percent of commercial freight ton-miles in 1944, down to 56 percent in 1950, and eroding to 44 percent by 1960. Trucks, inland waterways, and pipelines all increased their transport market shares in this period. Freight shippers made their analyses based not just on costs but, increasingly, on the more trustworthy delivery dates offered by other modes. In the imperfectly predictable movement of boxcars from yard to yard along their routes, railroads came up short in schedule-keeping.

Simultaneously, railroad managers faced a painful situation regarding their physical plant. The Depression of the 1930s had curtailed track maintenance, and few new locomotives had been acquired. Although the war had generated an influx of new locomotives, both steam and diesel, and although track work had picked up, most of the physical plant – locomotives, cars, rails, communication systems, maintenance facilities, shops – coped with the avalanche of war traffic with only limited renewals. By 1945, the locomotive fleet was mostly old and worn out.

Then other problems descended in the wake of peace. Strikes in the Appalachian coalfields, the result of long-simmering labor issues which the war had only temporarily preempted, caused coal prices to rise. More-expensive coal helped push rail transport costs up, especially for Eastern and Midwestern roads dependent on coal for fuel. (Many steam locomotives in the West ran on oil.) Haulage rates, however, stayed artificially low, as the Interstate Commerce Commission maintained its control over fares and tariffs. Railroad workers demanded higher wages. Workers in various crafts walked out, and every railroad union bargained hard for higher pay. Though the trains kept running under the "cooling-off" and arbitration provisions of the Railway Labor Act, labor's pressure meant real trouble for railroad costs.

Payroll represented more than half of all expenses, and there were a lot of people to pay. From 1944's 1.4 million, rail employment still held at almost 1.3 million in 1951 even though traffic was way off. At the same time, wages per employee shot up an unprecedented 53 percent. Railroad managers at all levels felt themselves in an unrelenting squeeze. The confident assumptions about business as usual after the war turned to ashes.

On every railroad, the locomotive fleet stood out as a major sinkhole of cost. The aging fleet was obviously jeopardizing the chances for economic survival. And the question was not just a simple one of steam versus diesel.

Momentum

Internal-combustion locomotives had been around since the 1920s as small transfer engines and switchers, and since the 1930s in such glamorous forms for passengers as the Union Pacific's distillate-fueled M-10000 and the Burlington's diesel-powered *Pioneer Zephyr*. General Motors subsidiaries Electro-Motive Corporation and Winton Engine Company had produced the prime movers for both of these articulated trains, and then began limited production of larger passenger diesels in the mid-1930s. The preferred designs incorporated a diesel prime-mover with an electric transmission. Under the hood, a big diesel engine turned an electric generator, which in turn supplied high current to several direct-current motors mounted directly on the locomotive's axles. Watching these developments, two of the traditional

Union Pacific's distillate-fueled M-10000 streamliner (TOP) and Burlington Route's diesel-fueled *Zephyr* 9900 were 1930s harbingers of American railroading's looming internal-combustion transformation.
Top, Gerald M. Best; Both, Courtesy Kalmbach Media

steam locomotive manufacturers hedged their bets. The American Locomotive Co. purchased diesel engine builder McIntosh & Seymour in 1931, and partnered with General Electric for locomotive electrical components; Baldwin Locomotive Works acquired De La Vergne Engine Co. in 1931, and partnered with Westinghouse for electrical components. Alco and Baldwin sold diesel switchers in various models from the early 1930s, going head to head with EMC's "NC," "NW," and "SW" series.

In 1939, EMC built a four-unit diesel-electric demonstrator, christened it the "FT" model, and gave it road number 103 for dispatching purposes. The locomotive then toured the country, covering 83,000 miles. The tour was a triumph. No. 103 pulled fast freights and heavy drags with equal facility and experienced no significant breakdowns. EMC's peripatetic demonstrator showed for the first time that a diesel freighter could stand the demands of rough, mainline duty.[6] Railroad executives expressed keen interest in 1939 and 1940. Contrary to long-accepted legend, however, there were only modest orders in those years for production locomotives. A few lines jumped: The tiny New York, Ontario & Western of upstate New York, trying desperately (and vainly, it turned out) to stave off bankruptcy, ordered several, and after the war became one of the first American railroads to fully dieselize. Southern Railway, Baltimore & Ohio, Rock Island, Great Northern, Santa Fe, and several other lines ordered some diesel freighters. But most railroads held back.

Then came American entry into the war in December 1941 and full mobilization. By early 1942, nearly every large railroad wanted to try the FT diesels as supplements to their steam fleets. As the War Production Board organized and began exerting its authority, it diverted the majority of GM diesel prime-mover production to submarines. Diesel-powered locomotives were allocated on a limited basis.

The Santa Fe made a cogent plea. Its lines connected Chicago and Los Angeles via the deserts of New Mexico, Arizona, and Southern California. The Santa Fe had always had problems with water in the desert for its steamers, not only with supply but with bad quality, which rapidly deposited scale inside locomotive boilers, enormously increasing maintenance. The railroad spent considerable sums on chemical treatment of its boiler water supplies, to mixed effect. Santa Fe had experimented with diesels in the 1930s and had developed expertise in their operation. With no timidity, Santa Fe had

LEFT Municipal smoke-abatement ordinances and a high degree of utility at lower cost than steam power were two incentives for railroads to sample early diesel models designed for yard and terminal switching. This is a Baldwin VO-1000, built in 1943; it represents that builder's biggest-selling model, with 540 produced.

Courtesy Kalmbach Media

MIDDLE Styled by Otto Kuhler, Alco's DL-109 series was sold to seven railroads between 1939 and 1945.

Courtesy Kalmbach Media

BELOW Electro-Motive's model FT gave America's railroads a glimpse of the future in 1939, and cemented General Motors' position as the leader in diesel-electric locomotive design and production.

Courtesy Kalmbach Media

ordered 68 of the FT diesels for delivery in 1940. In the crush of war traffic to the West Coast in 1942, the Santa Fe was a logical choice for a concentrated assignment of diesels. The WPB agreed and authorized additional purchases.

The diesels shone. Santa Fe president Fred Gurley became a true believer. "Time does not permit a discussion of all [the diesel's] virtues," he declared in a speech in 1946. "Sufficient to say it is the best which man's ingenuity has produced for our service."[7] EMC sales people must have glowed. The public, too, took a lively interest. *Life* magazine ran a big photo spread on the Santa Fe's diesels in 1947 and correctly observed that 90 percent of new locomotive orders the previous year had been for diesels.

Against this onslaught, the steam locomotive manufacturers spoke up bravely. They meant to compete in the postwar market. At war's end, U.S. railroads counted 40,000 active steam locomotives and just 3,000 diesels. Railroads were heavily invested in steam maintenance facilities and backshops. Hundreds of thousands of employees worked as boilermakers, steamfitters, foundrymen, machinists, and in other trades tied to steam technology. Other thousands fueled, watered, handled ash, lubricated, inspected, and performed running repairs. Roundhouses, coaling towers, and water towers stood as prominent landmarks in towns large and small. A few railroads, such as the Pennsylvania, the Norfolk & Western, the Reading, and the Canadian Pacific owned engineering and shop facilities so extensive that they could still design and produce their own steam locomotives. Every large railroad had the staff and resources to rebuild steam locomotives entirely, as well as to develop complete mechanical and design specifications for new models in cooperation with the builders. If railroads were still the core of overland transportation, steam was the core of railroad operations.

Total costs were the issue, however, and in that context, the old age and limited capacity of most steam locomotives in use at the time stood out. Despite the improved steam designs introduced in the 1930s and early '40s, newer steam constituted a small proportion of the total roster. The average steamer had been purchased in the early 1920s, long before the Depression, and had undergone major repairs many times. Locomotive repair costs rose sharply with increased age. Even though the robust construction inherent to steam locomotives allowed useful service lives of three or four decades, there was no way around the maintenance/age cost curve. To managers, the answer was obvious: New engines, whatever their type, had to replace the older ones, and soon.

The established steam builders – Baldwin, Alco, and Lima – intended to provide as large a share of those new engines as possible. A few diesels might enter the mix, and despite the rush of postwar orders to Electro-Motive, the bulk of the new business should be steam. Lima's voluble design director, Albert Townsend, expressed his view to a convention of the Master Boiler Makers' Association:

> Whenever you hear that the steam locomotive is all done, washed up, and ready to be put away, just remember the old story of the hammer and the anvil. It was the hammer that wore out.[8]

Improved technology developed for steam since the 1920s promised increases in fuel efficiency and reductions in maintenance cost. And steam possessed a significant advantage: purchase price. Compared to new diesels, new steam built commercially cost about half as much per horsepower, and in many applications, less than half.[9]

A marketing blitz began before the war started. In the advertising tradition of its corporate parent, EMC polished its trade-ad campaigns in the 1930s, touting the diesels' savings in fuel and other operating costs. High purchase price compared to steam was a definite problem, but EMC literature claimed that operating savings could offset the price differential in relatively short order.[10]

EMC got an early foothold with diesel switchers. Since steam switching locomotives were often among the oldest engines in a railroad's fleet, they became an easy target. Switchers were also notorious for consuming a lot of fuel while standing idle for long periods between switching moves in the yard, so the operating savings of diesel switchers could be easily demonstrated. (A steamer has to burn fuel when standing just to keep the boiler hot; a diesel consumes a relatively small amount of fuel at idle.) In addition, many cities had begun to limit the use of steam locomotives as an anti-pollution measure.

For mainline passenger trains, Electro-Motive catered to the railroads' worry over chronic passenger losses. In colorful trade ads – and in ads for the traveling public, too – EMC capitalized on the fresh, modern look of brashly painted, streamlined diesels. Fast, smooth-pulling, and clean – no more rain of cinders down the back of the neck or smoke blowing through coach ventilators – diesels gave hope of attracting travelers back out of their automobiles.

The establishment fights back

Steam builders responded to the diesel manufacturers in kind: Their own trade ads pointed up the reliability and dependability of modern steam. To catch the public's eye, railroads installed streamlined, Art Deco casings on passenger steamers in the late 1930s and early 40s in an effort to address steam's image problem. The public enjoyed the show, but while the new streamliners – steam and diesel – often ran sold out before the war, overall passenger numbers fell after the war.[11] Railroaders winced when travelers sometimes referred to the streamlined steamers as "diesels" anyway. In the public mind, modernity was more associated with internal combustion than with steam.

A streamlined covering had nothing to do with the underlying technology of steam, and the builders knew it. Designers realized that of all the parts of the thermodynamic cycle affecting reciprocating steam performance – drafting, combustion, heat exchange, evaporation, steam pressure, superheating, valve timing, steam expansion in the cylinders – only increased boiler pressure, better drafting, and improved valves offered any practical improvement in overall efficiency. Increased boiler pressure required a watertube boiler, which in numerous applications in the U.S. and Europe had proven too costly to maintain. Better drafting had defied analysis. So, in the view of many engineers, only the valves were left.

Engineers for Lima and one of its associated companies, Franklin Railway Supply, worked hard on a solution: cam-operated poppet valves. The Franklin system of poppet valves gave fuel savings of 15 to 25 percent, with best efficiency at high engine rpm. The Franklin Type B rotary-cam variant, developed after the war, gave the same fuel saving at lower maintenance cost.

On other postwar fronts, Lima engineers experimented with a form of boiler they called the "double Belpaire." It had the traditional Belpaire bulge at the top, but it was mirrored by the novelty of a bulge at the bottom, resulting in more tubes and flues, and thus, more heating surface.

Chesapeake & Ohio engineers at Huntington, W.Va., tried a proprietary drafting device that lowered cylinder backpressure and improved locomotive power, the "Giesl ejector." The steam builders pushed the ICC to approve all-welded boiler construction, which could reduce boiler maintenance. The Baltimore & Ohio studied a multiple-cylinder locomotive, with several small, two-cylinder "vee" steam engines driving directly on the powered axles. The trade press, led by *Railway Age*, was full of editorials championing steam's cause, and ran articles suggesting forced boiler water circulation, improved feedwater heating, and other design proposals. "Come what may," declared a Lima ad in the trade magazines, "steam designs are ready to meet every demand of our railroads. ... Steam [will be] the dominating power for railroad transportation for a long, long time to come."

Builders and operators also recognized that more than the machine itself needed attention. Maintenance facilities – the infrastructure of steam – had to be redesigned and substantially upgraded if steam was to compete economically. Locomotive manufacturers by themselves could do little to effect change in the maintenance arena. A railroad led the effort: the Norfolk & Western. In the heavy flow of coal and commerce on the N&W, daily operations required many locomotives to be "turned" – inspected, fires cleaned, lubricated, given minor repairs, fueled, and re-dispatched – at Shaffers Crossing terminal in Roanoke, Va. At this key location, N&W staff designed and built two "lubritoriums." These were modern, run-through servicing bays unlike anything railroads had ever seen. Instead of taking a half day or more to turn a locomotive, N&W servicing crews could do it in about an hour. And N&W added a couple of steps. At every turning, workers flushed the locomotive's boiler completely in a few minutes with clean hot water, and other workers applied pressure lubrication throughout the chassis and running gear. The new servicing philosophy, in turn, let N&W designers re-imagine lubrication systems on the locomotive, adding dozens of pressure lubrication points to extend running-gear life. The rapid, semi-automated cycling of engines through the bays, the almost daily boiler flushing that each engine received (instead of only once a month as required by federal regulation) and the improved lubrication let N&W set new records for locomotive reliability and utilization, while cutting per-mile repair costs in half compared to some other big roads.

A new playing field

The postwar "war" between diesel and steam looked like a donnybrook. But there was a subtle point missed by many railroaders and observers of the fray. The battle was not fought *mano-a-mano*, machine against machine. A host of factors were to be decisive, and railroaders only vaguely appreciated the significance of most of these factors. The result would transform an industry beyond the imagining of most of the participants.

The insurgent was certainly GM, in a classic case of an outsider forcing change. Aggressive, backed by huge resources, and uninhibited by traditional ideas of how railroads and locomotive builders worked together, GM refused to play by the rules. A watershed departure was in design collaboration

Norfolk & Western "lubritoriums" brought modern methods to steam-locomotive servicing.
Courtesy Kalmbach Media

with customers. Charles Kettering had been instrumental in the creation of EMC, and Kettering was of the Alfred P. Sloan school of market penetration, as articulated by Chevrolet Division head William Knudsen in the 1920s. That is, study the market thoroughly, but get beyond what customers think; produce a product that customers didn't think they needed but is so attractive that it generates its own need.[12] When the Baltimore & Ohio, which wanted to help design a diesel locomotive in the late 1930s, offered to underwrite GM's expenses for testing on its lines, EMC design chief Richard Dilworth declined. Why? asked the B&O. "So you fellows won't tell us how to build it."[13]

Railroad company motive-power engineers had always been intimately involved in the design of their commercially-purchased locomotives, working closely with the manufacturer's staff. Railroad officers rightly insisted on customized steam locomotives suited specifically to the unique topography and operational circumstances of their railroad. Different prevailing conditions of grades, operating speeds, traffic density, and train size required entirely different designs – for steam engines. And, given the batch-style production methods used by steam builders – production runs usually amounted to only ten to 50 engines at a time – purchase price was not much reduced by the size of the order, and the railroad received engines best tailored to its specific needs. Real standardization was not a priority.

To GM, on the other hand, thoroughgoing standardization had always been part of its engineering and production approach. Standardization in high-volume production meant more efficient production methods, reduced materials costs, and, for GM's automotive and trucking customers, lower unit purchase prices and reduced parts inventories to support repair and maintenance. Based on its prewar experience, GM's renamed Electro-Motive Division (EMD) saw no good reason for collaboration on custom designs. The inherent operational flexibility of its electric transmission – high torque at low speed and high horsepower at all other speeds – suggested that a standard, general-purpose diesel locomotive might handle successfully a much wider variety of train sizes, grades, and speeds than could any steam locomotive. The need for custom design should not apply.

In a celebrated incident in the late 1930s, a railroad interested in new passenger diesels kept insisting on changes to the GM design. Finally, in exasperation, EMD founder Hal Hamilton made an offer:

> We'll build you a locomotive. You tell us what color you want it painted and we'll be responsible for everything else. We'll send you the locomotive without charge, with one of our men to supervise. ... You run the locomotive for six months. At the end of that time, you send us either the locomotive or the money.[14]

Six months later, the railroad paid up – and also ordered five more engines.

So EMD stuck to its guns, and design head Dilworth decreed: No departure from mass-produced, strictly standardized locomotives. The only options were lower gearing for freight service, and higher gearing with trucks (bogies) of longer wheelbase for passenger service. (The longer wheelbases provided better riding stability at high speed.) But with its savvy marketing sense, EMD offered to paint its customers' new diesels in stylish, color-coordinated schemes, unique to each railroad. The idea caught on quickly, and EMD established a styling studio, led by graphic designer Leland Knickerbocker. It should not be lost on readers that even for locomotives, GM reversed Ford's supposed dictum, "any color, as long as it's black." GM's answer was, "Any color you want."

GM's customer relations did not end there. EMD set up a network of parts-and-service depots across the country and trained a corps of field staff to deliver new locomotives, to help establish training programs for its customers' crews and mechanics, and to act as technical consultants and trouble-shooters. No steam builder had ever done such a thing; it was a need that railroads, so long wedded to steam, had never had before. EMD's managers knew, however, that their success depended heavily on railroads adapting to the new locomotives with a minimum of teething trouble.

Baldwin, meanwhile, catered to tradition. Hoping to secure the Pennsylvania Railroad as a diesel customer, for example, Baldwin poured resources into a collaborative, custom design for a mainline locomotive built only in limited numbers. Baldwin's diesel designs were mechanically inferior and, in vain hope, the old company merged in 1950 with Lima (which had joined with diesel-engine maker Hamilton in 1947) to create Baldwin-Lima-Hamilton, or BLH. Alco, in partnership with General Electric in Schenectady, N.Y., brought forth some diesel designs in the 1940s that were initially quite successful. Alco (and its Montreal Locomotive Works affiliate) became EMD's only serious competitor in the North American diesel market.

With its close links to the financial community, GM helped cash-strapped railroads in the critical arena of credit. In response to the issue of higher purchase price compared to steam, EMD pointed out that its standardized diesels were far more acceptable as security to prospective lenders. In the past, railroads had usually financed purchases of locomotives from revenues or from bank lines of credit secured by assets of the company. The locomotive builders were indifferent to the financing arrangements, but the diesel introduced a new wrinkle: Since the mass-produced diesel models were completely interchangeable from one railroad to another, the locomotives themselves could be accepted readily as full security for their own financing. Such security had been rarely used for steam locomotive sales, as a repossessed steamer could not easily be resold. The arrangement became common for diesels, and a railroad in bankruptcy or in weak financial condition could acquire a fleet of new locomotives this way, as in the case of the New York, Ontario & Western.

There is another aspect of financing that is often misunderstood by historians, graduate engineers, and popular writers alike. That is how a large corporation, such as a railroad, approaches major investment decisions, either in the 1940s or today. Investments, such as in new equipment, always involve interest. Even if the company uses its own cash, that cash has alternative uses. Such cash has an interest rate associated with it, based on the alternative investment uses that might be made of the funds. When a company borrows from a bank, it is often because the net interest rate is cheaper than if the company used its own cash. In all events, the decision to borrow is based on a fundamental calculation: The rate of return anticipated from using the borrowed funds – to invest in new equipment, facilities, technologies – will more than offset the debt service.

This is probably the most important insight to understand railroad dieselization. Every railroad that tried diesels reached a point where the purchase of additional diesels, using borrowed money, generated such operational savings that those savings covered the debt and then some. Put another way, the railroad was better off financially the faster it borrowed to put diesels into service. The only historical question is when a given railroad discovered that situation to be true, from its own experience in its initial operation of diesels vs. its existing steam. No proprietary bank or financial records are known to the author from the 1940s bearing on that precise financing question. (Such records would be among the most sensitive, both to a railroad and its bank, and so are among the least likely to survive.) That each railroad discovered its own diesel investment threshold, however, is historically moot.

In the end it was not a question of EMD's hype or GM's sales acumen. At some point each railroad's financial vice president and banker looked at their own numbers privately and made that startling discovery: Borrow as much as possible, buy diesels with the proceeds as fast as possible, and both banker

Known colloquially as a "Centipede," officially this customized Baldwin model was a BP60a to the Pennsylvania Railroad, and a DR-12-8-30 (meaning Diesel Road, 12 axles, 8 powered, 3,000 h.p.) to its builder. The "60" in PRR's nomenclature derived from the fact that the railroad ran them in semi-permanently coupled pairs.

Courtesy Kalmbach Media

and railroad would benefit. The steady erosion in rail traffic and depressed rail revenues only increased the incentives. Diesels would certainly not solve all the railroads' financial problems, but the faster they came into use, the more black ink would go to the balance sheets.

Standardized diesel locomotives ushered in change on many levels. The changes and cost impacts can be grouped into two basic categories: operations on the one hand, and maintenance and heavy repairs on the other. In both categories, diesel and steam differed acutely.

Railroad operations demand adaptability from a railroad's locomotive fleet. Passenger trains run on fixed schedules; fast freights, too, may run to schedule. Many freights, however, run as unscheduled "extras," slotted by dispatchers into the complex flow of other trains. Traffic on a line usually does not come at a steady rate and is not entirely predictable; there is wide variation in seasonal, weekly, and daily traffic movement.

Topography is another variable affecting operations. Truly flat sections of track are rare. Most track runs up and down hill, even in gentle terrain, with grades varying in severity. Often a relatively steep section will impose on an otherwise flat profile. Mountain districts place special demands, the more serious of which is not ascending the grades – which is tough enough – but descending grades safely. Trains coming down long grades must stay in full control, within the limitations of locomotive and car braking systems. On all sections, flat or steep, a locomotive must alter its power output frequently – from maximum power, to partial, to idle with braking, to maximum again, in a continuously changing response to load and grade. All of these changes in power output keep the train steady at the posted speed (which may vary from signal to signal), with heavy tonnage in tow (which varies from day to day), over track with many changes in curve and profile. All these variables require highly skilled engine crews, but they also require dispatchers and locomotive fleet managers to cooperate closely on the careful matching of both scheduled and unscheduled trains to the capabilities of locomotives available for each day's duty.

In the 1940s and early 1950s, operations reflected some fundamental characteristics of the steam locomotive, characteristics that had been an inherent part of railroading for over 100 years. First, there was a basic mechanical limitation: A steamer's cylinders, rods, and driving wheels are fixed in size and mechanical relationship. The locomotive is, in effect, locked in one "gear," with cycles of the pistons fixed to the rpm of the wheels. This is not as limiting as it sounds, because along with the throttle, the locomotive engineer varies the cutoff, which, as discussed, alters the timing as well as the quantity of steam flowing to the cylinders. In skilled hands, the power output of the engine can be managed very effectively and smoothly at any speed, from starting up to the maximum speed limit.

But the catch lies in the power available at different speeds. The fixed geometry of any steamer's drive means that maximum power and efficiency occur within a very narrow band of rpm or speed. Although a thoroughly accepted characteristic, this narrow band severely limited the flexibility of assigning locomotives to trains. The maximum raw pull of a steamer (tractive effort, or torque at the rims of the wheels) occurs at starting and decreases as speed rises; therefore the heaviest trains on the steepest grades run at slow speed. Maximum horsepower and efficiency, on the other hand, occur only at a defined rpm. The smaller-diameter driving wheels of freight engines give maximum power at around 25 to 40 mph. The larger driving wheels on passenger engines give maximum power at 45 to 65 mph, but with very poor low-speed performance. At speeds slower or faster than its peak-power zone, any steamer is terribly inefficient, wasting fuel out of all proportion to the tonnage to be pulled. Depending on terrain and other factors, steam designers specified driving-wheel sizes and various numbers of driving wheels, arranged in many different configurations. The welter of specific wheel arrangements was inherent. Variety in the size, power, and speed-range of a railroad's steam locomotives was a precondition to the adaptability and economic flexibility of the locomotive fleet as a whole.

The new diesels rewrote the honored, ancient rules. A diesel locomotive's direct current transmission included a control feature known as "transition." Transition connects the traction motors in varying combinations of series and parallel circuits to best match motor rpm and current, thus achieving the diesel's characteristic wide range of high horsepower at the rail. A diesel can run efficiently at speeds both faster and slower than a steamer. Like steam, the diesel also puts its maximum available pull to the rail at starting and slow speed, but the diesel's horsepower and efficiency reach maximum quickly – at around eight mph – and stay high as speed increases. Horsepower does not begin to fall off until 40 to 60 mph, depending on axle gearing. The upshot is this: When any locomotive, steam or diesel, operates at peak horsepower, its economic and operating productivity for its owner is also at its peak. To a railroad manager, the diesel is the dream locomotive because it maximizes productivity regardless of speed.

The implications of a "universal" locomotive went a vital step further. As GM's demonstrator No. 103 had shown , diesel locomotives could be designed in "units," each individual chassis self-contained with a complete engine/transmission/driving wheel package. Each fully standardized locomotive unit could be built to a convenient size. No. 103 had four such units of 1,350 horpower each, for a total of 5,400 horsepower, all answering to a set of controls in a cab at either end. For a short time, GM engineers did not appreciate what they had done, billing No. 103 as "a 5,400-hp locomotive" that was arranged in four units for flexibility around curves and for convenience in maintenance. Each of the two pairs of 1,350-hp units was connected with drawbars, not couplers. Eventually, however, the logic dawned: Forget the drawbars. If four locomotive units could be put together under one set of controls, so could three or six – or any number that was needed for the train to be pulled. All that was required to assemble a locomotive of almost any horsepower quickly were couplers and plug-in electrical cables. Thus was born the "modular locomotive," an unsung but momentous innovation in railroading.

To better appreciate this aspect of diesel flexibility with multiple units, consider that the largest modern steam locomotives had eight driving axles. In practical terms, each driving axle on a big steamer or on an early road diesel could exert reliably about the same low-speed pull – about 7½ tons of tractive pull for each axle. The steamer's pull was limited by uneven torque. The diesel's pull was limited by the amount of current that could be sustained in each axle-mounted electric motor. Thus, only two standard diesel units, of four axles each, could generate almost the pull of the largest steamers at slow speed. Put four diesel units together, such as GM No. 103, and the tractive pull is nearly equal to two of the largest steamers ever built. Six diesel units equaled three such steamers, and so forth. And all with just one engine crew – engineer and fireman – instead of two or three such crews.

The comparison is actually more complex. Compared to diesels, steamers had greater horsepower per driving axle at high speed, and early diesels often burned up traction motors at slow speed with too much current. Therefore at least three (and usually four) diesel units were needed to replace the very largest steamers, and steam could better compete on flat topography or with high-speed passenger trains. But the bread-and-butter of railroading was then, and remains today, heavy freight. Steam locomotives with eight driving axles were in fact rare. The preponderance of freight steamers had only four or five driving axles, not eight. Therefore, four diesel freight units with one engine crew could replace not just two steam freighters, but often three or four – and three or four locomotive crews. With diesels, furthermore, freight trains could actually run slower when long, steep grades required, at top efficiency, making the best of a diesel's higher horsepower at slow speeds. The use of "helper" or "pusher" locomotives – extra engines and crews assigned to help boost trains over steeper grades – could be eliminated in all but a very few locations.

Power for pulling, however, was just half of the operations equation. Safe speed control descending long grades had always been the primary limitation on the size of trains that could be dispatched in mountain territory. Air-brake systems on locomotives and cars were capable and highly sophisticated, having been developed over three-quarters of a century. Nevertheless, such systems required considerable skill on the part of the locomotive engineer in managing a train's air brakes on a long descent. And there was the unavoidable frictional heating of brake shoes and car wheels. The heat and wear of friction were the most serious problems, necessitating high replacement rates for wheels and shoes, with associated labor costs and downtime for the car.

Diesels came with a valuable device: the dynamic brake. Running downgrade, the locomotive engineer engaged a switch, and a simple set of relays functionally changed the electric traction motors on every driving axle into electric generators. The high turning resistance of these temporary "generators" slowed the locomotive and poured out electrical current, which dissipated as heat from fan-cooled grids on the locomotive's roof. The engineer could vary resistance to keep train speed steady as grades changed. Dynamic brakes were not a new idea. Straight-electric locomotives often had a similar system (called "regenerative braking"), with the current going back into the overhead wire. Air brakes on engines and cars were still essential, since dynamic brakes applied only to the locomotive driving axles. But electrical braking had never been available on non-electrified railroads before.

Mountain railroading radically changed. Freight trains no longer had to stop before coming down long grades to let brakemen set up air-brake retaining valves on the cars. Freight trains could become considerably heavier, yet engineers could control their speed of descent with greater assurance. Wheel and brake shoe wear sharply decreased.

Dispatchers and operating officers quickly perceived the advantages of locomotives having frictionless braking plus high horsepower in a wide range of speeds. Oddly, however, the operating flexibility from the "modular" idea was much slower in being perceived. During the Second World War and for a while thereafter, operating departments commonly regarded multi-unit freight and passenger locomotives as such: single locomotives for dispatching purposes, whose two, three, or four units remained coupled together unless an individual unit needed rotating for repairs. Only after a sufficient number of units had entered the fleet, so that dispatchers and locomotive maintenance officers could cooperate in assigning engine units daily in random, building-block style, were the advantages of modularity fully realized. Unit utilization rates rose significantly. Higher utilization – the percent of time a locomotive is actually out on the road on assignment – meant that fewer units were needed to cover a given traffic level. Compared to steam's 60 to 70 percent availability, average diesel utilization rates of 75 to 80 percent were normal in the 1940s, since diesels needed less downtime for daily maintenance or repair. After modularity became the norm in the 1950s, however, railroads frequently reported rates up to 90 percent. Any price advantage steam might have had was thus negated. (A cheaper locomotive needing a lot more downtime than another is not cheaper.) By 1950, though, the steam-diesel contest had already been decided, based on clear cost advantages, even before the added savings from modularity became fully apparent.

Impact on the workforce

The combination of the features above, rather than any single one, was revolutionary. All the old bugbears affecting freight operations – topography and varying traffic – still applied. Yet now, from a common fleet of standard engine units, all trains on the railroad could be handled. Freight trains in any territory could become longer. In both mountainous and flat terrain, much more horsepower could be assigned to a single crew. In the hilly districts, dynamic brakes permitted the longer trains safely to descend long grades as well as climb them. Longer trains in turn meant fewer trains. That eased dispatching, and having fewer trains compounded the crew savings. A single engine crew could often do the work of two or three as diesels simply substituted for steam, and with fewer trains, the rest of the operating crew roster – brakemen and conductors – could also be trimmed.

The operating unions perceived the threat and tried to fight back. The number of available crew assignments began dropping as both freight and passenger train movements fell off. Under long-agreed union-railroad work rules, however, there was nothing the union could do about the disappearing assignments. The protection that individual operating crew members had was seniority. Older men could bid the available jobs, but younger men often could not retain steady work, remaining on the "extra board" for years. As attrition took its inevitable toll, there was little or no new hiring.

Fearing for their declining numbers, the Brotherhood of Locomotive Engineers (BLE) and the Brotherhood of Locomotive Firemen & Enginemen (BLFE) focused their energy on saving the fireman's job. To railroad managers, firemen were redundant on diesels. BLE and BLFE spokesmen countered that a second person in the engine cab was still vital for safety, just as a co-pilot was on an airliner. Unions representing the brakemen and conductors supported the firemen, trying to maintain union agreements and some state laws ("full-crew" statutes) that required a five-person minimum on freight or passenger trains: conductor, two brakemen or trainmen, and two on the engine. The brouhaha over "featherbedding" consumed time and editorial ink for years. The merits on all sides of the argument are forever open to inconclusive debate. For the railroads, as employers, the featherbedding issue was a magnificent red herring that diverted public attention from the real story: Railroads were slashing payrolls anyway. From 1.4 million in 1946 (and still almost 1.3 million in 1951), railroad employment withered to 700,000 by 1962 – a reduction of half.

The bulk of this reduction came not from the operating crews but from the backshops – the army of workers needed to keep steam running. The steam locomotive had developed from an industrial era of inch-and-a-half-thick steel plate rolled and bull-riveted together; of huge forgings beaten into shape by colossal steam hammers; of one-piece steel castings 70 feet long; of huge lathes, planers, vertical boring mills, and other machine tools for huge piece-work. High precision came in limited doses: in axle bearings, rod bearings, frame alignment, cylinders, valves, and valve setting, for example. But precisely machined fits wore away quickly, and the locomotive was designed to accommodate the imprecision and to operate tolerably until the next cycle of major repair. Interchangeability of parts on steamers was very limited, even within individual locomotive classes, and machinery parts always required a great amount of hands-on fitting up by skilled mechanics. The diesel, on the other hand, came from a different industrial time: the era of machine design for internal combustion, where high precision characterizes nearly every working part, where close tolerances must be maintained for the life of the engine, and where genuine interchangeability of identical parts is the rule.

A diesel is designed as an array of standardized components arranged on a standard chassis. Big components such as diesel prime-movers, electric generators, and traction motors can be directly removed and replaced, with the removed parts sent to separate shops for heavy repair. Likewise, smaller components like blowers, pumps, and controls are readily replaceable with a minimum of downtime. A steam locomotive, in contrast, was designed as a complex structural unity: A steamer's frame and boiler were more or less permanently bolted together and shared in carrying the locomotive's weight and working stresses. Boiler and frame were not separated except for complete boiler replacement, which was rare. For machinists to bore its cylinders, replace its axle bearings, or turn its axles and wheels, or for boilermakers to repair or replace its firebox or reset flues, the entire locomotive had to be handled as a whole. There was no component modularity; even light repairs to auxiliary appliances required custom fitting of yards of piping for steam, water, air, and lubrication.

The difference between the two technologies, diesel and steam, was no more starkly apparent than in their railroad-shop layouts. The great variety of types and sizes of steam locomotives, coupled with the high labor intensity for every repair, prevented significant routinization or production-style repair procedures. The diesel, with its common, interchangeable, standardized parts, lent itself to enormous improvement in shop efficiency. There was, truly, no way the two technologies could coexist in the same shop building, for either light or heavy repair.

And no matter how well designed the steam shop, the availability statistics (availability is the percent of time ready for assignment, as distinct from utilization) told the tale. Rarely could a steam locomotive exceed 80 percent availability, due to the monthly interior boiler wash (usually one or two days downtime itself) and the continuous demands of "running repairs" – staybolt replacements, axle-box wedge adjustments, pump repairs, air-brake adjustments, electrical work, etc. – performed by various crafts, not in the backshop but in the steam locomotive's basic terminal building, the roundhouse. Diesels, best handled in a building with tracks in parallel and with elevated, deck-height walkways for the mechanics, posted availability rates of 90 to 95 percent. Fewer locomotives could therefore do more work, with labor hours cut drastically, simply because maintenance was so much easier.

At railroad repair centers, the new diesel shop buildings arose. Men skilled in internal combustion engines and in heavy electrical equipment hired on. The numbers of boilermakers, foundrymen, and machinists dropped rapidly, mostly by attrition and steam shop closings. Younger workers took eagerly to the new skills. For supervisors and old steam hands, the restructuring was wrenching. Union Pacific master mechanic Frank Acord, who worked up from an apprentice machinist at Cheyenne, Wyo., to chief of UP motive power in the diesel era, put it this way: "I felt like I was a steam-engine expert. I knew my business, but I get up one morning and ... I have to learn from scratch." Acord's associate Charlie Spicka, a shop superintendent, saw his first diesels and declared, "You're not bringing those steetcars in my shop." He was overruled. Said Acord of his friend, "It was like they shot him."[15]

Older steam mechanics still assumed that their skills would be needed for years to come. In the worst case, workers hoped, it would take several decades for diesels to replace steam entirely. After all, those 40,000 steamers at war's end could not be replaced overnight. For a while, even some railroad managers felt that the two technologies might coexist for some time. It was a vain thought. Railroad finance officers again ran the numbers: The expense of maintaining two parallel sets of shop facilities and shop staff could not long continue. One set of facilities would have to go.

Smaller steam terminals closed. The largest backshops converted. Fewer staff, concentrated at a few centralized locations, could handle heavy diesel repair. Some infrastructure changes were publicly visible: The big water tanks and coaling towers that symbolized steam came down. Other changes were not so apparent: Boiler-water chemical treatment and ash handling operations could cease. For daily servicing of diesels – inspection, fuel, sand, and small repairs – new, compact facilities sprang up, in a network of fewer locations than steam needed. With some exceptions for the most modern designs, steam locomotives on average had to stop every 50 miles for water and every 100 miles for fuel, rod greasing, and ashing; The latter usually meant changing a train's engine and putting on a fresh one. Diesels could run for several hundred miles before refueling or inspection.

That change – the ability of diesels to bypass traditional engine-change points – made another impact on railroad operating costs that was unexpected but profound. The traditional railroad administrative "division" – headed by a superintendent and including a major engine terminal and a major yard for classifying freight cars – was usually about 100 miles long, a length that had been determined by the characteristic need of a typical steam locomotive for full service after such a run.[16] The divisional structure also fit well with rail freight distribution patterns in the steam era. When railroads carried nearly every commodity and manufactured good to nearly every city and town, freight yards were needed in a thick network. Establishing such yards and engine terminals together made for an efficient management and distribution structure.

Each yard is analogous to a modern airline hub. Freight cars are collected from several different routes, merged, and ordered into new groups for sending on to many different destinations. When railroads were in the business of "retail" freight distribution – i.e., delivering goods all the way to customers' loading docks – a lot of hubs were required. As the freight market shifted between 1945 and 1965, railroads lost most retail to trucks but developed the "wholesale" or bulk trade, including unit trains of coal and grain; and dedicated carload service for large-scale industrial shippers of chemicals, foodstuffs and feed, autos and auto parts, wood products, paper, and ore. The diesel, with its normal operating range of several hundred miles, could run right by the traditional yards. The diesel thus permitted yard consolidations. The effect was a big reduction in the number of hubs to fit the new freight market. Said former company officer Al Eggerton of the Southern Railway:

> The restructuring of yards was among the most important savings the diesels made. We simply couldn't have done it with steam. Only diesels could run the distance without needing fuel, inspections, and a lot of other attention.[17]

Small and medium-sized yards were closed or trimmed back, and big yards were "streamlined" – that is, rebuilt for smoother operation with a larger numbers of cars (cars that would have been classified at the yards now closed). In these changes, not just yards but many route-miles became redundant, especially on secondary lines. Thousands of track workers lost jobs as work on such track was curtailed and as track work itself became heavily mechanized.[18] In the 1960s, a wave of railroad mergers began to consolidate yards, shops, and routes even further.

From the 1930s, crewmen who ran the locomotives saw the diesels threatening not only their numbers but their working traditions. Engineers and firemen were a close-knit fraternity that had developed during more than a century. Firemen not only stoked the coal, they were acolytes in a system that promised them eventual promotion to engineers. Engineers saw themselves at the top of this supporting social hierarchy. The BLFE acted early. In 1937, the union demanded that firemen continue to be assigned to diesels. The Union Pacific and the Burlington, which were then running some of the early diesel streamliners, reluctantly agreed. Managers saw merit in the argument that two sets of eyes were wise to have in the cab of a fast-moving passenger train. Moreover, only a few trains were involved. There was no thought in 1937 that diesels would ever fully replace steam on passenger trains, let alone be used on freight trains.

Ten years later, the acrimony over the fireman's position was in full cry. During the war, the BLFE and BLE had argued that a second fireman, and even a second engineer, should be assigned to every set of multiple locomotive units assigned to a train. A presidential board rejected those ideas. By 1947 the firemen were on strike for the survival of their profession, and the engineers supported them. Even with firemen on every train, railroads still saved on engine-crew payroll. An example is the Western Maryland Railway, which in steam days assigned four to six steam locomotives to each coal train it wrestled over the spine of the Alleghenies. One four-unit set of diesels could handle the same train or a longer one, with assistance from a two-unit pusher set on the most difficult stretch. Hence four crewmen (the road-engine crew and pusher crew) did the work of eight or twelve, even without confronting the fireman issue.

Steam's last gasp

Railroad orders for new steam locomotives evaporated in the late 1940s. Alco built its last steamer in 1948. The great Baldwin plant at Eddystone, Pa., made its last one for a U.S. road in 1949. And Lima turned out the last commercially built reciprocating steamer in the U.S. in the same year, a 2-8-4 Berkshire-type, much like the one Will Woodard created two and a half decades earlier. Thousands of skilled workers at these plants lost careers. By 1956, most railroads had made their last runs with steam, and by 1958 only a handful of steamers were left. The Norfolk & Western held out with steam for two more years, as did Grand Trunk Western, a U.S. subsidiary of Canadian National. N&W built its own superbly designed engines at Roanoke until 1953. Soon that railroad, too, threw in the towel. On many railroads, locomotives that were only a few years old, and had decades of service remaining, joined the ranks of more elderly engines in dead lines, awaiting scrap. In 1960, some 27,000 diesel units had entirely replaced those 40,000 steamers.

Communities large and small were drastically affected. From Hornell and Binghamton, N.Y., to Los Angeles and San Jose, Calif.; from Cheyenne and Green River, Wyo., to Baltimore and Hagerstown, Md.; from Livingston and Havre, Mont., to St. Louis and Sedalia, Mo.; from Pine Bluff and Little Rock, Ark., to Denver and Durango, Colo.; from Bangor and Pittsfield, Maine, to Miami and Jacksonville, Fla.; from Spencer and Asheville, N.C., to Chicago and

In the spring of 1949, Lima delivered its final steam locomotives – and the last commercially built steam locomotives in the U.S. – to the Nickel Plate Road. Class S-3 2-8-4 Berkshires Nos. 770-779 were younger than the Alco PA-1 diesels acquired by Nickel Plate for its passenger trains, and all were retired before those Alco "Bluebirds" ran their last miles.

Left, Don Wood; Both, Courtesy Kalmbach Media

Centralia, Ill. – and from Vancouver, British Columbia, to Montreal; Winnipeg, Manitoba, to Toronto; and Calgary, Alberta, to Quebec City – the geographic extent of the upheaval was unlike anything in American or Canadian industrial history. In about 3,000 communities across the continent, steam facilities, watering stations, and servicing depots closed, came down, or were abandoned between 1955 and 1960. Thousands of lives were wrenchingly altered.

It was a time of pain for many. Sons could no longer follow fathers into well-loved trades; fathers saw their trades disappear as sophisticated skills, acquired over lifetimes, became worthless. Families moved on. Communities adjusted.

An example is Altoona, a city of medium size in central Pennsylvania. Altoona owed its existence to the Pennsylvania Railroad. When the railroad was first surveyed in the late 1840s, planners saw that the foot of the Allegheny Mountains would make a logical place for major locomotive and car shops, and so Altoona was born. As the PRR grew, eventually connecting New York, Philadelphia, and Washington with Chicago and St. Louis, and carrying freight, travelers, and commuters in 14 states, the shops at Altoona grew as well. At its peak, 16,000 people and their families gained their livelihoods at Altoona's three-mile-long complex, and these citizens built a cultivated city. The PRR helped to foster the community by underwriting sports teams, bands, an accomplished orchestra, a library, and a major hospital. (Other railroads, in their shop towns, did the same.) The diesel locomotive upset all of this. In 15 short years, 1955 to 1970, Altoona's social and economic fabric had to be reconstructed. Rail employment shrank by three-quarters. In 1968, the PRR itself ended its history in the city, as "the P comp'ny" merged with its former archrival, the New York Central, to become Penn Central. It took time for the wounds to heal, but Altoona prospered again, its economy moving to a diversified base. Said a long-time Altoona resident:

> When the Pennsylvania gave up on steam, something in this town died, too. It's a great little city, but it took ages for us to recover. In many ways, we never have. That intense loyalty, that's gone.[19]

As the diesel revolution swept on, EMD led the field. The source of its dominance can be traced to more than marketing. It had a much superior product and an army of field technicians to train railroad shopmen and help ease the transition to diesels. From its predecessor, the Winton Engine Co., EMD inherited a valuable formula, which it protected with many patents for locomotive applications: the two-cycle, "V" engine configuration. Two-cycle operation made for a simple design and eliminated exhaust valves; the "V" layout allowed multiple small cylinders in a short block for a given engine displacement. Alco and Baldwin, meanwhile, had to make do with diesel prime-mover designs adapted from marine use. These had fewer, bigger pistons laid out in-line, and Alco's engines based on McIntosh & Seymour designs were four-cycle, necessitating exhaust valves. Anyone who had to work with both Alco and EMD engines knows the difference: EMD's smaller pistons and "power assemblies" (cylinder-and-piston units for mounting in an engine block) were easy to handle in the shop. Alco's huge pistons and extra valves were by contrast much more cumbersome and harder to deal with.

Alco's four-stroke cycle gave significantly better fuel economy than EMD. But in an era of 10-cent-per-gallon diesel fuel, comparative thermal efficiency was not critical. Ease of maintenance was. In fact, despite heavy emphasis by Alco and EMD on fuel cost savings over steam, such savings were undoubtedly the least consequential of the economies diesels entailed. The biggest saving was in labor.

Also affecting relative maintenance cost was the reliability of auxiliaries: pumps, generators, blowers, electrical controls. As GM did, EMD controlled its product quality by integration: Nearly all auxiliaries were produced along with frames, prime movers, and electrical gear on the grounds of EMD's plant at La Grange, Ill., west of Chicago. Alco, meanwhile, relied on numerous outside suppliers. Despite the high quality of Alco's generators, traction motors, and other electrical gear from GE, other auxiliaries gave more trouble than EMD's. And even GE's components weren't always reliable: Its air-cooled turbocharger, so successful on the P-38 Lightning of World War II, overheated in the down-to-earth confines of a locomotive engine room.[20] On such details market superiority turned.

The electric alternative

And what of the straight electric locomotive? While the U.S. dieselized, much of Europe's railway network went electric. Why wasn't electrification considered more widely here?

The only large-scale electrification project in the U.S. that is considered a long-term economic success was that of the Pennsylvania Railroad, completed in the mid-1930s between New York and Washington, with extensions between the Northeast Corridor and Harrisburg. Without loans and financing guarantees from the federal government through the Works Progress Administration (WPA), the project would never have been realized.[21] The one-time capital requirement was simply too large. European governments provided financial backing to electrification in their countries as well. The fundamental financial hurdle for any electrification is that the entire motive-power system – locomotives, substations, power distribution, overhead catenary structure and wires, and special shop facilities – must all be installed at once. Until the whole infrastructure is in place over an operating district long enough to give economies of scale, not a single electrified wheel can turn. Diesels, on the other hand, could be brought into use incrementally, with capital expenditures spread out in manageable doses. Operating savings began immediately to support the financing.

PRR's GG1 electric locomotive was highly successful, but high entry costs and low traffic densities meant that widespread electrification was limited elsewhere in North America.

Courtesy Kalmbach Media

Another factor basic to North America is its extended geography. Unless traffic densities – numbers of trains per day – are high enough, electrification cannot return enough to pay for its installation. Even today, few long-haul routes in the U.S. have sufficient traffic densities to pay off the huge initial investment required to electrify. In Europe in the 1950s and today, sufficient densities exist, the result of frequent, government-subsidized passenger service maintained on a highly compact route structure. In the U.S., only a few non-urban electrifications have been tried. The short Virginian Railway electrified its high-density coal train movement, and the Great Northern electrified its Cascade Tunnel, both before 1910. The Milwaukee Road strung more than 600 miles of low-voltage, direct-current wires across Montana, Idaho, and Washington on parts of its Chicago-Seattle route and began running its famous "bi-polar" locomotives in 1916, but the railroad entered bankruptcy later on. Great Northern de-energized its wires in 1956 and the Milwaukee Road in 1973. The locomotives and infrastructure were worn out and too expensive to replace compared to the alternative: diesels. The Milwaukee Road's traffic fell to such low densities that upgrading its electrified line to a modern, higher-voltage, a.c. system was out of the question.[22]

Diesels for passengers

Passenger trains were not neglected in the early diesel years; quite the contrary. It is a myth that that U.S. railroads did not try to recapture the elusive rail passenger. Fabulous new streamliners rolled out after the war. The *20th Century Limited* and the *Broadway Limited*, the *Hiawatha* and the *Daylight*, the *City of San Francisco* and the *City of Los Angeles*, the *Chief* and the *Super Chief*, the *Texas Eagle* and the *Texas Special*, the *Sunset Limited* and the *Crescent*, the *Silver Meteor* and the *Florida Special*, the *North Coast Limited* and the *Empire Builder*, *The Canadian* and the *Super Continental* – all these and many more were revamped in new, improved editions with brand-new cars. Entirely new trains such as the *California Zephyr*, *Phoebe Snow*, *Southerner*, and the *San Francisco Chief* debuted. These were all full-size, commodious trains, not compact affairs with low seating capacities like the experimental *Pioneer Zephyr* and M-10000 of the 1930s. Marketing to the public was intense, and schedules were speeded up to take full advantage of diesel run-through capabilities. Many of these trains used coaches, diners, and sleepers designed by the Budd Co., the same firm that had designed the *Pioneer Zephyr*. Budd cars were built almost entirely of stainless steel, a major innovation in durability and light weight using aircraft-style "monocoque" construction. The material and reduced weight cut maintenance and operating cost per seat. The unpainted, fluted exteriors of these beautiful cars gleamed in the sun and created a completely new architecture for rail travel.[23]

Two trains in particular epitomized the attempt to recapture the long-distance traveler: the *Super Chief* and the *California Zephyr*. Both operated on popular routes where, their railroads hoped, the public would regard auto travel as too long and air travel (in the piston age) too uncomfortable and expensive. Santa Fe's *Super Chief* ran between Chicago and Los Angeles via Albuquerque, beginning operation before the war. Its splashy look of polished stainless steel and scarlet-nosed diesels painted in the so-called "warbonnet" motif became a Southwestern icon. The train quickly picked up the nickname,

Santa Fe's *Super Chief* – seen here at Fullerton, Calif., behind Electro-Motive E1 diesels delivered in 1937 – was emblematic of the rise of streamlined, diesel-powered passenger trains in the U.S.
Courtesy Kalmbach Media

"Train of the Stars," from its frequent patronage by Hollywood's elite. The *California Zephyr* began in 1949, running daily between Chicago and Oakland, Calif., opposite San Francisco, as a cooperative venture of the Burlington, the Denver & Rio Grande Western, and the Western Pacific railroads.

The *Super Chief* was the posh, upscale train, with the finest dining in the celebrated "Turquoise Room" decorated with original Navajo and Hopi art. The *California Zephyr*, on the other hand, aimed at the vacationer on a budget and was launched at a time when rail passengers were disappearing in droves. The planners who conceived the new *CZ* realized that some attention-grabbers were in order. Fares in those years were regulated by the ICC, and so price competition was forbidden. To cater to families who could not afford compartment space, the coaches were given large, fully reclining seats to accommodate sleeping. Then came the virtual trademark of this train: the Vista-Dome car. A strictly diesel-era innovation, pioneered by the Burlington Route in 1945, such a car was impractical for steam-hauled trains; the dome's glass would have been dirtied quickly by smoke.

Seats in the dome were unticketed and open to all. The *California Zephyr* was not the first all-new train with a dome car (that was GM's *Train of Tomorrow*, a special demonstration train that toured to extensive press coverage in 1947), but other trains in the U.S. and Canada introduced dome cars of their own after the *CZ's* initial success. For lesser trains, however, a dome car was an add-on. For the *CZ* – which traversed by daylight the Rocky Mountains west of Denver and the Feather River Canyon of the Sierra Nevada – the Vista-Dome was the main event. And the train didn't have just one such car; the regular complement was five of these splendid sightseeing conveyances. With these bright bubble-tops in tow, the *California Zephyr* was dubbed "The Silver Lady." It passed "through the Rockies, not around them," as the old D&RGW slogan said.

For an all too brief time, both the *Super Chief* and the *CZ* brought a renewed public interest in train travel. A few other named trains (as distinct from the many anonymous numbered trains), such as New York Central's ever-famous *20th Century Limited* and the Milwaukee's *Hiawatha*, prospered briefly with new cars and engines of fresh design. But lasting economic success eluded them. By 1960, almost every passenger train in North America was struggling under a crushing burden of high labor costs and evaporating patronage.[24] Some commentators babbled that railroads "were not doing enough" to recapture the passenger trade. A look at the record is sobering. Railroads did try, and very hard, investing millions in locomotives, cars, and marketing.

In 1962, freight ton-miles on railroads fell to their lowest level since the Great Depression. Passenger-miles kept on their downward spiral well past the creation of Amtrak in 1971. In 1963, a long-term recovery began in freight. Only with the economies brought by the new diesel fleet would railroads have been positioned to survive a radically reordered transportation market. Of all the economies that diesels brought, fuel-cost saving was only a small fraction of the story. Thirty years later, by 1993, railroads were prospering, carrying all-time record levels of freight – well over a trillion ton-miles per year. Market share of all intercity freight ton-mileage approached 40 percent. (In comparison, intercity trucks carried 27 percent.)[25] The stage was set in the 1945-1960 period.

Those 15 years marked the end of "the Railroad Age." The vast business enterprise of railroading had been the physical connection between every other business in the land. Trains were the way one came and went, and the way one received and sent all one's goods. Early in the 20th century and into the 1920s, trains employed 15 percent of all industrial workers, spread throughout thousands of small towns and principal cities. Every American citizen interacted with railroaders, as ticket and express agents, porters and conductors, freight agents, friends, or family members. Into the 1930s, railroads were the social network that physically linked every other human and cultural enterprise on the continent. Trains were basic. Somewhere between 1945 and 1960, railroads became just another industry.

Jervis Langdon, former president of the Baltimore & Ohio and an architect of the diesel transition, summed up railroaders' mixed emotions:

> We had to realize that the diesel was a lifesaver. If we had to compete against trucks with steam engines, I doubt if the economics would have permitted a competitive operation. But there were many in management who were very reluctant to get rid of the steam engines. ... The hard facts of business can be tough when you're dealing with emotions. ... As a kid, I lived in the country, up on a hill overlooking Elmira, N.Y. Down below were the old Delaware, Lackawanna & Western Railroad and the Erie Railroad. I remember I'd wake up in the night and hear those steam-engine whistles coming down the valley. I still hear them in my dreams.[26]

Chapter 17 Notes

1. Quoted in *The American Heritage Dictionary of the English Language*, 1973 ed., p. 441.
2. Association of American Railroads statistics, quoted at http://www.aar.org.
3. Anecdotal but probably typical: Nearly every GI had experienced wartime train journeys under abominably crowded conditions. As an uncle and a vet related to the author after the war, "Given the choice of driving my car, *I'd never ride a train again!*" (Emphasis most definitely in the original.) The editor's father, another World War II vet, commuted by rail but never rode another intercity train after he was mustered out in 1945.
4. Statistics provided by Dr. F. Robert van der Linden, chairman of the aeronautics department at the Smithsonian Institution's National Air and Space Museum.
5. These facts clearly undermine various notions that the postwar transport picture might have been different if only the railroads had marketed better, or if Washington had produced a more equitable transportation policy – as though policy is made in ivory towers, divorced from the real world. At its heart, changing U.S. transportation preferences were the result, not of railroad industry failure, but of a popular-cum-political juggernaut that demanded a heavy emphasis on roads. Once that process got underway, plain old marginal economics took care of the rest, as both travelers and shippers made their individual decisions, one by one and at the margin, to choose their modes of transport. See Alfred Kahn, "The Tyranny of Small Decisions," *Kyklos*, February 1966.

6. Franklin M. Reck, *On Time: The History of Electro-Motive Division of General Motors Corporation*, 1948.
7. *Railway Age*, September 28, 1946. The occasion was the introduction of Alco's PA-1 locomotive, a model that would prove less reliable than EMD's products.
8. David P. Morgan, "Super Power," *Trains*, January 1952, pp. 13-21.
9. P.W. Keifer, *A Practical Evaluation of Railroad Motive Power*, 1948.
10. Reck, *On Time* (Note 6).
11. Mark Reutter, "The Lost Promise of the American Railroad," *Wilson Quarterly*, Winter 1994. Reutter contends that the lightweight diesel passenger trains of the late 1930s, if better marketed and if supported by a more even-handed governmental policy on passenger travel, might have developed into a competitive mode. But these trains were few, small, and of very limited seating – typically only 70 to 100 people per train. Literally hundreds of such trains, utterly beyond the ability of railroads to finance, would have been needed to support a large enough ridership to have made a significant difference. And even assuming huge government support, whether the public would have responded by patronizing such an enlarged fleet is open to question. Cheap gasoline, uncrowded highways, and the personal freedom associated with auto travel in the 1950s and 60s created a potent context. In that context, individual travelers made their own choices, one by one.
12. Charles E. Edwards, *Dynamics of the United States Automobile Industry*, 1965. See also John B. Rae, *The American Automobile: A Brief History*, 1965.
13. Franklin M. Reck, *The Dilworth Story: The Biography of Richard Dilworth, Pioneer of the Diesel Locomotive*, 1954.
14. Quoted in Reck, *On Time*.
15. Maury Klein, "The Diesel Revolution," *American Heritage Invention and Technology*, Winter 1991, p. 20.
16. There was a lot of variation in that number, but nearly all divisions were within the 80-200 mile range. Shorter divisions were more common in the East and South; longer in the Midwest and West.
17. Author's interview with Eggerton, former Southern Railway corporate relations vice president, April 1998.
18. It is important to note here that railroads could not simply abandon secondary lines. ICC abandonment regulations, unchanged until the mid-1970s, applied. Years of notices, hearings, and appeals kicked in if a railroad sought to abandon even a few miles of secondary route that would result in any town or community losing rail access. On the other hand, railroads could reduce yards or simply not maintain them, and a railroad could tear up track on multi-track mainlines (reducing double track to single track, for example), so as to cut track maintenance budgets.
19. Author's interview with Fred E. Long, May 20, 1987.
20. Peter A. Hansen, "The First PAs: The Agony, the Ecstasy, and the Legacy," *Classic Trains*, Winter 2008, p. 30.
21. Michael Bezilla, *Electric Traction on the Pennsylvania Railroad, 1895-1968*, 1980.
22. Electrification of U.S. railroads is another perpetual and inconclusive debate. But the huge initial burden of financing, and the difficulty of repaying the financing in a reasonable period of time from revenues earned by the line in question is, without doubt, the primary difficulty. See William L. Withuhn, "Risk and the Real Cost of Electrification," *Railroad History*, Autumn 1999, pp. 80-91.
23. *The Official Guide of the Railways*, published monthly since 1868, provides timetables and equipment for most of the premier trains.
24. Passenger losses cannot be disaggregated from annual revenue and expense statistics compiled by the Association of American Railroads for the industry as a whole. Passenger and freight revenues were separately compiled in accordance with ICC reporting rules, but "transportation," "maintenance of way," and other expenses were a mix of all such expenses in running all trains. Accounting rules often made it difficult for railroads to publicly justify passenger losses: how could track maintenance expenses, for example, be allocated between freight and passenger? Or dispatching expenses? (Dispatchers on shift integrated both types of trains into the flow; ceasing passenger service would not necessarily alter the number of dispatchers needed.) The best data, from the railroads' perspective, is in Congressional hearing testimony in 1969-1970, on legislation that created Amtrak on May 1, 1971.
25. Association of American Railroads, *Railroad Facts*, 1994.
26. Quoted from oral histories compiled by Stuart Leuthner in *The Railroaders*, 1983, p. 129.

Chapter 18

Big Boy and Allegheny:

The Most Powerful of All

EVER SINCE RICHARD TREVITHICK'S audacious little "high-pressure" locomotive ran in Wales in 1804, steam locomotives had grown in size and power. Almost a century and a half later, designers stretched what would become the final, restrictive limits of both weight and dimensions, achieving 6,000 to 7,500 horsepower in gargantuan locomotives. Trevithick's first machine exerted perhaps five horsepower; in 1941, an approximately 1,200-fold increase in useful output had been managed successfully on pretty much the same gauge of track.

By the early 1940s, however, some railroaders suspected that the evident ingenuity was nearing a dead end, at least in terms of sheer size. The context was not simply the incipient incursion of new diesels having competitive performance, but the fact that oversize, heavy, high-power locomotives appropriate only to the largest carriers were irrelevant to the needs of the great majority of railroads, while no satisfactory improvement seemed evident for steam locomotives of more generally useful sizes.[1] Nevertheless, railroaders both in the U.S. and abroad took keen interest in the new designs.

The Union Pacific's 4-8-8-4 Big Boy type debuted in 1941 with an initial batch of 20 from the American Locomotive Co. of Schenectady, N.Y. (UP hadn't settled on a name for the locomotives – "Wahsatch" was one contender – before an Alco employee decided the question for them. He scrawled "Big Boy" on the smokebox of the first locomotive in the class, and the name stuck.) The new locomotives garnered considerable public notoriety for the railroad, which operated them on a portion of its Omaha, Neb.-Ogden, Utah, route, a vital artery that was heavily used for shipping manufactures, fruit and vegetables, express, and other freight between the Far West, Midwest, and East. An energetic Union Pacific publicity department promoted the new locomotive not only to the railroad trade press but to the public via newspapers, newsreel coverage, and in magazine ads. Operating success of the type, together with increased wartime traffic, led to an order for five more Big Boys in 1944.

A Union Pacific 4-8-8-4 Big Boy type singlehandedly leads a long westbound train at Dale, Wyo., in May 1958.
Richard F. Lind, Courtesy Kalmbach Media

The author gratefully acknowledges William W. Kratville and Eugene L. Huddleston for data and quotations used in this chapter.

The Chesapeake & Ohio Railway's 2-6-6-6 Allegheny type, with the first ten delivered from the Lima Locomotive Works in December 1941, was much less celebrated in the contemporary trade and public media, given its introduction in the same month as Pearl Harbor. Eventually, the Lima Works built 60 for C&O; the locomotives hauled 160-car coal trains and other traffic in Virginia, West Virginia, Kentucky, and Ohio. Both the UP and C&O designs vied for the honorifics of "world's largest," "world's heaviest," or "world's most powerful." Which locomotive could factually claim which title turned out to be far from clear-cut and turned on a surprisingly complex set of questions.

Of the two locomotives, the Union Pacific's seemed, in the long run, to be the more carefully conceived as part of an explicit corporate strategy. Huge in size though it was, the Big Boy was an extrapolation of a previous design which had well-proven itself in fleet use, the 4-6-6-4 Challenger. For the new, larger design, an integrated approach prevailed, from initial specification through application. Mechanical engineers' decisions were governed throughout by the high speed that UP managers required of their freight trains; civil engineers and track gangs eased curves and widened right-of-way clearances specifically to accommodate the engines' greater size; operations planners worked out new dispatching criteria to take full advantage of the engines' power; and maintenance planners made improvements to selected facilities, so that servicing and repair for the Big Boys blended seamlessly into that for the existing fleet of Challengers.

The Allegheny, on the other hand, had a more idiosyncratic genesis and problematic career. The C&O hauled immense quantities of coal out of West Virginia and over the spine of the Allegheny Mountains. The waning of the Depression and increasing war-related production accelerated mine output. (This was true, even before Pearl Harbor, as the U.S. ramped up production for its European allies, and also in anticipation of possible direct involvement in the war.) Just as at UP, C&O's managers defined a need for new locomotives based on increased traffic. In contrast to the Union Pacific situation, however, neither of the C&O's most-recently designed heavy freight locomotive types – the T-1 class of 1930 and the H-7/H-7a classes of 1923 and 1926 – were capable of "extrapolation." And, rather than working within a centrally planned effort integrating locomotive design with improved train operations as part of an overall corporate strategy, evidence suggests that the

Builder's photos of a Union Pacific 4-8-8-4 Big Boy and a Chesapeake & Ohio 2-6-6-6 Allegheny.
Courtesy Kalmbach Media

Allegheny's mechanical engineers made design decisions based on their own, often conflicting criteria. In the end, the Allegheny set records for horsepower that were never equaled – at least 1,000 more horsepower than Big Boy. The C&O's biggest could run at speeds both low and high, and yet it was horribly botched in fundamental ways.

By mid-1940, Union Pacific's freight volume was climbing out of its Depression-era doldrums, especially on the railroad's Omaha-Ogden "Overland Route." Although the U.S. was not yet a combatant in the rapidly escalating world war that had begun in 1939, and although the phrase "national defense" was still a subject of hot debate between isolationist commentators and others, U.S. industrial output was slowly responding.[2]

Union Pacific had weathered the 1930s in good financial condition. Corporate belt-tightening included the purchase of only a limited number of new locomotives, and none from 1931 until 1936. Even accounting for its corporate size and mileage, however, Union Pacific ordered proportionately more locomotives in the 1930s than many big railroads. Beginning in 1936, the railroad began expanding its department for locomotive engineering and design, and initiated a fleet modernization program. Of the new locomotives added between 1930 and 1939 (including the last 25 of the 4-12-2 "Union Pacific" types and the first 40 of the 4-6-6-4 Challengers), most were built specifically to increase the average speeds of UP's heaviest freight trains, part of an explicit business strategy designed to attract as much long-distance traffic as possible in a troubled economy.

UP President William Jeffers convened a series of planning meetings in the spring and summer of 1940. Looking at all operations on the main line, operations people identified a growing bottleneck: the arduous, 65-mile grade east from Ogden through Echo Canyon up to Wahsatch, Utah. This had been historically the most troublesome part of UP's entire system, limiting train capacity and requiring helper locomotives to assist every eastbound freight train. This procedure added enormously to costs, given the unusual length of the Wahsatch helper district, especially costs for labor (each helper locomotive needed a separate crew), extra locomotives, locomotive fleet maintenance, and fuel. As important, in view of UP's revenue-enhancing fast freight philosophy, the coupling and uncoupling of helpers and attendant delay increased transit times by as much as 30 minutes. In this context, Jeffers

With "Big Boy" scrawled in chalk on its smokebox, an Alco employee bestowed an enduring name on UP's 4-8-8-4s in 1941.
Courtesy Kalmbach Media

asked the mechanical engineering staff, headed by Otto Jabelmann, to begin design studies for a new class of engine for the Wahsatch grade, to operate without helper assistance on heavy freights between Ogden, Wahsatch, and the engine terminal at Green River, Wyo.[3]

Otto Jabelmann had been promoted to head UP's reorganized Motive Power and Machinery Department in 1936 and then to vice president of research and mechanical standards in 1939. A bright engineer and an excellent manager, he rose to prominence from within UP ranks in the 1920s, supervising locomotive repair. Born in Cheyenne, Wyo., in 1891, where UP had its largest repair shops, Jabelmann hired on as a crew caller at age 15 and later became a machinist. After learning engineering at Stanford and the University of Michigan, he returned to Cheyenne and worked his way up in traditional fashion, albeit swiftly, becoming by 1933 UP's general superintendent of motive power and machinery at the company headquarters in Omaha. Although UP's mechanical engineering department was large, only a few on the staff were university-trained, and Jabelmann brought in more such graduates, notably from Purdue and the University of Illinois, (both of which had specialties in railway mechanical design), beginning in 1936.

In early summer 1940, before any engineering work began, Jeffers and Jabelmann agreed on the basic performance specification: 3,600 trailing gross tons on the maximum Wahsatch grade of 1.14 percent (1.14-foot rise in 100 feet of travel), with no helpers.[4] Additionally, Jabelmann knew that speed capability on level track would need to be 60 mph or higher if the engine was to mesh smoothly with other mainline traffic elsewhere on the system. Such a combination of pulling power and speed had never before been attempted anywhere.

Within a few days, Jabelmann's core design team decided the engine's fundamental architecture. To meet Jeffers' tonnage dictum on the maximum grade, the locomotive would need four cylinders and 135,000 pounds of tractive pull from starting up to 10 mph. To maintain adhesion, it would therefore require at least 540,000 pounds of weight (four times the rated pull) on the driving wheels. To reach the desired speed within inertial limits on the rotating machinery, it might need driving wheels of 68 inches or more in diameter. To maintain vehicle stability at high speed, a four-wheel leading truck was called for. Based on rough estimation of the weight of cast-steel frames, with some basic boiler and furnace dimensions calculated for adequate steam generation using UP's available coal (relatively low in BTU or heating value) and adding steam pipes, pumps, and other appliances, all-up weight, less tender, would approach 385 tons. Loading limits of no more than 35 tons per driving axle, dictated by the normal weight-carrying capacity of rails and track structure, closed the specification circle. The resulting initial calculations were utterly straightforward: UP needed a brand-new locomotive configuration, a 4-8-8-4. Based on the success of the 4-6-6-4 Challengers of 1936 and 1937, Jabelmann concluded that the new configuration was feasible. Jeffers, who took an active interest throughout the project, concurred.

Then came the hard part: sweating the details. The Union Pacific's favored builder, the American Locomotive Company, contracted to construct the design when finished, and so Alco assigned four teams of engineers and draftsmen to the project, led by Vice President of Engineering Joseph Ennis and his star designer, Alfred W. Bruce. In traditional fashion, the design project was a collaboration between manufacturer and railroad, with the railroad's own engineering staff equal in talent and research base to that of the builder. The railroad was primary as arbiter on design decisions.

An early design parameter related to speed. From their own recent research in road tests, UP engineers knew that maximum stress on connecting rods, wristpins, crankpins, and other rotating or reciprocating parts often occurred when a locomotive's engineman abruptly reduced the throttle while running and decelerated the engine with improper control of valve gear. The resulting combination of poorly controlled steam pressure within the cylinders and high rotational inertia could create stresses far in excess of the steam thrust forces indicated by ordinary calculations for the highest working power. Taking these insights into account, and adding a margin for safety, Jabelmann fixed the design top speed for the locomotive at 80 mph, unheard of for an engine of such weight and size.

Boiler pressure also was stretched to the practical limit. Three-hundred psi was relatively rare in contemporary practice, but the higher pressure would allow the new engine's cylinders to be as small in diameter as possible, with a long stroke. Smaller-diameter pistons would be lighter, thus reducing reciprocating stresses at speed, while the long stroke would give smoother torque. At the same time, however, higher boiler pressure meant a heavier boiler, since thicker steel for the boiler shell would be required. Also, the larger the diameter of the boiler (or the larger the diameter of any pressure vessel), the thicker its shell must be for any given pressure. A big boiler diameter was essential in order to pack in all the tubes needed for high steam evaporation and output. Additionally, an extremely large firebox would be a necessary feature – a firebox having both an extensive grate and great furnace volume, so as to provide sufficient heat release from UP's specific variety of low-to-medium-BTU coal, most of which came from mines near Rock Springs, Wyo.

Here was a classic engineering conundrum: Certainly the designers could have the boiler dimensions and pressure desired, but the boiler easily could become too heavy. Jabelmann set 380 tons as the total target engine weight (*i.e.*, weight without tender). Both Alco and UP staffs went laboriously through many combinations of boiler pressure, boiler diameter and length, number and size of tubes, boiler plate thickness, firebox dimensions, and resulting weight. Provisionally, a successful combination emerged: Specifications included 300 psi, 107 inches maximum boiler diameter, maximum boiler plate thickness of 1⅜ inches – which would be the heaviest yet used in a locomotive – and a firebox grate area of 150 square feet. To compound the boiler designers' problem, however, the other engineering teams working on frames, cylinder assemblies, running gear, and other components would have to be further along in design to be sure the total target weight was not exceeded.[5]

The running gear and frame design presented a special set of demands, primarily because of the 80-mph speed and the fact that the articulated (*i.e.*, hinged) frames were to be so long. Jabelmann specified roller bearings for all axles and lightweight, hollow-cast driving wheels. (The latter to help improve balancing for high rpm by providing more room within each driving wheel for its counterweights.) Facing another perennial conundrum, engineers wrestled with a decision on driving-wheel size, a sensitive parameter that affected rpm and piston speed, and thereby steam consumption and power. The 80-mph criterion called for a large-diameter wheel to keep piston speed down, but the need for high power at low, sustained speeds of 15 to 25 mph on the grade called for as small a diameter as possible. Finally, a diameter of 68 inches (combined with a piston stroke of 32 inches) gave adequate calculated performance while keeping the engine wheelbase within practical length.

A key element was the articulation hinge between front and rear engine frames; this hinge joined the swiveling front engine unit to the rear engine unit, which was fixed to the boiler. An important innovation in the design of this hinge had been introduced on the Norfolk & Western Railway's 2-6-6-4 of 1936 and was subsequently adopted by Alco for Challengers with cast-steel frames. The innovation involved a large-diameter pin, set vertically, connecting a tongue at the back of the front unit's subframe into a great socket in the rear unit's frame. This arrangement made a dramatic difference in locomotive stability and, in fact, was the hidden but vital secret behind the Challengers' unparalleled ability as heavy, four-cylinder freight locomotives that could run at passenger-train speeds.

Gerald Blunt had been Alco's suspension and running gear specialist for the Challengers, and now as Alco's chief mechanical engineer, he supervised the design of Big Boy's suspension. The genius in the Norfolk & Western-style articulation hinge, though deceptively simple, was that it permitted no appreciable vertical motion of the front unit; the big pin permitted the front unit to move only laterally, in the horizontal plane. All previous types of articulation permitted the front unit to move in at least two planes, laterally and vertically. Designers once thought this freedom of motion was unquestionably necessary, both for Mallets and for simple-expansion articulateds, so that the front unit could respond properly to track irregularities and maintain adhesion.

With such a full-freedom hinge, the suspension of an articulated locomotive resolved into two tripods, according to the classical three-point suspension method developed since Joseph Harrison's invention of the equalizer in 1838 and William S. Hudson's refinement of 1864.[6] In all Mallets and articulateds prior to 1936, the front engine unit formed one independent tripod, and the rear engine unit plus trailing wheels formed the second tripod, with the second tripod's forward suspension point being the front of the boiler bearing down on the front unit. (The three-point, or tripod principle of locomotive suspension and spring-rigging is discussed in Chapters 1 and 4.) The configuration might be called "a tripod on a tripod." With such a suspension and the requisite hinge, an articulated locomotive ran well at slow and moderate speed with good adhesion, but at high speed, the front engine unit frequently banged around in disconcerting motions and oscillations, it lost traction, and it sometimes damaged both itself and the track. Simple-expansion articulateds built in the 1920s were often little faster than their supposedly slower Mallet cousins.

The revised hinge, acting together with a waist support under the boiler ahead of the hinge, changed the dynamics entirely. With vertical motion of the front engine unit suppressed to a minimum, the locomotive's complete suspension system could be arranged as a single tripod and so, in effect, share the high-speed stability of a fast, two-cylinder engine having no articulation.

Both Challenger and Big Boy shared the single-tripod suspension: An equalizer set lengthwise under the front cylinder saddle, linked with a cross-equalizer connecting the springs of the left and right sides, joined all of the front unit's spring rigging together. Since the front engine unit's lead truck and all drivers were thus equalized together – equalized across as well as front-to-back – the front unit resolved to a single suspension point. The rear unit's springing, with no cross-equalization, formed the two other suspension points. Vertical irregularities in the track were absorbed entirely by the front and back springs. UP's staff determined the final geometry of the springs and gave them very generous travel so they would not overload on small humps or depressions.

When describing the locomotive's behavior in negotiating curves, UP and Alco designers often referred to the suspension and articulation hinge as incorporating a "lever principle," with the front engine unit swinging horizontally and pulling the rear unit around a pivot point several feet forward of the last driving axle. Stability in all planes of motion was uncanny. The American articulated locomotive had been reinvented.

Due to Big Boy's total wheelbase being some 12 feet longer than a Challenger's, both UP and Alco designers worried that Jerry Blunt's hinge, successful on the smaller locomotive, might not work on the larger. The static shearing forces on the hinge pin would be immense, more than seven tons, and more if the pin were misaligned. But the hinge worked as predicted. It had to be modified slightly in later years; UP did field studies in early 1945 to solve problems of binding, which were remedied by some dimensional changes that gave the tongue and pocket a bit more clearance. Blunt went on to design trucks and spring rigging for Alco diesels, a design since known as the Blunt truck.

Big Boy's boiler, though long, was conventional in layout. The firebox grate area was determined by the firing rate per square foot required to burn Rock Springs coal with relative efficiency at the power output demanded. As discussed in Chapter 11, locomotive designers for a time regarded grate area as the primary determinant of combustion efficiency. University and industrial research work on combustion chemistry in the 1930s yielded fresh insights, and by 1940, the governing relationship of total firebox volume, rather than grate area, to combustion efficiency was well understood.[7] The Alco team in Schenectady designed a cavernous firebox eight feet wide and just shy of 20 feet long, which included the combustion chamber.

Length of tubes was set at 22 feet; even in such a large boiler, additional tube length would not have added appreciably to evaporation capacity. Turbulent water flow inside the boiler and especially around the firebox was known to improve evaporation, so Alco staff configured the firebox with seven "circulators," each of which forced water by convection from the two sides up a vertical neck through the crown sheet. Though the firebox crown sheet was 19 feet long, an ample 32-inch clearance above the sheet enabled the Big Boys to scale 2.2 percent grades safely.[8]

As the design project entered its final stages, both Alco and UP engineers worked out final performance and total weight calculations. Performance would be more than adequate. (Tests of drawbar pull and horsepower two years later verified that calculated and actual performance were very close.)

TOP Boiler and firebox of a Union Pacific Big Boy, at Alco's Schenectady, N.Y., plant. Thimbles in firebox sides reduced smoke without cooling the fire.
Courtesy Kalmbach Media

ABOVE Big Boy firebox, with seven circulators to force water by convection up to the crown sheet.
Courtesy Kalmbach Media

Total design weight of the engine – including water, sand, lubricants, and steam pipes and other plumbing – came to about 772,000 lbs., or slightly more than the goal of 380 tons.[9]

Smoke abatement had become an increasing concern for railroads since the 1920s. Even in Wyoming and Utah, public annoyance at locomotive smoke concerned UP managers. Several railroads in the 1930s, including UP, experimented with "secondary air" (*i.e.*, air added above the firebed) to improve oxygenation and reduce carbon loss. As with much in locomotive engineering, a frustrating trade-off between irreconcilable goals was apparent: A little secondary air reduced smoke somewhat, but more secondary air cooled the furnace temperature and radically reduced boiler efficiency and therefore power. Senior UP management wanted as much smoke reduction in the new locomotive as was practical, so based on recently conducted tests on an older UP locomotive, the railroad's designers asked Alco for 20 small openings, or "thimbles," through each of the two firebox sidewalls to provide a modest amount of secondary air.

The tender design was derived from that used on a 1939 order of passenger locomotives, UP's second series of 4-8-4 Northerns. The "pedestal" or "centipede" tender spread weight over seven axles arranged in an equalized, three-point suspension. This configuration permitted 28 tons of coal and 24,000 gallons of water to be carried at high speed with improved stability and without exceeding a total weight of slightly more than 30 tons per axle (less than the axle-loading for the engine). Incorporating the steam-driven stoker, the tender would supply enough coal and water so that, eastbound, one refueling stop would be taken between Ogden and Green River. As an integral part of the completed locomotive, the loaded tender added some 215 tons to the total in-service weight, for a total of 596 tons. The entire locomotive, engine and tender together, would be just shy of 133 feet long.

Civil engineers worried about clearances: vertical clearances within tunnels and shop buildings and on truss bridges, lateral clearances at platforms and between locomotives passing on adjacent tracks, clearances between trains passing each other on sharp curves in yards or on main tracks. The entire line between Omaha and Ogden needed checking. By April 1941, locomotive design was well along, and thus civil and mechanical engineers consulted regularly on clearance issues.

Excessive lateral overhang by the locomotive on sharp curves was a concern. The wheelbase of the engine alone was almost 73 feet. To reduce overhang on this long vehicle, designers trimmed walkways and arranged steam piping so as to taper the overall width at the front from 11 feet near the first pair of driving wheels down to 9 feet 6 inches at the pilot. With locomotive-width dimensions agreed upon, civil engineers then planned realignments of curves and passing tracks between Ogden and Green River. By early summer 1941, track crews began toiling with transits, cranes, jacks, tampers, and mauls, pulling track sideways several feet and then reballasting and retamping it into precise, wider-radius curves. Crews also realigned approaches to switches, and — between Ogden and Wahsatch – installed new, 131-pounds-per-yard rails. Other crews installed longer, 135-foot turntables at the Ogden and Green River terminals. In anticipation of possible emergency operation of the new engines beyond their assigned territory, UP staff checked clearances between Ogden and Pocatello, Idaho, and from Ogden to Los Angeles.

Besides articulation, Big Boy's designers tapered the boiler and running boards to facilitate clearance on sharp curves.

Robert Hale, Courtesy Kalmbach Media

At last, in late August 1941, and after a brief fire-up and inspection test, the first Big Boy, UP road number 4000, left Alco's Schenectady plant. The price tag was $265,174.00, plus shipping. Carried dead-in-tow in regular freight trains, with an Alco employee as riding inspector camping in the cab, No. 4000 traveled the Delaware & Hudson, the New York Central, and the Chicago & North Western to Omaha. The journey inspired dozens of news stories along the way; radio and newspaper reporters seemed intrigued with the "world's largest" accolade and the insouciant nickname, Big Boy. After arrival in Omaha on September 5, UP machinists unblocked the four pistons and installed the main rods; hostlers filled the boiler and prepared a fire. The next day, a UP test crew then took the 4000 west, with a dormitory car spliced between the tender and a train of empty refrigerator cars, followed by a wake of more press coverage and admiring crowds at every station across Nebraska and Wyoming.

During the run west, the 4000 reached 72 mph and rode well. After arriving in Ogden, performance trials began up the Wahsatch grade, with Jabelmann supervising. For the first eastward run, the test crew agreed on a load of 3,500 tons, a bit less than design capacity, and yard crews assembled a train as requested. The locomotive seemed somewhat slow in getting underway, but it marched up the hill. Speed fell to 12 mph a few miles west of the summit. The run was judged a complete success, although some on the test crew wondered about the weight of the train. With the consist sheets in hand, a couple of the research department engineers checked the addition of the car weights. The trailing tonnage had been 3,800.

It was not until 1943 that the Big Boys ran performance tests with an instrumented dynamometer car. Detailed tests measured horsepower and fuel and water consumption on each of three locomotives over six runs on the grade, April 2-3. By that time, the fleet of 20 had been in service for more than a year; the three tested locomotives had accumulated about 100,000 miles apiece, with a major shopping at around 50,000 miles.

Engine 4016 set the record during these tests, hitting 6,290 horsepower at 41 mph, measured at the drawbar, while pulling upgrade near the Henefer passing track, 36 miles east of Ogden. Between 25 and 45 mph, all of the three engines achieved 5,500 to 6,000 drawbar hp, with trains of 3,500 to 3,880 tons. As a result of these tests and 18 months of operating experience with the class, tonnage rating for Big Boys out of Ogden was increased to 4,200 – 600 tons or 17 percent more than the originally intended capacity.

Sadly, Otto Jabelmann could not enjoy these results. He died in January 1943, assisting W. Averell Harriman on a wartime economic assistance project for Britain directed by President Franklin D. Roosevelt.[10] (Averell Harriman, son of the legendary E.H. Harriman, had himself become UP chairman in 1932. Though he would always be a significant voice in UP affairs, his greatest notoriety was earned as a diplomat and elder Democratic Party statesman.)

Five more Big Boys joined the roster in 1944. The operating department staff determined that locomotive utilization could be improved if all 25 engines were given an expanded territory, so longer turntables and stalls were added to the roundhouses in Cheyenne and Laramie, Wyo. And despite the original intent not to use helper locomotives with Big Boys, wartime traffic often required helpers; Big Boys occasionally doubleheaded with each other and with Challengers.

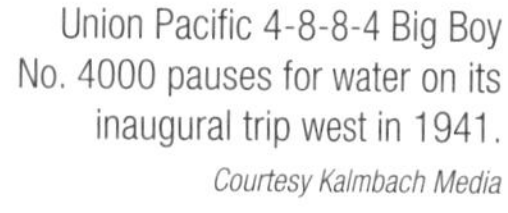
Union Pacific 4-8-8-4 Big Boy No. 4000 pauses for water on its inaugural trip west in 1941.
Courtesy Kalmbach Media

In truth, UP managers regarded the Big Boys as a supplement to the Challengers in the context of the company's fleet modernization program. In that program, the 40 Challengers built in the 1930s were supplemented by 65 more between 1942 and 1944. During those wartime years, Roosevelt's War Production Board oversaw locomotive orders by all U.S. railroads, restricting use of steel alloys in short supply, asking (for a short time) that no new locomotive designs be undertaken, strictly allocating locomotive production to railroads based on war traffic priorities, and diverting some locomotive manufacturing capacity to tanks and other vehicles.[11]

The Big Boy design of 1940 and 1941 led straight to an improved Challenger which, fortunately for UP, slipped in under the WPB wire. Even as Big Boy was in process, the UP and Alco design teams worked almost simultaneously on a fresh Challenger design that shared many identical and near-identical features. Both UP designs were complete when WPB restrictions came into being. The 65 new Challengers, built in three series, and the five additional Big Boys were among Alco's largest orders during the war, and yet UP was so stretched for locomotives that early in 1945 it also bought some used, almost-20-year-old articulated freighters from two Eastern railroads that weren't so strapped.[12]

By the late 1950s, both Big Boys and Challengers were nearing the end of their service lives, overrun by both new diesels and declining rail traffic. UP employees, however, spoke with almost universal fondness for the two types. Good riding, more than capable, with few mechanical ills, these locomotives engendered great pride on the part of enginemen, firemen, shopmen, and dispatchers.

For their part, enginemen learned the Big Boys' quirks. These enginemen became consummate specialists in how to set throttle in concert with precise setting of valve-gear cutoff to get maximum power without slipping the wheels, how to trade momentum for speed on changing grades, and how best to handle trains of various tonnage at every point along the assigned route

UP Big Boy No. 4024, westbound west of Medicine Bow, Wyo.
Courtesy Kalmbach Media

that the crews traveled week in and week out. In the mid-1950s, enginemen regularly brought 4,450 tons up the Wahsatch grade without helper engines, 24 percent more than the Big Boys' original design capacity. What portion of that excess was the result of remarkable design and what portion was the result of human skill cannot be known.

The Allegheny

The Allegheny story stands in contrast. The Chesapeake & Ohio Railway had a distinctly different set of issues facing it in 1940, compared to Union Pacific. Like UP, the C&O possessed a talented mechanical engineering staff, reputed as one of the best among U.S. railroads. The nature of C&O's traffic, route geography and topography, existing locomotive fleet, organizational context affecting the engineering staff, and working relationship with locomotive manufacturers, however, were all different than on UP.

In 1940, as coal traffic grew from West Virginia mines along its lines, C&O's top executives reconsidered their locomotive needs. C&O had not ordered any new freight locomotives for ten years. The 1930 engines, though, were universally admired by railroaders across the country as being among the most successful fast-freighters ever built: C&O's Class T-1, 40 especially massive and powerful 2-10-4s built by the Lima Locomotive Works. These engines worked between Russell, an important C&O terminal in northeastern Kentucky, and Toledo, Ohio, handling both fast freight trains and coal drags. The serious limitation on traffic capacity was not on the Kentucky-Ohio lines, however, but on C&O's route between West Virginia's Pocahontas mining region and northern Virginia.

Between the C&O division points at Handley, W.Va., in the heart of the coal country, and Clifton Forge, Va., ponderous freighters of Class H-7 hauled 125-car coal trains over the Alleghany Summit.[13] Loaded trains went eastward, and up the 45-mile grade from Hinton, W.Va., to the top of the grade just beyond the Alleghany Tunnel, standard practice put one H-7 at the front of the train and one helping at the back. On other C&O divisions across southern West Virginia, H-7s ran singly, doubleheaded, or with helpers on coal and other freight trains. Grades varied from steep to moderate, with frequent curves.

The H-7 locomotives were four-cylinder, 2-8-8-2 articulateds, 45 of which had been built for C&O between 1923 and 1926. Like the later T-1, the H-7 had been path-breaking in its design. The H-7 was the first simple-expansion articulated manufactured in quantity, and its success led to the virtual abandonment of compound expansion on American railroads. The C&O was a pioneering user of articulated locomotives, having bought 266 compound-expansion Mallets between 1910 and 1923; all of these were of the 2-6-6-2 type, for slow freight. The larger, sixteen-drivered H-7 was originally intended to incorporate compounding, but the low-pressure cylinders would have been too big to fit through C&O's numerous tunnels. Four equally sized cylinders dispensed with the compounding, solved the clearance problem, and produced a somewhat more stable-riding locomotive in the bargain. But by 1940, the H-7s had proven too slow, even compared to the Mallets, and lower in useful train-hauling power than the two-cylinder T-1s.

In the meantime, in a development that would deeply affect C&O's locomotive decisions, a competing railroad in the Appalachian coal region, the

Norfolk & Western, had developed an improved simple-expansion, articulated engine for fast freight: the N&W Class A 2-6-6-4 (the same design mentioned earlier that had affected the suspension layout for Challengers and Big Boys). In May 1936, N&W test engineers ran road tests with a dynamometer car on the first Class A and quickly touted the unprecedented result to the railroad trade press: 6,000 horsepower at the drawbar had been registered between 32 and 57 mph, with a peak of 6,300 at 45 mph. No locomotive had ever exceeded 6,000 drawbar horsepower before; none had gone much beyond 5,000. The Class-A tests were widely discussed by locomotive designers, both in the U.S. and Europe.

Pondering new locomotive purchases, C&O's management referred the matter in late 1940 to the Advisory Mechanical Committee, the senior mechanical engineers who oversaw locomotive purchases for the railroads controlled by Cleveland's Van Sweringen brothers. (Recall that the AMC had been instrumental in refining the 2-8-4 Berkshire type for Van Sweringen roads C&O, Erie, Nickel Plate, and Pere Marquette.) The AMC, formed in 1929, exercised dictatorial control over all design issues for new locomotives.

The AMC in 1940 consisted of chairman Daniel S. Ellis and members A.G. Trumbull, Edward Haurer, Richard Vining, and Michael J. Donovan. These five men were of varied engineering backgrounds: Ellis had joined the committee in 1933 from a major supplier of locomotive auxiliary systems, the Worthington Pump and Machinery Co.; he became chairman when William G. Black (who had headed design for the T-1) died three years later. Trumbull, formerly in C&O's locomotive department, served as AMC's chief mechanical engineer. Richard Vining was an expert in engineering calculation, and gave precision to the committee in its design decisions. Donovan, an Englishman who had been a junior engineer for North British Locomotive Works in Glasgow, Scotland, brought expertise on British and European design practice. Since its formation in 1929, the only changes to the committee had been Black's death and the addition of Donovan. A powerful ally of AMC chairman Ellis was Frank D. Beale, assistant to the president for C&O in Cleveland.

No traffic expert served on the AMC. For a locomotive specification by a participating railroad, the pattern seems to have been as follows: The railroad's managers defined only the most general requirements to the top of the executive hierarchy, with little engineering input. Then the request was referred for design to the AMC, which worked independently. In the case of C&O, no new engines had been purchased for ten years, and so no substantive relationship between C&O traffic managers and AMC existed. In the 1930s, the AMC developed important new designs for other Van Sweringen railroads, but for C&O, the AMC's engineers concerned themselves only with locomotive repair standards, working exclusively with C&O's mechanical engineering department in Richmond, Va. Based on how the Allegheny design was subsequently deployed in C&O operations, it seems clear that there was no collaboration between the Allegheny's designers and C&O traffic people.

An important and well-exercised relationship for AMC members was with the design and engineering staff of the Lima Locomotive Works. As peers, AMC and Lima engineers frequently discussed locomotive performance issues, especially for the various orders placed with Lima on

AMC recommendation. After Lima's co-development of the C&O T-1 with AMC, Lima became one of the committee's favored builders.

Performance of the Norfolk & Western Class A was the talk of the locomotive design community, so Lima had suggested an even more-powerful 2-6-6-6 to Indiana's Monon Railroad in 1936.[14] Lima's engineering chief, William E. Woodard, championed what Lima called Super Power – locomotives with greatly increased combustion capacity and hence incorporating four- and six-wheel trailing trucks to support the enormous fireboxes required. The C&O T-1 had been explicitly a Super Power design, and the largest up to 1930. The N&W Class A, designed and built in N&W's own shops in Roanoke, Va, and the Alco-Union Pacific Challenger had both stolen a march on Lima in 1936, with Lima-inspired firebox size, four-wheel trailing trucks, and high-horsepower performance, but without Lima as the builder. Monon demurred; the 2-6-6-6 would have been too expensive in the depths of the Depression. But Lima was hungry for orders, and recapturing the horsepower crown would help its marketing efforts.

Like Lima, AMC chairman Ellis was a partisan of high horsepower. In 1933-1934, his first task with the AMC was a new 2-8-4 design for the Nickel Plate, extrapolated from the Lima-originated Super Power 2-8-4 and incorporating ideas from the later T-1. Lima men no doubt smarted when the first orders for the new AMC 2-8-4 went to Alco. In early 1941, Ellis repaid the implicit debt by calling on Lima to help develop C&O's new engine. After conferring with C&O mechanical department people in Richmond and talking to Lima designers, Ellis decided what he wanted: a 2-6-6-6.

It is unrecorded whether Lima engineers or AMC members took the creative lead in suggesting a 2-6-6-6 for C&O. James Cunningham, a Lima staff engineer assigned to the project at its inception, wrote later that the "original preliminary design specifications for the 2-6-6-6 were from the Advisory Mechanical Committee" and were quite detailed, with basic features of the locomotive spelled out and a weight limit in working order, less tender, given as 695,000 lbs. Often, Lima would be aggressive in its recommendations to potential clients; both Woodard and his principal deputy, Albert J. (Bert) Townsend, were conspicuous throughout the railroad industry as articulate and persuasive advocates of Super Power design as best meeting railroads' present and future needs. Cunningham was not privy to the first discussions in late 1940 or early 1941 between the AMC and Lima, but he recalled that at the earliest stage of a new project at Lima, its design staff either worked up a detailed proposal for a potential customer or "the railroad would send in their own designs and specs and ask our opinion. ... The C&O 2-6-6-6 was one of this type."

The initial specification was not in the form of a tonnage rating for a particular grade, or framed in other operational or traffic terms, with the major design choices left for solution, as was done at Union Pacific. Even before the weight or performance of the new C&O engine could be sensibly estimated, its basic configuration was unalterably set.

Within five days of receipt at Lima, AMC's weight requirement turned out to be defective. AMC calculations had inadvertently left three feet of length out of the boiler and combustion chamber. After a week's work, Cunningham came to his own comprehensive weight estimates from the AMC initial design.

Engine weight without tender would be at least 724,500 lbs., almost 15 tons more than the AMC figure. AMC-member Donovan soon visited Lima. After resolving (apparently) the weight issue, AMC modified the design in Cleveland and, a few weeks later, sent a formal specification to Lima. The formal design agreement included the revised engine weight of 724,500 lb. – a figure that would haunt the project.[15]

Under the direct supervision of Bert Townsend, the Lima engineers went to work. Boiler design received priority. From the fact that the detailed AMC specification included specific weights worked out with Lima engineers, the boiler configuration was probably fixed by the AMC. Compared to the Big Boy, the boiler of the Allegheny would be quite different.

Big Boy's Alco and UP engineers designed their boiler to fit over sixteen driving wheels. The boiler's firebox grate had to be placed over the top of the last four drivers, so that within the overall boiler length available, the firebox could be sufficiently large. Lima and AMC designers, on the other hand, placed their firebox entirely behind the drivers, so as to place the grate as low as possible. This placement gave increased furnace volume within a given length; the added volume would greatly improve combustion efficiency and hence

LEFT Union Pacific Big Boy, showing arrangement of firebox grate above the four rear drivers.
Courtesy Kalmbach Media

BELOW C&O Allegheny, showing the firebox located entirely behind the drivers.
Philip R. Hastings, Courtesy Kalmbach Media

locomotive power. The grate would actually be somewhat smaller than Big Boy's, but grate area was determined by the heat release from C&O's higher-BTU coal, one of the highest-BTU varieties of stoker coal in North America.

The firebox placement necessitated the Allegheny's hallmark, its six-wheel trailing truck. Such a trailing truck had been used a couple of years earlier on a one-off, experimental engine designed by the Pennsylvania Railroad, but in that application the truck's reliability on engines for general use was unproven. Safe tracking of the truck, especially in yards and at switches on the main line, was a concern, as well as the extreme lateral overhang at the rear of the engine on curves; the back of the cab and the rear engine buffer would be more than 25 feet behind the last driving axle, the rearmost point of fixed wheelbase. The buffer interface between engine and tender was especially critical; improper lateral movement of this interface while the locomotive negotiated sharp curves could derail the tender as well as the engine.

Albert Townsend.
Courtesy Kalmbach Media

Since the advent of the first four-wheel trailing truck, designed in 1925 by Lima's William Woodard and James Smith, such a truck had been much improved in design and had become standard on Lima's Super Power engines, as well as on high-horsepower locomotives from other builders. The four-wheel trailing truck on C&O's T-1 of 1930 was among the longest anywhere. Lima designers on the Allegheny worked out the geometry and expected behavior of their truck, and in consultation with C&O mechanical engineers at Richmond under J.B. Blackburn, ensured that the locomotive when swinging through curves would fit clearance limits.

With the design of the trailing truck settled, the boiler layout could be completed. Lima's designers in Ohio worked independently of the Alco staff that was engaged simultaneously on the UP project and produced a different result. A combustion chamber – slightly longer and about ten percent larger in volume than Big Boy's – dominated the forward end of the firebox. The firebox was made as wide as possible: nine feet wide at the grate – compared to eight feet on the UP design – in order to gain volume. Boiler diameter, 109 inches at the widest point, and boiler tube length, at 23 feet, were each slightly more than the Alco-UP design. Thermic syphons provided water circulation.

The relationship of boiler capacity and weight now came forcefully into play. C&O staff desired a boiler pressure similar to that of the T-1: 265 psi. (C&O's mechanical department in Richmond believed that this rather conservative pressure had several benefits: Firebox steel with a given amount of boiler scale buildup on the waterside was less prone to small thermal cracks at the staybolts, and cylinder lubrication was more reliable, since working steam at lower pressure and thus lower temperature was less prone to break down the lubricant.) For use in calculating the weight of the boiler, the thickness of the boiler shell was determined utterly by the boiler pressure and shell diameter. A federal rule required a safety factor of four for boiler pressure; that is, if a working pressure of 250 psi was desired, the boiler must be designed to withstand 1,000 psi. With weight clearly a major consideration, and needing to keep the 109-inch maximum diameter to ensure both a generous combustion volume and high evaporative power, Bert Townsend's staff set the maximum shell thickness at 1 11/32 inches. Allowable boiler pressure could then be no higher than 260. Only if the boiler diameter and/or boiler pressure were reduced could shell thickness be reduced.

Taking into account the predicted weight of all the other engine components and the design features the AMC wanted, Cunningham soon found that the engine would weigh seven tons more than the revised limit. Townsend assured his young staff engineer that adjustments would be made later in design.

Drawings for frames, cylinders, running gear, and major steam piping went along with those for the boiler. For many of the details, Lima draftsmen used their firm's "standard-practice sheets" as guides. So-called draftsmen, however, were in fact talented and creative engineers; standard-practice sheets were often of little help in working out design problems such as placement of potentially interfering parts in close proximity, providing adequate mechanical support for parts subject to high stress, and in routing the maze of steam piping so that steam flow was nowhere restricted.

Steam piping to the Allegheny's swiveling front engine unit involved an especially creative solution. On previous articulated locomotives, flexible joints that incorporated a total of four swiveling connections and two sliding sleeves allowed superheated boiler steam to reach the two front cylinders. Exhaust steam from the front cylinders passed via another flexible connection to the exhaust nozzle in the smokebox. These flexible joints sometimes gave trouble in service, by leaking or binding. Since the two rear cylinders were fixed to the boiler, steam going to and from the rear engine unit needed no flexible joints. Routing all the necessary pipes to both front and back was always a design headache on a big articulated, due to the close clearances under and alongside the large-diameter boiler.

The Allegheny's engineers worked out a piping system that needed only one flexible joint and no sliding sleeves in the high-pressure steam pathway. Large pipes, one on each side, carried the steam for both pairs of cylinders back alongside the boiler. After feeding the rear cylinders, boiler steam then flowed to a junction in the rear cylinder saddle and to a single, large flexible joint located immediately above and in exact line with the articulation hinge between the front and rear frames. High-pressure steam then ran in one line forward to feed the front cylinders. Exhausted steam from all four cylinders was routed in a more-or-less conventional manner to the smokebox.

One might wonder if the unusually long high-pressure path to the front cylinders would result in a drop in efficiency, with too much heat being lost along the way. But it is a characteristic of superheated steam that it gives up its heat reluctantly. Lima designers knew that their innovative system would work well, with the added benefit of reduced maintenance.

The Allegheny's suspension followed the same plan originated on the Norfolk & Western A-class. No vertical play was given to the front engine unit, which reduced motion at the high-pressure steam connection to the front cylinders, and the locomotive was sprung and suspended as a single tripod.

The tender, specified to carry 25 tons of coal and 25,000 gallons of water in order to mesh with C&O's normal water stops on the West Virginia divisions, needed careful layout of trucks and truck centers to ensure the right behavior of the tender and engine buffers in curves and to distribute weight. Otherwise, the tender was conventional. The tender would add about 215 tons to overall locomotive weight.

On a tight schedule, construction got underway in the fall of 1941, with some detail design changes still being made to the engine. Writer Eugene

Huddleston has documented the insidious fiasco that then developed, based on interviews and the notes of engineer Cunningham:[16]

> In rotation each week, one of the AMC officials, D.S. Ellis, A.G. Trumbull, Ed Haurer, or Mitch [*sic*] Donovan, would come [to Lima] and review progress and approve drawings, frequently increasing sizes which were according to specifications simply because they 'looked too small.' [For example,] the main and side rods were overdesigned originally, but were increased in size four times, once by each of those mentioned. With the additional weight in [driving wheel] counterbalance, the added weight was somewhere in the range of 2,000-3,000 lbs., just for the main and side rods.

Cunningham's worry increased:

> During construction I kept track of other weight increases by AMC officials until 35,000 lbs. more [beyond the contracted 724,500 lbs.] had been added, bringing the total to 759,500 lbs. When I pointed this out to Bert Townsend, I was told, 'Forget it,' which I did. Still more was added, but I do not know how much. Before the first locomotive was built, the second order was placed [for the 11th through 20th engines] and the drawing room started cutting weight – steel tubes for main steam pipes vs. cast steel, etc.

Axle loading on the driving wheels was not supposed to exceed 40 tons per axle, which would already be the highest in the world. (Compare to Big Boy's 33.75 tons. The C&O T-1 driver-axle loading – regarded as very heavy – was a bit more than 37 tons.) With the added weight he was charged with keeping track of, plus inferences that he drew from the detailed suspension engineering, Cunningham realized that the maximum axle loading on the first order of locomotives could reach 43 tons and the total engine weight could be as high as 778,000 lbs. – a 53,500 lb. overrun.

Then came the day of expected truth: the official weighing of the first locomotive, including weight on each axle, in the Lima scale house. Cunningham remembered the day:

> When first weighed, Art Fowler [another Lima engineer] and I put the wheel scales under the wheels, but were told by Bert Townsend not to balance them. Only [AMC chairman] Dan Ellis and Bert were in the scale house to balance and read the scales; the rest of us [including AMC's Trumbull] were in the laboratory office.

BELOW LEFT A C&O Class H-8 2-6-6-6 Allegheny inside Lima's scale house.
Courtesy Kalmbach Media

BELOW RIGHT C&O and Lima officials, including Dan Ellis (second from right) and A.J. Townsend (right) pose with their new 2-6-6-6 behemoth.
Courtesy Kalmbach Media

When Townsend and Ellis returned to the lab office with a list of weights, Cunningham's boss, Lima Chief Calculating Engineer Ralph Schmitt, took the sheet. It is unknown what numbers Schmitt added up, but in Cunningham's view, numbers were subtracted which should have been added. Schmitt gave a figure: 724,500 lbs. Trumbull asked, "What did you say?" Schmitt repeated the number. "That's what I thought you said," replied Trumbull, at which point the group concluded its business and dispersed. The bogus weight was soon published by Lima and accepted by C&O as the actual, recorded weight.

It would be three years before senior managers in C&O's operating and civil engineering departments learned of the discrepancies. By 1944, Ellis had left the AMC and was working for Lima. C&O filed a lawsuit against Lima and later collected a reported $3 million, a major financial setback for the builder. Since the prices at the factory for the Alleghenies from 1941 through 1944 were $231,000 to $284,000 each, with a margin of no more than $25,000 each, the judgment more than wiped out Lima's profit on those orders as well as the profits on many other orders.[17]

The enginemen's union, the Brotherhood of Locomotive Engineers, learned about the weight dispute before the filing and demanded a new weighing by C&O, to be witnessed by BLE representatives. An engineman's daily pay rate in part derived from the weight on drivers of his assigned locomotive. As a result of the weighing, many BLE members on C&O collected back pay. C&O civil engineers, meanwhile, recalculated bridge stresses and no doubt wondered about wear and tear on rails. Track ballasting standards had to be changed after the true weight was learned, so as to better anchor the crossties.

In the course of the suit, many of Lima's weight records went to the Philadelphia law firm that handled Lima's affairs; these and other weight records are no longer available. What official data exist show the second order of Alleghenies weighing 771,300 lbs. with successive reductions on each additional order; the last engines came in at 751,830 lbs.

Despite the missteps, C&O ordered more Alleghenies in 1944 and 1948. In the last batch, the lightest driving-wheel axle loading was achieved: 42 tons, but still excessive. (Big Boys had 17 tons on each driving axle.) Few railroads could tolerate such axle loadings without considerably heavier rails installed, upgraded track construction and maintenance standards, and some bridges replaced. Diesels would later resolve such potential difficulties with maximum axle loadings on all wheels of 30 to 35 tons, to the great relief of civil engineers on railroads across the country.

The 60 Alleghenies certainly performed well for C&O. Operating staff set tonnage ratings based on estimated performance before the first engines arrived. As the fleet grew in the war years under the press of accelerating traffic, Alleghenies ranged beyond the Handley-Clifton Forge route to serve also in Ohio on the north-south run connecting Russell, Ky., Columbus, and Toledo.

Tests with a dynamometer car occurred in July and August 1943, in both West Virginia and Ohio. Tests were made with trains up to 14,000 tons, on level track and on grades, with helper locomotives and without, and including several tests of acceleration from standing starts on the level and on grades. As reported soon afterward and repeated so many times since, the most spectacular result occurred on August 6, 1943, when an Allegheny pulling

160 cars hit the highest drawbar horsepower ever recorded by a single steam locomotive: 7,498, at 46 mph.

As described in the C&O report, this was an "instantaneous" reading, made at a spot on the run with undulating, up-and-down grades. The train was stretching out on a moderate upgrade, after having descended a somewhat steeper downgrade. Any recording of drawbar horsepower is a product of drawbar pull times speed, and readings may be spurious due to varying momentum within the train affecting the instantaneous pull on the locomotive. The C&O test engineers' plot of numerous horsepower readings taken over several tests in August 1943 (including the August 6 runs) takes account of the "scatter" in the raw recordings and gives a curve peaking at 7,000 drawbar horsepower. This curve gives a more accurate indication of sustained power capacity at the different speeds.

For comparison, Union Pacific test engineers plotted a curve of sustained horsepower from their April 1943 Big Boy tests. This curve shows a top drawbar hp of about 6,100, reached between 30 and 40 mph.

Such data are often discussed in secondary accounts, usually with the thought that steam locomotive horsepower ratings were perhaps too conservative. Test engineers, however, knew what the objective was: to find the power levels that could be produced reliably in pulling regular trains, day in and day out. One-shot, unrepeated power readings were irrelevant to establishing reliable performance.

In August 1943, however, one man was deeply thrilled by his locomotive's showing. Daniel Ellis was riding along in the dynamometer car on several of the Allegheny's test runs. A few months before, he had left the AMC and C&O after a falling-out with Robert Young, C&O's recently appointed, charismatic chairman. Ellis's new title as a Lima vice president was perhaps some vindication, but he knew that his career as a designer was over. Aboard the test car, there was animated talk about beating the record of 6,300 drawbar horsepower set in 1936 by the Norfolk & Western Class A. The Allegheny smashed that mark repeatedly. A C&O officer on the test, J.C. Nelson, told writer Huddleston:

> I don't remember any figures, but we beat the record made by the N&W's test of the class A type. ... I remember the tears that rolled down [Dan Ellis's] cheeks when his record was the best of these two monarchs; he was very elated.

As the Alleghenies were deployed throughout much of the C&O's system, their impact on existing practices of train dispatching was practically nil. Yardmasters in West Virginia and Ohio assembled C&O coal trains based only partly on tonnage. The operating department set a governing restriction on the number of cars: 140 in West Virginia and 160 in Ohio. Trains breaking in two was the concern. With the varying slack action that affected a long train on the hilly, up-and-down grade profiles involved, inexpert handling of air brakes on downgrades could cause forces near the middle of a train so extreme that cars derailed or couplers snapped. Maximum train weights for the Alleghenies were 11,500 tons in West Virginia and 13,500 tons in Ohio. Those ratings were the same as those for, respectively, the H-7A 2-8-8-2s and the T-1 2-10-4s. For H-7 and T-1 alike, helper engines were needed on long or sharp upgrades, and this practice continued with the H-8 Alleghenies.

The Alleghenies also pulled other types of freight trains and, during the war, passenger trains. The latter were most often troop trains with Pullman sleeping cars of about 80 tons each. An Allegheny could handle long passenger trains with 25 or more Pullmans and, where grades and curves were not too severe, could speed them at more than 60 mph. Enginemen praised the high-speed riding quality of the Alleghenies and often told stories of hitting 60-70 mph – which was usually against the rules.

Where Alleghenies served, about 70 percent of the traffic was loaded or empty coal trains cycling from the mines. Other traffic included scheduled passenger trains (pulled by passenger-type locomotives) and merchandise freight trains of boxcars, refrigerator cars, tankers, and other non-coal cars. A number of these merchandise trains ran on regular schedules, as fast as track and grades allowed. Such scheduled fast-freight trains were called "manifests" on the C&O. In contrast to the coal trains, the manifests were dispatched so as not to require helpers.

A coincidence of topography provides a comparison of Big Boy and Allegheny locomotives in quite similar use. Westbound from Clifton Forge to Alleghany, Va., the coal trains ran empty; the maximum grade of 1.14 percent was twice as steep as for the eastward climb of loaded trains to the same summit. Manifest trains running west, however, were limited in tonnage by the steeper ascent. Without a helper, maximum tonnage for an Allegheny westbound on a manifest was 2,950. As we have seen, a Big Boy climbing the Wahsatch grade – also a maximum of 1.14 percent – could handle more than 4,400 tons of merchandise cars without helpers. In both cases, normal train speed ranged from 10 or 15 mph on the steepest stretches, to 60 mph.

What could explain the enormous disparity in tonnage rating on the same grade with a similar type of train? If a Big Boy was reliably capable of 6,100 horsepower and an Allegheny 7,000, why would the more powerful engine be given so much less tonnage?

Chesapeake & Ohio Class H-8 2-6-6-6 Allegheny No. 1603, in its element with a coal train.
Courtesy Kalmbach Media

A part of the answer has to do with track engineering. The C&O grades were "uncompensated;" that is, the actual grade was the same on curves as well as on the straight. Train resistance is higher on curves, and on the Alleghany climb there are a lot of curves. The extra train resistance from curvature can be calculated readily, and on Union Pacific, curves were "compensated." That is, the actual gradient was reduced in curves to give the same net resistance on straight and curved track. About 800 tons of the disparity is explained by the track design and generally sharper curves on C&O.

The rest of the answer has to do with the fundamental relationship of horsepower to speed. So-called fast freight trains still had to slog up the steepest parts of either the Wahsatch or the Alleghany climb. At lower speeds, neither Big Boy's 6,100 horsepower nor an Allegheny's 7,000 applied. In the former case, top horsepower was not available until 30 mph was reached; in the latter case, 40-45 mph. At 15 mph, Big Boy's available drawbar hp was 4,500, an Allegheny's only 4,000.

For low speed on train-capacity-limiting grades, comparative steam locomotive performance can be assessed equally well using either horsepower or tractive effort; the two measures are inextricably linked. Tractive effort is the pull, measured in pounds, at the locomotive's driving wheels. TE is the more common rating and was always published by locomotive builders and railroads. Published TE figures can be misleading to both historians and enthusiasts, however, since published numbers are always given for TE at starting and not for other speeds.

Tractive effort comparisons are generally valid for comparing locomotive pull at very low speed. Here, Big Boy's TE at starting of 135,375 lbs. can be compared to an Allegheny's 110,200 lbs. In fact, Big Boy's actual drawbar pull exceeds an Allegheny's all the way up to 30 mph.

This analysis points directly to one of the Allegheny's limiting flaws in basic design compared to actual use. The real reason Big Boy performs so much better at tonnage-limiting speeds is that it has more driving wheels: 16 instead of 12. At a given axle loading, only so much pull can be exerted before the wheels slip. Union Pacific and Alco designers, using the usual 4:1 ratio of weight-on-drivers to tractive effort, chose 16 driving wheels primarily to be certain of low-speed performance on difficult grades. AMC and Lima designers, on the other hand, put their record-setting boiler on just 12 driving wheels; they knew very well that low-speed performance would thus be constrained. Because they chose to limit the number of driving wheels, Lima and AMC people knew that exorbitant axle loads would go hand in hand. Big Boy and Allegheny were originally supposed to have engine weights of 380 tons and 350 tons, respectively; even then, the Allegheny design was two axles short for spreading total weight. Adding 35 tons to Allegheny's originally intended engine weight didn't help.

With its excessive load on driving axles, the Allegheny had unusual adhesion. That is, weight on drivers was 4.6 times the tractive effort, rather than 4 times. As a result, an Allegheny rarely slipped. One engineman told an amazing story of running an Allegheny up the approach to the Sciotoville bridge over the Ohio River. Unknown to him, his long coal train, without a helper engine, was more than 2,000 tons too heavy, with too many cars assembled into the train by mistake. When the inevitable stall occurred after a long struggle, there was no great crash of spinning wheels, in the fashion customary to most steam locomotives at stalling. Despite throttle completely open and valve-gear cutoff at maximum, the Allegheny just ... stopped. Steam at full force against its pistons could not move it further, but neither did it slip. C&O enginemen praised the Allegheny for its adhesion, especially in rain and wet snow, when slipping is endemic; if an Allegheny could start a heavy train, it could generally keep it moving in even the worst conditions.

Whether, as has been asserted by several authors including this one, the Alleghenies were "misused in drag service" by C&O is too simplistic a judgment. The operating department did not change coal train weights or length, either before or after the Alleghenies arrived. Other concerns, legitimate ones given the air-brake technology of the era, governed coal train size. Helper districts could not be eliminated. (Even UP found that helpers or double-heading were often demanded by wartime traffic.) Based on the performance tests of 1943, Alleghenies could have pulled heavier trains than they did. A virtue of C&O sticking to its prevailing tonnage ratings, however, was that the Alleghenies could pull their trains at faster average speeds when they were on gentler grades. That extra speed improved the economics of their operation.

To understand this last point, the horsepower/speed curves are again relevant. Any steam locomotive produces its best economics (fuel, crew costs, total tonnage moved per hour or per week) when it can be operated as close as possible to its maximum-horsepower speed. For an Allegheny, this would be 40 to 50 mph. At maximum-horsepower speed, any locomotive produces its maximum possible gross ton-miles per train-hour (GTMTH). This relation is true because GTMTH, a standard measure of railway operating productivity, is exactly the same measure mathematically as horsepower: a unit of weight, times distance, per unit of time. (Horsepower is defined in foot-pounds per minute; only the units are different.) Just as on any railroad, the steepest, tonnage-limiting sections were only part of any given run. Elsewhere, speed could be higher – often up to 45 mph or more, where Alleghenies were at their best.

The conclusion is not that the Alleghenies were "misused;" they were simply the wrong design for C&O. For either coal drags or manifest freight trains, C&O could have better used a 16-drivered engine. Such an engine, designed to conventional 1941 technology, would have hauled at least 30 percent more tonnage on the manifest trains and would have given high adhesion and capable service on the drags. In 1940, AMC members may have assumed that a new 16-drivered design would have been undesirable for two reasons: Either it would have been too slow and could not have supplemented the fast T-1, or, if built with larger-diameter drivers for the higher speed needed, its wheelbase would have been too long for the twisting track in West Virginia.

AMC members did not realize that the extra stability given by the N&W-type articulation hinge and single-tripod suspension rendered their dilemma moot. First, while the AMC dismissed a 16-drivered design out of hand based on their old H-7, Union Pacific and Alco engineers did a careful analysis of 16 drivers in a new chassis. Secondly, driving wheels larger than those on C&O's H-7 but smaller than on the Allegheny or Big Boy would have given speed/pull performance better matched to C&O's traffic and well within wheelbase limits. Again in view of the actual traffic and topography, a boiler providing steam for 6,000 drawbar horsepower rather than 7,000 would have been entirely adequate.[18] The near rail-bending, per-axle weight of the Allegheny might have been avoided. Daniel Ellis, however, would probably not have achieved his dream of breaking the horsepower record. The Allegheny design makes little sense, unless one assumes that the objective was to beat the N&W Class A at 35 to 50 mph.

Writer Huddleston has speculated at length that raising the Allegheny's boiler pressure would have produced still more horsepower – which is doubtless true.[19] But such a change would have been impossible without increasing boiler-shell thickness and hence weight. More horsepower from the Alleghenies would not have helped C&O, in either tonnage ratings or ton-mile productivity, given the train-length restrictions that applied, which were rational. Nor could higher-power Alleghenies have eliminated helper districts, due to the limit on low-speed tractive effort imposed by having just 12 drivers.

As to the "world's most powerful" or the "world's heaviest" descriptors, Big Boy and Allegheny split the titles. In trade literature and in hundreds of articles, the claim is long-standing that Big Boy was the heavier. For engine weight alone, the question is complicated by the varying weight of both designs over several orders. In the 1944 order, Big Boy got a little heftier due to the use of heavier steels mandated by War Production Board restrictions. Allegheny, on the other hand, lost pounds as engineers tried to trim the fat. The result shows a virtual tie. For locomotive weight, ready for service (which is the more relevant measure), the second order of Big Boys added 1,000 gallons of water and four tons more coal to reach 608 tons, edging the heaviest Alleghenies by an eyelash. The charts below add up the applicable weights. As to horsepower, there is no doubt as to Allegheny's priority, but only for speeds above 30 mph. Enthusiasts have often speculated as to what additional power Big Boy might have produced at higher speeds, running on high-grade, Eastern coal. But the question is immaterial, since the design of furnace and boiler is affected by fuel type, and Big Boy's firebox was proportioned for the fuel at hand. Even the much lighter N&W Class A could put out more horsepower than a Big Boy – on the high-heat coal the Class A was designed for.

Alleghenies ran until 1956; Big Boys until 1959. Multiple-unit diesels – running at slower average freight-train speeds on UP and C&O than the steam

Class. "Four Cylinder Simple" 4884 S 772 — Road Number, 4022

BUILT FOR THE UNION PACIFIC.

GAUGE OF TRACK	CYLINDERS Diam.	CYLINDERS Stroke	DRIVING WHEEL DIAMETER	BOILER Inside Dia.	BOILER Pressure	FIRE BOX Length	FIRE BOX Width	TUBES Number	TUBES Diameter	TUBES Length
4'-8½"	23¾"	32"	68"	95"	300 lbs.	235 1/32"	96 3/16"	212 73	2¼" 5½"	22'-0"

WHEEL BASE Driving	WHEEL BASE Engine	WHEEL BASE Engine & Tender	WEIGHT IN WORKING ORDER—POUNDS Leading	Driving	Trailing	Engine	Tender (⅔ Load)
18'-3" & 18'-3"	72'-5½"	117'-7"	99800	545000	127200	772000	348000

FUEL Kind	EVAPORATING SURFACES. SQUARE FT. Tubes	Flues	Fire Box	Circulators	Total	SUPERHEATING SURFACE SQUARE FT.	GRATE AREA SQ.FT. 225 x 96 3/16	MAXIMUM TRACTIVE POWER	FACTOR OF ADHESION
Soft Coal	2734	2301	595	125	5755	2043	150.3	135375 lbs.	4.02

TOP Alco summary of weights and dimensions for Union Pacific Big Boy order S-1936, built in 1944.

Author's Collection

Class: 2666-S-752 — Built for THE CHESAPEAKE AND OHIO RAILWAY CO. — Road No. 1650

R. R. Class: H-8 — Order Covers 15 Locos. Nos. 1645 to 1659

GAUGE OF TRACK	DRIVING WHEEL DIAMETER	FUEL KIND	CYLINDERS DIAMETER	CYLINDERS STROKE	BOILER O.D. FRONT	BOILER PRESSURE	FIREBOX LENGTH	FIREBOX WIDTH
4'-8½"	67"	SOFT COAL	22½"	33"	100 8/16"	260 LBS.	180"	108¼"

WHEEL BASE DRIVING	WHEEL BASE ENGINE	WHEEL BASE ENGINE AND TENDER	MAXIMUM TRACTIVE POWER	FACTOR OF ADHESION	TUBES AND FLUES NUMBER	TUBES AND FLUES DIAMETER	TUBES AND FLUES LENGTH
34'-8"	62'-6"	112'-11"	110200	4.57	58 219	2¼" 4"	23'-0"

AVERAGE WEIGHT IN WORKING ORDER, POUNDS ON DRIVERS	TRUCK	TRAILER	TOTAL ENGINE	TENDER ⅔ LOAD	GRATE AREA SQ. FT.	HEATING SURFACES, SQUARE FEET TUBES & FLUES	SYPHONS	FIREBOX & COMB.CHAM.	TOTAL	SUPER-HEATER
504010	65570	182250	751830	346710	135.3	6032	162	600	6794	2922

BOTTOM Lima Locomotive Works summary of weights and dimensions for Chesapeake & Ohio Allegheny Nos. 1645-1659, built in 1948.

Author's Collection

engines ran – redefined all the economic questions of locomotive operations. Two Alleghenies and eight Big Boys are preserved: the former type at the Henry Ford Museum in Dearborn, Mich., and at the B&O Railroad Museum in Baltimore; the latter type at eight sites around the country, including Scranton, Pa., Green Bay, Wis., and in six cities on Union Pacific lines.

As this book was being prepared for print, Union Pacific was restoring Big Boy No. 4014 to operation. This locomotive had been donated decades earlier to the Railway & Locomotive Historical Society's Southern California Chapter, for display at its Rail Giants exhibit in Pomona. When UP began assessing the feasibility of operating a Big Boy, No. 4014 was deemed to be in the best condition among the eight survivors, thanks largely to a dry climate and regular lubrication. The R&LHS chapter graciously gave up its prize possession in order to share it with the world.

In 1963, Arthur E. Stoddard, Union Pacific president when the Big Boys were retired, summed up the thoughts of many:

> [They] were more than tools of an era – they were a symbol of the finest in transportation. Everyone on the line was proud of their performance and talked about it.

People are still talking about it – and about the Alleghenies, too.

Chapter 18 Notes

1. Compare the D&H high-pressure experiments, the Pennsylvania Railroad's S1 (for its size), and Franklin's poppet valve project. Collectively, by 1940, these experiments provided little indication of practical increases in efficiency, either for the boiler or "transmission."
2. United States Department of Commerce, *Statistical Abstract of the United States*, 1941.
3. William Kratville and Harold E. Ranks, *Motive Power of the Union Pacific*, 1982, pp. 197-204.
4. Kratville, *Big Boy*, 1963.
5. Alfred W. Bruce, *The Steam Locomotive in America: Its Development*, 1952, pp. 328-30.
6. John H. White Jr., *American Locomotives: An Engineering History, 1830-1880*, 1968, pp. 62-64, 152-53.
7. Bruce, p. 328.
8. Ibid., p. 329.
9. Ibid.
10. *New York Times*, January 7, 1943, p. 19.
11. Eugene L. Huddleston, "War Production Board," *Railfan & Railroad*, March 1985, p. 41. See also George Drury, *Guide to North American Steam Locomotives*, 2015, pp. 50-51.
12. Kratville and Ranks, pp. 137-40.
13. "Alleghany" and "Allegheny" are alternate spellings for the same general region, but they're not used interchangeably. Various places in Appalachia use one spelling or the other, and in the case of Alleghany Summit/Tunnel, the spelling that's given here is correct. Alleghany Tunnel is correct in Virginia, but 200 miles to the north, the Pennsylvania Turnpike has an Allegheny Tunnel.
14. Drury, p. 132.
15. Eric Hirsimaki, *Lima: The History*, 1986, pp. 212-13.
16. Huddleston interviewed and corresponded with Cunningham and other Lima and C&O officials in the course of research for the former's *Allegheny: Lima's Finest*, 1984. Huddleston also incorporated quotes from these interviews, correspondence, and notes in "Doctoring the Scales: The Case of the Overweight Alleghenies," *Trains*, December 1998, pp. 78-85, and *World's Greatest Steam Locomotives*, 2001.
17. Hirsimaki, *Lima: The History*, 1986, pp. 212-13.
18. Duluth, Missabe & Iron Range 2-8-8-4s provide a good example. They were also intended for similar service to C&O's H-8s: hauling heavy mine products (in this case, iron ore).
19. Huddleston, Note 16.

5505

Chapter 19

The T1 and Poppet Valves:

The Last Important Innovation

IN APRIL 1942, AN EXOTIC-LOOKING locomotive emerged from the erecting halls of the Baldwin Locomotive Works at Eddystone, Pa., south of Philadelphia. Built to a mechanical design developed by Baldwin and Pennsylvania Railroad engineers, this was the first of the PRR's T1 class, with showy streamlining by Raymond Loewy. In contrast to previous rollouts of innovative locomotives, press notice was subdued for the first T1 and for the second engine completed a few weeks later: National attention was riveted on the country's recent entry into World War II. Nevertheless, both Baldwin and PRR engineers were confident that they had made a fundamental advance in locomotive efficiency and performance.[1]

That confidence was perhaps reflected in the radical shape of the two engines: they looked like horizontal spaceships. The T1 was Loewy's fourth locomotive commission from the Pennsylvania Railroad. The company had engaged him on an exclusive retainer for railroad-related industrial design work in 1935, after the success of his stylistic improvements to the GG1 electric locomotive.[2] In 1936 and 1939, his streamlining of Pennsy's K4s locomotive No. 3768 and of its experimental S1-class 6-4-4-6, respectively, had gained the railroad a wealth of publicity in newspapers and newsreels. The 3768 even starred in a 1941 Hollywood movie, "Broadway Limited," and the huge S1 was a popular highlight of the 1939 New York World's Fair, steaming away on rollers at a special outdoor site near the Hall of Railroads.

The engineers knew that the real significance of the T1 to the future of steam locomotion lay apart from Loewy's art. Two features in particular elicited comment among railroaders: the "divided" or "duplex" drive, in which the piston thrust of a conventional, rigid-frame engine of similar size and tractive force was spread over four cylinders instead of two – essentially a Northern with four cylinders, oxymoronic as that sounds – and the use of poppet valves to distribute steam to the cylinders.

Baldwin's chief designer, Ralph P. Johnson, had been promoting the notion of divided drive for several years. The idea was first tried, however, by George H. Emerson, the Baltimore & Ohio's long-time head of locomotive engineering, in 1938. The B&O 5600, a high-speed passenger engine designed and built at

The futuristic front end of Pennsylvania Railroad Class T1 4-4-4-4 duplex-drive locomotive No. 5505.

Courtesy Kalmbach Media

George Emerson's Baltimore & Ohio 4-4-4-4 No. 5600. Its water-tube firebox was problematic, but its death blow was struck by Electro-Motive EA-model diesels, which B&O purchased in 1937.
Courtesy Kalmbach Media

the Mt. Clare Shops, Baltimore, used a 4-4-4-4 wheel arrangement in lieu of the 4-8-4 layout that would have been the usual practice for a locomotive of 5600's weight and type of service. Four simple-expansion cylinders instead of two powered the drivers – two cylinders for each pair of driving axles – and, unlike many larger freight locomotives with four cylinders arranged on articulated frames, Emerson's 4-4-4-4 carried its two sets of drivers in a common frame. Compared to a two-cylinder design of the same tractive effort, each of 5600's pistons had half the surface area, exerted half the thrust on its associated crankpin, and was significantly lighter in weight. The 5600 also had an experimental water-tube firebox, which Emerson championed but which was never used on a production steamer in the U.S. because of its high maintenance.

Johnson's first crack at divided drive had come with the PRR's experimental S1 of 1939, in whose design all three major builders had participated. The objective of the S1 project had been to build an engine capable of sustaining 100 mph or more with a 1,000-ton passenger train, or about 13 to 15 standard-weight cars. Although the S1 later proved impractical in normal service due to its exceptionally long wheelbase, its duplex arrangement proved well-suited to reaching high horsepower with four driving axles. A divided drive cut mechanical forces on individual rods and crankpins. The resulting lighter-weight reciprocating parts promised lower running-gear repair costs and better driving-wheel counterbalancing for high speed.

Pennsylvania Railroad Class S1 of 1939, seen here with its skirts removed for easier wartime maintenance, represented PRR's proof-of-concept for duplex drives. Significantly, its design did not include poppet valves.
Courtesy Kalmbach Media

PRR amassed a fleet of 52 T1s. Poppet valves helped to make them fast, but contributed to reliability problems.

Courtesy Kalmbach Media

The incorporation of poppet valves was the most controversial feature of the T1. Instead of piston (or spool) valves, whose sliding motion was derived from an eccentric, poppet valves opened and closed like the valves in an automobile engine, with the valves actuated by cams. Such valves had been used with mixed success on locomotives in Europe since the mid-1920s, although their use through the 1930s was limited to a few locomotive classes in France, Italy, and Austria, and some individual engines in England.

In theory and sometimes in practice, poppet valves greatly improved steam economy, since they solved several problems of valve timing and steam flow that were inherently intractable with any other form of valve or valve gear. In 1927, the Baldwin Works had bought the U.S. rights to a promising type of poppet valve gear invented in 1921 by an Italian, Arturo Caprotti, and subsequently developed by him for the Italian State Railways. Baldwin engineers worked with the Baltimore & Ohio to install a set of Caprotti valves on a medium-sized freight locomotive in 1927 and on a new high-speed passenger engine the following year. A number of other U.S. railroads applied the Caprotti gear to a few existing locomotives. An alternative form

Application of poppet valves on a French National Railways locomotive.

Courtesy Kalmbach Media

of poppet valves – the Lentz type marketed by the French firm Dabeg S.A. – was tried by the Delaware & Hudson on a handful of locomotives, notably on the high-pressure *L.F. Loree* of 1933, using a rotary-cam drive.[3]

Baldwin's installation of poppet valves on the T1 depended, ironically, on developmental work by a firm controlled by the Lima Locomotive Works, one of Baldwin's chief rivals. The story of that development is important to understanding the genesis of the T1 and its subsequent history.

Franklin Railway Supply Co., a firm in the Coffin-Allen management group (Chapter 11), had initiated a special project in late 1936 to develop a form of poppet valve tailored specifically for the North American market. Lima's William Woodard was the principal architect of the Franklin project. Woodard knew, as did every locomotive designer, that the largest proportional loss in locomotive efficiency occurred not in the boiler but in the cylinders. In a conventional locomotive with the best in cylinder and valve design, only some 10 to 12 percent of the energy in the steam delivered to the cylinders was converted to work at the drawbar. And since boiler design had reached practical limits in grate area, furnace volume, and steam pressure in the pursuit of better boiler performance and fuel economy, the only hope for major improvement in overall efficiency in a reciprocating locomotive lay in the valves.[4]

As had Baldwin engineers before him, Woodard saw promise in the poppet-valve concept. But the Caprotti valves on U.S. engines had proven too fragile, especially in high-speed use. The problem was that North American locomotives were much larger, were more powerful per driving axle, and were worked closer to maximum output in daily service than locomotives in any of the European countries; unit stresses on mechanical parts were much higher than in European practice. Woodard realized that if poppet valves were to fulfill their promise, whether in the U.S. or in Europe, they would require thoroughgoing redesign.[5]

Woodard researched all the existing forms. He corresponded with all the railroads and manufacturing firms on both sides of the Atlantic that had had any experience in the design or application of such valves. He concluded that the Lentz type had the best reliability record and the greatest potential. Consulting with his friend Paul Synnestvedt, senior partner at

Caprotti valve gear on restored British Railways Standard Class 8 4-6-2 Pacific-type locomotive *Duke of Gloucester*. *Wikimedia Commons*

the Philadelphia law firm that handled Lima's patent affairs, Woodard evolved a strategy. Rather than buying rights from Dabeg S.A., as Baldwin had done with Caprotti, Woodard recommended to Lima chairman Sam Allen that Lima – or a Lima-controlled firm – "invent" its own valves. Rather than buying rights, Lima should buy the services of one or more engineers with the deepest experience in the subject, put them together with a specially assembled team of talented colleagues who could contribute fresh thinking, give them a generous budget, and let patent rights take care of themselves. (Woodard was an acknowledged expert in patent matters; Paul Synnestvedt loved nothing better than to get Woodard on the witness stand in patent infringement proceedings, which were fairly frequent among locomotive manufacturers and suppliers.) Woodard was convinced that by the time the proposed team finished its work, there would be enough genuine, new invention to earn a set of patents.[6]

TOP Built in 1933, Delaware & Hudson 4-8-0 No. 1403, *L.F. Loree*, was equipped with rotary-cam poppet valves; the drive shaft is visible emerging from the cylinder cover.

Harold K. Vollrath Collection

ABOVE Closeup of rotary cam on right side of D&H No. 1403.

Courtesy Kalmbach Media

Woodard recalled a young Austrian engineer who had worked with George Edmonds and John Muhlfeld on two of the Delaware & Hudson's poppet-valve projects, the installation on 4-6-2 No. 653 and, later, the design of rotary-cam valves for the high-pressure *L.F. Loree*. Julius Kirchhof, as chief field engineer for Dabeg, had made quite an impression on Edmonds for his creativity and tenacity in resolving practical difficulties and in modifying the initial Dabeg designs to better suit the two D&H machines. After conferring with Edmonds, Woodard, who was based in New York, exchanged several letters with Kirchhof in Paris. At that point, it seemed to Woodard that Kirchhof might be the ideal person to lead the Franklin engineering team, and so told the Lima board. Lima Vice President J.E. Dixon went to Paris to meet with Kirchhof. It was summer 1937.

Kirchhof jumped at the invitation to lead the Lima-Franklin project. In Kirchhof's mind, Nazi Germany clearly threatened his homeland, Austria. Although he tried to hide his delight, emigrating to America under the circumstances Dixon proposed was a godsend. Kirchhof and Dixon discussed possible management structures for the proposed project team, negotiated a starting salary, and sealed an agreement. A month later, Kirchhof arrived in New York.[7] (The Anschluss – Germany's annexation of Austria – took place in March 1938.)

Dixon, Woodard, and Kirchhof met in the Lima offices at 17 East 42nd Street in New York. After a week, the project had a shape: Some half-dozen of the best engineers and a dozen draftsmen then working in the Coffin-Allen group of companies would be chosen by Woodard, with Kirchhof participating in the interviews. As finally approved by Allen and the Franklin board, the project would be part of Franklin Railway Supply but would occupy a separate building in Baltimore and be answerable only to Kirchhof, who would report to Woodard.

"The meetings amazed me," Kirchhof later recalled. "Allen and Dixon had such confidence in Woodard. They made decisions together so quickly."[8] Within another week, Kirchhof and Woodard were on a train to Lima, Ohio, to begin interviews.

Woodard seemed to know whom he wanted. Of those to whom Woodard made offers, few at Lima, and later at Franklin, turned him down. Among the engineers who signed on were Jim Smith and Vernon L. Smith (no relation) from Lima, and a young man who had worked at Franklin only about a year, Raymond H. Delano. One of the most talented draftsmen at Franklin, William Forker, also accepted. Woodard stressed to each that, except for Kirchhof in the role of team leader, there would be no ranks among the engineers and draftsman; all would be expected to contribute. Said Kirchhof,

> Later, in the 1950s, I heard about [aeronautical engineer] Kelly Johnson and his famous 'Skunk Works' at Lockheed [Aircraft Co.], and there were those NASA special design teams in the 1960s. Well, we set up our own group like that in 1937. We had no chain-of-command or administrators to deal with. If we needed our budget changed, we got it. We were independent, and we had backing from the top. All we had to do was produce.[9]

Kirchhof's group began with the basic valve and valve-gear design as manufactured by Dabeg. In contrast to the Caprotti gear, which had the poppet valves arranged vertically, the Dabeg valves were set horizontally, which simplified the cam drive and dispensed with the Caprotti's elongated bellcrank-shaped tappets, which occasionally fractured in use. The new challenge was to size the valves for the greater rates of steam flow typical in North American practice, as compared to European, and to keep the drive simple and rugged. The valves would need to be larger and therefore heavier than those made by Dabeg, and the valves, tappets, cams, and other associated mechanism would need to be reliable at high rpm. Kirchhof set the maximum-rpm target at 500, equivalent to about 120 mph for an engine with 80-inch-diameter driving wheels or 105 mph with 70-inch drivers – in either case somewhat higher than such locomotives would likely see in service.[10]

To understand the work of Kirchhof and his associates, an understanding of some basic features of poppet valves is needed. Unlike an automotive valve, which has a single, circular seat, a locomotive poppet valve was hollow and "double ported," with two circular seats. This configuration gave one of the poppet valve's main virtues, an extremely generous port opening with steam flowing both around and right through the valve, immediately upon the valve's lifting off its twin seats. Therefore, in contrast to a conventional, reciprocating piston valve, the flow through a poppet valve was virtually unobstructed between the moment of opening to the moment of closing:

> The conventional reciprocating valve is always in motion, although at variable speeds, and on one side or the other is constantly engaged in restricting the port opening. Poppet valves on the contrary, are fixed in their open and closed positions, having movement only at the action points between 'open' and 'closed,' with quick transition from one to the other.[11]

Little force was needed to move the valve, since it was "balanced;" *i.e.*, its double-ported configuration meant that steam pressure did not resist its opening or closing.

The greatest virtue of poppet valves was their separate timing of steam admission and exhaust. With a conventional, reciprocating valve, steam inlet and exhaust timing are inherently tied to one another, since one valve controls both, "thus mechanically binding two separate and distinct phases to the disadvantage of both."[12] At a given stroke of the locomotive piston, the valve controls duration of steam admission to the cylinder; that duration can be made longer or shorter, by varying the point at which the valve "cuts off" the flow of steam into the cylinder. (When running, the locomotive engineer adjusts the cutoff by a lever in the cab.) Reducing the cutoff – having cutoff occur earlier during a given piston stroke, so that the steam can then expand on its own to produce work – is essential to economy in steam consumption.

But with a conventional valve, adjusting the cutoff to occur earlier also results in two highly detrimental events. First, there is an earlier release: the exhaust ports on the working side of the piston open prematurely, before steam expansion is complete. And there is an earlier closure of the exhaust ports on the exhaust side of the piston, trapping steam, so that the piston must literally work against itself. At cutoffs shorter than 20 percent – steam admitted for less than 20 percent of the piston stroke – the premature exhaust release and premature exhaust closure cause rough running and substantially degraded locomotive performance.

With poppet valves, separate valves with separate actuation controlled inlet and exhaust. Hence very short cutoffs could be set without affecting exhaust release or closure, and all valve events (admission, cutoff, release, closure) could be optimally timed for maximum economy and smooth running at any cutoff setting a locomotive engineer might make on the road. Cutoffs as short as five percent could be set in practice, dramatically improving cylinder expansion ratios and thus significantly improving steam-to-mechanical efficiency.[13]

Kirchhof applied his decade of experience in the design and application of such valves in Europe, combining that experience with a group of designers who knew intimately the demands of the heavier service – and generally inferior maintenance – characteristic of American railroads. Even Kirchhof knew that his experience on the Delaware & Hudson was a special case: The D&H 653 and *L.F. Loree* were pampered prototypes that got better care than engines in ordinary pool service.[14]

Arranging a geared drive for the valves was initially considered, but Woodard's research had indicated that the gear drive for the Caprotti valves tried in the U.S. was a source of trouble. Woodard suspected that this was because the Caprotti's drive required some care in lubrication and occasional

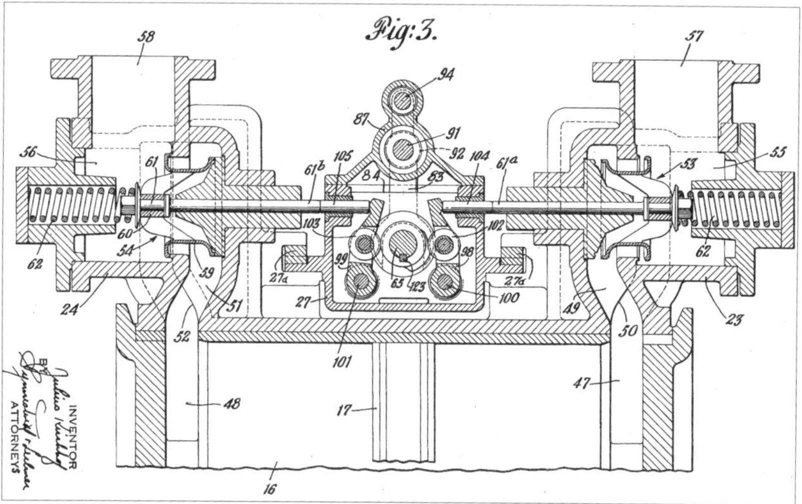

Kirchhof's patent drawing. The double-ported design provides a free flow of steam from valve opening to closing. The"Woodard box," a swap-able module containing the valve actuation gear, is clearly visible at center. *United States Patent Office*

adjustment for which ordinary roundhouse staff lacked the skills and experience. Woodard suggested another approach for the team to consider: a self-contained box that would house all the needed actuation gear. The idea was that the box would normally be sealed, reducing daily maintenance to a simple checking of lubricant level. Repairs, when needed, would consist of removing the box, substituting another, and sending the reparable box to the backshop where skilled machinists could handle the precision parts inside. It was an idea new to steam locomotives: modularization.[15]

Kirchhof was skeptical at first, but set the group to work. Many possible arrangements of box and internal working were considered and rejected. Kirchhof remembered the spirited discussions:

> Everybody spoke up. Everybody had their own ideas. But they all knew how important the final result would be – that the box work, and it had to work well.[16]

Engineer Ray Delano (who, years later, went to Du Pont and rose to become its top manager of special facilities projects) also recalled:

> It was the most exciting time I ever had as an engineer. Julius brought out the best in all of us. He had an elegant style; it was his European way, I guess. Quiet, polite, forceful. You had to respect him. And he respected you. We all had our say at every step. That respect is what did it. He listened, we listened, and then we made decisions.[17]

Finally, an approach began to emerge that combined tradition and innovation. What if the workings in the box were based on the Walschaerts valve gear, certainly one of the most reliable valve gears ever developed and the overwhelming favorite on railroads around the world? (See Chapters 1 and 2.) The team members agreed that if they could provide for separate actuation of admission and exhaust, they could obtain the valve timing required with a very dependable drive mechanism. Various ideas for layout of the gear were thrashed out. The Franklin pattern shop made a wooden model to some preliminary sketches. After some adjustments to the model, design work began for a full-size prototype.

As design proceeded, Delano noted the habits of one of the senior draftsmen, Bill Forker:

That guy was amazing. It's the only way to describe it. Bill would take on a detail design issue, where the parts had to relate in a particular way and nobody was sure how to provide [mechanical] support, or lubrication, or an arrangement [of parts] that a mechanic could actually take apart and put back together. Bill would spend two or three days gazing out the window, smoking his cigarettes. He'd make a few notes. People would mutter that he was just goofing off. But then he would unroll a fresh sheet of vellum, clean his pens, get a new bottle of [India] ink, and start drawing lines. I rarely saw him with a pencil. He had it all worked out in his head. In a few days, out would come a beautiful, finished sheet. And it was always a brilliant solution.[18]

After a couple of months, drawings were complete for building the prototype. Although Woodard, in New York, signed off on preliminary drawings in periodic review sessions with Kirchhof, the Lima office took little part in the design work in Baltimore. Nonetheless, the team dubbed their creation the "Woodard box." Inside were four small versions of the tried-and-true Walschaerts valve gear. Each pair of Walschaerts gear in the box controlled valve events for one cylinder, one gear for the inlet valve and one gear for the exhaust valve. Cutoff was adjusted by means of a rotary shaft running to the locomotive cab. As the engineer varied cutoff for various conditions of speed and power, the two separate valve gears for each cylinder kept inlet and exhaust events in the correct relationship.

A conventional valve gear uses an eccentric, so that the gear operates 90 degrees out of phase with the piston for which admission and exhaust are being controlled. (When the piston is at end-of-stroke in its cylinder, the valve is at mid-stroke, and vice versa.) In the "Woodard box," each pair of valve gear also had to run 90 degrees out of phase with each piston, so a rocker from the opposite crosshead provided the necessary synchronized motion for each pair of Walschaerts links. The whole arrangement ran in a bath of light oil. It was an ingenious solution.

The patenting implications particularly pleased Woodard. Because of the way the new valve-gear box operated, the cams that actually timed inlet and exhaust valves oscillated rather than rotated. The cams, located in a separate housing in each steam chest, were actuated by means of short, lateral shafting from the box. The cams, in turn, operated the valves by means of conventional tappets. The oscillating motion of the cams contrasted with the rotary cam motion of most poppet valve gear produced by Caprotti or Dabeg. The whole arrangement of new gear-box, shafting, cams, tappets, and valves got around nearly all the relevant existing patents. Woodard was pleased indeed.[19]

Bill Forker then supervised several Franklin machinists in fabricating a prototype of the box, while the rest of the group designed the associated valves. In developing these double-ported valves, the team studied all the literature they could find on fluid dynamics, on single- and double-ported valves, and on gas flows through valves and cylinders of both steam and internal combustion engines. The goals were to achieve smooth and generous passageways, minimal restriction through the ports, and light weight for the valves so they could be actuated without excessive force.

The last two goals set up a classic design conflict: "minimal restriction" meant large-diameter, elongated valves with a high lift off the valve seats; "light weight" meant small-diameter, compact valves with a short lift. Two more factors complicated matters: Space was at a premium in any locomotive steam chest (where the valves would be eventually fitted) and steam-flow rates were different between high-pressure, high-density steam coming through the inlet ports and low-pressure, high-volume steam going out the exhaust ports.

Finally, the team decided on an approach that gave reasonable valve weight and allowed flexibility in handling different steam flow rates: multiple valves. Caprotti valves had used only one inlet and one exhaust valve at each end of a cylinder; in the Franklin team's system, up to two inlet and three exhaust valves, with diameters of five to seven inches, could be arrayed in suitable combination at each end of a cylinder. Locomotives of all sizes thus could be accommodated. To Woodard, this was a major virtue: The new Franklin system could be applied to any locomotive with an assortment of standard parts, thus enhancing marketability.[20]

Some minor modifications were needed in laying out the box, and Forker beefed up some of the actuation levers. Kirchhof wanted the design strength of every part of the mechanism to be twice the actual stress at 500 rpm. Based on Dabeg experience, Kirchhof also specified cast steel for the valves, so Delano negotiated with Bethlehem Steel at Sparrows Point in Baltimore to cast some valve blanks from patterns made by the Franklin pattern shop. Franklin machinists turned them to final shape. By early spring 1938, box and valves were ready for bench testing.

Only three horsepower were needed to run the box at 500 rpm, while actuating two inlet valves and two exhaust valves. On the bench, the gear in the box ran smoothly and cutoff could be adjusted easily. But an unexpected difficulty arose. The valves, each weighing two to two-and-a-half pounds, seemed to vibrate on their seats at higher rpm; when closed, the valves were not staying closed.

Vern Smith and Ray Delano constructed a crude stroboscope. Their idea, not used before in steam engine design, was to study the behavior of gear and valves with the stroboscope "freezing" their motion at various rpm. What they discovered under the flickering light of the strobe was that the valves were literally bouncing on the seats. Certain rpm values seemed to produce resonant frequencies, which magnified the bounce. Resulting high stress on valves, tappets, and seats was bad enough; were steam to be flowing through, the bouncing would destroy a clean cutoff, leak steam into the cylinder at the wrong time, and ruin cylinder efficiency.

The first thought was to stiffen the valve springs. But that would put extra stress on cams and tappets. A search of engineering literature disclosed some work on combining springs to create self-damping, and the team tried various combinations of inner and outer springs. Some combinations made the problem worse, not better. The trick turned out to be winding each spring with its coils differently spaced from end to end, and combining inner and outer springs of different spring rates. "Those springs were the hardest part of the whole project," said Delano. "There were some awful days when we thought we might not solve it. We were worried."

Eventually the valve springs were sorted out. The valves then behaved as they should, opening and closing cleanly, even up to 550 rpm. Drawing began for production versions of all the components. The box became an intricate steel casting of two pieces, a body and a lid, with placement inside for needle bearings to hold all links and shafts. Cams and tappets, in their separate housing in each locomotive steam chest, were provided with pressure lubrication. Recalling the Franklin group's labors, Delano observed:

> I can't say who contributed the most. Woodard's early ideas were important, but it was Julius who made us a team. We were so committed to working things out that we thought of it as 'our' project. The final design reflected big contributions from everyone in the room.

In fall 1938, after patent applications were filed, Woodard told Pennsylvania Railroad's head of motive power, F.W. Hankins, what the Franklin group had been up to. Hankins was familiar with both the possibilities and pitfalls of poppet valves. The PRR had designed an enlarged Pacific-type locomotive in 1929, the K5. Baldwin built the second of two prototypes, the 5699, with Caprotti valves. Performance was only marginally better than sister 5698 with conventional valves, and the ensuing Depression halted any further production of the K5 or development of the valves.[21]

Although the PRR's standard passenger engine, the K4s type, had been improved over the years, new tests on the Altoona dynamometer in 1937 and 90-mph road tests in 1938 demonstrated the K4s' limitations in hauling the increasing weight and speed of passenger trains. Double-headed K4s locomotives had been the rule for years on most premier trains from Harrisburg west to Chicago – and expensive practice – with a third K4s

LEFT K5 No. 5699 of 1929 was an early PRR experiment with poppet valves. It was only marginally successful.

Courtesy Kalmbach Media

BELOW PRR K4s No. 5399, with its "Woodard box" on the pilot deck.

Courtesy Kalmbach Media

required over Horseshoe Curve west of Altoona.[22] Hankins and Woodard discussed a proposal to try out the Franklin poppet-valve system, partly to see if the K4s might be further improved, but primarily to test the valves for later application to newly designed engines.

By early 1939, a deal was approved. The PRR mechanical engineering staff chose No. 5399, the last of a K4s batch constructed at Juniata in 1924, for modification. The Franklin team worked out an installation of four six-inch diameter inlet valves and four seven-inch diameter exhaust valves per cylinder, with the oscillating cams on the centerline of each steam chest and the valve-gear box (the "Woodard box") on the locomotive pilot deck. Along with the poppet valves, Hankins also agreed to the addition of other devices from Lima-associated suppliers: a new form of Type-E superheater with tubular elements bent into a sinuous "sine wave" form (the idea was to improve heat transfer into the superheated steam) and a multiple-valve, head-end throttle. Kirchhof appointed Ray Delano as chief field engineer for Franklin, and so Delano accompanied 5399 from Altoona, where the modifications were installed, to Fort Wayne, Ind., where the PRR had a large locomotive shop from which road tests would be conducted. The Fort Wayne Division had some of the flattest and straightest track between New York and Chicago, and so made for an ideal road-testing ground.

On his first day at Fort Wayne, Delano had an experience that, in retrospect, he regarded as prophetic. The 5399 and crew, accompanied by a Franklin engineer, had just come in from Altoona running light (*i.e.*, without a train), after overnight stops at Pittsburgh and Crestline, Ohio; Delano had followed by automobile. The valve gear had run well, but after three days breaking-in, Delano thought he should inspect the valves, cams, gear, and box and make any needed adjustments. It was evening and so he located the roundhouse night supervisor, asking if he might have the assistance of a couple of skilled mechanics. The foreman was cheerful to oblige, and Delano waited by the locomotive in the poorly lit roundhouse stall. Years later, he recalled to the author:

> Around the corner came a pair of guys in greasy overalls, pulling a little wooden wagon. They had two oil lamps, those inspection lamps that look like teapots. On the wagon were a bunch of tools, big steam wrenches mostly. There wasn't anything lighter than a two-pound maul. I remember this sinking feeling: our poppet valves were high-precision machinery, and in this roundhouse, the idea of real precision was completely foreign. And this was one of the Pennsy's best roundhouses. So I told the two guys to wait. I went out to my car, got my socket set, and did the [unbolting of inspection covers] and the adjustments myself. I remember thinking: steam engines and high-precision might not be able to mix.

Nevertheless, the 5399 ran off some 50,000 miles on the Fort Wayne Division in 1939, east to Crestline and as far west as Chicago, mostly pulling the railroad's regularly scheduled high-speed trains. In test runs, the engine's increased power over a normal K4 was noticeable at lower speed and phenomenal at higher speed: 20 percent to 30 percent more drawbar power at 50 to 70 mph, and 40 percent or more at 80 mph and above. In regular service on heavier trains, the 5399 often substituted for two locomotives.[23]

The high point came on a special run with a 1,000-ton, 15-car train. The objective was to reach the highest possible speed. On a slight downgrade, 5399 and train hit 94.7 mph, producing more than twice the cylinder horsepower of a standard K4s at that speed. For 100 miles, the train averaged more than 80 mph. Valves and valve gear worked flawlessly. "Riding on that engine that day," said Delano decades later, "was the thrill of a lifetime."[24]

On the Altoona test plant later that year, the 5399 recorded a cylinder horsepower of nearly 4,300 and a drawbar horsepower of 3,860, both at 75 mph. The cylinder horsepower was almost 800 more than a standard but improved K4s. Kirchhof recalled that PRR Engineer of Tests Lloyd B. Jones, was deeply impressed. "Jones said maybe we could beat the diesels after all. We all felt he might be right."[25]

Pennsy's S1 and T1

In the meantime, the huge S1, designed as a four-cylinder, 6-4-4-6 duplex by participating Baldwin, Alco, Lima, and Pennsylvania Railroad engineers, was already at the World's Fair. There had been no consideration of putting an unproven valve system on the S1. Shakedown runs on regular trains in early 1939, before the Fair, were successful, and in late 1940, road testing of the S1 began on the Fort Wayne Division. The results led straight to development of the T1 by PRR and Baldwin.

That the S1 was too big for the sharper curves and tighter clearances on PRR lines east of Pittsburgh was clear to designers and operating staff, even

PRR T1 poppet valves. One person's complexity is another person's precision: Each side of each cylinder had two five-inch-diameter inlet valves and two six-inch-diameter exhaust valves, for a total of 32. Performance in tests, however, was beyond debate, as the poppet valves enabled the T1 to produce unprecedented high horsepower.

Courtesy Kalmbach Media

if it could handle a 1,000-ton train at 100 mph. So, to permit a more usefully sized locomotive, PRR motive power chief Hankins in 1941 approved a final specification calling for an 880-ton trailing load at 100 mph. Hankins and Jones wanted the Franklin poppet valves; sources conflict on whether Baldwin's Ralph Johnson desired them. Based on the S1's performance with normal piston valves, Johnson may have felt that the performance specification for the smaller T1 could be reached without using valves that were, after all, untried in long-term service.[26] Or, the notion that the Franklin poppet-valve system had apparently succeeded where the Baldwin-licensed Caprotti system had failed may have galled some Baldwin staff. Johnson certainly appreciated the potential value of the poppets and knew that they would make the attainment of the desired performance easier to achieve. The final design called for two five-inch diameter inlet valves and two six-inch diameter exhaust valves at each end of each cylinder, or 32 valves in all, actuated by two valve-gear boxes, one box for each cylinder/driving wheel set.

After running in service pulling some of the PRR's top trains, one of the two prototype T1 engines went to Altoona. An extension had to be added to the test plant building to accommodate the T1 and another large, newly designed engine (the Q class, discussed later in this chapter). The T1 registered the highest cylinder and drawbar horsepower ratings – 6,100 and 5,400, respectively – ever recorded at the plant for a passenger locomotive, and its average fuel and water rates were even lower than Baldwin's high-efficiency, compound-expansion No. 60000 of 1926. At speeds above 40 mph, the T1 horsepower curves were significantly flatter than any engine tested before; the poppet valves greatly reduced power losses at higher rpm, with the biggest improvement at the highest speeds. And the lighter weight of main and side rods, reciprocating parts, and driving-wheel counterweights made for smooth operation, as the duplex concept promised. Vertical imbalance in the drivers was only 4,170 pounds at 80 mph, far less than the 5,000- to 7,000-pound imbalance common in other eight-drivered engines of similar size at that speed.

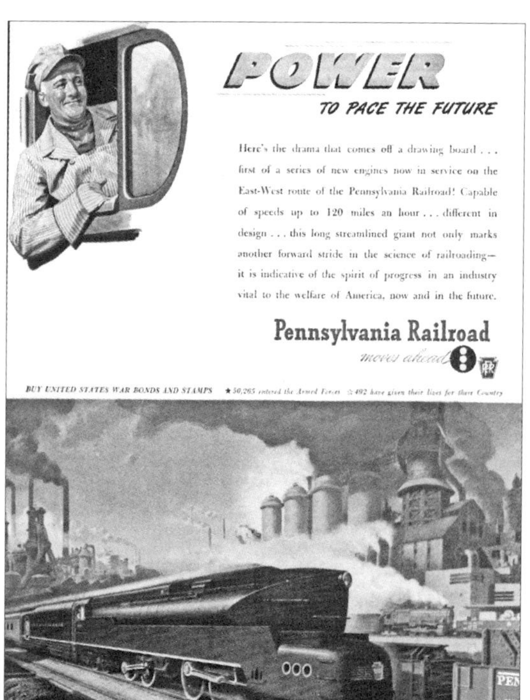

The rakish T1 was featured in patriotic PRR advertising, where the vital role of the locomotives and their owner on the World War II home front was highlighted.
Author's Collection

In everyday use the two T1s ran well, hauling the *Broadway Limited* and other trains between Harrisburg (the westerly end of PRR electrified lines) and Chicago. The engines' rakish image began to appear in PRR advertising. Franklin staff trained roundhouse mechanics in the proper care of the valves and valve gear. The only sour note was comment from locomotive crewmembers that the driving wheels were prone to slip at starting and sometimes at high speed as well; a light hand was needed on the throttle to prevent such slipping.[27]

When wartime demands eased in 1945, the PRR ordered a production run of 50 T1s, with half built at Altoona and half at Baldwin. After 15 years of Depression and war, this new fleet was intended at last to take over most of the mainline passenger trains west of Harrisburg from the K4s, whose design was three decades old. Compared to the two T1 prototypes, the production locomotives were slightly shorter and their streamlined casing was somewhat altered. To address the slipping, Baldwin and PRR designers agreed on a significant change to the T1 suspension and equalization system. The initial engines had been suspended as a standard 4-8-4 would be, with the lead truck independent and all drivers and trailing wheels on each side equalized together. In the production version of the T1, the lead truck was equalized with the first set of drivers, as on the earlier E6-class 4-4-2 and first K4s, with the suspension divided between the two driver sets. Both suspension systems provided a three-point or tripod equalization, but the hope was that the revised plan would better resist fore-and-aft surging, thus alleviating the driving-wheel slippage.[28]

The first T1s had been assigned to the flagship trains and had therefore been run by the most experienced crews. As production T1s entered regular pool service in 1945 and 1946, the slipping problems came to the fore. Enginemen repeatedly complained that the T1s slipped easily at starting. But more serious

LEFT Duplex drive of PRR's T1 prototype 6110, with its oscillating-cam valve gear. Essentially a four-cylinder 4-8-4, the T1's divided drive made for lighter rods and machine parts.
Courtesy Kalmbach Media

BELOW PRR's T1 gained a reputation for being slippery at starting and could be unwieldy at speed. No. 5548 leads a passenger train at Lewistown, Pa., in October 1947.
J.P. Ahrens, Courtesy Kalmbach Media

were instances of slipping at speed: one cylinder/driver set would slip, usually the one in front, as dampness on the rails or some other track irregularity was encountered; this would cause a sudden deceleration of the locomotive, which would take weight off the rear cylinder/driver set and cause it to slip. As weight was thrown to the forward drivers, they might or might not regain their grip. But a common occurrence was "hobby horsing," as first one cylinder/driver set and then the other lost and partially regained footing, in a terrific, wheel-spinning, back-and-forth oscillation. At 60 to 80 mph, this was scary to say the least, and the only cure was to reduce throttle immediately and then to try to ease the throttle back on without losing too much train speed or slipping all over again. Passengers felt the longitudinal lurching, and there were a few instances of people being knocked down in the aisles.[29]

At about the same time, the first reports of broken valves began to come in. It is a widespread myth, prevalent in enthusiast literature, that the T1 experienced trouble with the gearboxes. Kirchhof and other Franklin engineers conferred with PRR locomotive staff at Altoona – where there were some new faces, since Hankins had retired in 1941 – while Delano and others traveled the railroad gathering information and looking at locomotive engineers' reports and shop records. According to both Delano and Kirchhof, there were no gearbox failures between 1945 and 1948 due to any flaw of the box; there were a few cases of gearbox failure because oil level had been neglected and the box had run dry. Delano himself changed one of those boxes.[30]

Breakage of the valves themselves was another matter. A few times each month, a T1 limped into a terminal with a broken valve, the valve body shattered against its seat. Maintenance practices and inspections were tightened up, but the breakages continued. Kirchhof and his colleagues were not only embarrassed but profoundly puzzled. Based on six years experience with the 5399 and elaborate bench testing in 1941 for the first T1s, Franklin had warranted the new T1 valves for sustained speeds up to 100 mph and short durations of 125 mph.[31]

By late 1946, elaborate analysis of production and maintenance records had yielded little insight, and nearly every valve in the T1 fleet had been individually inspected for flaws. The valve breakages seemed to occur randomly, but they were concentrated on the high-speed line between Crestline and Fort Wayne where the authorized speed was 100 mph. Kirchhof decided to send out a "spy" – a Franklin staffer to ride trains anonymously for a month on the Fort Wayne Division and to clock their actual speed.

In telephone and letter reports, the staffer verified the not-infrequent slipping at speed, as well as numerous milepost timings of 100 mph and above. Some of his reports seemed unbelievable, including some instances of speeds up to 140 mph.[32] When he returned to Baltimore, he met with the group and presented his findings, and he gave his log and watch to Kirchhof for verification. Once or twice per week in the recorded month, when a train was ten cars or less in length and running behind schedule, the engineer had made up time by exceeding 125 mph. Twice that month, with short trains of six or seven cars, speed had reached 135 to 142 mph, as clocked over several miles. Careful inspection of logged entries and watch, as well as the consistency of successive time intervals between mileposts on all the timed runs, attested to the veracity of the log.[33]

Kirchhof was at a loss as to what to do with this information. There were PRR enginemen grossly exceeding speed limits, beyond Franklin's warrant. (PRR locomotives in those days had speedometers but not speed recorders, instruments used generally from the 1950s to keep track of speed for later audit.) By performance calculation, there was no doubt that a T1 was capable of such speeds. Yet the frequent slipping, even well below 125 mph, could easily explain most of the rpm overruns on the valves and machinery. Franklin was not responsible for the slipperiness, but that flaw implicated partner Baldwin and client PRR. Kirchhof's old friends Kiesel and Hankins were gone, and there was no one at the PRR mechanical department in whom Kirchhof thought he could confide.[34]

Kirchhof decided on an approach that would preserve good customer relations and also get to the bottom of the valve breakage problem. He notified the PRR that Franklin would continue to honor its warranty, cautioned against the hazards of overspeeds on the valves, and disclosed that Franklin was commissioning a study by the Battelle Institute to find the best alloy for the valves, in the hope that a better material would provide a cure.[35]

The future of Lima and Franklin was at stake. If poppet valves failed, in the view of both Kirchhof and Lima's executives, steam's rearguard action against diesels was doomed. No other technology for reciprocating steam promised enough improvement in operating economy, and other alternatives – such as building a steam-turbine drive – were judged by Lima managers as longshots in which the company had no expertise. While Franklin's engineers worked on the valve issue, Lima engineers under new chief designer Albert J. Townsend worked on a better boiler. In terms of potential improvement in overall locomotive efficiency, however, the engineers in both firms knew that better valves were the *sine qua non*.[36]

Battelle investigated both the metallurgy and the manufacturing methods for the valves. Franklin supplied samples of new valves, used valves, and the broken ones returned by PRR. Franklin also lent its bench-testing apparatus so mechanical tests could be made at various rpm and valve-spring settings. Impact stress of the valves on their seats was studied. Numerous alloys of steel were tried, with valves both cast and machined out of solid billets. Even bronze alloys were tried. Design of the valves was reexamined, to see if a different configuration might handle working stresses better.

After months of analysis, Battelle's verdict, as interpreted by Kirchhof, was disappointing in the extreme. Because of the geometric increases in impact stress in normal operation at high rpm, the material almost did not matter: The best possible, high-density, cast-steel valves, made with proper technique to relieve internal stress and installed with springs of optimal stiffness, could provide sustained, reliable operation up to 125-130 mph with the T1's 80-inch diameter drivers (525-545 rpm) as both Kirchhof and Delano recalled the report. Beyond the equivalent of 130 mph, however, breakage rates increased quickly. Good quality cast iron valves – thicker, somewhat heavier, and considerably cheaper – did almost as well, according to Delano, operating reliably up to about 100-110 mph.[37]

For the T1 problems, it was grim news. For even if a 100-mph speed limit were rigidly observed, the high-speed slipping tendency of the T1 would likely take rpm above 550 fairly often. Delano vividly recalled Kirchhof's reaction

Altoona's largest-ever freight locomotive design was the 4-4-6-4 Q2 class of 1944-1945 (RIGHT), an evolution of the one-of-a-kind, semi-streamlined 4-6-4-4 Q1-class engine No. 6130 of 1942 (ABOVE).
Courtesy Kalmbach Media

to someone's suggestion that cast iron might be used, if not for the T1, then for other locomotives. "It was the only time I ever saw Julius lose his temper. He blew up: 'We cannot make poppet valves out of s--t!' His remark became a watchword for the group; people would repeat it with an imitation of Julius's elegant Austrian accent."[38]

Pennsy's Q2

While Franklin engineers struggled with the T1 valves, the PRR was dealing with the wheel-slip problems of another class of duplex locomotive. The Q2 was introduced in 1944, considerably altered from a prototype Q1 of 1942. PRR's Juniata Works turned out 26 Q2s through 1945. These were the largest steam locomotives for freight duty ever designed at Altoona, and they stretched boiler and running gear capacity to the utter limits within their 69 feet of total engine length.

Having ten driving wheels arranged on a rigid frame with four cylinders, and an immense, 300-psi boiler (with 122 square feet of grate area and 922 cubic feet of firebox/combustion-chamber volume) capable of evaporating 140,000 pounds of steam per hour, the Q2 exerted an amazing peak of 6,645 drawbar horsepower on the Altoona test plant – more than the 6,300 of Union Pacific's Big Boy of 1941. Rather than poppet valves, the Q2 employed standard piston valves actuated by a conventional form of Walschaerts valve gear. PRR designers chose the conventional valves for two reasons: Poppet valves were as yet untested in fleet use (the Q2s were built before the production T1s), and the Q2, as a fast freighter, was intended to develop maximum drawbar horsepower at 35 to 50 mph, a speed range in which poppet valves gave only slight advantage.

From the moment the Q2s entered pool service with enginemen of average ability handling heavy trains, driving-wheel slip became a daily occurrence. Yet even in the hands of highly skilled crews, a Q2 often slipped in the same manner later experienced with the T1. First one cylinder/driver set would slip, followed by a longitudinal surge, followed by a slipping of the other cylinder/driver set. The engineer's only recourse, as later found for the T1s, was to reduce throttle quickly to stop the runaway drivers and then snap the throttle back on before too much train speed was lost. For a Q2 pulling heavy freight, however, the loss of momentum from repeated slips while working upgrade at 20 to 40 mph could result in stalling the train altogether.[39]

Working with the American Brake Shoe Co., PRR developed a "slip arrestor" that shut off steam automatically to the offending cylinder/driver set when a slip occurred. Four special air-actuated, steam shutoff valves were installed, one in the steam path supplying each of the four cylinders. Small rollers monitored the rpm of each set of driving wheels, and when a difference in rpm above a small threshold was detected by an electric circuit, the shut-off valves curtailed steam flow to the higher-speed cylinders until equal rpm was reestablished. Indication lights in the cab told the engineer which pair of shutoff valves was operating. The electrical design was a precursor of wheel-slip systems later used on modern diesels.[40]

As one author has noted, however, the system "did not prevent slip, it simply checked a slip that had developed." That, and a reported "fore-and-aft surging when both [cylinder/driver] groups were in phase" made the Q2 extremely hard for crews to handle at high power output. Why the slipping and surging tendencies were so much more pronounced than, say, a similar-size, high-horsepower 4-6-6-4 articulated freight locomotive, which also had four cylinders driving two separate wheelsets, is a mystery. A popular claim that reciprocating masses in the Q2 were left sufficiently "unbalanced" by PRR's driving-wheel counterbalancing techniques is unlikely, given comparable balancing techniques for other large, four-cylinder freighters.[41]

Any interest other railroads had in duplex locomotives was killed off by the Pennsy's experience, although Baldwin continued to promote the idea for a few years.[42] In Kirchhof's strongly-held opinion, the fallacy of the duplex idea was having two independent drive-systems in the same frame. Rather, the two cylinder pairs and all the driving wheels should have been synchronized as one mechanical group, not two. Invariably, in any locomotive, the leading set of drivers slips first when the locomotive encounters reduced adhesion on the rails. If the locomotive has a jointed frame (as in a standard American articulated freight locomotive), the slippage of one cylinder/driver set does not so directly affect the traction of the other set. In Kirchhof's view, Baldwin should have borrowed some of the principles common in European design, whereby smooth running and high tractive adhesion were obtained with four cylinders in a single frame, so long as the four pistons drove on one coupled (*i.e.*, mechanically connected) set of drivers.[43]

Oscillating cam applications

The Franklin team went on to apply their valves to seven other locomotives or locomotive classes, involving four other railroad customers besides the PRR. The oscillating-cam valve gear such as used on the T1, termed the "Type A" by Franklin, was fitted to single locomotives on the New York Central and the Missouri Pacific and to a small class of passenger locomotives on the Chesapeake & Ohio. In all cases, the valve gear worked well and produced significant economies in steam consumption at higher rpm. Since none of these locomotives ran much faster than 80 or 90 mph, nor had any undue slipping problems, there were no valve breakages except for a couple due to manufacturing flaws.[44]

Kirchhof persuaded New York Central's chief of motive power, Paul W. Kiefer (who was well noted in the trade as the principal designer of the NYC's famous 4-6-4 Hudsons), to try a set of poppet valves and Type A valve gear on one of his company's new 4-8-4s, built by Alco. The resulting locomotive was No. 5500, NYC class S-2a. The single S-2a was identical in nearly all respects except for its valves to the production version, the very successful NYC class S-1 Niagara. The road number of the modified engine perhaps reflected the drawbar horsepower Kiefer hoped to achieve, fully equal to or exceeding the T1 of NYC's great competitor.[45]

The S-2a ran well, did not slip unduly, and became a reliable member of the Niagara fleet. But its performance, both in top horsepower and in steam economy, was a disappointment to both Kirchhof and Kiefer. The Franklin team worked with Alco designers under Alfred W. Bruce and with

Missouri Pacific 4-6-2 No. 6001 was retrofitted with poppet valves in 1942, when it was 17 years old. They performed well, but weren't pushed to the speeds of PRR's T1s.
Courtesy Kalmbach Media

Closeup of the valve gear and cylinder on New York Central class S-2a 4-8-4 No. 5500.
Courtesy Kalmbach Media

Kiefer's staff. In pursuit of maximum exhaust-steam flow rates out of the cylinders, which would improve cylinder efficiency as well as lower exhaust backpressure, NYC engineers insisted on six exhaust valves per cylinder, rather than the four per cylinder used on the T1. The Franklin team agreed. As a result, the exhaust passages into and out of the steam chests became convoluted and, in Kirchhof's later judgment, too restricted. In retrospect, said Kirchhof, "The decision to add more exhaust valves was a mistake."[46]

Calculated drawbar horsepower was 5,600 to 5,700, yet the S-2a produced about 5,400 at about 70 mph – hardly an embarrassment, but not much better than the 5,000 drawbar horsepower at 65 mph of a regular S-1. Fuel and steam economy was also better than the S-1, but not much better. Poppet valves, when added to an old design like the K4s, had made dramatic changes in power and economy. Added to a locomotive of sophisticated, up-to-date design, the incremental improvements were not as great. New York Central managers did not judge the improvement worth the poppet valves' extra purchase cost.[47]

Kirchhof felt that Franklin now must make its valve-gear system simpler and cheaper. A rotary drive had long been part of Dabeg's catalog. Such a drive made for easy access for maintenance and adjustment, since it was all external, and was less costly, with fewer moving parts. A rotary cam, however, was far more elaborate than the relatively simple oscillating cams of the Type A. The rotary cam itself was long – about 12 inches – with one installed at each cylinder. To achieve different cutoffs, the rotating cam translated side-to-side so that valve tappets could intersect different profiles on the cam: long-duration valve lifts at one end of the cam (long cutoffs) and short-duration valve lifts at the other (short cutoffs), with infinitely variable cutoffs in between. Delano called such a cam "the sassafrass root" for its shape.

Rotary cam developments

The PRR offered a test bed for the Franklin rotary-cam system: K4s No. 3847. PRR later tried the system out on a lone T1, primarily to let Franklin

Santa Fe 4-8-4 No. 3752, shown at Denver in 1946, was the recipient of Franklin Type B rotary-cam valve gear.
R.H. Kindig, Courtesy Kalmbach Media

test the gear up to 100 mph. The Santa Fe also experimented with it, by means of an installation designed by Franklin engineer Vern Smith. Franklin termed its rotary-cam system the "Type B."

The Chesapeake & Ohio had had good results with Type A poppet valve-gear on its L-1 class of 4-6-4s. These were rebuilt at C&O's Huntington, W.Va., shops from heavy 4-6-2s. Poppet valves added to this essentially older design markedly improved performance. C&O locomotive managers were impressed and asked for Type B poppet valve gear on the new L-2 class 4-6-4s to be built by Baldwin in 1948.[48]

The five L-2-As were among the last steam locomotives built in the U.S. They were Franklin's penultimate valve-gear project. Big and heavy, the L-2s

RIGHT PRR K4s No. 3847, equipped with Franklin Type B rotary-cam poppet valves.
Courtesy Kalmbach Media

BELOW PRR T1 No. 5500, at St. Louis Union Station in 1948.
Paul Gibbs, Courtesy Kalmbach Media

were intended for high power at speeds of 50 to 80 mph with passenger trains on C&O's difficult topography, which spanned tidewater flats, hills, and steep Allegheny ridges.

As soon as the first L-2-As went into service, problems cropped up with the valve gear. A transverse shaft involved in adjusting the position of both cams for different cutoffs snapped on two different engines. As he had done on every other field problem with Franklin valves, Delano headed out, this time to Huntington. What he found was a total puzzle. He could find no apparent reason for the shaft breakages. Each cam was driven by its own gear; the two cams were set 90 degrees apart (since the cylinders on a two-cylinder steam locomotive are also set 90 degrees apart). If the cams and driving wheels on each side of the locomotive were 90 degrees from those on the other side, there should be virtually no stress on the cutoff-adjusting shaft, which was the only tie between the valve gears on either side. That observation suggested a thought to Delano, but one he at first discounted: Could the drivers on the affected engines be improperly set on their axles – "out of quarter" (not at the prescribed 90 degrees)? Given the way a driving-wheel pair is mounted on a new axle at the shop and the crankpins machined using a "quartering machine," such a thing was nearly impossible. By careful measurement, however, it turned out to be true. Inexplicably, each pair of drivers on the two locomotives was out of quarter, by the same few degrees. It was enough to do the damage.[49]

"The C&O boys were furious. At least they couldn't be upset with us [at Franklin]." But to Delano, it was an ignominious end to work with C&O.

There was one last valve-gear project. The U.S. Army responded favorably to a Franklin proposal to develop a simplified gear for use in military locomotives. The design was Delano's brainchild. The rotary cam had only three positions: forward, neutral, and reverse. Cutoff in forward and reverse was fixed. Carefully restricted inlet ports produced an effect similar to reduced cutoff at higher locomotive speed. As steam flow increased with increasing rpm, the fixed-inlet restriction limited the quantity of steam consumed. One of the military 2-8-0s at Fort Eustis, Va., was modified with the new "Type B-1" gear. The gear proved highly reliable, with steam economy similar to conventional piston valves. According to Delano, the Army mechanics at Fort Eustis deemed the B-1 gear easier to repair and adjust than conventional valves. "Valve setting" – the normally elaborate procedure of aligning valves and valve gear to produce the same cylinder power on both sides of the piston at different cutoffs – was reduced to a couple of minutes of checking cam installation; most repairs involved a quick and simple exchange of parts.[50]

There would be no repeat orders from the Army or from any railroad. On a morning in 1948, Kirchhof was on an early train from Baltimore to Philadelphia. He had been invited by PRR motive-power staff to discuss

Chesapeake & Ohio Class L-1 4-6-4 Hudson No. 490, rebuilt from a 4-6-2, is another example of an older locomotive that was successfully retrofitted with poppet valves.

Courtesy Kalmbach Media

U.S. Army 2-8-0 No. 2628, with Franklin Type B-1 valve gear.
Courtesy Kalmbach Madia

further Type B applications. At Wilmington, he got a newspaper. There was an article about the House Committee on Un-American Activities. And there was another article: A short piece on an inside page carried the news that the Pennsy board of directors had voted to give up on steam locomotives and purchase only diesels instead. Gracious as always, Kirchhof went to his appointment, exchanged a few regrets, and went home.[51]

Delano remembered Kirchhof's breaking the news to the now much-reduced Franklin staff. If the mighty PRR, innovator and coal-hauler, had thrown in the towel on steam, so eventually would every other railroad. Kirchhof had recently been made president of Franklin, but now he had to preside over its inevitable decline.

> We all so admired Julius. I knew I would soon be looking for other work. But I felt I might never have another boss like Julius, or have as much fun as an engineer as I did with this group of people. Well, I was right.[52]

Chapter 19 Notes

1. *Baldwin Locomotives* (BLW client magazine), May 1942. Also, Ralph P. Johnson, *The Steam Locomotive: Its Theory, Operation, and Economics*, 1942, especially chapters 9, 15, 25, and 29. Johnson was chief engineer at BLW.
2. Raymond Loewy, *Never Leave Well Enough Alone: The Personal Record of an Industrial Designer*, 1951, pp. 135-41.
3. Jim Shaughnessy, *Delaware & Hudson*, 1967, pp. 334-43.
4. Johnson (note 1), chapters on boiler evaporation, valves, and cylinders.
5. Interviews with George H. Woodard, son of William E. Woodard, at Bryn Athyn, Pa., summer 1973. GHW was a noted engineer in his own right, having worked on the first successful commercially produced U.S. diesel locomotives, the Alco-GE-Ingersoll Rand joint venture of 1925, and at Westinghouse on the first U.S. jet fighter, the XP-59A of 1942. (GHW quoted his father's response to GHW's chiding on sticking with steam locomotives: "If I can get ten more good years out of the old steam horse, then I can retire happy.") In the following text, wherever description or interpretation is written regarding William E. Woodard's thinking and actions, the source is GHW interviews.
6. George Woodard interview. Also, interview with Charles Synnestvedt (son of Paul Synnestvedt of the patent law firm of Synnestvedt & Lechner), at Tanglewood, Mass., fall 1980.
7. Interview with Julius Kirchhof at Towson, Md., spring 1973.
8. Ibid. The Kirchhof interview was recorded and transcribed, after which Kirchhoff reviewed the transcripts and made necessary corrections for accuracy.
9. Ibid.
10. Ibid. Also based on a 1974 interview with Raymond H. Delano at Rising Sun, Md. As with the Kirchhoff interview, the Delano session was recorded and transcribed, and the subject reviewed the transcript for accuracy.

11. W.A. Austin, "Caprotti Poppet Valve Gear: Important Economies Derived From Its Application to Steam Locomotives," *Proceedings of the New York Railroad Club*, October 1928, p. 8673.
12. Ibid., p. 8671.
13. Kirchhof interview.
14. Ibid.
15. Ibid., and Delano interview.
16. Kirchhof interview.
17. Delano interview.
18. Ibid.
19. Kirchhof and Delano interviews.
20. George Woodard interview.
21. Delano interview.
22. Vernon L. Smith, "The Case for the American Steam Locomotive," *Trains*, August 1967, pp. 22-28.
23. Ibid.
24. Ibid. See also Raymond P. Delano, "Riding K4s 5399 - to 94.7 mph," *Trains*, May 1973, pp. 46-47.
25. Kirchhof interview. See also Brian Reed, *Locomotives in Profile*, vol. 2, 1972, which has a chapter on "Pennsylvania Pacifics."
26. Kirchhof interview. See also Reed (Note 25), which also includes a chapter on "Pennsylvania Duplexii."
27. Delano and Kirchhof interviews. See also Vernon L. Smith, "And the Case for the T1," *Trains*, August 1967, pp. 26-27.
28. Kirchhof interview.
29. Delano and Kirchhof interviews. Also, interviews with James Smith, Lima engineer, by telephone to his home in Orleans, Mass., 1975.
30. Delano and Kirchhof interviews.
31. Kirchhof interview.
32. Both Delano and Kirchhof, independently, offered this story without prompting from the interviewer. Note that the established speed record for steam locomotives is 126 mph, by the London & North Eastern Railway's *Mallard*. (The 127-mph claim for the PRR 7002 in 1904 is subject to dispute, being an informal timing only.)
33. Kirchhof interview.
34. Kiesel had retired in 1936, and Hankins in 1941. Woodard was no longer available for counsel, either, having died in 1942.
35. Kirchhof interview.
36. Delano and Kirchhof interviews.
37. Kirchhof and Delano interviews. In 1981, author tried to obtain a copy of the report from Battelle. The institute confirmed the existence of the report, but would not provide a copy, asserting that it was proprietary and possibly contained commercially useful information. (The ACE 3000 steam locomotive design project, of which the author was a principal participant, was then underway. The owners of the project did not wish to purchase rights to the report.)
38. Delano interview. Delano was an eyewitness, but the story was also confirmed by James Smith in his interview, though Smith was in Lima and heard the story second-hand.
39. Delano interview. Although the Q2s were not equipped with poppet valves, the operating problems they experienced were extensively discussed at Franklin because of the parallels with the T1's problems.
40. Delano interview.
41. Quotation from Reed (Note 26), p. 286. Note that the author's interpretation in this paragraph does not agree with Reed's.
42. *Railway Age*, May 19, 1945.
43. Kirchhof interview.
44. Kirchhof and Delano interviews.
45. Kirchhof interview.
46. Ibid.
47. Delano interview.
48. Kirchhof and Delano interviews.
49. Delano interview.
50. Ibid.
51. Kirchhof interview.
52. Delano interview.

NORFOLK AND WESTERN
NORFOLK AND WESTERN

Chapter 20

Norfolk & Western's Big Three:

Standardization Too Late

O Winston Link was an industrial photographer who gained nationwide fame in the 1980s for the night shots he took along the Norfolk & Western Railway in the late 1950s. The Museum of Modern Art's photography curator called Link "a legitimate American genius."[1] Link's subject was the last several years of steam operations on the N&W – mostly captured in elaborately staged night scenes of its locomotives. He sought to make a visual document; instead he made a dreamlike world. The same qualities that attract people to the photographs – carefully crafted composition, a blaze of artificial light from hundreds of flashbulbs that creates a world neither in day nor night – render the locomotives as strange antiques. Once, however, those antiques were part of a modern transportation system, one of the most efficient and productive railroads in the world.

At 2,100 miles of road, the Norfolk & Western was not one of the largest U.S. railroads, but it was dependably profitable. Between its reorganization from receivership in 1896 and its merger as part of Norfolk Southern in 1982, the line never had a year without a solid net income, even through the Depression. In the mid-1950s, ten to 11 percent of U.S. coal originated on the N&W.[2] In 1955, just three locomotive types, all steam – the A, Y, and J classes – produced 94 percent of the N&W's freight ton-miles and 84 percent of its passenger train miles.[3] These standardized locomotives operated with extraordinarily high utilization, serviced in advanced "lubritoriums" for rapid turnaround from runs.

Most extraordinary of all, the railroad originated its "Big Three" locomotive types in its own offices and then manufactured them in its own Roanoke Shops. They were exemplary designs, superbly efficient in comparison to other steamers, and admired in their time by railroaders both in the U.S. and overseas. N&W didn't buy any road diesels, and then just a few, until the fall of 1955. President Robert Smith explained that "[t]his does not mean that we have changed our view that our modern ... steam locomotives can handle the major part of our traffic economically." The internal-combustion

Norfolk & Western Class Y6 2-8-8-2 No. 2129 at Waynesboro, Va., in June 1956. Auxiliary water tenders extended these locomotives' range.
Courtesy Kalmbach Media

The author acknowledges his debt to E.W. King for his original research on N&W locomotive engineering history and for his counsel on this chapter.

Before embracing its legendary Big Three classes, N&W motive power was reliable but unremarkable, like this 1905 Richmond product.
Courtesy Kalmbach Media

interlopers – eight, four each from Alco and EMD – were for use only on the long Lynchburg, Va.-Durham, N.C., branch line, "where, because of comparatively thin traffic, we are not able to get out of [our large steam] power the full service of which it is capable."[4]

N&W's home-built Y2 came in 1918, the Y6 model and A-class in 1936, and the J in 1941. Before the 1930s, N&W accumulated a mix of locomotive types that was not unusual for a medium-sized railroad having to carry heavy mainline tonnage over mountainous topography as well as reach many coal-mine branch lines. Most of N&W's engines had come from commercial builders. Beginning in the 1880s, however, the railroad began constructing some of its own engines. In 1883 the company's Roanoke Machine Works installed a major foundry and machine-shop complex on part of 800 recently purchased acres and began work on a few light locomotives. The "Works" produced 152 engines through 1895.[5]

In the Depression of the 1930s, developmental funds were limited because of shrunken traffic. But the N&W maintained its employment of fine designers and a capable shop staff. Locomotive repair and construction facilities (by then called the Roanoke Shops) had been extensively expanded in the flush years of 1926-27 to do the heaviest boiler, frame, and machinery work. In 1932, the railroad posted its leanest profit of the decade (just under $17 million, a respectable figure at a time when over 30 percent of U.S. rail mileage was in bankruptcy). The railroad kept out of deficit by cutting total employment from 21,000 to 19,000 through layoffs and putting everyone else – including office and engineering staff – on short hours. Net income in 1935 improved to $25 million. Ten-percent wage-rate cuts, agreed nationally by rail unions three years before, came off. The mechanical engineering office – which in 1932 had unanimously voted for a four-day workweek rather than job losses – resumed work full-time.[6]

At the instigation of top management in late 1934 and early 1935, the office re-analyzed locomotive capabilities based on operational needs. A thought shared by Superintendent of Motive Power Russell Henley and Mechanical Engineer John Pilcher was that fewer engine classes might do the bulk of mainline work.

Implicitly there was an even more daring thought: Rather than a time to "hunker down" as every other railroad was doing, perhaps the Depression was a unique opportunity for the N&W to restructure its fleet. Expensive shopping of older engines, many standing idle and needing repairs of varying severity, could be avoided, while resources of money and shop capacity thus freed-up could be redirected to new construction. Assuming that hard times one day lifted, N&W could have a pruned and markedly upgraded fleet for the central trunk lines that its branches fed. As a piece of business sense, it was a remarkable approach.

In 1930, N&W operated 788 locomotives. In 1934 alone, 115 of those went under the torch, including 4-6-2s, some ancient 4-8-0s, and 37 Z-class 2-6-6-2s. In 1930 the fatter engine roster moved 40 million tons of coal; in 1940, a leaner and redirected roster of 572 would haul 45 million tons.[7] Every railroad inevitably improved its productivity per locomotive decade by decade, as newer, more powerful engines replaced older ones. N&W, however, made a dramatic such jump and simultaneously began the radical consolidation of its classes that reached such an obvious conclusion in the early 1950s.

There is continued speculation as to whether and how much the Pennsylvania Railroad might have affected N&W's business decisions. From 1901, when it bought up 39 percent of N&W stock, through the 1960s, the PRR owned a controlling interest in the N&W.[8] PRR appointees to the N&W board surely participated in strategic development. From the evidence of manifest practices, however, it is clear that Roanoke maintained a fierce independence in motive power and operations matters. PRR's long-standing policy of locomotive standardization, begun by Alexander Cassatt in the 1870s, perhaps influenced N&W's own approach to standardization in subtle ways. The design results, however, were starkly different, and the PRR was one of those companies whose Depression policy was simply to stop engine acquisitions and to weather the storm.[9]

John A. Pilcher was by all accounts an effective leader as well as a brilliant engineer. In the early 1930s he reported to Henley and supervised 22 people on the third floor of N&W's Motive Power Building in Roanoke: a chief draftsman, 19 holding the title of draftsman, and two "tracers." Many of the draftsmen were in fact engineers, and all of them participated in engineering design. The office kept close ties to Virginia Polytechnic Institute at Blacksburg; Alexander Kearney, who Henley succeeded as SMP in 1928, was a graduate. Kearney had instituted an unusual procedure for gathering wisdom from the field when design began on a new class. Once a preliminary specification had been drawn up, Kearney formally solicited the recommendations of master mechanics in the shops and of road foremen (head locomotive engineers in charge of engine crew training and promotion) in the operating department as to design features and details they wished to see incorporated or improved.[10] Pilcher supported that rather democratic process and continued it under Henley. According to Voyce Glaze, a Virginia Tech graduate who was a junior draftsman in 1934, Pilcher definitely ran the office but insisted that his group work as a team on major design issues. There were frequent meetings in which everyone was expected to contribute ideas. As detailed work was divided among the staff, he encouraged development of several alternative approaches to design problems. He insisted that his draftsmen take drawings of major parts at mid-stage out to shop and roundhouse staff for critique as to whether the part would be economical to make and maintain.[11] Loyalty among colleagues in the office was high. One has the sense that John Pilcher understood "quality circles" and "team play" long before such things became fashionable in the 1970s. Work on the Y6 and A classes began in late 1934.

ABOVE N&W Class Y2 2-8-8-2 No. 1700 was built in 1918.
Courtesy Kalmbach Media

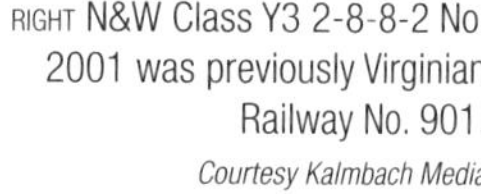

RIGHT N&W Class Y3 2-8-8-2 No. 2001 was previously Virginian Railway No. 901.
Courtesy Kalmbach Media

To better understand N&W's locomotive designs, a look at its demanding topography is helpful. Eastbound coal trains faced three daunting grades: Iaeger, W.Va., to Bluefield, Va.; Walton, Va., to Christiansburg; and Roanoke over Blue Ridge. East of Blue Ridge, Va., was high-speed track to Lynchburg and to tidewater at Norfolk. Westbound from the coal region between Walton and Williamson, grades were moderate, with fast track to Portsmouth and Columbus, Ohio. Coal trains on the different mainline sections needed either very high tractive effort and horsepower at around 15-25 mph, or high horsepower at 50 mph or more. General freight and merchandise trains, lighter than the coal trains, needed to make 30-40 mph up the grades and faster on the Piedmont and west of Williamson. Finally, mainline passenger trains had to be able to traverse any of the terrain effectively. Each of the Big Three was specifically matched to these requirements. As the number of Y-class 2-8-8-2s rose, mine runs were well taken care of by the 2-6-6-2s. The many local passenger trains and yard switching duties were done with much smaller engines, but again specific to those tasks.

The Y class, destined to dominate the slow, slogging role, began in 1910. Five Y1 engines, compound-expansion 2-8-8-2s, arrived from Baldwin that year. But a compound 2-6-6-2 design was then judged better sized to the average tonnage on mainline grades. N&W therefore acquired its large fleet of these from Alco's Richmond Works and from Baldwin beginning in 1912. In 1918 traffic had increased such that a revamped 2-8-8-2 was in order. Under Kearney, John Pilcher's team at that time worked up plans for a Y2. To keep cylinders from fouling lateral clearance limits, boiler pressure was set at 230 psi, unprecedented for a Mallet. The two inches thus shaved off the diameter of the low-pressure pistons (39 inches compared to the 41 then common in 16-drivered Mallets) also reduced the weight of the piston, helping dynamic balance. The higher pressure improved economy. Roanoke Shops turned out five, while Baldwin manufactured 20. Then came U.S. entry into World War I and the federal seizure of railroads by the USRA. John Pilcher found himself on the USRA locomotive design committee.[12]

N&W's proven Y2 became the basis of both USRA Mallets, the 2-6-6-2 as well as the 2-8-8-2. The two types shared a number of common parts; the USRA 2-8-8-2 followed the Y2 closely, with the same-size cylinders, a larger grate, similar combustion chamber, ten more psi of boiler pressure, and a five-inch smaller boiler diameter to keep weight at the desired axle loads. N&W itself bought 50 USRA duplicates in 1919 from Alco-Schenectady and Baldwin, calling them class Y3. The operating department was well satisfied. Alco-Richmond delivered 30 more Y3s in 1923-1924, while Roanoke Shops built six more Y2s with existing tooling, designating them as the Y2a subclass.

Roanoke Shops completed its expansion in 1927. N&W bought 10 heavier Y4s that year from Richmond, the last large steam locomotives the railroad did not produce for itself. Major improvements in the Y4 were the addition of feedwater heating, in the form of the Worthington BL open-type heater, and a boost to 270 psi boiler pressure, a benchmark step in pressure for a Mallet. In 1927 as well, Pilcher's staff did some reengineering for the Y2 and Y3 classes, and the shops started a program to raise the boiler pressure safely on those engines to 270 psi.

Another 101 Y-class engines were to come, beginning with 20 Y5s. Constructed in 1931-1932 as the nation's economy plummeted, they kept Roanoke Shops open on a drastically curtailed workweek. The Y5 went the limit on boiler pressure – 300 psi – and included two improvements intended to solve a Mallet's backpressure problems once and for all. The four valves on a Y's cylinders had always been equally sized at 14 inches in diameter, regarded as generous. In the Y5, the high-pressure valves stayed the same, but the low-pressure valves' diameter went to an unheard-of 18 inches, permitting enlarged ports and freer steam passage both in and out of the cylinders. To move these much heavier valves, the valve gear was beefed up. At the same time, based on experiments on a Y3, N&W designers completely rearranged the exhaust-steam piping from the low-pressure valve chests to the smokebox exhaust stand. What the designers called a "bridge pipe" provided a cross-connection of increased volume between the exhaust passages of both low-pressure chests, creating a large plenum. The swiveling pipe to the exhaust stand, also of increased internal size, connected at the bottom of the bridge. The effect was to remove restrictions and to approximately double the internal volume available to exhaust steam on its way to the smokebox.

BELOW N&W Class Y4 2-8-8-2 No. 2087. Built by Alco's Richmond, Va., works in 1927, the ten Y-4s were the last large steam locomotives built commercially for N&W.

Courtesy Kalmbach Media

BOTTOM N&W Class Y5 2-8-8-2 No. 2092, built at the railway's Roanoke, Va., shops.

Courtesy Kalmbach Media

The performance improvement was so good that Y3s were retrofitted during major machinery overhauls.

Specific drawings for the Y6 went ahead in 1935. The Y5s had shown themselves to be highly efficient – if they could be kept in repair. Parts of their conventionally fabricated frames, similar to those in all other Y classes, worked loose or broke under terrific forces amplified by the Y5's maximum starting tractive effort, raised to 152,200 lbs. from a Y4's 137,000. Top management approved Pilcher's proposal to add two quite expensive features to the Y6 design: one-piece, cast-steel frames and roller bearings. The goals were reduced maintenance and higher dependability. A new type of multiple-valve, commercially available front-end throttle was also included, to improve locomotive responsiveness to throttle changes. To fit the enlarged superheater header with throttle into the smokebox, but without extending the smokebox and thus interfering with necessary clearances around the bridge pipe and its connections, the stack was angled forward. This change is an example of the hundreds of such details which Pilcher and staff decided in collective meetings, with detailed work assigned to various individual members.

General Steel Castings provided the one-piece frames for the Y6, produced at its Granite City (Ill.) Works. Rather than a cast clone of a fabricated frame, a cast frame used boxed-in spaces to add rigidity without more weight, and added fillets of material at high-stress points. Roller bearings came from the Timken Co. A General Steel engineer and a Timken engineer worked with the staff in Roanoke. The high initial costs for these components soon proved their economic worth in fewer breakdowns and in higher engine utilization.[13] Roanoke shopmen made the initial five Y6s in 1936, the first completed in September, with 35 produced through 1940.[14]

Hand in hand with the Y6, N&W designers considered an altogether new freight locomotive in 1934-35, one that would put the N&W in the forefront of American railroads in ton-miles-per-train-hour productivity. The new design was the A-class, a single-expansion 2-6-6-4.

The Seaboard Air Line Railway (SAL) acquired five 2-6-6-4s, then a new wheel arrangement, from Baldwin in 1935. These were high-speed locomotives with the remarkably light axle-loading of 27½ tons on each driver pair. They had demonstrated a propensity to move freight at passenger-train speeds, with enough tractive force to move a train normally handled by a pair of light 2-8-2s. SAL, a relatively small carrier, ordered five more in 1937. Locomotive designers usually anticipated new wheel arrangements years in advance of their realization. No one needed to suggest the 2-6-6-4 plan to Roanoke. The success of the first five SAL engines must nevertheless have added to Pilcher's confidence as his design work progressed.

The reduced backpressure of the Y5 showed that a Mallet compound need not be altogether slow.[15] Without a train or downhill with one, the Y5s (and Y6s) ran easily at 50 mph, blistering for a Mallet. Their 58-inch-diameter drivers, however, were sized for piston speeds and steam flow to give maximum horsepower at 20-25 mph on the three tough eastbound grades to the summits at Bluefield, Christiansburg, and Blue Ridge. The A class, on the other hand, was intended for highest horsepower at 30-60 mph – with emphasis on the latter speed. To run that fast at maximum power, compound steam locomotives with three or more cylinders needed all valves

TOP N&W Class Y6 2-8-8-2 No. 2137, near Christiansburg, Va., in June 1953.

Courtesy Kalmbach Media

ABOVE N&W Class Y6b 2-8-8-2 No. 2197.

Courtesy Kalmbach Media

and cylinders to cycle in perfect concert on one set of inter-connected driving wheels so that valve timing for all cylinders could be synchronized. In a Mallet, pressure in the receiver (from high-pressure exhaust to low-pressure inlet) could vary in unpredictable ways, since the two engine units were independent.[16] For the four-cylinder articulated arrangement, high-speed steam utilization was effective only with simple expansion.

By having a truly high-speed articulated, N&W could vastly improve operations in western West Virginia, in Ohio, and east of Blue Ridge to Norfolk. Through trains of coal would not need to be broken down nor engines doubleheaded, and train speeds could be raised significantly. The result would be to handle greater traffic flow with fewer locomotives. That N&W invested in this notion in the economic trough of the 1930s reflected a degree of forward thinking that would have been a credit to any American corporation. That the company's shop workers benefited from the resulting employment was not lost on anyone at N&W either. Together with a policy for all employees that attempted to keep furloughs limited, a pioneering safety program begun in 1912 that reduced injuries far below the norm, and its practice of seeking employee input on new design, the human result for N&W was a high level of employee loyalty – probably among the highest on any American railroad.[17]

N&W Class A 2-6-6-4 No. 1212.
Courtesy Kalmbach Media

For the high-speed power curve desired for the A-class, Pilcher and company chose a 70-inch driver diameter, within an inch of the Seaboard engine. Similarity to SAL ended there. Cylinders, grate, combustion chamber, boiler diameter, heating surfaces – all were made far bigger. Boiler pressure was put at 275 psi, compared to the SAL's modest 230, with the A's boiler shell plate thickness chosen to accommodate 300 psi, within the ICC boiler-pressure safety factor of 4.0.[18] Weight on drivers increased from the SAL's 165 tons to 215 tons, a 30-percent jump. Axle load became just under 36 tons, which N&W's heavy mainline rail, mostly 130- and 131-lbs. per yard, could well tolerate. Everything the N&W design staff had learned in the previous decades about steam flow and steam utilization was brought to bear, such as long lap valves set to run at 75 percent maximum cutoff. Cast-steel frame, roller bearings, front-end throttle, running gear and suspension improvements – and suggestions from blue-collar staff – were included.

A component worth describing is the N&W approach to exhaust and boiler drafting. N&W's "waffle iron" steam exhaust-jet arrangement was unique to that railroad. Pilcher had studied all the literature on drafting and exhaust, including William Kiesel's "star" nozzle used on the PRR. The N&W design, perfected over several years of experiments, was a blend of conventional jet and multiple nozzles that in some ways anticipated the Giesl exhaust (Chapter 21). The several openings around the circumference of the "waffle iron" created jets of steam that better sealed the stack from air "leakage" (counterflows of air) down its internal wall. A somewhat larger total cross-sectional area of jets and stack reduced the amount of backpressure for a given amount of draft generated through the flues.

The first two Class As emerged from Roanoke Shops in May 1936. By the end of the year they had proven to be all that the N&W staff had hoped for, and more. In road trials with a dynamometer car conducted by the testing staff of N&W Engineer of Tests Robert M. Pilcher (John's son), the A recorded 6,300 drawbar horsepower at around 45 mph. Likely this was a short-duration figure, since the railroad later put the A's sustained dbhp at 5,300 at 40-45, implying an indicated (cylinder) hp of about 5,800 at such speeds. Any of those numbers was sensational and the highest yet set by any four-cylinder locomotive. Better still, the locomotive was able to sustain more than 5,000 dbhp at any speed between 25 and 60 mph. The engine could easily reach 75, track and trailing load permitting, with no riding instabilites. The front unit behaved well and caused no crew complaints as to undue "hunting" or slipping.[19]

Eight more As rolled out in 1937, as did two additional Y6s. From 1938 (in which a sharp economic dip countered optimism about the Depression ending soon) through 1940, the shops concentrated on new Y6s and the rebuilding of 19 Y5s with cast-steel frames and roller bearings. In September

1941, N&W operated 54 engines of Y6 standard and ten As, in addition to the many Y2s, Y3s, and Y4s. Z1a 2-6-6-2s and a variety of other locomotives (including the famous little 4-8-0s for branchline locals, 4-6-2s for secondary passenger trains on the main line, 4-8-2s for heavy passenger and fast-freight duty, and yard switchers) rounded out the list, all in good repair.

That September, Roanoke had five more engines in various stages of construction. The first – with a spectacular "bullet" nose and a red stripe down each skirted side – came forth in October. This was the first J-class 4-8-4. Simply as a 4-8-4, the new J was hardly noteworthy. Its specific features, however, caught the attention of the railroading community.

The design staff evidently began planning for the J about 1937, but the slump of 1938 put things off. When revenues rebounded somewhat in 1939, work resumed. N&W had considered a 4-8-4 in the mid-1920s, a proposed class-N with low, 63-inch-diameter driving wheels for freight and passenger work on the railroad's demanding grades.[20] That idea had been part of the process that turned into ten K3 4-8-2s in 1926.

In the 1920s, locomotive designers generally were beginning to understand the contribution of furnace volume to boiler power. Instead of either a 4-8-4 or a 2-8-4 for higher horsepower, Pilcher's office created in the K3 an engine with increased furnace volume from a 4-foot-long combustion chamber and a grate area of 85 square feet, in contrast to the bigger grate and lack of a combustion chamber in the Lima A-1 2-8-4. N&W had access to the finest, high-BTU coal, which could release just as much heat per hour as lesser coal on the Lima's grate. The K3 carried an engine weight similar to the A-1 on the same number of axles, but with a better-tracking four-wheel lead truck up front.

The K3 was a flop.[21] The design difficulty was not because of the K3's free-steaming boiler. The engines ran roughly at any decent speed, nosing side-to-side and pounding vertically. Their 63-inch drivers (the same size as the A-1's), combined with their long and heavy main rods connected to the third driver-pair, contributed to an imbalance of pistons, rods, and counterweights. (See Chapter 4.) With little room in the small but heavily cast drivers, the engines were apparently underbalanced – that is, there was insufficient room for enough lead weights to properly balance the reciprocating masses. The problem must have been more complex, however, because attempts at obvious corrective strategies helped only partly.[22]

The design staff never forgot the lesson of the K3s. It was a classic situation of failure leading to path-breaking success later. When the new J was being planned, the staff knew that relatively small-diameter drivers would be needed for highest horsepower at 40-50 mph. N&W's mountains imposed that limitation. Yet in the Piedmont and in Ohio, a front-rank passenger

N&W Class J 4-8-4 No. 600 rolled out of Roanoke Shops in October 1941.

Courtesy Kalmbach Media

Decades before its second career in excursion service, N&W Class J 4-8-4 No. 611 leads a train beside the New River. *Norfolk & Western*

engine should be able to roll at 80. This combination of speeds had never before been well tolerated by any single steam design.

John Pilcher had retired in December 1938. His successor as head mechanical engineer was H.W. Reynolds. Gordon McGavock, a senior draftsman in the early 1930s, had become chief draftsman (number two in the mechanical engineering department) in 1936. Most of the staff had begun under Pilcher. Exactly how the approach to the J was conceived by the restructured team isn't known, but the decisions the designers made resulted in a locomotive whose performance ranked among the best 4-8-4s. Doubtless the staff studied every treatise on wheel and machinery balance available. They were not about to repeat the mistakes in the K3. So in its perverse way the K3 helped lead to the J.

The J's boiler was derived from that for the A-class. The J's boiler was so big that concave slots had to be provided in the lower portion of the boiler jacketing over the third and fourth drivers so the wheels would have room to move vertically. Overall boiler size exceeded any other 4-8-4 and exceeded that of a Y6. As in the A, boiler pressure was first set at 275 psi and later raised to 300. The design team responded to N&W's stress on serviceability by incorporating an enlarged system of automatic pressure lubrication to 220 points in its roller-bearing-equipped machinery, with oil reservoirs good for 1,300 miles. The As and many Y6s were retrofitted with such systems.

Of all 4-8-4s, only the New York Central S-1a Niagara and the N&W J-class exceeded 5,000 drawbar horsepower in well-documented tests. Their published drawbar horsepowers are close at about 5,200, peaking in the J at 45-50 mph and in the S-1a at 65; the speed difference was due to their significant differences in driver size, piston speed, and steam evaporation and flow at the given speeds. Its dynamic balance characteristics made the J truly amazing to locomotive designers. Driver-size selected was the same as for the A: 70 inches. In a test in 1944 on tires worn to 68½ inches diameter, a J hit 110 mph.[23] A PRR T-1 or a Milwaukee Road F-7 could do 110 mph or more but on slower-turning 80-inch and 84-inch drivers respectively. At the speed attained, the J's machinery was spinning at 540 rpm. (The centrifugal and other forces involved rise proportional to the square of speed. Any rotative imbalance – the so-called "dynamic augment" – in a wheel at 50 mph becomes four times worse at 100.[24]) Locomotive drivers of 70-inch diameter or less rarely ran at more than 400 rpm. The K3's imbalance was severe at less than 200 rpm; the well-balanced A at 65 mph was turning at just over 310 rpm. The J's achievement marked something new in two-cylinder balancing.

The secret was actually no secret in principle. The laws of motion and force were not repealed. The J's drivers had an utter minimum of overbalance mass added to the counterweights, probably about 50 lbs. or less in any wheel, with perhaps less in the main driver. Even with lightweight reciprocating parts, including the J's alloy-steel Timken rods, the J's overbalance was much less than would have been added using then-accepted rules.[25] All revolving masses were therefore in excellent balance, with comparatively little dynamic augment at high rpm. The unavoidable penalty was less balance for the reciprocating parts. The designers decided to pay for that reciprocating imbalance by changing the lateral resistance in lead and trailing trucks.

By altering rocker and lateral-device geometry to provide higher-resistance centering in both trucks, the whole locomotive was made extremely stiff longitudinally, absorbing the reciprocating imbalances. The most lateral resistance was in the lead truck, per usual practice, so that the rear truck's force in sideward deflection didn't entirely counteract the leading wheels in easing the drivers into curves. The lead truck's initial lateral resistance was probably 50 percent or more of the weight on the truck, or about 45,000 lbs., though the actual figure is not known.[26] Lateral cushioning devices were used across the driving-axle boxes. As expected, the J did not like sharp curves in yard track or on branchlines. Occasional derailments on substandard yard tracks occurred. But the J ran wonderfully on straight track and on mainline curves. With 15-car trains like the *Pocahontas* or the streamlined *Powhatan Arrow*, the relatively small-diameter drivers exerted high power for mountain climbs and yet could spin smoothly at 80 mph on the flats.

The attack on Pearl Harbor wrenched the nation before the fifth J was finished in January 1942. The designs and tooling for the railroad's three new locomotive classes were complete, however, and the N&W geared up to produce them at an accelerated rate from 1942. (Roanoke built 16 copies of an improved Y6a that year, 25 more As in 1943 and 1944, and six Js without streamlined shrouding in 1943 – the shrouding was put on after war's end.) As on all railroads throughout the country, traffic demands stretched resources. N&W's coal tonnage rose from 38½ million tons in 1939 to 54 million tons by 1943. N&W's revenue tonnage of all freight – coal, merchandise, and military shipments – shot up from 48 million tons in 1939 to 71½ million tons in 1944. The number of passengers multiplied from one million in 1939 to five million in 1944; passenger-miles increased more than ten-fold.[27]

Postwar coal strikes cut tonnages in 1946, but coal traffic rebounded to higher levels in 1947-48 than at any time during the war. Passenger traffic fell off rapidly. N&W kept up its steam locomotive production, building eight more As in 1949-1950, 30 of the Y6b variant between 1948 and 1952, and a final three Js in 1950. A Y6b tested at 5600 drawbar hp at 25 mph – 300 more than an A at 40. The Y6b produced its power at the highest thermal efficiency of any production-model steam locomotive ever to run in North

"Lubritoriums" at key locations on the N&W system ensured that the company's well-designed steam locomotives were readily maintained to a high standard.
Courtesy Kalmbach Media

America, proving the economic wisdom of compound expansion.[28] Roanoke wasn't done making steam engines, however; the shops turned out 45 0-8-0 switchers from 1951 through 1953 after buying 30 from the C&O in 1948 (no doubt cheaply). Meanwhile, in 1947, 90 percent of orders for new locomotives to other U.S. railroads were for diesels, with no steam orders to the major commercial builders after 1948. Railroaders elsewhere shook their heads at N&W's switcher acquisitions especially. Compared to steam, diesel switching locomotives had persuasively established their unassailable economies in fuel and maintenance for all to see in the late 1930s and early '40s.

But the N&W operated its steam fleet in a manner unlike any other railroad in the world. Rather than stick with time-consuming practices in roundhouses and at fueling stops, N&W studied its infrastructural arrangements carefully. Right after the war, it designed and erected four revamped servicing stations at the engine terminals in Williamson, W.Va., Shaffers Crossing in Roanoke, Portsmouth, Ohio, and Bluefield, W.Va., with a smaller one at Pulaski, Va. In assembly-line style, support crews at each of these places added fuel and water to tenders, sand to sand domes, cleaned fires and dropped ashes, pressure-washed the locomotives (much of this work done simultaneously), and then ran the engines into a special, newly built two-track shed N&W

called a "lubritorium." There, several men topped off lube-oil reservoirs and injected grease to numerous fittings. Mechanics did minor repairs at the same time, and, in a later refinement, boiler water was entirely replaced with fresh, heated water (a tactic to cut internal boiler scaling and corrosion). The whole affair was distinctly comparable to a "Jiffy Lube." But far larger and more complex vehicles than autos moved through, and N&W's service centers were conceived and established in the seemingly archaic 1940s.[29]

A typical J ran more than 15,000 miles per month and accumulated more than 230,000 miles before machinery repairs were needed. At that rate, and accounting for other downtime, a J could go nearly 700,000 miles before boiler teardown and internal inspection, as required by the ICC after 48 months of continuous service. The As posted somewhat smaller numbers since average speeds were slower due to the heavy tonnages they moved. The As and Y6s hauled 11,000 to 13,000-ton trains, with Y6s in pusher duty on the steepest climbs. The As ran free with those huge trains at 50 mph downgrade and up to 65 mph on the long, gentler stretches to Norfolk and Columbus.

In 1952 the N&W invited a competitive test to compare an A, a Y6b, and a four-unit General Motors/EMD F7 freight diesel in haulage capacity and fuel costs between Portsmouth and Bluefield. The EMD representatives were ecstatic; here was a chance to take on the last bastion of steam in the U.S. The test was a bit rigged on both sides, however. Information that came to light long after the test was publicly described revealed that EMD engineers had adjusted the diesel engines in their four-unit set to put out 6,800 hp rather than the nominal 6,000. Like Southern stock-car racers, the Roanoke people were not above some mechanical ploys, either. Their two steam locomotives operated at 315 psi, their frames had extra lead ballast, and the A had its cylinders and driver tires "re-trued," which somehow added a quarter-inch

In a gathering of giants, N&W Class Y6b Nos. 2189, 2176, and 2188 await assignments at Grundy, W. Va.

Bruce Meyer, Courtesy Kalmbach Media

to the cylinder diameter (with specially cut new rings) and removed a half-inch from the drivers' diameter. These modifications improved low-speed drawbar pull – a few percent for the Y6 and perhaps nine percent for the A.[30]

The runoff, conducted in September, was a virtual tie. Running times with similar tonnages were almost identical. Only pennies – and sometimes tenths of pennies – per thousand ton-miles separated diesel and steam in fuel costs. Interestingly, the diesels shaved more fuel cost the steeper the grade, probably reflecting the high carbon loss of steamers as their boilers worked harder at lower speeds. Not regarded in the tests were long-term maintenance costs, which N&W felt were similar, as shown by conventional but antiquated ICC accounting rules, which had little to do with modern cost-accounting.

In 1955, the N&W philosophy of engine standardization and sophisticated servicing reached its highest economic performance before diesels became a factor, with just 441 steam locomotives moving nearly all trains. Coal originated was 52 million tons. (Compare to 1930: 788 locomotives and 40 million tons.) N&W employees were confident that steam would still predominate on their railroad for a decade or more, even if antiquated steam-maintenance practices and a hodge-podge of engines had hastened a capitulation to diesels by the mid-1950s on other lines.

Exactly three years to the month after the EMD/steam contest, diesels began coming to N&W, first as a trickle and then, in 1957, by the hundred. Through the spring of 1958 a "dieselized" 240-mile branch showed per-ton-mile locomotive costs – including labor, applicable overheads, and all repairs – slashed by almost a third.[31] Fuel costs were only part of the story, especially compared to shop and roundhouse labor. The intensely loyal employees of N&W throughout its system, and the citizens of Roanoke, faced the prospect of enormous change.

Chapter 20 Notes

1. John Szarkowski, quoted in *The Washington Post*, March 18, 1984, p. L6 (continued from p. L1). Rail buffs have appreciated Link's work in his well-publicized photography and sound recordings since the early 1960s. The actress Diane Keaton was said to have helped in Link's "discovery" by the art and photography *cognoscenti* in the 1980s. Link's exhibition in the mid-1980s, titled *Ghost Trains*, was shown in New York, London, Washington, and other cities. A 1987 book of Link photographs, *America's Last Steam Railroad – Steam, Steel & Stars* (text by Tim Hensley and afterword by Thomas Garver) describes Link's methods. Link died in 2001, and a museum in his honor has been established in the Norfolk & Western's "hometown" of Roanoke, Va.
2. E.F. Pat Striplin, *The Norfolk & Western: A History* (N&W Historical Society, revised ed., 1997), p. 124.
3. Philip Atkins, *Dropping the Fire* (Irwell Press, U.K., 1999), p. 24.
4. Quoted in ibid., p. 25.
5. Striplin (Note 2), pp. 42, 46, 111.
6. Ibid., pp. 92-93; Ed King, *The A: Norfolk & Western's Mercedes of Steam* (Trans-Anglo, 1991), pp. 37, 56. Net income (profit) in 1936 was $33 million, the highest of the 1930s. (Next to 1932, the worst year was 1938 at $20 million; the latter figure was a sharp drop of ⅓ from that of the previous year, due to the late-1930s recession before World War II.)
7. Locomotive aggregate numbers and coal tonnages from Striplin (Note 2), pp. 91, 92, 101-02. Scrapping in 1934 from King (Note 6), p. 55. The 286 M-class 4-8-0s of 1906-12 and the 190 Z1 and Z1a engines of 1912-18 were the largest classes N&W owned.
8. Striplin (Note 2), pp. 70, 147-48.
9. The giant PRR developed no new engines for production between 1930 and 1941, relying instead on its locomotive legions built at Altoona in the 'Teens and '20s, most of which

were relatively young in age at the onset of the Depression. (Discussion in Chapter 9.)

10. King (Note 6), p. 30.
11. Ibid., pp. 34-37. King's description of the office is based on several interviews with former members.
12. King, p. 34; George H. Drury, *A Guide to North American Steam Locomotives* (Kalmbach Books, 1993) p. 299. Data in Drury and in Ron Rosenberg and Eric Archer, *Norfolk & Western Steam (The Last 25 Years)*, Quadrant Press, 1973, which compiles official N&W roster information. The Y4 class was first designated as Y3b; the Y5 as Y4a.
13. See King, pp. 52 ff., and Chapter 12.3.
14. Rosenberg and Archer (Note 12), p. 41.
15. See Chapter 5 for a discussion of speed and compounding.
16. See Chapter 5. Underway, Mallet cylinders tended to get "in step" over time as small slippages accumulated in either engine unit, while pressure variations in the receiver slightly affected the tractive force developed by the front pistons. Without a mechanical linkage between the units, however, performance of the front unit at any given piston stroke was impossible to predict precisely.
17. Testimony of numerous former N&W employees, as gathered, *e.g.*, by the Virginia Museum of Transportation (established at Roanoke in the 1960s).
18. "Safety Factor" for a boiler is its bursting strength, expressed as a multiple of the boiler's designed working pressure. Effective in 1923, the ICC "*Rules & Instructions for Inspection ... of Locomotive Boilers ...*" set the minimum factor at 4.0. When the ICC regulation was first promulgated in 1912 (Chapter 8), the minimum factor was set at 3.25. Earlier, 3.0 was common and such engines had to have their boiler pressure lowered. The larger the boiler diameter, the higher the working pressure, and/or the higher the safety factor, the thicker must be the boiler plate. A working pressure of 275 psi, under ICC regulation effective in 1923, required a bursting pressure no less than 1100 psi anywhere in the boiler. 300 psi required a 1200-psi bursting pressure, which was the design parameter for the A's boiler.
19. . King, pp. 99.
20. Drawing in Ibid., p. 165.
21. Cf. Pilcher's 16 very successful, home-built K1s of 1916, which helped make his reputation, and the N&W's 22 USRA K2s from Alco-Brooks and Baldwin of 1919-1923, which also performed well.
22. Balance problems in King, pp. 30-31. The ten K3s served (their speed usually limited by their balance problems to 30 mph or so) until 1944, when N&W sold them at bargain prices to two roads stressed by wartime traffic and short of motive power. Denver & Rio Grande Western bought six, and Richmond, Fredericksburg & Potomac bought four.
23. Atkins, p. 24.
24. Ralph P. Johnson (Baldwin Locomotive Works), *The Steam Locomotive* (Simmons-Boardman, 1945 ed.), Chap. 16, pp. 275-79.
25. Ibid., Chap. 16, pp. 266-69.
26. According to an N&W engineer who worked on the A-class, the initial lateral resistance of that design's two-wheel lead truck was 30 percent of the vertical load on the truck. Thus on a four-wheel truck, a lateral resistance of 50 percent of the weight on the truck would be taken by two flanges on each side of the truck, or 25 percent on each flange. Using the same lateral-to-vertical ratio (in current terminology, the L/V ratio) as for the A, a J's lead truck may have had a resistance of 60 percent.

    When diesels finally bumped the Js off mainline trains in the late 1950s, Js were found to be hopeless on branch lines and were retired before the last As and Y6s.
27. Striplin, pp. 92, 102.
28. In a personal communication to the author in 1970, former N&W motive-power superintendent Clarence E. Pond put the Y6b's thermal efficiency at eight percent. This figure may seem modest, but it would result in a fuel economy 33 percent better than a thermal efficiency of six percent, which is about the best ever achieved by a simple-expansion engine. The Y6b variant had a Worthington SA open-type feedwater heater and a "booster" valve that allowed the engineman, when underway in compound-working, to admit superheated steam at reduced pressure directly from the boiler to the low-pressure cylinders for added tractive force. That device required lead ballast added in the front-unit frame, so that its drivers wouldn't slip at the shot of extra steam.
29. *Railway Age*, October 11, 1947, pp. 56(610)-59(613).
30. Atkins, pp. 24-25; King, pp. 96-98.
31. *Railway Age*, April 1958.

Chapter 21

Resisting the Revolution

BY THE MID-1930S, IT WAS EVIDENT TO most motive-power experts that the steam locomotive's century-old place in railroading was deeply threatened. A popular view today is that there was widespread recalcitrance in the face of change or a failure of imagination in sticking too long with an old, reliable technology. Such a view is uninformed. In fact, designers, their employers, and their customers could well imagine a world without the old ways. Spirited discussions on such thoughts filled the trade press.

The press was a mirror to industry concerns. There was a broadly shared perception that change was fast approaching. As usual, though, no one had a monopoly on accurate prediction. Response by suppliers, worried about their markets, took a variety of forms. As we saw in Chapter 17, both Baldwin and Alco offered diesel locomotives in the 1930s. Of the three major steam suppliers, only Lima – the smallest and the most severely drained financially by the Depression – put all its limited resources into research on reciprocating steam in the late 1930s and early 1940s. Baldwin teamed with Westinghouse and diesel-engine maker De La Vergne; Alco purchased diesel-engine builder McIntosh & Seymour in 1931, and teamed with General Electric. Designers considered other alternatives as well. It was not imprudent to think that, if an alternative kind of locomotive was to be economic in the long term, perhaps it should make some use of the huge investment that railroads already had in the steam infrastructure: fuel provisioning, shop facilities, and skilled labor. A total and complete overthrow of that infrastructure, when railroads were so thin on investment capital, was certainly the hardest thing to conceive.[1]

Throughout the second half of the 1930s, railroads received reams of good publicity as new or revamped streamliners and their locomotives debuted before an interested public. Some of these trains were diesel-powered, and reporters avidly remarked how exciting they seemed to be; they represented a ray of hope to a nation striving to recover from hard times. These new trains, emblematic of optimism, were clean, colorful, fast, shaped like nothing before, and – if diesel – almost smokeless. The shock of the new, in many ways, looked like a big plus to railroad managers.

Chesapeake & Ohio Class M-1 steam-turbine-electric locomotive No. 501, near Afton, Va., in July 1948.
August A. Thieme, Courtesy Kalmbach Media

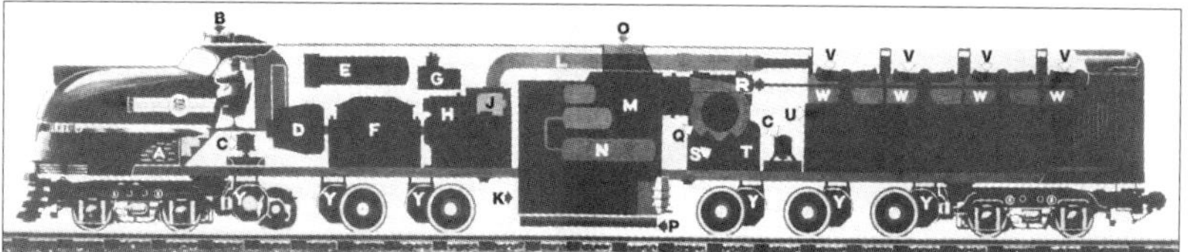

General Electric completed two "Steamotive" oil-fired steam-turbine-electric locomotives in 1938. Over the next five years they were evaluated by Union Pacific, New York Central, and Great Northern. Mechanical components shown in the cutaway rendering include water tanks (A); traction-motor blowers (C); air-conditioning alternator (D); train-heating evaporator (E); main generators (F); reduction gear (H); main turbine (J); boiler (M); feedwater heater (N); boiler draft fan (Q); condenser fan turbine (R); feedwater pump (S); boiler auxiliary set turbine (T); fuel tanks (U); air-cooled condensers (W); and traction motors (Y). *Courtesy Kalmbach Media*

In the midst of this, another experimental locomotive appeared. It looked like a contemporary diesel but it ran on steam. It was an oil-fired, steam turbine-electric. It had been suggested not by a railroad but by a railroad supplier. Nevertheless the railroad concerned was an enthusiastic partner and agreed to underwrite road testing on its system.

The Union Pacific Railroad and General Electric began cooperating in 1936 on the locomotive's development. The leading maker of high-efficiency stationary boilers, Babcock & Wilcox, and a firm specializing in automatic controls, the Bailey Meter Co., also participated. A few years before then, GE had considered the marketability of compact electrical generating units, with the steam and electrical gear packaged together, and having outputs of between 1,000 and 10,000 horsepower. Such relatively lightweight packaged units could incorporate the latest steam technology from stationary practice, it could be oil-fired for convenience, and it could be appropriate in many industrial uses. A locomotive was high on the list of such possible applications, for which use the concept got a name: the "Steamotive" Unit.[2]

At GE's Schenectady, N.Y., plant, the company completed a boiler-turbine-generator unit for tests in late 1934. After Union Pacific signed on, GE completed a prototype locomotive at its Erie, Pa., facility in January 1938. It was a streamlined, chrome-trimmed unit rated at 2,500 horsepower, the first of two identical such units intended to operate back-to-back (in later diesel locomotive terminology, as an "A-A" set, the "A" denoting units with cabs, as opposed to cabless boosters, or "B" units). To support its weight of 274 tons, each unit carried ten axles, arranged on two "4-6-0" articulated subframes in the style of many straight-electric locomotives. Within each subframe, electric motors drove the three major axles; a two-axle lead truck served to spread weight and to perform a guiding function. Accommodating all the electrical-generation gear – semi-flash boiler, fuel tank, turbine and generator set, air-cooled condenser, hot well, water tank, auxiliaries, and crew cab – meant that each unit was more than 85 feet long between coupler faces, close to the maximum that permitted passage around the sharp curves found in most yards without sideswiping something.

The boiler was nothing like those ever used before on locomotives. It was generically a water-tube type, but bore no resemblance to the water-tube fireboxes tried on several North American railroads.[3] In the Steamotive boiler, Babcock & Wilcox engineers included all the thermodynamic features that characterized stationary plants: an air preheater and an economizer to heat feedwater (both of these devices recovering heat from exhaust gases), high steam pressure (1,500 psi), and high superheat (to a total steam temperature of 900-1,000° F). The boiler was a "flashwall" type (a watertube boiler in which the tubes are so hot that water flashes instantly to steam), laid horizontally to fit on a locomotive, with five feedwater-to-steam evaporative circuits which also formed the walls of the furnace – floor, sides, and roof, together with two loops forming a boiler "screen." The superheater tube banks were in the upper part of the furnace. Air was supplied to the furnace not by induced draft but by a blower, delivering combustion air at 450 to 500 degrees out of the air heater at boosted pressure. Dampers controlled airflow to regulate excess air to about 15 percent at high boiler output, so that high combustion efficiency was maintained with minimum carbon loss. Such a boiler, when hot, responded relatively quickly to wide swings in steam demand. When cold, the boiler could be brought up to full working pressure in ten minutes.

Automatic controls for fuel, feedwater, and combustion-air rates were cleverly designed. These three rates were made proportional to steam output. A small auxiliary turbine drove a shaft which, in turn, drove the "auxiliary set" – fuel pump; five-cylinder, piston-type feedwater pump; centrifugal air compressor; and lube oil pump. Critically important was that water feed rate, at any steam output, ensured an excess of water coming out of the evaporative circuits. In a flash-type boiler, this spillover assured that all furnace surfaces were always wet. (Such spillover water went into the bottom of a separating drum, which was essentially the steam dome. From the drum, saturated boiler steam passed to the superheater banks.) For the Steamotive unit, feedwater rate was governed in two ways: proportional to steam output and, at a minimum, to maintain a fixed water level in the separating drum "regardless of variations in steam or water pressure, feed-pump efficiency [e.g., leakage], or other variables."[4] In the event of low water in the drum or other emergency, fuel was automatically shut off to the burner, protecting the boiler.

The locomotive went into trial service on Union Pacific in March 1938, pulling a test train from Omaha, Neb., to Los Angeles and return. Up the 2.2 percent grade to California's Cajon Pass with 1,000 tons behind it, the two-unit, 5,000-hp Steamotive could make 22 mph, and on level stretches it could cruise at 90 or more. After a few months running on UP, sometimes pulling the *Challenger* and other long-distance trains, the railroad sent the engines on a publicity tour. (Assigning the turbines to the *Challenger* is significant: It had a demanding schedule, but it was an all-coach train that wasn't targeted at the road's business customers.) Various mechanical ailments caused UP to return the engines to GE in 1939. The units ran also on the New York Central and, in 1943, on Great Northern.[5]

In some respects, operating characteristics were good. Dynamic braking through the axle-hung electric motors controlled speed downhill, which no steam locomotive had ever been able to do. Each boiler could supply all the steam needed for locomotive power and steam heat for passenger cars, generating more than 22,000 pounds of steam per hour, at 375,000 BTU per cubic foot of furnace volume. The design maximum steam rate of 21,000 pounds per hour to produce 2,500 horsepower at the main turbine in each unit (or 42,000 pounds per hour to produce 5,000 horsepower in the locomotive pair) showed that, when its main turbine was running steadily at its optimal speed, the Steamotive was roughly two to two-and-a-half times more efficient than a conventional, reciprocating steamer in turning steam into mechanical power.[6]

In other respects, there were some apparently intractable problems. The flashwall boiler was a bit delicate for the shocks and jolts of railroad duty, and it developed leaks. The condenser performed well but also developed leaks, causing unplanned losses of water from the closed evaporation-condensation loop. When that happened, makeup water – which needed to be chemically treated to prevent scale formation – had to be added earlier than scheduled on a given run. When such unplanned servicing occurred, timetables went in the trashbasket.[7]

Aside from maintenance headaches, there were distinct performance limitations that would bedevil all steam turbines. When GE glowingly discussed the boiler's ability to follow swings in power demand, not mentioned was the loss of efficiency of the main turbine when it was not operating within a tight range of rpm. When the turbine could operate very close to design rpm and steam flow rate, it was very efficient in extracting the most mechanical work from a given quantity of steam. At higher rpm (seldom) or at any lower rpm (often), the turbine lost efficiency. At medium steam output from the boiler, with medium power in the traction motors, and with turbine rpm therefore below optimal, overall fuel and steam usage rates were poor.

Turbine limitations

There is a fundamental reason for these inefficiencies. The Steamotive and all the steam turbines to follow were affected, as were all the gas turbines that Union Pacific operated in the 1960s and 1970s. The utility of turbines in high-horsepower applications on railroads is always debated, so it is important to review this inherent problem briefly.

Turbine blades cannot change pitch or shape. Blades are designed and shaped in order to deliver the desired horsepower to the turbine shaft at highest efficiency. By nature, turbines are extremely efficient at converting gas flow into mechanical energy, but only when they're running at their design rpm, often termed "full rpm," but not at other times. As any pilot can testify, jet engines – gas turbines – guzzle fuel when the engines run at less or more than their designed cruising rpm. This limitation is endemic to turbines, and it explains why such engines are well-suited to aircraft and ocean-going vessels, which cruise for hours at a more-or-less constant speed, but not to locomotives, which encounter speed restrictions, changing topography, etc.

It is important to remember that torque is not the same as power. A gas turbine can "spool up" rapidly, albeit with high fuel consumption. A steam turbine turning a shaft can produce high torque at low rpm, but with a great waste of steam. Full horsepower is reached at about 90 percent of full rpm and best efficiency at 100 percent rpm. A steam or gas turbine makes a superlative power source when it can operate at a fixed, steady output for long periods – such as in a stationary power plant, in a ship at sea, or in a commercial airplane. In such uses, turbines can run at optimal rpm and load for 90 percent or more of their working lives.[8]

Most locomotives spend their lives in a radically different environment. On a given trip, speed and power must be set for various durations at many different levels, dictated by track speed limits or curves (say, 30, 45, 70, or 90 mph, as fixed by employees' timetable for various subsections of line or as governed by signals en route). Accelerations and decelerations are frequent. Between required speed changes, an engineman attempts to maintain a steady speed on each part of the line. But the grade varies considerably and almost continually along almost any section of main line. A train might encounter a one percent upgrade for a mile, then .3 percent up for two miles, .3 percent down for a mile, and .5 percent up for three miles. As grade varies, an engineman holds train speed within a tight range, varying throttle and air brake as necessary.[9] Downhill there is little opportunity to "sling-shot" for climbs ahead; speed can't exceed the track limit, even downhill. (In fact, braking rules for heavy trains may require less than the speed permissible for lighter trains down the same hill.) Uphill, with a train of capacity tonnage, a locomotive may be a struggle to maintain even drag speed. A locomotive may work 80 percent of its time at maximum power on a steep upgrade trip, but only 20 percent of its time at top power on a trip over a relatively moderate low-grade line. Then, to complicate matters further, train weight varies considerably from day to day, even as required speeds and the prevailing grades on various sections stay the same.

In such an environment, it is no accident that "positive displacement" engines – *i.e.*, piston engines, whether steam or diesel – have prevailed since the early 19th century. Piston engines have much lower efficiency at designed maximum output than a turbine, but a piston engine sustains its moderate efficiency over a much wider range of rpm and power output. And a piston engine responds much more quickly to changes in power demand. That characteristic, rapid response, is critical for a good locomotive.

The type of transmission can ameliorate part, but only part, of getting a turbine's output to the rail within its narrow optimal rpm range. In a reciprocating steamer, the transmission is "direct," and changes to cutoff are the way steam flow is matched to different power requirements at different speeds. The steam engine's piston-and-cylinder design keeps its comparatively poor efficiency over an extremely wide range of rpm and power, such that a separate transmission is not cost effective. For an internal-combustion engine, however, or for a turbine, a separate transmission can better match power output and vehicle speed to an optimal rpm for the prime mover.

The electrical transmission – such as used in diesel locomotives – is just about ideal: It can take tremendous power changes without stripping any gears or blowing any hydraulic lines, and it easily incorporates features that tailor power (amperage at different motor rpm) in the axle-hung electric motors to locomotive speed, while permitting the prime mover to run most of the time at its best rpm.[10] A good transmission, however, cannot entirely solve a turbine's steep efficiency loss when the turbine is running at anything less than top power.

The Steamotive ran at part load (*i.e.*, part throttle) for long stretches. Climbing up Cajon Pass was one thing; long runs across Nebraska or Kansas required peak power only during accelerations. Existing records don't include fuel consumption per ton-mile per hour (actual performance data over the road was never publicized), but undoubtedly consumption was high while cruising at part-load on mostly level track, or on grades requiring only part throttle.

Peculiar to the Steamotive were serious lags in acceleration due to the boiler. Reported GE data from simulated station stops tell the tale. When the engineman closed the throttle, steam flow was shut off. A few seconds later, the oil-fuel burner shut off and the fire went out. After another 45 seconds or so, the fire relighted automatically and the unit continued at a low load. Then came starting. From the moment the throttle was opened, it took almost 30 seconds to reach half-power and 2½ minutes to reach full power.

Such a long delay is an eternity in trying to accelerate a train. The 1937 report doesn't discuss it, but such power-response delays constituted a fatal Achilles heel. Apart from inadequate acceleration from station stops, there are many situations – say, running downhill at idle power, with an immediate demand for smoothly applied power just prior to the foot of a grade, in which a 2½-minute lag in power would be grossly unacceptable. If the engineman powered up just a few seconds too soon, he would violate a speed limit. If the train was heavy, such an inordinate lag would stall the train on the upgrade. The Great Northern tried the steam turbine locomotives on freight a few times in 1943 – and it was a short-lived experiment. A diesel responds within a few seconds to the widest power swings and its throttle can be notched up as quickly as proper train handling might dictate. A conventional steam locomotive with a big reservoir of boiler steam always ready to tap responds with virtually no delay to such swings. The Steamotive and its semi-flash boiler had no such reservoir.

Albert Bruce summarized his account of the Steamotive by saying it "had all the excellent characteristics of the electric locomotive"[11] Unfortunately, that judgment was hardly the case. An electric locomotive, too, has a huge reservoir of power ready for rapid application – voltage in overhead wires instantly convertible to as much amperage through motor windings as they can take.

The two turbine-electric units went back to GE for good in 1943. They were disposed of as wartime scrap soon after, the high hopes of 1936 unrealized. Even if the Steamotive had not done so poorly, it perhaps begged a deeper question: If a new type of locomotive were to run on liquid fuel, wasn't internal combustion more efficient and practical? GE would produce electrical gear for Alco diesel locomotives – and the machines were marketed under the Alco-GE name – but GE would abandon the partnership in 1952. It emerged as a locomotive builder in its own right in the 1960s.

Coal vs. oil

After the Steamotive's unhappy experience, steam-turbine work turned entirely to using coal as fuel. Railroads – particularly in the Middle Atlantic region – were dependent on coal for much of their traffic and wanted to keep good relations with coal suppliers.

About the same time that the Steamotive appeared, the Baltimore & Ohio's irrepressible locomotive chief, George Emerson, suggested a possible improvement to the reciprocating steam locomotive. Designers at B&O's headquarters began work on a 4-8-4 geared locomotive with 16 cylinders. Each driving axle was to have a four-cylinder, V-type steam engine driving directly on cranks set into the axle. How far design got in the late 1930s is unclear. One of the four-cylinder steam engines was built and bench-tested in 1940. How the whole concept was supposed to reduce steam locomotive costs is mysterious. The maintenance downtime would have been excessive at best, with 16 pistons and cylinders and attendant valve gear, all buried within the locomotive frames and inaccessible except if a driving unit was removed by means of a drop table in a major shop. The valve gear arrangement that was practical within the tight space available gave mediocre regulation of steam cylinder efficiency. Steam and coal rates would have been disappointing. For B&O, the U.S. entry into World War II apparently stopped any further development on projects of such marginal value.

The Pennsylvania Railroad, Baldwin Locomotive Works, and Westinghouse made the next foray into the turbine locomotive arena, beginning before the GE units were cut up. By 1940, designers saw that the flash boiler presented acute developmental difficulties. Designers were also aware of steam turbine locomotives in Europe built with direct drive (*i.e.*, not having transmissions) and conventional, coal-burning boilers, including the London, Midland & Scottish Railway's "Turbomotive" of 1935 and similar locomotives in Germany and Sweden.

In 1941, engineers for the three U.S. firms agreed on a prototype locomotive. It was to have a direct steam-turbine drive, geared to driving axles arranged in a 4-8-4 layout. The advent of war delayed further work until 1944. Due to wartime restrictions on domestic use of high-tensile steels, the locomotive became a 6-8-6 to spread the greater weight attendant in using ordinary carbon steel.[12] Westinghouse designed the turbines, one for forward movement and one for backing. The forward, 6,900-hp turbine turned the middle two driving axles through a double-reduction gear set. A flexible "cup drive," similar to those used on electric locomotives with big motors, made the

PRR Class S2 steam-turbine No. 6200, with its 6-8-6 wheel arrangement, outwardly resembled a conventional steam locomotive.
Courtesy Kalmbach Media

Driving-axle gear before installation on PRR Class S2 steam-turbine No. 6200.
Courtesy Kalmbach Media

final connection to these axles. Connection to the first and fourth pairs of drivers was via side rods. The reverse-movement, 1,500-horsepower turbine drove the propulsion gears through an additional reduction gear and a clutch. This clutch could only be engaged if the locomotive was not moving.

The form of the turbines – impulse type, a general form usually used for water turbines – was interesting. Westinghouse engineers adapted it from a small but powerful steam turbine for marine use. The impulse design gave the turbines a wider range of rpm, with better pickup at lower rpm compared to normal turbine blades. The penalty with a compressible gas like steam was lower peak efficiency.

The coal-burning, firetube boiler was big and well-proportioned: 120 square feet of grate, 310 psi, and capable of more than 95,000 pounds of steam output per hour. There was no condenser. Exhaust steam directed up the stack induced firebox draft in the usual way. The finished prototype rolled out of Baldwin's Eddystone, Pa., plant in October 1944. In road tests that fall and in early 1945, initially between Chicago and the division point at Crestline, Ohio, No. 6200 churned out 6,550 horsepower at the rail at 70 mph – the highest horsepower ever reached by a steam locomotive at speeds above 50. Initial press was optimistic, and in March 1945 a PRR release stated the railroad's intent to design (again in association with Baldwin and Westinghouse) a 9,000-horsepower, twin-turbine, direct geared locomotive having a 4-8-0+4-8-0 configuration.

Meanwhile, Lionel Corp., marketer of electric toy trains to legions of American boys since 1900, tooled up to manufacture a model version of No. 6200 at a scale of about 1/5 of an inch to the foot. Lionel advertised it as the postwar "locomotive of the future." (And the 6200's lack of pistons and thus of main rods and valve gear made the miniature engine cheaper to produce in quantity.) Made for O-scale track, it soon became Lionel's most popular steam locomotive type. Through the 1960s, fathers and sons ran thousands of them as part of electric-train sets sold all over the country.

The fates of the real 6200 and of the announced follow-on design were less exciting. The latter was canceled before construction. Though the 6200 ran with enormous power at 30 mph or better, had about 20 percent better fuel efficiency at its highest speeds, and ran smoothly with none of the dynamic imbalance characteristic of reciprocating steam locomotives, the engine had unexpected difficulties. Starting tractive effort was good: 70,000 pounds. But at low speed, which for 6200's geared turbine was at low rpm, steam passed through the turbine at a high rate, with comparatively little of the steam's potential energy converted to mechanical power. At speeds up to about 40, overall efficiency was worse than for a conventional reciprocating steamer. As one report put it,

> Its steam rate is high at starting, which makes it necessary to dispatch the engine with a hot fire, but as the turbine gains speed the steam rate steadily improves until it reaches maximum economy at approximately 70 mph.[13]

In the workaday railroad world of 30-mph average speeds, more or less, no statement could have been as damning with respect to general operational usefulness.

The phrase above, "necessary to dispatch the engine with a hot fire," masks another severe problem. Any fireman on a coal-burning locomotive in steam days prepared a hot fire just before train departure, with boiler pressure just below the safety-valve relief pressure. He added coal carefully in the minutes before departure to build up the firebed without excess smoke, in order to get a high firebox temperature and to ensure plenty of reserve heat energy when the heavy draft of starting hit the fire.

The 6200's unique failing, described more candidly in an in-house report, was that its high and wasteful steam flow at starting and at low speed rapidly drained the huge boiler, no matter how hot or well-prepared the fire. When the engineer opened the throttle even moderately to start, boiler pressure dropped precipitously – often by more than 50 psi within less than a minute. The result was an excessive rate of broken firebox staybolts.

In any boiler, pressure and internal steam/water temperature are inextricably tied together by the laws of physics. Rapid pressure changes, and thus rapid internal temperature changes, cause rapid increases in mechanical stresses on internal boiler structure: If temperature drops, contracting steel pulls on adjacent contracting steel. The most problematic points of stress when temperatures change are on the staybolts, as firebox sheets literally move in response.

A fireman on 6200 no doubt struggled doggedly to keep boiler pressure up by firing at the fastest fuel rate possible without literally smothering the fire with too much coal. Given its excessive volume of steam exhaust at low speed, the locomotive did not lack for draft. Immediately, however, if there was a great and sudden pressure drop, the temperature change overstressed numerous staybolts, which broke after a few such experiences. If just two adjacent stays broke, revealing themselves to casual observers by spraying hot steam out their so-called "telltale" holes to the engine's exterior, the locomotive had to be removed from service at the next terminal having repair facilities. But it was far worse than that. If pressure and temperature swings were bad enough, several stays broke on a single trip. The 6200 was a wonderful boon to boilermakers' overtime.[14]

Through May 1948, the 6200 totted up three and a half years of operational service, mostly on passenger trains and express or mail trains for which its power at high rpm was useful. Enginemen learned to open the throttle gingerly at starting, allowing the fireman to "catch up" on boiler pressure. Acceleration was therefore slow with a heavy train. Pullman conductor William Moedinger remembered a run west out of Harrisburg on a night train with 6200; the engine could indeed fly once speed built up.[15] The gears gave little trouble. After 40,000 miles the gears were "in excellent condition."[16] Baldwin designers suggested a replacement boiler (perhaps with welded stays?), which was never constructed. In 1952, the 6200 met the cutting torches at PRR's Conway Yard, west of Pittsburgh.

Hard on the heels of PRR's 6200, Chesapeake & Ohio engineers at Huntington, W.Va., Baldwin designers, and Westinghouse electrical engineers began work on a turbine concept in early 1944, spurred on by

ABOVE Baldwin builder's photo of Chesapeake & Ohio Class M-1 steam-turbine-electric locomotive No. 500, one of three built in 1947-1948 to pull C&O's ill-starred *Chessie* streamliner. *Courtesy Kalmbach Media*

RIGHT The boiler, firebox, and frame of a C&O M-1 steam-turbine-electric under construction at Baldwin. *Courtesy Kalmbach Media*

C&O's flamboyant chairman, Robert R. Young. The C&O research group was initially headed by an aeronautical engineer, K.A. Browne. Young had taken his chair in 1942 and immediately began steering the traditionalist C&O in new directions. Among other things, he wanted to introduce a new passenger train as soon as the war was over: a new, daytime-running, ultra-posh train with dome cars between Cincinnati and Washington, D.C. For the new *Chessie* streamliner, he wanted headline-capturing motive power, and it had to burn coal. A railroad so wedded to coal traffic was not going to offend the mine owners and companies it catered to.

The result was a radical looking, streamlined, 6,000-horsepower monster, 106 feet long, and with an engine weight of 428 tons – about 42 tons heavier than one of Union Pacific's 4-8-8-4 Big Boys. A 48-foot tender, also streamlined, brought up the rear. Bright orange trim set off polished stainless steel. Actually, there were three of these ponderous locomotives, steam-turbine-electrics numbered by C&O as 500 to 502, ordered off the drawing boards with no developmental prototype. Baldwin finished the first in late 1947 and the other two in early 1948.

At the same time, the Budd Company worked on an order for 46 stainless cars to equip three trainsets, plus cars for a connecting train to Richmond and Hampton Roads, Va. The railroad put up two special coaling towers, one at Clifton Forge, Va., and the other at Hinton, W.Va., specifically for the *Chessie's* refueling. The architecturally stylish towers, with slanting lines and portholes, echoed the C&O's new image and slogan, "For Progress."

The turbine-electric's wheels were grouped in a 4-8-0+4-8-4 arrangement. The layout was more complex than it might first appear: Three of the four larger wheelsets in each subframe were powered with electric traction motors; the fourth wheelset simply spread weight. The trailing truck was powered, however, for a total of eight traction motors. From front to rear on each locomotive came the coal bunker, crew cab, an altogether conventional firetube boiler set with firebox facing the rear of the cab (and ashpan placed in the gap between the front subframe and the second lead truck), and the steam turbine/electrical generating set (over the powered trailing truck). As in the PRR 6200, there was no condensing. Exhaust steam up the stack provided draft. The C&O tender was devoted exclusively to carrying 25,000 gallons of water.

The three 500s were an unmitigated disaster. According to Claude Howdyshell, a junior C&O engineer in the late 1940s who later became Chessie System's chief mechanical officer, "They never made a single trip that I'd call successful."[17]

The least problem was that big clinkers regularly formed in the firebed, which Howdyshell felt were mostly the result of the boiler's draft characteristics. Clinkers are caused by incombustible impurities in coal, such as silicates, which melt at temperatures above 2,000° F and can fuse together on a grate, blocking air flow to the layer of coal immediately above and severely retarding combustion. Air flow accelerating around the edges of the clinker, however, raises combustion heat locally around the clinker and causes it to grow as more impurities melt. Soon a good portion of the grate can be blocked from adequate air, the furnace temperature falls, and boiler pressure drops. The pulsing draft of a reciprocating steam locomotive tends to keep a coal firebed well-agitated, which may break up clinkers before they become serious. Poor grades of coal with a high percentage of impurities can clinker in any locomotive.

A 500's draft, from exhaust steam out of the turbine, was not pulsing but steady. When accelerating, the steady draft was abnormally forceful, which caused the coal in the firebed to reach clinker-forming temperatures quickly. When mechanics readjusted draft appliances in the smokebox, the changes only partly reduced the problem. The only sure remedy for the clinkering was to use high-cost coal having minimum non-carbon content, close to the quality of metallurgical coal.

The insoluble problem was that, even when draft appliances were adjusted for better performance, adequate draft unavoidably came at the expense of high backpressure against the steam-turbine exhaust, cutting the turbine's net output. The 6,000-shaft-horsepower turbine, which should have given 5,000-5,500 horsepower at the drawbar through the electric motors (net of various losses), could provide only about 3,500 shaft horsepower, and 3,000 at the drawbar. The locomotive's power-to-weight ratio was probably the worst in the 20th century. Few episodes in the whole history of steam locomotive engineering were as embarrassing to all concerned.

The PRR's 6200 had not experienced such extreme clinkering or backpressure defects, but it did not have a ratio-changing transmission. As seen above, its required method of operation – minimum and careful throttle up to 40 mph or so to avoid boiler-pressure swings – apparently kept draft within effective bounds. A C&O 500, though, having an electric transmission, could use high boiler output and high turbine rpm at low track speeds, just as a diesel can use maximum engine power at low speeds. In fact, because of the excessive backpressure, the C&O locomotive had to start and accelerate at high boiler output, just to get enough horsepower to move its train. Steam and fuel efficiencies were poor. Steam flow rate and rpm in combination were rarely at ideal flow and speed. Two ordinary, 1,500-horsepower EMD diesels could have done as well, without all the hassles.

C&O engineers, including Howdyshell, vainly worked on solutions. An Austrian engineer, Dr. Adolph Giesl-Gieslingen, offered to install his patented form of low-backpressure drafting device in the steam exhaust pathway. (See pages 417-18.) By late 1948, it was clear to everyone that no solution promised any cost-effective improvement. In 1950, the C&O withdrew the locomotives entirely from their sporadic use, in which they had pulled the railroad's *George Washington*, *Sportsman*, and other trains. All three of the M-1 class steam-turbine-electric engines went back to Baldwin for salvage the following year. Said Howdyshell, "Nobody on C&O wanted to see or hear of a turbine again – ever."[18]

An irate stockholder wrote in a March 1948 letter to C&O president Robert Bowman, mailing a copy to the ICC,

> A recent engineering report on the new steam-turbine-electric locomotive indicates that a dependable commercial locomotive is at least five years off. I understand that a large eastern coal carrier who collaborated ... has become so discouraged about the project that it has placed orders for ... Diesel-electric motive power. Is the C.&O. going to be influenced by [chairman Robert R.] Young's personal, arbitrary views on this subject and delay modernizing its motive power?[19]

The stockholder's views on modernity obviously conflicted with those of the chairman.

And what happened to the *Chessie*? It never ran. After the war there was no appreciable market for a daytime, luxury Cincinnati-Washington train.[20] Other economic concerns also intruded. By spring 1948, in the midst of a coal miners' strike, the C&O had furloughed nearly 14,000 employees, the most of any of the 23 railroads affected by the United Mine Workers action.[21]

Jawn Henry

The most successful steam-turbine-electric was Norfolk & Western's experimental No. 2300, semi-officially dubbed the *Jawn Henry*. After research beginning in 1948, N&W placed a firm order in 1949. The ever-optimistic Westinghouse did the electrical gear. Baldwin-Lima-Hamilton completed the locomotive at Eddystone, Pa., in May 1954.[22]

The 2300's creators pulled out all the stops. Babcock & Wilcox, which had made the Steamotive's semi-flash, oil-fired boilers, designed and installed a 600-psi, watertube, coal-burning boiler this time around. Unlike most previous watertube installations on locomotives, which married a watertube firebox to a conventional barrel enclosing firetubes, B&W's 1954 boiler was a full watertube design. Except for lacking a condenser, the boiler took advantage of B&W's expertise, coupled with lessons learned from previous turbine and watertube locomotive failures.

The lack of a condenser simply recognized the universal experience with the few condensers tried on steam locomotives overseas: They took up a great deal of scarce room and developed unavoidable leaks due to the pounding and vibration of railroad duty. B&W's boiler was designed to deliver ample steam for a sustained 4,500 shaft-horsepower at the Westinghouse impulse turbine. That horsepower was perhaps conservative, but the 2300 was unlike any steam-turbine locomotive in the U.S. before it, being designed for heavy freight service. Intended to generate top drawbar power at 15 to 40 mph speeds, 4,500 horsepower translated into great tractive effort.

Norfolk & Western steam-turbine-electric locomotive No. 2300, *Jawn Henry*, at Christiansburg, Va., in July 1954.
Rev. LeRoy A. Scott, Courtesy Kalmbach Media

Originally conceived as a 4-8-0+4-8-0 superficially similar to the firetube-boilered C&O 500s, *Jawn Henry* emerged in 1954 as an engine 111½ feet long over couplers with a 49½-foot water tender, longer than the C&O design. The N&W locomotive rode on four, six-wheel trucks derived straight from diesel locomotive practice. Twelve axle-hung traction motors propelled all wheels. Weight, less tender, was 409 tons. The general layout – front-to-back of coal bunker, crew cab, boiler, turbine-generator set, and water carried in a separate tender – was the same as C&O's. An addition in the N&W tender was a small water-softening unit to prevent scale build-up in the locomotive's boiler.

An interesting device was the 2300's "shuffle"-type grate. Coal, fed automatically at one end of the grate, was kept in constant agitation by the moving grate bars, which also leveled the whole coal bed. The cyclic action constantly cleaned the fire of ash and clinkers, which dropped in a steady rain into the ashpan below. Though there was a fireman on board, essential to monitoring boiler function, experience showed that the firebed was self-tending. Automatic features regulated feedwater rate, fuel rate, and draft in proportion to boiler power demand, using philosophies similar to those applied in the GE Steamotive. A draft fan, driven by an auxiliary turbine, provided furnace draft, saving considerable horsepower by virtually eliminating backpressure in the steam exhaust pathway from the main turbine.

In tests against one of N&W's famed Y6b-class 2-8-8-2 Mallets, the turbine produced a peak of 4,000 drawbar horsepower at 17 to 20 mph, versus 5,600 drawbar horsepower by the Y6b at 25 mph. Tractive effort – with 12 smooth-torque driving axles – surpassed the Mallet. Whereas the highly developed Y6 exerted 152,000 pounds of tractive effort when starting in simple expansion, No. 2300 could exert a stupefying 200,000 lbs. up to a couple of mph. Through spring of 1955, N&W affirmed that "the future of this type locomotive is bright."[23]

That January, I.N. Moseley, an N&W research engineer, described the 2300's first 19,000 miles of testing to a meeting of the American Society of Mechanical Engineers. Though running about 12 percent slower than its reciprocating cousins, the turbine showed remarkable power and fuel economy. Taking eastbound coal from Bluefield, W.Va., to Roanoke, Va., the turbine handled 11,500 to 13,000 tons, compared to a Y6b Mallet's rating of 10,300. The average tonnage increase was 13 percent while using 23 percent less fuel. Hauling maximum-size trains of 175 cars on the gentler grades from Portsmouth, Ohio, to the terminal at Williamson, W.Va., the 2300 saved 30 percent on fuel compared to an N&W Class-A. Moseley elaborated:

> It [the 2300] is very easy to fire, ... is exceptionally responsive to load changes, and can be fired with a clear stack at all steam demands. ... [All operating difficulties] have been corrected.[24]

N&W President R.H. Smith separately told a group of Wall Street securities analysts that the turbine had "shown a fuel cost per unit of traffic moved lower than that of any other type of locomotive we have tested, including the diesels.[25]

Jawn Henry ran fairly regularly for more than three years. By 1956, however, maintenance began to increase. The boiler acquitted itself well, needing little more than the monthly washout and inspection required by ICC locomotive safety rules. Automatic controls for the main turbine and boiler gave occasional trouble, and failure of the centrifugal feedwater pump was apparently chronic. There was some erosion to the hardened stainless steel draft-fan blades from cinders, but this was not mentioned as a major difficulty in contemporary reporting. Accumulated problems persisted, and after a time the 2300 was assigned exclusively to pusher duty on coal trains over the Blue Ridge eastbound from Roanoke, where it could be close to the Roanoke Shops. In early 1957, an N&W engineer told a reporter that 2300's "dependability, like most experimental locomotives, leaves something to be desired."[26] In December 1957, N&W sent *Jawn* to the scrapping line at Roanoke. A release held out some optimism, stating that, based on the experience with the 2300, "a more economic and dependable steam-turbine locomotive could be designed and built."[27]

The biggest factor leading to the 2300's demise was that, from 1955 through 1957, no other railroad expressed any serious interest in the turbine concept. Most railroads had already decided to dieselize completely, and for them, the costs of maintaining two supporting infrastructures, one for diesel and one for steam, could not be paid by the fuel savings Jawn had posted. Moreover, without orders for such locomotives from more than one railroad, there were no economies from volume production to bring purchase cost down or to support a spare-parts market. Westinghouse, for its part, ceased working on any locomotive development in 1954, dropping out of its partnership with Baldwin that summer.[28] N&W simply couldn't go it alone on a motive-power technology that no other railroad shared, no matter how fine that technology might have proven to be, and no matter how devoted N&W was to coal.

As for the 2300 itself, it was clearly too big in sheer size for most railroads to deal with; few shops and yards could have handled it. The 2300 was a highly specialized machine in the railroad context, suitable only for unusually heavy trains on profiles, like N&W's, where the locomotive could labor uphill at its flat-out maximum power for long periods. N&W engineer Moseley had praised the 2300's good response to throttle changes, but the fact is that the locomotive had been tested and used primarily in duty that was well suited to a turbine's nature of performing best under sustained, full load.

In mid-1958, under new president Stuart T. Saunders, N&W announced that all future purchases would be diesels, and it began ordering an initial fleet of Alco RS-11 road freight units. The last N&W steamer to operate in road service, a Y6 on Pocahontas Division mine runs, had its fire dropped in May 1960.

Final developments

Turbine-electric proposals did not end with *Jawn Henry's* demise. Even before then, in 1956, the Association of American Railroads' Locomotive Development Committee (formed in 1937 as the Committee on Further Development of the Steam Locomotive) drew up a coal-fired gas-turbine-electric. "Fluidized" coal (ground-up coal mixed with fuel oil) would run through an onboard pulverizer to reduce the coal particles to extremely fine size. The final coal-oil mixture, from a storage tank, would feed a 2,470-horsepower English Electric gas turbine turning a generator. The whole arrangement fit into a single Alco DL-600 locomotive hood, with the trucks and traction motors unchanged.[29]

The committee's proposal was never realized, but Union Pacific tried a related idea as part of its extensive development of a fleet of oil-fired gas-turbine-electrics. UP and Alco cooperated on a locomotive fired on dry coal, the No. 80. The main turbine was powered by pressurized gases from a furnace. Since the products of combustion – including cinders – passed at high velocity through the main turbine, there was considerable scoring of the turbine blades. Better filtration impeded the gas flow from the furnace, sharply lowering power and efficiency. No. 80 was quickly deemed unsuccessful.

Apart from turbines, intriguing initiatives trying to "save steam" emerged in the late 1940s and early 1950s. Since the two large American steam builders (Alco and the merged Baldwin and Lima) manufactured their last domestic steam locomotives in 1948 and 1949, nothing after those years had any long-term significance. A late innovation, however, one that received a lot of attention in Europe where steam continued in flagging production into the 1960s, deserves discussion.

Recall that in 1948, Dr. Gieslingen was trying to sell his idea for the "Giesl Oblong Exhaust Ejector" to the C&O. Gieslingen saw a simple way to improve draft effectiveness. His essential idea, startling in its insight considering the 140-odd years that locomotive designers had tinkered with draft devices, was to recreate the high ratio of smokestack height to stack diameter that was characteristic of early locomotives of the 19th century.

UP No. 80, a one-of-a-kind coal-fired gas-turbine-electric, was an operational failure.

Courtesy Kalmbach Media

Designers long knew that a tall stack abetted draft, with less backpressure in the cylinders needed for a given draft force on the fire. On some of its late-design steamers, the Santa Fe used "stack extensions," which could be raised and lowered to clear overhead obstacles. Such extensions improved draft efficiency. In 1947, an assistant superintendent for the Wabash observed that "some 200 to 1,000 horsepower is wasted in back pressure through the exhaust nozzle on large locomotives working at or near full power. That is [a great deal of power to] produce draft when it probably could be done with not over 75 horsepower driving an exhaust fan."[30] The observation on wasted power may have been accurate, and a draft fan was later incorporated in *Jawn Henry's* design. But in a conventional firetube boiler burning coal, a draft fan would have been continually pelted by a high volume of cinders, most of them containing hard silicates, at 250 to 300 mph. Designers had never deemed existing steels capable of withstanding such a beating for very long. Jawn's fan was subject to lower velocities and fewer cinders, due to an altogether different combustion-gas pathway through the boiler.

Gieslingen's in-line exhaust jets and funnel, designed as an assembly of rather simple castings of different overall size, depending on the size and steam output of the locomotive to which the device might be applied.
Courtesy Kalmbach Media

Gieslingen knew that if good draft could be provided while cutting the power wasted through the exhaust, the net power at the locomotive drawbar could be increased by a similar amount, all on the same amount of fuel. He thought to divide the exhaust-steam nozzle into a row of in-line jets, usually five to seven of them, depending on volume of exhaust steam. These jets vented fanwise into an "oblong ejector." An essential trick, as in any locomotive exhaust, was that the ascending exhaust steam and captured flue gas, despite all their turbulence, had to entirely fill the smokestack (in this case the ejector), leaving no gaps between the high-velocity exhaust and the smokestack wall. Such gaps, even momentary, tend to destroy the effectiveness of a stack in creating a partial vacuum in the smokebox, by allowing counterflows downward along the stack wall. (Taller smokestacks and chimneys are efficient largely due to their better prevention of such counterflows. Turbulence up the stack has less opportunity to open momentary counterflows downward.)

Gieslingen's in-line jets exhausted into a carefully sized, flattened funnel. The effective ratio of height in the funnel for each jet, divided by jet diameter, was increased up to five-fold. The steam/gas flow along the stack wall was better "sealed" thereby. The same partial vacuum was created in the smokebox at much less backpressure.

The C&O put an "oblong ejector" into one of its 0-8-0 switchers in 1949. Staff marveled at the little locomotive's quicker acceleration, increased power, and softer exhaust noise. Gieslingen – whom everyone called "Dr. Giesl" – noted that lots of exhaust noise merely indicated high exhaust inefficiency, betraying the high average backpressure. But by 1949, there was no turning back in the in the U.S. rush to dieselize, so Gieslingen returned to Europe, where he applied his ejectors to engines in Britain, France, Germany, and Spain.[31] In all events, Claude Howdyshell thought that the man was a little hard to deal with, insisting on "pretty steep" royalties on his patent.[32] In Giesl exhaust applications in Europe, power increases of 10 to 15 percent, with overall fuel efficiency increases of up to 20 percent, were claimed. As might be expected, locomotives with poor draft qualities benefited the most.

As we have seen, in the 1940s U.S. engineers debated a number of other ideas. Among these were poppet valves, improved driving-wheel counterbalance, maintenance techniques to increase locomotive availability and utilization, boilers for pulverized coal, higher boiler pressures, forced water circulation within the boiler using supplementary pumps, "double-Belpaire" configuration for firetube boilers, and welded boiler construction.

Lima Locomotive Works' chief designer, Albert J. Townsend, proposed the double-Belpaire boiler in 1946, and the company built a large working model to test its behavior under expansion and contraction. Lima claimed that tests on the model showed stress changes under varying pressures and temperatures to be less than in a normal firetube boiler. Comparing performance indicators to a radial-stayed boiler of the same diameter, the double-Belpaire's superheating surface (with the same type of superheater) jumped more than 18 percent. Cross-sectional gas area through tubes and flues was 10½ percent better. Townsend stressed the latter increase. Compared to relatively efficient locomotive boilers in Europe, cross-sectional gas area in large American designs was regarded as low. Inadequate gas area created higher resistance through the tubes and thereby required higher cylinder backpressure to generate a needed level of draft and evaporation rate.[33] Lima proposed a 4-8-6 locomotive in 1949 with Franklin rotary-driven poppet valves and the new form of boiler. It was too late. Lima had already received its last steam locomotive order, ten 2-8-4s for the Nickel Plate Road.

Welded boilers had long been resisted by the Bureau of Locomotive Inspection of the ICC because of the notorious failures in fireboxes repaired by poor welding techniques in the 1910s. Finally, in 1937, after welded firebox construction had proven itself over several years, the Bureau relented and let the Delaware & Hudson install an all-welded boiler experimentally on a 2-8-0 in 1937. Ten years later, no leaks had ever developed and no repairs to the shell had ever been needed.[34] The advantage over riveted construction was greatly reduced boiler maintenance, especially of the outer-wrapper sheets around the firebox, where changing mechanical stresses in service concentrated.

In 1947, railroads were planning about 25 welded boilers in new locomotives. Two years before, Alco built an annealing furnace at Schenectady to stress-relieve the largest boilers and began design of an all-welded boiler that was installed on a Delaware & Hudson J-class 4-6-6-4. The boiler's seams were all radiographed to prove their integrity.[35] Few other welded boilers were built; dieselizing railroads dropped their previous plans for such vessels. Combustion Engineering, a firm specializing in compact stationary boilers, manufactured some all-welded replacement boilers for large Santa Fe locomotives in 1949 and 1950.[36] Alco delivered no more steam locomotives after 1948.

One can certainly assert that the replacement of external combustion by internal combustion was inevitable – but the actual story, and its historical timing, are far more interesting. The Great Depression and the World War II years hampered steam locomotive research and development for a decade and a half. The lag could never be made up. Steam manufacturers closed their doors for a time in the 1930s; any largesse for research and development, either from railroads or builders, disappeared. Even in the late 1930s, economically strapped railroads ordered few locomotives of any type. The deep pockets of General Motors, meanwhile, financed the creation of a fully practical diesel. Rapid war expansion caused a wave of new steam orders, leaving little time for research. Then the severe demands of surging wartime traffic proved the diesels' dependability in a way no other experience could have done during so compressed a time. Accepted steam technology in 1946, however, was insignificantly different from what it had been in 1930. As we have seen, that fact was not for lack of the experimental spirit, which persisted all along within the bounds of the economics to support it.

Despite any dreamed-of advances, however, the unacknowledged but overwhelming issue for steam was its labor intensity. No change in construction technique and no add-on device to radically cut fuel consumption would have materially cut the labor hours needed to service and repair steam locomotives. From 1946 to 1962, railroads chopped their employment in half – from 1.4 million to 700,000 – with about half that decrease coming from the backshops and engine terminals.[37] The diesel's thermodynamic economy was secondary to the diesel's ultimate impact on shop labor. Steam was dead, as legions of boilermakers, pipefitters, machinists, valvesetters, and other skilled tradesmen and their families knew too well.

Chapter 21 Notes

1. For financial precariousness of many Class I railroads in the mid-1930s, see "Net Income Summary of Large Steam Railways [1936, 1937]," *Railway Age*, February 12, 1938, p. 311. Of 47 such railroads, 24 were in deficit in 1936, and 27 were in deficit in 1937. Union Pacific was among the most profitable lines, along with Chesapeake & Ohio, Norfolk & Western, and Pennsylvania, though 1937 net income for all of them was lower than in 1936.
2. Complete description in E.G. Bailey (B&W Co.), A.R. Smith (GE), and P.S. Dickey (Bailey Meter), "The 'Steamotive' Unit for a Union Pacific Locomotive," *Mechanical Engineering*, December 1936. See also *Railway Age*, March 20, 1937, pp. 468-72.
3. For example, on Delaware & Hudson, Baltimore & Ohio, Baldwin 60000, New York Central No. 800, Canadian Pacific No. 8000. See Chapters 11 and 13.
4. Bailey, Smith, and Dickey in *Railway Age*, March 20, 1937, p. 468.
5. Alfred W. Bruce, *The Steam Locomotive in America: Its Development in the Twentieth Century*, 1952, p. 338.
6. Bailey, Smith, and Dickey in *Railway Age*, March 20, 1937, p. 471.
7. Bruce (p. 337) says that water was distilled, which may have been the case initially but could not be maintained in normal service. Steam for heating passenger cars alone lost several percent of the water/steam per hour from the otherwise closed cycle, not to mention losses from safety valves, leaks, etc.
8. For steam-turbine horsepower and torque characteristics, see C.A. Atwell and C.E. Baston, "Steam-Electric Locomotives," *Railway Mechanical Engineer*, April 1949, p. 214.
9. An engineman's control of speed, since the advent in the 1930s of speed recorders on locomotives, is taken dead seriously. An incident of willful overspeeding by even five mph might result in a suspension without pay for a week or more, depending on circumstances. Other violations, such as missing a signal, could result in a 30-day suspension. If there was an accident in which excessive speed was found to be a contributing factor, an engineman could lose his job. More forceful than sanctions was the fact that, for most engineers, precise control of speed is a mark of professionalism. Engineers take pride in smooth train-handling. Proper speed control downhill with a heavy freight train is a mark of skill – and enginemen well know that, because of the weight and momentum of a heavy freight running downgrade, excess speed can rapidly lead to loss of control and a runaway.
10. See G.F. McGowan, *Diesel-Electric Locomotive Handbook: Electrical Equipment*, Simmons-Boardman, 1951, for a full explanation of such features. One such is "transition," as commonly used for DC traction motors in General Motors' Electro-Motive Division diesels through the 1960s (before DC locomotives were equipped with advanced-technology alternators). Locomotives with Westinghouse and GE electrical equipment used different electrical control circuits and devices to integrate prime-mover output, traction-motor amperage, and traction-motor rpm. In essence, transition (done manually in early EMC/EMD models; automatically in most models

built after the 1940s) changed the basic way circuits were connected between the DC output to the motors and the motors themselves. Transition traded amperage for voltage, appropriate to the speed of the electric motor and the electrical resistance within it, which increased with speed. In this way, high horsepower could be developed in the electric motor at low locomotive speed or high. At each traction motor, low road speed requires high torque and high amperage at low voltage, while high road speed requires low torque, high voltage, and amperage proportional to power. Control circuits in EMD locomotives connected the traction motors in series for slow speed, series-parallel for medium speed, and full parallel for high speed. A diesel-electric locomotive could thus exert maximum horsepower at the rail at 10 to 12 mph as well as at 40 to 50 mph. The biggest danger was too much amperage in the traction motors, which could occur at low motor rpm. Below about 10 mph, enginemen had to keep an eye on the ammeter. EMD published time limits for running the motors in a yellow zone shown on the meter. Too much time there, or any time in the red zone, risked heat build-up in the motor windings that would break down insulation and short the motor.

11. Bruce, p. 338.
12. "Steam Locomotive Development," *Railway Age*, June 26, 1947, p. 1294. For a description by a consulting transportation engineer to Westinghouse, including tractive effort/horsepower curves, see Charles Kerr, Jr., "The Steam Turbine: Coal's New Hope" in *Trains*, June 1947, pp. 14-18. See also Bruce, pp. 336-37; and Philip Atkins, *Dropping the Fire* (Irwell Press/National Railway Museum, York, U.K.: 1999), pp. 92-94.
13. Ibid., "Steam Locomotive Development."
14. Atkins (Note 12), pp. 93-94. The rule regarding two adjacent broken staybolts was, and remains, part of federal regulation.
15. As told to the author by son Linn Moedinger in 1998.
16. "Steam Locomotive Development" (Note 12). There is also a repeated claim that 6200's *coup-de-grace* came in 1948 when an engineman or hostler running 6200 "light" (without a train) reversed direction too quickly and destroyed the clutch to the backward turbine. The author could not confirm this.
17. Author's interview with Howdyshell, March 1981. The former Chesapeake & Ohio became part of the Chessie System in 1973, along with Baltimore & Ohio and Western Maryland. In 1987, Chessie was merged into CSX Transportation.
18. Ibid. See also Atkins, p. 94.
19. George S. Jackson to Robert J. Bowman, March 22, 1948, quoted in *Railway Age*, April 3, 1948, p. 61.
20. Geoffrey H. George, "This Was The Train That Was (But Never Was)," *Trains*, July 1968, pp. 38-47. Geoffrey H. George is a *nom de plume* of author Herbert H. Harwood.
21. George S. Jackson to Robert J. Bowman, March 22, 1948, quoted in *Railway Age*, April 3, 1948, p. 61.
22. *Railway Age*, August 20, 1949, pp. 70-71; *Railway Mechanical Engineer*, September 1949, p. 530.
23. *Trains*, May 1955, p. 49.
24. Quotes in *Trains* (from ASME address), February 1955, pp. 10-11.
25. Ibid.
26. *Trains*, May 1957, p. 54.
27. *Railway Age*, January 1958.
28. *Trains*, August 1954, p. 12.
29. "Motive Power Survey," *Trains*, May 1956, p. 29. In the atomic-minded 1950s, there was even a proposal for a nuclear-powered locomotive, first seriously suggested in 1953 by an academic. (See *Trains*, May 1955, p. 49.) A 1956 concept drawing appeared to show a turbine receiving compressed, superheated air that cooled a small reactor. Unmentioned were the weight of adequate shielding or the hazards that would result from high-speed collisions.
30. W.A. Pownall, quoted in Railway Age, June 26, 1947, p. 1294.
31. Atkins, (Note 12), pp. 96-97.
32. Author's interview with Howdyshell, (Note 17).
33. Atkins, pp. 12-13.
34. *Railway Age*, June 26, 1947, p. 1294.
35. Ibid. Radiography of boiler seams involves taping down a sheet of film (within a light-opaque sleeve) on the seam and exposing the film for a prescribed brief time to an X-ray source at a prescribed distance.
36. Atkins, p. 12.
37. Rail employment data by employee group is found in ICC annual reports, 1947-1963.

"Be certain that it is an architecture that has its own customs, standards, and appeals." – *H. Stafford Bryant Jr.*[1]

Chapter 22

Industrial Beauty and the Beholder:

Aesthetics of Locomotives in the 20th Century

BEAUTIFUL," "HANDSOME," "TRIM," "GRACEFUL," and similar adjectives can be found in commentary about steam locomotives from the mid-19th century on. Such praise is distinguished from "powerful," "potent," "impressive," "majestic," or other adjectives intended to convey a sense of the awesome mechanical prowess of a locomotive. In the last third of the 19th century, locomotives dominated much of the industrial landscape. Many people regarded them as an unwanted intrusion into a former garden; others welcomed them as the embodiment of human progress. Both camps could agree on some of the "power" adjectives, perhaps, but probably not on any of the words implying grace and beauty. Nonetheless, Currier & Ives lithographs of locomotives as then-modern objects – "Lightning Express," "American Express Train," and others – decorated the walls of modest 19th-century homes, hung as if they were prints of potted flowers, bucolic landscapes, or other scenes reflective of aesthetic sensibility.[2]

That is a reason for curiosity: What transforms a functional iron-and-steel thing, lacking any obvious visual connection to accepted canons of sculpture or architecture, into – for some – a composition having an artistic form? Is it embellishment or decoration? Machine designers once incorporated classical architectural elements such as Corinthian columns into cast iron in order to make a connection to accepted art. Such shapes stated clearly the maker's assertion, "This machine is art, too, and as heroic as anything made in ancient times." In the late 19th century, elements of art nouveau were eagerly added to machines. Later, embellishment was stripped away. Machines, shaped in ways untreated in classic texts and before the 20th-century era of streamlining and industrial design, came to be regarded as having strong aesthetic content.[3]

In the 20th century, locomotives became an accepted part of the domestic landscape. People complained about their smoke, about rates and fares that many saw as high, and about the still-monopolistic ways of the locomotives' owners, who had become fat and dominant in American life in the 1880s. People did not complain about the travel and adventure that locomotives propelled. Even to the most deprived of citizens, even for those whose actual mobility was limited, the locomotive symbolized escape, new horizons, new

Two legendary Canadian National steam locomotive designs – the bullet-nosed U-1-f class 4-8-2 of 1944 and the fully streamlined U-4-a class 4-8-4 of 1936 – are represented by Nos. 6079 and 6404 at Toronto, Ontario, in March 1957, with yellow-trimmed green striping relieving their expanses of black paint.

Jim Shaughnessy

The steam locomotive as aesthetic object was an accepted part of American popular culture in the 19th century, thanks to widely circulated lithographs produced by Currier & Ives and other publishers.
Author's Collection

possibilities. The locomotive whistle was a haunting call to the evergreen valley over a distant hill.

> The railroad track is miles away,
> And the day is loud with voices speaking,
> Yet there isn't a train goes by all day
> But I hear its whistle shrieking.
> All night there isn't a train goes by,
> Though the night is still for sleep and dreaming,
> But I see its cinders red on the sky,
> And hear its engine steaming.
> My heart is warm with friends I make,
> And better friends I'll not be knowing;
> Yet there isn't a train I wouldn't take,
> No matter where it's going.

Edna St. Vincent Millay, "Travel," first published in Second *April, 1921.*

Reaction to a thing's supposed aesthetics cannot be disentangled from one's other emotional responses to it. The perceived beauty of a bridge, for example, cannot be separated from the other engagements the viewer may have with bridges. A bridge soars to the extent that one can soar with it, gaining access to places once difficult of access. One's reaction to a car cannot be divorced from one's sense of possible adventure in it. People employed by a machine can despise it – but they can also admire it and see a beauty there that others miss. Craftspeople who are skilled with machines, who turn the machines to their human purposes, regularly speak of their machines' beauty, as a carpenter does of a finely made woodworking tool.

Today, one's reaction to a steam locomotive – in a museum, say, or at a living history site that operates one – takes place in an entirely different context. If one has had no other experience with the thing, trying to recapture the aesthetic qualities one's forebears may have seen in it is difficult at best. For industrial things particularly, aesthetic response cannot be separated from historical context, any more than from personal experience – which of course is historical as well, if in a more immediate frame.

Few 20th-century American writers have ever tried to explain steam locomotive form as an aesthetic exercise.[4] Those who made the attempt note that people continually disagree in their opinions about mechanical beauty. "One man's Datsun 280ZX is another man's Hudson Terraplane," wrote Ed King (the 280ZX has itself become dated since he wrote those words in 1985). He then took the innovative tack of discussing what makes a locomotive ugly – an approach that throws good looks into relief by analyzing their opposite. In what follows, I take the approach of looking for those qualities of form and relationship that seem to have pleased railroaders in the steam era. My purpose here is not to assert any intrinsic principles, but rather to sensitize a modern reader – who may rightly regard the locomotive's image as functional at best – to an appreciation that's pretty well extinct today.

H. Stafford Bryant tried a bit of sampling in the 1940s and 1950s:

> It is curious how ... there is a sort of consensus of taste. How often the New York Central Hudson-type is described as lovely – by professional [railroader], fan and casually interested amateur alike. ... I have several times placed [comparative photographs] one above the other ... of the Central locomotive and a[nother] particularly ugly [locomotive] and set them before an observer who is conscious of classical architecture but largely indifferent to railroads. The picture of the Central is favored every time.[5]

Bryant certainly reveals his bias by the adjective "lovely." Apart from the "consensus" of which he is trying to persuade us, I think his emphasis on architecture is partly right but I'll pursue it differently than he did.

His book, *The Georgian Locomotive*, argued that the most stylish steam locomotives after about 1920 shared qualities reminiscent of Georgian architecture, which "trade[s] heavily in complicated applications of simple geometric shapes."[6] The book uses locomotives in the region from Northern Virginia to West Texas as exemplars and draws parallels between their "complicated applications" of shapes and the uses of rectangles, circular fan

Even without the 1938 Dreyfuss-designed streamlined shrouding of rostermates Nos. 5445-5454, New York Central Class J-3a 4-6-4 No. 5435 was, arguably, a more aesthetically pleasing locomotive than Great Northern Class O-8 2-8-2 No. 3378, with multiple air pumps cluttering the front of the latter's smokebox. No. 3378's Vanderbilt tender was also considered by some to be an aesthetic liability.

Courtesy Kalmbach Media

ABOVE Union Pacific 4-6-2 No. 112, a classic Harriman Pacific, exemplifies the early 20th century locomotive design aesthetic, with a Vanderbilt tender its only distraction. *Courtesy Kalmbach Media*

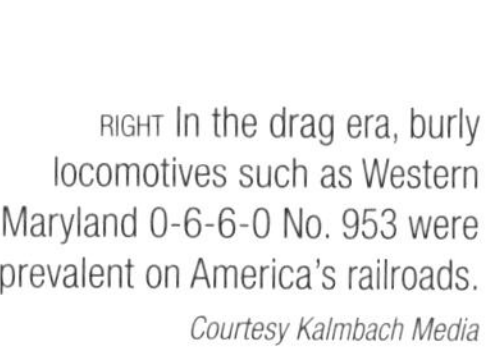

RIGHT In the drag era, burly locomotives such as Western Maryland 0-6-6-0 No. 953 were prevalent on America's railroads. *Courtesy Kalmbach Media*

shapes, and other geometric elements in the stolid symmetry of "grand neo-Georgian" buildings and other "correct traditional styles."[7]

David P. Morgan takes a more historical approach and divides steam locomotive engineering and style into five periods since 1900: "Early 20th Century, Drag Era, U.S.R.A., Superpower Age, and Streamlined Superpower."[8] In the first period, says Morgan, "American builders produced some of our finest examples of trim steam power." There was little clutter and complexity apparent, "and the usual construction followed simple, clean-limbed lines."

In the "Drag Era ... graceful lines were discarded with the advent of big-boilered, low-drivered 2-8-2s, Santa Fe types, Mallets, and Decapods." But "passenger power achieved a high standard. ... One only has to recall Alco's remarkable 50000 Pacific. ... Or consider the fleet-footed 4-6-2s of the New York Central."

Then, "the standardized plans prepared for the United States Railroad Administration" had a "widespread effect" on aesthetics. These engines had a "degree of symmetrical beauty. Many roads in the South and Southwest centralized their future construction about the theme introduced by these government prime movers." Included was the Southern Railway. "Special reference is made to the pleasing appearance of the mighty Ps-4 Pacifics."

In the "Superpower Age ... [h]orsepower at high speed was the watchword as driver size increased. ... Some of our finest engine contours appeared in company with most of our ugliest." Morgan points out the New York Central Hudsons and the Louisville & Nashville M-1 class 2-8-4s as evidencing "careful designing." These engines are particularly "handsome" and "clean-limbed" with "concealed piping, long tender, and well balanced arrangement of leading, driving, and trailing wheels." Morgan's point is reinforced perhaps by comparing two other Super-Power locomotives separated by just five years:

ABOVE Southern Railway Class Ps-4 4-6-2 No. 1401 – enshrined in the Smithsonian's National Museum of American History since its opening in 1964 – was built to a USRA design.

R.E. Prince, Courtesy Kalmbach Media

LEFT Louisville & Nashville Class M 2-8-4 No. 1970 was a product of Super Power originator Lima Locomotive Works.

Courtesy Kalmbach Media

the first 2-10-4 Texas type of 1925 and the Chesapeake & Ohio's larger version of the same type in 1930. Or one might compare Lima's first 2-8-4 with the Nickel Plate S-class of 1934.

"With the swift flight of the [diesel] Burlington *Zephyr* ... the final era to date was introduced, as the reciprocating steam locomotive was sheathed in a streamlined cowl to combat the wide acclaim of the Diesel-electric." Bryant despises streamlining; Morgan finds it attractive, within limits, extolling the Norfolk & Western's J-class with its "torpedo nose, handsome boiler and cab outline complete with gracefully planned tender" as "visually pleasing" and "easily the most impressive single locomotive I have ever laid eyes on." However, in a view shared by many contemporary railroaders, Morgan says that "*semi-streamlining* has produced a far better effect than *complete streamlining* [italics in original]."

In the realm of "well-balanced" and "pleasing" appearance, Morgan makes an important observation concerning the design engineer:

> His paramount thought in the creation of a new horsepower producer must needs be one of efficiency. Often, all hope of a handsome result has been sacrificed by the time such mechanical requirements have been solved.[9]

Boston & Maine Class P4a 4-6-2 No. 3710 qualifies as a partially streamlined locomotive, thanks to a skyline casing concealing its steam and sand domes and other appurtenances. "Elephant ear" smoke lifters, in a variety of configurations, were employed by many railroads to direct air upwards beside the exhaust stack in an effort to improve crew visibility at moderate speed.
Courtesy Kalmbach Media

Not mentioned is that a few designers, Francis Cole and Paul Kiefer among them, were known to be openly concerned with aesthetics, though they left little in the written record of their precise ideas of good looks following form. Their works are the record. The forceful insistence of a senior designer that the final result come out well-proportioned or handsome (as he saw those qualities) probably was key when that occurred. Bryant's point that a pleasing appearance did not happen accidentally is undoubtedly astute.

Morgan wrote his brief tour through locomotive aesthetics in 1947. As a leading editor and writer in the trade – one who grew up in the 1920s and '30s avidly train-watching and absorbing the folklore of railroading, and who then indelibly affected the way railroaders and enthusiasts perceived the railroad industry – his views give insight into a shared language. To get beyond the adjectives that Morgan and Bryant use, which have no explicit visual connection for the modern reader, let's try some comparative visual analysis. The two locomotives below are not mentioned in the spare literature on aesthetics and so make a good beginning here.

These two passenger designs are separated by 19 years, before and after the USRA influence. The latter engine is an example of Super Power, defined as a locomotive with a firebox big enough to require a four-wheel trailing truck. For the visual comparison, let's consider a number of attributes in turn. The evaluations are of course the author's, but they try to keep good faith with the sensibilities of Morgan, Bryant, and the trade of the time.

Proportion/'masses in balance': Both engines score high. The masses of cylinders and front-end on the one hand, and of firebox and cab on the other, seem well-distributed about the boiler and over the running gear. To

Rock Island Class P-33 4-6-2 Pacific No. 931 of 1910 provides a useful comparison with Super Power designs like the Nickel Plate 4-6-4 on the next page.
Harold K. Vollrath Collection

The stepped boiler taper of Southern Pacific 2-6-0 No. 1681 was particularly obvious.

Courtesy Kalmbach Media

a railroader, as to an artist using different forms and perceived masses to balance a composition, the cab is a large element, but known to be hollow; its perceived visual mass balances the cylinders and front, which are known to be heavy.

Boiler contour: Both locomotives have conical boilers. The largest diameter is just ahead of the firebox, tapering gently to smaller diameters (or semi-diameters) to the front and back. The effect is much like that of a Doric column, which appears at first glance to be strictly cylindrical but actually is tapered to a slightly larger diameter toward the middle, giving it a subtle sense of elasticity as it bears its weight. The horizontal boiler, known to be containing great pressure, appears more graceful in this tapered form, compared to a straight boiler like the Union Pacific light 4-6-2 pictured on page 426, which somehow lacks equivalent grace. But the taper should not be too severe; a boiler with a pronounced diameter-difference from main course to front course looks awkward, as would a misshapen column.

Cab: Cabs were perhaps the single most important part of a locomotive's conscious styling since their function of sheltering the crew could be accommodated with the widest variation of perhaps any other component.

In the two locomotives pictured, both cabs are rectangular. The Nickel Plate cab is the USRA style in proportion, windows, and details. The Rock Island cab appears to be a little taller in appearance (though this is actually

Nickel Plate Road Class L-1b 4-6-4 Hudson No. 176 of 1929 is typical of locomotive aesthetics in the Super-Power era.

Courtesy Kalmbach Media

ABOVE LEFT Kansas City Southern 2-8-0 No. 480 was distinguished by its small cab windows.
Courtesy Kalmbach Media

ABOVE RIGHT New Haven 2-6-0 No. 163 had arched cab windows.
Courtesy Kalmbach Media

RIGHT Erie 4-6-2 No. 2524 was built with a curved – almost gambrel – cab roof.
Harold K. Vollrath Collection

Southern Pacific 4-10-2 No. 5048, with slanted cab front.
Harold K. Vollrath Collection

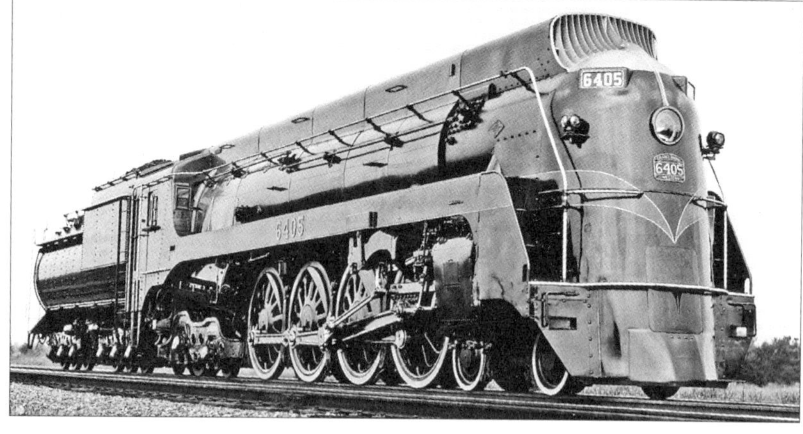

Grand Trunk Western U-4-b No. 6405's all-weather cab was a feature shared with large locomotives – streamlined and unstreamlined – of parent Canadian National.
Courtesy Kalmbach Media

an illusion deriving from the fact that it's shorter from front to back). The USRA cab, being just a little longer, looks better proportioned and also seems to blend more comfortably into the back of the boiler. The small turret cover just ahead of the cab at the top, flush with the roof, helps in the blending. On both engines, the cab windows look well proportioned in size relative to the full rectangular sidewall of the cab. This is a proportion that Bryant calls "Georgian," in which window and sidewall seem to relate in size to one another in a way that suggests neoclassical architecture. The point is seen by comparison with other cab-window arrangements, which take up far more or far less of the sidewall space. Some railroads specified an arched window, which clearly indicated a stylistic intention since the arch served no other purpose. Bryant saw what he called a "Gothic" element in such an arched shape, but the very gentle arch possible under the roofline is too flattened to be Gothic.

The cab roof is a stylistic element. The overhang at the back protects the crew from rain, but its lines also suggest a sense of speed. There was great variation in roof styles: wooden cabs of the 1880s and 1890s sometimes had clerestories; post-1900 steel cabs had rounded roofs, severely rounded roofs, and roofs slightly gambrel in form. Roof overhangs could be long or short, their lower edges (over the cab gangway) straight or slanted or shaped with gentle reverse curves. A straight lower edge on the overhang seems ordinary; a slanted lower edge looks a bit racier. An upward-turned deflector at the overhang's back edge (there to deflect flying cinders) also adds an accent.

The cab's forward edge, at the sides, could be vertical (as in the two engines here discussed) or slanted. If vertical, the cab keeps a strict rectangular shape, which Bryant regarded as a Georgian element. If slanted at the front, or sometimes notched out, the reason was to give better access for repair of firebox staybolts in the area thus uncovered.

The "all-weather" cab, so-called because it was closed-in at the rear and usually had a door on either side, came into wide use in the 1920s by Canadian railroads and U.S. railroads operating in regions with severe winters. This kind of cab was indeed functional, since it was better protection for the crew. Visually, however, it created a heavy look at the rear of the locomotive: the cab took up a bigger proportion of the length of the locomotive, upsetting the perceived balance fore-and-aft, and eliminated the roof overhang. For purely aesthetic reasons, therefore, three classes of Union Pacific engines, including Big Boy, had all-weather cabs with rear-entry doors; the classic lines of cab design were thus retained, complete with a carefully shaped roof overhang.

Elements on top of the boiler: The stack, domes, and various devices atop the boiler can be arranged in great variety of ways. In North America, the alignment of the stack exactly over the vertical centerline of the cylinders was universal. The reason was to align the steam exhaust jet in the smokebox exactly equidistant from the exhaust passages in each side of the cylinder saddle. To American engineers, this alignment was only natural. (European and British engineers weren't so inflexible and sometimes put cylinders and stack in altogether different alignments, but to Americans this was an extremely awkward-looking feature.) Note in both the Rock Island and Nickel Plate designs how the stack and cylinders, in vertical line, seem to unify boiler and cylinders.

The stack itself is taller on one engine than the other. This is simply the result of the larger boiler diameter of the more powerful 1927 design. Both locomotives had to meet similar overhead clearance limits, so the over-stack height on each, from the rail, is a few inches above 15 feet. For a "tall" stack, the Rock Island's has a customary, slightly tapered shape. The slight taper and curves make an otherwise mundane feature look a bit more interesting. The Nickel Plate's "short" stack (ignoring the latter-day stack extension seen in the photo) is also tapered.

Nashville, Chattanooga & St. Louis 4-8-4 No. 566, with decorative "capped" stack. *Courtesy Kalmbach Media*

The shape of the stack (both visible and not visible) depended a great deal on the theories about draft efficiency held by the reigning chief mechanical engineering officer or superintendent of motive power. Since exhausting and drafting constituted such a problematic science, there was plenty of room for variation in precise design. A few railroads, notably the Delaware & Hudson and the Nashville, Chattanooga & St. Louis, liked the "capped" stack as an overtly decorative element and applied it to even their most modern designs.

Next on top of the boiler for the two engines pictured, front to rear, is the sand dome, or sand box in 19th-century terms. The location is determined in part functionally, since sand piping must take a direct route to the front of the first pair of drivers, with sand piping to other drivers and for backing having somewhat less priority. Hence the sand dome is usually forward; in the Rock Island it is well forward. (Railroads varied as to how much sanding to provide. The Rock Island has two pipes on each side; the Nickel Plate just one. Later, the NKP went to four on each side for its freight locomotives.)

On top of the largest-diameter course of the boiler is the steam dome, followed by other devices: an early form of electric dynamo on the Rock Island and a housing for safety valves on both. The Nickel Plate has a turret cover ahead of the cab bulkhead; the Rock Island's turret is in the cab behind the bulkhead. The outside location for the turret came to be favored since, in an emergency involving a blown valve in the turret, a steam eruption was better separated from the crew.

The distribution of domes and appliances looks better balanced on the Nickel Plate. Intervals between the elements don't seem as harmonious on the Rock Island; the bell, for example, looks a little lonely between the widely spaced domes. But as Morgan warned, function has dictated dome locations. The form of the domes on the Rock Island – tall, "upside-down thunder mugs" in King's fine term – are classic but hardly as graceful as on the Nickel Plate. From a 1920s-1940s perspective, when the ever-larger boilers of bigger engines had forced the domes to squash down – and to visually smooth down – under the overhead clearance limit, the Rock Island might have been derided as "a tall-domed scald pot."[10] But the Rock Island 931 was a flashy speedster in its day. Its domes have complex curves (that are not functional except aesthetically) to blend the domes into the boiler. The visible steam dome on each locomotive is merely a sheet-metal cover over the structural boiler dome and cap underneath; the sand dome is of thicker sheet, has its own bottom welded to its circular wall, and is held in place by studs and nuts.]

Other forms of domes on U.S. steamers were curved in different ways depending on taste. Sand domes could be huge, for generous sand capacity, and latter-day engines sometimes hid the steam dome within the sand dome – Delaware & Hudson 4-8-4s exemplify both of these features. The New York Central Niagara 4-8-4 had no steam dome at all – the 100-inch-diameter boiler, combined with NYC's tight overhead clearances left no room for a dome, and a slotted drypipe was used instead. The resulting external appearance was sleek indeed. The Lackawanna, to create the most lateral space possible in the sand dome, slanted the sides of the dome outward.

The Front: This is the face of the locomotive, a combination of boiler front and headlight, with the front deck and pilot – cowcatcher to non-railroaders – below. The composition of those elements, for most contemporary Americans, was the distilled symbol of the railroad and all it represented. No one, anywhere in the nation, could mistake even the most sketchy suggestion of the front of a locomotive for what it was.

The headlight, smokebox and door, number plate if present, and pilot are the crucial elements. Contributing are the cylinders, which provide low, symmetrical masses balancing the boiler front, but slightly in the background. The headlight can be high-mounted or centered. The headlight up high is imposing, dominant. A high headlight looks good with a tall stack behind it. The centered headlight is concentric with the other circular elements of the boiler and its door. A subtlety is locating the headlight slightly below center, which to many gave a more pleasing arrangement than strict concentric centering. (That aesthetic touch is related to the attractiveness of a gently tapered column or boiler, vs. a straight, perfectly cylindrical column or boiler. Strict linearity or concentricity can be boring.) The smokebox door can take many specific forms. If it is shaped in relief, with the depth of a cameo, it is attractive. If it is too flat, it is not.

Classification lights, front steps, and front deck suggest a frame for the boiler front. The absence of class lights makes for a rather "bald" appearance.[11] Other frontal elements up top can be number boards or a feedwater heater. All of these can add interesting accents or symmetrical touches. The deck, below the boiler front, can be plain or set with devices. If such devices are placed symmetrically, such as twin air compressors behind shields, the effect can be to fill in a seeming gap below the smokebox. If the devices are asymmetric – a single compressor or a feedwater pump – the effect is disconcerting, like an auto with half its front grille badly distorted.

The pilot defines the base of the locomotive's frontal composition. The Rock Island has a satisfying pilot, large enough to be noticed, with a rakish slant. The Nickel Plate's pilot, from the side, is weak looking, like an afterthought under the front coupler. In front view it seems more appropriate.

The pilot's function was to deflect obstructions on the track from getting under the locomotive and derailing it. It wasn't to save the cow but to save

LOWER LEFT PRR Class I-1 2-10-0 No. 4628, with high-mounted headlight and symmetrical pilot-mounted air tanks.
Richard J. Cook, Courtesy Kalmbach Media

LOWER RIGHT Southern Pacific 4-10-2 No. 5021, wtih below-center headlight and shaped front on its "silvered" smokebox.
Stan Kistler, Courtesy Kalmbach Media

ABOVE LEFT Union Pacific cast-steel pilot with swing-away coupler. *Art Stensvad, Courtesy Kalmbach Media*

ABOVE RIGHT PRR drop-coupler pilot. *Don Wood, Courtesy Kalmbach Media*

the engine. Pilots were made of wood in the 19th century, and into the 1920s on some roads; wooden pilots were generally made of oak, for strength. Early in the century a form that became popular was made from steel tubing, sometimes cut from used boiler tubes; the Reading 4-8-4 is one such. Pilots got smaller in the 1910s, for reasons that aren't clear. Some roads, like the Santa Fe and the Great Northern, kept them big, which was a matter of bolting the top of each tube to the pilot beam and not to a separate crossbar beneath the beam. By the 1930s, companies marketing steel castings offered cast pilots. Some of these looked particularly stylish and seemed more in keeping with the rest of the frontal mass of the locomotive.

In the 1930s, the Pennsylvania Railroad, the Milwaukee Road, the Norfolk & Western, and a few other lines devised large pilots formed of sheet steel, with couplers that could be lowered, raised, or swung out of the way. These huge pilots did nothing for the engines' frontal aspect, but the objective was to keep a larger obstruction (that is, an automobile) out from under the locomotive in a high-speed road-crossing accident. Grade-crossing collisions were becoming a greater problem for railroads. A front coupler that could be folded away, so it would be less prone to impale an automobile, plus the large expanse of sheet steel made a more effective deflector. The large cast-steel pilot adopted by Union Pacific, with a swing-away coupler, served the same function with an obvious nod toward aesthetics: the vertical slots served to give a more traditional appearance to the engine.

Bryant and Morgan both preferred the bell to be placed as a frontal ornament, rather like a piece of jewelry on the locomotive's brow. Railroads were entirely divided on the matter. Each railroad generally had its own practice. A railroad that specified the headlight to be mounted high most often put the bell up on the boiler; a railroad that placed the headlight lower could specify the bell to be almost anywhere. Whatever the arrangement at the front – headlight, markers, bell if present, number plate if present – was

ABOVE LEFT Smokebox-mounted compressors on non-articulated locomotives – such as Chesapeake & Ohio 4-8-2 No. 546 – were unusual but not unknown.

Courtesy Kalmbach Media

ABOVE RIGHT Duluth, Missabe & Iron Range 2-8-8-4 No. 223 illustrates a more common application of such hardware, on an articulated locomotive.

Courtesy Kalmbach Media

a studied one and gave a railroad's locomotives a kind of family appearance. The aesthetic taste involved was entirely that – taste.

Sometimes the steam locomotive front was hung with twin air compressors. On many articulated freighters, there was no place else to put the compressors because space over the front deck was too confined and all the room along both sides of the boiler was taken with steam pipes, air tanks, and plumbing. Some non-articulated locomotives, notably on the C&O, had twin compressors on the boiler front. The thought was to distribute weight – each compound compressor weighs several tons. To some eyes, the visage created was bold and visually arresting. Others found it cluttered. Placing the pumps in front found a more popular solution in the 1920s by tucking them down behind the pilot beam and under the smokebox.

Driving Wheels: In any side- or broad three-quarter view of a locomotive in motion, the driving wheels are the focus of attention, by far the most important visual feature. An architectural interpretation of the locomotive tends to stress the engine's design as an imposing, complex, solid structure – like a building. But a locomotive is also a moving vehicle – one that could shake the earth or blaze past at 80 miles an hour. Its motion is its sensory reality. Its great wheels function not only as propulsion but as the central aesthetic component in our response to its image, either static or in action.

Thus the architectural view can leave out the greater part of a locomotive's meaning. There may be circles occasionally in architecture, but there are no wheels. And no other everyday transport vehicle ever had such audacious wheels – five, six, and even seven feet in diameter.

In the 19th century, therefore, a visual parallel to fine, high-wheeled carriages is relevant. To the 19th-century eye, tall, light-looking wheels meant speed. Locomotives of the period – as depicted in the Currier & Ives print on page 424 – incorporated classical architecture overtly in the details of their beautifully crafted wooden cabs, but their graceful wheels echoed the design of fast carriages. In the first decades of the 20th century, locomotive wheels symbolized the fastest thing on land. In movies, audiences had only to see a brief, tight close-up of fast-revolving engine wheels to sense that a dramatic change in the story was about to unfold.

"Fleet-footed," "high-wheeled," "tall-drivered," "long and tall" – these were common descriptions of passenger locomotives with big drivers. "Muscular," "husky," "brawny," "mountain battler" – such words described freight locomotives with low drivers that denoted great power at lower speeds, "wrestling" a long train uphill, "fighting" the grade. The words painted a verbal picture that readers or listeners could see immediately. What they saw in their minds' eye were the drivers – spinning in a blur or slowly churning.

The Rock Island 4-6-2 and the Nickel Plate 4-6-4 have drivers exactly the same diameter: 73 inches. Yet, in their proportion, such drivers look taller and more graceful on the Rock Island. On the Nickel Plate, the fatter boiler looks a little top heavy on the same-size wheels.

Trucks: The wheels in leading and trailing trucks play a supporting role – literally and aesthetically. On four-wheel lead trucks, the pair of lead wheels on each side frames the cylinder, completing a composition of stack, cylinder, and wheels balanced around the stack centerline. Two-wheel lead trucks don't have that appearance; the single wheel on each side nestles comfortably between pilot and cylinder, clearly displaying its guiding function.

Two-wheel trailing trucks often had a light appearance that seemed appropriate to the weight they carried. Four-wheel trucks, a product of Super-Power design principles, were expected to carry large fireboxes, and the trucks are commensurately heavier. The Nickel Plate 4-6-4's trailer is a Delta truck (so-called because it carries the rear of the locomotive on the truck's extreme rear corners; the forward pivot for the cast-steel yoke is the third point. In actuality the Delta is also a complex affair, but equalizers and springs are hidden behind the outer cast frame. The frame itself is a sculpture. When seen in a casting shop photo, its wonderful play of shapes and curves is shown to advantage. Under the firebox, it blends with the Nickel Plate's hefty quality, the drivers with their heavier counterweights, and the spokeless lead wheels.

Inside-bearing trailing trucks were common at the turn of the century. On the light engines of the period spoked trailing wheels fit in well with all the other spoked wheels. On later, heavier engines a spoked trailer could look inappropriate. The outside truck frame filled-in the lateral space under the wide firebox and cab immediately above. The outside-bearing forms provided not only the reality of greater lateral stability but also the tangible appearance of it.

Outside-bearing lead trucks facilitated inspection and repair of bearings but hid the leading wheels from view. One senses that the rarity of such trucks was strictly a matter of tradition since the 1840s. If leading wheels

TOP Inside-bearing trailing trucks were common at the turn of the century, but usually were fitted with spoked wheels. *Courtesy Kalmbach Media*

BELOW LEFT Delta trailing trucks supported a larger firebox. They looked more substantial, and they were. *Courtesy Kalmbach Media*

BELOW RIGHT Outside-bearing lead trucks were never common, either because of aesthetics or because there wasn't much space under the cylinders. *Courtesy Kalmbach Media*

were visible, as with inside-bearing trucks, their guiding function was openly displayed. The locomotive somehow looked more agile, better able to race down the track, to negotiate the curves. The reality, of course, was that the location of the truck bearings made no difference to tracking function. Fitting an outside-bearing, four-wheel truck within the tight clearances under the cylinders was no small trick, however.

Symmetry of Wheels: To many in the steam era, an engine wheeled symmetrically fore-and-aft, such as a 2-8-2, 4-6-4 or 4-8-4, or even a 4-6-6-4 or 4-8-8-4, was more aesthetically arranged around the drivers. Super-Power locomotives with two-wheel lead trucks and extended fireboxes over four trailing wheels sometimes looked rear-end heavy. But to other observers, the greater number of rear wheels compensated visually as well as actually for the rearward weight distribution.

Rods and Counterweights: The main and side rods, balanced literally by the driving wheel counterweights, are the intricately dynamic parts that grab the eye as the locomotive moves. The Rock Island and Nickel Plate engines have crescent-shaped counterweights, which not only put the most real mass closest to the rims of the drivers, but look more pleasing than other forms. The weights themselves bothered early designers. To their sensibility, visible weights upset the lacy look of carriage wheels that were their model, so they hid the needed mass in hollow spokes or blended it as unobtrusively as possible into the rims.

As locomotives grew in power, and visible weights on the drivers became unavoidable, the weights took on an aesthetic of their own, always in visual balance with the rods. The rhythm created by the swirling masses, parallel rotation of the side rods, and the back-and-forth plus round-and-round gyration of the main rod produced an effect like kinetic sculpture – long before that became an art form.

In the photo of the Nickel Plate 4-6-4, the rods have been set in a position that railroaders thought attractive – the "rods down" position. Although static, the rods' position suggests motion, as if the engine is poised for starting. Of course the engine can start easily from other rod-positions, so the deliberate posing in the photos is an artistic convention. A "rods up" position, as with the Rock Island 4-6-2, could look attractive to some. If an external eccentric crank was present, the relationship among the rods suggested what a modern viewer might see as an artistic "tension."

Most of the rods on both engines are fluted, giving them an overtly sculptural appearance. "Flat" rods, those without fluting, seem crude by comparison. A fluted rod gains strength from shape, like a girder, but is wider in cross-section. To keep the distance across the cylinders to an utter minimum, side rods were often flat, especially on freight locomotives that exerted very high piston thrust. Each inch of inter-cylinder distance added greatly to the colossal stresses on the cylinder saddle and forward engine frame.

Crossheads looked light or heavy: The Rock Island and Nickel Plate engines pictured on pages 428-29 both have the "alligator" style crossheads, which were the most common, with upper and lower guides. Later forms called the Laird (after its designer) and the multiple-bearing crosshead used one upper guide. More of the first driver was visible. The choice had an aesthetic result though function governed: Many railroads felt the alligator form gave better lateral stability to the piston rods under high thrust.

The flutes of main and side rods were painted black on some railroads, as a visual accent. Later, railroad and ICC inspectors looking for hairline cracks discouraged any painting of rods. A fine polish to all the rods, so that the steel gleamed, was always admired. Whether there was time in the roundhouse and shop to do such a nicety depended on whether the railroad could afford the labor. Roundhouse mechanics wiped and polished the rods as an extra mark of pride.

Valve Gear: For many 19th century railroaders, the Walschaerts valve gear, hung on the outside of the engine for easy access in setting valves in the shop and lubrication on the road, ruined the visual simplicity of just main rod and side rods connected to the drivers. As with previous necessary mechanical changes, such as visible counterweights, outside valve gear soon became an accepted part of the action sculpture. Morgan's adjective of "clean-limbed" certainly could refer to either of the locomotives pictured, complete with Walschaerts valve gear.

The angle of the eccentric crank was universally thought to be prettier if it angled forward on the crankpin backstroke, as it does on the Nickel Plate engine. Also, the proportions in the sizes of the main rod, side rod, and eccentric rod were visually important. On both the Rock Island and the Nickel Plate, those proportions are agreeable. On freight locomotives needing massive main rods, the eccentric rod can look too dainty – even on so formidable a beast as a Big Boy. The rod designer could do little about the matter: the various cross-sectional sizes were determined strictly from stress calculations, and one wanted the eccentric rod to be as lightweight as possible, to help in dynamic wheel-balance calculations.

The improbably delicate eccentric rod of a Union Pacific 4-8-8-4 Big Boy.
Courtesy Kalmbach Media

Many other forms of outside-hung valve gear gained various degrees of acceptance in the early part of the 20th century, and each form had its partisans. The Walschaerts was the most favored, followed by the Baker, with all the others together holding a distant third place. Some railroaders preferred the comparatively direct relationships of the Walschaerts. Others were entirely indifferent between the two leading types.

Running Boards, Piping: Both the Rock Island and Nickel Plate locomotives have straight running boards, which for many railroaders looked cleaner. Such boards were also safer, since one was less apt to trip at a height-change on the narrow footway seven or eight feet above the ground, especially on a dark night next to the hot boiler. But the running board must be located above air tanks and above other devices that can interfere with a straight alignment, such as the power reverse on the right side and the air compressor hung on the left side. The Nickel Plate has its air compressors on the front deck, which removes them from the left side, and the engine's air tanks are hidden under the boiler between the frame rails, a less convenient position clearly intended for appearance.

On both engines, air piping is not visible on the right side. Sand piping is exposed, so that boiler jacketing doesn't have to be removed to replace a seriously plugged-up pipe (from moisture getting into the pipe). Feedwater piping is also exposed. Such piping needs to be as straight as possible, with shallow bends to avoid excessive resistance in the water's rapid pathway from each injector to its check valve. The Nickel Plate has a top check valve, which takes feedwater from either side.[12] Most locomotives had air piping in a visible array on the left or both sides, which could look cluttered, or be aesthetically arranged.[13] Locomotives like the two illustrated, and those with neatly arranged piping under the running board, would certainly be called "clean and trim," as a yacht is with all its sail-handling and dock lines well stowed.

'Extras': Feedwater heaters, feedwater-heater pumps, and various appliances could challenge notions of appearance, especially on the left side of the locomotive where components of the main feedwater delivery system were always located, so that the fireman could control the system.

Such components could include the pump for an Elesco feedwater heating system, or the combined pumps and heater of the massive Worthington BL system, or the hot water and cold water pumps of the Worthington SA system, plus the air compressor, which was usually on the left as well. Placing these items could result in a jagged running board, with step-ups and -downs to clear it all. To some observers, all the plumbing and fixtures held a fascination, implying that all the complexities added more efficiency and greater power to the locomotive – which they did.

The feedwater heater itself was located on or in the forward part of the smokebox. The curving brow of a Coffin heater, as seen on the Milwaukee Road 2-6-6-2, obscured the engine's front altogether. The Elesco – jutting forward over the front, set back just ahead of the stack, or partially buried – altered the locomotive's face in different ways, adding to a look denoting power. The large-diameter exhaust steam pipes to an externally mounted heater also made for some highly noticeable frontal plumbing. The Worthington SA heater, mostly inside the smokebox with a small rectangular cover jutting up ahead of the stack, was probably the most pleasing visually.[14]

Tenders: A locomotive was not a locomotive without its tender, and the tender was not just an attachment but was a carefully designed part of the whole. From the late 19th century, tenders grew larger, not only as bigger locomotives hauling heavier trains ingested more fuel per mile, but also as railroads endeavored to reduce the number of service stops over a given division. In the 20th century's first decade, even some rather large locomotives had relatively small tenders. That soon changed.

LOWER LEFT Elesco feedwater heater on Canadian National Class U-2-e 4-8-4 No. 6167.
Courtesy Kalmbach Media

CENTER Worthington Type SA feedwater heater on UP Class FEF-3 4-8-4 No. 844.
Courtesy Kalmbach Media

LOWER RIGHT Coffin feedwater heater on Milwaukee Road Class N-3 2-6-6-2 No. 9307.
Courtesy Kalmbach Media

ABOVE The flat-top profile of Santa Fe 4-8-4 No. 2919's tender reflects provision for large volumes of fuel oil and water.
Courtesy Kalmbach Media

RIGHT Great Northern 2-8-2 No. 3390 employed a Vanderbilt tender, with its distinctive cylindrical water tank.
N.F. Priebe, Courtesy Kalmbach Media

RIGHT The welded tender of Milwaukee Road 4-8-4 No. 268 was curved at top and bottom.
Henry J. McCord, Courtesy Kalmbach Media

FAR RIGHT Tenders on switching locomotives – such as Norfolk & Western 0-8-0 No. 253 – often had tapered coal-bunker sides to improve crews' rearward visibility.
Courtesy Kalmbach Media

As tender dimensions expanded, function suggested a form with raised cowling around the coal space forward and a lower deck around the water-filling hatch at the back, as seen on the Rock Island and Nickel Plate engines. The high cowl maximized coal capacity; the lower rear deck enabled a crewman to walk safely for access to water-crane spouts and to the tender's hatch or hatches. The proportion of fuel space to water space was determined such that, in its planned service, the locomotive would take fuel once every 100 to 150 miles (the length of a division), and take water about twice as often,[15] depending on the topographic profile. Running upgrade always meant far greater consumption rates of both fuel and water.

Aesthetically, a proportion of about 2/3 raised cowling to 1/3 lower rear deck was most preferred. In the 1930s, the necessity to add water space sometimes forced a return to a full-rectangular shape with the rear deck as high as the fuel space. Older tenders could be modified in later years with raised coal cowling, which added coal capacity at the expense of looks.

An adroit blending of the lines of the cab into the front of the tender made for an improved visual relationship between engine and tender. A fuel-space cowling that curved inward along its top edge could help make that visual connection. In such shaping, clearance considerations applied, affecting not only the height limit but also the precise clearances at the top corners of all railway cars and locomotives, but exact configuration was up to the designer. A Vanderbilt-style tender, with cylindrical water tank, pleased some observers: The tender's combined shapes echoed those of the engine's flat-sided cab and round boiler.

Greater structural rigidity with somewhat lighter weight came from curving the tender sides at top and bottom. All-welded tenders came into use in the 1930s. Welded construction eliminated rivet lines and gave a smooth appearance. Tenders on switching locomotives were often "slope-backed" and/or had the cowling around the coal stepped inward . Such a configuration gave improved rearward visibility for the engine crew in backing movements in congested yards.

Tender trucks came in weltering variety. The number of wheels per truck was strictly a function of the tender's loaded weight. Ordinary freight-car trucks, which gave no styling benefit at all, were commonly found under freight-engine tenders. Four-wheel tender trucks on faster locomotives were often an "express" type with a long wheelbase for running stability. Six-wheel trucks for heavier tenders had long wheelbases inherently; their cast-steel truck sideframes were marvelous sculptures. The pedestal- or "centipede"-type tender maximized fuel and water capacity. Opinions were diverse as to whether any tender-truck arrangement added or subtracted from visual appearance. Most agreed that more-modern trucks looked better on the biggest tenders.

Decorations: A few railroads lined and striped their locomotives. The Southern Railway and the Frisco (St. Louis-San Francisco Railway) had attractive patterns. Striping was usually confined to passenger locomotives, but not always. The simplest touch was to edge running boards in white, perhaps with a similar-width white line down the tender. In the 1920s through the 1940s, the Richmond, Fredericksburg & Potomac applied surely the most elaborate striping of any latter-day steam railroad.

On the Southern, management approved the permanent attachment of brass eagles and "candlesticks" to the smokebox front by motivated roundhouse staff or engine crews. This was done to relatively few locomotives but added a classy touch.

Color was rare on unstreamlined locomotives. The most common accent was medium-green paint on the woodwork of cab windows (and also on the woodwork in cab interiors). Graphite-gray was often seen on the bare steel of smokeboxes and sometimes fireboxes; it appears on the Rock Island 4-6-2. Graphite powder mixed with oil, applied to such surfaces, produced a heat-resistant coating. Most paints, under the intense heat inherent to those unjacketed areas, just peeled away leaving rusty patches. Aluminum-based paint was also heat-resistant, more expensive, but favored by several far-Western lines. The Southern Pacific adopted bright aluminum paint for smokebox fronts in the 1930s, primarily to make its locomotives more visible to motorists.

Even in the 20th century, the Baltimore & Ohio, Canadian National, Canadian Pacific, Delaware & Hudson, Great Northern, Southern Pacific, and a few others painted some of their front-rank passenger engines in

ABOVE A cast-metal eagle, perched aboved the headlight of Southern Railway Class Ps-4 4-6-2 No. 1395.

Courtesy Kalmbach Media

BELOW Richmond, Fredericksburg & Potomac 2-8-4 No. 574 displays that road's affinity for fine striping detail, even on a freight locomotive.

Courtesy Kalmbach Media

blue, dark green, dark red, or olive shades. (Great Northern and Kansas City Southern even had some green freight locomotives.) On some railroads, cab roofs and tender decks on passenger and freight locomotives were red, which could be bright red but was usually a dark, red-oxide paint, which was a rust preventive. The Southern's Ps-4 passenger locomotives were the most colorful, in "Sylvan" green with gold or yellow striping, and with or without a red roof. On tenders, a few railroads put on spots of color, limited in size so they could be easily cleaned of the ever-flying soot. Rock Island, Katy (the Missouri-Kansas-Texas Railroad) and the Great Northern painted company heralds – or applied separate plates with their heralds – on tenders in an age when such décor was extremely rare on locomotives. The Western Maryland added a bright-red "fireball" logo on tenders to signify its fast-freight service.

After a major shopping, painters sometimes trimmed driving-and truck-wheels in white or aluminum. In builder photos, driver tires are almost always white. Keeping wheels that clean was impossible in daily service, so the white on wheels generally disappeared after a few weeks on the road. Passenger locomotives, and their driver- and lead-truck wheels, received more cleaning attention, at least through the 1920s, and white rims were standard for a few companies. To many observers, whitened tires accented the drivers and running gear, attractively setting them off.

Railroaders debated whether added decoration was aesthetically important. The consensus seemed to be that fine striping, while universally admired and elegant, was not essential. For a locomotive, the lines created by the steel shapes themselves, the engine's overall proportions, and a good-looking front visage were the most significant things, even though taste about those aspects varied.

Articulated Locomotives: Railroaders agreed that most Mallets would not win any beauty contests. Articulateds built in the 1920s were somewhat improved; as boilers grew larger in diameter, domes and steam pipes got pushed into the clearance limits. The second series of Union Pacific Challengers (and their close cousins on Delaware & Hudson), the Big Boys, and the B&O EM-1 2-8-8-4s, however, were unusually handsome despite their great size.

Railroad Design Practices: Each railroad had mechanical standards for its locomotives that resulted in distinctive touches that combined to give a characteristic appearance, often markedly so. Railroaders could easily identify a locomotive as being from a particular railroad in a particular era, even if the railroad's name was entirely obscured. Simple tradition, or successive top officers managing the engineering of locomotives, put a stamp on proportions and details. Belpaire boilers, front-mounted compressors, and Vanderbilt tenders were Great Northern hallmarks; Santa Fe's boiler-tube pilots, stack extensions, and two-sided number boards betrayed their identities; while Belpaire boilers and keystone number plates bespoke the Pennsylvania Railroad.

Canadian railroads also expressed a different aesthetic sense. One feature of the Canadian Pacific's later standards was skirted running boards, which were a fine decorative touch. The skirting made room for tasteful striping and an engine's road number specially framed. In comparison, the running boards of U.S. engines looked "weak" and rather puny along immense boilers. When such thin-edged running boards lost their straightness, bent from years of banging around the shops, a locomotive looked forlorn indeed.

This extended tour of outward, external design – for a machine shaped so much by function – is revealing. Engineering function plays a clear and strong role, but it is not the final determinant. Human beings leave their own remarkable and varying imprints on steel crafted for economic purposes, just as they do on clay, wood, and marble for art's sake.

Chapter 22 Notes

1. H. Stafford Bryant Jr., "The Architecture of the Locomotive," *Trains*, April 1956, p. 26.
2. In such popular art, it was the locomotive itself that was the central focus, rather than the artist's rendition of an aspect of the railway scene in larger context or as impressionist or expressionist statement. The subject of the railroad itself in art is discussed in Ian Kennedy and Julian Treuherz (co-authors) *The Railway: Art in the Age of Steam*, Yale University Press, 2008. See also Susan Danly and Leo Marx (eds. and co-authors), *The Railroad in American Art*, MIT Press, 1988. The discussion in the present chapter is the exterior shape and design of the locomotive, *per se*.
3. John Kouwenhoven and Siegfried Giedion treat this phenomenon in their respective classics on American industrial taste and aesthetics, *Made in America* and *Mechanization Takes Command*. See also Lewis Mumford, *Technics and Civilization*.
4. David P. Morgan, "What is a Good-Looking Locomotive?" *Railroad Magazine*, March 1948, pp. 46-58; H. Stafford Bryant Jr., "Ps-4" (the class of locomotive that includes the Smithsonian's 4-6-2 No. 1401), *Trains*, Oct. 1950, pp. 20-26; H. Stafford Bryant Jr., *The Georgian Locomotive*, Barre Gazette Press, 1962; and Ed W. King, "The Rolling Mud Fence," *Trains*, Feb. 1985, pp. 29-35. The quotation is from King, p. 29.
5. Bryant, p. 30.
6. *The Georgian Locomotive*, p. xv.
7. Ibid., p. xvi.
8. Morgan (Note 4), p. 49 (two lines of typography reversed in the original. Quotes in the paragraphs following are all from Morgan, pp. 49-54.
9. Ibid., p. 54.
10. A phrase from steam locomotive fireman Lloyd Arkinstall (Chapter 8 Notes).
11. Toy train manufacturers are forever making these marker lights red, which is silly. In the steam era, markers were either not illuminated for scheduled trains, white for extra (*i.e.*, non-scheduled) movements, or green to indicate following sections of passenger trains. On any locomotive, red was only used for "rear markers" when the engine ran light or in reverse.
12. The top check valve was favored by many roads, since the incoming feedwater, cooler than water in the boiler, entered the boiler as a spray. The spray hitting the surface of the boiler water caused less thermal shock than feedwater entering below the waterline at the sides, as in the Rock Island. In either method, the check valve is well forward, so that water enters in the relatively cooler end of the boiler.
13. Whether hidden or not, air piping leaving the air compressor(s) needed to have a sufficiently long run partially to cool the air, heated by the compression that is required to maintain between 120 and 150 psi in the air reservoirs.
14. Many roads came to prefer the Worthington open-type heater – which actively mixed condensed cylinder exhaust with the incoming cold water – for its free-oxygen-reducing quality, which helped to reduce internal boiler corrosion. The Worthington was also valued for its better heating at high feedwater delivery volumes. Many latter-day locomotives incorporated the Worthington SA type in various capacity sizes.
15. There was a lot of variation in such a rule of thumb. Large tenders on passenger locomotives in the 1930s and '40s, running without change over several divisions often had enough coal to traverse at least two divisions. On heavily trafficked segments of the New York Central and the Pennsylvania Railroad, passenger engines scooped water on the fly from track pans at designated spots in order to eliminate service stops – that's why the Hudsons assigned to the *20th Century Limited* had huge coal bunkers and comparatively small water cisterns. On the Union Pacific in steam days, Challengers and Big Boys westbound from Cheyenne, Wyo., took both coal and water just 25 miles out of town, at Harriman, due to the prodigious fuel consumption entailed in climbing Sherman Hill with a heavy freight train.

Index

William L. Withuhn (1941–2017) was the long-time transportation curator at the Smithsonian Institution's National Museum of American History. He was a licensed locomotive engineer who ran dozens of steam engines, from saddle-tankers to Northerns. Withuhn was also the chairman of the Federal Railroad Administration's Engineering Standards Committee, which re-wrote regulations for the 21st century and thus helped ensure continued operation of heritage locomotives. He was author of *The Spirit of Steam* and *Rails Across America*.